THE ULTIMATE DIETARY REFERENCE

Whether you're on a low-cholesterol, low-fat, or salt-restricted diet, trying to watch your calories or add fiber, here is the book specially tailored to your needs.

Did you know that . . .

ZUCCHINI CAN BE A LOW-CALORIE DELIGHT—OR A CALORIC DISASTER: frozen zucchini: 3.2 oz. 15 calories vs. frozen zucchini sticks in batter: 3 oz. 180 calories.

NOT ALL STEAKS ARE EQUAL IN FAT: broiled club steak, 4 oz. = 46.0 gm. fat vs. broiled round steak, lean (fat trimmed) 4 oz. = 6.9 gm. fat.

FAST FOODS—THERE IS A LOWER CHOLESTEROL CHOICE: Enjoy Wendy's potato stuffed with sour cream and chives, 11 oz. = 15 mg. cholesterol

YOU CAN BOOST YOUR FIBER INTAKE: Try wheat bran, crude, commercially milled, 4 oz. = 10.3 gm. vs. wheat germ, crude, commercially milled, 4 oz. = 2.8 gm.

What you don't know may be damaging to your health! Discover all the data you need right here, and plan the diet that's exactly right—for you!

THE COMPLETE BOOK OF FOOD COUNTS

THE BOOK THAT NO HEALTH-CONSCIOUS PERSON SHOULD BE WITHOUT!

THE
COMPLETE
BOOK
OF
FOOD COUNTS

Corinne T. Netzer

A DELL BOOK

Published by
Dell Publishing
a division of
The Bantam Doubleday Dell Publishing Group, Inc.
1 Dag Hammarskjold Plaza
New York, New York 10017

Dell ® TM 681510, Dell Publishing, a division of the Bantam Doubleday Dell Publishing Group, Inc.

ISBN: 0-440-20062-8

Printed in the United States of America

March 1988

10 9 8 7 6 5 4 3 2 1

KRI

To Pat Ladew

Introduction

The Complete Book of Food Counts is the largest, most complete compilation of essential food data ever published. It contains figures (calories, protein, carbohydrates, fat, cholesterol, sodium and fiber) for basic generic foods, brand-name foods, and fast-food chains. Whether you are interested in dieting or nutrition—or both—you will find this book unique and invaluable as a reference.

Since this book is alphabetized, you should have no difficulty finding whatever food you wish to look up. There are, however, times when you may have to look in more than one place. If you are searching for a particular food and cannot find it immediately, look for it under a category—such as cakes, puddings, cookies, soups. Wherever appropriate, I have cross-referenced listings, but the pressure of space has made it impossible to do that for every item.

Compare only foods listed in similar measures. This rule particularly applies to the confusion between measures by capacity and measures by weight. Eight ounces is not necessarily equivalent to eight fluid ounces or one cup. Eight ounces is a measure of how much something weighs; one cup is a measure of how much space it occupies. For instance, a cup of lightweight food, such as puffed rice or popcorn, weighs about one ounce, and eight ounces of the same product would fill many cups. Naturally, you can convert a similar unit of measure into a smaller or larger amount. The following table may be useful in making such conversions.

Equivalents by Capacity
(all measures level)
1 quart = 4 cups
1 cup = 8 fluid ounces
= ½ pint
= 16 tablespoons
2 tablespoons = 1 fluid ounce
1 tablespoon = 3 teaspoons

Equivalents by Weight

1 pound = 16 ounces
3.57 ounces = 100 grams
1 ounce = 28.35 grams

All the material contained in *The Complete Book of Food Counts* is based on information from the United States government, from producers and processors of brand-name foods, and from fast-food chains. The data contained herein are the most complete and accurate information available as this book goes to press. Please bear in mind that the food industry often changes recipes and sizes and may discontinue a product or add new ones. In the future I will revise and update this book to keep you completely informed.

Good luck and good dieting.

CORINNE T. NETZER

Abbreviations in this book

cal. calories

carbo. . . . . carbohydrates

chol. . . . . cholesterol

diam. . . . . diameter

fl. . . . . fluid

gms. . . . . grams

" . . . . inch

< . . . . less than

mgs. . . . . milligrams

lb. pound

n.a. . . . . not available

oz. . . . . ounces

pkg. . . . . package

prot. . . . . protein

sod. . . . . sodium

tbsp. . . . . tablespoon

tsp. . . . . teaspoon

tr. trace

A

Food and Measure	cal.	prot. (gms)	carbo. (gms)	fat (gms)	chol. (mgs)	sod. (mgs)	fiber (gms)
Abalone:							
raw, meat only, 4 oz.	119	19.4	6.8	.9	96	341	0
Acapulco dip:							
with American cheese							
(Ortega), 1 oz. . .	60	3.7	1.1	4.6	24	172	.1
with cheddar (Ortega),							
1 oz.	64	3.9	1.2	4.9	24	106	.1
with Monterey Jack							
(Ortega), 1 oz. . .	59	3.3	1.4	4.5	15	124	.1
without cheese							
(Ortega), 1 oz. . .	8	.3	1.8	.1	0	1	.3
Acerola, fresh:							
10 cherries	2	.2	3.7	.1	0	0	.2
juice, 1 cup	51	1.0	11.6	.7	0	7	.7
A la king sauce, mix:							
(Durkee), 1.1-oz. pkg.	133	1.3	14.0	8.0	n.a.	1384	n.a.
Albacore:							
raw, meat only, 4 oz.	201	28.7	0	8.6	n.a.	45	0
canned, see "Tuna"							
Alcoholic beverages,							
see specific list-							
ings							
Ale, see "Beer, ale							
and malt liquor"							
Alewife:							
raw, meat only, 4 oz.	144	22.0	0	5.6	n.a.	n.a.	0
Alfalfa seeds,							
sprouted:							
1 cup	10	1.3	1.3	.2	0	2	.5
1 tbsp.	1	.1	.1	<.1	0	0	.1

Food and Measure	cal.	prot. (gms)	carbo. (gms)	fat (gms)	chol. (mgs)	sod. (mgs)	fiber (gms)
Allspice:							
ground (all brands), 1 tsp.	5	.1	1.4	.2	0	1	.4
Almond:							
blanched, natural *(Planters)*, 1 oz.	170	6.0	6.0	15.0	0	0	n.a.
dried:							
shelled, 4 oz. . . .	668	22.6	23.2	59.3	0	12	3.1
chopped, 1/2 cup	383	13.0	13.3	33.9	0	7	1.8
slivered, 1/2 cup	277	9.4	9.6	24.5	0	5	1.3
dry-roasted *(Planters)*, 1 oz.	170	6.0	6.0	15.0	0	0	n.a.
dry-roasted, smoked flavor *(Laura Scudder's)*, 1 oz. . . .	181	6.8	4.3	15.6	0	191	1.1
oil-roasted, 1 oz. . .	176	5.8	4.5	16.4	0	3	1.4
smoked *(Planters)*, 1 oz.	170	5.0	6.0	15.0	0	160	n.a.
Almond butter:							
raw *(Hain)*, 2 tbsp.	190	8.0	3.0	18.0	0	5	n.a.
raw, blanched *(Hain)*, 2 tbsp.	190	7.0	3.0	18.0	0	5	n.a.
toasted, blanched *(Hain)*, 2 tbsp. . .	210	8.0	3.0	19.0	0	5	n.a.
Almond meal:							
partially defatted, 1 oz.	116	11.2	8.2	5.2	0	2	.7
Almond paste:							
1 oz.	127	3.4	12.4	7.7	0	3	1.7
Amaranth:							
raw, 1 cup	7	.7	1.1	.1	0	5	.3
boiled, drained, 1 cup	28	2.8	5.4	.2	0	28	1.7
Anchovies:							
canned *(Granadaisa Brand)*, 2 oz. . . .	80	9.0	.1	5.0	n.a.	3175	n.a.
Anise seed:							
(all brands), 1 tsp.	7	.4	1.1	.3	0	tr.	.3

Food and Measure	cal.	prot. (gms)	carbo. (gms)	fat (gms)	chol. (mgs)	sod. (mgs)	fiber (gms)
Apple:							
fresh:							
whole, 1 apple (2¾" diam.). . .	81	.3	21.1	.5	0	1	1.1
pared, 1 apple (2¾" diam.) . .	72	.2	19.0	.4	0	0	.7
canned:							
sliced *(Comstock)*, 4 oz.	40	0	10.0	0	0	10	.7
sliced *(White House)*, 4 oz.	54	0	14.0	0	0	10	n.a.
spiced rings *(Comstock)*, 1 ring . .	20	0	5.0	0	0	5	<.1
dehydrated (sulphured):							
uncooked, 1 cup	208	.8	56.1	.4	0	74	2.5
cooked, 1 cup . .	142	.5	38.4	.2	0	51	1.7
dried, uncooked *(Del Monte)*, 2 oz. . . .	140	0	37.0	0	0	<50	n.a.
dried (sulphured), uncooked, 10 rings	155	.6	42.2	.2	0	56	1.8
Apple, escalloped, frozen:							
(Stouffer's), 4 oz. . .	140	0	28.0	3.0	n.a.	20	n.a.
Apple butter:							
(Bama), 2 tsp. . . .	25	0	6.0	0	0	5	n.a.
natural or cider *(Smucker's)*, 2 tsp.	25	0	6.0	0	0	0	n.a.
Apple cider:							
(Mott's), 6 fl. oz. . .	80	0	20.0	0	0	0	n.a.
Apple criss-cross pastry, frozen:							
(Pepperidge Farm), 2-oz. piece	180	1.0	24.0	9.0	n.a.	140	n.a.
Apple croissant, frozen:							
(Sara Lee Le Pastrie), 3.3-oz. piece. . . .	260	4.0	36.0	11.0	n.a.	400	n.a.

Food and Measure	cal.	prot. (gms)	carbo. (gms)	fat (gms)	chol. (mgs)	sod. (mgs)	fiber (gms)
Apple danish:							
(Hostess), 1 piece	360	4.0	43.0	20.0	19	410	n.a.
frozen (Sara Lee), 1.3-oz. piece	120	2.0	15.0	6.0	n.a.	120	n.a.
refrigerated (Pillsbury Best), 1 piece . .	240	3.0	33.0	11.0	n.a.	260	n.a.
Apple drink:							
(Hawaiian Punch), 6 fl. oz.	90	0	22.0	0	0	13	n.a.
(Hi-C), 6 fl. oz. . . .	94	<.1	23.0	<.1	0	15	tr.
(Hi-C Candy Apple Cooler), 6 fl. oz.	93	<.1	23.0	<.1	0	16	tr.
(Sunkist), 8.45 fl. oz.	140	0	34.0	0	0	0	n.a.
mix* (Wyler's Crystals), 8 fl. oz. . . .	90	0	22.0	0	0	25	n.a.
Apple dumpling, frozen:							
(Pepperidge Farm), 3-oz. piece	260	2.0	33.0	14.0	n.a.	240	n.a.
Apple fritter, frozen:							
(Mrs. Paul's), 2 fritters	280	3.0	33.0	15.0	n.a.	770	n.a.
Apple juice:							
(Kraft Pure 100%), 6 fl. oz.	80	0	20.0	0	0	5	n.a.
(Minute Maid), 6 fl. oz.	90	<1.0	23.0	<1.0	0	16	tr.
(Mott's Juice Pak Aseptic), 8.5 fl. oz.	110	0	27.0	0	0	20	n.a.
(Mott's Natural/Clear), 6 fl. oz.	80	0	20.0	0	0	0	n.a.
(Ocean Spray), 8 fl. oz.	126	<1.0	30.0	<1.0	0	18	n.a.
(Red Cheek), 8 fl. oz.	111	.2	28.3	tr.	0	2	.2
(S&W), 6 fl. oz. . . .	85	0	20.0	0	0	5	n.a.
(Seneca), 6 fl. oz.	90	0	22.0	0	0	10	n.a.
(Thank You), 6 fl. oz.	90	0	21.0	0	0	35	0
(Tree Top), 6 fl. oz.	90	0	22.0	0	0	10	n.a.
(Tropicana), 6 fl. oz.	87	.3	21.3	.2	0	13	n.a.

* Prepared according to package directions

Food and Measure	cal.	prot. (gms)	carbo. (gms)	fat (gms)	chol. (mgs)	sod. (mgs)	fiber (gms)
(White House), 6 fl. oz.	87	0	22.0	0	0	5	n.a.
frozen*:							
(A&P), 6 fl. oz. . . .	90	4.0	22.0	<1.0	0	0	n.a.
(Minute Maid), 6 fl. oz.	90	<1.0	23.0	<1.0	0	2	tr.
(Seneca), 6 fl. oz.	90	0	22.0	0	0	10	n.a.
Apple fruit square, frozen:							
(Pepperidge Farm), 1 piece	230	1.0	27.0	12.0	n.a.	180	n.a.
Apple roll or bar:							
(Flavor Tree), .75-oz. roll	80	0	18.0	<1.0	0	15	n.a.
(Fruit Roll-Ups), 1/2-oz. roll	50	0	12.0	<1.0	0	5	n.a.
(Nature's Choice), 1/2-oz. bar	50	0	11.0	0	0	0	n.a.
(Pocket Fruit), .7-oz. bar	70	0	17.0	0	0	n.a.	n.a.
(Stretch Island Leather), 1/2-oz. bar	40	0	10.0	0	0	<1	n.a.
Apple sticks, breaded, fried, frozen:							
(Farm Rich), 4 oz.	260	2.0	44.0	8.0	n.a.	565	n.a.
(Chill Ripe/Gold King Fries), 4 oz.	261	2.8	43.3	6.2	5	397	n.a.
Apple strudel, frozen:							
(Pepperidge Farm), 3 oz.	240	1.0	35.0	11.0	n.a.	220	n.a.
Apple turnover:							
frozen *(Pepperidge Farm)*, 1 piece . .	310	3.0	35.0	17.0	n.a.	220	n.a.
refrigerated *(Pillsbury)*, 1 piece	170	2.0	23.0	8.0	n.a.	320	n.a.
Apple-cranberry drink:							
(Hi-C), 6 fl. oz. . . .	83	<.1	21.0	<.1	0	15	tr.

* Prepared according to package directions

Food and Measure	cal.	prot. (gms)	carbo. (gms)	fat (gms)	chol. (mgs)	sod. (mgs)	fiber (gms)
Apple-cranberry juice:							
(Mott's 100%), 6 fl. oz.	80	0	20.0	0	0	16	n.a.
(Mott's Juice Pak Aseptic), 8.5 fl. oz.	110	0	27.0	0	0	25	n.a.
Apple-grape juice:							
(Mott's 100%), 6 fl. oz.	84	0	20.0	0	0	15	.7
(Mott's Juice Pak Aseptic), 8.5 fl. oz.	120	0	30.0	0	0	25	n.a.
(Welch's Orchard), 6 fl. oz.	100	0	24.0	0	0	15	n.a.
frozen* (Welch's Orchard), 6 fl. oz.	100	0	24.0	0	0	5	n.a.
Apple-raspberry juice:							
(Mott's Juice Pak Aseptic), 8.5 fl. oz.	110	0	27.0	0	0	65	n.a.
Applesauce, canned or in jars:							
unsweetened, 1 cup	106	.4	27.6	.1	0	5	1.3
(A&P), 1/2 cup . . .	110	<1.0	25.0	<1.0	0	15	n.a.
(A&P Natural Style), 1/2 cup	50	<1.0	13.0	<1.0	0	0	n.a.
(Del Monte), 1/2 cup	90	0	24.0	0	0	<5	n.a.
(Del Monte Lite), 1/2 cup	50	0	13.0	0	0	<10	n.a.
(Mott's/Mott's Chunky), 4 oz. . .	119	0	29.0	0	0	0	n.a.
(Mott's Natural), 4 oz.	53	0	12.0	0	0	0	n.a.
(S&W), 1/2 cup . . .	90	0	24.0	0	0	10	n.a.
(S&W Unsweetened), 1/2 cup	55	0	14.0	0	0	5	n.a.
(Seneca), 1/2 cup . .	90	0	22.0	0	0	20	n.a.
(Seneca Natural Style), 1/2 cup . .	50	0	12.0	0	0	20	n.a.

* Prepared according to package directions

Food and Measure	cal.	prot. (gms)	carbo. (gms)	fat (gms)	chol. (mgs)	sod. (mgs)	fiber (gms)
(Stokely's Finest), 1/2 cup	90	0	23.0	0	0	30	n.a.
(Stokely's Finest No Salt or Sugar), 1/2 cup	45	0	12.0	0	0	5	n.a.
(Thank You), 1/2 cup	90	0	22.0	0	0	25	0
(Thank You Un-sweetened), 1/2 cup	60	0	13.0	0	0	15	0
(White House Regular or Chunky), 1/2 cup	80	0	22.0	0	0	10	n.a.
(White House Natural Style), 1/2 cup . .	50	0	13.0	0	0	5	n.a.
cinnamon *(Mott's)*, 4 oz.	119	0	29.0	0	0	0	n.a.
cinnamon, golden deli-cious, or McIntosh *(Seneca)*, 1/2 cup	90	0	22.0	0	0	20	n.a.
Apricot:							
fresh:							
3 apricots, about 12 per lb.	51	1.5	11.8	.4	0	1	.6
pitted, halves, 1 cup	74	2.2	17.2	.6	0	1	.9
candied, 1 oz. . . .	96	.2	24.5	.1	0	n.a.	.2
canned, 1/2 cup:							
whole, peeled *(Del Monte)*	100	0	27.0	0	0	<10	n.a.
halves *(Del Monte)*	100	0	26.0	0	0	<10	n.a.
halves *(Del Monte Lite)*	60	0	16.0	0	0	<10	n.a.
halves *(Stokely's Finest)*	80	0	20.0	0	0	5	n.a.
canned, in heavy syrup with liquid, 1/2 cup:							
unpeeled *(A&P)*	110	<1.0	28.0	<1.0	0	15	n.a.
whole, peeled *(S&W)*	100	0	26.0	0	0	15	n.a.
halves, unpeeled *(S&W)*	110	0	28.0	0	0	15	n.a.

Food and Measure	cal.	prot. (gms)	carbo. (gms)	fat (gms)	chol. (mgs)	sod. (mgs)	fiber (gms)
Apricot *(cont.)*							
dehydrated:							
uncooked, 1 cup	381	5.8	98.6	.7	0	15	4.7
cooked, 1 cup ..	314	4.8	81.2	.6	0	13	3.9
dried:							
uncooked, halves, 1							
cup	310	4.8	80.3	.6	0	13	3.8
uncooked, 10							
halves	83	1.3	21.6	.2	0	3	1.0
uncooked, diced							
(Del Monte), 2 oz.	140	2.0	35.0	0	0	< 10	n.a.
frozen, sweetened, 1							
cup	237	1.7	60.7	.2	0	10	1.5
Apricot nectar,							
canned:							
(Del Monte), 6 fl. oz.	100	1.0	26.0	0	0	< 10	n.a.
(S&W), 6 fl. oz. ...	120	1.0	29.0	0	0	10	n.a.
Apricot roll or bar:							
(Fruit Roll-Ups), 1/2-oz.							
roll	50	0	12.0	< 1.0	0	5	n.a.
(Nature's Choice), 1/2-							
oz.	50	0	11.0	0	0	0	n.a.
(Pocket Fruit), .7-oz.							
bar	60	0	16.0	0	0	n.a.	n.a.
(Stretch Island							
Leather), 1/2 oz.	45	1.0	10.0	0	0	< 1	n.a.
Apricot-pineapple							
nectar, canned:							
(S&W), 6 fl. oz. ...	120	1.0	29.0	0	0	10	n.a.
Arby's:							
sandwiches, 1 serving:							
bac 'n cheddar							
deluxe, 8 oz. ...	561	28.0	36.0	34.0	78	1385	n.a.
beef 'n cheddar, 6.7							
oz.	490	24.0	51.0	21.0	51	1520	n.a.
chicken breast, 7.4							
oz.	592	28.0	56.0	27.0	57	1340	n.a.
hot ham 'n cheese,							
5.7 oz.	353	26.0	33.0	13.0	50	1655	n.a.

Food and Measure	cal.	prot. (gms)	carbo. (gms)	fat (gms)	chol. (mgs)	sod. (mgs)	fiber (gms)
roast beef, regular, 5.2 oz.	353	22.0	32.0	15.0	39	590	n.a.
roast beef, junior, 3 oz.	218	12.0	22.0	8.0	20	345	n.a.
roast beef, king, 6.7 oz.	467	27.0	44.0	19.0	49	765	n.a.
roast beef, super, 8.3 oz.	501	25.0	50.0	22.0	40	800	n.a.
turkey deluxe, 7 oz.	375	24.0	32.0	17.0	39	850	n.a.
potato, baked, plain, 11-oz. serving. . .	290	8.0	66.0	.5	0	12	n.a.
potato cakes, 3-oz. serving	201	2.0	22.0	14.0	13	425	n.a.
potato, superstuffed, 1 serving:							
broccoli and cheddar, 12 oz. . . .	541	13.0	72.0	22.0	24	475	n.a.
deluxe, 11 oz. . .	648	18.0	59.0	38.0	72	475	n.a.
mushroom and cheese, 10.5 oz.	506	16.0	61.0	22.0	21	635	n.a.
taco, 15 oz.	619	23.0	73.0	27.0	145	1065	n.a.
French fries, 2.5-oz. serving	211	2.0	33.0	8.0	6	30	n.a.
shakes, 1 serving:							
chocolate, 10.6 oz.	384	9.0	62.0	11.0	32	300	n.a.
jamocha, 10.8 oz.	424	8.0	76.0	10.0	31	280	n.a.
vanilla, 8.8.	295	8.0	44.0	10.0	30	245	n.a.
Arrowhead, fresh:							
raw, 1 medium corm (25/8″ diam.) . . .	12	.6	2.4	<.1	0	3	.1
boiled, drained, 1 medium corm	9	.5	1.9	<.1	0	2	.2
Arthur Treacher's:							
chicken, 2 pieces or 5.2 oz.	369	27.1	16.5	21.6	<65	495	n.a.
chicken sandwich, 5.5-oz. piece	413	16.2	44.0	19.2	32	708	n.a.
chips, 4-oz. serving	276	4.0	34.9	13.2	<1	39	n.a.
chowder, 6-oz. serving	112	4.6	11.2	5.4	9	835	n.a.

Food and Measure	cal.	prot. (gms)	carbo. (gms)	fat (gms)	chol. (mgs)	sod. (mgs)	fiber (gms)
Arthur Treacher's *(cont.)*							
cod, bake 'n broil, 5-oz. serving	245	19.6	9.7	14.2	n.a.	144	n.a.
cole slaw, 3-oz. serving	123	1.0	11.1	8.2	<6	266	n.a.
fish, 2 pieces or 5.2 oz.	355	19.2	25.4	19.8	<56	450	n.a.
fish sandwich, 5.5-oz. piece	440	16.4	39.4	24.0	<42	836	n.a.
Krunch Pup, 2-oz. piece	203	5.4	12.0	14.8	25	446	n.a.
Lemon Luv, 3-oz. piece	276	2.6	35.1	13.9	<1	314	n.a.
shrimp, 7 pieces or 4 oz.	381	13.1	27.2	24.4	93	538	n.a.
Artichoke, globe or French:							
fresh:							
raw, 1 large, 14.3 oz.	83	4.3	19.3	.3	0	130	1.7
raw, 1 medium, 11.3 oz.	65	3.4	15.3	.2	0	102	1.4
boiled, drained, 1 medium	53	2.8	12.4	.2	0	79	1.1
boiled, drained, hearts, 1/2 cup	37	1.9	8.7	.1	0	55	.8
canned, hearts, marinated *(S&W)*, 3.5 oz.	225	2.0	6.0	26.0	0	15	n.a.
frozen, hearts *(Birds Eye* Deluxe), 3 oz.	30	2.0	7.0	0	0	40	.8
Artichoke, Jerusalem, see "Jerusalem artichoke"							
Asparagus:							
fresh:							
raw, whole or cut, 1 lb.	54	7.3	8.9	.5	0	5	2.0
raw, cut, 1 cup . .	30	4.1	5.0	.3	0	2	1.1

Food and Measure	cal.	prot. (gms)	carbo. (gms)	fat (gms)	chol. (mgs)	sod. (mgs)	fiber (gms)
boiled, drained, 4 medium	15	1.6	2.6	.2	0	3	.5
boiled, drained, cut, 1 cup	44	4.7	7.9	.6	0	8	1.5
canned, 1/2 cup:							
(Stokely's Finest)	20	2.0	3.0	0	0	380	n.a.
spears (Le Sueur)	30	3.0	4.0	0	0	390	n.a.
spears (S&W) . .	18	2.0	3.0	0	0	320	n.a.
spears, colossal (S&W)	20	2.0	4.0	0	0	320	n.a.
spears and tips (Del Monte)	20	2.0	3.0	0	0	355	n.a.
green tipped (Del Monte)	20	2.0	3.0	0	0	355	n.a.
cuts (Green Giant)	20	3.0	2.0	0	0	450	n.a.
cuts (Joan of Arc)	30	3.0	4.0	<1.0	0	340	n.a.
frozen, 3.3 oz.:							
whole or cut (Frosty Acres)	25	3.0	4.0	0	0	<7	1.0
spears (Birds Eye)	25	3.0	4.0	0	0	0	.7
cuts (Birds Eye)	25	3.0	4.0	0	0	0	.8
Asparagus with mornay sauce in pastry:							
frozen (Pepperidge Farm), 1 piece . .	240	5.0	19.0	16.0	n.a.	250	n.a.
Au jus gravy:							
canned (Franco-American), 2 oz.	5	0	1.0	0	0	290	n.a.
mix:							
(Durkee), 1-oz. pkg.	62	3.7	13.0	.3	0	1826	n.a.
(Durkee Roastin' Bag), 1-oz. pkg.	64	.5	14.0	1.0	0	2628	n.a.
(French's), 1/4 cup*	10	0	2.0	0	0	260	n.a.
Avocado, fresh:							
California:							
8 oz. or 1 average	306	3.6	12.0	30.0	0	21	3.7

* Prepared according to package directions

Food and Measure	cal.	prot. (gms)	carbo. (gms)	fat (gms)	chol. (mgs)	sod. (mgs)	fiber (gms)
Avocado, California *(cont.)*							
puree, 1 cup . . .	407	4.8	15.9	39.9	0	28	4.9
Florida:							
whole, 1 lb. or 1 average	339	4.8	27.1	27.0	0	14	6.4
puree, 1 cup . . .	257	3.7	20.5	20.4	0	11	4.9
Avocado dip, see "Guacamole dip"							

B

Food and Measure	cal.	prot. (gms)	carbo. (gms)	fat (gms)	chol. (mgs)	sod. (mgs)	fiber (gms)
Bacon, cooked:							
4.48 oz. (yield from 1 lb. raw)	732	38.7	.8	62.5	107	2026	0
(Armour Star), .3-oz. slice	38	2.5	<.1	3.1	6	185	0
(Armour Lower Salt), .3-oz. slice	38	2.5	<.1	3.2	6	127	0
(Armour Star), .2-oz. slice	29	1.9	<.1	2.4	5	147	0
(Armour Lower Salt), .2-oz. slice	29	1.9	<.1	2.5	5	100	0
(Hormel Black Label), 2 slices	60	4.0	0	5.0	n.a.	298	0
(Hormel Range Brand), 2 slices	110	6.0	0	9.0	n.a.	392	0
(Hormel Red Label), 3 slices	110	6.0	0	10.0	n.a.	n.a.	0
(Oscar Mayer), 1/5-oz. slice	35	1.7	.1	3.1	5	115	0
(Oscar Mayer Center Cut), 1/6-oz. slice	21	1.2	.1	1.7	4	83	0
thick sliced (Oscar Mayer), 1/4 oz. . .	64	3.0	.2	1.0	10	208	0
Bacon, Canadian, cooked:							
grilled, 2 slices (6 per 6-oz. pkg.)	86	11.3	.6	3.9	27	719	0
(Armour 1877), 2 oz.	80	10.0	1.0	4.0	40	850	0
(Eckrich Calorie Watcher), 1 oz. . .	35	6.0	1.0	1.0	n.a.	460	0
(Hormel), 1 oz. . . .	45	6.0	0	2.0	n.a.	315	0

Food and Measure	cal.	prot. (gms)	carbo. (gms)	fat (gms)	chol. (mgs)	sod. (mgs)	fiber (gms)
Bacon, Canadian *(cont.)*							
(Jones Dairy Farm), 1 oz.	37	6.4	tr.	1.4	n.a.	290	0
(Light & Lean), 2 slices	35	6.0	0	1.0	n.a.	n.a.	0
(Oscar Mayer), 1-oz. slice	35	5.6	.1	1.4	12	391	0
Bacon, substitute, cooked:							
beef:							
(Oscar Mayer Breakfast Strips), 2/5-oz. strip . . .	46	2.9	.2	3.8	13	182	0
(Sizzlean/Fire-brand), 2 strips	50	4.0	<1.0	4.0	15	260	0
pork:							
(Oscar Mayer Breakfast Strips), 2/5-oz. strip . . .	52	2.8	.1	4.5	14	196	0
(Sizzlean), 2 strips	70	4.0	0	6.0	20	380	n.a.
Bacon bits:							
(Bac*Os), 1 tbsp. . .	30	3.0	2.0	1.0	0	130	n.a.
(Durkee), 1 tsp. . . .	8	.7	.5	.4	0	229	n.a.
real bacon:							
(Hormel), 1 tbsp.	30	3.0	0	2.0	n.a.	313	n.a.
(Oscar Mayer), 1/4 oz.	21	2.6	.2	1.0	6	181	0
Bacon chips:							
(Durkee), 1 tbsp. . .	44	3.0	4.0	2.0	n.a.	279	n.a.
Bacon and horserad-ish dip:							
(Kraft), 2 tbsp. . . .	60	1.0	3.0	5.0	0	200	n.a.
(Kraft Premium), 1 oz.	50	1.0	2.0	4.0	10	250	n.a.
Bacon and onion dip:							
(Nalley), 1 oz.	113	5.7	1.1	11.9	25	359	n.a.
Bacon-onion season-ing:							
(Lawry's), 1 tsp. . .	10	.5	1.5	.2	n.a.	275	<.1

Food and Measure	cal.	prot. (gms)	carbo. (gms)	fat (gms)	chol. (mgs)	sod. (mgs)	fiber (gms)
Bagels, frozen, 1 piece:							
plain:							
(Lender's), 2 oz.	150	6.0	30.0	1.0	0	320	n.a.
(Lender's Bagelettes), .9 oz. . .	70	3.0	13.0	<1.0	0	170	n.a.
(Sara Lee), 3 oz.	230	9.0	45.0	1.0	n.a.	500	n.a.
cinnamon and raisin (Sara Lee), 3 oz.	240	8.0	47.0	2.0	n.a.	260	n.a.
egg:							
(Lender's), 2 oz.	150	7.0	29.0	1.0	5	360	n.a.
(Sara Lee), 3 oz.	240	9.0	46.0	2.0	n.a.	390	n.a.
garlic (Lender's), 2 oz.	160	6.0	32.0	1.0	0	340	n.a.
onion:							
(Lender's), 2 oz.	160	7.0	31.0	1.0	0	290	.1
(Lender's Bagelettes), .9 oz. . .	70	3.0	14.0	<1.0	0	135	<.1
(Sara Lee), 3 oz.	220	9.0	44.0	1.0	n.a.	560	n.a.
poppy seed:							
(Lender's), 2 oz.	160	7.0	29.0	1.0	0	370	n.a.
(Sara Lee), 3 oz.	230	9.0	45.0	1.0	n.a.	560	n.a.
pumpernickel (Lender's), 2 oz.	160	6.0	31.0	1.0	0	330	.3
raisin 'n honey (Lender's), 2 oz.	200	8.0	40.0	1.0	0	310	.1
raisin 'n wheat (Lender's), 2 oz.	190	6.0	39.0	1.0	0	310	.6
rye (Lender's), 2 oz.	150	6.0	30.0	1.0	0	310	n.a.
sesame seed (Lender's), 2 oz.	160	7.0	31.0	1.0	0	320	n.a.
Baking powder:							
SAS, 1 tsp.	4	tr.	.9	tr.	0	329	tr.
phosphate, 1 tsp. . . .	5	tr.	1.1	tr.	0	304	tr.
tartrate, 1 tsp. . . .	2	tr.	.5	tr.	0	204	tr.
Balsam pear, fresh:							
leafy tips:							
raw, 1 cup	14	2.5	1.6	.3	0	6	1.1
boiled, drained, 1 cup	20	2.1	3.9	.1	0	7	1.1

Food and Measure	cal.	prot. (gms)	carbo. (gms)	fat (gms)	chol. (mgs)	sod. (mgs)	fiber (gms)
Balsam pear *(cont.)*							
pods, raw:							
1 pod (9½″ × 1½″)	21	1.2	4.6	.2	0	6	1.7
½″ pieces, 1 cup	16	.9	3.4	.2	0	5	1.3
pods, boiled, drained,							
pieces, 1 cup . . .	24	1.0	5.4	.2	0	8	1.3
Bamboo shoots:							
fresh:							
cuts, 1 cup	42	4.0	7.9	.5	0	6	1.1
boiled, drained,							
pieces, 1 cup	15	1.8	2.3	.3	0	5	.8
canned, drained *(Chun King)*, 8.5 oz. . . .	65	6.3	12.5	.7	0	0	1.7
Banana:							
fresh:							
whole, 1 lb.	271	3.1	69.1	1.4	0	3	1.5
whole, 1 average (8¾″ long) . . .	105	1.2	26.7	.6	0	1	.6
mashed, 1 cup . .	207	2.3	52.7	1.1	0	2	1.1
dehydrated, 1 oz. . .	98	1.1	25.0	.5	0	1	.5
Banana, baking, see "Plantain"							
Banana, red:							
fresh, 1 average (7¼″ long)	135	1.8	.3	35.1	0	1	n.a.
Banana chips, freeze-dried:							
(Mountain House), ¼ cup	310	2.0	36.0	19.0	0	n.a.	n.a.
Banquet loaf:							
beef *(Eckrich Smorgas Pac)*, 1 slice . . .	50	2.0	1.0	4.0	n.a.	250	0
Barbados cherry, see "Acerola"							
Barbecue dip:							
(Nalley), 1 oz.	111	.6	1.1	11.9	16	414	n.a.
Barbecue loaf:							
(Armour), 1 oz. . . .	50	n.a.	n.a.	3.0	10	n.a.	0
(Eckrich Calorie Watcher), 1 oz. . .	35	4.0	1.0	2.0	n.a.	370	0

Food and Measure	cal.	prot. (gms)	carbo. (gms)	fat (gms)	chol. (mgs)	sod. (mgs)	fiber (gms)
(Oscar Mayer Bar-B-Q), 1-oz. slice . .	47	4.5	1.9	2.5	13	353	0
Barbecue sauce, in jars:							
(Chris' & Pitt's), 1 tbsp.	15	.2	4.0	.1	0	141	n.a.
(French's), 1 tbsp.	14	0	3.0	0	0	250	n.a.
(French's Dip'Um), 2 tbsp.	45	1.0	10.0	0	0	390	n.a.
(Heinz Thick and Rich), 1 tbsp. . . .	20	0	5.0	0	0	230	n.a.
(Hunt's All Natural Original), 1 tbsp.	20	0	5.0	0	0	200	n.a.
(Kraft), 2 tbsp. . . .	40	0	9.0	1.0	0	510	n.a.
(Kraft Thick'n Spicy), 2 tbsp.	50	0	11.0	1.0	0	510	n.a.
(Open Pit), 1 tbsp.	25	0	6.0	0	0	250	.1
(Open Pit Hot 'n Tangy), 1 tbsp. . .	25	0	5.0	0	0	210	.1
(Open Pit Sweet 'n Tangy), 1 tbsp. . .	25	0	6.0	0	0	190	tr.
chunky:							
(Heinz Thick and Rich), 1 tbsp. . .	20	0	5.0	0	0	230	n.a.
(Kraft Thick'n Spicy), 2 tbsp.	50	0	12.0	1.0	0	500	n.a.
garlic flavored *(Kraft)*, 2 tbsp.	40	0	9.0	0	0	530	n.a.
hickory:							
(Heinz Thick and Rich), 1 tbsp. . .	20	0	5.0	0	0	220	n.a.
(Hunt's All Natural), 1 tbsp.	25	0	6.0	0	0	200	n.a.
(Kraft), 2 tbsp. . .	40	0	9.0	1.0	0	510	n.a.
(Kraft Thick'n Spicy), 2 tbsp.	50	0	11.0	1.0	0	510	n.a.
hickory, with onion *(Kraft)*, 2 tbsp. . .	50	0	10.0	1.0	0	420	n.a.
honey *(Kraft* Thick'n Spicy), 2 tbsp. . .	60	0	13.0	1.0	0	380	n.a.

Food and Measure	cal.	prot. (gms)	carbo. (gms)	fat (gms)	chol. (mgs)	sod. (mgs)	fiber (gms)
Barbecue sauce *(cont.)*							
hot:							
(Heinz Thick and Rich), 1 tbsp.	20	0	5.0	0	0	220	n.a.
(Kraft), 2 tbsp. . .	40	0	8.0	1.0	0	630	n.a.
hot hickory *(Kraft),* 2 tbsp.	40	0	8.0	1.0	0	460	n.a.
mushroom *(Heinz* Thick and Rich), 1 tbsp.	20	0	5.0	0	0	220	n.a.
onion *(Heinz* Thick and Rich), 1 tbsp.	20	0	5.0	0	0	200	n.a.
onion bits *(Kraft),* 2 tbsp.	50	0	11.0	1.0	0	420	n.a.
smoky *(French's),* 1 tbsp.	14	0	3.0	0	0	280	n.a.
Western *(Sauceworks),* 2 tbsp.	50	0	11.0	1.0	0	510	n.a.
Barley, pearled:							
light, uncooked, 8 oz.	791	18.6	178.7	2.3	0	7	1.1
pot or scotch, un-cooked, 8 oz. . . .	789	21.7	175.1	2.5	0	n.a.	2.0
medium or quick *(Quaker Scotch Brand)* 1/4 cup . .	172	5.5	36.3	.5	0	5	.4
Barracuda, Pacific:							
raw, meat only, 4 oz.	128	23.8	0	2.9	n.a.	n.a.	0
Basil leaves:							
ground (all brands), 1 tsp.	4	.2	.9	.1	0	tr.	.3
Baskin-Robbins:							
ice, 1 junior scoop (2.5 oz.):							
daiquiri	84	0	20.9	0	n.a.	11	n.a.
pineapple	94	.6	22.8	<.1	n.a.	83	n.a.
ice cream, 1 junior scoop (2.5 oz.):							
butter pecan . . .	136	4.0	16.2	10.2	n.a.	81	n.a.

Food and Measure	cal.	prot. (gms)	carbo. (gms)	fat (gms)	chol. (mgs)	sod. (mgs)	fiber (gms)
chocolate	165	2.8	20.4	7.9	n.a.	80	n.a.
chocolate fudge	178	2.7	21.3	9.1	n.a.	122	n.a.
chocolate mint . .	162	3.0	16.7	9.2	n.a.	60	n.a.
chocolate mousse royale	183	3.8	22.7	8.5	n.a.	94	n.a.
jamoca	146	2.8	15.8	8.0	n.a.	64	n.a.
pralines'n cream	177	2.4	23.7	8.2	n.a.	166	n.a.
rocky road	182	3.0	26.7	7.0	n.a.	77	n.a.
strawberry	141	7.7	15.6	6.0	n.a.	68	n.a.
vanilla	147	2.6	15.6	8.2	n.a.	57	n.a.
vanilla, French . .	181	2.9	15.9	11.8	n.a.	60	n.a.
ice cream cone, 1 cone:							
cake	19	.5	3.7	.3	n.a.	26	n.a.
sugar	57	1.3	10.7	1.0	n.a.	45	n.a.
sherbet, 1 junior scoop (2.5 oz.):							
orange	99	1.6	20.9	1.5	n.a.	29	n.a.
raspberry sorbet	134	0	34.2	0	0	42	n.a.
Bass, fresh, raw, meat only:							
sea, black, 4 oz. . .	105	21.8	0	1.4	n.a.	n.a.	0
sea, white, 4 oz. . .	109	24.3	0	.6	n.a.	n.a.	0
smallmouth and largemouth, 4 oz.	129	21.4	0	4.2	77	79	0
striped, 4 oz.	110	20.1	0	2.6	91	78	0
Bass, sea, entree, in lemon butter:							
frozen *(Certi-Fresh),* 9 oz.	280	28.0	12.0	14.0	n.a.	n.a.	n.a.
Bay leaves:							
crumbled (all brands), 1 tsp.	2	.1	.5	.1	0	tr.	.2
Bean curd, see "Soybean curd"							
Bean dip:							
hot *(Hain),* 4 tbsp.	100	7.0	6.0	5.0	0	n.a.	n.a.
jalapeño bean, see "Jalapeño dip"							

Food and Measure	cal.	prot. (gms)	carbo. (gms)	fat (gms)	chol. (mgs)	sod. (mgs)	fiber (gms)
Bean dip *(cont.)*							
onion *(Hain)*, 4 tbsp.	90	5.0	5.0	6.0	0	n.a.	n.a.
Bean flour:							
lima, 1 oz.	97	6.1	17.9	.4	0	n.a.	.6
Bean salad, canned, ½ cup:							
four bean *(Joan of Arc)*	120	2.0	26.0	<1.0	0	850	n.a.
green bean, German *(Joan of Arc)* . . .	90	2.0	15.0	2.0	0	730	n.a.
marinated *(S&W)* . .	90	4.0	17.0	1.0	0	730	n.a.
three bean:							
(Green Giant) . .	80	2.0	18.0	<1.0	0	540	n.a.
(Joan of Arc) . . .	90	2.0	20.0	<1.0	0	920	n.a.
Bean sprouts:							
kidney:							
mature seeds, raw, 1 cup	53	7.7	7.5	.9	0	n.a.	n.a.
mature seeds, boiled, drained, 4 oz.	37	5.5	5.4	.7	0	n.a.	n.a.
mung:							
raw, 1 cup	32	3.2	6.2	.2	0	6	.8
boiled, drained, 1 cup	26	2.5	5.2	.1	0	12	.6
navy:							
mature seeds, raw, 1 cup	70	6.4	13.6	.7	0	n.a.	2.6
boiled, drained, 4 oz.	88	8.0	17.0	.9	0	n.a.	3.3
pinto:							
mature seeds, raw, 4 oz.	70	6.0	13.2	1.0	0	174	3.1
mature seeds, boiled, drained, 4 oz.	25	2.1	4.6	.4	0	58	1.1
soy:							
raw, 1 cup	90	9.2	7.8	4.7	0	10	1.6
steamed, 1 cup	76	8.0	6.1	4.2	0	10	1.8

Food and Measure	cal.	prot. (gms)	carbo. (gms)	fat (gms)	chol. (mgs)	sod. (mgs)	fiber (gms)
Bean sprouts, canned:							
drained *(Chun King)*, 28-oz. can	222	25.4	41.3	1.6	0	32	5.6
Beans and franks dinner, frozen:							
(Banquet American Favorites), 10¼ oz.	500	19.0	64.0	19.0	n.a.	1377	n.a.
Beans, baked, canned:							
(Campbell's Home Style), 8 oz. . . .	270	11.0	48.0	4.0	n.a.	1130	n.a.
(Campbell's Old Fashioned), 8 oz. . . .	270	11.0	49.0	3.0	n.a.	1160	n.a.
(Grandma Brown's Home Baked), 8 oz.	289	14.3	54.1	1.7	n.a.	n.a.	n.a.
(S&W Brick Oven), ½ cup	160	7.0	28.0	2.0	n.a.	560	n.a.
and bacon *(Hormel Short Order)*, 7½ oz.	330	16.0	40.0	12.0	n.a.	813	n.a.
barbecue *(B&M)*, 8 oz.	310	15.0	48.0	6.0	n.a.	1000	n.a.
brown sugar *(Van Camp's)*, 1 cup . .	284	11.6	47.8	5.1	n.a.	692	3.2
and franks:							
(Campbell's), 7⅞ oz.	360	14.0	43.0	14.0	n.a.	1140	n.a.
(Heinz), 7¾ oz.	330	14.0	34.0	15.0	n.a.	905	n.a.
(Nalley), 3½ oz.	130	6.0	15.0	5.0	5	325	n.a.
(Van Camp's Beanee Weenee), 1 cup	326	15.2	31.7	15.4	n.a.	990	2.7
and ham *(Hormel Short Order)*, 7½ oz.	360	16.0	32.0	18.0	n.a.	1182	n.a.
kidney, red *(B&M)*, 8 oz.	326	15.0	50.0	7.0	n.a.	620	n.a.
maple sugar *(S&W)*, ½ cup	150	6.0	28.0	1.0	0	586	n.a.

Food and Measure	cal.	prot. (gms)	carbo. (gms)	fat (gms)	chol. (mgs)	sod. (mgs)	fiber (gms)
Beans, baked *(cont.)*							
pea, small *(B&M)*, 8 oz.	330	16.0	49.0	8.0	n.a.	770	n.a.
and pork:							
(A&P), 1/2 cup or 4.6 oz.	150	7.0	25.0	2.0	n.a.	440	n.a.
(Campbell's), 8 oz.	240	9.0	42.0	3.0	n.a.	820	n.a.
(Hunt-Wesson), 4 oz.	140	6.0	26.0	1.0	n.a.	400	n.a.
(Joan of Arc), 1/2 cup	130	7.0	23.0	<1.0	n.a.	660	n.a.
(S&W), 1/2 cup	130	5.0	22.0	2.0	n.a.	135	n.a.
(Van Camp's), 1 cup	216	10.9	38.8	1.9	n.a.	1011	2.4
with tomato or molasses sauce *(Libby/ Seneca)*, 1/2 cup	140	7.0	25.0	2.0	n.a.	320	n.a.
smoked *(S&W Smokey Ranch)*, 1/2 cup	130	6.0	20.0	2.0	n.a.	569	n.a.
vegetarian:							
(A&P), 1/2 cup or 4.6 oz.	130	7.0	25.0	<1.0	0	420	n.a.
(B&M), 8 oz.	280	15.0	50.0	2.0	0	770	n.a.
(Heinz), 8 oz.	230	11.0	43.0	1.0	0	910	n.a.
(Libby/Seneca), 1/2 cup	130	7.0	25.0	1.0	0	300	n.a.
(Van Camp's), 1 cup	206	10.9	39.2	.6	0	987	2.4
western style *(Van Camp's)*, 1 cup	207	11.1	32.0	3.8	n.a.	1006	2.4
and wieners *(Hormel Short Order)*, 71/2 oz.	280	12.0	29.0	14.0	n.a.	1342	n.a.
yelloweye *(B&M)*, 8 oz.	326	15.0	50.0	7.0	n.a.	770	n.a.
Beans, barbecue, canned:							
(Campbell's Barbecue), 77/8 oz.	250	10.0	43.0	4.0	n.a.	1110	n.a.
and beef *(Nalley)*, 31/2 oz.	130	7.0	18.0	4.0	5	500	n.a.

Food and Measure	cal.	prot. (gms)	carbo. (gms)	fat (gms)	chol. (mgs)	sod. (mgs)	fiber (gms)
in sauce *(S&W* Texas Style), 1/2 cup . .	135	7.0	24.0	1.0	n.a.	550	n.a.
Beans, black turtle, canned:							
(Progresso), 8 oz.	205	14.0	37.0	1.0	0	n.a.	n.a.
Beans, black-eye, see "Black-eye peas"							
Beans, broad, see "Broad beans"							
Beans, burrito filling mix:							
canned *(Del Monte),* 1/2 cup	110	6.0	20.0	1.0	n.a.	900	n.a.
Beans, butter, see "Butterbeans"							
Beans, cannellini, see "Beans, kidney, white"							
Beans, chili:							
(Hunt's), 4 oz. . . .	100	6.0	18.0	1.0	n.a.	460	n.a.
(Joan of Arc), 1/2 cup	100	6.0	16.0	1.0	n.a.	660	n.a.
(Van Camp's Mexican Style), 1 cup . . .	210	11.4	35.8	2.4	n.a.	718	2.6
hot, canned *(A&P),* 1/2 cup	140	8.0	24.0	1.0	0	440	n.a.
in sauce:							
(Hormel), 5 oz. . .	130	6.0	19.0	3.0	n.a.	453	n.a.
(S&W), 1/2 cup . .	130	7.0	23.0	1.0	0	520	n.a.
Beans, fava:							
canned *(Progresso),* 8 oz.	180	14.0	31.0	1.0	0	n.a.	n.a.
Beans, great northern:							
dry:							
uncooked, 8 oz.	771	50.6	139.0	3.6	0	43	9.8
cooked, 8 oz. . . .	268	17.7	48.1	1.4	0	16	3.4
cooked *(A&P),* 1 cup	210	14.0	38.0	1.0	0	0	n.a.

Food and Measure	cal.	prot. (gms)	carbo. (gms)	fat (gms)	chol. (mgs)	sod. (mgs)	fibe (gms
Beans, great northern *(cont.)*							
canned *(Joan of Arc),* 1/2 cup	90	5.0	17.0	<1.0	0	420	n.a.
Beans, green:							
fresh:							
raw, 1 lb.	123	7.3	28.5	.5	0	23	4.4
boiled, drained, 1 cup	44	2.4	9.9	.4	0	4	1.8
canned, 1/2 cup:							
all cuts:							
(A&P)	20	1.0	4.0	<1.0	0	350	n.a.
(A&P No Salt Added)	20	1.0	4.0	<1.0	0	10	n.a.
(Joan of Arc) ..	25	2.0	5.0	<1.0	0	380	n.a.
(Libby/Seneca)	20	1.0	4.0	0	0	340	n.a.
(Libby/Seneca Natural)	20	1.0	4.0	0	0	10	n.a.
(S&W Blue Lake)	20	1.0	4.0	0	0	385	n.a.
(Stokely's Finest)	20	1.0	4.0	0	0	360	n.a.
(Stokely's Finest No Salt or Sugar)	20	1.0	4.0	0	0	5	0
whole or French, with liquid *(Del Monte)*	20	1.0	4.0	0	0	355	n.a.
whole, stringless *(S&W Fancy)* ..	20	1.0	4.0	0	0	385	n.a.
cut *(Green Giant)*	20	1.0	3.0	<1.0	0	310	n.a.
cut, kitchen style *(Green Giant)*	20	2.0	3.0	0	0	260	n.a.
dilled *(S&W)* ...	60	1.0	15.0	0	0	385	n.a.
French cut *(Green Giant)*	18	1.0	3.0	0	0	270	n.a.
Italian cut, with liquid *(Del Monte)*	24	1.0	6.0	0	0	355	n.a.
seasoned, French cut, with liquid *(Del Monte)* ..	20	1.0	4.0	0	0	355	n.a.
freeze-dried *(Mountain House)*	35	1.0	6.0	0	0	n.a.	n.a.

Food and Measure	cal.	prot. (gms)	carbo. (gms)	fat (gms)	chol. (mgs)	sod. (mgs)	fiber (gms)
frozen:							
(Green Giant), 1/2 cup	20	1.0	4.0	0	0	10	n.a.
whole (Birds Eye Deluxe), 3 oz.	25	1.0	5.0	0	0	0	.8
cut (A&P), 3 oz.	25	1.0	6.0	<1.0	0	0	n.a.
cut (Birds Eye), 3 oz.	25	1.0	6.0	0	0	0	.9
cut (Frosty Acres), 3 oz.	25	1.0	6.0	0	0	3	n.a.
cut (Green Giant Harvest Fresh), 1/2 cup	20	1.0	4.0	0	0	150	n.a.
cut (Southland), 3.2 oz.	25	1.0	6.0	0	0	0	n.a.
French cut (A&P), 3 oz.	25	1.0	6.0	<1.0	0	3	n.a.
French cut (Birds Eye), 3 oz. . . .	25	1.0	6.0	0	0	0	1.0
French cut (Frosty Acres), 3 oz. . .	25	1.0	6.0	0	0	3	n.a.
French cut (Southland), 3.2 oz. . .	25	1.0	6.0	0	0	0	n.a.
Italian cut (Birds Eye), 3 oz. . . .	30	2.0	7.0	0	0	0	.9
Italian cut (Frosty Acres), 3 oz. . .	30	2.0	7.0	0	0	3	n.a.
boiled, drained, 1 cup	36	1.8	8.3	.2	0	17	1.4
in butter sauce, cut (Green Giant), 1/2 cup	35	1.0	5.0	1.0	n.a.	300	n.a.
in butter sauce, French cut (Green Giant), 1/2 cup	40	1.0	6.0	1.0	n.a.	360	n.a.
Beans, green, combinations, frozen:							
and corn, carrots, and pearl onions (Birds Eye), 3.2 oz. . . .	45	2.0	10.0	0	0	15	.8

Food and Measure	cal.	prot. (gms)	carbo. (gms)	fat (gms)	chol. (mgs)	sod. (mgs)	fiber (gms)
Beans, green, combinations *(cont.)*							
and spaetzle, Bavarian style *(Birds Eye)*, 3.3 oz. . . .	110	2.0	11.0	6.0	n.a.	420	.5
French, and cauliflower, and carrots *(Birds Eye)*, 3.2 oz.	25	1.0	6.0	0	0	20	1.0
French, with toasted almonds *(Birds Eye)*, 3 oz.	50	3.0	8.0	2.0	0	340	1.0
Beans, green, and mushroom casserole:							
frozen *(Stouffer's)*, 4¾ oz.	170	3.0	12.0	12.0	n.a.	640	n.a.
Beans, green, with mushroom sauce, in pastry:							
frozen *(Pepperidge Farm)*, 1 piece . .	250	4.0	20.0	17.0	n.a.	270	n.a.
Beans, green and wax:							
canned, cut *(S&W)*, ½ cup	20	1.0	5.0	0	0	385	n.a.
Beans, kidney:							
red, dried:							
uncooked, 8 oz.	778	51.0	140.4	3.4	0	23	9.5
cooked, 8 oz. . . .	268	17.7	48.5	1.1	0	7	3.4
cooked *(A&P)*, 1 cup	230	17.0	41.0	1.0	0	5	n.a.
red, canned:							
(A&P), ½ cup . .	110	7.0	20.0	<1.0	0	440	n.a.
(Hunt's), 4 oz. . .	120	7.0	21.0	0	0	400	n.a.
(Progresso), 8 oz.	190	12.0	34.0	1.0	0	1080	n.a.
(S&W Premium), ½ cup	120	6.0	22.0	1.0	0	596	n.a.
(S&W Lite), ½ cup	120	7.0	22.0	0	0	355	n.a.
(Stokely's Finest), ½ cup	110	7.0	20.0	1.0	0	360	n.a.

Food and Measure	cal.	prot. (gms)	carbo. (gms)	fat (gms)	chol. (mgs)	sod. (mgs)	fiber (gms)
(Van Camp's New Orleans), 1 cup	178	12.1	31.0	.6	0	793	2.4
dark *(Joan of Arc)*, 1/2 cup	110	7.0	20.0	<1.0	0	340	n.a.
dark *(Van Camp's)*, 1 cup	182	11.7	32.6	.5	0	732	2.3
light *(Joan of Arc)*, 1/2 cup	90	6.0	17.0	<1.0	0	390	n.a.
light *(Van Camp's)*, 1 cup	184	11.5	33.4	.5	0	688	2.2
white, canned:							
(Progresso Cannellini), 8 oz.	180	12.0	30.0	1.0	0	717	n.a.
Beans, lima:							
dry:							
raw, in pods, 1 lb.	226	13.7	40.2	1.7	0	16	3.8
raw, shelled, 1 cup	176	10.7	31.5	1.3	0	13	3.0
boiled, drained, 8 oz.	278	15.5	53.6	.7	0	39	4.7
boiled, drained, 1 cup	208	11.6	40.2	.5	0	29	3.5
baby, cooked *(A&P)*, 1 cup	230	16.0	40.0	1.0	0	15	n.a.
large, cooked *(A&P)*, 1 cup ..	230	15.0	35.0	1.0	0	0	n.a.
canned, 1/2 cup:							
(Libby/Seneca) ..	80	5.0	15.0	0	0	230	n.a.
(Stokely's Finest, 81/2 oz.)	80	5.0	16.0	0	0	300	n.a.
(Stokely's Finest No Salt or Sugar)	80	5.0	16.0	0	0	5	n.a.
Fordhook *(Stokely's Finest)*	75	5.0	15.0	1.0	0	315	n.a.
green *(A&P)* ...	80	5.0	15.0	<1.0	0	320	n.a.
green, with liquid *(Del Monte)* ..	70	4.0	14.0	0	0	355	n.a.
green, small *(S&W* Fancy)	80	6.0	16.0	0	0	390	n.a.

Food and Measure	cal.	prot. (gms)	carbo. (gms)	fat (gms)	chol. (mgs)	sod. (mgs)	fiber (gms)
Beans, lima *(cont.)*							
frozen:							
(Green Giant), 1/2 cup	100	6.0	19.0	0	0	30	n.a.
(Green Giant Harvest Fresh), 1/2 cup	70	5.0	11.0	1.0	0	210	n.a.
baby *(A&P)*, 3.3 oz.	130	7.0	24.0	<1.0	0	130	n.a.
baby *(Birds Eye)*, 3.3 oz.	130	7.0	24.0	0	0	115	1.9
baby *(Frosty Acres)*, 3.3 oz.	130	7.0	24.0	0	0	125	2.0
baby, in butter sauce *(Green Giant)*, 1/2 cup . .	110	5.0	18.0	2.0	n.a.	460	n.a.
Fordhook, boiled, drained, 1/2 cup	85	5.2	16.0	.3	0	45	1.6
Fordhook *(A&P)*, 3.3 oz.	100	6.0	19.0	<1.0	0	70	n.a.
Fordhook *(Birds Eye)*, 3.3 oz. . .	100	6.0	19.0	0	0	100	1.8
Fordhook *(Frosty Acres)*, 3.3 oz.	100	6.0	19.0	0	0	71	2.0
Beans, lima, and ham, canned:							
(Nalley), 31/2 oz. . .	115	6.0	15.0	3.0	n.a.	345	n.a.
Beans, mung:							
dry, uncooked, 8 oz.	771	54.9	136.8	2.9	0	14	10.0
Beans, pea or navy:							
dry:							
uncooked, 8 oz.	771	50.6	139.0	3.6	0	43	9.8
cooked, 8 oz. . . .	268	17.7	48.1	1.4	0	16	3.4
cooked *(A&P Michigan #1)*, 1 cup	220	15.0	40.0	1.0	0	15	n.a.
canned *(Joan of Arc)*, 1/2 cup	100	6.0	17.0	<1.0	0	550	n.a.
Beans, pinto:							
dry, cooked *(A&P)*, 1 cup	230	17.0	42.0	1.0	0	5	n.a.

Food and Measure	cal.	prot. (gms)	carbo. (gms)	fat (gms)	chol. (mgs)	sod. (mgs)	fiber (gms)
canned:							
(Joan of Arc), 1/2 cup	100	6.0	18.0	<1.0	0	400	n.a.
(Progresso), 8 oz.	165	10.0	31.0	1.0	0	n.a.	n.a.
Beans, red, canned:							
(A&P), 1/2 cup . . .	120	7.0	23.0	<1.0	0	400	n.a.
(Van Camp's), 1 cup	194	11.5	35.6	.6	0	928	2.4
small *(Joan of Arc)*, 1/2 cup	100	5.0	19.0	<1.0	0	450	n.a.
Beans, refried:							
canned:							
(Del Monte), 1/2 cup	130	6.0	20.0	2.0	n.a.	530	n.a.
(Rosarita), 4 oz.	130	7.0	20.0	2.0	n.a.	460	n.a.
with green chilis *(Rosarita)*, 4 oz.	120	7.0	19.0	2.0	n.a.	430	n.a.
spicy *(Del Monte)*, 1/2 cup	130	6.0	20.0	2.0	n.a.	480	n.a.
spicy *(Rosarita)*, 4 oz.	120	7.0	19.0	2.0	n.a.	440	n.a.
vegetarian *(Rosarita)*, 4 oz.	120	7.0	19.0	2.0	0	430	n.a.
frozen *(Patio Boil-in-Bag)*, 4 oz.	190	8.0	23.0	7.0	n.a.	n.a.	n.a.
Beans, Roman, canned:							
(Progresso), 8 oz.	210	14.0	36.0	1.0	0	n.a.	n.a.
Beans, shelled, canned:							
(Stokely's Finest, 8 oz.), 1/2 cup . . .	35	2.0	7.0	0	0	360	n.a.
(Stokely's Finest, 16 oz.), 1/2 cup . . .	35	2.0	7.0	0	0	470	n.a.
Beans, yellow or wax:							
fresh, see "Beans, green"							
canned, 1/2 cup:							
(Joan of Arc) . . .	25	2.0	5.0	<1.0	0	330	n.a.
(Libby/Seneca) . .	20	1.0	5.0	0	0	340	n.a.

Food and Measure	cal.	prot. (gms)	carbo. (gms)	fat (gms)	chol. (mgs)	sod. (mgs)	fiber (gms)
Beans, yellow or wax, canned *(cont.)*							
(Stokely's Finest)	20	1.0	4.0	0	0	360	n.a.
(Stokely's Finest, No Salt or Sugar)	20	1.0	4.0	0	0	5	n.a.
cut *(A&P)*	20	1.0	5.0	<1.0	0	340	n.a.
golden, cut or French, with liquid *(Del Monte)* . .	20	0	4.0	0	0	355	n.a.
golden, cut *(S&W Premium)*	20	1.0	5.0	0	0	385	n.a.
frozen, cut *(Frosty Acres),* 3 oz. . . .	25	2.0	5.0	0	0	1	1.0
Beans, white:							
dry, uncooked, 8 oz.	771	50.6	139.0	3.6	0	43	9.8
Bearnaise sauce:							
dehydrated, .9-oz. packet	90	3.5	14.8	2.2	tr.	841	.1
Beaver:							
roasted, meat only, 8 oz.	281	33.1	0	15.5	n.a.	n.a.	0
Beechnuts:							
shelled, 4 oz.	656	7.0	38.0	56.8	0	n.a.	4.2
Beef, choice grade, retail trim, meat only:							
brisket, whole, braised:							
lean with fat, 4 oz.	443	26.1	0	36.8	105	69	0
lean (fat trimmed), 4 oz.	273	33.3	0	14.6	105	82	0
chuck, arm roast, braised:							
lean with fat, 4 oz.	401	30.6	0	30.1	112	67	0
lean (fat trimmed), 4 oz.	265	37.4	0	11.7	113	75	0
chuck, blade roast, braised:							
lean with fat, 4 oz.	440	28.8	0	35.2	117	71	0

Food and Measure	cal.	prot. (gms)	carbo. (gms)	fat (gms)	chol. (mgs)	sod. (mgs)	fiber (gms)
lean (fat trimmed), 4 oz.	312	35.2	0	17.9	120	81	0
flank steak, braised, lean (fat trimmed), 4 oz.	277	31.8	0	15.7	81	82	0
ground, raw:							
extra lean, 4 oz.	265	21.1	0	19.3	78	75	0
lean, 4 oz.	298	20.0	0	23.4	85	78	0
regular, 4 oz. . . .	351	18.8	0	30.0	96	77	0
ground, broiled, medium:							
extra lean, 11.9 oz., yield from 1 lb. raw	859	85.3	0	54.9	281	234	0
extra lean, 3-oz. patty	217	21.6	0	13.9	71	59	0
lean, 11.4 oz., yield from 1 lb. raw	876	79.6	0	59.4	280	248	0
lean, 3-oz. patty	231	21.0	0	15.7	74	65	0
regular, 10.7 oz., yield from 1 lb. raw	880	73.2	0	62.9	273	251	0
regular, 3-oz. patty	246	20.5	0	17.6	76	70	0
porterhouse steak, broiled:							
lean with fat, 4 oz.	339	28.5	0	24.1	94	69	0
lean (fat trimmed), 4 oz.	248	31.9	0	12.2	91	75	0
rib, whole (ribs 6–12), roasted:							
lean with fat, 4 oz.	438	24.8	0	36.8	96	71	0
lean (fat trimmed), 4 oz.	279	30.9	0	16.3	92	84	0
rib, eye, small end (ribs 10–12), broiled:							
lean with fat, 4 oz.	335	28.8	0	23.4	94	73	0
lean (fat trimmed), 4 oz.	255	31.8	0	13.2	91	78	0

Food and Measure	cal.	prot. (gms)	carbo. (gms)	fat (gms)	chol. (mgs)	sod. (mgs)	fiber (gms)
Beef *(cont.)*							
rib, large end (ribs 6–9), roasted:							
lean with fat, 4 oz.	422	25.7	0	34.5	96	73	0
lean (fat trimmed), 4 oz.	281	31.2	0	16.3	92	83	0
rib, small end (ribs 10–12), broiled:							
lean with fat, 4 oz.	376	27.2	0	28.8	95	70	0
lean (fat trimmed), 4 oz.	255	31.8	0	13.2	91	78	0
round, bottom round, braised:							
lean with fat, 4 oz.	299	33.8	0	17.2	109	57	0
lean (fat trimmed), 4 oz.	255	35.8	0	11.3	109	58	0
round, eye of round, roasted:							
lean with fat, 4 oz.	277	30.4	0	16.3	83	67	0
lean (fat trimmed), 4 oz.	209	32.9	0	7.6	78	70	0
round, full cut, broiled:							
lean with fat, 4 oz.	311	29.0	0	20.7	95	68	0
lean (fat trimmed), 4 oz.	220	32.3	0	9.1	93	73	0
round, tip round, roasted:							
lean with fat, 4 oz.	288	30.0	0	17.8	94	70	0
lean (fat trimmed), 4 oz.	219	32.6	0	8.8	92	74	0
round, top round:							
broiled, lean with fat, 4 oz.	242	35.0	0	10.2	96	68	0
fried, lean (fat trimmed), 4 oz.	257	39.8	0	9.7	110	81	0
shank, crosscuts, simmered:							
lean with fat, 4 oz.	277	35.8	0	13.7	90	70	0

Food and Measure	cal.	prot. (gms)	carbo. (gms)	fat (gms)	chol. (mgs)	sod. (mgs)	fiber (gms)
lean (fat trimmed), 4 oz.	228	38.2	0	7.2	88	73	0
short loin, tenderloin, broiled:							
lean with fat, 4 oz.	307	29.3	0	20.2	98	68	0
lean (fat trimmed), 4 oz.	235	32.0	0	10.9	95	71	0
short loin, top loin, broiled:							
lean with fat, 4 oz.	324	29.1	0	22.2	90	71	0
lean (fat trimmed), 4 oz.	235	32.5	0	10.7	86	77	0
shortribs, braised:							
lean with fat, 4 oz.	534	24.5	0	47.6	107	57	0
lean (fat trimmed), 4 oz.	335	34.9	0	20.6	105	66	0
sirloin steak, broiled:							
wedge bone, lean with fat, 4 oz.	321	31.0	0	20.9	102	70	0
wedge bone, lean (fat trimmed), 4 oz.	239	34.4	0	10.3	101	75	0
T-bone steak, broiled:							
lean with fat, 4 oz.	367	27.2	0	27.9	95	68	0
lean (fat trimmed), 4 oz.	243	31.9	0	11.8	91	75	0
Beef, corned:							
cooked, brisket, 4 oz.	285	20.6	.5	21.5	111	1286	0
(Carl Buddig), 1 oz.	42	5.7	.3	2.0	16	380	0
(Dinty Moore), 2 oz.	130	15.0	0	8.0	n.a.	n.a.	0
(Eckrich Calorie Watcher), 1-oz. slice	40	6.0	1.0	2.0	n.a.	340	0
(Oscar Mayer), 3/4-oz. slice	20	4.1	0	.4	8	248	0
Beef, corned, hash, canned:							
8 oz.	411	20.0	24.3	25.6	n.a.	1225	1.1
(Mary Kitchen), 7 1/2 oz.	360	20.0	17.0	24.0	n.a.	1368	n.a.

Food and Measure	cal.	prot. (gms)	carbo. (gms)	fat (gms)	chol. (mgs)	sod. (mgs)	fiber (gms)
Beef, corned, hash *(cont.)*							
(Mary Kitchen, 15 oz.),							
7½ oz.	360	20.0	19.0	24.0	n.a.	1386	n.a.
(Nalley), 3½ oz. . .	180	12.0	9.0	11.0	35	630	n.a.
Beef, corned, spread:							
(Hormel), ½ oz. . .	35	2.0	0	3.0	n.a.	n.a.	n.a.
Beef, dried (chipped):							
uncooked, 2.5 oz.	145	24.0	0	4.0	46	3053	0
sliced *(Hormel),* 1 oz.	45	8.0	0	1.0	n.a.	822	0
Beef, freeze-dried, steak, rib eye:							
(Mountain House), 1 steak	260	35.0	0	9.0	n.a.	n.a.	0
Beef, frozen:							
rib eye *(Snow King),* 2 oz.	90	12.0	0	40.0	n.a.	35	0
steak:							
chip *(Snow King),* 2 oz.	75	13.0	0	2.0	n.a.	35	0
flake *(Snow King),* 2 oz.	160	9.0	0	14.0	n.a.	35	0
Beef, Italian style:							
(Oscar Mayer), ¾-oz. slice	22	3.9	.3	.6	9	259	0
Beef dinner, frozen:							
(Banquet American Favorites), 10 oz.	345	23.0	19.0	19.0	n.a.	1009	n.a.
(Banquet Extra Helpings), 16 oz. . . .	864	40.0	72.0	46.0	n.a.	1731	n.a.
(Morton), 11 oz. . .	272	26.7	28.9	5.5	n.a.	700	n.a.
(Swanson), 11½ oz.	320	27.0	35.0	8.0	n.a.	870	n.a.
Burgundy *(Dinner Classics),* 10½ oz.	330	30.0	23.0	14.0	95	990	n.a.
chopped:							
(Banquet American Favorites), 11 oz.	434	19.0	23.0	30.0	n.a.	1199	n.a.
(Banquet Extra Helpings), 18 oz.	1028	40.0	70.0	67.0	n.a.	1792	n.a.

Food and Measure	cal.	prot. (gms)	carbo. (gms)	fat (gms)	chol. (mgs)	sod. (mgs)	fiber (gms)
sirloin (Le Menu), 12¼ oz.	410	26.0	28.0	23.0	n.a.	1080	n.a.
sirloin (Swanson), 11½ oz.	350	21.0	29.0	17.0	n.a.	930	n.a.
steak (Swanson Hungry-Man), 17¼ oz.	600	36.0	48.0	29.0	n.a.	1640	n.a.
Oriental (Lean Cuisine), 8⅝ oz. . .	270	20.0	30.0	8.0	35	1150	n.a.
pepper steak:							
(Classic Lite), 10 oz.	240	16.0	28.0	7.0	60	1020	1.4
(Le Menu), 11½ oz.	360	27.0	32.0	14.0	n.a.	1110	n.a.
Salisbury steak, see "Salisbury steak dinner"							
short ribs, boneless (Dinner Classics), 10½ oz.	460	26.0	31.0	25.0	95	1180	n.a.
sirloin tips:							
(Dinner Classics), 11 oz.	380	33.0	28.0	17.0	100	1180	n.a.
(Le Menu), 11½ oz.	390	30.0	26.0	18.0	n.a.	840	n.a.
sliced:							
(Morton Lite), 11 oz.	260	28.0	20.0	7.0	n.a.	850	n.a.
(Swanson Hungry-Man), 16 oz. . .	470	40.0	49.0	12.0	n.a.	1150	n.a.
and broccoli (Classic Lite), 10¼ oz.	280	25.0	29.0	7.0	n.a.	1480	n.a.
steak Diane mignonettes (Classic Lite), 10 oz.	290	29.0	23.0	9.0	90	770	n.a.
steak teriyaki (Dinner Classics), 10 oz.	360	24.0	33.0	16.0	95	1440	n.a.
Stroganoff:							
(Dinner Classics), 11¼ oz.	370	31.0	23.0	17.0	90	1330	n.a.
(Le Menu), 9¼ oz.	430	28.0	24.0	24.0	n.a.	930	n.a.
Swiss steak (Swanson), 10 oz. . . .	350	23.0	33.0	14.0	n.a.	830	n.a.

Food and Measure	cal.	prot. (gms)	carbo. (gms)	fat (gms)	chol. (mgs)	sod. (mgs)	fiber (gms)
Beef dinner, frozen *(cont.)*							
Szechuan *(Classic Lite)*, 10 oz. . . .	280	23.0	26.0	9.0	70	1010	n.a.
Yankee pot roast, see "Pot roast"							
Beef dinner, mix, pepper steak:							
(La Choy), 1/5 pkg.	40	2.0	8.0	0	n.a.	890	n.a.
Beef enchilada, see "Enchilada"							
Beef entree, canned: chow mein:							
(Chun King Stir-Fry), 6 oz. with beef	286	17.8	11.0	19.4	52	541	.6
(La Choy), 3/4 cup	60	6.0	5.0	1.0	n.a.	890	n.a.
drained *(Chun King Divider Pak—2 Servings)*, 8.11 oz.	104	10.3	13.3	1.7	19	639	.8
drained *(Chun King Divider Pak—4 Servings)*, 7.14 oz.	91	9.1	11.6	1.5	17	560	.7
pepper Oriental, drained *(Chun King Divider Pak)*, 7.05 oz.	103	6.7	11.0	4.2	15	875	1.1
goulash:							
(Heinz), 71/2 oz.	240	13.0	22.0	11.0	n.a.	920	n.a.
(Hormel Short Order), 71/2 oz. . .	230	14.0	17.0	12.0	n.a.	n.a.	n.a.
pepper steak *(Chun King Stir Fry)*, 6 oz. with meat	249	16.4	8.6	16.6	51	1003	.7
stew:							
(Dinty Moore), 71/2-oz. can	180	12.0	14.0	9.0	n.a.	939	n.a.
(Dinty Moore, 24 oz.) 8 oz.	220	12.0	15.0	12.0	n.a.	980	n.a.

Food and Measure	cal.	prot. (gms)	carbo. (gms)	fat (gms)	chol. (mgs)	sod. (mgs)	fiber (gms)
(Dinty Moore, 40 oz.), 8 oz. . . .	210	13.0	16.0	11.0	n.a.	971	n.a.
(Heinz), 7 1/2 oz.	210	12.0	19.0	9.0	n.a.	1245	n.a.
(Nalley), 3 1/2 oz.	110	5.0	8.0	6.0	20	400	n.a.
(Wolf), 7 1/2 oz. . .	179	9.6	18.3	7.5	n.a.	1043	.6
chunky (Nalley Big Chunk), 3 1/2 oz.	83	5.0	11.0	3.0	20	360	n.a.
Beef entree, freeze-dried:							
almondine (Mountain House), 1 cup . .	230	15.0	20.0	8.0	n.a.	n.a.	n.a.
and rice, with onions (Mountain House), 1 cup	330	11.0	42.0	12.0	n.a.	n.a.	n.a.
stew (Mountain House), 1 cup . .	260	16.0	26.0	9.0	n.a.	n.a.	n.a.
Stroganoff (Mountain House), 1 cup . .	270	10.0	26.0	13.0	n.a.	n.a.	n.a.
Beef entree, frozen:							
barbecue sauce and (Banquet Cookin' Bag), 4 oz.	133	9.0	13.0	5.0	n.a.	929	n.a.
Burgundy:							
(Freezer Queen Single Serve), 9.5 oz.	280	28.0	22.0	8.0	n.a.	n.a.	n.a.
(Light & Elegant), 9 oz.	230	23.0	25.0	4.0	n.a.	1235	n.a.
chipped, creamed:							
(Banquet Cookin' Bag), 4 oz. . . .	125	11.0	8.0	5.0	n.a.	1082	n.a.
(Freezer Queen Cook-in-Pouch), 5 oz.	80	9.0	2.0	4.0	n.a.	n.a.	n.a.
(Stouffer's), 5 1/2 oz.	240	13.0	8.0	17.0	n.a.	890	n.a.
chop suey (Stouffer's), 12 oz.	340	19.0	38.0	12.0	n.a.	1590	n.a.
chow mein Mandarin (Van de Kamp's Chinese Classics), 11 oz.	310	20.0	40.0	10.0	n.a.	1700	n.a.

Food and Measure	cal.	prot. (gms)	carbo. (gms)	fat (gms)	chol. (mgs)	sod. (mgs)	fiber (gms)
Beef entree, frozen *(cont.)*							
gravy and *(Banquet Family Entrees)*, 8 oz.	344	13.0	6.0	13.0	n.a.	890	n.a.
gravy with *(Banquet Cookin' Bag)*, 4 oz.	136	9.0	4.0	9.0	n.a.	492	n.a.
julienne *(Light & Elegant)*, 8½ oz. . .	260	21.0	27.0	7.0	n.a.	990	n.a.
mushroom gravy and charcoal patties:							
(Banquet Family Entrees), 5⅓ oz.	168	n.a.	6.0	13.0	n.a.	715	n.a.
(Freezer Queen, 2 lb.), 10.67 oz.	380	19.0	13.0	28.0	n.a.	n.a.	n.a.
(Freezer Queen Cook-in-Pouch), 5 oz.	150	10.0	7.0	9.0	n.a.	n.a.	n.a.
onion gravy, toasted, and patties *(Freezer Queen, 2 lb.)*, 8 oz.	270	15.0	7.0	24.0	n.a.	n.a.	n.a.
Oriental *(The Budget Gourmet)*, 10 oz.	290	17.0	35.0	9.0	n.a.	850	n.a.
pepper Oriental:							
(Chun King Boil-in-Bag), 10 oz. . .	244	13.9	39.2	8.8	23	1257	1.1
(La Choy), ⅔ cup	80	7.0	11.0	1.0	n.a.	820	n.a.
pepper steak:							
(Stouffer's), 10½ oz.	340	22.0	38.0	11.0	n.a.	1470	n.a.
Oriental, with rice *(Dining Lite)*, 9.3 oz.	267	21.1	32.5	6.4	n.a.	1400	1.0
with rice *(The Budget Gourmet)*, 1 serving	300	15.0	39.0	9.0	n.a.	800	n.a.
and peppers *(Freezer Queen Single Serve)*, 9.5 oz. . .	280	19.0	43.0	3.0	n.a.	n.a.	n.a.
pizza patties *(Banquet Entree Express)*, 3 oz.	255	14.0	3.0	20.0	n.a.	349	n.a.

Food and Measure	cal.	prot. (gms)	carbo. (gms)	fat (gms)	chol. (mgs)	sod. (mgs)	fiber (gms)
roast, hash (Stouffer's), 5¾ oz. . . .	250	18.0	11.0	15.0	n.a.	710	n.a.
short ribs (Stouffer's), 5¾ oz.	280	24.0	2.0	20.0	n.a.	510	n.a.
sirloin, in herb sauce (The Budget Gourmet), 10 oz. . . .	290	21.0	26.0	12.0	n.a.	920	n.a.
sirloin tips, with country vegetables (The Budget Gourmet), 1 serving	310	16.0	21.0	18.0	n.a.	570	n.a.
sliced:							
(Swanson Hungry-Man), 12¼ oz.	330	40.0	24.0	8.0	n.a.	1040	n.a.
gravy and (Freezer Queen, 2 lb.), 8 oz.	150	18.0	8.0	5.0	n.a.	n.a.	n.a.
gravy and (Freezer Queen Cook-in-Pouch), 5 oz.	90	12.0	6.0	2.0	n.a.	n.a.	n.a.
gravy and (Morton Lite), 8 oz. . . .	280	20.0	30.0	9.0	n.a.	490	n.a.
gravy and (Swanson), 8 oz. . . .	200	18.0	18.0	6.0	n.a.	760	n.a.
steak, breaded (Hormel), 4 oz.	370	14.0	13.0	30.0	n.a.	n.a.	n.a.
stew:							
(Banquet Family Entrees), 8 oz. . . .	254	12.0	21.0	13.0	n.a.	977	n.a.
(Freezer Queen, 2 lb.), 8 oz.	115	12.0	13.0	2.0	n.a.	n.a.	n.a.
(Freezer Queen Single Serve, 9 oz.	260	15.0	36.0	5.0	n.a.	n.a.	n.a.
(Stouffer's), 10 oz.	310	22.0	19.0	16.0	n.a.	1460	n.a.
Stroganoff:							
(Light & Elegant), 9 oz.	260	24.0	27.0	6.0	n.a.	785	n.a.
(Stouffer's), 9¾ oz.	410	25.0	29.0	21.0	n.a.	1180	n.a.

Food and Measure	cal.	prot. (gms)	carbo. (gms)	fat (gms)	chol. (mgs)	sod. (mgs)	fiber (gms)
Beef entree, frozen, Stroganoff *(cont.)*							
and vegetable *(Van de Kamp's* Chinese Classics), 11 oz.	370	20.0	35.0	15.0	n.a.	940	n.a.
teriyaki:							
(Dining Lite), 8 5/8 oz.	230	20.0	33.0	3.0	n.a.	980	n.a.
(Light & Elegant), 8 oz.	240	18.0	37.0	3.0	n.a.	625	n.a.
(Stouffer's), 9 3/4 oz.	330	22.0	35.0	9.0	n.a.	1260	n.a.
Beef gravy, canned:							
(Franco-American), 2 oz.	25	1.0	3.0	1.0	n.a.	310	n.a.
Beef, ground, see "Beef"							
Beef, ground, seasoning mix:							
(Durkee), 1.1-oz. pkg.	91	3.0	18.0	.9	n.a.	1314	n.a.
with onion *(Durkee),* 1.1-oz. pkg.	102	3.0	13.0	n.a.	n.a.	1914	n.a.
Beef loaf, jellied:							
(Hormel Perma-Fresh), 2 slices	90	14.0	0	4.0	n.a.	900	n.a.
Beef luncheon meat:							
(Eckrich Calorie Watcher), 1-oz. slice	40	5.0	1.0	2.0	n.a.	560	n.a.
(Hormel), 1-oz. slice	50	5.0	0	3.0	n.a.	382	n.a.
roasted *(Boar's Head),* 2-oz. slice	70	15.0	1.0	1.0	n.a.	70	n.a.
Beef pie, frozen:							
(Banquet), 8 oz. . .	557	15.0	47.0	34.0	n.a.	964	n.a.
(Stouffer's), 10 oz.	560	21.0	36.0	37.0	n.a.	1300	n.a.
(Swanson), 8 oz. . .	400	11.0	42.0	21.0	n.a.	900	n.a.
(Swanson Chunky), 10 oz.	530	19.0	53.0	28.0	n.a.	900	n.a.
(Swanson Hungry-Man), 16 oz.	670	23.0	68.0	34.0	n.a.	1750	n.a.

Food and Measure	cal.	prot. (gms)	carbo. (gms)	fat (gms)	chol. (mgs)	sod. (mgs)	fiber (gms)
steak burger (Swanson Hungry-Man), 16 oz.	750	27.0	61.0	44.0	n.a.	1520	n.a.
Beef, roast, hash, canned:							
(Mary Kitchen), 7½ oz. can	360	20.0	18.0	23.0	n.a.	1156	n.a.
(Mary Kitchen, 15 oz.), 7½ oz.	350	20.0	18.0	22.0	n.a.	1142	n.a.
Beef, roast, croissant, in wine sauce:							
frozen (Sara Lee Le San"Wich), 4 oz.	300	14.0	26.0	15.0	n.a.	570	n.a.
Beef, roast spread:							
(Hormel), ½ oz. . .	31	2.0	0	2.0	n.a.	n.a.	n.a.
Beef, smoked:							
(Carl Buddig), 1 oz.	42	5.7	.3	2.0	16	425	0
Beef stew, see "Beef entree, canned and frozen"							
Beef stew seasoning mix:							
(Durkee), 1.7-oz. pkg.	99	.7	22.0	.5	n.a.	6953	n.a.
(French's), ⅙ pkg.	25	0	5.0	0	n.a.	770	n.a.
Beef sticks, see "Sausage sticks"							
Beer, ale and malt liquor, 12 fl. oz.:							
(Beck's)	143	1.8	11.0	0	0	<1	0
(Black Horse)	158	1.2	14.9	0	0	26	0
(Blatz)	142	1.1	11.8	0	0	14	0
(Bud Lite)	108	1.1	8.8	0	0	tr.	0
(Budweiser)	144	1.4	11.7	0	0	tr.	0
(Busch)	144	1.1	11.8	0	0	tr.	0
(Champale Extra Dry Malt Liquor) . . .	169	.5	14.3	0	0	32	0
(Classic)	144	1.0	12.8	0	0	10	0
(Colt 45 Malt Liquor)	156	1.2	11.1	0	0	14	0

Food and Measure	cal.	prot. (gms)	carbo. (gms)	fat (gms)	chol. (mgs)	sod. (mgs)	fiber (gms)
Beer, ale and malt liquor *(cont.)*							
(Coqui Malt Liquor)	208	1.7	9.8	0	0	13	0
(Heileman Black La-bel)	136	1.2	11.2	0	0	17	0
(Heileman Old Style)	146	1.1	11.5	0	0	10	0
(Heileman Special Ex-port)	155	1.1	11.1	0	0	14	0
(King Cobra)	160	1.4	9.5	0	0	tr.	0
(Knickerbocker) . . .	140	.9	12.3	0	0	9	0
(LA)	112	.9	15.6	0	0	tr.	0
(McSorley's Ale) . .	166	1.7	14.7	0	0	8	0
(Metbrau)	71	1.3	14.8	0	0	16	0
(Michelob)	160	1.6	14.3	0	0	tr.	0
(Michelob Classic Dark)	164	1.7	15.0	0	0	tr.	0
(Michelob Light) . .	134	1.1	12.4	0	0	tr.	0
(Mickeys Malt Liquor)	156	1.2	11.1	0	0	14	0
(Nordik Wolf Light)	110	1.0	3.3	0	0	n.a.	0
(Ortlieb's)	140	.9	12.3	0	0	9	0
(Pabst Blue Ribbon)	144	1.0	12.4	0	0	8	0
(Prior Double Dark)	171	1.4	15.4	0	0	10	0
(Rheingold)	148	1.0	12.9	0	0	9	0
(Rheingold Light) . .	96	.7	2.8	0	0	9	0
(Schmidt's)	148	1.0	12.9	0	0	9	0
(Schmidt Light) . . .	96	.7	2.8	0	0	7	0
(Tiger Head Ale) . .	166	1.7	14.7	0	0	8	0
non-alcoholic *(Birell)*	77	.8	15.5	0	0	7	0
Beerwurst, see "Sa-lami, beer"							
Beet:							
fresh:							
raw, whole, 1 me-dium (2″ diam.)	36	1.2	8.2	.1	0	59	.7
boiled, drained, 2 medium (2″ diam.) . .	31	1.1	6.7	.1	0	49	.9
boiled, drained, sliced, 1 cup . .	52	1.8	11.4	.1	0	84	1.4

Food and Measure	cal.	prot. (gms)	carbo. (gms)	fat (gms)	chol. (mgs)	sod. (mgs)	fiber (gms)
canned, 1/2 cup:							
all cuts (Libby/Seneca)	35	1.0	8.0	0	0	270	n.a.
all cuts (Stokely's Finest No Salt or Sugar)	40	1.8	8.0	0	0	40	n.a.
whole, small (S&W)	40	1.0	9.0	0	0	270	n.a.
whole or sliced (A&P)	40	1.0	9.0	<1.0	0	300	n.a.
whole, tiny or sliced, with liquid (Del Monte)	35	1.0	8.0	0	0	290	n.a.
whole, sliced or cut (Stokely's Finest)	40	1.0	8.0	0	0	300	n.a.
diced (Stokely's Finest)	35	1.0	7.0	0	0	300	n.a.
diced or julienne (S&W)	40	1.0	9.0	0	0	270	n.a.
sliced (A&P No Salt Added)	35	1.0	8.0	<1.0	0	50	n.a.
sliced, small (S&W Premium)	40	1.0	9.0	0	0	270	n.a.
Harvard (Comstock/Greenwood)	100	1.0	18.0	0	0	350	.5
Harvard (Libby/Seneca)	80	1.0	20.0	0	0	270	n.a.
Harvard (Stokely's Finest)	70	1.0	18.0	0	0	135	n.a.
pickled (Comstock/Greenwood)	90	1.0	22.0	0	0	500	.6
pickled, regular or with onion (Libby/Seneca)	80	0	18.0	0	0	270	n.a.
pickled, whole, extra small (S&W)	70	1.0	16.0	0	0	215	n.a.
pickled, small (Stokely's Finest)	90	1.0	22.0	0	0	280	n.a.
pickled, crinkle (Del Monte)	80	1.0	19.0	0	0	375	n.a.

Food and Measure	cal.	prot. (gms)	carbo. (gms)	fat (gms)	chol. (mgs)	sod. (mgs)	fiber (gms)
Beet, canned *(cont.)*							
pickled, red wine vinegar, *(S&W Regular or Party)*	70	1.0	16.0	0	0	215	n.a.
Beet greens, fresh:							
raw, 1" pieces, 1 cup	8	.7	1.5	<.1	0	76	.5
boiled, drained, 1" pieces, 1 cup . . .	40	3.7	7.9	.3	0	346	1.5
Berliner:							
pork and beef, 1 oz.	65	4.3	.7	4.9	13	368	0
Berry drink:							
canned *(Hi-C Wildberry),* 6 fl. oz.	90	<.1	23.0	<.1	0	17	0
citrus, chilled *(Five Alive),* 6 fl. oz. . .	88	<1.0	22.0	<.1	0	15	tr.
citrus, frozen* *(Five Alive),* 6 fl. oz. . .	88	<1.0	22.0	<.1	0	1	n.a.
Biscuit, 2 biscuits, except as noted:							
(Wonder), 1 biscuit	80	2.0	14.0	1.0	<5	140	.1
refrigerated:							
(Ballard Ovenready)	100	3.0	20.0	1.0	n.a.	360	n.a.
(1869 Brand Butter Tastin')	210	4.0	25.0	10.0	n.a.	590	n.a.
(Pillsbury Big Country Butter Tastin')	190	4.0	27.0	8.0	n.a.	650	n.a.
(Pillsbury Country)	100	3.0	20.0	1.0	n.a.	360	n.a.
baking powder *(1869 Brand)* . .	210	4.0	25.0	10.0	n.a.	590	n.a.
baking powder, dinner *(Pillsbury Tenderflake)* . .	110	2.0	14.0	5.0	n.a.	340	n.a.
butter *(Pillsbury)*	100	3.0	20.0	1.0	n.a.	360	n.a.
buttermilk *(Ballard Ovenready)* . .	100	3.0	20.0	1.0	n.a.	360	n.a.
buttermilk *(1869 Brand)*	210	4.0	25.0	10.0	n.a.	590	n.a.

* Prepared according to package directions

Food and Measure	cal.	prot. (gms)	carbo. (gms)	fat (gms)	chol. (mgs)	sod. (mgs)	fiber (gms)
buttermilk (Hungry Jack Extra Rich)	110	2.0	19.0	3.0	n.a.	350	n.a.
buttermilk (Pillsbury)	100	3.0	20.0	1.0	n.a.	360	n.a.
buttermilk (Pillsbury Big Country) . .	200	4.0	29.0	8.0	n.a.	650	n.a.
buttermilk (Pillsbury Deluxe Heat'n Serve)	280	5.0	32.0	15.0	n.a.	610	n.a.
buttermilk (Pillsbury Heat'n Serve)	170	4.0	27.0	5.0	n.a.	530	n.a.
buttermilk (Pillsbury Tenderflake) . .	110	2.0	14.0	5.0	n.a.	340	n.a.
buttermilk, flaky (Hungry Jack)	170	3.0	25.0	7.0	n.a.	590	n.a.
buttermilk, flaky (Pillsbury Extra Lights)	110	2.0	18.0	4.0	n.a.	340	n.a.
buttermilk, fluffy (Hungry Jack)	180	3.0	24.0	8.0	n.a.	560	n.a.
flaky (Hungry Jack)	170	3.0	24.0	7.0	n.a.	590	n.a.
flaky (Hungry Jack Butter Tastin')	180	3.0	23.0	9.0	n.a.	310	n.a.
fluffy (Pillsbury Good 'n Buttery) . . .	180	3.0	21.0	10.0	n.a.	730	n.a.
southern style (Big Country)	200	4.0	29.0	8.0	n.a.	650	n.a.
Biscuit dough, frozen:							
buttermilk:							
(Bridgford), 1-oz. piece	100	2.0	15.0	3.0	n.a.	377	n.a.
(Bridgford), 2-oz. piece	190	4.0	29.0	6.0	n.a.	716	n.a.
Biscuit mix:							
(Bisquick), 2 oz. . .	240	4.0	37.0	8.0	n.a.	700	n.a.
(Martha White Bixmix), 1 pkg.	640	14.0	96.0	22.0	n.a.	n.a.	n.a.
Blackberry:							
fresh, 1 cup	74	1.0	18.4	.6	0	0	5.9

Food and Measure	cal.	prot. (gms)	carbo. (gms)	fat (gms)	chol. (mgs)	sod. (mgs)	fiber (gms)
Blackberry *(cont.)*							
canned, in heavy							
syrup, 1 cup . . .	236	3.4	59.1	.4	0	7	11.8
frozen, unsweetened,							
1 cup	97	1.8	23.7	.7	0	2	4.1
Blackberry bar or							
roll:							
(Stretch Island							
Leather), 1/2-oz. bar	45	0	11.0	0	0	<1	n.a.
Black-eye peas:							
raw, see "Cowpeas"							
dried, cooked *(A&P)*, 1							
cup	230	15.0	41.0	1.0	0	15	n.a.
canned:							
(A&P), 1/2 cup . .	120	7.0	20.0	1.0	0	410	n.a.
(Joan of Arc), 1/2							
cup	90	6.0	15.0	<1.0	0	350	n.a.
(Progresso), 8 oz.	165	11.0	29.0	1.0	0	n.a.	n.a.
frozen:							
(Frosty Acres), 3.3							
oz.	130	9.0	23.0	0	0	6	n.a.
(Southland), 3.3 oz.	130	9.0	23.0	1.0	0	5	n.a.
Blackfish, see "Tau-							
tog"							
Blintz, frozen, 1							
piece:							
apple *(Golden)* . . .	100	2.0	24.0	.5	28	115	n.a.
apple raisin *(Golden)*	110	2.0	25.0	.5	28	131	n.a.
blueberry *(Golden)*	110	2.0	25.0	.5	27	116	n.a.
cheese *(Golden)* . .	110	7.0	20.0	.5	32	126	n.a.
cherry *(Golden)* . . .	110	2.0	25.0	.5	28	105	n.a.
potato *(Golden)* . . .	130	3.0	21.0	4.0	19	224	n.a.
Blood sausage:							
1 oz.	107	4.1	.4	9.8	34	n.a.	0
Bloody Mary drink							
mixer:							
(Holland House							
Smooth N'Spicy), 1							
fl. oz.	1	0	0	0	0	106	n.a.
(Rose's), 1 fl. oz. . .	3	0	0	0	0	102	n.a.

Food and Measure	cal.	prot. (gms)	carbo. (gms)	fat (gms)	chol. (mgs)	sod. (mgs)	fiber (gms)
Blue cheese dip:							
(Kraft Premium), 1 oz.	45	1.0	2.0	4.0	10	200	0
(Nalley), 1 oz.	106	.6	.9	11.6	13	360	0
Blueberry:							
fresh, 1 cup	82	1.0	20.5	.6	0	9	1.9
canned:							
in water (Thank You), 1/2 cup . .	50	0	12.0	0	0	1	0
in heavy syrup (A&P), 1/2 cup	110	<1.0	28.0	<1.0	0	25	n.a.
in heavy syrup (S&W), 1/2 cup	111	0	30.0	0	0	<10	n.a.
in heavy syrup (Thank You), 1/2 cup	100	0	26.0	0	0	10	1.2
frozen:							
unsweetened, 1 cup	78	.7	18.9	1.0	0	1	2.3
sweetened, 1 cup	187	.9	50.5	.3	0	3	2.1
Blueberry fruit square:							
frozen (Pepperidge Farm), 1 piece . .	220	1.0	29.0	11.0	n.a.	190	n.a.
Blueberry turnover:							
frozen (Pepperidge Farm), 1 piece . .	320	3.0	32.0	19.0	n.a.	240	n.a.
refrigerated (Pillsbury), 1 piece	170	2.0	22.0	8.0	n.a.	310	n.a.
Bluefish fillets:							
raw, meat only, 4 oz.	141	22.7	0	4.8	67	68	0
Bockwurst:							
1 link, about 2.3 oz.	200	8.7	.3	17.9	n.a.	n.a.	0
Bologna:							
(Armour), 1 oz. . . .	90	3.0	n.a.	8.0	15	285	0
(Ballpark), 1 slice . .	107	4.0	0	10.1	n.a.	363	0
(Boar's Head), 1 oz.	74	4.0	.3	6.3	n.a.	n.a.	0
(Boar's Head Lower Salt), 1 oz.	74	4.0	.3	6.3	n.a.	220	0
(Eckrich), 1 slice . .	90	3.0	2.0	8.0	n.a.	290	0
(Eckrich Ring), 1 oz.	90	3.0	2.0	8.0	n.a.	280	0

Food and Measure	cal.	prot. (gms)	carbo. (gms)	fat (gms)	chol. (mgs)	sod. (mgs)	fiber (gms)
Bologna *(cont.)*							
(Eckrich German Brand), 1 slice . .	80	4.0	1.0	7.0	n.a.	350	0
(Eckrich German Brand Chub), 1 oz.	80	4.0	1.0	7.0	n.a.	360	0
(Eckrich Smorgas Pac), 1 slice . . .	90	3.0	2.0	8.0	n.a.	310	0
(Eckrich Thick Slice, 12 oz.), 1 slice . .	160	5.0	3.0	14.0	n.a.	490	0
(Eckrich Thick Slice, 1 lb.), 1 slice	160	5.0	3.0	14.0	n.a.	510	0
(Eckrich Thin Slice, 8 oz.), 2 slices . . .	110	4.0	2.0	9.0	n.a.	320	0
(Eckrich Thin Slice, 12 oz.), 2 slices . . .	110	3.0	2.0	10.0	n.a.	320	0
(Grillmaster), 1 slice	89	4.5	1.3	7.3	n.a.	454	0
(Hormel Coarse Ground), 2 oz. . .	160	8.0	1.0	14.0	n.a.	578	0
(Hormel Fine Ground), 2 oz.	170	7.0	1.0	16.0	n.a.	596	0
(Light & Lean), 2 slices	140	6.0	2.0	12.0	n.a.	n.a.	0
(Light & Lean Thin Slice), 2 slices . .	70	3.0	1.0	6.0	n.a.	n.a.	0
(Oscar Mayer), 4/5-oz. slice	74	2.6	.5	6.8	13	243	0
beef:							
(Armour), 1 oz. . .	90	3.0	n.a.	8.0	15	285	0
(Eckrich, 8 oz./1 lb.), 1 slice . . .	90	3.0	2.0	8.0	n.a.	280	0
(Eckrich, 12 oz.), 1 slice	90	3.0	2.0	8.0	n.a.	270	0
(Eckrich Smorgas Pac), 1 slice . .	70	2.0	1.0	6.0	n.a.	230	0
(Eckrich Thick Sliced), 1 slice	140	5.0	2.0	12.0	n.a.	400	0
(Hormel Coarse Ground), 2 oz.	160	8.0	1.0	14.0	n.a.	576	0

Food and Measure	cal.	prot. (gms)	carbo. (gms)	fat (gms)	chol. (mgs)	sod. (mgs)	fiber (gms)
(Hormel Perma-Fresh), 2 slices	170	6.0	1.0	16.0	n.a.	592	0
(Kahn's), 1 oz. . . .	88	3.1	1.4	8.2	n.a.	309	0
(Oscar Mayer), 4/5-oz. slice	74	2.5	.5	6.9	12	253	0
Lebanon *(Oscar Mayer)*, 1.6 oz.	50	4.7	.4	3.3	16	296	0
beef and pork, 1-oz. slice	89	3.3	.8	8.0	16	289	0
with cheese *(Eckrich)*, 1 slice	90	3.0	2.0	8.0	n.a.	290	0
cheese *(Oscar Mayer)*, 4/5-oz. slice	74	2.7	.6	6.7	14	242	0
chicken, see "Chicken bologna"							
garlic:							
(Eckrich), 1 slice	90	3.0	2.0	8.0	n.a.	290	0
(Oscar Mayer), 4/5-oz. slice	73	2.6	.4	6.8	13	235	0
lunch, chub *(Eckrich)*, 1 oz.	100	3.0	2.0	9.0	n.a.	290	0
meat:							
(Armour), 1 oz. . .	90	3.0	n.a.	8.0	15	285	0
(Hormel Perma-Fresh), 2 slices	180	7.0	0	16.0	n.a.	599	0
pickled, ring *(Eckrich)*, 1 oz.	90	3.0	2.0	8.0	n.a.	290	0
sandwich *(Eckrich)*, 1 slice	90	3.0	2.0	8.0	n.a.	310	0
turkey, see "Turkey bologna"							
Bonito:							
raw, meat only, 4 oz.	191	27.2	0	8.3	n.a.	n.a.	0
Borage, fresh:							
raw, 1" pieces, 1 cup	19	1.6	2.7	.6	0	71	.8
boiled, drained, 4 oz.	28	2.4	4.0	.9	0	100	1.2
Bouillon (see also "Soup"):							
beef:							
(Herb Ox), 1 packet	8	.8	.9	.1	n.a.	1040	n.a.

Food and Measure	cal.	prot. (gms)	carbo. (gms)	fat (gms)	chol. (mgs)	sod. (mgs)	fiber (gms)
Bouillon, beef *(cont.)*							
(Herb Ox Low Sodium), 1 packet	11	1.0	1.7	.1	n.a.	10	n.a.
cube *(Herb Ox)*, 1 cube	6	.6	.6	.1	n.a.	840	n.a.
cube *(Steero)*, 1 cube	6	0	1.0	n.a.	n.a.	1000	n.a.
instant *(Herb Ox)*, 1 serving	6	.6	.6	.1	n.a.	n.a.	n.a.
instant *(Steero)*, 1 tsp.	6	0	1.0	n.a.	n.a.	1000	n.a.
instant *(Wyler's)*, 1 tsp.	6	<1.0	1.0	<1.0	n.a.	930	n.a.
chicken:							
(Herb Ox), 1 packet	12	.7	1.9	.1	n.a.	960	n.a.
(Herb Ox Low Sodium), 1 packet	12	.9	2.0	.2	n.a.	5	n.a.
cube *(Herb Ox)*, 1 cube	6	.7	.6	.1	n.a.	960	n.a.
cube *(Wyler's)*, 1 cube	8	<1.0	1.0	<1.0	n.a.	850	n.a.
instant *(Herb Ox)*, 1 serving	6	.7	.6	.1	n.a.	n.a.	n.a.
onion:							
(Herb Ox), 1 packet	14	.9	1.9	.2	0	800	n.a.
cube *(Herb Ox)*, 1 cube	10	.6	1.3	.1	0	560	n.a.
instant *(Herb Ox)*, 1 serving	10	.6	1.3	.1	0	n.a.	n.a.
instant *(Wyler's)*, 1 tsp.	10	<1.0	1.0	<1.0	0	n.a.	n.a.
vegetable:							
(Herb Ox), 1 packet	12	.5	2.2	.1	0	880	n.a.
cube *(Herb Ox)*, 1 cube	6	.6	.7	.1	0	920	n.a.
instant *(Herb Ox)*, 1 serving	6	.6	.7	.1	0	n.a.	n.a.
Bourbon, see "Liquor"							

Food and Measure	cal.	prot. (gms)	carbo. (gms)	fat (gms)	chol. (mgs)	sod. (mgs)	fiber (gms)
Boysenberry:							
fresh, see "Black- berry"							
canned, in heavy syrup, 1 cup . . .	225	2.5	57.1	.3	0	9	4.9
frozen, unsweetened, 1 cup	66	1.5	16.1	.4	0	2	3.6
Boysenberry juice:							
(Smucker's), 8 fl. oz.	130	0	32.0	0	0	5	n.a.
Brains, beef, fresh:							
raw, 4 oz.	142	11.1	0	10.5	1890	116	0
pan fried, 4 oz. . . .	222	14.3	0	18.0	2262	179	0
Bran, see "Wheat bran"							
Brandy, unflavored, see "Liquor"							
Bratwurst:							
(Kahn's), 2-oz. link	180	6.0	2.0	17.0	n.a.	n.a.	0
cooked (Hillshire Farms), 1 oz. . . .	87	3.4	1.0	7.7	8	195	0
Braunschweiger (liver sausage):							
(Hormel), 1 oz. . . .	80	4.0	0	7.0	n.a.	322	0
(Oscar Mayer), 1-oz. slice	95	3.9	.5	8.6	50	321	0
chub:							
(Eckrich), 1 oz. . .	70	4.0	1.0	6.0	n.a.	400	0
(Jones Dairy Farm), 1 oz. . . .	87	4.2	0	7.7	n.a.	267	n.a.
(Oscar Mayer), 1 oz.	94	3.9	.5	8.4	46	341	0
sliced (Jones Dairy Farm), 1 oz. . . .	87	4.3	0	7.9	n.a.	222	n.a.
tube (Oscar Mayer), 1 oz.	96	3.8	.8	8.7	41	319	0
Brazil nuts:							
in shell, 1 lb.	1428	31.2	28.9	144.2	0	2	5.0
shelled, 6 large nuts	186	4.1	3.6	18.8	0	0	.7
Bread, 2 slices, ex- cept as noted:							
(Arnold Bran'nola)	180	7.0	31.0	3.0	0	355	.7

Food and Measure	cal.	prot. (gms)	carbo. (gms)	fat (gms)	chol. (mgs)	sod. (mgs)	fiber (gms)
Bread *(cont.)*							
(Brownberry Bran'nola)	200	9.0	36.0	2.0	n.a.	355	.7
(Brownberry Great Grains)	140	6.0	26.0	1.0	n.a.	n.a.	n.a.
(Brownberry Sandwich Dark)	150	6.0	29.0	1.0	n.a.	365	n.a.
bran:							
honey *(Pepperidge Farm)*	190	5.0	36.0	2.0	n.a.	350	n.a.
honey *(Roman Meal)* 1 slice . .	70	3.0	13.0	<1.0	0	140	.9
whole *(Brownberry)*	150	5.0	30.0	1.0	n.a.	395	n.a.
brown, see "Bread, canned"							
cinnamon *(Pepperidge Farm)*	170	4.0	27.0	4.0	n.a.	200	n.a.
corn, see "Bread, mix"							
date nut loaf *(Thomas')*, 1 oz.	90	1.4	16.6	1.4	n.a.	138	.2
French:							
(DiCarlo Parisian), 1 slice	70	3.0	13.0	1.0	<5	180	.1
(Francisco), 2 oz.	160	6.0	29.0	2.0	n.a.	325	n.a.
(Gonnella), 1 oz.	70	2.5	14.0	.5	0	260	n.a.
(Wonder)	140	6.0	26.0	2.0	0	360	.2
Vienna *(Francisco)*, 2 oz.	160	6.0	29.0	2.0	n.a.	340	n.a.
(Hillbilly), 1 slice . .	70	3.0	14.0	1.0	<5	140	.1
(Hollywood Dark), 1 slice	70	3.0	13.0	1.0	<5	160	.3
(Hollywood Light), 1 slice	70	3.0	13.0	1.0	<5	150	.1
Italian *(Wonder* Family), 1 slice	70	2.0	13.0	1.0	<5	160	.1
(Monk's Hi-Fibre), 1 oz.	50	3.0	10.0	1.0	0	n.a.	n.a.

Food and Measure	cal.	prot. (gms)	carbo. (gms)	fat (gms)	chol. (mgs)	sod. (mgs)	fiber (gms)
multi-grain:							
(Home Pride 7 Grain), 1 slice	70	3.0	13.0	1.0	<5	140	.1
(Roman Seven Grain), 1-oz. slice	70	3.0	13.0	<1.0	0	140	.5
very thin *(Pepperidge Farm)* . . .	80	3.0	14.0	1.0	n.a.	150	n.a.
nut *(Brownberry Health Nut)*	170	6.0	30.0	3.0	n.a.	405	n.a.
oat:							
(Arnold Bran'nola Country)	220	8.0	38.0	4.0	<5	405	.3
(Brownberry Bran'nola) . . .	220	9.0	38.0	4.0	n.a.	405	n.a.
oatmeal *(Brownberry)* . .	160	5.0	30.0	2.0	n.a.	400	n.a.
oatmeal *(Pepperidge Farm)* . . .	140	4.0	25.0	3.0	n.a.	370	n.a.
pita:							
(Sahara Mini), 1-oz. piece	80	3.0	16.0	1.0	0	190	.4
(Toufayan's), 1/2 piece or 1 oz.	80	4.0	15.0	1.0	n.a.	n.a.	n.a.
whole wheat *(Sahara)*, 1-oz. piece	75	3.5	13.7	.7	0	170	.3
protein:							
(Thomas' Fresh)	93	6.9	14.7	.8	0	180	.2
(Thomas' Frozen)	114	8.2	18.1	1.0	0	220	.2
pumpernickel:							
(Arnold)	150	5.0	28.0	1.0	0	460	.5
(Levy)	170	6.0	31.0	2.0	0	385	.4
(Pepperidge Farm Family)	160	6.0	30.0	2.0	n.a.	610	n.a.
raisin:							
(Arnold Tea) . . .	140	3.0	26.0	3.0	<5	225	.3
(Monk's), 1 oz. . .	70	2.0	10.0	1.0	0	n.a.	n.a.
cinnamon *(Brownberry)* . .	170	4.0	33.0	2.0	n.a.	320	n.a.
cinnamon *(Pepperidge Farm)* . . .	150	4.0	28.0	3.0	n.a.	190	n.a.

Food and Measure	cal.	prot. (gms)	carbo. (gms)	fat (gms)	chol. (mgs)	sod. (mgs)	fiber (gms)
Bread, raisin *(cont.)*							
nut *(Brownberry)*	190	5.0	29.0	6.0	n.a.	235	n.a.
(Roman Meal), 1 slice	70	3.0	13.0	1.0	<5	140	.4
rye:							
(Arnold Melba Thin)	100	4.0	19.0	1.0	0	270	.5
(Brownberry Extra Thin)	130	5.0	24.0	1.0	n.a.	260	n.a.
(Pepperidge Farm Family)	170	6.0	31.0	2.0	n.a.	490	n.a.
Dijon *(Pepperidge Farm)*	110	4.0	18.0	2.0	n.a.	340	n.a.
dill *(Arnold)*	150	6.0	27.0	2.0	0	405	1.7
Jewish, seeded *(Arnold)*	150	5.0	28.0	2.0	<5	425	.6
Jewish, seeded *(Levy)*	160	6.0	29.0	2.0	0	370	2.0
Jewish, unseeded *(Arnold)*	150	5.0	28.0	2.0	0	415	.3
seedless *(Pepperidge Farm)* . . .	160	6.0	31.0	2.0	n.a.	500	n.a.
sourdough, French:							
(Boudin), 2 slices or 1³/₄ oz.	137	5.1	27.7	.7	tr.	325	tr.
(DiCarlo)	140	6.0	24.0	2.0	0	280	.2
(Parisian), 1.8 oz.	138	5.1	27.9	.6	tr.	290	.1
wheat:							
(Arnold Bran'nola Hearty)	210	8.0	35.0	4.0	<5	445	.7
(Brownberry Bran'nola) . . .	210	8.0	35.0	4.0	n.a.	445	.7
(Brownberry Natural)	170	6.0	35.0	1.0	n.a.	530	n.a.
(Fresh Horizons)	100	6.0	20.0	2.0	0	280	4.2
(Fresh & Natural)	140	6.0	26.0	2.0	0	280	.8
(Home Pride Butter Top), 1 slice . .	70	3.0	13.0	1.0	<5	140	.2
(Home Pride Wheatberry), 1 slice	70	3.0	12.0	1.0	<5	160	.4

Food and Measure	cal.	prot. (gms)	carbo. (gms)	fat (gms)	chol. (mgs)	sod. (mgs)	fiber (gms)
(Monk's), 1 oz. . .	70	3.0	13.0	1.0	0	n.a.	n.a.
(Pepperidge Farm)	190	6.0	35.0	3.0	n.a.	390	n.a.
(Roman Meal Light), 1 slice	40	3.0	7.0	0	<5	105	n.a.
(Roman Wheatberry), 1-oz. slice	70	3.0	12.0	<1.0	0	140	1.0
(Wonder Family), 1 slice	70	3.0	13.0	1.0	<5	140	.2
apple honey *(Brownberry)* . .	130	5.0	27.0	1.0	n.a.	n.a.	n.a.
cracked *(Pepper- idge Farm)* . . .	140	4.0	26.0	2.0	n.a.	290	n.a.
cracked *(Roman Meal)*, 1-oz. slice	70	3.0	12.0	1.0	0	140	1.1
cracked *(Wonder)*, 1 slice	70	3.0	13.0	1.0	<5	180	.2
honey *(Arnold Wheatberry)* . .	180	6.0	32.0	2.0	<5	410	n.a.
sprouted *(Arnold)*	130	5.0	24.0	2.0	<5	265	1.4
whole *(Arnold Brick Oven)*	120	4.0	19.0	3.0	<5	190	.6
whole *(Arnold Brick Oven, 32 oz.)*	160	6.0	26.0	4.0	0	420	.5
whole *(Arnold Mea- sure Up)*	80	3.0	13.0	2.0	<5	140	.4
whole *(Pepperidge Farm)*	130	5.0	24.0	3.0	n.a.	250	n.a.
whole *(Roman Meal 100% Whole Grain)*, 1-oz. slice	70	3.0	13.0	<1.0	0	150	n.a.
whole *(Wonder 100%)*, 1 slice	70	3.0	12.0	1.0	<5	160	.4
whole, soft *(Wonder 100%)*, 1 slice	70	4.0	10.0	1.0	0	140	.4
whole, very thin *(Pepperidge Farm)*	80	3.0	15.0	2.0	n.a.	160	n.a.

Food and Measure	cal.	prot. (gms)	carbo. (gms)	fat (gms)	chol. (mgs)	sod. (mgs)	fiber (gms)
Bread (cont.)							
white:							
(Arnold Bran'nola							
Old Style) . . .	210	7.0	38.0	2.0	0	415	.2
(Arnold Brick Oven)	130	4.0	22.0	2.0	<5	205	.1
(Arnold Brick Oven,							
32 oz.)	170	5.0	29.0	3.0	<5	370	.2
(Arnold Country)	190	6.0	34.0	3.0	<5	490	.4
(Arnold Hearth-							
stone)	170	4.0	30.0	3.0	0	450	.3
(Arnold Measure							
Up)	80	3.0	14.0	2.0	<5	135	.1
(Brownberry) . . .	150	5.0	31.0	1.0	n.a.	355	n.a.
(Brownberry Extra							
Thin)	140	4.0	27.0	2.0	n.a.	260	n.a.
(Brownberry Sand-							
wich)	150	5.0	31.0	1.0	n.a.	355	n.a.
(Fresh Horizons)	100	6.0	20.0	2.0	0	280	4.2
(Home Pride Butter							
Top), 1 slice . .	70	3.0	13.0	1.0	<5	160	.1
(Monk's), 1 oz. . .	60	3.0	10.0	1.0	0	n.a.	n.a.
(Pepperidge Farm)	150	4.0	25.0	3.0	n.a.	270	n.a.
(Pepperidge Farm							
Sandwich) . . .	130	4.0	23.0	2.0	n.a.	270	n.a.
(Pepperidge Farm							
Toasting)	170	6.0	32.0	2.0	n.a.	460	n.a.
(Roman Meal Light),							
1 slice	40	2.0	7.0	<1.0	<5	105	n.a.
(Wonder), 1 slice	70	3.0	13.0	1.0	<5	140	.1
very thin (Pepper-							
idge Farm) . . .	80	3.0	16.0	1.0	n.a.	170	n.a.
with buttermilk							
(Wonder), 1 slice	70	2.0	13.0	1.0	<5	160	.1
Vienna (Gonnella), 1							
oz.	70	3.0	14.0	<1.0	0	125	n.a.
Bread, canned,							
brown:							
(S&W New England),							
2 slices, 12 per can	76	2.0	17.0	0	n.a.	172	n.a.

Food and Measure	cal.	prot. (gms)	carbo. (gms)	fat (gms)	chol. (mgs)	sod. (mgs)	fiber (gms)
plain or raisin (B&M), 1/2" slice	80	2.0	18.0	n.a.	n.a.	220	n.a.
Bread, mix:							
applesauce spice (Pillsbury), 1/12 loaf*	150	2.0	28.0	3.0	n.a.	150	n.a.
apricot nut (Pillsbury), 1/12 loaf*	160	2.0	27.0	4.0	n.a.	150	n.a.
banana:							
(Duncan Hines), 1/2" slice*	160	2.0	27.0	5.0	n.a.	205	n.a.
(Pillsbury), 1/12 loaf*	160	3.0	26.0	5.0	n.a.	210	n.a.
blueberry nut (Pillsbury), 1/12 loaf* ..	150	2.0	26.0	4.0	n.a.	150	n.a.
carrot nut:							
(Duncan Hines), 1/2" slice*	160	2.0	27.0	5.0	n.a.	205	n.a.
(Pillsbury), 1/12 loaf*	150	2.0	27.0	4.0	n.a.	180	n.a.
cherry nut (Pillsbury), 1/12 loaf*	180	3.0	29.0	5.0	n.a.	150	n.a.
corn:							
(Dromedary), 2"×2" piece*	130	3.0	20.0	3.0	n.a.	480	n.a.
(Aunt Jemima), 1.7 oz. dry	205	3.6	33.9	6.1	n.a.	519	.1
Mexican (Martha White), 1/4 bread*	220	6.0	33.0	7.0	n.a.	n.a.	n.a.
cranberry (Pillsbury), 1/12 loaf*	160	2.0	30.0	3.0	n.a.	150	n.a.
date (Pillsbury), 1/12 loaf*	160	2.0	31.0	3.0	n.a.	150	n.a.
date-nut roll (Dromedary), 1/2" slice*	80	1.0	13.0	2.0	n.a.	160	n.a.
French (Home Hearth), 2 slices, 3/8"*	170	6.0	29.0	3.0	n.a.	480	n.a.
honey granola (Pillsbury), 1/12 loaf* ..	170	3.0	29.0	4.0	n.a.	180	n.a.

* Prepared according to package directions

Food and Measure	cal.	prot. (gms)	carbo. (gms)	fat (gms)	chol. (mgs)	sod. (mgs)	fiber (gms)
Bread, mix (cont.)							
nut:							
(Duncan Hines), 1/2" slice*	170	2.0	27.0	6.0	n.a.	190	n.a.
(Pillsbury), 1/12 loaf*	170	3.0	27.0	6.0	n.a.	150	n.a.
raisin cinnamon (Duncan Hines), 1/2" slice*	150	2.0	27.0	4.0	n.a.	190	n.a.
rye (Home Hearth), 2 slices, 3/8"*	150	6.0	29.0	1.0	n.a.	360	n.a.
white (Home Hearth), 2 slices, 3/4"* . .	150	6.0	28.0	1.0	n.a.	260	n.a.
Bread crumbs:							
seasoned:							
(Contadina), 1 cup	426	16.5	81.5	3.6	0	3150	.7
(Contadina), 1 tbsp.	35	1.0	7.0	<1.0	0	265	.1
toasted (Old London), 2 oz.	210	7.0	40.0	2.0	0	n.a.	n.a.
Bread cubes:							
(Brownberry), 1 oz.	110	3.0	20.0	2.0	n.a.	n.a.	n.a.
Bread dough:							
frozen:							
French (Bridgford), 2 slices	150	7.0	26.0	1.0	n.a.	328	n.a.
honey wheat (Bridgford), 2 slices	150	6.0	27.0	2.0	n.a.	304	n.a.
white (Bridgford), 2 slices	150	5.0	28.0	2.0	n.a.	325	n.a.
white (Rich's), 2 slices	116	3.9	22.7	1.1	0	300	n.a.
refrigerated:							
French (Pipin' Hot), 1" slice	60	2.0	11.0	1.0	n.a.	120	n.a.
wheat (Pipin' Hot), 1" slice	80	3.0	12.0	2.0	n.a.	170	n.a.

* Prepared according to package directions

Food and Measure	cal.	prot. (gms)	carbo. (gms)	fat (gms)	chol. (mgs)	sod. (mgs)	fiber (gms)
white *(Pipin' Hot)*, 1″ slice	80	2.0	13.0	2.0	n.a.	170	n.a.
Bread stuffing, see "Stuffing"							
Breadfruit:							
fresh, peeled, seeded, 1 cup	227	2.4	59.7	.5	0	4	3.3
Breadfruit seeds, shelled:							
raw, 1 oz.	54	2.1	8.3	1.6	0	n.a.	.5
boiled, 1 oz.	48	1.5	9.1	.7	0	n.a.	.5
roasted, 1 oz.	59	1.8	11.4	.8	0	n.a.	.6
Breadnut tree seeds:							
raw, 1 oz.	62	1.7	13.1	.3	0	n.a.	.7
dried, 1 oz.	104	2.5	22.6	.5	0	n.a.	1.6
Breadsticks:							
plain *(Stella D'Oro)*, 1 piece	41	1.0	6.0	1.3	n.a.	n.a.	n.a.
onion *(Stella D'Oro)*, 1 piece	38	1.1	5.8	1.1	n.a.	n.a.	n.a.
salt sticks, plain, 1 oz.	109	3.4	21.3	.8	n.a.	475	.1
sesame *(Stella D'Oro)*, 1 piece	50	1.4	6.2	2.2	n.a.	n.a.	n.a.
soft *(Pillsbury)*, 1 piece	100	3.0	17.0	2.0	n.a.	230	n.a.
Vienna, 1 oz.	86	2.7	16.4	.9	n.a.	444	.1
wheat *(Stella D'Oro)*, 1 piece	41	1.3	6.0	1.3	n.a.	n.a.	n.a.
Breakfast bar (see also "Granola and similar snack bars"):							
chocolate *(Carnation Slender)*, 2 bars	270	11.0	26.0	14.0	n.a.	285	n.a.
chocolate chip:							
(Carnation), 1 bar	200	6.0	20.0	11.0	n.a.	180	n.a.
(Carnation Slender), 2 bars	270	11.0	26.0	14.0	n.a.	315	n.a.

Food and Measure	cal.	prot. (gms)	carbo. (gms)	fat (gms)	chol. (mgs)	sod. (mgs)	fiber (gms)
Breakfast bar *(cont.)*							
chocolate crunch							
(*Carnation*), 1 bar	190	6.0	20.0	10.0	n.a.	145	n.a.
chocolate peanut butter (*Carnation Slender*), 2 bars	270	11.0	24.0	15.0	n.a.	285	n.a.
honey nut (*Carnation*), 1 bar	190	6.0	18.0	11.0	n.a.	155	n.a.
peanut butter crunch or chocolate chip (*Carnation*), 1 bar	200	6.0	20.0	11.0	n.a.	170	n.a.
vanilla (*Carnation Slender*), 2 bars	270	11.0	24.0	15.0	n.a.	320	n.a.
Breakfast strips, see "Bacon, substitute"							
Broad beans:							
raw, 1 cup	79	6.1	12.8	.7	0	55	2.4
boiled, drained, 4 oz.	64	5.4	11.5	.6	0	46	2.2
Broccoli:							
fresh:							
raw, 1 spear, 8.7 oz.	42	4.5	7.9	.5	0	40	1.7
boiled, drained, 1 spear, 6.3 oz.	53	5.4	10.0	.5	0	19	2.2
boiled, drained, chopped, 1 cup	46	4.6	8.7	.4	0	16	1.9
frozen:							
spears (*A&P*), 3.3 oz.	25	3.0	5.0	<1.0	0	20	n.a.
spears (*Birds Eye*), 3.3 oz.	25	3.0	5.0	0	0	20	.9
spears (*Frosty Acres*), 3.3 oz.	25	3.0	5.0	0	0	20	1.0
spears (*Green Giant Harvest Fresh*), 1/2 cup	30	3.0	4.0	0	0	200	n.a.
spears, baby (*Birds Eye* Deluxe), 3.3 oz.	30	3.0	5.0	0	0	15	1.1

Food and Measure	cal.	prot. (gms)	carbo. (gms)	fat (gms)	chol. (mgs)	sod. (mgs)	fiber (gms)
spears, mini *(Green Giant* Frozen Like Fresh), 1/2 cup	16	1.0	3.0	0	0	10	n.a.
florets *(Birds Eye Deluxe)*, 3.3 oz.	25	3.0	5.0	0	0	20	.9
florets *(Frosty Acres)*, 3.3 oz.	30	3.0	5.0	0	0	14	1.0
cuts *(Birds Eye)*, 3.3 oz.	25	3.0	4.0	0	0	25	1.0
cuts *(Frosty Acres)*, 3.3 oz.	25	3.0	5.0	0	0	50	1.0
cuts *(Green Giant)*, 1/2 cup	16	2.0	2.0	0	0	10	n.a.
cuts *(Green Giant Harvest Fresh)*, 1/2 cup	25	2.0	4.0	0	0	200	n.a.
cuts or chopped *(A&P)*, 3.3 oz.	25	3.0	5.0	<1.0	0	25	n.a.
chopped *(Birds Eye)*, 3.3 oz. . .	25	3.0	5.0	0	0	20	1.0
chopped *(Frosty Acres)*, 3.3 oz.	25	3.0	5.0	0	0	18	1.0
with almonds *(Birds Eye)*, 3.3 oz. . .	50	4.0	6.0	3.0	0	220	1.0
in butter sauce, spears *(Green Giant)*, 1/2 cup . .	45	2.0	5.0	2.0	n.a.	340	n.a.
with cheddar cheese sauce *(Stouffer's)*, 41/2 oz.	150	8.0	7.0	10.0	n.a.	480	n.a.
with cheese sauce *(Birds Eye)*, 5 oz.	120	5.0	13.0	7.0	n.a.	510	.7
in cheese flavored sauce *(Green Giant)*, 1/2 cup . .	70	3.0	9.0	2.0	n.a.	530	n.a.
with creamy Italian cheese sauce *(Birds Eye)*, 4.5 oz.	110	5.0	8.0	7.0	n.a.	280	.9

Food and Measure	cal.	prot. (gms)	carbo. (gms)	fat (gms)	chol. (mgs)	sod. (mgs)	fiber (gms)
Broccoli, frozen (cont.)							
in white cheddar cheese flavored sauce (Green Giant), 1/2 cup . .	60	3.0	6.0	3.0	n.a.	450	n.a.
Broccoli combinations, frozen:							
and baby carrots and water chestnuts (Birds Eye), 3.2 oz.	30	2.0	6.0	0	0	25	.9
and carrots:							
in butter sauce (Green Giant), 1/2 cup	30	1.0	4.0	1.0	n.a.	340	n.a.
in cheese flavored sauce (Green Giant), 1/2 cup . .	70	3.0	9.0	2.0	n.a.	490	n.a.
and carrot fanfare (Green Giant Valley Combination), 1/2 cup	20	1.0	4.0	0	0	30	n.a.
and carrots and pasta twists (Birds Eye), 3.3 oz.	90	2.0	11.0	4.0	n.a.	270	.8
and cauliflower, with creamy Italian cheese sauce (Birds Eye), 4.5 oz. . . .	110	5.0	8.0	7.0	n.a.	280	.8
and cauliflower medley:							
(Green Giant Harvest Get Togethers), 1/2 cup	60	2.0	10.0	1.0	n.a.	470	n.a.
with sauce (Green Giant Valley Combination), 1/2 cup . . .	60	2.0	9.0	2.0	n.a.	430	n.a.

Food and Measure	cal.	prot. (gms)	carbo. (gms)	fat (gms)	chol. (mgs)	sod. (mgs)	fiber (gms)
and cauliflower supreme *(Green Giant Valley Combination)*, 1/2 cup	18	1.0	3.0	0	0	30	n.a.
and cauliflower and carrots *(Birds Eye)*, 3.2 oz.	25	2.0	5.0	0	0	25	.9
and cauliflower and carrots, with cheese sauce *(Birds Eye)*, 5 oz.	110	4.0	12.0	7.0	n.a.	500	.6
and corn and red peppers *(Birds Eye)*, 3.2 oz.	50	3.0	11.0	0	0	10	.7
fanfare *(Green Giant Harvest Get Togethers)*, 1/2 cup	70	3.0	12.0	1.0	n.a.	470	n.a.
fanfare, with sauce *(Green Giant Valley Combination)*, 1/2 cup	80	3.0	13.0	2.0	n.a.	430	n.a.
and green beans, pearl onions and red peppers *(Birds Eye)*, 3.2 oz. . . .	25	2.0	5.0	0	0	15	.9
and water chestnuts *(Birds Eye)*, 3.3 oz.	30	3.0	6.0	0	0	220	.9
Broccoli with cheese, in pastry, frozen:							
(Pepperidge Farm), 1 piece	230	5.0	18.0	16.0	n.a.	380	n.a.
croissant *(Sara Lee Le San*Wich)*, 4-oz. piece	320	10.0	30.0	18.0	n.a.	610	n.a.
Brown gravy:							
canned:							
(Heinz Home Style)*, 2 oz.	29	.7	1.4	2.3	n.a.	130	n.a.

Food and Measure	cal.	prot. (gms)	carbo. (gms)	fat (gms)	chol. (mgs)	sod. (mgs)	fiber (gms)
Brown gravy (cont.)							
with onions (Franco-American), 2 oz.	25	0	4.0	1.0	n.a.	340	n.a.
mix:							
(Durkee), .8-oz. pkg.	59	2.5	10.0	.4	n.a.	1037	n.a.
(French's), 1/4 cup*	20	1.0	4.0	1.0	n.a.	250	n.a.
(Pillsbury French's), 1/4 cup*	15	<1.0	3.0	0	0	300	n.a.
(Spatini Family Style), 1 fl. oz.*	8	0	2.0	0	0	205	n.a.
with mushrooms (Durkee), .8-oz. pkg.	59	.3	11.0	.5	n.a.	1402	n.a.
with onions (Durkee), .8-oz. pkg.	66	2.0	13.0	.5	n.a.	1356	n.a.
Brownie (see also "Cookies"):							
fudge walnut (Tastykake), 1 piece	394	3.9	52.9	18.5	n.a.	169	n.a.
mix*:							
(Duncan Hines Moist Regular Size), 1 piece	160	2.0	22.0	7.0	n.a.	105	n.a.
(Duncan Hines Moist Family Size), 1 piece	160	2.0	23.0	7.0	n.a.	105	n.a.
black forest (Pillsbury), 2" square	160	2.0	25.0	6.0	n.a.	100	n.a.
chocolate chip (Betty Crocker, 1/24 pkg.	130	1.0	20.0	5.0	n.a.	75	n.a.
fudge (Betty Crocker Regular Size), 1/16 pkg.	150	1.0	23.0	6.0	n.a.	100	n.a.
fudge (Betty Crocker Family Size), 1/24 pkg.	130	1.0	21.0	5.0	n.a.	95	n.a.

* Prepared according to package directions

Food and Measure	cal.	prot. (gms)	carbo. (gms)	fat (gms)	chol. (mgs)	sod. (mgs)	fiber (gms)
fudge (Betty Crocker Supreme), 1/24 pkg.	120	1.0	21.0	3.0	n.a.	85	n.a.
fudge (Pillsbury), 2" square	150	2.0	21.0	6.0	n.a.	100	n.a.
fudge (Pillsbury Family Size), 2" square	150	1.0	20.0	7.0	n.a.	95	n.a.
fudge, double (Pillsbury), 2" square	160	2.0	24.0	6.0	n.a.	105	n.a.
fudge, frosted (Betty Crocker Family Size), 1/24 pkg.	160	1.0	27.0	5.0	n.a.	105	n.a.
golden (Betty Crocker), 1/24 pkg.	130	1.0	19.0	5.0	n.a.	30	n.a.
rocky road, fudge (Pillsbury), 2" square	170	2.0	24.0	7.0	n.a.	100	n.a.
walnut (Betty Crocker Regular Size), 1/16 pkg.	160	1.0	22.0	7.0	n.a.	105	n.a.
walnut (Betty Crocker Family Size), 1/24 pkg.	130	1.0	19.0	6.0	n.a.	85	n.a.
walnut (Pillsbury Family Size), 2" square	150	2.0	19.0	8.0	n.a.	90	n.a.
refrigerated, fudge (Pillsbury), 1 bar	140	1.0	22.0	5.0	n.a.	115	n.a.
Browning sauce:							
(Gravymaster), 1 tsp.	12	.5	2.4	<.1	0	<1	<.1
Brussels sprouts:							
fresh:							
raw, 4 average . .	32	2.6	6.8	.2	0	20	1.2
boiled, 4 average	32	2.1	7.3	.4	0	16	1.2
frozen:							
(A&P), 3.3 oz. . . .	35	3.0	7.0	<1.0	0	15	n.a.
(Birds Eye), 3.3 oz.	35	3.0	7.0	0	0	15	1.2

Food and Measure	cal.	prot. (gms)	carbo. (gms)	fat (gms)	chol. (mgs)	sod. (mgs)	fiber (gms)
Brussels sprouts, frozen *(cont.)*							
(Frosty Acres), 3.3 oz.	35	3.0	7.0	0	0	12	1.0
(Green Giant), 1/2 cup	30	2.0	6.0	0	0	10	n.a.
in butter sauce *(Green Giant)*, 1/2 cup	60	3.0	9.0	1.0	n.a.	320	n.a.
baby, with cheese sauce *(Birds Eye)*, 4.5 oz.	120	5.0	13.0	6.0	n.a.	440	1.0
baby, in cheese fla- vored sauce *(Green Giant)*, 1/2 cup	80	3.0	13.0	2.0	n.a.	470	n.a.
and cauliflower and carrots *(Birds Eye)*, 3.2 oz. . .	30	2.0	7.0	0	0	20	1.0
Bulgur (parboiled wheat):							
club wheat, dry, 8 oz.	814	19.7	180.0	3.2	0	n.a.	3.9
hard red winter wheat, dry, 8 oz.	803	25.4	171.7	3.4	0	n.a.	3.9
white wheat, dry, 8 oz.	810	23.4	177.1	2.7	0	n.a.	2.9
canned, hard red win- ter wheat:							
unseasoned, 8 oz.	381	14.1	79.4	1.6	0	1359	1.8
seasoned, 8 oz.	413	14.1	74.4	7.5	0	1043	1.8
Buns, honey, 1 bun:							
glazed *(Hostess)* . .	450	5.0	49.0	27.0	24	650	n.a.
frozen:							
plain or maple nut *(Morton)*, 2.3 oz.	240	3.0	31.0	12.0	n.a.	150	n.a.
chocolate *(Morton)*, 2.3 oz.	240	3.0	31.0	12.0	n.a.	170	n.a.
coconut or orange *(Morton)*, 2.3 oz.	240	3.0	31.0	12.0	n.a.	155	n.a.

Food and Measure	cal.	prot. (gms)	carbo. (gms)	fat (gms)	chol. (mgs)	sod. (mgs)	fiber (gms)
Burdock root, fresh:							
raw:							
1 root, 7.3 oz. . . .	112	2.4	27.1	.2	0	8	3.0
1" pieces, 1 cup	85	1.8	20.5	.2	0	6	2.3
boiled, drained, 1"							
pieces, 1 cup . . .	110	2.6	26.4	.2	0	5	2.3
Burger King:							
sandwiches, 1 serving:							
bacon double							
cheeseburger,							
7.13 oz.	600	35.0	36.0	35.0	n.a.	985	n.a.
cheeseburger, 4.7							
oz.	360	18.0	35.0	16.0	n.a.	705	n.a.
cheeseburger,							
double, 6.7 oz.	520	32.0	35.0	28.0	n.a.	865	n.a.
chicken, 7.8 oz.	690	26.0	52.0	42.0	n.a.	775	n.a.
ham and cheese,							
7.8 oz.	550	29.0	43.0	30.0	n.a.	1550	n.a.
hamburger, 4.3 oz.	310	16.0	35.0	12.0	n.a.	560	n.a.
hamburger, double,							
5.8 oz.	430	26.0	35.0	21.0	n.a.	585	n.a.
Whaler, 7.23 oz.	540	24.0	57.0	24.0	n.a.	745	n.a.
Whaler with cheese,							
7.66 oz. . . .	590	26.0	58.0	28.0	n.a.	885	n.a.
Whopper, 9.9 oz.	670	27.0	56.0	38.0	n.a.	975	n.a.
Whopper with							
cheese, 10.8 oz.	760	33.0	56.0	45.0	n.a.	1260	n.a.
Whopper double							
beef, 12.6 oz.	890	46.0	56.0	53.0	n.a.	1015	n.a.
Whopper double							
beef, with cheese,							
13.5 oz.	980	51.0	56.0	61.0	n.a.	1295	n.a.
Whopper Jr., 5.3 oz.	370	16.0	35.0	18.0	n.a.	545	n.a.
Whopper Jr. with							
cheese, 5.7 oz.	410	19.0	35.0	21.0	n.a.	685	n.a.
side dishes, 1 serving:							
French fries, regu-							
lar, 2.4 oz. . . .	210	3.0	25.0	11.0	n.a.	230	n.a.

Food and Measure	cal.	prot. (gms)	carbo. (gms)	fat (gms)	chol. (mgs)	sod. (mgs)	fiber (gms)
Burger King, side dishes *(cont.)*							
onion rings, regular, 2.7 oz.	270	3.0	29.0	16.0	n.a.	450	n.a.
dessert and shakes, 1 serving:							
apple pie, 4.5 oz.	330	3.0	48.0	14.0	n.a.	385	n.a.
chocolate shake, 10 oz.	340	8.0	57.0	10.0	n.a.	280	n.a.
vanilla shake, 10 oz.	340	8.0	52.0	11.0	n.a.	320	n.a.
Burrito, frozen, 1 piece:							
beef *(Hormel)*	205	9.0	31.0	8.0	n.a.	780	n.a.
beef and bean:							
(Patio), 1 oz. . . .	190	5.0	21.0	9.0	n.a.	n.a.	n.a.
(Patio), 6 oz. . . .	450	13.0	49.0	22.0	n.a.	n.a.	n.a.
with red chili *(Patio),* 1 oz.	190	5.0	22.0	8.0	n.a.	n.a.	n.a.
with red chili *(Patio),* 6 oz.	440	13.0	53.0	19.0	n.a.	n.a.	n.a.
with green chili *(Patio),* 1 oz.	190	6.0	23.0	8.0	n.a.	n.a.	n.a.
with green chili *(Patio),* 6 oz.	450	15.0	54.0	20.0	n.a.	n.a.	n.a.
cheese *(Hormel)* . .	210	9.0	32.0	5.0	n.a.	792	n.a.
chicken and rice *(Hormel)*	200	9.0	32.0	4.0	n.a.	594	n.a.
chili, hot *(Hormel)*	240	9.0	33.0	8.0	n.a.	619	n.a.
Burrito dinner, frozen:							
bean and beef *(Swanson),* 15¼ oz. . .	720	21.0	88.0	32.0	n.a.	1630	n.a.
Grande, with rice and corn *(Van de Kamp's* Combinations), 14¾ oz.	530	20.0	70.0	20.0	n.a.	1210	n.a.
Burrito entree, frozen:							
fried, crispy *(Van de Kamp's* Mexican Classics), 6 oz. . .	365	10.0	40.0	15.0	n.a.	823	n.a.

Food and Measure	cal.	prot. (gms)	carbo. (gms)	fat (gms)	chol. (mgs)	sod. (mgs)	fiber (gms)
Grande *(Hormel)*, 5½ oz.	380	14.0	45.0	16.0	n.a.	877	n.a.
sirloin Grande *(Van de Kamp's* Mexican Classics), 11 oz.	440	25.0	45.0	15.0	n.a.	1120	n.a.
Burrito sauce:							
(Del Monte Salsa), ¼ cup	20	0	4.0	0	0	355	n.a.
Butter:							
regular, salted:							
4 oz., 1 stick or ½ cup	813	1.0	.1	92.0	248	937	0
1 tbsp.	102	.1	.1	11.5	31	140	0
1 tsp.	34	tr.	tr.	3.8	10	46	0
1 pat, 1″ × ⅓″ . .	36	<.1	tr.	4.1	11	41	0
regular, unsalted:							
4 oz., 1 stick or ½ cup	813	1.0	.1	92.0	248	13	0
1 tbsp.	102	.1	.1	11.5	31	1	0
1 tsp.	34	tr.	tr.	3.8	10	<1	0
1 pat, 1″ × ⅓″ . .	36	<.1	tr.	4.1	11	1	0
whipped, salted:							
½ cup or 1 stick	542	.6	<.1	61.3	165	625	0
1 tbsp.	67	.1	tr.	7.6	20	93	0
1 tsp.	23	tr.	tr.	2.6	7	32	0
1 pat, 1¼″ × ⅓″	27	<.1	tr.	3.1	8	31	0
whipped, unsalted:							
½ cup or 1 stick	542	.6	<.1	61.3	165	13	0
1 tbsp.	67	.1	tr.	7.6	20	1	0
1 tsp.	23	tr.	tr.	2.6	7	<1	0
1 pat, 1¼″ × ⅓″	27	<.1	tr.	3.1	8	1	0
Butter oil:							
1 tbsp.	112	<.1	0	12.7	33	n.a.	0
Butterbeans:							
canned:							
(A&P), ½ cup . .	110	7.0	20.0	<1.0	0	380	n.a.
(Joan of Arc), ½ cup	100	6.0	18.0	<1.0	0	420	n.a.

Food and Measure	cal.	prot. (gms)	carbo. (gms)	fat (gms)	chol. (mgs)	sod. (mgs)	fiber (gms)
Butterbeans, canned *(cont.)*							
(Ritter Golden), 1/2 cup	140	9.0	25.0	0	0	430	n.a.
(Van Camp's), 1 cup	162	11.0	28.4	2.8	0	752	2.8
dry, cooked *(S&W Tender)*, 1/2 cup	100	6.0	19.0	1.0	0	440	n.a.
frozen *(Frosty Acres)*, 3.3 oz.	120	7.0	23.0	0	0	180	n.a.
Butterbur (fuki), fresh:							
raw, 1 cup	13	.4	3.4	<.1	0	7	1.2
boiled, drained, 4 oz.	9	.3	2.4	<.1	0	5	.9
Butterfish, raw:							
meat only, 4 oz. . .	166	19.6	0	9.1	74	101	0
Buttermilk dip:							
(Kraft), 2 tbsp. . . .	70	1.0	3.0	6.0	n.a.	240	n.a.
Butternuts:							
dried, shelled, 4 oz.	696	28.3	13.7	64.7	0	0	2.1

C

Food and Measure	cal.	prot. (gms)	carbo. (gms)	fat (gms)	chol. (mgs)	sod. (mgs)	fiber (gms)
Cabbage, fresh:							
raw:							
whole, 1 lb.	86	4.4	19.5	.7	0	65	2.9
one head (5¾"							
diam.)	215	11.0	48.8	1.6	0	164	7.3
shredded, 1 cup	16	.8	3.8	.1	0	12	.6
boiled:							
shredded, 1 cup	32	1.4	7.1	.4	0	28	.9
¼ of 5¾" head	68	3.0	15.0	.8	0	60	1.9
Cabbage, Chinese, fresh:							
bok-choy:							
raw, whole, 1 lb.	52	6.0	8.7	.8	0	257	2.4
raw, shredded, 1 cup	9	1.1	1.5	.1	0	45	.4
boiled, shredded, 1 cup	20	2.7	3.0	.3	0	57	1.0
pe-tsai:							
raw, whole, 1 lb.	68	5.1	13.6	.8	0	38	2.5
raw, shredded, 1 cup	12	.9	2.5	.2	0	7	.5
boiled, shredded, 1 cup	16	1.8	2.9	.2	0	11	.6
Cabbage, red:							
fresh:							
raw, whole, 1 lb.	100	5.0	22.2	.9	0	38	3.6
raw, shredded, 1 cup	19	1.0	4.3	.2	0	7	.7
boiled, shredded, 1 cup	32	1.6	7.0	.3	0	12	1.1

Food and Measure	cal.	prot. (gms)	carbo. (gms)	fat (gms)	chol. (mgs)	sod. (mgs)	fiber (gms)
Cabbage, red *(cont.)*							
canned, sweet and sour *(Greenwood)*, 1/2 cup	60	1.0	13.0	0	0	480	.4
Cabbage, savoy, fresh:							
raw:							
whole, 1 lb.	100	7.3	22.1	.4	0	102	2.9
shredded, 1 cup	19	1.4	4.3	.1	0	20	.6
boiled, drained, shredded, 1 cup	35	2.6	7.8	.1	0	34	1.0
Cabbage, stuffed, dinner, frozen:							
(Classic Lite), 12 oz.	290	13.0	43.0	8.0	40	600	n.a.
(Lean Cuisine), 103/4 oz.	220	15.0	20.0	9.0	40	830	n.a.
Cabbage, swamp, see "Swamp cabbage"							
Cake, frozen:							
black forest *(Sara Lee)*, 2.5 oz. . . .	190	2.0	28.0	8.0	n.a.	100	n.a.
Boston cream *(Pepperidge Farm)*, 27/8 oz.	290	3.0	39.0	14.0	n.a.	190	n.a.
butter pound *(Pepperidge Farm)*, 1 oz.	130	1.0	16.0	7.0	n.a.	110	n.a.
butterscotch pecan layer *(Pepperidge Farm)*, 15/8 oz. . .	160	1.0	23.0	7.0	n.a.	110	n.a.
carrot, with cream cheese icing *(Pepperidge Farm)*, 13/8 oz.	140	1.0	17.0	8.0	n.a.	150	n.a.
cheese cake:							
(Sara Lee Classic Elegant Endings), 4 oz.	350	10.0	29.0	22.0	n.a.	250	n.a.

Food and Measure	cal.	prot. (gms)	carbo. (gms)	fat (gms)	chol. (mgs)	sod. (mgs)	fiber (gms)
chocolate chip (Sara Lee Elegant Endings), 4 oz.	420	7.0	38.0	27.0	n.a.	390	n.a.
cream cheese, French (Sara Lee), 3 oz. . . .	260	4.0	23.0	17.0	n.a.	150	n.a.
pecan praline (Sara Lee Elegant Endings), 4 oz. . . .	430	7.0	32.0	30.0	n.a.	410	n.a.
strawberry, French (Sara Lee), 3.3 oz.	250	3.0	23.0	16.0	n.a.	170	n.a.
chocolate: (Pepperidge Farm Supreme), 2⅞ oz.	310	3.0	37.0	17.0	n.a.	140	n.a.
Dutch (Pepperidge Farm Supreme), 1¾ oz.	190	1.0	25.0	10.0	n.a.	115	n.a.
fudge layer (Pepperidge Farm), 1⅝ oz.	180	1.0	23.0	10.0	n.a.	140	n.a.
German, layer (Pepperidge Farm), 1⅝ oz.	180	1.0	23.0	10.0	n.a.	170	n.a.
mint layer (Pepperidge Farm), 1⅝ oz.	170	1.0	22.0	9.0	n.a.	140	n.a.
mousse (Sara Lee), 2.7 oz.	250	3.0	23.0	16.0	n.a.	140	n.a.
coconut layer (Pepperidge Farm), 1⅝ oz.	180	1.0	25.0	9.0	n.a.	120	n.a.
coffee cake: pecan (Sara Lee), 1.45 oz.	160	3.0	19.0	8.0	n.a.	240	n.a.
walnut (Sara Lee), 1.45 oz.	170	3.0	18.0	9.0	n.a.	160	n.a.
devil's food layer (Pepperidge Farm), 1⅝ oz.	180	1.0	24.0	9.0	n.a.	135	n.a.

Food and Measure	cal.	prot. (gms)	carbo. (gms)	fat (gms)	chol. (mgs)	sod. (mgs)	fiber (gms)
Cake, frozen *(cont.)*							
golden layer *(Pepperidge Farm)*, 1 5/8 oz.	180	1.0	24.0	9.0	n.a.	115	n.a.
Grand Marnier *(Pepperidge Farm Supreme)*, 1 1/2 oz.	160	1.0	22.0	18.0	n.a.	85	n.a.
lemon coconut *(Pepperidge Farm Supreme)*, 3 oz. . . .	280	2.0	38.0	13.0	n.a.	220	n.a.
peach Melba *(Pepperidge Farm Supreme)*, 3 1/8 oz.	270	2.0	50.0	7.0	n.a.	135	n.a.
pineapple cream *(Pepperidge Farm Supreme)*, 2 oz. . . .	190	2.0	28.0	7.0	n.a.	130	n.a.
pound cake:							
all butter *(Sara Lee)*, 1.1 oz. . .	130	2.0	14.0	7.0	n.a.	85	n.a.
chocolate chip *(Sara Lee)*, 1.3 oz.	130	2.0	19.0	5.0	n.a.	150	n.a.
walnut raisin *(Sara Lee)*, 1.4 oz. . .	140	3.0	20.0	5.0	n.a.	170	n.a.
raspberry mocha *(Pepperidge Farm Supreme)*, 3 1/8 oz.	310	3.0	43.0	14.0	n.a.	170	n.a.
strawberry cream *(Pepperidge Farm Supreme)*, 2 oz.	190	1.0	30.0	7.0	n.a.	120	n.a.
strawberry shortcake *(Sara Lee)*, 2.5 oz.	190	2.0	26.0	8.0	n.a.	90	n.a.
vanilla layer *(Pepperidge Farm)*, 1 5/8 oz.	190	1.0	25.0	8.0	n.a.	120	n.a.
Cake, mix:							
angel food:							
(Duncan Hines), 1/12 cake*	140	3.0	30.0	0	0	130	n.a.

* Prepared according to package directions

Food and Measure	cal.	prot. (gms)	carbo. (gms)	fat (gms)	chol. (mgs)	sod. (mgs)	fiber (gms)
chocolate (Betty Crocker), 1/12 pkg.	150	3.0	34.0	0	0	300	n.a.
confetti (Betty Crocker), 1/12 pkg.	160	3.0	36.0	0	0	310	n.a.
lemon custard (Betty Crocker), 1/12 pkg.	150	3.0	35.0	0	0	260	n.a.
strawberry (Betty Crocker), 1/12 pkg.	150	3.0	35.0	0	0	160	n.a.
white (Betty Crocker), 1/12 pkg.	150	3.0	34.0	0	0	300	n.a.
white, traditional (Betty Crocker), 1/12 pkg.	140	3.0	31.0	0	0	160	n.a.
apple: (Duncan Hines Deluxe), 1/12 cake*	260	3.0	34.0	12.0	n.a.	285	n.a.
cinnamon (Betty Crocker Supermoist), 1/12 pkg.	180	1.0	36.0	3.0	n.a.	260	n.a.
Dutch (Betty Crocker Cake Lovers Collection), 1/12 pkg.	210	1.0	42.0	4.0	n.a.	290	n.a.
Dutch (Streusel Swirl), 1/16 cake*	260	3.0	38.0	11.0	n.a.	200	n.a.
applesauce-raisin (Betty Crocker Snackin' Cake), 1/9 pkg.	190	2.0	33.0	6.0	n.a.	260	n.a.
applesauce-spice (Pillsbury Plus), 1/12 cake*	250	3.0	36.0	11.0	n.a.	300	n.a.
banana: (Pillsbury Plus), 1/12 cake*	250	3.0	36.0	11.0	n.a.	290	n.a.

* Prepared according to package directions

Food and Measure	cal.	prot. (gms)	carbo. (gms)	fat (gms)	chol. (mgs)	sod. (mgs)	fiber (gms)
Cake, mix, banana *(cont.)*							
supreme *(Duncan Hines Deluxe)*, 1/12 cake* . . .	260	3.0	36.0	11.0	n.a.	285	n.a.
walnut *(Betty Crocker Snackin' Cake)*, 1/9 pkg.	200	2.0	31.0	7.0	n.a.	260	n.a.
Boston cream *(Pillsbury Bundt)*, 1/16 cake*	270	3.0	43.0	10.0	n.a.	310	n.a.
Boston cream pie *(Betty Crocker Classics)*, 1/8 pkg. . . .	230	1.0	48.0	4.0	n.a.	370	n.a.
butter *(Betty Crocker Supermoist Brickle)*, 1/12 pkg.	190	2.0	38.0	3.0	n.a.	260	n.a.
butter pecan *(Betty Crocker Supermoist)*, 1/12 pkg.	180	2.0	35.0	4.0	n.a.	300	n.a.
butter recipe *(Pillsbury Plus)*, 1/12 cake*	260	3.0	34.0	12.0	n.a.	370	n.a.
carrot:							
(Betty Crocker Supermoist), 1/12 pkg.	180	2.0	34.0	4.0	n.a.	240	n.a.
(Betty Crocker Cake Lovers Collection), 1/12 pkg.	210	2.0	40.0	5.0	n.a.	290	n.a.
(Duncan Hines Deluxe), 1/12 cake*	250	3.0	34.0	11.0	n.a.	265	n.a.
with cream cheese frosting *(Betty Crocker Stir 'N Frost)*, 1/6 pkg.	230	2.0	43.0	6.0	n.a.	210	n.a.
and spice *(Pillsbury Plus)*, 1/12 cake*	260	3.0	36.0	11.0	n.a.	330	n.a.

* *Prepared according to package directions*

Food and Measure	cal.	prot. (gms)	carbo. (gms)	fat (gms)	chol. (mgs)	sod. (mgs)	fiber (gms)
cheese:							
(Royal No Bake), 1/8 cake*	210	5.0	23.0	10.0	n.a.	380	n.a.
real (Royal No Bake), 1/8 cake*	280	5.0	31.0	9.0	n.a.	370	n.a.
cherry:							
chip (Betty Crocker Supermoist), 1/12 pkg.	180	2.0	37.0	3.0	n.a.	250	n.a.
supreme (Duncan Hines), 1/12 cake*	260	3.0	36.0	11.0	n.a.	285	n.a.
chocolate:							
almond (Betty Crocker Cake Lovers Collection), 1/12 pkg.	260	3.0	41.0	9.0	n.a.	260	n.a.
dark (Pillsbury Plus), 1/12 cake*	250	3.0	32.0	12.0	n.a.	380	n.a.
deep (Duncan Hines Deluxe), 1/12 cake*	280	4.0	33.0	15.0	n.a.	375	n.a.
double (Betty Crocker Cake Lovers Collection), 1/12 pkg.	240	2.0	43.0	7.0	n.a.	250	n.a.
fudge (Betty Crocker Supermoist), 1/12 pkg.	180	2.0	35.0	3.0	n.a.	440	n.a.
fudge, with vanilla frosting (Betty Crocker Stir 'N Frost), 1/6 pkg.	230	2.0	43.0	5.0	n.a.	270	n.a.
fudge chip (Betty Crocker Snackin' Cake), 1/9 pkg.	190	2.0	33.0	6.0	n.a.	210	n.a.

* Prepared according to package directions

Food and Measure	cal.	prot. (gms)	carbo. (gms)	fat (gms)	chol. (mgs)	sod. (mgs)	fiber (gms)
Cake, mix, chocolate (cont.)							
German (Betty Crocker Supermoist), 1/12 pkg.	180	2.0	37.0	3.0	n.a.	410	n.a.
German (Pillsbury Plus), 1/12 cake*	250	3.0	36.0	11.0	n.a.	340	n.a.
German, coconut pecan (Betty Crocker Snackin' Cake), 1/9 pkg.	190	2.0	33.0	5.0	n.a.	270	n.a.
milk (Betty Crocker Supermoist), 1/12 pkg.	180	2.0	35.0	3.0	n.a.	270	n.a.
mousse (Pillsbury Bundt), 1/16 cake*	230	3.0	36.0	9.0	n.a.	310	n.a.
pudding (Betty Crocker Classics), 1/6 pkg.	220	2.0	44.0	4.0	n.a.	240	n.a.
Swiss (Duncan Hines Deluxe), 1/12 cake* . . .	280	4.0	33.0	15.0	n.a.	375	n.a.
chocolate chip:							
(Betty Crocker Supermoist), 1/12 pkg.	180	1.0	36.0	4.0	n.a.	280	n.a.
(Duncan Hines Deluxe), 1/12 cake*	260	3.0	34.0	12.0	n.a.	265	n.a.
(Pillsbury Plus), 1/12 cake*	270	3.0	33.0	14.0	n.a.	290	n.a.
with chocolate frosting (Betty Crocker Stir 'N Frost), 1/6 pkg.	230	2.0	41.0	6.0	n.a.	200	n.a.
chocolate (Betty Crocker Supermoist), 1/12 pkg.	180	2.0	34.0	4.0	n.a.	410	n.a.

* Prepared according to package directions

Food and Measure	cal.	prot. (gms)	carbo. (gms)	fat (gms)	chol. (mgs)	sod. (mgs)	fiber (gms)
chocolate, with chocolate choco- late chip frosting (Betty Crocker Stir 'N Frost), 1/6 pkg.	230	2.0	41.0	6.0	n.a.	260	n.a.
chocolate macaroon (Pillsbury Bundt), 1/16 cake*	250	3.0	37.0	11.0	n.a.	300	n.a.
chocolate-mint (Pills- bury Plus), 1/12 cake*	250	3.0	32.0	12.0	n.a.	370	n.a.
cinnamon (Streusel Swirl), 1/16 cake*	260	3.0	38.0	11.0	n.a.	200	n.a.
coconut macaroon (Betty Crocker Clas- sics), 1/24 pkg. . .	80	1.0	10.0	4.0	n.a.	15	n.a.
coffee:							
(Aunt Jemima Easy), 1.3 oz. dry	162	1.8	28.7	4.4	n.a.	685	.7
(Pillsbury), 1/8 cake*	240	3.0	40.0	7.0	n.a.	160	n.a.
date bar (Betty Crocker Classics), 1/32 pkg.	60	<1.0	9.0	2.0	n.a.	40	n.a.
devil's food:							
(Betty Crocker Supermoist), 1/12 pkg.	190	2.0	35.0	5.0	n.a.	410	n.a.
(Duncan Hines Deluxe), 1/12 cake*	280	4.0	33.0	15.0	n.a.	375	n.a.
(Pillsbury Plus), 1/12 cake*	270	4.0	32.0	14.0	n.a.	370	n.a.
chocolate, with chocolate frosting (Betty Crocker Stir 'N Frost), 1/6 pkg.	230	2.0	41.0	6.0	n.a.	260	n.a.

* Prepared according to package directions

Food and Measure	cal.	prot. (gms)	carbo. (gms)	fat (gms)	chol. (mgs)	sod. (mgs)	fiber (gms)
Cake, mix *(cont.)*							
fudge:							
(Duncan Hines But-ter Recipe), 1/12 cake*	270	4.0	34.0	13.0	n.a.	350	n.a.
(Pillsbury Bundt Tunnel of Fudge), 1/16 cake*	270	3.0	37.0	12.0	n.a.	310	n.a.
marble (Duncan Hines Deluxe), 1/12 cake*	260	3.0	36.0	11.0	n.a.	285	n.a.
marble *(Pillsbury Plus)*, 1/12 cake*	270	4.0	36.0	12.0	n.a.	300	n.a.
peanut butter chip *(Betty Crocker Snackin' Cake)*, 1/9 pkg.	200	3.0	32.0	7.0	n.a.	250	n.a.
gingerbread:							
(Betty Crocker Clas-sics), 1/9 pkg.	200	2.0	35.0	6.0	n.a.	320	n.a.
(Dromedary), 2"×2" piece*	100	1.0	19.0	2.0	n.a.	190	n.a.
(Pillsbury), 3" square*	190	2.0	36.0	4.0	n.a.	310	n.a.
golden:							
(Duncan Hines But-ter Recipe), 1/12 cake*	270	3.0	36.0	13.0	n.a.	270	n.a.
chocolate chip *(Betty Crocker Snackin' Cake)*, 1/9 pkg.	190	2.0	34.0	5.0	n.a.	260	n.a.
pound *(Betty Crocker Classics)*, 1/12 pkg.	190	1.0	28.0	8.0	n.a.	150	n.a.
vanilla *(Duncan Hines Deluxe)*, 1/12 cake*	260	3.0	36.0	11.0	n.a.	285	n.a.

* Prepared according to package directions

Food and Measure	cal.	prot. (gms)	carbo. (gms)	fat (gms)	chol. (mgs)	sod. (mgs)	fiber (gms)
lemon:							
(Betty Crocker Supermoist), 1/12 pkg.	180	2.0	37.0	3.0	n.a.	280	n.a.
(Pillsbury Bundt Tunnel of Lemon), 1/16 cake* . . .	270	2.0	45.0	9.0	n.a.	300	n.a.
(Pillsbury Plus), 1/12 cake*	220	3.0	31.0	9.0	n.a.	260	n.a.
(Streusel Swirl), 1/16 cake*	270	3.0	39.0	11.0	n.a.	340	n.a.
chiffon (Betty Crocker Classics), 1/12 pkg.	180	3.0	35.0	3.0	n.a.	180	n.a.
pudding (Betty Crocker Classics), 1/6 pkg.	220	1.0	45.0	4.0	n.a.	260	n.a.
supreme (Duncan Hines Deluxe), 1/12 cake* . . .	260	3.0	36.0	11.0	n.a.	285	n.a.
lemon-blueberry (Pillsbury Bundt), 1/16 cake*	200	3.0	28.0	8.0	n.a.	270	n.a.
marble (Betty Crocker Supermoist), 1/12 pkg.	180	1.0	36.0	3.0	n.a.	280	n.a.
mocha (Pillsbury Plus), 1/12 cake*	250	3.0	33.0	12.0	n.a.	380	n.a.
oats'n brown sugar (Pillsbury Plus), 1/12 cake*	260	3.0	35.0	12.0	n.a.	310	n.a.
orange supreme (Duncan Hines Deluxe), 1/12 cake*	260	3.0	36.0	11.0	n.a.	285	n.a.
pecan brown sugar (Streusel Swirl), 1/16 cake*	260	3.0	37.0	11.0	n.a.	200	n.a.

* Prepared according to package directions

Food and Measure	cal.	prot. (gms)	carbo. (gms)	fat (gms)	chol. (mgs)	sod. (mgs)	fiber (gms)
Cake, mix *(cont.)*							
pineapple:							
cream *(Pillsbury Bundt)*, 1/16 cake*	260	2.0	40.0	10.0	n.a.	300	n.a.
supreme *(Duncan Hines Deluxe)*, 1/12 cake* . . .	260	3.0	36.0	11.0	n.a.	285	n.a.
upside-down, with topping *(Betty Crocker Classics)*, 1/9 pkg.	230	1.0	43.0	6.0	n.a.	200	n.a.
pound:							
(Dromedary), 1/2" slice*	150	2.0	21.0	6.0	n.a.	340	n.a.
(Pillsbury Bundt), 1/16 cake* . . .	230	3.0	33.0	9.0	n.a.	260	n.a.
sour cream:							
chocolate *(Betty Crocker Supermoist)*, 1/12 pkg.	180	2.0	36.0	3.0	n.a.	430	n.a.
chocolate *(Duncan Hines Deluxe)*, 1/12 cake* . . .	280	4.0	33.0	15.0	n.a.	375	n.a.
white *(Betty Crocker Supermoist)*, 1/12 pkg.	180	2.0	36.0	3.0	n.a.	280	n.a.
spice:							
(Betty Crocker Supermoist), 1/12 pkg.	180	1.0	36.0	4.0	n.a.	300	n.a.
(Duncan Hines Deluxe), 1/12 cake*	260	3.0	36.0	11.0	n.a.	285	n.a.
with vanilla frosting *(Betty Crocker Stir 'N Frost)*, 1/6 pkg.	280	2.0	48.0	9.0	n.a.	310	n.a.

* Prepared according to package directions

Food and Measure	cal.	prot. (gms)	carbo. (gms)	fat (gms)	chol. (mgs)	sod. (mgs)	fiber (gms)
strawberry:							
(Pillsbury Plus), 1/12 cake*	260	3.0	37.0	11.0	n.a.	300	n.a.
supreme *(Duncan Hines* Deluxe), 1/12 cake* . . .	260	3.0	36.0	11.0	n.a.	285	n.a.
Vienna dream bar *(Betty Crocker* Classics), 1/24 pkg. . .	80	1.0	10.0	4.0	n.a.	40	n.a.
white:							
(Betty Crocker Supermoist), 1/12 pkg.	190	2.0	37.0	4.0	n.a.	230	n.a.
(Duncan Hines Deluxe), 1/12 cake*	250	3.0	36.0	10.0	n.a.	260	n.a.
(Pillsbury Plus), 1/12 cake*	240	3.0	35.0	10.0	n.a.	290	n.a.
yellow:							
(Betty Crocker Supermoist), 1/12 pkg.	180	1.0	36.0	4.0	n.a.	280	n.a.
(Betty Crocker Supermoist Butter Recipe), 1/12 pkg.	170	2.0	37.0	2.0	n.a.	260	n.a.
(Duncan Hines Deluxe), 1/12 cake*	260	3.0	36.0	11.0	n.a.	285	n.a.
(Pillsbury Plus), 1/12 cake*	250	3.0	34.0	11.0	n.a.	290	n.a.
with chocolate frosting *(Betty Crocker Stir 'N Frost)*, 1/6 pkg.	230	2.0	37.0	8.0	n.a.	210	n.a.
Cake, snack, 1 piece:							
banana:							
(Hostess Suzy Q's)	240	2.0	38.0	9.0	21	195	n.a.

* *Prepared according to package directions*

Food and Measure	cal.	prot. (gms)	carbo. (gms)	fat (gms)	chol. (mgs)	sod. (mgs)	fiber (gms)
Cake, snack, banana (cont.)							
(Tastykake Banana Treats)	147	1.2	25.9	4.3	n.a.	99	n.a.
butterscotch (Tastykake Krimpets)	129	1.3	19.9	5.0	n.a.	94	n.a.
chocolate or devil's food:							
(Hostess Big Wheels)	170	1.0	21.0	9.0	6	130	n.a.
(Hostess Chip Flips)	330	2.0	47.0	16.0	25	165	n.a.
(Hostess Choco-Diles)	240	2.0	35.0	11.0	22	280	n.a.
(Hostess Ding Dongs)	170	1.0	21.0	9.0	6	130	n.a.
(Hostess Ho-Hos)	120	1.0	17.0	6.0	13	90	n.a.
(Hostess Suzy Q's)	240	2.0	37.0	10.0	16	300	n.a.
(Tastykake Creamie)	195	1.6	25.1	9.2	n.a.	114	n.a.
(Tastykake Kandy Kake)	95	1.0	12.4	4.3	n.a.	64	n.a.
(Tastykake Tempty)	97	1.0	14.7	3.7	n.a.	76	n.a.
coconut covered (Hostess Sno Balls)	150	1.0	28.0	4.0	2	170	n.a.
creme filled (Drake's Devil Dogs)	170	2.0	22.0	8.0	n.a.	165	n.a.
creme filled (Drake's Ring Ding Jr)	160	1.0	20.0	9.0	n.a.	120	n.a.
creme filled (Drake's Yankee Doodles)	110	1.0	15.0	5.0	n.a.	130	n.a.
creme filled (Tastykake Junior)	354	4.3	56.0	11.5	n.a.	292	n.a.
creme filled (Tastykake Krimpets)	148	1.4	20.5	6.7	n.a.	122	n.a.
fudge bar (Tastykake)	266	3.0	38.1	10.5	n.a.	144	n.a.

Food and Measure	cal.	prot. (gms)	carbo. (gms)	fat (gms)	chol. (mgs)	sod. (mgs)	fiber (gms)
coconut:							
(Tastykake Junior)	330	4.4	60.0	7.1	n.a.	327	n.a.
(Tastykake Kandy Kake)	106	1.1	13.9	4.8	n.a.	44	n.a.
coffee:							
(Tastykake Koffee Kake)	329	4.0	49.4	11.8	n.a.	314	n.a.
creme filled (Tastykake Koffee Kake)	147	1.7	21.2	5.7	n.a.	135	n.a.
small (Drake's) . .	220	3.0	32.0	9.0	n.a.	220	n.a.
cupcake:							
buttercream, creme filled (Tastykake)	129	1.3	19.6	5.1	n.a.	121	n.a.
chocolate (Hostess)	170	2.0	29.0	6.0	3	250	n.a.
chocolate (Tastykake)	113	1.3	19.1	3.5	n.a.	111	n.a.
chocolate, creme filled (Tastykake)	137	1.5	19.6	5.8	n.a.	131	n.a.
creme (Tastykake Kreme Kups) . .	115	1.4	15.3	5.4	n.a.	134	n.a.
(Hostess Dessert Cups)	60	1.0	14.0	0	9	120	n.a.
orange (Hostess)	150	1.0	28.0	5.0	13	175	n.a.
vanilla (Tastykake)	116	1.5	17.2	4.6	n.a.	129	n.a.
(Drake's Funny Bones)	160	2.0	18.0	9.0	n.a.	130	n.a.
(Hostess L'il Angels)	90	1.0	14.0	2.0	2	95	n.a.
(Hostess O's) . .	240	3.0	33.0	11.0	14	265	n.a.
(Hostess Tiger Tails)	210	2.0	38.0	6.0	25	240	n.a.
(Hostess Twinkies)	160	1.0	26.0	5.0	20	150	n.a.
jelly (Tastykake Krimpets)	112	1.3	22.0	2.1	n.a.	85	n.a.
oatmeal raisin bar (Tastykake)	239	3.6	36.8	8.0	n.a.	269	n.a.
orange (Tastykake Junior)	347	3.6	58.4	11.0	n.a.	258	n.a.

Food and Measure	cal.	prot. (gms)	carbo. (gms)	fat (gms)	chol. (mgs)	sod. (mgs)	fiber (gms)
Cake, snack *(cont.)*							
peanut *(Hostess Peanut Putters)*	410	7.0	43.0	21.0	4	240	n.a.
peanut, filled *(Hostess Peanut Putters)*	360	5.0	46.0	15.0	4	240	n.a.
peanut butter *(Tastykake Kandy Kake)*	105	2.0	10.8	5.6	n.a.	48	n.a.
vanilla:							
(Tastykake Creamie)	209	1.3	27.6	9.8	n.a.	126	n.a.
creme filled *(Tastykake Krimpets)*	149	1.2	21.3	6.6	n.a.	83	n.a.
Candy, 1 oz., except as noted:							
(Baby Ruth)	130	2.0	18.0	6.0	n.a.	60	n.a.
(Black Cow Sucker)	127	.9	23.8	3.2	n.a.	52	n.a.
(Black Jack Kisses)	116	.1	25.6	1.5	n.a.	71	n.a.
bridge mix:							
(Nabisco)	140	1.0	20.0	6.0	n.a.	15	n.a.
(Deran)	130	1.0	20.0	5.0	n.a.	25	n.a.
(Butterfinger)	130	2.0	19.0	6.0	n.a.	50	n.a.
(Butternut), 2-oz. bar	270	6.0	32.0	13.0	n.a.	100	n.a.
butterscotch chips *(Nestlé Morsels)*	150	1.0	19.0	7.0	0	15	n.a.
caramel:							
(Kraft), 1 piece . .	35	0	6.0	1.0	0	20	n.a.
(Pearson's Caramel Nip)	120	1.0	23.0	3.0	n.a.	70	n.a.
(Sugar Babies), 15/8-oz. pkg. . .	180	1.0	40.0	2.0	n.a.	85	n.a.
(Sugar Daddy), 13/8-oz. pop	150	1.0	33.0	1.0	n.a.	85	n.a.
(Sugar Mama), 3/4-oz. piece	90	0	17.0	3.0	n.a.	30	n.a.
chocolate coated *(Milk Duds)* . . .	129	1.0	21.4	4.4	n.a.	43	n.a.
chocolate coated *(Pom Poms)* . .	100	1.0	15.0	3.0	n.a.	70	n.a.
chocolate coated *(Rolo)*, 8 pieces or 1.55 oz.	220	2.0	30.0	10.0	n.a.	85	n.a.

Food and Measure	cal.	prot. (gms)	carbo. (gms)	fat (gms)	chol. (mgs)	sod. (mgs)	fiber (gms)
chocolate coated, with cookies *(Twix Bar)*	140	2.0	19.0	7.0	n.a.	60	n.a.
cherries, dark or milk chocolate coated *(Cortina)*, 2 pieces	180	1.0	32.0	5.0	n.a.	20	n.a.
chocolate (see also "Chocolate, baking"):							
(Chocolaty Pay Day), 2-oz. bar	290	7.0	30.0	15.0	n.a.	130	n.a.
(Pearson's Chocolate Parfait) . .	120	1.0	23.0	3.0	n.a.	70	n.a.
with almonds *(Cadbury)*, 2 oz.	310	6.0	31.0	18.0	n.a.	80	n.a.
with Brazil nuts *(Cadbury)*, 2 oz.	310	5.0	32.0	18.0	n.a.	80	n.a.
candy coated *(M&M's)*, 1.7-oz. pkg.	240	3.0	33.0	10.0	n.a.	70	n.a.
with caramel *(Cadbury Caramello)*, 2 oz.	280	4.0	37.0	13.0	n.a.	110	n.a.
dark *(Hershey's Special Dark)*, 1.35-oz. bar . .	210	2.0	23.0	12.0	n.a.	5	n.a.
with fruit and nuts *(Cadbury)*, 2 oz.	300	5.0	33.0	16.0	n.a.	80	n.a.
fudge bar *(Nabisco)*, 2 pieces	170	1.0	29.0	5.0	n.a.	40	n.a.
fudgie *(Kraft)*, 1 piece	35	0	6.0	1.0	0	20	n.a.
with hazelnuts *(Cadbury)*, 2 oz.	310	5.0	32.0	17.0	n.a.	90	n.a.
milk *(Andes* Petite)	156	1.9	15.6	9.0	<4	24	0
milk *(Cadbury Dairy Milk)*, 2 oz.	300	4.0	34.0	16.0	n.a.	90	n.a.
milk *(Hershey's)*, 1.45-oz. bar . .	230	3.0	24.0	13.0	n.a.	30	n.a.

Food and Measure	cal.	prot. (gms)	carbo. (gms)	fat (gms)	chol. (mgs)	sod. (mgs)	fiber (gms)
Candy, chocolate *(cont.)*							
milk *(Hershey's Kisses)*, 8 pieces or 1.3 oz.	200	3.0	21.0	11.0	n.a.	30	n.a.
milk *(Nestlé)* . . .	150	2.0	17.0	9.0	n.a.	20	n.a.
milk *(Nabisco* Stars)	160	2.0	19.0	8.0	n.a.	35	n.a.
milk, with almonds *(Hershey's)*, 1.45-oz. bar	230	4.0	22.0	14.0	n.a.	35	n.a.
milk, with almonds *(Nestlé)*	160	3.0	15.0	10.0	n.a.	15	n.a.
milk, with crisps *(Krackel)*, 1.45-oz. bar	220	3.0	25.0	12.0	n.a.	75	n.a.
milk, with crisps *(Nestlé Crunch)* 1¹/₁₆ oz.	160	2.0	19.0	8.0	5	50	n.a.
milk, with crisps *(Ting-A-Ling)* . .	150	1.7	16.8	8.0	3	43	0
milk, with fruit and nuts *(Chunky)*	150	3.0	16.0	8.0	n.a.	15	n.a.
milk, with fruit and nuts (Deluxe Nut Chunky)	160	3.0	14.0	10.0	n.a.	15	n.a.
milk, with peanuts *(Mr. Goodbar)*, 1.65-oz. bar . .	270	6.0	22.0	17.0	n.a.	20	n.a.
white, with almonds *(Nestlé Alpine)*	170	3.0	13.0	12.0	n.a.	20	n.a.
(Clark Bar)	134	2.0	20.2	5.0	n.a.	26	n.a.
coconut, chocolate coated *(Mounds)*, 1.65 oz.	230	2.0	28.0	12.0	n.a.	90	n.a.
coconut, chocolate coated, with almonds *(Almond Joy)*, 1.55 oz. . . .	220	2.0	26.0	12.0	n.a.	90	n.a.

Food and Measure	cal.	prot. (gms)	carbo. (gms)	fat (gms)	chol. (mgs)	sod. (mgs)	fiber (gms)
coffee:							
(Pearson's Coffee Nip)	120	1.0	23.0	3.0	n.a.	70	n.a.
(Pearson's Coffioca Parfait)	120	1.0	23.0	3.0	n.a.	70	n.a.
cough drops:							
(Beech-Nut), 1 piece	10	0	3.0	0	n.a.	0	n.a.
all flavors (Pine Bros.)	130	0	31.0	0	n.a.	0	n.a.
creme eggs (Cadbury)	136	1.3	19.2	6.0	n.a.	n.a.	n.a.
creme eggs, mini (Cadbury)	140	2.0	20.0	7.0	n.a.	n.a.	n.a.
fruit flavored:							
all flavors (Bonkers!), 1 piece	20	0	5.0	0	n.a.	0	n.a.
(Skittles), 2 oz. . .	230	tr.	52.0	2.0	n.a.	30	n.a.
chews (Starburst), 2.1 oz.	240	tr.	50.0	5.0	n.a.	30	n.a.
(Good Stuff), 1.8-oz. bar	250	4.0	29.0	14.0	n.a.	90	n.a.
granola bars, see "Granola and similar snack bars"							
gum:							
(Big Red), 1 piece	<10	0	2.3	1.5	0	<1	n.a.
(Doublemint), 1 piece	<10	0	2.3	1.5	0	<1	n.a.
(Extra), 1 piece . .	8	0	0	0	0	0	n.a.
(Freedent), 1 piece	<10	0	2.3	1.5	0	<1	n.a.
(Juicy Fruit), 1 piece	<10	0	2.3	1.5	0	<1	n.a.
(Wrigleys Spearmint), 1 piece	<10	0	2.3	1.5	0	<1	n.a.
all flavors (Beech-Nut), 1 piece . .	10	0	2.0	0	0	0	n.a.
all flavors (Care*Free), 1 piece	8	0	2.0	0	0	0	n.a.

Food and Measure	cal.	prot. (gms)	carbo. (gms)	fat (gms)	chol. (mgs)	sod. (mgs)	fiber (gms)
Candy, gum *(cont.)*							
all flavors *(Fruit Stripe)*, 1 piece	9	0	2.0	0	0	0	n.a.
bubble, all flavors *(Bubble Yum)*, 1 piece	25	0	7.0	0	0	0	n.a.
bubble, all flavors, sugarless *(Bubble Yum)*, 1 piece	20	0	5.0	0	0	0	n.a.
bubble, all flavors *(Care*Free)*, 1 piece	10	0	2.0	0	0	0	n.a.
bubble, all flavors *(Fruit Stripe)*, 1 piece	10	0	2.0	0	0	0	n.a.
bubble, original and fruit flavors *(Hubba Bubba)*, 1 piece	23	0	5.8	.3	0	<1	n.a.
candy coated, all flavors *(Beechies)*, 1 piece	6	0	2.0	0	0	0	n.a.
halvah *(Sahadi)* . . .	150	3.0	13.0	10.0	0	45	n.a.
hard candy:							
butter creme mint *(Life Savers)*, 1 piece	<10	0	3.0	0	0	5	n.a.
butter rum *(Life Savers)*, 1 piece	<10	0	3.0	0	0	10	n.a.
butterscotch *(Life Savers)*, 1 piece	<10	0	3.0	0	0	10	n.a.
cherry, wild *(Life Savers)*, 1 piece	<10	0	3.0	0	0	0	n.a.
cinnamon *(Life Savers* Cin-O-Mon)*, 1 piece	<10	0	3.0	0	0	0	n.a.
fruit, all flavors *(Life Savers)*, 1 piece	<10	0	3.0	0	0	0	n.a.

Food and Measure	cal.	prot. (gms)	carbo. (gms)	fat (gms)	chol. (mgs)	sod. (mgs)	fiber (gms)
mint (Life Savers Cryst-O-Mint), 1 piece	<10	0	3.0	0	0	0	n.a.
mint (Life Savers Pep-O-Mint), 1 piece	7	0	3.0	0	0	0	n.a.
mint (Life Savers Spear-O-Mint), 1 piece	7	0	3.0	0	0	0	n.a.
mint (Life Savers Stik-O-Pep), 1 piece	<10	0	3.0	0	0	0	n.a.
mint (Life Savers Wint-O-Green), 1 piece	7	0	3.0	0	0	0	n.a.
root beer (Life Savers), 1 piece . .	<10	0	3.0	0	0	0	n.a.
sour (Life Savers), 1 piece	<10	0	3.0	0	0	0	n.a.
honey (Bit-O-Honey) 1.7 oz.	200	1.0	41.0	4.0	n.a.	130	n.a.
(Hot Tamales) . . .	109	0	27.0	0	0	9	0
jellied candy:							
(Chuckles JuJubes)	110	0	25.0	0	0	15	n.a.
(Chuckles JuJu Softees)	100	0	25.0	0	0	15	n.a.
all fruit flavors (Chuckles) . . .	100	0	23.0	0	0	10	n.a.
bar (Chuckles) . .	100	0	25.0	0	0	10	n.a.
beans (Chuckles)	110	0	26.0	0	0	10	n.a.
beans (Maillard's Teenee Beanees)	109	0	27.0	0	0	9	0
berries (Chuckles)	110	0	25.0	0	0	15	n.a.
cinnamon (Chuckles Softees)	100	0	23.0	0	0	10	n.a.
drops, spiced (Chuckles) . . .	110	0	24.0	1.0	0	15	n.a.
eggs (Chuckles)	110	0	26.0	0	0	10	n.a.

Food and Measure	cal.	prot. (gms)	carbo. (gms)	fat (gms)	chol. (mgs)	sod. (mgs)	fiber (gms)
Candy, jellied candy (cont.)							
eggs (Maillard's Petite Pectin) . . .	109	0	27.0	0	0	9	0
eggs, nougat center (Chuckles) . . .	110	0	26.0	0	0	10	n.a.
leaves, spearmint (Chuckles) . . .	110	0	15.0	1.0	0	15	n.a.
licorice (Chuckles)	100	0	23.0	0	0	10	n.a.
licorice (Chuckles Softees)	100	0	26.0	0	0	25	n.a.
mint (Chuckles Softees)	100	0	23.0	1.0	n.a.	10	n.a.
nougat center (Chuckles) . . .	110	0	26.0	0	0	10	n.a.
orange slices (Chuckles) . . .	110	0	24.0	0	0	10	n.a.
rabbits (Chuckles)	100	0	23.0	0	0	10	n.a.
rabbits (Chuckles JuJu)	110	0	25.0	0	0	15	n.a.
rings (Chuckles)	100	0	22.0	0	0	10	n.a.
strings, spiced (Chuckles) . . .	110	0	24.0	1.0	0	10	n.a.
(Jolly Joes)	109	0	27.0	0	0	9	0
licorice:							
(Pearson's Licorice Nip)	120	1.0	23.0	3.0	n.a.	70	n.a.
(Switzer)	94	1.3	22.1	<.1	n.a.	128	n.a.
black or strawberry (Y&S Twizzlers)	100	1.0	23.0	<1.0	0	95	n.a.
black or strawberry (Y&S Bites) . .	100	1.0	23.0	<1.0	0	85	n.a.
candy coated (Good & Fruity)	106	.6	25.7	.1	0	8	n.a.
candy coated (Good & Plenty)	106	1.0	25.9	<.1	0	52	n.a.
lollipops, all flavors:							
(Life Savers), 1 piece	45	0	11.0	0	0	10	n.a.

Food and Measure	cal.	prot. (gms)	carbo. (gms)	fat (gms)	chol. (mgs)	sod. (mgs)	fiber (gms)
assorted (Tootsie Pops)	111	.1	26.4	.6	<1	1	n.a.
lollipops, chocolate (Tootsie Pops) . .	110	.1	26.2	.6	<1	2	n.a.
lozenges, mint (Canada), 1 piece . . .	12	0	3.0	0	0	n.a.	0
malted milk balls, chocolate coated (Deran)	140	1.0	20.0	6.0	n.a.	70	n.a.
(Mars), 1.8-oz. bar	240	4.0	30.0	11.0	n.a.	80	n.a.
marshmallow: (Campfire), 2 large or 24 mini pieces	40	0	10.0	0	0	10	n.a.
(Funmallows), 1 piece	25	0	5.0	0	0	0	n.a.
(Kraft/Funmallow Miniatures), 10 pieces	18	0	4.0	0	0	0	n.a.
(Kraft Jet-Puffed), 1 piece	25	0	6.0	0	0	10	n.a.
all shapes (Rodda)	99	1.0	24.0	0	0	7	0
eggs (Chuckles)	110	0	27.0	0	0	0	n.a.
toasted coconut (Rodda)	97	1.0	19.0	2.0	n.a.	19	n.a.
(Mike & Ike)	109	0	27.0	0	0	9	0
(Milkshake), 2-oz. bar	250	2.0	43.0	8.0	n.a.	140	n.a.
(Milky Way), 2.1-oz. bar	270	3.0	41.0	10.0	n.a.	110	n.a.
mint: (Andes Creme de Menthe)	150	1.5	15.6	9.3	<1	18	0
(Andes Mint Parfait)	162	1.6	16.2	9.6	<2	18	0
(Breath Savers), 1 piece	8	0	2.0	0	0	0	n.a.
(Cortina Thin Mints), 3 pieces	120	1.0	23.0	2.0	n.a.	10	n.a.
(Junior Mints) . . .	120	1.0	24.0	3.0	n.a.	10	n.a.
(Kraft Party Mints), 1 piece	8	0	2.0	0	0	0	n.a.

Food and Measure	cal.	prot. (gms)	carbo. (gms)	fat (gms)	chol. (mgs)	sod. (mgs)	fiber (gms)
Candy, mint *(cont.)*							
(Nabisco Peppermint Patties) . .	110	1.0	25.0	0	0	10	n.a.
(Pearson's Mint Parfait)	120	1.0	23.0	3.0	n.a.	70	n.a.
anise *(Richardson)*	120	0	30.1	0	0	1	n.a.
butter *(Kraft)*, 1 piece	8	0	2.0	0	0	0	n.a.
butter *(Richardson)*	135	0	30.1	7.5	n.a.	4	n.a.
chocolate coated *(Royals)*, 2.1 oz.	290	4.0	41.0	13.0	n.a.	50	n.a.
chocolate coated *(York* Peppermint Pattie)*, 1.25 oz.	160	1.0	28.0	4.0	n.a.	15	n.a.
jelly *(Richardson)*	172	0	44.8	0	0	9	n.a.
sugar *(Richardson)*	90	0	22.4	0	0	1	n.a.
(My Buddy), 1.8-oz. bar	250	5.0	30.0	13.0	n.a.	60	n.a.
(Necco Sky Bar), 1.38-oz. bar . . .	176	n.a.	26.0	7.8	n.a.	n.a.	n.a.
nougat, all flavors, chocolate coated *(Charleston Chew)*	120	1.0	22.0	3.0	n.a.	40	n.a.
(Nutcracker)	161	2.2	15.3	10.1	n.a.	30	n.a.
nut and fruit bars: almond/apricot *(Planters)*	140	3.0	17.0	7.0	n.a.	75	n.a.
almond/pineapple *(Planters)*	140	2.0	18.0	6.0	n.a.	80	n.a.
peanut/raisin *(Planters)*	140	3.0	17.0	7.0	n.a.	70	n.a.
walnut/apple *(Planters)*	150	2.0	16.0	8.0	n.a.	90	n.a.
nut fudge square *(Nabisco)*, 2 pieces	130	1.0	21.0	5.0	n.a.	25	n.a.
(Oh Henry!), 2 oz.	280	6.0	32.0	14.0	n.a.	95	n.a.
(100 Grand), 1.5-oz. bar	200	2.0	31.0	8.0	n.a.	75	n.a.

Food and Measure	cal.	prot. (gms)	carbo. (gms)	fat (gms)	chol. (mgs)	sod. (mgs)	fiber (gms)
(Park Avenue), 1.8-oz. bar	230	3.0	34.0	9.0	n.a.	120	n.a.
(Pay Day), 1.9-oz. bar	250	9.0	28.0	12.0	n.a.	200	n.a.
peanut:							
(Andes Peanut Parfait)	161	3.0	14.0	10.0	<4	63	0
(Munch), 1.4-oz. bar	220	5.0	21.0	14.0	n.a.	110	n.a.
(Peanut Blossom Kisses)	115	1.5	24.0	1.4	n.a.	85	n.a.
(Planters)	140	4.0	13.0	9.0	n.a.	70	n.a.
(Planters Bar), 1.6-oz. bar	240	8.0	21.0	14.0	n.a.	110	n.a.
(Sahadi Peanut Crunch), 3/4 oz. bar	110	4.0	9.0	6.0	0	10	n.a.
chocolate coated *(Goobers)* . . .	160	5.0	13.0	10.0	n.a.	10	n.a.
chocolate coated *(Nabisco)*	160	4.0	14.0	9.0	n.a.	15	n.a.
chocolate coated, candy covered *(M&M's)*, 1.7-oz. pkg.	240	5.0	28.0	12.0	n.a.	60	n.a.
cluster *(Deran)*, . .	150	5.0	13.0	9.0	n.a.	15	n.a.
plank *(Tom's)*, 1.7 oz.	230	7.0	28.0	11.0	n.a.	30	n.a.
roll *(Tom's)*, 13/4-oz. roll	230	6.0	29.0	11.0	n.a.	120	n.a.
peanut brittle *(Kraft)*	140	3.0	20.0	5.0	0	140	n.a.
peanut butter:							
(Pearson's Peanut Butter Parfait) . . .	120	1.0	23.0	3.0	n.a.	70	n.a.
(Tom's Pals), 1.3-oz. piece	200	5.0	19.0	12.0	n.a.	100	n.a.
candy coated *(Reese's Pieces)*, 1.75-oz. pkg. . .	240	7.0	30.0	10.0	n.a.	85	n.a.
chips *(Nestlé* Morsels)	160	5.0	12.0	10.0	n.a.	60	n.a.

Food and Measure	cal.	prot. (gms)	carbo. (gms)	fat (gms)	chol. (mgs)	sod. (mgs)	fiber (gms)
Candy, peanut butter *(cont.)*							
chips *(Reese's)*, 1.5 oz. or ¼ cup	230	9.0	19.0	13.0	n.a.	90	n.a.
chocolate coated *(Reese's* Cups), 2 pieces or 1.6 oz.	250	6.0	23.0	15.0	n.a.	170	n.a.
chocolate coated, with cookies *(Twix* Bar)*, .9 oz. . . .	140	3.0	15.0	8.0	n.a.	80	n.a.
popcorn, plain or flavored, see "Popcorn"							
popcorn, caramel coated:							
(Laura Scudder's)	122	2.1	21.9	3.1	0	102	.3
(Orville Redenbacher's Gourmet Crunch)	130	1.0	19.0	6.0	n.a.	100	n.a.
(Tom's), 1.6 oz.	180	1.0	41.0	2.0	n.a.	120	n.a.
with peanuts *(Laura Scudder's)*, 1.5 oz.	180	3.0	34.0	4.0	0	105	.6
with peanuts *(Cracker Jacks)*	120	2.0	22.0	3.0	n.a.	85	n.a.
(Powerhouse), 2 oz.	260	4.0	38.0	11.0	n.a.	195	n.a.
raisin, chocolate coated:							
(Deran)	120	1.0	20.0	4.0	n.a.	35	n.a.
(Nabisco)	130	1.0	21.0	5.0	n.a.	20	n.a.
(Raisinets)	120	2.0	20.0	4.0	n.a.	10	n.a.
rum water *(Deran)*	150	1.0	20.0	7.0	n.a.	15	n.a.
(Slo-Poke Sucker)	124	.9	24.6	2.4	n.a.	51	n.a.
(Snickers), 2-oz. bar	270	6.0	33.0	13.0	n.a.	140	n.a.
(3 Musketeers), 2.1-oz. bar	260	2.0	46.0	8.0	n.a.	130	n.a.
toffee:							
(Kraft), 1 piece . .	30	0	5.0	1.0	0	20	n.a.
(Skor), 1.2-oz. bar	200	2.0	20.0	12.0	n.a.	100	n.a.
(Tootsie Roll)	112	.3	22.8	2.5	<1	6	n.a.

Food and Measure	cal.	prot. (gms)	carbo. (gms)	fat (gms)	chol. (mgs)	sod. (mgs)	fiber (gms)
(Treasure), 2-oz. bar	270	6.0	32.0	13.0	n.a.	100	n.a.
wafer *(Necco)*, 1 piece	5	0	1.4	0	0	n.a.	0
wafer bar, chocolate covered *(Kit Kat)*, 1.5-oz. bar	230	3.0	26.0	12.0	n.a.	55	n.a.
(Whatchamacallit), 1.4-oz. bar	210	4.0	22.0	12.0	n.a.	115	n.a.
(Wispa)	150	2.0	17.0	8.0	n.a.	45	n.a.
(Zagnut)	131	2.0	20.8	4.4	n.a.	29	n.a.
(Zero), 2-oz. bar . .	250	3.0	38.0	10.0	n.a.	120	n.a.
Cannelloni dinner, frozen:							
beef and pork *(Lean Cuisine)*, 95/8 oz.	270	19.0	25.0	10.0	50	940	n.a.
cheese *(Lean Cuisine)*, 91/8 oz. . .	270	22.0	24.0	10.0	45	900	n.a.
Cannelloni entree, frozen:							
cheese *(Dining Lite)*, 9 oz.	261	16.1	35.5	6.8	n.a.	940	1.7
veal and vegetable *(Dining Lite)*, 9 oz.	255	16.7	30.5	8.0	n.a.	790	1.6
Cantaloupe: fresh:							
1/2 melon, 5" diam.	94	2.3	22.3	.7	0	23	1.0
cubed, 1 cup . . .	57	1.4	13.4	.4	0	14	.6
Capocollo:							
(Hormel), 1 oz. . . .	80	5.0	0	6.0	n.a.	273	n.a.
Carambola:							
fresh, raw, cubed, 1 cup	45	.8	10.7	.5	0	2	1.3
Caraway seeds:							
(all brands), 1 tsp.	7	.4	1.1	.3	0	tr.	.3
Cardamom seeds:							
ground (all brands), 1 tsp.	6	.2	1.4	.1	0	tr.	.2
Cardoon, fresh:							
raw, shredded, 1 cup	36	1.3	8.7	.2	0	303	n.a.
boiled, drained, 4 oz.	25	.9	6.0	.1	0	200	n.a.

Food and Measure	cal.	prot. (gms)	carbo. (gms)	fat (gms)	chol. (mgs)	sod. (mgs)	fiber (gms)
Carissas, raw:							
1 average carissa	12	.1	2.7	.3	0	1	.2
sliced, 1 cup	92	.8	20.5	2.0	0	4	1.4
Carp, raw:							
meat only, 4 oz. ..	144	20.2	0	6.4	75	56	0
Carrot:							
fresh:							
raw, 1 average (7½" × 1⅛" diam.)	31	.7	7.3	.1	0	25	.8
raw, shredded, 1 cup	48	1.1	11.2	.2	0	38	1.1
boiled, drained, sliced, 1 cup ..	70	1.7	16.4	.3	0	104	2.3
canned, ½ cup:							
all cuts:							
(Libby/Seneca) ..	20	0	5.0	0	0	250	n.a.
(Stokely's Finest)	35	1.0	7.0	0	0	300	n.a.
(Stokely's Finest, No Salt or Sugar)	35	1.0	7.0	0	0	35	n.a.
(S&W Fancy) ...	30	1.0	7.0	0	0	240	n.a.
with liquid (Del Monte)	30	0	7.0	0	0	265	n.a.
sliced:							
(A&P)	30	1.0	6.0	<1.0	0	300	n.a.
(A&P No Salt) ..	25	<1.0	6.0	<1.0	0	40	n.a.
frozen, 3.3 oz.:							
(A&P)	40	1.0	9.0	<1.0	0	45	n.a.
baby, whole (Birds Eye Deluxe) ..	40	1.0	9.0	0	0	45	1.2
sliced (Frosty Acres)	40	1.0	9.0	0	0	44	1.0
baby, and peas and pearl onions (Birds Eye Deluxe)	50	2.0	10.0	0	0	60	1.2
Carrot juice:							
canned, 6 fl. oz. ..	73	1.7	17.1	.3	0	54	1.8

Food and Measure	cal.	prot. (gms)	carbo. (gms)	fat (gms)	chol. (mgs)	sod. (mgs)	fiber (gms)
Carrot-raisin salad:							
dairy pack (Knudsen), 1/2 cup	110	2.0	14.0	5.0	n.a.	n.a.	n.a.
Casaba melon:							
cubed, 1 cup	45	1.5	10.5	.2	0	20	.9
Cashew, 1 oz. except as noted:							
(Beer Nuts)	170	5.0	8.0	13.0	0	65	n.a.
(Eagle Honey Roast)	150	4.0	9.0	12.0	0	175	n.a.
(Frito Lay's)	170	4.0	9.0	14.0	0	115	n.a.
(Planters Honey Roast)	170	4.0	11.0	12.0	0	170	n.a.
(Tom's), .9 oz. . . .	160	5.0	7.0	13.0	0	110	n.a.
dry-roasted:							
salted (Flavor House)	170	6.0	7.0	13.0	0	200	n.a.
salted (Planters)	160	5.0	9.0	13.0	0	230	n.a.
salted (Laura Scudder's)	170	5.8	7.8	13.1	0	261	.5
unsalted (Planters)	160	5.0	9.0	13.0	0	0	n.a.
oil-roasted:							
salted (Laura Scudder's)	159	4.9	8.3	13.0	0	57	.4
salted (Planters)	170	5.0	8.0	14.0	0	135	n.a.
unsalted (Planters)	170	5.0	8.0	14.0	0	0	n.a.
and peanuts (Planters Honey Roast) . .	170	5.0	9.0	12.0	0	170	n.a.
Cashew butter:							
raw, unsalted (Hain), 2 tbsp.	190	6.0	8.0	15.0	0	5	n.a.
toasted, unsalted (Hain), 2 tbsp. . .	190	6.0	8.0	16.0	0	5	n.a.
Cassava:							
raw, 4 oz.	136	3.5	30.5	.4	0	9	2.8
Catfish:							
channel, raw, fillets, 4 oz.	132	20.6	0	4.8	66	71	0

Food and Measure	cal.	prot. (gms)	carbo. (gms)	fat (gms)	chol. (mgs)	sod. (mgs)	fiber (gms)
Catfish *(cont.)*							
frozen:							
fillets *(Taste O' Sea)*, 4 oz. . . .	100	21.0	0	2.0	n.a.	290	0
breaded *(Mrs. Paul's)*, 1 fillet	215	13.0	14.0	12.0	n.a.	243	n.a.
breaded, fingers *(Mrs. Paul's)*, 4 oz.	250	15.0	17.0	14.0	n.a.	260	n.a.
Catsup:							
(Del Monte), 1/4 cup	60	1.0	16.0	0	0	675	n.a.
(Heinz), 1 tbsp. . . .	18	.2	4.0	tr.	0	180	n.a.
(Heinz Lite), 1 tbsp.	8	.2	2.0	tr.	0	110	n.a.
(Heinz Lite Low Sodium), 1 tbsp. . .	8	.2	2.0	tr.	0	90	n.a.
(Hunt's), 1 tbsp. . .	16	0	4.0	0	0	160	n.a.
(Smucker's), 2 tsp.	14	0	3.0	0	0	90	n.a.
hot *(Heinz)*, 1 tbsp.	18	.2	4.0	tr.	0	180	n.a.
Cauliflower:							
fresh:							
raw, 3 flowerets	13	1.1	2.8	.1	0	8	.5
raw, pieces, 1 cup	24	2.0	4.9	.2	0	14	.8
boiled, drained, 1 cup	30	2.3	5.7	.2	0	8	1.0
frozen:							
(A&P), 3.3 oz. . .	25	2.0	5.0	<1.0	0	20	n.a.
(Birds Eye), 3.3 oz.	25	2.0	5.0	0	0	20	.8
(Frosty Acres), 3.3 oz.	25	2.0	5.0	1.0	0	16	1.0
(Kohl's), 3 oz. . .	20	2.0	4.0	<1.0	0	15	n.a.
cuts *(Green Giant)*, 1/2 cup	12	1.0	2.0	0	0	15	n.a.
with almonds *(Birds Eye)*, 3.3 oz. . .	40	3.0	5.0	2.0	0	270	.8
in butter sauce *(Green Giant)*, 1/2 cup	30	1.0	4.0	1.0	n.a.	310	n.a.
with cheese sauce *(Birds Eye)*, 5 oz.	120	4.0	12.0	7.0	n.a.	500	.6

Food and Measure	cal.	prot. (gms)	carbo. (gms)	fat (gms)	chol. (mgs)	sod. (mgs)	fiber (gms)
in cheese flavored sauce *(Green Giant)*, 1/2 cup	60	2.0	10.0	2.0	n.a.	450	n.a.
in white cheddar cheese flavored sauce *(Green Giant)*, 1/2 cup	70	3.0	7.0	3.0	n.a.	420	n.a.
Cauliflower combinations, frozen:							
and carrot bonanza *(Green Giant Harvest Get Togethers)*, 1/2 cup	60	2.0	7.0	3.0	n.a.	290	n.a.
and green bean festival *(Green Giant Valley Combination)*, 1/2 cup	16	1.0	3.0	0	0	30	n.a.
and green beans and corn *(Birds Eye)*, 3.2 oz.	35	2.0	8.0	0	0	10	.7
Cauliflower and cheese sauce, in pastry:							
frozen *(Pepperidge Farm)*, 1 piece	210	5.0	19.0	13.0	n.a.	450	n.a.
Caviar, (see also "Roe"):							
black and red, granular, 1 oz.	71	6.9	1.1	5.0	165	420	0
Celeriac, fresh:							
raw:							
whole, with skin, 1 lb.	154	5.9	35.9	1.2	0	390	5.1
pared, 1 cup	62	2.3	14.4	.5	0	156	2.0
boiled, drained, 4 oz.	28	1.1	6.7	.2	0	69	.9
Celery, fresh:							
raw:							
1 stalk, 71/2″ × 11/4″ diam.	6	.3	1.5	.1	0	35	.3

Food and Measure	cal.	prot. (gms)	carbo. (gms)	fat (gms)	chol. (mgs)	sod. (mgs)	fiber (gms)
Celery, raw *(cont.)*							
diced, 1 cup . . .	18	.8	4.4	.1	0	106	.8
boiled, drained, diced,							
1 cup	22	.8	5.3	.2	0	97	1.0
Celery seed:							
(all brands), 1 tsp.	8	.4	.8	.5	0	3	.2
Celtus:							
fresh, raw, trimmed, 4							
oz.	25	1.0	4.1	.3	0	12	.5
Cereal, ready-to-eat,							
1 oz. except as							
noted:							
(Booberry)	110	1.0	24.0	1.0	0	210	n.a.
bran:							
(All Bran)	70	4.0	22.0	1.0	0	260	2.0
(All Bran Extra Fi-							
ber)	60	3.0	22.0	1.0	0	270	n.a.
(Bran Buds) . . .	70	3.0	22.0	1.0	0	150	2.0
(Kellogg's Bran							
Flakes)	90	3.0	23.0	0	0	220	n.a.
(Loma Linda) . . .	60	4.0	19.0	1.0	0	115	2.0
(Nabisco 100%)	70	3.0	21.0	2.0	0	190	n.a.
(Post 40% Bran							
Flakes)	90	3.0	23.0	0	0	230	1.0
with fruit *(Kellogg's*							
Fruitful Bran) . .	120	3.0	30.0	0	0	230	n.a.
with raisins *(Kel-*							
logg's Raisin							
Bran)	120	3.0	30.0	1.0	0	220	1.1
with raisins *(Post*							
Raisin Bran) . .	80	2.0	22.0	0	0	160	1.0
with raisins and							
honey *(Post*							
Honey Nut							
Crunch)	90	2.0	22.0	1.0	0	150	1.0
with raisins and nuts							
(Raisin Nut Bran)	110	2.0	21.0	3.0	0	150	n.a.
(Bran Muffin Crisp),							
1.4 oz.	130	3.0	30.0	1.0	0	250	n.a.

Food and Measure	cal.	prot. (gms)	carbo. (gms)	fat (gms)	chol. (mgs)	sod. (mgs)	fiber (gms)
(Cinnamon Toast Crunch)	120	1.0	23.0	3.0	0	220	n.a.
(Cocoa Pebbles) . .	110	1.0	25.0	1.0	0	160	tr.
corn:							
(Cocoa Puffs) . . .	110	1.0	25.0	1.0	0	200	n.a.
(Country Corn Flakes)	110	2.0	25.0	<1.0	0	310	n.a.
(Honeycomb) . . .	110	1.0	25.0	1.0	0	195	tr.
(Kellogg's Corn Flakes)	110	2.0	25.0	0	0	290	.1
(Kellogg's Corn Pops)	110	1.0	26.0	0	0	90	n.a.
(Kellogg's Frosted .Flakes)	110	1.0	26.0	0	0	200	.1
(Kellogg's Honey & Nut Corn Flakes)	110	2.0	24.0	1.0	0	200	.1
(Kix)	110	2.0	24.0	1.0	0	310	n.a.
(Nutri-Grain) . . .	100	2.0	24.0	1.0	0	170	.5
(Post Toasties) . .	110	2.0	24.0	0	0	280	tr.
(Total Corn Flakes)	110	2.0	24.0	1.0	0	310	n.a.
brown sugar and honey *(Body Buddies)*	110	2.0	24.0	<1.0	0	290	n.a.
fruit flavor, natural *(Body Buddies)*	110	2.0	24.0	1.0	0	280	n.a.
corn bran *(Quaker)*	109	2.2	23.3	.9	0	244	1.2
(Dairy Crisp) . . .	120	3.0	19.0	4.0	0	140	n.a.
(Fiber One)	60	4.0	21.0	1.0	0	230	n.a.
(Fruity Pebbles) . .	110	1.0	25.0	1.0	0	150	tr.
(Golden Grahams)	110	2.0	24.0	1.0	0	280	n.a.
granola or natural style:							
(C.W. Post Hearty)	130	2.0	21.0	4.0	0	85	tr.
(Heartland)	130	3.0	18.0	4.0	0	80	n.a.
(Quaker 100%) . .	136	3.7	17.8	5.6	0	11	.3
apple and cinnamon *(Cream of Wheat Mix 'n Eat)*, 1¼ oz.	130	2.0	30.0	0	0	240	n.a.

Food and Measure	cal.	prot. (gms)	carbo. (gms)	fat (gms)	chol. (mgs)	sod. (mgs)	fiber (gms)
Cereal, ready-to-eat, granola or natural style *(cont.)*							
with apples and cinnamon *(Fruit & Fibre)*	90	2.0	23.0	0	0	160	1.0
apple and cinnamon *(Quaker* 100%)	130	3.2	18.2	5.3	0	15	.5
with almonds *(Sun Country)*	130	3.0	19.0	5.0	0	10	n.a.
with blueberries and milk, freeze-dried *(Mountain House)*, 1 cup	290	8.0	44.0	8.0	n.a.	n.a.	n.a.
brown sugar cinnamon *(Cream of Wheat* Mix 'n Eat), 1¼ oz. . .	130	2.0	30.0	0	0	180	n.a.
cinnamon raisin *(Nature Valley)*, ⅓ cup	130	3.0	19.0	5.0	0	35	n.a.
coconut *(Heartland)*	130	3.0	18.0	5.0	0	80	n.a.
coconut honey *(Nature Valley)*, ⅓ cup	150	3.0	18.0	7.0	0	35	n.a.
with dates, raisins and walnuts *(Fruit & Fibre)*	90	2.0	22.0	1.0	0	170	1.0
with fruit, tropical *(Fruit & Fibre)*	90	2.0	21.0	1.0	0	160	1.0
fruit and nut *(Nature Valley)*, ⅓ cup	130	3.0	19.0	5.0	0	35	n.a.
maple brown sugar *(Cream of Wheat* Mix 'n Eat), 1¼ oz	130	2.0	30.0	0	0	180	n.a.
oat, toasted *(Nature Valley)*, ⅓ cup	130	3.0	19.0	5.0	0	35	n.a.
original *(Cream of Wheat* Mix 'n Eat), 1¼ oz. . .	100	3.0	21.0	0	0	180	n.a.

Food and Measure	cal.	prot. (gms)	carbo. (gms)	fat (gms)	chol. (mgs)	sod. (mgs)	fiber (gms)
with raisins (C.W. Post Hearty) ..	120	2.0	21.0	4.0	0	80	tr.
with raisins (Heart-land)	130	3.0	18.0	4.0	0	80	n.a.
with raisins (Sun Country)	130	3.0	20.0	5.0	0	10	n.a.
raisin and date (Quaker 100%)	132	3.5	18.2	5.0	0	11	.3
with raisins and dates (Sun Country)	130	3.0	20.0	4.0	0	10	n.a.
strawberry (Cream of Wheat Mix 'n Eat), 1¼ oz. . . .	140	2.0	29.0	2.0	0	200	n.a.
(Halfsies)	113	1.8	24.0	1.1	0	243	.1
(Kaboom)	110	2.0	23.0	1.0	0	370	n.a.
(Mr. T)	121	1.3	23.1	2.6	0	189	.1
mixed grain:							
(Apple Jacks) . .	110	2.0	26.0	0	0	125	.1
(Cap'n Crunch) . .	121	1.4	22.9	2.6	0	185	.1
(Cap'n Crunch's Choco Crunch)	116	1.5	23.8	1.7	0	172	.2
(Cap'n Crunch's Crunchberries)	120	1.4	22.9	2.6	0	166	.1
(Cap'n Crunch's Peanut Butter)	127	2.3	20.9	3.8	0	250	.2
(Circus Fun) . . .	110	1.0	25.0	1.0	0	160	n.a.
(Count Chocula)	110	2.0	24.0	1.0	0	210	n.a.
(Frankenberry) . .	110	1.0	24.0	1.0	0	210	n.a.
(Grape Nuts) . . .	110	3.0	23.0	0	0	190	tr.
(Grape Nuts Flakes)	100	3.0	23.0	1.0	0	170	1.0
(Kellogg's Crispix)	110	2.0	25.0	0	0	220	n.a.
(Kellogg's Just Right)	100	3.0	24.0	0	0	190	n.a.
(King Vitamin) . .	112	2.2	23.4	1.1	0	250	.2
(Loma Linda 7 Grain No Sugar)	110	5.0	20.0	1.0	0	75	<1.0
(OJ's)	120	2.0	23.0	2.0	0	135	n.a.
(Product 19) . . .	110	2.0	24.0	0	0	320	.1

Food and Measure	cal.	prot. (gms)	carbo. (gms)	fat (gms)	chol. (mgs)	sod. (mgs)	fiber (gms)
Cereal, ready-to-eat, mixed grain *(cont.)*							
(Quisp)	121	1.3	23.1	2.6	0	189	.1
(Raisins, Rice & Rye)	140	2.0	31.0	0	0	235	.4
(Roman Meal Original)	110	4.0	19.0	1.0	0	10	4.3
(Special K)	110	6.0	20.0	0	0	230	.1
(Team Flakes) . .	110	2.0	24.0	1.0	0	190	.3
crunchy (Loma Linda 7 Grain)	110	2.0	21.0	2.0	0	90	<1.0
with fruit (Kellogg's Apple Raisin Crisp), 2/3 cup	140	2.0	35.0	0	0	220	n.a.
with fruit (Kellogg's Just Right), 3/4 cup	140	3.0	30.0	1.0	0	190	n.a.
with raisins (Raisin Grape Nuts) . .	100	3.0	22.0	0	0	140	tr.
with raisins and almonds (Nutri-Grain), 2/3 cup	150	3.0	32.0	2.0	0	220	n.a.
oats:							
(Alpha-Bits)	110	2.0	24.0	1.0	0	180	tr.
(Cheerios)	110	4.0	20.0	2.0	0	290	n.a.
(Cinnamon Life)	110	5.2	18.8	1.6	0	150	.3
(Froot Loops) . . .	110	2.0	25.0	1.0	0	125	.3
(Honey Nut Cheerios)	110	3.0	23.0	1.0	0	250	n.a.
(Life)	111	5.2	18.6	1.8	0	150	.3
(Post Fortified Oat Flakes)	100	6.0	20.0	1.0	0	250	tr.
with marshmallow (Lucky Charms)	110	2.0	24.0	1.0	0	180	n.a.
with raisins (Raisin Life), 1 1/3 oz. . .	105	5.5	16.8	1.8	0	161	.5
oat bran (Cracklin' Oat Bran), 1/2 cup . .	110	3.0	20.0	4.0	0	150	n.a.
(Pac-Man)	110	1.0	25.0	<1.0	0	200	n.a.
rice:							
(Kellogg's Frosted Krispies)	110	1.0	25.0	0	0	210	.1

Food and Measure	cal.	prot. (gms)	carbo. (gms)	fat (gms)	chol. (mgs)	sod. (mgs)	fiber (gms)
(Kellogg's Rice Krispies)	110	2.0	25.0	0	0	290	.1
(Quaker Puffed Rice), 1/2 oz. . .	55	.9	12.7	.1	0	1	.1
chocolate flavor (Cocoa Krispies)	110	1.0	25.0	0	0	190	.1
with marshmallow (Kellogg's Marshmallow Krispies), 1 1/4 cup	140	2.0	33.0	0	0	290	n.a.
(Rocky Road)	120	1.0	23.0	3.0	0	120	n.a.
(S'mores Crunch) . .	120	1.0	24.0	2.0	0	250	n.a.
(Smurf-Berry Crunch)	110	1.0	25.0	1.0	0	75	tr.
(Super Golden Crisp)	110	2.0	26.0	0	0	45	tr.
wheat: (Honey BucWheat Crisp)	110	2.0	24.0	<1.0	0	250	n.a.
(Honey Smacks)	110	2.0	25.0	0	0	70	n.a.
(Nutri-Grain) . . .	100	3.0	24.0	0	0	170	.5
(Quaker Puffed Wheat), 1/2 oz.	50	2.2	10.8	.2	0	1	.3
(Total)	110	3.0	23.0	1.0	0	280	n.a.
(Wheaties)	110	3.0	23.0	1.0	0	370	n.a.
with raisins: (Crispy Wheats'n Raisins) . . .	110	2.0	23.0	1.0	0	180	n.a.
(Nutri-Grain), 2/3 cup	130	3.0	32.0	0	0	170	n.a.
raisin filled (Kellogg's Raisin Squares), 1/2 cup	90	2.0	22.0	0	0	0	n.a.
shredded: (Frosted Mini-Wheats Regular or Apple Flavor), 4 pieces	100	3.0	24.0	0	0	5	.5
(Nabisco), 5/6-oz. biscuit	90	2.0	19.0	1.0	0	0	3.0
(Nabisco Spoon Size)	110	3.0	23.0	0	0	0	3.0

Food and Measure	cal.	prot. (gms)	carbo. (gms)	fat (gms)	chol. (mgs)	sod. (mgs)	fiber (gms)
Cereal, ready-to-eat, wheat, shredded *(cont.)*							
(Quaker), 2 biscuits	104	3.1	22.0	.4	0	1	.6
(Sunshine), 1 biscuit	90	2.0	19.0	1.0	0	0	n.a.
(Sunshine Bite Size)	110	3.0	22.0	1.0	0	0	n.a.
and bran (Nabisco) . .	110	3.0	23.0	1.0	0	0	4.0
(Toasted Wheat and Raisins)	100	2.0	23.0	1.0	0	0	3.0
Cereal, cooking:							
cooked*, oats or oatmeal, 3/4 cup, except as noted:							
(Instant Quaker)	105	4.5	18.1	1.7	n.a.	281	.3
(Quaker Quick/Old Fashioned), 2/3 cup	109	4.6	18.4	1.9	n.a.	1	.3
apples & cinnamon (Instant Quaker)	134	3.9	26.0	1.6	n.a.	181	.4
bran & raisins (Instant Quaker)	153	5.2	29.2	1.7	n.a.	240	1.0
cinnamon & spice (Instant Quaker)	176	5.0	34.8	1.8	n.a.	258	.4
honey & graham (Instant Quaker)	136	3.6	26.6	1.7	n.a.	224	.3
maple & brown sugar flavor (Instant Quaker)	163	4.6	31.9	1.9	n.a.	228	.3
peaches & cream flavor (Instant Quaker)	136	3.5	26.0	2.0	n.a.	134	.4
raisins, dates & walnuts (Instant Quaker)	150	4.0	25.4	3.6	n.a.	155	.4

* Prepared according to package directions

Food and Measure	cal.	prot. (gms)	carbo. (gms)	fat (gms)	chol. (mgs)	sod. (mgs)	fiber (gms)
raisins & spice (Instant Quaker)	159	4.5	31.4	1.8	n.a.	217	.3
strawberries & cream flavor (Instant Quaker)	136	3.4	26.3	1.9	n.a.	172	.4
cooked, wheat:							
(Wheat Hearts), 3/4 cup	110	4.0	21.0	1.0	n.a.	190	n.a.
farina (Pillsbury), 2/3 cup	80	2.0	17.0	<1.0	n.a.	270	n.a.
whole (Quaker Natural), 2/3 cup . .	106	3.4	21.8	.6	n.a.	1	.1
uncooked, 1 oz., except as noted:							
farina, regular or chocolate flavor (Malt-O-Meal Quick)	100	3.0	22.0	<1.0	n.a.	0	.1
farina, creamy (Quaker Quick), 2½ tbsp.	101	3.1	21.7	.2	0	1	.1
oatmeal (Maypo 30-Second)	123	4.0	19.0	1.0	0	0	.3
oat bran (Quaker), 1/3 cup	110	5.7	16.2	2.5	0	1	.5
oats, maple flavored (Maypo Vermont Style)	122	4.0	20.0	1.0	0	0	.4
rice (Cream of Rice)	100	2.0	23.0	0	0	0	n.a.
wheat (Cream of Wheat Instant or Regular)	100	3.0	22.0	0	0	0	n.a.
wheat (Cream of Wheat Quick)	100	3.0	22.0	0	0	130	n.a.
wheat (Wheatena)	120	3.0	21.0	<1.0	0	0	n.a.
wheat and barley (Maltex)	117	3.0	21.0	<1.0	0	0	n.a.

Food and Measure	cal.	prot. (gms)	carbo. (gms)	fat (gms)	chol. (mgs)	sod. (mgs)	fiber (gms)
Cereal beverage:							
mix* (*Postum Regular or Coffee Flavor*), 6 fl. oz.	12	0	3.0	0	0	0	tr.
Cervelat, see "Thuringer cervelat"							
Champagne, see "Wine"							
Chard, Swiss, fresh:							
raw, chopped, 1 cup	6	.6	1.3	.1	0	76	.3
boiled, drained, chopped, 1 cup	35	3.3	7.2	.1	0	313	1.6
Chayote, fresh:							
raw, 1 chayote, 5³/₄″×2⁷/₈″ . . .	49	1.8	11.0	.6	0	8	1.4
boiled, drained, pieces, 1 cup . . .	38	1.0	8.2	.8	0	1	.9
Cheddarwurst:							
(*Hillshire Farms*), 1-oz. slice	98	4.3	.3	8.9	9	259	n.a.
Cheese, 1 oz., except as noted:							
American, processed:							
(*Borden*)	110	6.0	1.0	9.0	n.a.	445	0
(*Dorman's*)	110	6.0	n.a.	9.0	n.a.	410	0
(*Kraft Deluxe* Loaf)	110	6.0	1.0	9.0	25	430	0
(*Kraft Deluxe* Slices)	110	6.0	1.0	9.0	25	460	0
(*Land O'Lakes*) . .	110	6.0	<1.0	9.0	25	405	0
(*Lite-line*)	50	7.0	1.0	2.0	n.a.	410	0
(*Lite-line* Reduced Sodium)	70	6.0	2.0	4.0	n.a.	90	0
(*Lite-line* Sodium Lite)	70	6.0	2.0	4.0	n.a.	200	0
hot pepper (*Sargento*) . . .	106	6.3	.5	8.9	27	406	0
sharp (*Old English* Loaf)	110	6.0	1.0	9.0	30	390	0

* Prepared according to package directions

Food and Measure	cal.	prot. (gms)	carbo. (gms)	fat (gms)	chol. (mgs)	sod. (mgs)	fiber (gms)
sharp *(Old English* Slices)	110	6.0	1.0	9.0	30	440	0
American-Swiss, processed *(Land O'Lakes)*	100	6.0	<1.0	9.0	25	445	0
asiago:							
medium *(Universal)*	110	7.0	1.0	9.0	30	290	0
old *(Universal)* . .	100	8.0	1.0	8.0	20	320	0
soft *(Universal)* . .	110	7.0	<1.0	9.0	33	290	0
bel dolce, Italian style *(Universal)*	110	7.0	1.0	9.0	33	290	0
(Bel Paese)	90	5.7	.3	7.4	n.a.	196	0
(Bel Paese Madallion Processed)	71	3.4	1.3	5.9	n.a.	193	0
blue:							
(Dorman's)	100	6.0	1.0	8.3	21	n.a.	0
(Frigo)	100	6.0	1.0	8.0	21	400	0
(Kraft)	100	6.0	1.0	9.0	30	330	0
(Sargento)	100	6.1	.7	8.2	21	396	0
blue and gorgonzola *(Universal)*	110	6.0	1.0	9.0	20	370	0
brick:							
(Dorman's)	105	6.5	n.a.	8.2	n.a.	n.a.	0
(Kraft)	110	7.0	0	9.0	30	170	0
(Land O'Lakes) . .	110	7.0	1.0	8.0	25	160	0
(Sargento)	105	6.6	.8	8.4	27	159	0
Brie *(Sargento)* . . .	95	5.9	.1	7.9	28	178	0
caljack *(Churny)* . .	100	6.0	1.0	8.0	n.a.	n.a.	0
Camembert *(Sargento)*	85	5.6	.1	6.9	20	239	0
caraway *(Kraft)* . . .	100	7.0	1.0	8.0	30	180	0
cheddar:							
(Armour)	110	7.0	1.0	9.0	30	180	0
(Armour Lower Salt)	110	7.0	1.0	9.0	30	106	0
(Dorman's)	110	7.0	1.0	9.2	29	n.a.	0
(Frigo)	110	7.0	1.0	9.0	n.a.	200	0
(Kraft)	110	7.0	1.0	9.0	30	180	0
(Land O'Lakes) . .	110	7.0	<1.0	9.0	30	175	0
(Sargento)	114	7.1	.4	9.4	30	176	0
(Universal)	110	7.0	1.0	9.0	30	176	0

Food and Measure	cal.	prot. (gms)	carbo. (gms)	fat (gms)	chol. (mgs)	sod. (mgs)	fiber (gms)
Cheese, cheddar *(cont.)*							
sharp *(Lite-line)*	50	7.0	1.0	2.0	n.a.	445	0
Cheshire, natural . .	110	6.6	1.4	8.7	29	198	0
colby:							
(Armour)	110	7.0	1.0	9.0	30	170	0
(Dorman's)	112	6.7	n.a.	8.6	27	n.a.	0
(Kraft)	110	7.0	1.0	9.0	30	180	0
(Land O'Lakes) . .	110	7.0	1.0	9.0	25	170	0
(Lite-line)	50	7.0	1.0	2.0	n.a.	470	0
(Sargento)	112	6.7	.7	9.1	27	171	0
colby jack *(Sargento)*	109	6.8	.5	8.8	27	162	0
cottage:							
dry curd *(Crowley)*, ½ cup	80	18.0	3.0	1.0	n.a.	15	0
large curd *(Knudsen Velvet)*, ½ cup	120	14.0	3.0	5.0	n.a.	490	0
4% fat *(Crowley)*, ½ cup	120	14.0	4.0	5.0	n.a.	390	0
low fat *(Knudsen)*, ½ cup	100	16.0	4.0	2.0	n.a.	490	0
low fat *(Lite-line)*, ½ cup	90	14.0	4.0	2.0	n.a.	375	0
low fat, 2% *(Land O'Lakes)*, 4 oz.	100	16.0	4.0	2.0	10	460	0
low fat, 1% *(Crowley)*, ½ cup . .	90	14.0	4.0	1.0	n.a.	390	0
low fat, 1% *(Crowley* Reduced Salt)*, ½ cup	90	14.0	4.0	1.0	n.a.	260	0
(Borden), ½ cup	120	14.0	4.0	5.0	n.a.	465	0
(Land O'Lakes), 4 oz.	120	14.0	3.0	5.0	15	460	0
chive *(Knudsen)*, ½ cup	120	14.0	2.0	5.0	n.a.	480	n.a.
fruit cocktail *(Knudsen)*, ½ cup . .	130	11.0	11.0	5.0	n.a.	390	n.a.
with fruit salad *(Crowley)*, ½ cup	140	11.0	15.0	4.0	n.a.	330	n.a.

Food and Measure	cal.	prot. (gms)	carbo. (gms)	fat (gms)	chol. (mgs)	sod. (mgs)	fiber (gms)
garden salad *(Crowley)*, 1/2 cup . .	110	14.0	2.0	4.0	n.a.	440	n.a.
with pineapple *(Crowley)*, 1/2 cup	140	11.0	15.0	4.0	n.a.	330	n.a.
with pineapple *(Knudsen)*, 1/2 cup	120	11.0	8.0	5.0	n.a.	380	n.a.
cream:							
(Armour Lower Salt)	110	7.0	1.0	9.0	30	120	0
(Knudsen)	110	3.0	1.0	10.0	n.a.	110	0
(Philadelphia Brand)	100	2.0	1.0	10.0	30	85	n.a.
with chives *(Philadelphia Brand)*	90	2.0	1.0	9.0	30	125	n.a.
with pimentos *(Philadelphia Brand)*	90	2.0	1.0	9.0	30	150	n.a.
cream, soft:							
(Philadelphia Brand)	100	2.0	1.0	10.0	30	105	0
with chives and onion *(Philadelphia Brand)*	100	2.0	2.0	9.0	30	100	n.a.
with peaches *(Philadelphia Brand)*	90	1.0	3.0	8.0	25	50	n.a.
with pineapple *(Philadelphia Brand)*	90	1.0	4.0	8.0	25	90	n.a.
with strawberries *(Philadelphia Brand)*	70	1.0	4.0	8.0	25	75	n.a.
cream, whipped:							
(Philadelphia Brand)	100	2.0	1.0	10.0	30	110	0
with bacon and horseradish *(Philadelphia Brand)*	90	2.0	1.0	9.0	20	130	n.a.
with blue cheese *(Philadelphia Brand)*	100	3.0	2.0	9.0	25	150	0
with chives *(Philadelphia Brand)*	90	2.0	1.0	9.0	25	140	n.a.
with onions *(Philadelphia Brand)*	90	2.0	2.0	8.0	20	160	n.a.

Food and Measure	cal.	prot. (gms)	carbo. (gms)	fat (gms)	chol. (mgs)	sod. (mgs)	fiber (gms)
Cheese, cream, whipped *(cont.)*							
with pimentos *(Phil-adelphia Brand)*	90	2.0	2.0	8.0	20	140	n.a.
with smoked salmon *(Philadelphia Brand)*	100	3.0	1.0	9.0	25	90	0
Edam:							
(Dorman's)	100	7.2	1.0	7.8	25	n.a.	0
(Kraft)	90	8.0	0	7.0	20	310	0
(Land O'Lakes) . .	100	7.0	<1.0	8.0	25	275	0
(Sargento)	101	7.1	.4	7.9	25	274	0
(Universal)	100	7.0	1.0	8.0	25	200	0
farmer's *(Sargento)*	102	6.8	.8	8.0	26	129	0
feta:							
(Churny)	75	4.0	1.2	6.0	25	316	0
(Frigo)	100	6.0	1.0	8.0	n.a.	400	0
(Sargento)	75	4.0	1.2	6.0	25	316	0
fontina:							
(Frigo)	110	7.0	1.0	9.0	33	400	0
(Sargento)	110	7.3	.4	8.8	33	n.a.	0
fontinella, Italian, sharp or mild *(Uni-versal)*	110	7.0	1.0	9.0	35	290	0
food, see "Cheese food"							
gjetost:							
(Sargento)	132	2.7	12.1	8.4	n.a.	170	0
(Ski Queen) . . .	130	3.0	12.0	8.0	20	110	0
Gorgonzola *(Sargento)*	100	6.1	.7	8.2	21	396	0
Gouda:							
(Kraft)	110	7.0	0	9.0	30	200	0
(Land O'Lakes) . .	100	7.0	1.0	8.0	30	230	0
(Red Rooster Re-duced Sodium)	105	8.0	1.0	8.0	30	59	0
(Sargento)	101	7.1	.6	7.8	32	232	0
(Universal)	100	7.0	1.0	8.0	32	210	0
Gruyere *(Sargento)*	117	8.5	.1	9.2	31	95	0
havarti:							
(Casino)	120	6.0	0	11.0	35	140	0

Food and Measure	cal.	prot. (gms)	carbo. (gms)	fat (gms)	chol. (mgs)	sod. (mgs)	fiber (gms)
(Sargento)	118	5.1	.3	10.6	31	200	0
hoop *(Knudsen)*, 1/2 cup	80	18.0	3.0	1.0	n.a.	n.a.	n.a.
Italian blend, grated *(Kraft)*	120	12.0	2.0	7.0	20	430	0
Italian style, grated *(Sargento)*	108	8.2	1.0	7.6	26	106	0
jalapeño, processed *(Kraft)*	80	5.0	2.0	6.0	20	470	n.a.
Jarlsberg:							
(Norseland)	100	7.0	1.0	7.0	16	130	0
(Sargento)	100	7.0	1.0	7.0	16	130	0
Limburger:							
(Mohawk Valley Little Gem)	90	6.0	0	8.0	25	250	0
(Sargento)	93	5.7	.1	7.7	26	227	0
Monterey Jack:							
(Armour)	110	7.0	1.0	9.0	30	160	0
(Armour Lower Salt)	110	7.0	1.0	9.0	30	111	0
(Dorman's)	100	6.0	1.0	8.0	n.a.	180	0
(Kraft)	110	6.0	0	9.0	30	190	0
(Land O'Lakes) . .	110	7.0	<1.0	9.0	20	150	0
(Lite-line)	50	7.0	1.0	2.0	n.a.	470	0
(Sargento)	106	6.9	.2	8.6	n.a.	152	0
with jalapeño peppers *(Kraft)* . . .	110	7.0	1.0	9.0	30	190	n.a.
with peppers, mild *(Kraft)*	110	7.0	0	9.0	30	180	n.a.
mozzarella:							
(Casino)	90	6.0	1.0	7.0	25	180	0
(Polly-O Lite) . . .	70	7.0	1.0	4.0	15	200	0
(Universal)	90	6.0	1.0	7.0	25	180	0
whole milk *(Frigo)*	90	6.0	1.0	7.0	26	190	0
whole milk *(Polly-O)*	90	5.0	1.0	6.0	20	280	0
whole milk *(Sargento)* . . .	90	6.1	.7	7.0	25	118	0
part skim *(Frigo)*	80	7.0	1.0	5.0	16	190	0
part skim *(Kraft)*	80	8.0	0	5.0	15	190	0

Food and Measure	cal.	prot. (gms)	carbo. (gms)	fat (gms)	chol. (mgs)	sod. (mgs)	fiber (gms)
Cheese, mozzarella *(cont.)*							
part skim *(Land O'Lakes)*	80	8.0	1.0	5.0	15	150	0
part skim *(Polly-O)*	80	6.0	1.0	5.0	15	280	0
part skim *(Sargento)*	79	7.8	.9	4.9	15	150	0
part skim, with jalapeño pepper *(Kraft)*	80	8.0	1.0	5.0	20	230	n.a.
with pizza spices *(Sargento)* ...	79	7.8	.9	4.9	15	150	0
shredded *(Weight Watchers)* ...	70	7.0	1.0	4.0	n.a.	150	0
Muenster:							
(Dorman's)	110	8.0	1.0	9.0	n.a.	190	0
(Dorman's Low Sodium)	110	6.0	0	8.0	n.a.	95	0
(Kraft)	110	7.0	0	9.0	30	180	0
(Land O'Lakes) ..	100	7.0	<1.0	9.0	25	180	0
(Lite-line)	50	7.0	1.0	2.0	n.a.	470	0
(Sargento Red Rind)	104	6.6	.3	8.5	27	178	0
nacho *(Sargento)* ..	106	8.3	.5	8.9	27	406	0
Neufchâtel *(Kraft)*	80	3.0	1.0	7.0	25	115	0
nokkelost *(Norseland)*	100	7.7	0	7.4	26	240	n.a.
Parmesan:							
(Frigo)	110	10.0	1.0	7.0	20	350	0
(Kraft Natural) ..	110	10.0	1.0	7.0	20	350	0
(Sargento)	111	10.1	.9	7.3	19	454	0
(Universal Loaf)	100	11.0	1.0	7.0	19	320	0
grated *(Frigo)* ...	130	12.0	1.0	9.0	23	510	0
grated *(Kraft)* ...	130	12.0	1.0	9.0	30	430	0
grated *(Sargento)*	129	11.8	1.1	8.5	22	528	0
grated *(Universal)*	100	13.0	1.0	8.0	25	500	0
zest *(Frigo)*	130	7.0	8.0	8.0	n.a.	460	0
Parmesan and Romano:							
grated *(Frigo)* ...	130	12.0	1.0	9.0	28	510	0
grated *(Sargento)*	111	9.6	1.0	7.5	24	397	0
pimento, processed *(Kraft Deluxe)* ..	100	6.0	1.0	8.0	25	440	n.a.

Food and Measure	cal.	prot. (gms)	carbo. (gms)	fat (gms)	chol. (mgs)	sod. (mgs)	fiber (gms)
pizza *(Frigo)*	90	7.0	1.0	6.0	n.a.	210	0
pot cheese *(Sargento)*	26	5.0	.8	.2	n.a.	1	0
Port du Salut	100	6.7	.2	8.0	35	151	0
provolone:							
(Dorman's)	90	7.3	1.0	7.3	19	n.a.	0
(Frigo)	100	7.0	1.0	7.0	n.a.	230	0
(Kraft)	100	7.0	1.0	7.0	25	260	0
(Land O'Lakes) . .	100	7.0	1.0	8.0	20	250	0
(Sargento)	100	7.3	.6	7.6	20	248	0
(Universal, 8-oz.							
Half Moon) . . .	95	7.0	1.0	8.0	25	260	0
(Universal, 7-oz.							
Stick or Slices)	100	7.0	1.0	7.0	25	260	0
queso blanco							
(Sargento)	104	6.6	.3	8.5	27	178	0
queso de papa							
(Sargento)	114	7.1	.4	9.4	30	176	0
ricotta:							
(Polly-O Lite), 2 oz.	80	7.0	3.0	4.0	15	65	0
(Universal)	50	3.0	1.0	4.0	15	60	0
whole milk *(Frigo)*	50	3.0	1.0	4.0	15	100	0
whole milk *(Polly-O),*							
2 oz.	100	7.0	2.0	7.0	20	45	0
whole milk							
(Sargento) . . .	53	3.2	1.0	4.0	15	35	0
whole milk and							
whey *(Sargento)*	40	3.0	1.1	2.6	13	26	0
part skim *(Frigo)*	45	3.0	1.0	3.0	10	100	0
part skim *(Polly-O),*							
2 oz.	90	7.0	2.0	6.0	20	45	0
part skim *(Sargento)*	32	2.6	1.1	1.9	10	27	0
Romano:							
(Casino Natural)	100	9.0	1.0	7.0	30	350	0
(Frigo)	110	9.0	1.0	8.0	30	350	0
(Sargento)	110	9.0	1.0	7.6	29	340	0
(Universal Loaf)	100	10.0	1.0	7.0	21	310	0
grated *(Frigo)* . . .	130	12.0	1.0	9.0	35	510	0
grated *(Kraft)* . . .	130	11.0	1.0	9.0	30	350	0
grated *(Universal)*	120	11.0	1.0	8.0	25	520	0

Food and Measure	cal.	prot. (gms)	carbo. (gms)	fat (gms)	chol. (mgs)	sod. (mgs)	fiber (gms)
Cheese (cont.)							
Roquefort	105	6.1	.6	8.7	26	513	0
Scamorze, part skim							
(Kraft)	80	8.0	0	5.0	15	190	0
Slim Jack (Dorman's)	90	6.0	1.0	7.0	n.a.	95	0
smoked (Sargento							
Smokestik)	103	7.0	.6	7.1	24	388	0
spread, see "Cheese spreads"							
string cheese, regular or smoked							
(Sargento)	79	7.8	.9	4.9	15	150	0
Swiss:							
(Dorman's)	100	8.0	0	8.0	24	80	0
(Dorman's No Salt							
Added)	110	8.0	1.0	8.0	n.a.	8	0
(Frigo)	110	8.0	1.0	8.0	n.a.	80	0
(Kraft)	110	8.0	1.0	8.0	25	40	0
(Land O'Lakes) . .	110	8.0	1.0	8.0	25	75	0
(Lite-line)	50	7.0	1.0	2.0	n.a.	330	0
(Sargento)	107	8.1	1.0	7.8	26	74	0
aged (Kraft) . . .	110	8.0	1.0	8.0	25	50	0
processed (Borden)	100	7.0	1.0	8.0	n.a.	355	0
processed (Deluxe)	90	7.0	1.0	7.0	25	420	0
taco cheese:							
(Frigo)	110	7.0	1.0	9.0	n.a.	200	0
(Sargento)	109	6.8	.5	8.8	27	162	0
shredded (Kraft) . .	110	7.0	1.0	9.0	30	180	0
Tilsit, whole milk . .	96	6.9	.5	7.4	29	213	0
Tilsiter (Sargento) . .	96	6.9	.5	7.4	29	213	0
Tybo (Sargento Red							
Wax)	98	7.1	.3	7.4	23	200	0
Cheese, imitation, 1 oz.:							
American:							
(Dorman's)	90	6.0	1.0	8.0	n.a.	490	0
(Sandwich-Mate)	90	5.0	2.0	7.0	<5	385	0
cheddar:							
(Ched-O-Mate) . .	90	6.0	1.0	7.0	5	435	0

Food and Measure	cal.	prot. (gms)	carbo. (gms)	fat (gms)	chol. (mgs)	sod. (mgs)	fiber (gms)
(Frigo)	70	5.0	1.0	5.0	0	310	0
(Sargento)	85	7.0	<1.0	6.0	2	350	0
mild *(Golden Image)*	110	7.0	0	9.0	5	150	0
(Cheez-Ola)	80	6.0	1.0	6.0	<5	415	0
(Cheez-Ola Reduced Sodium)*	80	6.0	1.0	6.0	<5	160	0
(Chef's Delight) . . .	70	4.0	4.0	4.0	<5	435	0
colby *(Golden Image)*	110	7.0	1.0	9.0	5	170	0
(Count Down)	40	6.0	3.0	1.0	<5	415	0
mozzarella:							
(Frigo)	90	6.0	6.0	1.0	0	240	0
(Pizza-Mate) . . .	90	6.0	1.0	7.0	<5	340	0
(Sargento)	80	7.0	<1.0	6.0	2	310	0
Parmesan *(Sargento)*	115	5.0	10.0	7.0	3	445	0
semi-soft *(Dorman's)*	105	6.0	0	9.0	4	130	0
Cheese, spreads, 1 oz., except as noted:							
American, pasteurized process:							
5-oz. jar	412	23.3	12.4	30.2	78	1910	0
(Easy Cheese) . .	80	4.0	2.0	6.0	n.a.	350	0
(Kraft)	80	5.0	2.0	6.0	20	450	0
(Sargento Sharp)	106	6.3	.5	8.9	27	406	0
pimiento *(Sargento)*	106	6.3	.5	8.8	27	405	0
and bacon:							
(Easy Cheese) . .	80	4.0	2.0	6.0	n.a.	350	0
(Kraft)	80	5.0	0	7.0	20	360	0
(Squeez-A-Snak)	90	5.0	1.0	7.0	20	320	0
blue *(Roka Brand)*	70	3.0	2.0	6.0	20	270	0
brick *(Sargento)* . .	95	5.7	.8	8.6	25	431	0
cheddar:							
(Easy Cheese) . .	80	4.0	2.0	6.0	n.a.	370	0
sharp *(Easy Cheese)*	80	4.0	2.0	6.0	n.a.	320	0
and chive *(Easy Cheese)*	80	4.0	2.0	6.0	n.a.	340	0
freeze-dried *(Mountain House)* . .	180	9.0	1.0	15.0	n.a.	n.a.	0

Food and Measure	cal.	prot. (gms)	carbo. (gms)	fat (gms)	chol. (mgs)	sod. (mgs)	fiber (gms)
Cheese, spreads *(cont.)*							
(Cheez Whiz)	80	4.0	2.0	6.0	20	470	0
cream cheese, see "Cheese"							
with garlic *(Kraft)* . .	80	5.0	2.0	6.0	15	340	n.a.
garlic flavor *(Squeez-A-Snak)*	90	5.0	1.0	7.0	20	280	n.a.
garlic and herb *(Pub Cheese)*	90	3.0	2.0	8.0	n.a.	190	n.a.
hickory smoke flavor *(Squeez-A-Snak)*	80	5.0	0	7.0	20	280	n.a.
with jalapeño peppers *(Cheez Whiz)* . . .	80	4.0	2.0	6.0	15	440	n.a.
jalapeño pepper *(Kraft)*	70	2.0	3.0	5.0	15	95	n.a.
(Land O'Lakes Golden Velvet)	80	5.0	2.0	6.0	15	380	0
Limburger *(Mohawk Valley* Brand) . . .	70	4.0	0	6.0	20	400	0
Mexican:							
(Velveeta Hot) . .	80	5.0	3.0	6.0	20	520	n.a.
(Velveeta Mild) . .	80	5.0	3.0	6.0	20	440	n.a.
nacho *(Easy Cheese)*	80	4.0	2.0	6.0	n.a.	340	0
olive and pimento *(Kraft)*	60	2.0	2.0	5.0	15	160	n.a.
pimento:							
(Cheez Whiz) . . .	80	5.0	2.0	6.0	15	370	n.a.
(Kraft)	70	2.0	3.0	5.0	15	120	n.a.
(Squeez-A-Snak)	90	5.0	1.0	7.0	20	280	n.a.
(Velveeta)	80	5.0	3.0	6.0	20	400	n.a.
pineapple *(Kraft)* . .	70	2.0	4.0	5.0	15	75	n.a.
relish *(Kraft)*	70	2.0	3.0	5.0	15	90	n.a.
sharp:							
(Old English) . . .	90	5.0	1.0	7.0	20	330	0
(Squeez-A-Snak)	80	5.0	0	7.0	20	280	0
(Velveeta)	80	5.0	2.0	6.0	20	450	n.a.
Swiss *(Sargento)* . .	95	7.0	.6	7.1	24	388	0
(Velveeta Loaf) . . .	80	5.0	2.0	6.0	20	430	0
(Velveeta Slices) . .	90	5.0	2.0	6.0	20	400	0

Food and Measure	cal.	prot. (gms)	carbo. (gms)	fat (gms)	chol. (mgs)	sod. (mgs)	fiber (gms)
Cheese and bacon dip:							
(Nalley), 1 oz.	116	.9	.9	12.5	17	347	n.a.
Cheese blintzes, see "Blintz"							
Cheese croissant, frozen:							
(Sara Lee L'Original), 1.5 oz. piece . . .	120	4.0	19.0	8.0	n.a.	260	n.a.
Cheese danish, frozen:							
(Sara Lee), 1.3 oz. piece	130	2.0	13.0	8.0	n.a.	130	n.a.
Cheese dip, see specific listings							
Cheese food, 1 oz.:							
American:							
(Borden)	90	5.0	3.0	7.0	n.a.	490	0
(Dorman's)	90	6.0	2.0	9.0	6	340	0
(Golden Image)	90	7.0	2.0	6.0	5	360	0
(Kraft Singles) . .	90	6.0	2.0	7.0	20	390	0
(Sargento Burger cheese)	106	6.3	.5	8.9	27	406	0
grated *(Kraft)* . . .	70	5.0	5.0	4.0	10	430	0
product *(Harvest Moon Brand)* . .	70	6.0	2.0	4.0	15	420	0
product *(Light 'N Lively)*	70	6.0	2.0	4.0	15	410	0
with bacon:							
(Cheez'N Bacon Singles)	90	6.0	2.0	7.0	20	390	n.a.
(Cracker Barrel)	90	5.0	3.0	7.0	20	280	n.a.
(Kraft)	90	5.0	2.0	7.0	20	260	n.a.
cheddar:							
(Land O'Lakes LaChedda) . . .	90	6.0	2.0	7.0	20	335	0
(Light 'N Lively)	70	6.0	2.0	4.0	15	380	0
cold pack *(Kaukauna)* . . .	100	6.0	3.0	7.0	25	250	0

Food and Measure	cal.	prot. (gms)	carbo. (gms)	fat (gms)	chol. (mgs)	sod. (mgs)	fiber (gms)
Cheese food, cheddar *(cont.)*							
extra sharp *(Cracker Barrel)*	90	5.0	3.0	7.0	20	270	0
port wine *(Cracker Barrel)*	90	5.0	4.0	7.0	20	260	0
sharp *(Cracker Barrel)*	90	5.0	4.0	7.0	20	260	0
with garlic *(Kraft)* . .	90	5.0	2.0	7.0	20	220	n.a.
jalapeño:							
(Kraft Singles) . .	90	5.0	2.0	7.0	25	440	n.a.
(Land O'Lakes) . .	90	6.0	2.0	7.0	20	360	n.a.
Monterey Jack *(Kraft* Singles)	90	5.0	2.0	7.0	25	390	0
onion *(Land O'Lakes)*	90	6.0	2.0	7.0	15	330	n.a.
pepperoni *(Land O'Lakes)*	90	6.0	1.0	7.0	20	395	n.a.
pimento *(Kraft* Singles)	90	5.0	2.0	7.0	20	380	n.a.
product *(Harvest Moon Brand)* . . .	70	6.0	2.0	4.0	15	420	0
salami *(Land O'Lakes)*	100	5.0	2.0	8.0	20	400	n.a.
sharp *(Kraft* Singles)	100	6.0	1.0	8.0	25	400	n.a.
smoked *(Smokelle)*	100	6.0	2.0	7.0	20	220	n.a.
Swiss:							
(Kraft Singles) . .	90	5.0	2.0	7.0	25	450	0
(Light 'N Lively)	70	6.0	2.0	4.0	15	350	0
substitute *(Lite-line)*	90	5.0	2.0	7.0	n.a.	450	0
Cheese nuggets, breaded, frozen:							
cheddar *(Banquet)*, 3 oz.	414	13.0	24.0	30.0	n.a.	1015	n.a.
mozzarella *(Banquet)*, 3 oz.	288	15.0	21.0	16.0	n.a.	750	n.a.
Cheese-nut balls or logs, 1 oz.:							
cheddar with almonds *(Sargento)*	97	5.5	2.6	7.5	18	252	n.a.
port wine with almonds:							
(Cracker Barrel)	90	5.0	4.0	6.0	15	410	n.a.
(Sargento)	97	5.5	2.6	7.5	18	252	n.a.

Food and Measure	cal.	prot. (gms)	carbo. (gms)	fat (gms)	chol. (mgs)	sod. (mgs)	fiber (gms)
sharp or smoky with almonds *(Cracker Barrel)*	90	5.0	4.0	6.0	15	410	n.a.
Swiss with almonds *(Sargento)*	94	6.1	1.6	7.4	21	349	n.a.
Cheese sauce:							
mix *(Durkee)*, 1.1-oz. pkg.	157	7.3	13.1	8.4	n.a.	796	n.a.
Cheese soufflé, frozen:							
(Stouffer's), 6 oz. . .	380	18.0	12.0	29.0	n.a.	950	n.a.
Cheese straws or sticks:							
(Farm Rich Fiesta), 3 oz.	270	8.0	18.0	18.0	n.a.	860	n.a.
with bacon *(Farm Rich)*, 3 oz.	300	11.0	21.0	19.0	n.a.	790	n.a.
cheddar:							
(Farm Rich), 3 oz.	300	10.0	19.0	21.0	n.a.	740	n.a.
(Flavor Tree), 1 oz.	160	3.0	12.0	11.0	n.a.	445	n.a.
hot pepper *(Farm Rich)*, 3 oz.	260	8.0	20.0	17.0	n.a.	700	n.a.
mozzarella *(Farm Rich)*, 3 oz.	240	10.0	19.0	13.0	n.a.	570	n.a.
Cherimoyas:							
fresh, 1 average . .	515	7.1	131.3	2.2	0	n.a.	12.0
Cherry:							
fresh:							
sour, whole with pits, 1 cup . . .	51	1.0	12.5	.3	0	3	.2
sour, whole, pitted, 1 cup	77	1.6	18.9	.5	0	5	.3
sweet, whole, 1 cup	104	1.7	24.0	1.4	0	1	.6
sweet, 10 cherries	49	.8	11.3	.7	0	0	.3
candied, 1 oz. . . .	96	.1	24.6	.1	0	n.a.	.1
canned, dark, sweet, with liquid, 1/2 cup:							
with pits *(Del Monte)*	90	0	23.0	0	0	<10	n.a.

Food and Measure	cal.	prot. (gms)	carbo. (gms)	fat (gms)	chol. (mgs)	sod. (mgs)	fiber (gms)
Cherry, canned, dark, sweet, with liquid *(cont.)*							
pitted *(Del Monte)*	90	0	24.0	0	0	<10	n.a.
in water *(Thank You)*	60	1.0	14.0	0	0	<5	0
in heavy syrup *(Thank You)* . .	100	1.0	23.0	0	0	10	tr.
canned, light, sweet, with pits *(Del Monte)*, 1/2 cup . .	100	0	26.0	0	0	<10	n.a.
canned, red tart, 1/2 cup:							
(A&P)	50	<1.0	12.0	<1.0	0	5	n.a.
in water *(Thank You)*	60	1.0	14.0	0	0	<5	0
in heavy syrup *(Thank You)* . .	120	1.0	30.0	0	0	15	0
frozen:							
sour, unsweetened, unthawed, 8 oz.	106	2.1	25.0	1.0	0	2	.7
sweet, sweetened, unthawed, 8 oz.	203	2.6	50.7	.3	0	3	.9
Cherry, maraschino, bottled:							
with liquid, 1 oz. . .	33	.1	8.3	.1	0	n.a.	.1
Cherry drink: canned:							
(Hawaiian Punch), 6 fl. oz.	90	0	23.0	0	0	17	n.a.
(Hi-C), 6 fl. oz. . .	99	<.1	25.0	<.1	0	18	tr.
mix*, 8 fl. oz.:							
black *(Wyler's)* . .	100	0	26.0	0	0	n.a.	n.a.
regular or black *(Kool-Aid)* . . .	100	0	25.0	0	0	0	tr.
presweetened *(Kool-Aid)* . . .	90	0	23.0	0	0	5	tr.
sugar free *(Funny Face)*	4	0	1.0	0	0	0	0

* Prepared according to package directions

Food and Measure	cal.	prot. (gms)	carbo. (gms)	fat (gms)	chol. (mgs)	sod. (mgs)	fiber (gms)
sugar free *(Kool-Aid)*	4	0	0	0	0	5	tr.
sugar sweetened *(Funny Face)* . .	88	0	22.0	0	0	0	0
wild *(Wyler's Crystals)*	90	0	22.0	0	0	n.a.	n.a.
Cherry fruit square, frozen:							
(Pepperidge Farm), 1 square	230	1.0	29.0	12.0	n.a.	190	n.a.
Cherry roll or bar:							
(Flavor Tree), .75-oz. roll	80	0	18.0	<1.0	0	15	n.a.
(Fruit Corners), 1 bar	90	<1.0	18.0	2.0	0	10	n.a.
(Fruit Roll-Ups), 1/2-oz. roll	50	0	12.0	<1.0	0	5	n.a.
(Nature's Choice), 1/2-oz. bar	50	0	11.0	0	0	0	n.a.
(Pocket Fruit), .7-oz. bar	60	0	15.0	0	0	n.a.	n.a.
(Sunkist Fruit Rolls), 1/2-oz. roll	50	0	12.0	<1.0	0	10	n.a.
Cherry turnover:							
frozen *(Pepperidge Farm)*, 1 piece . .	310	3.0	32.0	19.0	n.a.	290	n.a.
refrigerated *(Pillsbury)*, 1 piece	170	2.0	24.0	8.0	n.a.	310	n.a.
Chervil:							
fresh, 1 oz.	16	1.0	3.3	.3	0	n.a.	n.a.
dried, 1 tsp.	1	.1	.3	<.1	0	tr.	.1
Chestnut flour:							
4 oz.	411	6.9	86.4	4.2	0	12	2.3
Chestnuts, Chinese:							
raw, shelled, 4 oz.	256	4.8	55.8	1.3	0	4	1.9
boiled or steamed, shelled, 4 oz. . . .	176	3.3	38.2	.9	0	4	1.3
roasted, 4 oz.	272	5.1	59.5	1.4	0	4	2.0
dried, 1 oz.	103	1.9	22.7	.5	0	2	.8

Food and Measure	cal.	prot. (gms)	carbo. (gms)	fat (gms)	chol. (mgs)	sod. (mgs)	fiber (gms)
Chestnuts, Chinese water, see "Water chestnuts"							
Chestnuts, European:							
raw, peeled, 4 oz.	224	1.8	50.2	1.4	0	4	1.1
boiled or steamed, peeled, 4 oz. . . .	148	2.3	31.5	1.6	0	32	.8
roasted, 4 oz.	280	3.6	60.2	2.5	0	4	2.2
dried, peeled, 1 oz.	105	1.4	22.3	1.1	0	11	1.4
Chestnuts, Japanese:							
boiled or steamed, 4 oz.	64	.9	14.4	.2	0	4	.4
roasted, 4 oz.	228	3.4	51.3	.9	0	n.a.	1.2
dried, 1 oz.	102	1.5	23.1	.4	0	10	.6
Chewing gum, see "Candy"							
Chick peas (garbanzos), canned:							
(Progresso), 8 oz.	200	10.0	32.0	4.0	0	691	n.a.
large:							
(S&W Premium), 1/2 cup	110	6.0	20.0	1.0	0	470	n.a.
(S&W Lite), 1/2 cup	110	6.0	21.0	0	0	295	n.a.
marinated *(S&W),* 1/2 cup	120	5.0	22.0	1.0	0	886	n.a.
Chicken, fresh:							
broilers or fryers, roasted:							
with skin, 1/2 chicken or 10.5 oz.	715	81.6	0	40.7	263	244	0
meat only, 4 oz.	215	32.8	0	8.4	101	98	0
breast, with skin, 1/2 breast or 3.5 oz.	193	29.2	0	7.6	83	69	0
drumstick, with skin, 1 drumstick or 1.8 oz.	112	14.1	0	5.8	48	47	0

Food and Measure	cal.	prot. (gms)	carbo. (gms)	fat (gms)	chol. (mgs)	sod. (mgs)	fiber (gms)
thigh, with skin, 1 thigh or 2.2 oz.	153	15.5	0	9.6	58	52	0
wing, with skin, 1 wing or 1.2 oz.	99	9.1	0	6.6	29	28	0
capon, roasted, with skin, 1/4 capon or 11.2 oz.	729	92.2	0	37.1	275	157	0
roaster, roasted: with skin, 1/2 chicken or 16.9 oz.	1071	115.0	0	64.3	365	349	0
meat only, 4 oz.	189	28.4	0	7.5	85	85	0
light meat only, 4 oz.	174	30.8	0	4.6	85	58	0
dark meat only, 4 oz.	202	26.4	0	9.9	85	108	0
stewing, stewed: with skin, 1/2 chicken or 9.2 oz.	744	70.2	0	49.2	205	190	0
meat only, 4 oz.	269	34.5	0	13.5	94	88	0
light meat only, 4 oz.	242	37.5	0	9.1	79	66	0
dark meat only, 4 oz.	293	31.9	0	17.3	108	108	0
Chicken, canned:							
breast, chunk (Hormel), 63/4 oz. . . .	350	41.0	0	20.0	n.a.	855	0
chunk style (Swanson Mixin'), 21/2 oz. . .	130	14.0	0	8.0	n.a.	225	n.a.
dark, chunk (Hormel), 63/4 oz.	327	42.0	0	18.0	n.a.	933	n.a.
white (Swanson), 21/2 oz.	90	17.0	0	2.0	n.a.	230	n.a.
white and dark (Swanson), 21/2 oz. . . .	100	16.0	0	3.0	n.a.	240	n.a.
white and dark, chunk: (Hormel), 63/4 oz.	340	39.0	0	20.0	n.a.	857	n.a.
(Hormel No Salt), 63/4 oz.	330	42.0	0	18.0	n.a.	75	n.a.

Food and Measure	cal.	prot. (gms)	carbo. (gms)	fat (gms)	chol. (mgs)	sod. (mgs)	fiber (gms)
Chicken, fried, frozen (see also "Chicken entree, frozen"):							
(Banquet), 6.4 oz.	325	18.0	20.0	19.0	n.a.	1201	n.a.
(Banquet Hot 'n Spicy), 6.4 oz. . .	325	18.0	20.0	19.0	n.a.	1201	n.a.
(Swanson), 3¼ oz.	270	15.0	13.0	17.0	n.a.	600	n.a.
(Swanson Take-Out), 3¼ oz.	270	17.0	13.0	17.0	n.a.	660	n.a.
(Weaver Crispy Light), 2.9 oz.	173	14.0	7.5	9.4	n.a.	265	n.a.
(Weaver Party Pack), 3.5 oz.	272	13.5	16.1	16.9	n.a.	440	n.a.
(Weaver Variety Pack), 3.5 oz.	246	14.8	12.9	15.0	n.a.	400	n.a.
in batter, breasts (Weaver), 3.5 oz.	255	17.0	11.2	15.5	n.a.	210	n.a.
in batter, drumsticks and thighs (Weaver), 3.5 oz.	255	15.1	11.9	16.0	n.a.	210	n.a.
breaded drum nuggets (Banquet), 12 oz.	806	57.0	55.0	38.0	n.a.	2126	n.a.
breaded nuggets (Banquet), 3 oz.	233	14.0	14.0	14.0	n.a.	169	n.a.
breaded winglets (Banquet), 12 oz.	806	57.0	55.0	38.0	n.a.	2126	n.a.
breast: (Swanson), 4½ oz.	350	22.0	19.0	21.0	n.a.	830	n.a.
(Weaver Dutch Frye), 3.5 oz. . .	246	16.5	13.1	14.2	n.a.	390	n.a.
cutlets (Swanson), 3½ oz.	230	14.0	14.0	13.0	n.a.	440	n.a.
dipsters (Swanson), 3 oz.	220	11.0	13.0	14.0	n.a.	480	n.a.
drumlets (Swanson), 3 oz.	220	11.0	15.0	13.0	n.a.	470	n.a.

Food and Measure	cal.	prot. (gms)	carbo. (gms)	fat (gms)	chol. (mgs)	sod. (mgs)	fiber (gms)
drumsticks and thighs *(Weaver* Dutch Frye), 3.5 oz. . . .	257	15.4	14.9	15.1	n.a.	390	n.a.
nibbles, wings *(Swanson)*, 3¼ oz. . . .	300	13.0	16.0	20.0	n.a.	550	n.a.
thighs and drumsticks:							
(Banquet), 5 oz.	277	16.0	16.0	16.0	n.a.	892	n.a.
(Swanson), 3¼ oz.	280	16.0	11.0	19.0	n.a.	550	n.a.
wings *(Banquet)*, 6¾ oz.	346	16.0	21.0	22.0	n.a.	1226	n.a.
Chicken bologna:							
(Weaver), 3 oz. . . .	559	12.1	3.6	24.9	n.a.	920	0
Chicken breast:							
(Eckrich Calorie Watcher), 2 slices	40	7.0	1.0	1.0	n.a.	420	n.a.
(Oscar Mayer), 1-oz. slice	27	5.3	.2	.5	11	385	0
oven roasted *(Louis Rich)*, 1-oz. slice	39	5.4	.2	1.8	14	165	n.a.
Chicken and broccoli croissant, frozen:							
(Sara Lee Le San*Wich), 4-oz. piece	360	17.0	29.0	19.0	n.a.	660	n.a.
Chicken and fish seasoning:							
(Lawry's Natural Choice for Chicken and Fish), 1 tsp.	11	.2	2.2	.2	0	4	.2
Chicken crepes, with mushroom sauce:							
frozen *(Stouffer's)*, 8¼ oz.	370	27.0	18.0	21.0	n.a.	930	n.a.
Chicken dinner, frozen:							
a la king *(Le Menu)*, 10¼ oz.	320	22.0	29.0	13.0	n.a.	1050	n.a.
a l'orange *(Lean Cuisine)*, 8 oz.	270	26.0	31.0	5.0	45	460	n.a.

Food and Measure	cal.	prot. (gms)	carbo. (gms)	fat (gms)	chol. (mgs)	sod. (mgs)	fiber (gms)
Chicken dinner (cont.)							
and vegetables (Lean Cuisine), 12¾ oz.	270	23.0	29.0	7.0	40	1120	n.a.
baked, and dressing (Banquet Extra Helpings), 19 oz.	808	38.0	89.0	34.0	n.a.	1817	n.a.
boneless:							
(Morton), 11 oz.	329	11.0	44.7	11.8	n.a.	500	n.a.
(Morton), 17 oz.	627	21.3	84.0	22.9	n.a.	1400	n.a.
(Morton Lite), 11 oz.	250	16.0	30.0	7.0	n.a.	1150	n.a.
(Swanson Hungry-Man), 17½ oz.	670	47.0	60.0	27.0	n.a.	1640	n.a.
breast, medallions Marsala (Classic Lite), 11 oz. . . .	270	22.0	28.0	7.0	85	970	n.a.
breast, roast (Classic Lite), 11 oz. . . .	270	22.0	26.0	9.0	85	1220	n.a.
Burgundy (Classic Lite), 11¼ oz. . .	230	21.0	26.0	5.0	70	1220	1.6
cacciatore (Lean Cuisine), 10⅞ oz. . .	280	23.0	25.0	10.0	40	950	n.a.
chow mein:							
(Classic Lite), 10½ oz.	220	20.0	25.0	4.0	60	1180	n.a.
(La Choy), 12 oz.	260	12.0	44.0	4.0	n.a.	1740	n.a.
(Lean Cuisine), 11¼ oz.	250	16.0	36.0	5.0	25	1160	n.a.
(Morton Lite), 11 oz.	260	11.0	43.0	5.0	n.a.	700	n.a.
cordon bleu (Le Menu), 11 oz. . .	460	26.0	47.0	19.0	n.a.	870	n.a.
Florentine (Le Menu), 12½ oz.	480	28.0	40.0	23.0	n.a.	880	n.a.
fricassee (Dinner Classics), 11¾ oz. . .	330	23.0	32.0	12.0	75	1210	n.a.
fried:							
(Banquet American Favorites), 11 oz.	359	18.0	46.0	11.0	n.a.	1831	n.a.
(Morton), 11 oz.	431	28.0	64.1	6.9	n.a.	900	n.a.

Food and Measure	cal.	prot. (gms)	carbo. (gms)	fat (gms)	chol. (mgs)	sod. (mgs)	fiber (gms)
barbecue (Swanson), 9¼ oz. . . .	560	24.0	49.0	30.0	n.a.	960	n.a.
breast (Swanson), 10¾ oz.	650	26.0	63.0	33.0	n.a.	1580	n.a.
breast (Swanson Hungry-Man), 14 oz.	880	37.0	73.0	49.0	n.a.	2120	n.a.
dark meat (Swanson), 10¼ oz.	610	24.0	55.0	32.0	n.a.	1390	n.a.
dark meat (Swanson Hungry-Man), 14 oz.	860	37.0	75.0	46.0	n.a.	1680	n.a.
glazed (Lean Cuisine), 8½ oz.	270	26.0	23.0	8.0	55	750	n.a.
Hawaiian (Dinner Classics), 11½ oz.	360	24.0	46.0	9.0	n.a.	700	n.a.
Milano (Dinner Classics), 11½ oz. . .	380	25.0	42.0	12.0	n.a.	1360	n.a.
Oriental (Classic Lite), 10½ oz.	250	24.0	26.0	6.0	65	880	.6
Parmigiana (Swanson Hungry-Man), 20 oz.	810	34.0	53.0	51.0	n.a.	2080	n.a.
Parmigiana, breast (Le Menu), 11½ oz.	380	27.0	28.0	18.0	n.a.	890	n.a.
sweet and sour:							
(Classic Lite), 11 oz.	250	23.0	33.0	3.0	70	640	n.a.
(Dinner Classics), 11 oz.	410	14.0	50.0	17.0	65	1240	n.a.
(Le Menu), 11¼ oz.	450	22.0	43.0	22.0	n.a.	980	n.a.
teriyaki (Dinner Classics), 10½ oz. . .	340	14.0	38.0	15.0	70	1340	n.a.
Chicken entree, canned:							
a la king (Swanson), 5¼ oz.	180	10.0	9.0	12.0	n.a.	690	n.a.
chow mein:							
drained (Chun King Divider Pak—4 Servings), 7.14 oz.	101	8.3	10.9	3.6	13	821	.7

Food and Measure	cal.	prot. (gms)	carbo. (gms)	fat (gms)	chol. (mgs)	sod. (mgs)	fiber (gms)
Chicken entree, canned, chow mein *(cont.)*							
drained *(Chun King Divider Pak—2 Servings)*, 8.11 oz.	110	7.7	12.7	3.8	11	937	.8
(Chun King Stir-Fry), 6 oz. with chicken	222	20.7	11.0	11.0	44	540	.6
(La Choy), 3/4 cup	70	7.0	5.0	2.0	n.a.	800	n.a.
(La Choy Bi-Pack), 3/4 cup*	80	7.0	7.0	3.0	n.a.	710	n.a.
and dumplings *(Swanson)*, 7 1/2 oz. . . .	220	11.0	19.0	12.0	n.a.	960	n.a.
stew:							
(Dinty Moore), 7 1/2 oz.	240	11.0	14.0	16.0	n.a.	1010	n.a.
(Swanson), 7 5/8 oz.	170	9.0	16.0	7.0	n.a.	960	n.a.
with dumplings *(Heinz)*, 7 1/2 oz.	210	9.0	22.0	9.0	n.a.	850	n.a.
Chicken entree, freeze-dried:							
(Mountain House), 1 cup	230	9.0	30.0	8.0	n.a.	n.a.	n.a.
Chicken entree, frozen:							
a la king:							
(Banquet Cookin' Bag), 5 oz. . . .	159	14.0	10.0	7.0	n.a.	645	n.a.
(Dining Lite), 9.5 oz.	290	18.4	33.8	9.6	n.a.	910	1.3
(Freezer Queen Boil-in-Pouch)*, 5 oz.	90	9.0	9.0	2.0	n.a.	n.a.	n.a.
(Freezer Queen Single Serve), 9.5 oz.	305	21.0	38.0	7.0	n.a.	n.a.	n.a.
(Morton Lite), 8 oz.	280	13.0	33.0	10.0	n.a.	600	n.a.
(Stouffer's), 9 1/2 oz.	320	19.0	37.0	11.0	n.a.	840	n.a.

* Prepared according to package directions

Food and Measure	cal.	prot. (gms)	carbo. (gms)	fat (gms)	chol. (mgs)	sod. (mgs)	fiber (gms)
almond Cantonese, with rice *(Van de Kamp's* Chinese Classics), 11 oz.	440	25.0	50.0	15.0	n.a.	1220	n.a.
au gratin *(The Budget Gourmet)*, 9.1 oz.	260	20.0	21.0	10.0	n.a.	950	n.a.
barbecue *(Light & Elegant)*, 8 oz.	300	26.0	35.0	6.0	n.a.	900	n.a.
breaded croquettes, gravy and *(Freezer Queen,* 2 lb.), 10.67 oz.	336	18.0	35.0	14.0	n.a.	n.a.	n.a.
breaded patties *(Banquet Entree Express)*, 3 oz.	225	13.0	13.0	14.0	n.a.	151	n.a.
breaded patties, barbecue *(Banquet Entree Express)*, 3 oz.	195	14.0	13.0	9.0	n.a.	652	n.a.
breaded sticks *(Banquet Entree Express)*, 3 oz. . . .	228	14.0	15.0	13.0	n.a.	166	n.a.
broccoli *(Light & Elegant)*, 9½ oz. . .	290	19.0	30.0	11.0	n.a.	805	n.a.
cacciatore:							
(Freezer Queen Single Serve), 9.5 oz.	275	26.0	30.0	5.0	n.a.	n.a.	n.a.
(Tyson), 10.5 oz.	300	30.0	18.0	12.0	n.a.	770	n.a.
cashew *(Stouffer's)*, 9½ oz.	410	31.0	33.0	17.0	n.a.	1240	n.a.
chow mein:							
(Chun King Boil-in-Bag), 10 oz. . .	227	13.1	32.6	4.8	28	1209	.9
(Dining Lite), 11.3 oz.	233	18.6	37.5	1.3	n.a.	1450	.9
(La Choy), ⅔ cup	90	8.0	11.0	2.0	n.a.	720	n.a.
(Morton Lite), 8 oz.	210	10.0	35.0	3.0	n.a.	500	n.a.
(Stouffer's), 8 oz.	140	12.0	11.0	5.0	n.a.	1170	n.a.
Mandarin *(Van de Kamp's* Chinese Classics), 11 oz.	340	20.0	40.0	10.0	n.a.	1180	n.a.

Food and Measure	cal.	prot. (gms)	carbo. (gms)	fat (gms)	chol. (mgs)	sod. (mgs)	fiber (gms)
Chicken entree, frozen (cont.)							
cordon bleu:							
(Beatrice International Entrees), 6 oz.	370	31.0	21.0	18.0	85	925	n.a.
(Tyson Chick'N Quick), 5 oz. . .	310	23.0	19.0	15.0	n.a.	n.a.	n.a.
creamed (Stouffer's), 6½ oz.	320	19.0	7.0	24.0	n.a.	700	n.a.
crepes, see "Chicken crepes"							
divan (Stouffer's), 8½ oz.	350	23.0	14.0	22.0	n.a.	850	n.a.
and dumplings (Banquet Family Entrees), 8 oz. . . .	430	18.0	31.0	25.0	n.a.	928	n.a.
escalloped (Stouffer's), 5¾ oz. . .	260	12.0	16.0	16.0	n.a.	720	n.a.
with fettuccine (The Budget Gourmet), 1 serving	400	23.0	29.0	21.0	n.a.	740	n.a.
fiesta (Tyson), 10.5 oz.	420	32.0	27.0	20.0	n.a.	1510	n.a.
Francais (Tyson), 8¾ oz.	320	28.0	16.0	16.0	n.a.	940	n.a.
French recipe (The Budget Gourmet), 10 oz.	270	23.0	20.0	11.0	n.a.	830	n.a.
fried (see also "Chicken, fried"):							
(Swanson), 7¼ oz.	390	19.0	30.0	21.0	n.a.	1070	n.a.
breast (Swanson Hungry-Man), 11¾ oz.	670	34.0	50.0	37.0	n.a.	1760	n.a.
dark meat (Swanson Hungry-Man), 11 oz.	620	33.0	42.0	36.0	n.a.	1370	n.a.
glazed:							
(Dining Lite), 8.5 oz.	243	22.5	25.8	6.0	n.a.	880	1.0
(Light & Elegant), 8 oz.	230	24.0	25.0	4.0	n.a.	655	n.a.

Food and Measure	cal.	prot. (gms)	carbo. (gms)	fat (gms)	chol. (mgs)	sod. (mgs)	fiber (gms)
kiev:							
(Beatrice International Entrees), 6 oz.	400	28.0	19.0	24.0	105	895	n.a.
(Tyson Chick'N Quick), 5 oz. . .	430	20.0	18.0	31.0	n.a.	n.a.	n.a.
l'orange *(Tyson)*, 8 1/4 oz.	300	26.0	31.0	8.0	n.a.	440	n.a.
Lucerne *(Beatrice* International Entrees), 6 oz.	340	22.0	24.0	18.0	50	1005	n.a.
Mandarin *(The Budget Gourmet)*, 10 oz.	290	20.0	38.0	7.0	n.a.	600	n.a.
marsala *(Tyson)*, 10.5 oz.	300	26.0	24.0	11.0	n.a.	760	n.a.
Mexican, Suiza, with rice *(Van de Kamp's* Combinations), 14 3/4 oz.	550	25.0	65.0	20.0	n.a.	1210	n.a.
nibbles *(Swanson)*, 5 oz.	390	13.0	28.0	25.0	n.a.	880	n.a.
and noodles, with broccoli *(The Budget Gourmet)*, 1 serving	450	23.0	31.0	26.0	n.a.	1110	n.a.
Oriental:							
(Chun King Boil-in-Bag), 10 oz. . .	267	13.9	45.0	3.7	26	1441	.6
with vegetables and rice *(Tyson)*, 10 1/4 oz.	300	26.0	31.0	8.0	n.a.	1050	n.a.
paprikash *(Stouffer's)*, 10 1/2 oz.	390	32.0	31.0	15.0	n.a.	1250	n.a.
Parmigiana:							
(Banquet Family Entrees), 6.4 oz.	143	14.0	10.0	5.0	n.a.	821	n.a.
(Beatrice International Entrees), 6 oz.	360	24.0	26.0	11.0	50	620	n.a.

Food and Measure	cal.	prot. (gms)	carbo. (gms)	fat (gms)	chol. (mgs)	sod. (mgs)	fiber (gms)
Chicken entree, frozen, Parmigiana *(cont.)*							
(Light & Elegant), 8 oz.	260	28.0	23.0	6.0	n.a.	685	n.a.
(Tyson), 11¾ oz.	450	34.0	38.0	18.0	n.a.	1100	n.a.
patties, Italian flavored *(Banquet Entree Express)*, 3 oz. . . .	195	14.0	13.0	9.0	n.a.	638	n.a.
picatta *(Tyson)*, 9 oz.	280	26.0	24.0	9.0	n.a.	660	n.a.
pie, see "Chicken pie"							
Romanoff *(Beatrice International Entrees)*, 6 oz.	340	23.0	26.0	16.0	55	705	n.a.
royale *(Beatrice International Entrees)*, 6 oz.	340	24.0	28.0	15.0	50	1040	n.a.
sliced, gravy and:							
(Freezer Queen Boil-in-Pouch), 5 oz.	80	6.0	6.0	4.0	n.a.	n.a.	n.a.
(Morton Lite), 8 oz.	240	7.0	32.0	9.0	n.a.	600	n.a.
sweet and sour:							
(The Budget Gourmet), 1 serving	350	18.0	53.0	7.0	n.a.	640	n.a.
(Chun King Boil-in-Bag), 10 oz. . .	335	15.6	63.0	2.3	26	1240	.9
(Freezer Queen Single Serve), 9.5 oz.	340	21.0	53.0	4.0	n.a.	n.a.	n.a.
(La Choy), ⅔ cup	190	11.0	33.0	<1.0	n.a.	1005	n.a.
(Tyson), 11 oz. . .	440	29.0	42.0	17.0	n.a.	840	n.a.
with vegetables *(Freezer Queen, 2 lb.)*, 8 oz.	132	11.0	15.0	3.0	n.a.	n.a.	n.a.
with vegetables, country style *(The Budget Gourmet)*, 1 serving	280	16.0	32.0	10.0	n.a.	495	n.a.
with vegetables and vermicelli *(Dining Lite)*, 12.8 oz. . .	280	24.4	32.3	6.8	n.a.	960	1.8

Food and Measure	cal.	prot. (gms)	carbo. (gms)	fat (gms)	chol. (mgs)	sod. (mgs)	fiber (gms)
walnut chicken, chunky (Chun King Boil-in-Bag), 10 oz.	315	15.6	42.0	9.9	31	1115	.6
Chicken entree, mix*, 1/5 pkg.:							
and dumpling (Chicken Helper)	530	34.0	41.0	26.0	n.a.	1320	n.a.
and mushrooms (Chicken Helper)	480	31.0	32.0	25.0	n.a.	1000	n.a.
potato and gravy (Chicken Helper)	600	34.0	45.0	32.0	n.a.	1050	n.a.
stuffing (Chicken Helper)	590	35.0	37.0	33.0	n.a.	1710	n.a.
teriyaki (Chicken Helper)	500	32.0	39.0	24.0	n.a.	1070	n.a.
Chicken frankfurter, 1 link:							
(Grillmaster)	130	7.4	2.0	11.0	n.a.	641	n.a.
(Weaver)	124	5.6	1.7	10.6	n.a.	513	n.a.
cheese (Grillmaster)	146	7.6	2.0	11.9	n.a.	683	n.a.
with cheese (Weaver)	170	7.7	2.2	13.0	n.a.	625	n.a.
Chicken gravy:							
canned:							
(Franco-American), 2 oz.	50	0	3.0	4.0	n.a.	320	n.a.
(Heinz Home Style), 2 oz.	35	.7	2.9	2.3	n.a.	110	n.a.
giblet, canned (Franco-American), 2 oz.	30	1.0	3.0	2.0	n.a.	320	n.a.
mix:							
(Durkee), 1-oz. pkg.	92	2.4	15.0	1.2	n.a.	1537	n.a.
(Durkee Roastin' Bag), 1.5-oz. pkg.	122	3.0	24.0	1.0	n.a.	3597	n.a.
(French's), 1/4 cup*	25	<1.0	4.0	1.0	n.a.	230	n.a.
(French's Gravy for Chicken), 1/4 cup*	25	1.0	4.0	1.0	n.a.	270	n.a.

* Prepared according to package directions

Food and Measure	cal.	prot. (gms)	carbo. (gms)	fat (gms)	chol. (mgs)	sod. (mgs)	fiber (gms)
Chicken gravy, mix *(cont.)*							
creamy *(Durkee)*, 1.2-oz. pkg.	156	3.0	14.0	9.0	n.a.	1528	n.a.
creamy *(Durkee Roastin' Bag)*, 2-oz. pkg.	242	4.0	22.0	12.0	n.a.	2528	n.a.
Italian style *(Durkee Roastin' Bag)*, 1.5-oz. pkg.	144	15.0	31.0	1.0	n.a.	3614	n.a.
Chicken pie, frozen:							
(Banquet), 8 oz.	520	16.0	45.0	30.0	n.a.	1027	n.a.
(Stouffer's), 10 oz.	530	21.0	34.0	34.0	n.a.	1210	n.a.
(Swanson), 8 oz.	420	13.0	39.0	24.0	n.a.	840	n.a.
(Swanson Chunky), 10 oz.	580	19.0	53.0	33.0	n.a.	850	n.a.
(Swanson Hungry-Man), 16 oz.	700	26.0	64.0	37.0	n.a.	1670	n.a.
Chicken sausage:							
(Grillmaster), 1 link	157	8.2	.4	13.6	n.a.	584	n.a.
(Grillmaster Rope), 4 oz.	306	15.2	3.7	25.6	n.a.	1142	n.a.
canned *(Hormel)*, 4 links	180	8.0	1.0	16.0	n.a.	n.a.	n.a.
Chicken, smoked:							
(Carl Buddig), 1 oz.	50	5.1	1.0	2.8	12	340	n.a.
Chicken spread, canned:							
(Hormel), 1/2 oz.	30	2.0	0	2.0	n.a.	n.a.	n.a.
(Swanson), 1 oz.	60	4.0	2.0	4.0	n.a.	140	n.a.
salad *(The Spreadables)*, 1.9 oz.	120	6.0	4.0	9.0	n.a.	230	n.a.
Chicory, witloof, see "Endive, French or Belgian"							
Chicory greens, fresh:							
untrimmed, 1 lb.	87	6.3	17.5	1.1	0	167	3.0
chopped, 1 cup	42	3.1	8.5	.5	0	81	1.4

Food and Measure	cal.	prot. (gms)	carbo. (gms)	fat (gms)	chol. (mgs)	sod. (mgs)	fiber (gms)
Chicory root, fresh:							
1 root, 2.6 oz. . . .	44	.8	10.5	.1	0	30	1.2
1" pieces, 1 cup . .	66	1.3	15.8	.2	0	46	1.8
Chili con carne, canned:							
(Heinz), 7³/4 oz. . .	350	15.0	27.0	21.0	n.a.	1000	n.a.
with beans:							
(Hormel, 15 oz.), 7¹/2 oz.	310	17.0	23.0	17.0	n.a.	1127	n.a.
(Hormel, 25 oz.), 8¹/3 oz.	350	18.0	26.0	20.0	n.a.	1202	n.a.
(Hormel, 40 oz.), 8 oz.	320	17.0	25.0	17.0	n.a.	1135	n.a.
(Hormel Short Order),* 7¹/2 oz. . .	280	17.0	23.0	14.0	n.a.	1134	n.a.
(Van Camp's), 1 cup	352	14.9	20.9	23.2	n.a.	1215	2.3
(Wolf), 7¹/2 oz. . .	345	15.0	21.8	22.0	n.a.	1013	2.3
hot *(Heinz),* 7³/4 oz.	330	15.0	30.0	16.0	n.a.	1140	n.a.
hot *(Hormel),* 7¹/2 oz.	310	16.0	24.0	16.0	n.a.	1121	n.a.
hot *(Hormel* Short Order),* 7¹/2 oz.	300	16.0	23.0	16.0	n.a.	1086	n.a.
spicy *(Wolf),* 7¹/2 oz.	324	14.1	20.6	20.6	n.a.	926	2.2
without beans:							
(Hormel), 10¹/2-oz. can	540	24.0	19.0	41.0	n.a.	1384	n.a.
(Hormel, 15 oz.), 7¹/2 oz.	370	17.0	12.0	28.0	n.a.	1012	n.a.
(Hormel, 25 oz.), 8¹/3 oz.	430	20.0	13.0	33.0	n.a.	1070	n.a.
(Hormel Short Order),* 7¹/2 oz. . .	360	18.0	11.0	27.0	n.a.	961	n.a.
(Nalley), 3¹/2 oz.	130	7.0	7.0	9.0	20	610	n.a.
(Nalley Big Chunk, 7¹/2 oz.), 3¹/2 oz.	170	9.0	9.0	12.0	30	555	n.a.
(Nalley Big Chunk, 15 oz.), 3¹/2 oz.	170	9.0	6.0	12.0	30	475	n.a.
(Van Camp's), 1 cup	412	15.4	12.1	33.5	n.a.	1499	1.6
(Wolf), 7¹/2 oz. . .	387	20.7	16.2	26.6	n.a.	1042	2.0

Food and Measure	cal.	prot. (gms)	carbo. (gms)	fat (gms)	chol. (mgs)	sod. (mgs)	fiber (gms)
Chili con carne, canned, without beans *(cont.)*							
hot *(Hormel)*, 7¹/2 oz.	370	17.0	12.0	28.0	n.a.	985	n.a.
spicy *(Wolf)*, 7¹/2 oz.	363	19.4	15.3	24.9	n.a.	926	1.9
and franks *(Van Camp's Chilee Weenee)*, 1 cup	309	14.4	27.6	15.7	n.a.	1057	2.2
and macaroni:							
(Heinz), 7¹/2 oz.	250	10.0	26.0	12.0	n.a.	860	n.a.
(Hormel Short Order)*, 7¹/2 oz. . . .	200	11.0	16.0	10.0	n.a.	1418	n.a.
(Wolf Chili Mac)*, 7¹/2 oz.	317	11.5	22.9	19.9	n.a.	854	1.1
mild and hot *(Nalley)*, 3¹/2 oz. . . .	130	8.0	11.0	6.0	15	490	n.a.
thick *(Nalley)*, 3¹/2 oz.	140	9.0	12.0	6.0	15	495	n.a.
Chili con carne, freeze-dried:							
with beans *(Mountain House)*, 1 cup . .	390	20.0	38.0	16.0	n.a.	n.a.	n.a.
with macaroni and beef *(Mountain House)*, 1 cup . .	250	12.0	31.0	8.0	n.a.	n.a.	n.a.
Chili con carne, frozen, with beans:							
(Stouffer's), 8³/4 oz.	280	21.0	23.0	11.0	n.a.	1190	n.a.
Chili con carne spread:							
concentrate *(Oscar Mayer)*, 1 oz. . . .	78	3.9	2.5	5.8	14	426	n.a.
Chili pepper, see "Pepper, chili"							
Chili powder:							
seasoned:							
1 oz.	89	3.5	15.5	4.8	0	286	6.3
1 tbsp.	24	.9	4.1	1.3	0	76	1.7
Chili sauce, canned or bottled:							
(Del Monte), ¹/4 cup	70	1.0	17.0	0	0	835	n.a.

Food and Measure	cal.	prot. (gms)	carbo. (gms)	fat (gms)	chol. (mgs)	sod. (mgs)	fiber (gms)
(Heinz), 1 tbsp. . . .	17	.2	3.8	tr.	0	191	n.a.
(S&W Chili Makins'), 1/2 cup	100	5.0	20.0	1.0	n.a.	782	n.a.
green, mild *(Del Monte* Chile Salsa), 1/4 cup	20	0	3.0	0	0	590	n.a.
hot dog sauce *(Wolf)*, 1/6 cup	44	1.5	4.4	2.3	n.a.	199	.4
Chili seasoning mix:							
(French's Chili-O), 1/6 pkg.	25	1.0	5.0	0	n.a.	630	n.a.
con carne *(Durkee)*, 1.7-oz. pkg.	148	2.0	33.0	1.6	n.a.	3239	n.a.
with onion *(French's Chili-O)*, 1/6 pkg.	35	1.0	7.0	0	n.a.	710	n.a.
Texas *(Durkee)*, 1.8-oz. pkg.	151	4.6	23.0	4.4	n.a.	2603	n.a.
Chinese snacks, crispy:							
(Mother's TV), 1 oz.	140	3.0	17.0	7.0	n.a.	n.a.	n.a.
Chives:							
fresh, chopped, 1 tbsp.	1	.1	.1	<.1	0	0	<.1
freeze-dried, 1 tbsp.	1	<.1	.1	<.1	0	n.a.	<.1
Chocolate, see "Candy"							
Chocolate, baking:							
(Nestlé Choco-Bake), 1 oz.	180	4.0	8.0	15.0	n.a.	n.a.	n.a.
milk *(Nestlé* Morsels), 1 oz.	150	2.0	17.0	9.0	5	20	n.a.
semi-sweet:							
(Borden Chips), 1 oz.	150	1.0	20.0	7.0	n.a.	5	n.a.
(Hershey's) regular and miniature, 1.5 oz. or 1/4 cup	220	2.0	26.0	12.0	n.a.	5	n.a.
(Nestlé Toll House Morsels), 1 oz.	150	2.0	18.0	8.0	n.a.	0	n.a.

Food and Measure	cal.	prot. (gms)	carbo. (gms)	fat (gms)	chol. (mgs)	sod. (mgs)	fiber (gms)
Chocolate, baking (cont.)							
unsweetened (Hershey's), 1 oz. . . .	190	4.0	7.0	16.0	n.a.	1	n.a.
Chocolate drink mix, see "Milk beverages, mix"							
Chocolate sauce, syrup or topping, see "Toppings, dessert"							
Chop suey seasoning mix:							
(Durkee), 1.5-oz. pkg.	128	1.8	19.0	2.1	n.a.	828	n.a.
Chow mein, see specific listings							
Chrysanthemum garland, fresh:							
raw, 1″ pieces, 1 cup	4	.4	1.1	<.1	0	13	.2
boiled, drained, 1″ pieces, 1 cup . . .	20	1.6	4.3	.1	0	53	1.2
Church's:							
catfish, fried, 3/4-oz. piece	67	3.9	3.8	4.0	n.a.	151	.1
chicken, fried:							
breast, 4.3-oz. piece	278	21.3	9.4	17.3	n.a.	560	0
breast-wing, 4.8-oz. piece	303	21.8	8.9	19.7	n.a.	583	0
leg (drumstick), 2.9-oz. piece	147	12.9	4.5	8.6	n.a.	286	0
thigh, 4.2-oz. piece	306	18.5	9.2	21.6	n.a.	448	0
chicken nuggets:							
regular, .63-oz. piece	55	3.0	3.7	3.1	n.a.	125	0
spicy, .63-oz. piece	52	3.1	3.4	2.9	n.a.	91	0
corn on cob, 6-oz. ear	237	4.2	32.9	9.3	n.a.	20	.6
French fries, 3-oz. serving	138	2.1	20.1	5.5	n.a.	126	.6
hush puppy, .82-oz. piece	78	1.3	11.6	2.9	n.a.	55	0

Food and Measure	cal.	prot. (gms)	carbo. (gms)	fat (gms)	chol. (mgs)	sod. (mgs)	fiber (gms)
Cinnamon:							
ground (all brands), 1 tsp.	6	.1	1.8	.1	0	1	.6
Cisco, see "Lake herring"							
Citron:							
candied, 1 oz. . . .	89	.1	22.7	.1	0	82	.4
Citrus drink:							
canned (*Hi-C* Citrus Cooler), 6 fl. oz.	94	<.1	23.0	<.1	0	17	tr.
chilled:							
(*Five Alive*), 6 fl. oz.	87	<1.0	22.0	<.1	0	16	tr.
tropical (*Five Alive*), 6 fl. oz.	88	<1.0	22.0	<.1	0	15	tr.
frozen*:							
(*Five Alive*), 6 fl. oz.	87	<1.0	22.0	<.1	0	2	tr.
tropical (*Five Alive*), 6 fl. oz.	85	<1.0	21.0	<.1	0	1	tr.
mix*, berry blend (*Sunkist* Light Crystals), 8 fl. oz. with ice.	6	0	2.0	0	0	20	n.a.
Citrus juice, tropical:							
(*Smucker's*), 8 fl. oz.	120	1.0	30.0	0	0	5	n.a.
Clam:							
fresh:							
mixed species, raw, meat only, 4 oz.	84	14.5	2.9	1.1	39	64	0
canned:							
chopped or minced (*S&W* Fancy), 2 oz.	28	5.0	2.0	0	n.a.	280	n.a.
chowder, whole, baby (*S&W*), 2 oz.	33	6.0	1.0	0	n.a.	n.a.	n.a.
minced (*Gorton's*), 1/2 can	70	12.0	4.0	1.0	n.a.	640	n.a.

* Prepared according to package directions

153

Food and Measure	cal.	prot. (gms)	carbo. (gms)	fat (gms)	chol. (mgs)	sod. (mgs)	fiber (gms)
Clam, canned *(cont.)*							
minced *(Snow's)*,							
6¹/₂ oz.	100	18.0	4.0	1.0	n.a.	920	n.a.
frozen:							
in batter *(Mrs. Paul's)*, 2¹/₂ oz.	230	9.0	20.0	13.0	n.a.	385	n.a.
French fried *(Taste O' Sea* Crispy Light), 5 oz. . .	400	17.0	40.0	20.0	n.a.	140	n.a.
strips, fried *(Gorton's* Crunchy), ¹/₂ pkg.	240	7.0	20.0	15.0	n.a.	460	n.a.
Clam chowder, see "Soup"							
Clam dinner, frozen:							
(Taste O' Sea Platter), 6¹/₂ oz.	540	15.0	55.0	29.0	n.a.	1130	n.a.
Clam dip:							
(Kraft), 2 tbsp. . . .	60	2.0	3.0	4.0	10	250	n.a.
(Kraft Premium), 1 oz.	45	1.0	2.0	4.0	20	210	n.a.
(Nalley), 1 oz.	99	.6	1.1	10.5	11	370	n.a.
Clam juice:							
canned *(Snow's)*, 3 fl. oz.	14	1.0	2.0	0	n.a.	470	n.a.
Cloves:							
ground, (all brands), 1 tsp.	7	.1	1.3	.4	0	5	.2
Coating mix, see "Seasoned coating mix"							
Cocktail drink mix*:							
(Bar-Tender's), 4 fl. oz. with alcohol	72	0	1.0	0	0	32	0
Cocktail sauce, in jars:							
(Nalley), 1 oz.	30	.6	7.1	.3	0	217	n.a.
(Sauceworks), 1 tbsp.	12	0	3.0	0	0	190	n.a.
(Stokely's Finest Seafood), 1 tbsp. . . .	18	n.a.	5.0	0	0	90	n.a.

* *Prepared according to package directions*

Food and Measure	cal.	prot. (gms)	carbo. (gms)	fat (gms)	chol. (mgs)	sod. (mgs)	fiber (gms)
Cocoa, dry:							
high fat or breakfast, plain, 1 oz.	85	4.8	13.7	6.7	n.a.	2	1.2
high-medium fat, plain, 1 oz.	75	4.9	14.6	5.4	n.a.	2	1.2
low-medium fat, plain, 1 oz.	62	5.4	15.3	3.6	n.a.	2	1.5
low fat, plain, 1 oz.	53	5.7	16.4	2.2	n.a.	2	1.6
(Alba), .7 oz.	62	5.4	10.2	.5	4	160	n.a.
(Carnation Sugar Free), 1 envelope or 4 heaping tsp. . .	50	4.0	8.0	<1.0	n.a.	160	n.a.
(Hershey's), 1 oz. or 1/3 cup	120	7.0	13.0	4.0	n.a.	5	n.a.
(Nestlé Superior Quality), 1.3 oz.	150	3.0	26.0	4.0	n.a.	110	n.a.
(Swiss Miss Lite),* 1 pkg.	70	2.0	15.0	<1.0	n.a.	210	n.a.
chocolate, double rich *(Swiss Miss),* 1 pkg.	110	2.0	19.0	3.0	n.a.	160	n.a.
chocolate, milk:							
(Carnation Instant), 1-oz. pkg. . . .	110	3.0	23.0	1.0	n.a.	115	n.a.
(Swiss Miss), 1 pkg.	110	1.0	20.0	3.0	n.a.	170	n.a.
(Swiss Miss Sugar Free),* 1 pkg. . . .	50	4.0	9.0	<1.0	n.a.	170	n.a.
chocolate, with mini marshmallows:							
(Carnation Instant), 1-oz. pkg. . . .	110	2.0	23.0	1.0	n.a.	115	n.a.
(Swiss Miss), 1 pkg.	110	1.0	20.0	3.0	n.a.	150	n.a.
chocolate, with marshmallow flavor *(Swiss Miss* Sugar Free), 1 pkg.	50	4.0	9.0	<1.0	n.a.	190	n.a.
chocolate, rich:							
(Carnation Instant), 1-oz. pkg. . . .	110	2.0	23.0	1.0	n.a.	115	n.a.
(Carnation 70 Calorie), 1 pkg. . . .	70	3.0	15.0	0	n.a.	125	n.a.

Food and Measure	cal.	prot. (gms)	carbo. (gms)	fat (gms)	chol. (mgs)	sod. (mgs)	fiber (gms)
Coconut:							
fresh:							
shelled, meat only, 4 oz.	401	3.8	17.3	38.0	0	23	4.9
shelled, meat only, 1 piece, 2″ × 2¹/2″	159	1.5	6.9	15.1	0	9	1.9
shredded or grated, 1 cup	283	2.7	12.2	26.8	0	16	3.4
canned, shredded *(Durkee)*, 1 cup	277	2.8	8.0	28.0	0	18	n.a.
Coconut cream:							
from grated coconut meat, 1 cup . . .	792	8.7	16.0	83.2	0	10	n.a.
from grated coconut meat, 1 tbsp. . . .	49	.5	1.0	5.2	0	1	n.a.
canned *(Coco Casa)*, 1 oz.	78	0	17.0	0	0	22	n.a.
Coconut milk:							
from grated coconut meat and coconut water, 1 cup . . .	552	5.5	13.3	57.2	0	37	n.a.
Coconut water:							
coconut liquid, 1 cup	46	1.7	8.9	.5	0	252	.1
Cod:							
fresh, Atlantic, raw, fillets, 4 oz.	93	20.2	0	.8	49	61	0
canned, 4 oz.	119	25.8	0	1.0	62	247	0
dried, salted, 4 oz.	328	71.2	0	2.7	172	7969	0
frozen:							
(Gorton's Fishmarket Fresh), 4 oz. . .	90	20.0	0	1.0	n.a.	70	0
(Van de Kamp's Today's Catch), 4 oz.	80	20.0	0	0	n.a.	150	0
fillets *(Booth Light & Tender)*, 4 oz.	89	20.0	0	1.0	n.a.	80	n.a.
fillets *(Taste O' Sea)*, 4 oz. . . .	80	18.0	0	1.0	n.a.	200	n.a.

Food and Measure	cal.	prot. (gms)	carbo. (gms)	fat (gms)	chol. (mgs)	sod. (mgs)	fiber (gms)
breaded (Van de Kamp's), 5 oz.	290	20.0	10.0	20.0	n.a.	371	n.a.
breaded, fillets (Certi-Fresh Light & Crunchy), 5 oz.	296	16.0	22.0	16.0	n.a.	n.a.	n.a.
seasoned (Booth Light & Tender), 3 oz.	150	11.0	18.0	4.0	n.a.	310	n.a.
uncooked (Taste O'Sea Calorie Watchers), 1 portion	60	13.0	0	1.0	n.a.	140	n.a.
Cod dinner, almondine, frozen: (Dinner Classics), 12 oz.	360	23.0	33.0	15.0	75	1440	n.a.
Cod entree, frozen: fillets (Dining Lite), 10 oz.	189	23.2	12.1	5.8	n.a.	570	n.a.
Florentine (Certi-Fresh), 9 oz. . . .	290	25.0	13.0	15.0	n.a.	n.a.	n.a.
in shrimp sauce (Certi-Fresh), 9 oz. . . .	290	27.0	12.0	15.0	n.a.	n.a.	n.a.
Coffee: (Folgers), 1 tbsp. . .	3	<1.0	<1.0	0	0	tr.	n.a.
instant: (Folgers), 1 tsp.	5	<1.0	1.0	0	0	tr.	n.a.
(High Point Decaffeinated), 1 tsp.	5	<1.0	1.0	0	0	1	n.a.
(Kava), 1 tsp. . . .	2	0	1.0	0	0	<5	n.a.
(Nescafé/Nescafé Decaffeinated), 1 cup	4	<1.0	1.0	<1.0	0	0	n.a.
(Sunrise), 1 cup	6	<1.0	1.0	<1.0	0	0	n.a.
instant, crystals (Folgers Decaffeinated), 1 tsp.	8	<1.0	1.6	<1.0	0	2	n.a.

Food and Measure	cal.	prot. (gms)	carbo. (gms)	fat (gms)	chol. (mgs)	sod. (mgs)	fiber (gms)
Coffee *(cont.)*							
flavored, prepared*, 6 fl. oz.:							
cafe Amaretto *(General Foods* International)	50	0	7.0	2.0	n.a.	25	tr.
cafe Amaretto *(General Foods* International Sugar Free)	35	0	3.0	3.0	n.a.	20	tr.
cafe Francais *(General Foods* International)	50	0	6.0	3.0	n.a.	25	tr.
cafe Irish creme *(General Foods International)* . .	60	0	8.0	3.0	n.a.	20	tr.
cafe Irish creme *(General Foods* International Sugar Free) . .	30	0	3.0	2.0	n.a.	15	tr.
cafe Vienna *(General Foods International)*	60	0	10.0	2.0	n.a.	105	tr.
cafe Vienna *(General Foods* International Sugar Free)	30	0	3.0	2.0	n.a.	95	tr.
Irish mocha mist *(General Foods International)* . .	50	0	8.0	2.0	n.a.	20	tr.
Irish mocha mist *(General Foods* International Sugar Free) . .	25	1.0	3.0	2.0	n.a.	20	tr.
orange cappuccino *(General Foods International)* . .	60	0	10.0	2.0	n.a.	105	tr.

* Prepared according to package directions

Food and Measure	cal.	prot. (gms)	carbo. (gms)	fat (gms)	chol. (mgs)	sod. (mgs)	fiber (gms)
orange cappuccino *(General Foods International Sugar Free)* . .	30	0	3.0	2.0	n.a.	50	tr.
Suisse mocha *(General Foods International)*	50	0	8.0	2.0	n.a.	25	tr.
Suisse mocha *(General Foods International Sugar Free)*	30	0	3.0	2.0	n.a.	20	tr.
freeze-dried *(Taster's Choice/Taster's Choice De-caffeinated)*, 1 cup	4	<1.0	1.0	<1.0	0	0	n.a.
Colada drink mixer:							
piña:							
(Freeze & Serve), 1 fl. oz.	31	0	7.0	0	0	7	n.a.
(Holland-House), 1 pouch	3	0	13.0	0	0	n.a.	n.a.
piña, bottled: *(Coco Casa)*, 1 fl. oz. . .	88	0	16.0	2.0	0	3	n.a.
(Holland House), 1 fl. oz.	33	0	8.0	0	0	7	0
piña, mix* *(Bar-Tender's)*, 5 fl. oz. with alcohol	254	3.0	24.0	3.0	12	45	0
strawberry, bottled *(Holland House)*, 1 fl. oz.	78	0	17.0	0	0	23	0
Coleslaw:							
dairy pack *(Knudsen)*, 1/2 cup	200	1.0	11.0	16.0	n.a.	n.a.	n.a.

* Prepared according to package directions

Food and Measure	cal.	prot. (gms)	carbo. (gms)	fat (gms)	chol. (mgs)	sod. (mgs)	fiber (gms)
Collard greens:							
fresh:							
raw, with stems, 1 lb.	49	4.1	9.7	.6	0	72	1.5
boiled, drained, chopped, 1 cup	27	2.1	5.0	.3	0	36	.8
frozen, chopped (Southland), 3.3 oz.	25	3.0	4.0	0	0	45	n.a.
Collins drink mix*:							
(Bar-Tender's), 6 fl. oz. with alcohol	177	0	18.0	0	0	32	0
Cookie:							
almond:							
(Pepperidge Farm Supreme), 2 pieces	140	2.0	13.0	10.0	n.a.	45	n.a.
toast (Stella D'Oro Breakfast Treats), 1 piece	102	1.6	15.5	3.7	n.a.	n.a.	n.a.
(Stella D'Oro Chinese Dessert), 1 piece	172	2.4	19.5	9.4	n.a.	n.a.	n.a.
(Stella D'Oro Mandel), 1 piece	56	1.2	10.0	1.2	n.a.	n.a.	n.a.
Amaretto (Stella D'Oro Amaretti), 1 piece	28	.7	4.8	.7	n.a.	n.a.	n.a.
animal crackers:							
(Barnum's Animals), 11 pieces or 1 oz.	130	2.0	21.0	4.0	n.a.	120	n.a.
(FFV), 7 pieces or ¾ oz.	85	.1	14.8	2.4	n.a.	87	tr.
(Sunshine), 7 pieces	60	1.0	10.0	2.0	0	90	n.a.
(Tom's), 1.7 oz.	210	4.0	37.0	5.0	n.a.	200	n.a.
anise:							
(Stella D'Oro Anisette Sponge), 1 piece	52	1.1	10.1	.8	n.a.	n.a.	n.a.

* Prepared according to package directions

Food and Measure	cal.	prot. (gms)	carbo. (gms)	fat (gms)	chol. (mgs)	sod. (mgs)	fiber (gms)
(Stella D'Oro Anisette Toast), 1 piece	46	.8	9.4	.5	n.a.	n.a.	n.a.
(Stella D'Oro Anisette Toast Jumbo), 1 piece	109	2.0	22.9	1.1	n.a.	n.a.	n.a.
apple:							
(Almost Home Fruit Sticks), 2/3-oz. piece	70	0	14.0	2.0	n.a.	30	n.a.
(Apple Newtons), 1 1/2 pieces or 1 oz.	110	1.0	21.0	2.0	n.a.	45	n.a.
(Tacoma Bar), 1 piece or 1/2 oz.	41	.4	9.0	.9	n.a.	37	.1
iced (Almost Home Dutch Fruit Sticks), 2/3-oz. piece	70	0	14.0	1.0	n.a.	40	n.a.
pastry, dietetic (Stella D'Oro), 1 piece	90	1.0	13.0	3.5	n.a.	<10	n.a.
applesauce-raisin iced (Nabisco), 2 pieces	140	2.0	17.0	8.0	n.a.	70	n.a.
apricot-raspberry (Pepperidge Farm Fruit Cookies), 3 pieces	150	1.0	23.0	6.0	n.a.	80	n.a.
arrowroot (National), 6 pieces or 1 oz. . .	130	2.0	21.0	4.0	n.a.	80	n.a.
assorted:							
(Pepperidge Farm Champagne), 3 pieces	95	1.0	12.0	5.0	n.a.	55	n.a.
(Pepperidge Farm Seville), 2 pieces	110	1.0	14.0	6.0	n.a.	50	n.a.
(Pepperidge Farm Southport), 2 pieces	150	1.0	18.0	9.0	n.a.	70	n.a.

Food and Measure	cal.	prot. (gms)	carbo. (gms)	fat (gms)	chol. (mgs)	sod. (mgs)	fiber (gms)
Cookie, assorted *(cont.)*							
(Stella D'Oro Hostess), 1 piece . .	41	.5	5.4	1.9	n.a.	n.a.	n.a.
(Stella D'Oro Lady Stella), 1 piece	42	.6	5.5	2.0	n.a.	n.a.	n.a.
blueberry:							
(Almost Home Fruit Sticks), 2/3-oz. piece	70	0	14.0	2.0	n.a.	90	n.a.
(Blueberry Newtons), 1 1/2 pieces or 1 oz.	110	1.0	21.0	2.0	n.a.	80	n.a.
(Pepperidge Farm Fruit Cookies), 3 pieces	170	2.0	27.0	6.0	n.a.	80	n.a.
brown edge wafer *(Nabisco)*, 5 pieces or 1 oz.	140	1.0	20.0	6.0	n.a.	80	n.a.
brownie:							
chocolate-nut *(Pepperidge Farm)*, 3 pieces	170	1.0	19.0	10.0	n.a.	80	n.a.
cream sandwich *(Pepperidge Farm* Capri), 2 pieces	160	1.0	20.0	9.0	n.a.	90	n.a.
fudge and nut *(Almost Home)*, 1 1/4-oz. piece	160	1.0	23.0	7.0	n.a.	75	n.a.
butter flavor:							
(Nabisco), 6 pieces	130	2.0	20.0	5.0	n.a.	140	n.a.
(Nabisco Danish), 5 pieces or 1 oz.	150	1.0	18.0	8.0	n.a.	70	n.a.
(Orbit), 4 pieces	60	<1.0	10.0	2.0	0	75	n.a.
(Pepperidge Farm Chessman), 3 pieces	130	1.0	18.0	6.0	n.a.	80	n.a.
(Sunshine), 2 pieces	60	1.0	9.0	2.0	0	75	n.a.
caramel *(FFV* Patties), 1 piece or 1.1 oz.	151	1.2	19.8	7.4	n.a.	109	tr.

Food and Measure	cal.	prot. (gms)	carbo. (gms)	fat (gms)	chol. (mgs)	sod. (mgs)	fiber (gms)
cherry:							
(Almost Home Fruit Sticks), 1 piece	70	0	14.0	2.0	n.a.	100	n.a.
(Cherry Newtons), 1½ or 1 oz. . . .	110	1.0	20.0	2.0	n.a.	80	n.a.
chocolate:							
(Famous Wafers), 5 pieces	130	2.0	21.0	4.0	n.a.	200	n.a.
(Nabisco Pure Middles), 2 pieces or 1 oz.	150	2.0	18.0	8.0	n.a.	65	n.a.
(Nabisco Snaps), 7 pieces	130	2.0	21.0	4.0	n.a.	140	n.a.
(Orbit), 4 pieces	60	1.0	9.0	2.0	0	85	n.a.
(Stella D'Oro Margherite), 1 piece	73	.9	10.1	3.2	n.a.	n.a.	n.a.
chocolate chip:							
(Almost Home Real), 2 pieces	130	1.0	20.0	5.0	n.a.	100	n.a.
(Chewy Chips Ahoy!), 2 pieces	130	1.0	18.0	6.0	n.a.	110	n.a.
(Chip-A-Roos), 1 piece	60	<1.0	8.0	3.0	0	50	n.a.
(Chips Ahoy! Pure), 3 pieces	140	2.0	18.0	7.0	n.a.	95	n.a.
(Chips 'n More), 2 pieces	150	2.0	18.0	7.0	n.a.	70	n.a.
(Duncan Hines), 1 piece	55	.5	7.0	2.5	n.a.	35	n.a.
(Grandma's), 3 oz.	400	5.0	55.0	18.0	n.a.	n.a.	n.a.
(Keebler Chips Deluxe), 1 piece	90	<1.0	10.0	4.0	n.a.	75	n.a.
(Keebler Rich 'n Chips), 1 piece	80	1.0	10.0	4.0	n.a.	70	n.a.
(Nabisco Snaps), 6 pieces	130	2.0	21.0	4.0	n.a.	100	n.a.
(Pepperidge Farm), 3 pieces	150	1.0	20.0	8.0	n.a.	75	n.a.

Food and Measure	cal.	prot. (gms)	carbo. (gms)	fat (gms)	chol. (mgs)	sod. (mgs)	fiber (gms)
Cookie, chocolate chip (cont.)							
(Sunshine Nuggets), 3 pieces	70	1.0	10.0	3.0	0	55	n.a.
(Tom's), 1.7 oz.	230	3.0	34.0	9.0	n.a.	120	n.a.
almond fudge (Duncan Hines), 1 piece	55	.5	7.0	2.5	n.a.	45	n.a.
butterscotch (Chippy Chews), 1 piece	50	<1.0	8.0	2.0	0	35	n.a.
butterscotch (Duncan Hines), 1 piece	55	.5	7.0	2.5	n.a.	35	n.a.
chocolate (Chip-A-Roos), 1 piece	60	<1.0	7.0	3.0	0	80	n.a.
chocolate (Pepperidge Farm), 3 pieces	160	1.0	19.0	9.0	n.a.	75	n.a.
coconut (Chips 'n More), 2 pieces	150	1.0	18.0	8.0	n.a.	95	n.a.
fudge (Almost Home), 2 pieces	130	1.0	20.0	5.0	n.a.	130	n.a.
fudge (Chippy Chews), 1 piece	50	<1.0	8.0	2.0	0	35	n.a.
fudge (Chips 'n More), 3 pieces	140	2.0	19.0	6.0	n.a.	90	n.a.
fudge raisin (Almost Home), 2 pieces	130	1.0	18.0	5.0	n.a.	85	n.a.
mint (Duncan Hines), 1 piece	55	.5	7.0	2.5	n.a.	35	n.a.
mocha (Pepperidge Farm), 3 pieces	120	1.0	16.0	6.0	n.a.	50	n.a.
peanut butter (Chippy Chews), 1 piece	50	<1.0	8.0	2.0	0	35	n.a.
peanut butter and fudge (Duncan Hines), 1 piece	55	.5	7.0	2.5	n.a.	45	n.a.

Food and Measure	cal.	prot. (gms)	carbo. (gms)	fat (gms)	chol. (mgs)	sod. (mgs)	fiber (gms)
raisin (Chippy Chews), 1 piece	50	<1.0	8.0	2.0	0	35	n.a.
chocolate chunk pecan (Pepperidge Farm), 2 pieces	130	1.0	15.0	7.0	n.a.	50	n.a.
chocolate macadamia (Pepperidge Farm), 2 pieces	120	2.0	13.0	7.0	n.a.	60	n.a.
chocolate sandwich (see also "creme sandwich"):							
(Giggles), 2 pieces or 1 oz.	140	1.0	17.0	6.0	n.a.	70	n.a.
(Pepperidge Farm Brussels), 3 pieces	160	1.0	20.0	8.0	n.a.	95	n.a.
(Pepperidge Farm Lido), 2 pieces	190	1.0	21.0	11.0	n.a.	85	n.a.
(Pepperidge Farm Milano), 3 pieces	180	1.0	21.0	10.0	n.a.	80	n.a.
(Tru Blu), 1 piece	80	1.0	11.0	3.0	0	75	n.a.
fudge (Gaiety), 3 pieces or 1 oz.	150	2.0	19.0	7.0	n.a.	120	n.a.
chocolate mint sandwich (Pepperidge Farm Brussels Mint), 3 pieces	200	1.0	25.0	10.0	n.a.	120	n.a.
cinnamon raisin (Almost Home), 2 pieces or 1 oz. ..	140	3.0	17.0	7.0	n.a.	95	n.a.
coconut:							
chocolate filled (Pepperidge Farm Tahiti), 2 pieces	170	1.0	17.0	11.0	n.a.	50	n.a.
dietetic (Stella D'Oro), 1 piece	50	.7	6.3	2.3	n.a.	<10	n.a.
macaroon (Nabisco), 1¹/₃-oz. piece	190	1.0	23.0	9.0	n.a.	65	n.a.

Food and Measure	cal.	prot. (gms)	carbo. (gms)	fat (gms)	chol. (mgs)	sod. (mgs)	fiber (gms)
Cookie, coconut (cont.)							
macaroon (Stella D'Oro), 1 piece	63	.7	6.8	3.7	n.a.	n.a.	n.a.
coffee, chocolate-praline filled (Pepperidge Farm Cappucino), 3 pieces	160	1.0	18.0	9.0	n.a.	60	n.a.
creme sandwich:							
(Baronet), 3 pieces or 1 oz.	140	1.0	20.0	6.0	n.a.	75	n.a.
(Frito-Lay's Duplex), 2¹/2 oz.	340	4.0	51.0	13.0	5	n.a.	n.a.
(Hydrox), 1 piece	50	<1.0	7.0	2.0	0	45	n.a.
(Vienna Fingers), 1 piece	70	<1.0	11.0	3.0	0	60	n.a.
chocolate (I Screams), 2 pieces or 1 oz.	150	1.0	20.0	7.0	n.a.	70	n.a.
chocolate (Oreo), 3 pieces or 1 oz.	140	1.0	20.0	6.0	n.a.	170	n.a.
chocolate (Oreo Double Stuf), 2 pieces or 1 oz.	140	1.0	19.0	7.0	n.a.	120	n.a.
fudge (Keebler), 1 piece	60	<1.0	8.0	3.0	n.a.	30	n.a.
fudge and chocolate (Almost Home), 1¹/8-oz. piece	140	2.0	20.0	6.0	n.a.	120	n.a.
fudge and vanilla (Almost Home), 1¹/8-oz. piece	140	1.0	20.0	6.0	n.a.	110	n.a.
mint (Oreo Mint Creme), 2 pieces or 1 oz.	140	1.0	20.0	6.0	n.a.	160	n.a.
oatmeal (Almost Home), 1¹/8-oz. piece	140	2.0	21.0	5.0	n.a.	150	n.a.
peanut butter (Almost Home), 1¹/8-oz. piece	140	2.0	20.0	6.0	n.a.	120	n.a.

Food and Measure	cal.	prot. (gms)	carbo. (gms)	fat (gms)	chol. (mgs)	sod. (mgs)	fiber (gms)
vanilla (Cameo), 3 pieces or 1 oz.	140	1.0	21.0	5.0	n.a.	85	n.a.
vanilla (Cookie Break), 3 pieces or 1 oz.	140	1.0	20.0	6.0	n.a.	95	n.a.
vanilla (I Screams), 2 pieces or 1 oz.	150	1.0	20.0	7.0	n.a.	70	n.a.
custard sandwich (Sunshine Cup Custard), 1 piece . . .	70	1.0	9.0	3.0	0	75	n.a.
date-nut:							
granola (Pepperidge Farm Kitchen Hearth), 3 pieces	160	1.0	20.0	9.0	n.a.	95	n.a.
pecan (Pepperidge Farm Kitchen Hearth), 3 pieces	160	1.0	22.0	8.0	n.a.	60	n.a.
devil's food (Nabisco Cakes), 1 1/3-oz. piece	140	1.0	30.0	1.0	n.a.	90	n.a.
egg biscuit:							
(Stella D'Oro), 1 piece	43	1.5	6.7	1.1	n.a.	n.a.	n.a.
(Stella D'Oro Anginetti), 1 piece	30	.5	4.8	1.1	n.a.	n.a.	n.a.
(Stella D'Oro Jumbo), 1 piece	46	1.0	9.0	.7	n.a.	n.a.	n.a.
dietetic (Stella D'Oro), 1 piece	40	1.5	6.5	1.0	n.a.	<10	n.a.
dietetic (Stella D'Oro Kichel), 1 piece	8	.2	.6	.5	n.a.	<10	n.a.
Roman, all flavors (Stella D'Oro), 1 piece	138	2.7	20.5	5.0	n.a.	n.a.	n.a.
sugared (Stella D'Oro), 1 piece	73	1.6	13.5	1.4	n.a.	n.a.	n.a.
(FFV T.C. Rounds), 2 pieces or 1.1 oz.	156	1.0	19.8	8.1	n.a.	61	.3

Food and Measure	cal.	prot. (gms)	carbo. (gms)	fat (gms)	chol. (mgs)	sod. (mgs)	fiber (gms)
Cookie *(cont.)*							
(FFV Tango), 2 pieces or 1.36 oz.	160	1.2	26.8	5.4	n.a.	59	tr.
(FFV Trolly Cakes), 2 pieces or 1.22 oz.	122	1.7	25.3	1.6	n.a.	80	.1
fig bars:							
(Fig Newtons), 2 pieces	100	1.0	20.0	2.0	n.a.	100	n.a.
(Sunshine Fig Chewies), 1 piece	50	<1.0	11.0	1.0	0	30	n.a.
(Tom's), 2 oz. . .	200	2.0	43.0	2.0	n.a.	140	n.a.
pastry, dietetic *(Stella D'Oro),* 1 piece	95	1.5	14.0	4.0	n.a.	<10	n.a.
whole wheat *(FFV),* 1 piece or .6 oz.	57	.9	10.7	1.2	n.a.	46	.2
fruit cakes *(Stella D'Oro* Miniatures), 1 piece	56	.7	7.3	2.7	n.a.	n.a.	n.a.
fudge *(Stella D'Oro* Swiss),* 1 piece . .	68	.8	8.4	3.4	n.a.	n.a.	n.a.
fudge bar, caramel and peanut *(Heyday),* 1-oz. piece	140	2.0	15.0	8.0	n.a.	45	n.a.
fudge sandwich:							
(Chips 'n Middles), 1 piece	70	<1.0	10.0	3.0	0	65	n.a.
(Sunshine), 1 piece	70	1.0	9.0	3.0	0	55	n.a.
fudge stripes *(Keebler),* 1 piece . . .	50	<1.0	7.0	3.0	n.a.	50	n.a.
jelly tarts *(FFV),* 2 pieces or 1 oz. . .	115	1.2	19.4	3.6	n.a.	90	tr.
ginger:							
(Nabisco Snaps), 4 pieces or 1 oz.	120	2.0	22.0	3.0	n.a.	200	n.a.
(Pepperidge Farm Gingerman), 3 pieces	100	1.0	15.0	4.0	n.a.	75	n.a.

Food and Measure	cal.	prot. (gms)	carbo. (gms)	fat (gms)	chol. (mgs)	sod. (mgs)	fiber (gms)
(Sunshine Snaps), 3 pieces	60	1.0	9.0	2.0	0	70	n.a.
graham crackers:							
(Bugs Bunny), 9 pieces or 1 oz.	120	2.0	20.0	4.0	n.a.	130	n.a.
(Keebler Honey Grahams), 4 pieces*	70	1.0	12.0	2.0	n.a.	85	n.a.
(Honey Maid), 2 pieces or 1/2 oz.	60	1.0	11.0	1.0	n.a.	90	n.a.
(Nabisco), 2 pieces or 1/2 oz.	60	1.0	11.0	1.0	n.a.	115	n.a.
(Party Grahams), 3 pieces or 1 oz.	140	1.0	19.0	7.0	n.a.	100	n.a.
(Regal), 2 pieces or .9 oz.	125	1.3	16.4	6.0	n.a.	105	.2
(Rokeach), 8 pieces	120	2.0	21.0	3.0	n.a.	n.a.	n.a.
(Sunshine Honey), 4 pieces	60	1.0	10.0	2.0	0	90	n.a.
chocolate (Nabisco), 3 pieces or 1 oz.	150	2.0	19.0	7.0	n.a.	70	n.a.
cinnamon (Keebler Crisp), 4 pieces*	70	1.0	11.0	2.0	n.a.	85	n.a.
cinnamon (Sun-shine), 1 piece*	70	1.0	14.0	1.0	0	40	n.a.
fudge (Keebler Deluxe), 2 pieces	80	<1.0	11.0	4.0	n.a.	50	n.a.
hazelnut (Pepperidge Farm), 3 pieces	170	1.0	22.0	9.0	n.a.	110	n.a.
lady fingers, 1 oz.	102	2.2	18.3	2.2	n.a.	20	<.1
lemon:							
(Sunshine Lemon Coolers), 3 pieces	90	1.0	13.0	4.0	0	65	n.a.
nut crunch (Pepper-idge Farm), 3 pieces	170	1.0	19.0	10.0	n.a.	75	n.a.

* Smallest piece after breaking on scoreline

Food and Measure	cal.	prot. (gms)	carbo. (gms)	fat (gms)	chol. (mgs)	sod. (mgs)	fiber (gms)
Cookie, lemon *(cont.)*							
sandwich *(Tru Blu)*,							
1 piece	80	1.0	11.0	3.0	0	75	n.a.
macaroons, see							
"Cookies, coconut"							
marshmallow:							
(Mallomars), 2							
pieces	130	1.0	18.0	6.0	n.a.	35	n.a.
(Mallo Puffs), 1							
piece	70	<1.0	12.0	2.0	0	60	n.a.
(Nabisco Puffs), 1							
piece	120	1.0	20.0	4.0	n.a.	55	n.a.
(Nabisco Twirls), 1							
piece	130	1.0	19.0	5.0	n.a.	55	n.a.
(Pinwheels), 1-oz.							
piece	130	1.0	20.0	5.0	n.a.	35	n.a.
sandwich *(Nabisco)*,							
4 pieces	120	1.0	22.0	3.0	n.a.	80	n.a.
mint sandwich:							
(FFV), 2 pieces or							
1.15 oz.	161	1.5	22.3	7.3	n.a.	95	n.a.
(Mystic), 2 pieces or							
1 oz.	150	1.0	19.0	8.0	n.a.	95	n.a.
chocolate-filled							
(Pepperidge Farm							
Mint Milano), 3							
pieces	230	0	25.0	13.0	n.a.	105	n.a.
molasses:							
(Grandma's Old							
Time), 3 oz. . .	350	4.0	63.0	9.0	10	n.a.	n.a.
(Pantry), 2 pieces or							
1 oz.	130	2.0	21.0	4.0	n.a.	130	n.a.
(Pepperidge Farm							
Crisps), 3 pieces	100	1.0	12.0	5.0	n.a.	75	n.a.
oatmeal:							
(Bakers Bonus), 2							
pieces or 1 oz.	130	2.0	20.0	5.0	n.a.	90	n.a.
(Drake's), 3 pieces	190	3.0	29.0	7.0	n.a.	200	n.a.

Food and Measure	cal.	prot. (gms)	carbo. (gms)	fat (gms)	chol. (mgs)	sod. (mgs)	fiber (gms)
(Keebler Old Fashioned), 1 piece	80	1.0	12.0	3.0	n.a.	115	n.a.
(Pepperidge Farm Irish), 3 pieces	140	1.0	20.0	7.0	n.a.	120	n.a.
(Sunshine Country Style), 1 piece	60	<1.0	8.0	2.0	0	60	n.a.
(Tom's Cake), 2.2 oz.	260	3.0	44.0	8.0	n.a.	220	n.a.
apple spice *(Grandma's)*, 3 oz. . .	350	6.0	55.0	12.0	10	n.a.	n.a.
peanut sandwich *(Sunshine)*, 1 piece	70	1.0	9.0	3.0	0	65	n.a.
raisin *(Almost Home)*, 2 pieces or 1 oz.	130	2.0	20.0	5.0	n.a.	100	n.a.
raisin *(Pepperidge Farm)*, 3 pieces	170	2.0	23.0	8.0	n.a.	170	n.a.
raisin, iced *(Almost Home)*, 2 pieces or 1 oz.	130	2.0	19.0	5.0	n.a.	80	n.a.
sandwich *(Keebler)*, 1 piece	80	<1.0	11.0	3.0	n.a.	60	n.a.
orange, chocolate-filled *(Pepperidge Farm* Orange Milano), 3 pieces . .	230	1.0	25.0	13.0	n.a.	105	n.a.
peach-apricot: bar *(Tacoma)*, 1 piece or 1 oz.	98	.7	20.3	1.8	n.a.	81	.3
pastry *(Stella D'Oro)*, 1 piece	96	1.2	13.7	4.0	n.a.	n.a.	n.a.
pastry, dietetic *(Stella D'Oro)*, 1 piece	90	1.5	12.5	4.0	n.a.	<10	n.a.
peanut, chocolate filled *(Pepperidge Farm* Nassau), 2 pieces	170	2.0	18.0	10.0	n.a.	90	n.a.

Food and Measure	cal.	prot. (gms)	carbo. (gms)	fat (gms)	chol. (mgs)	sod. (mgs)	fiber (gms)
Cookie *(cont.)*							
peanut butter:							
(Almost Home), 2 pieces or 1 oz.	166	2.1	21.2	8.1	n.a.	110	n.a.
(Grandma's Big), 3 oz.	410	9.0	49.0	19.0	n.a.	n.a.	n.a.
(Sunshine Wafers), 2 pieces	80	2.0	10.0	4.0	0	35	n.a.
chocolate chip *(Pepperidge Farm)*, 3 pieces	140	2.0	16.0	8.0	n.a.	125	n.a.
creme patties *(Nutter Butter)*, 4 pieces or 1 oz.	150	3.0	17.0	8.0	n.a.	95	n.a.
fudge *(Almost Home)*, 2 pieces or 1 oz.	140	3.0	16.0	7.0	n.a.	90	n.a.
sandwich *(Chips 'n Middles)*, 1 piece	70	1.0	9.0	3.0	0	70	n.a.
(FFV), 2 pieces or 1.15 oz.	166	2.1	21.2	8.1	n.a.	110	tr.
(Nutter Butter), 2 pieces or 1 oz.	140	3.0	18.0	6.0	n.a.	100	n.a.
(Pitter Patter), 1 piece	90	1.0	11.0	4.0	n.a.	120	n.a.
prune pastry, dietetic *(Stella D'Oro)*, 1 piece	90	1.5	13.0	4.0	n.a.	<10	n.a.
raisin:							
(Grandma's Soft), 3 oz.	350	4.0	59.0	11.0	10.0	n.a.	n.a.
(Stella D'Oro Golden Bars), 1 piece	111	1.6	15.9	4.5	n.a.	n.a.	n.a.
(Sunshine Golden Fruit), 1 piece*	70	1.0	14.0	1.0	0	40	n.a.
bran *(Pepperidge Farm* Kitchen Hearth), 3 pieces	160	1.0	20.0	8.0	n.a.	80	n.a.

* Smallest piece after breaking on scoreline

Food and Measure	cal.	prot. (gms)	carbo. (gms)	fat (gms)	chol. (mgs)	sod. (mgs)	fiber (gms)
sesame (Stella D'Oro Regina), 1 piece	48	.9	6.2	2.2	n.a.	n.a.	n.a.
sesame, dietetic (Stella D'Oro Regina), 1 piece . . .	43	.7	5.7	2.0	n.a.	<10	n.a.
(Social Tea Biscuit), 6 pieces or 1 oz. . .	130	2.0	21.0	4.0	n.a.	105	n.a.
shortbread:							
(Lorna Doone), 4 pieces or 1 oz.	140	2.0	18.0	7.0	n.a.	130	n.a.
(Pepperidge Farm), 2 pieces	150	1.0	17.0	8.0	n.a.	85	n.a.
fudge striped (Nabisco), 3 pieces or 1 oz.	150	1.0	19.0	7.0	n.a.	110	n.a.
pecan (Nabisco), 2 pieces or 1 oz.	150	2.0	16.0	9.0	n.a.	80	n.a.
pecan (Pecan Sandies), 1 piece	80	<1.0	9.0	5.0	n.a.	75	n.a.
striped (FFV), 2 pieces or .82 oz.	118	1.2	14.4	6.1	n.a.	92	.2
vanilla (Tastykake), 1 piece	49	.5	6.1	2.4	n.a.	23	n.a.
spice drops (Stella D'Oro Pfeffernusse), 1 piece	34	.4	6.6	.7	n.a.	n.a.	n.a.
sprinkled (Sunshine Sprinkles), 1 piece	70	<1.0	12.0	2.0	0	65	n.a.
(Stella D'Oro Angel Bars), 1 piece . .	74	1.0	7.1	4.7	n.a.	n.a.	n.a.
(Stella D'Oro Angel Wings), 1 piece	74	1.0	7.0	4.7	n.a.	n.a.	n.a.
(Stella D'Oro Angelica Goodies), 1 piece	104	1.7	15.5	4.0	n.a.	n.a.	n.a.
(Stella D'Oro Como Delight), 1 piece	141	2.0	17.0	7.2	n.a.	n.a.	n.a.
(Stella D'Oro Love Cookies), 1 piece	110	1.5	14.0	5.5	n.a.	<10	n.a.

Food and Measure	cal.	prot. (gms)	carbo. (gms)	fat (gms)	chol. (mgs)	sod. (mgs)	fiber (gms)
Cookie (cont.)							
(Stella D'Oro Royal Nuggets), 1 piece	1	<.1	.1	.1	n.a.	<10	n.a.
strawberry (Pepperidge Farm Fruit), 3 pieces	150	1.0	23.0	7.0	n.a.	70	n.a.
sugar:							
(Bakers Bonus Rings), 2 pieces or 1 oz.	130	2.0	20.0	5.0	n.a.	100	n.a.
(Bisco Wafers), 8 pieces or 1 oz.	150	1.0	20.0	7.0	n.a.	35	n.a.
(Bisco Waffle Cremes), 3 pieces or 1 oz.	150	1.0	20.0	7.0	n.a.	30	n.a.
(Pepperidge Farm), 3 pieces	150	1.0	20.0	8.0	n.a.	115	n.a.
(Sunshine Wafers), 2 pieces	90	<1.0	12.0	4.0	0	25	n.a.
(Super Heros), 11 pieces or 1 oz. . .	135	2.0	20.0	5.0	n.a.	120	n.a.
toy cookies (Sunshine), 5 pieces	60	1.0	10.0	2.0	0	90	n.a.
vanilla:							
(Nilla Wafers), 7 pieces or 1 oz.	130	1.0	21.0	4.0	n.a.	95	n.a.
(Pepperidge Farm Bordeaux), 3 pieces	110	1.0	16.0	5.0	n.a.	70	n.a.
(Pepperidge Farm Pirouettes), 3 pieces	110	0	13.0	7.0	n.a.	55	n.a.
(Sunshine Wafers), 4 pieces	90	1.0	12.0	4.0	5	65	n.a.
(Tom's Wafers), 1.7 oz.	220	2.0	35.0	8.0	n.a.	160	n.a.
chocolate coated (Pepperidge Farm Orleans), 3 pieces	90	0	11.0	6.0	n.a.	30	n.a.

Food and Measure	cal.	prot. (gms)	carbo. (gms)	fat (gms)	chol. (mgs)	sod. (mgs)	fiber (gms)
chocolate-laced *(Pepperidge Farm Pirouettes)*, 3 pieces	110	0	13.0	7.0	n.a.	45	n.a.
chocolate nut coated *(Pepperidge Farm Geneva)*, 3 pieces	170	2.0	19.0	10.0	n.a.	65	n.a.
vanilla sandwich:							
(Giggles), 2 pieces or 1 oz.	140	1.0	17.0	6.0	n.a.	50	n.a.
(Tru Blu), 1 piece	80	1.0	11.0	3.0	0	75	n.a.
Cookie, mix*, 2 pieces:							
chocolate chip:							
(Betty Crocker Big Batch)	120	1.0	16.0	6.0	n.a.	100	n.a.
(Duncan Hines)	150	1.0	19.0	8.0	n.a.	95	n.a.
double *(Duncan Hines)*	140	1.0	19.0	7.0	n.a.	80	n.a.
oatmeal raisin *(Duncan Hines)*	130	2.0	18.0	6.0	n.a.	70	n.a.
peanut butter *(Duncan Hines)*	140	3.0	15.0	7.0	n.a.	120	n.a.
sugar:							
(Betty Crocker Big Batch)	120	1.0	18.0	5.0	n.a.	95	n.a.
golden *(Duncan Hines)*	130	1.0	17.0	6.0	n.a.	70	n.a.
Cookie, refrigerator, 3 pieces:							
chocolate chip *(Pillsbury)*	210	2.0	29.0	10.0	n.a.	150	n.a.
oatmeal raisin *(Pillsbury)*	200	3.0	28.0	8.0	n.a.	190	n.a.
peanut butter *(Pillsbury)*	200	3.0	28.0	8.0	n.a.	190	n.a.

* *Prepared according to package directions*

Food and Measure	cal.	prot. (gms)	carbo. (gms)	fat (gms)	chol. (mgs)	sod. (mgs)	fiber (gms)
Cookie, refrigerator *(cont.)*							
sugar *(Pillsbury)* . .	200	2.0	30.0	8.0	n.a.	190	n.a.
Cookie crumbs, graham cracker:							
(Nabisco), 2 tbsp. or							
1/2 oz.	60	1.0	11.0	1.0	0	90	n.a.
(Sunshine), 2 tbsp.	69	1.1	11.9	1.8	0	124	n.a.
Corlander:							
fresh, raw, 1/4 cup	1	.1	.1	<.1	0	1	<.1
Corlander seed:							
ground (all brands), 1							
tsp.	5	.2	1.0	.3	0	1	.5
Corn:							
fresh:							
kernels, cut from 1							
average ear,							
boiled, drained	83	2.6	19.3	1.0	0	13	.5
boiled, drained, cut,							
1 cup	178	5.4	41.2	2.1	0	28	.0
canned, kernel, 1/2							
cup:							
(A&P)	80	2.0	20.0	1.0	0	330	n.a.
(A&P No Salt							
Added)	80	2.0	18.0	<1.0	0	10	n.a.
(LeSueur)	80	2.0	18.0	0	0	290	n.a.
(Libby/Seneca) . .	80	2.0	18.0	1.0	0	300	n.a.
(S&W Premium)	90	2.0	20.0	1.0	0	295	n.a.
golden *(Del Monte)*	70	2.0	17.0	1.0	0	355	n.a.
golden *(Joan of*							
Arc)	90	2.0	18.0	<1.0	0	190	n.a.
golden *(Stokely's*							
Finest)	90	2.0	20.0	0	0	300	n.a.
golden shoepeg							
Green Giant) . .	90	2.0	18.0	1.0	0	270	n.a.
golden, vacuum							
pack *(Del Monte)*	90	3.0	22.0	1.0	0	355	n.a.
vacuum pack *(A&P)*	100	2.0	25.0	1.0	0	300	n.a.
vacuum pack							
(Green Giant)	90	2.0	20.0	0	0	230	n.a.

Food and Measure	cal.	prot. (gms)	carbo. (gms)	fat (gms)	chol. (mgs)	sod. (mgs)	fiber (gms)
white (Del Monte)	70	2.0	16.0	0	0	355	n.a.
white (Stokely's Finest)	90	3.0	21.0	0	0	290	n.a.
white shoepeg, vacuum pack (Green Giant)	90	2.0	20.0	0	0	270	n.a.
canned, cream style, 1/2 cup:							
(A&P)	100	2.0	25.0	1.0	0	330	n.a.
(Green Giant) . .	100	2.0	21.0	1.0	0	320	n.a.
(Joan of Arc) . . .	120	3.0	27.0	<1.0	0	360	n.a.
(Libby/Seneca) . .	80	2.0	16.0	0	0	260	n.a.
(S&W Homestyle, Starch Added)	105	2.0	25.0	1.0	0	435	n.a.
(S&W Homestyle, No Starch) . . .	120	3.0	24.0	1.0	0	285	n.a.
golden (Del Monte)	80	2.0	18.0	1.0	0	355	n.a.
golden (Stokely's Finest), 8 oz. . .	100	2.0	23.0	0	0	375	n.a.
white (Del Monte)	90	2.0	21.0	0	0	355	n.a.
with peppers (Green Giant Mexicorn)	80	2.0	18.0	0	0	330	n.a.
freeze-dried (Mountain House), 1/2 cup . .	80	2.0	16.0	1.0	0	n.a.	n.a.
frozen:							
(A&P), 3.3 oz. . .	80	3.0	18.0	<1.0	0	0	n.a.
(Birds Eye Deluxe), 3.3 oz.	80	3.0	20.0	1.0	0	0	.5
(Frosty Acres), 3.3 oz.	80	3.0	20.0	1.0	0	3	1.0
(Green Giant Harvest Fresh), 1/2 cup	90	2.0	18.0	1.0	0	150	n.a.
(Green Giant Niblets), 1/2 cup	80	2.0	17.0	1.0	0	5	n.a.
on cob (A&P), 1 ear	120	4.0	28.0	1.0	0	0	n.a.
on cob (A&P Corn Treats), 2 ears	130	5.0	28.0	1.0	0	5	n.a.

Food and Measure	cal.	prot. (gms)	carbo. (gms)	fat (gms)	chol. (mgs)	sod. (mgs)	fiber (gms)
Corn, frozen *(cont.)*							
on cob *(Birds Eye)*, 1 ear	120	4.0	29.0	1.0	0	0	.5
on cob *(Birds Eye Big Ears)*, 1 ear	160	5.0	37.0	1.0	0	0	1.5
on cob *(Birds Eye Little Ears)*, 2 ears	130	4.0	30.0	1.0	0	0	1.2
on cob *(Frosty Acres)*, 1 ear . .	120	4.0	29.0	0	0	0	n.a.
on cob *(Green Giant Niblets, 4 ear)*, 1 ear . . .	150	4.0	32.0	1.0	0	20	n.a.
on cob *(Green Giant Niblets, 6 ear)*, 1 ear . . .	75	2.0	16.0	.5	0	10	n.a.
on cob *(Ore-Ida)*, 4½-oz. ear . .	150	4.0	32.0	1.0	0	35	n.a.
cream style *(Green Giant)*, ½ cup	120	3.0	25.0	1.0	0	370	n.a.
and broccoli bounty *(Green Giant Valley Combination)*, ½ cup	45	2.0	8.0	1.0	0	15	n.a.
in butter sauce *(Green Giant)*, ½ cup	100	2.0	18.0	2.0	n.a.	280	n.a.
and green beans and pasta curls *(Birds Eye)*, 3.3 oz.	110	3.0	15.0	5.0	0	280	.5
white shoepeg *(Green Giant)*, ½ cup	80	2.0	16.0	1.0	0	0	n.a.
white shoepeg *(Green Giant Harvest Fresh)*, ½ cup	100	2.0	20.0	1.0	0	270	n.a.

Food and Measure	cal.	prot. (gms)	carbo. (gms)	fat (gms)	chol. (mgs)	sod. (mgs)	fiber (gms)
white shoepeg, in butter sauce *(Green Giant)*, 1/2 cup	110	3.0	19.0	2.0	n.a.	340	n.a.
Corn chips and similar snacks, 1 oz., except as noted:							
(Bachman)	150	2.0	15.0	9.0	0	190	n.a.
(Diggers Corn Snack)	150	2.0	17.0	8.0	n.a.	260	n.a.
(Flavor Tree)	150	2.0	17.0	8.0	n.a.	260	n.a.
(Frito's Corn Chips)	150	2.0	16.0	10.0	0	220	n.a.
(Frito's Corn Chips Light)	150	2.0	16.0	10.0	0	210	n.a.
(Frito's King Size Dip Chips)	150	2.0	16.0	9.0	0	190	n.a.
(Laura Scudder's)	158	1.8	15.2	10.1	n.a.	235	.3
(Planters Corn Chips)	160	2.0	15.0	10.0	n.a.	160	n.a.
(Tom's), 2 oz.	310	4.0	34.0	17.0	0	400	n.a.
(Wise Corn Crunchies), ...	160	2.0	16.0	10.0	n.a.	n.a.	n.a.
bacon and cheddar fries *(Tom's)*, 15/8 oz.	150	2.0	16.0	9.0	n.a.	260	n.a.
barbecue flavored:							
(Bachman)	150	2.0	15.0	9.0	0	170	n.a.
(Frito's)	150	2.0	16.0	9.0	0	310	n.a.
(Tom's), 15/8 oz.	250	3.0	27.0	15.0	0	400	n.a.
(Bugles)	150	2.0	18.0	8.0	n.a.	300	n.a.
cheese flavored:							
(Cheese 'N Crunch)	160	2.0	15.0	11.0	n.a.	190	n.a.
(Chee•Tos)	160	2.0	15.0	10.0	tr.	300	n.a.
(Chee•Tos Balls)	160	2.0	15.0	10.0	tr.	350	n.a.
(Chee•Tos Rods)	160	2.0	15.0	10.0	tr.	370	n.a.
(Cheez Doodles, Regular or Crunchy)	160	2.0	16.0	10.0	n.a.	n.a.	n.a.
(Cheez Waffies)	140	3.0	14.0	8.0	n.a.	n.a.	n.a.
(Doo Dads), 1/2 cup or 1 oz.	140	3.0	18.0	6.0	n.a.	400	n.a.
(Guys Cheese Balls)	160	2.0	14.0	11.0	n.a.	320	n.a.

Food and Measure	cal.	prot. (gms)	carbo. (gms)	fat (gms)	chol. (mgs)	sod. (mgs)	fiber (gms)
Corn chips and similar snacks, cheese flavored *(cont.)*							
(Jax)	150	2.0	17.0	8.0	0	340	n.a.
(Jax Crunchy) . .	160	2.0	14.0	11.0	0	280	n.a.
(Laura Scudder's Cheese Puffs)	144	2.5	17.1	7.4	n.a.	326	.2
(Lite-line Puffed)	130	2.0	19.0	5.0	n.a.	n.a.	n.a.
(Planters Cheez Balls)	160	2.0	14.0	11.0	n.a.	270	n.a.
(Planters Curls) . .	160	2.0	14.0	11.0	n.a.	290	n.a.
(Tom's Puffed), 1 1/8 oz.	180	2.0	18.0	11.0	n.a.	300	n.a.
(Tom's Crunchy), 1 5/8 oz.	280	3.0	25.0	18.0	n.a.	270	n.a.
cheddar:							
(Chee•Tos)	160	3.0	15.0	10.0	tr.	270	n.a.
sharp *(Chee•Tos* Cheddar Valley)	150	3.0	15.0	9.0	tr.	260	n.a.
zesty *(Doo-Dads)*	140	3.0	18.0	6.0	n.a.	420	n.a.
and bacon *(Doo-Dads)*	140	3.0	18.0	6.0	n.a.	350	n.a.
and herb *(Doo-Dads)*	140	3.0	18.0	6.0	n.a.	400	n.a.
chili cheese *(Frito's)*	160	2.0	16.0	10.0	tr.	320	n.a.
nacho rings *(Tom's)*	160	2.0	15.0	11.0	n.a.	330	n.a.
hot fries *(Tom's)* . .	140	2.0	17.0	8.0	n.a.	280	n.a.
onion flavored *(Fun-yuns)*	140	2.0	18.0	6.0	0	275	n.a.
pizza flavored *(Plant-ers* Crunchies) . .	160	2.0	15.0	10.0	n.a.	160	n.a.
sour cream and onion *(Planters* Puffs) . .	160	1.0	16.0	10.0	n.a.	300	n.a.
sticks, buttered, popped *(Flavor Tree)*	160	2.0	15.0	10.0	n.a.	220	n.a.
toasted:							
(Cornnuts)	120	2.0	19.0	4.0	0	200	2.7
(Cornnuts Unsalted)	120	2.0	19.0	4.0	0	30	2.7
(Frito-Lay's Nug-gets), 1.38 oz.	170	3.0	29.0	5.0	n.a.	265	n.a.

Food and Measure	cal.	prot. (gms)	carbo. (gms)	fat (gms)	chol. (mgs)	sod. (mgs)	fiber (gms)
barbecue flavored							
(Cornnuts) ...	110	3.0	16.0	4.0	0	290	2.5
nacho (Cornnuts)	110	3.0	16.0	4.0	0	200	2.4
tortilla chips:							
(Bachman)	140	2.0	16.0	8.0	0	105	n.a.
(Doritos)	140	2.0	19.0	7.0	0	190	n.a.
(Eagle)	150	2.0	17.0	8.0	0	115	n.a.
(Laura Scudder's)	140	2.0	17.0	7.0	0	90	.4
(Laura Scudder's							
Strips)	140	2.0	18.0	7.0	0	140	.4
(Nalley), 3½ oz.	497	7.0	62.0	27.0	n.a.	600	n.a.
(Planters)	150	2.0	18.0	8.0	0	150	n.a.
(Tom's), 1½ oz.	210	2.0	27.0	10.0	0	260	n.a.
(Tostitos Crispy							
Round)	140	2.0	18.0	8.0	0	180	n.a.
nacho (Bachman)	140	3.0	17.0	6.0	0	180	n.a.
nacho (Bravos) ..	150	2.0	17.0	8.0	n.a.	n.a.	n.a.
nacho (Eagle) ..	150	2.0	17.0	8.0	0	160	n.a.
nacho (Laura Scud-							
der's)	140	2.0	17.0	7.0	0	240	.4
nacho (Lite-line)	130	2.0	19.0	5.0	n.a.	165	n.a.
nacho (Planters)	150	2.0	18.0	8.0	0	160	n.a.
taco (Doritos) ...	140	2.0	18.0	7.0	0	260	n.a.
taco (Laura Scud-							
der's Mini-Taco)	132	2.2	19.0	5.4	0	281	.4
Corn fritter:							
frozen (Mrs. Paul's), 2							
fritters	250	5.0	30.0	12.0	n.a.	725	n.a.
Corn grits:							
dry:							
white (Quaker/Aunt							
Jemima Regular							
or Quick), 3 tbsp.	101	2.4	22.4	.2	0	1	.1
white (Quaker In-							
stant), 1 packet	79	1.9	17.7	.1	0	385	.1
yellow (Quaker/Aunt							
Jemima Quick), 3							
tbsp.	101	2.4	22.4	.2	0	1	.1

Food and Measure	cal.	prot. (gms)	carbo. (gms)	fat (gms)	chol. (mgs)	sod. (mgs)	fiber (gms)
Corn grits, dry *(cont.)*							
with imitation bacon bits *(Quaker Instant)*, 1 packet	101	2.7	21.6	.4	0	544	.1
with imitation ham bits *(Quaker Instant)*, 1 packet	99	2.7	21.3	.3	0	665	.1
with real cheddar flavor *(Quaker Instant)*, 1 packet	104	2.2	21.6	1.0	n.a.	497	.1
canned:							
(Van Camp's Golden Hominy), 1 cup	128	2.7	27.9	.6	0	701	.8
(Van Camp's White Hominy), 1 cup	138	3.0	30.0	.7	0	708	.8
with red and green pepper *(Van Camp's Golden)*, 1 cup	129	2.6	28.5	.5	0	685	.7
Corn meal, dry:							
white:							
(Aunt Jemima Self-rising), 1/6 cup	98	2.3	21.1	.5	0	381	.2
(Quaker/Aunt Jemima), 3 tbsp.	102	2.4	22.2	.5	0	1	.2
bolted *(Aunt Jemima Mix)*, 1/6 cup	99	2.4	20.8	.7	0	337	.2
bolted *(Aunt Jemima Self-rising)*, 1/6 cup	99	2.3	20.4	.9	0	382	.3
buttermilk *(Aunt Jemima Self-rising Mix)*, 3 tbsp. . .	101	2.5	20.2	1.1	n.a.	439	.3
yellow:							
(Quaker/Aunt Jemima), 3 tbsp.	102	2.4	22.2	.5	0	1	.2

Food and Measure	cal.	prot. (gms)	carbo. (gms)	fat (gms)	chol. (mgs)	sod. (mgs)	fiber (gms)
bolted *(Aunt Je-mima* Mix), 1/6 cup	97	2.4	20.9	.4	0	369	.1
Corn salad:							
fresh, whole, 1 cup	12	1.1	2.0	.2	0	n.a.	.5
Corn soufflé:							
frozen *(Stouffer's),* 4 oz.	150	5.0	16.0	7.0	n.a.	540	n.a.
Corn syrup:							
dark *(Karo),* 1 tbsp.	60	0	15.0	0	0	40	n.a.
light *(Karo),* 1 tbsp.	60	0	15.0	0	0	30	n.a.
Cornstarch:							
(Argo/Kingsford's), 1 tbsp.	30	0	7.0	0	0	0	n.a.
Cough drops, see "Candy"							
Cottonseed kernels:							
roasted, 1 cup . . .	754	48.6	32.6	54.1	0	37	3.0
Cottonseed flour:							
partially defatted:							
1 cup	337	38.5	38.1	5.8	0	33	1.9
1 tbsp.	18	2.1	2.0	.3	0	2	.1
lowfat, 4 oz.	376	56.6	41.1	1.6	0	40	2.8
Cottonseed meal:							
partially defatted, 4 oz.	416	55.8	43.6	5.4	0	40	2.8
Couscous, Pilaf, mix:							
(Casbah), 1 oz. . . .	100	4.0	20.0	0	0	n.a.	n.a.
Cowpeas:							
raw, shelled, 1 cup	184	13.1	31.6	1.2	0	6	2.6
boiled, drained, 1 cup	179	13.4	29.9	1.3	0	7	2.9
young pods:							
with seeds, raw, 1 cup	42	3.1	8.9	.3	0	4	1.6
with seeds, boiled, drained, 1 cup	32	2.5	6.7	.3	0	3	1.6
Cowpeas, leafy tips, fresh:							
raw, chopped, 1 cup	10	1.5	1.7	.1	0	2	.5

Food and Measure	cal.	prot. (gms)	carbo. (gms)	fat (gms)	chol. (mgs)	sod. (mgs)	fiber (gms)
Cowpeas, leafy tips *(cont.)*							
boiled, drained, chopped, 1 cup	12	2.5	1.5	.1	0	3	1.4
Crab:							
fresh:							
Alaska King, steamed, meat only, 4 oz. . . .	110	21.9	0	1.7	60	1216	0
blue, steamed, meat only, 4 oz. . . .	116	22.9	0	2.0	113	316	0
canned:							
(Louisiana Brand), 4 oz.	115	19.0	1.0	3.0	n.a.	n.a.	n.a.
Dungeness *(S&W)*, 3¼ oz.	81	18.0	1.0	2.0	n.a.	920	n.a.
frozen:							
au gratin *(Gorton's Light Recipe)*, 1 pkg.	280	22.0	18.0	13.0	n.a.	810	n.a.
deviled *(Mrs. Paul's)*, 3-oz. piece	170	8.0	20.0	6.0	n.a.	385	n.a.
deviled, miniature *(Mrs. Paul's)*, 3½ oz.	220	15.0	18.0	10.0	n.a.	195	n.a.
king *(Wakefield)*, 3 oz.	60	14.0	<1.0	<1.0	n.a.	520	n.a.
snow *(Wakefield)*, 3 oz.	60	13.0	0	<1.0	n.a.	270	n.a.
stuffed, Imperial *(Gorton's Light Recipe)*, 1 pkg.	360	16.0	29.0	20.0	n.a.	670	n.a.
Crab and shrimp, frozen:							
(Wakefield), 3 oz. . .	60	13.0	0	<1.0	n.a.	210	n.a.
Crabapple, fresh:							
whole, 1 lb.	316	1.7	83.2	1.3	0	4	2.5
with skin, sliced, 1 cup	83	.4	21.9	.3	0	1	.7

Food and Measure	cal.	prot. (gms)	carbo. (gms)	fat (gms)	chol. (mgs)	sod. (mgs)	fiber (gms)
Cracker:							
appetizer *(FFV)*, 9 pieces or 1 oz. . . .	127	2.0	18.0	5.0	n.a.	195	n.a.
bacon flavored:							
(Great Crisps! Real), 9 pieces or 1/2 oz.	70	2.0	8.0	4.0	n.a.	230	n.a.
(Nabisco Thins), 7 pieces or 1/2 oz.	70	1.0	8.0	4.0	n.a.	210	n.a.
butter flavor:							
(Escort), 3 pieces or 1/2 oz.	80	1.0	9.0	4.0	n.a.	110	n.a.
(Hi-Ho), 4 pieces	80	1.0	8.0	5.0	0	125	n.a.
(Keebler Club), 4 pieces	70	1.0	11.0	2.0	n.a.	85	n.a.
(Pepperidge Farm Thins), 4 pieces	80	1.0	10.0	3.0	n.a.	100	n.a.
(Ritz), 4 pieces or 1/2 oz.	70	1.0	9.0	4.0	n.a.	120	n.a.
(Ritz Low Salt), 4 pieces or 1/2 oz.	70	1.0	9.0	4.0	n.a.	60	n.a.
(Town House), 5 pieces	80	1.0	9.0	5.0	n.a.	145	n.a.
(Tuc), 3 pieces . . .	70	1.0	8.0	4.0	n.a.	85	n.a.
and cheese *(Handi-Snacks)*, 1 pkg.	130	4.0	8.0	9.0	15	440	n.a.
cheese:							
(A & Eagle), 1 oz.	140	3.0	18.0	6.0	n.a.	195	n.a.
(Cheese Nips), 13 pieces or 1/2 oz.	70	1.0	9.0	3.0	n.a.	130	n.a.
(Cheese Tid-Bit), 16 pieces or 1/2 oz.	70	1.0	8.0	4.0	n.a.	200	n.a.
(Cheez-It), 12 pieces	70	1.0	7.0	4.0	n.a.	135	n.a.
(Pepperidge Farm Snack Sticks), 8 pieces	140	3.0	18.0	6.0	n.a.	350	n.a.
(Pepperidge Farm Thins), 4 pieces	70	1.0	8.0	3.0	n.a.	105	n.a.
(Planters), 1 oz.	140	4.0	15.0	7.0	n.a.	270	n.a.

Food and Measure	cal.	prot. (gms)	carbo. (gms)	fat (gms)	chol. (mgs)	sod. (mgs)	fiber (gms)
Cracker, cheese *(cont.)*							
(Ritz Cheese), 5 pieces or 1/2 oz.	70	1.0	8.0	3.0	n.a.	120	n.a.
(Tom's Cheese Crisp), 11/4 oz.	170	5.0	18.0	9.0	n.a.	330	n.a.
(Tom's Cheezer), 11/4 oz.	160	3.0	21.0	7.0	n.a.	470	n.a.
(Tom's Cheese Bites), 11/2 oz.	200	5.0	26.0	9.0	n.a.	540	n.a.
(Wheat Thins Cheese), 9 pieces 1/2 oz.	70	2.0	9.0	3.0	n.a.	220	n.a.
blue cheese *(Better Blue)*, 10 pieces or 1/2 oz.	70	1.0	8.0	4.0	n.a.	260	n.a.
cheddar *(American Heritage)*, 5 pieces	80	2.0	8.0	4.0	5	150	n.a.
cheddar *(Better Cheddar)*, 11 pieces or 1/2 oz.	70	2.0	8.0	4.0	n.a.	220	n.a.
cheddar *(FFV Thins)*, 13 pieces or 1 oz.	127	3.0	19.0	4.0	n.a.	405	n.a.
cheddar *(Pepperidge Farm Goldfish)*, 45 pieces	140	3.0	18.0	6.0	n.a.	180	n.a.
and chive *(Dip In A Chip)*, 8 pieces or 1/2 oz.	70	1.0	8.0	4.0	n.a.	130	n.a.
and chive *(Great Crisps!)*, 9 pieces or 1/2 oz.	70	2.0	8.0	4.0	n.a.	170	n.a.
nacho *(Better Nacho)*, 9 pieces or 1/2 oz.	70	1.0	8.0	4.0	n.a.	220	n.a.
nacho *(Great Crisps!)*, 8 pieces or 1/2 oz.	70	1.0	8.0	4.0	n.a.	250	n.a.

Food and Measure	cal.	prot. (gms)	carbo. (gms)	fat (gms)	chol. (mgs)	sod. (mgs)	fiber (gms)
Parmesan *(American Heritage)*, 4 pieces	70	2.0	7.0	4.0	n.a.	180	n.a.
Parmesan *(Pepperidge Farm Goldfish)*, 45 pieces	140	3.0	18.0	6.0	n.a.	250	n.a.
sandwich *(Nabisco)*, 2 pieces or 1/2 oz.	70	2.0	8.0	3.0	n.a.	150	n.a.
cheese-peanut butter sandwich *(Nabisco)*, 2 pieces or 1/2 oz.	70	2.0	8.0	3.0	n.a.	150	n.a.
chicken flavored *(Chicken In A Biskit)*, 7 pieces or 1/2 oz.	70	1.0	8.0	4.0	n.a.	115	n.a.
cinnamon *(Nabisco Treats)*, 2 pieces or 1/2 oz.	60	1.0	11.0	1.0	n.a.	80	n.a.
(Finn Crisp Dark/Dark with Caraway), 4 pieces	80	2.0	17.0	0	n.a.	238	n.a.
(Finn Crisp Light), 4 pieces	70	5.0	14.0	1.0	n.a.	186	n.a.
garlic:							
(Great Crisps! Savory), 8 pieces or 1/2 oz.	70	1.0	9.0	3.0	n.a.	190	n.a.
(Manischewitz Garlic Tams), 10 pieces	153	2.0	19.0	8.0	0	165	n.a.
graham crackers, see "Cookies"							
ham and cheese *(FFV)*, 10 pieces or 1.1 oz.	135	3.0	21.0	5.0	n.a.	320	n.a.
(Ideal Crisp Bread Extra Thin), 3 pieces	36	1.0	8.0	0	n.a.	52	.1
(Ideal Fiber Crisp Bread), 2 pieces	34	1.0	8.0	0	n.a.	78	.1

Food and Measure	cal.	prot. (gms)	carbo. (gms)	fat (gms)	chol. (mgs)	sod. (mgs)	fiber (gms)
Cracker *(cont.)*							
(Kavli Norwegian Thick), 2 pieces	70	2.0	15.0	0	0	n.a.	n.a.
(Kavli Norwegian Thin), 2 pieces ..	40	1.0	8.0	.3	0	32	n.a.
malted milk-peanut butter sandwich *(Nabisco)*, 2 pieces or 1/2 oz.	70	2.0	9.0	3.0	n.a.	150	n.a.
(Manischewitz Tam Tams), 10 pieces	147	2.0	17.0	8.0	0	171	n.a.
(Manischewitz Tam Tams, No Salt), 5 pieces	70	2.0	18.0	3.5	0	<5	n.a.
matzo:							
(Manischewitz Passover), 1 piece	129	3.3	27.0	.4	0	0	n.a.
(Manischewitz Unsalted), 1 oz. ...	110	3.0	24.0	.3	0	<5	.1
American *(Manischewitz)*, 1-oz. piece	115	2.9	22.0	1.9	0	n.a.	n.a.
egg *(Manischewitz* Passover), 10 pieces	108	3.0	20.0	2.0	20	<5	n.a.
egg *(Manischewitz* Passover), 1.2-oz. piece	132	4.0	27.0	2.0	25	0	n.a.
egg and onion *(Manischewitz)*, 1-oz. piece ...	112	3.1	23.0	1.0	15	180	n.a.
miniature *(Manischewitz)*, 1 piece	9	2.0	20.0	<1.0	0	0	n.a.
tea, thin *(Manischewitz)*, .9-oz. piece	103	3.0	22.0	.3	0	<1	.1
thins, dietetic *(Manischewitz)*, .8-oz. piece ..	91	2.6	19.0	.4	0	<1	n.a.

Food and Measure	cal.	prot. (gms)	carbo. (gms)	fat (gms)	chol. (mgs)	sod. (mgs)	fiber (gms)
wheat *(Manis-chewitz)*, 10 pieces	90	3.0	18.0	1.0	0	<10	n.a.
whole wheat with bran *(Manis-chewitz)*, 1.1-oz. piece	110	4.0	24.0	1.0	0	<5	.6
melba:							
bacon or cheese *(Old London* Rounds), 5 pieces	60	2.0	9.0	2.0	n.a.	n.a.	n.a.
garlic or onion *(Old London* Rounds), 5 pieces	50	2.0	9.0	1.0	n.a.	n.a.	n.a.
pumpernickel *(Old London)*, 3 pieces	50	2.0	10.0	0	n.a.	n.a.	n.a.
rye *(Old London)*, 3 pieces	50	2.0	10.0	0	n.a.	n.a.	n.a.
rye, salty *(Old London* Rounds), 5 pieces	50	2.0	9.0	1.0	n.a.	n.a.	n.a.
sesame *(Old London* Rounds), 5 pieces	60	2.0	8.0	2.0	n.a.	n.a.	n.a.
white *(Old London)*, 3 pieces	50	2.0	10.0	0	n.a.	n.a.	n.a.
white *(Old London* Unsalted)*, 3 pieces	50	2.0	10.0	0	n.a.	5	n.a.
whole grain *(Old London)*, 3 pieces	60	2.0	10.0	1.0	n.a.	n.a.	n.a.
(Mountain House), 2 pieces	110	2.0	20.0	3.0	n.a.	n.a.	n.a.
(Nabisco Country Crackers), 5 pieces or 1/2 oz.	80	1.0	9.0	4.0	n.a.	120	n.a.
onion:							
(Great Crisps! French), 7 pieces or 1/2 oz.	70	1.0	8.0	4.0	n.a.	90	n.a.

Food and Measure	cal.	prot. (gms)	carbo. (gms)	fat (gms)	chol. (mgs)	sod. (mgs)	fiber (gms)
Cracker, onion *(cont.)* *(Manischewitz Onion Tams)*, 10 pieces	150	2.0	18.0	8.0	0	157	n.a.
oyster and soup: *(Dandy)*, 20 pieces or 1/2 oz.	60	1.0	10.0	1.0	n.a.	220	n.a.
(FFV), 66 pieces or 1 oz.	121	2.6	20.6	3.1	n.a.	415	.1
(Oysterettes), 18 pieces or 1/2 oz.	60	1.0	10.0	1.0	n.a.	130	n.a.
(Sunshine), 16 pieces	60	1.0	10.0	2.0	0	190	n.a.
peanut butter sandwich, toasted *(Nabisco)*, 5 pieces or 1/2 oz.	80	1.0	8.0	2.0	n.a.	150	n.a.
peanut butter and cheese sandwich *(Handi-Snacks)*, 1 pkg.	190	6.0	11.0	13.0	n.a.	250	n.a.
(Pepperidge Farm Goldfish), 45 pieces	140	2.0	18.0	7.0	n.a.	160	n.a.
(Pepperidge Farm Snack Sticks), 8 pieces	130	2.0	20.0	5.0	n.a.	320	n.a.
pizza flavored: *(FFV)*, 11 pieces or 1 oz.	127	2.0	20.0	4.0	n.a.	280	n.a.
(Pepperidge Farm Goldfish), 45 pieces	140	2.0	18.0	7.0	n.a.	180	n.a.
poppy seed *(FFV)*, 13 pieces or 1 oz. . .	137	3.0	16.0	7.0	n.a.	80	n.a.
pumpernickel *(Pepperidge Farm* Snack Sticks), 8 pieces	130	2.0	20.0	5.0	n.a.	380	n.a.
rice *(FFV)*, 8 pieces or 1 oz.	104	3.2	16.9	2.9	n.a.	520	.1

Food and Measure	cal.	prot. (gms)	carbo. (gms)	fat (gms)	chol. (mgs)	sod. (mgs)	fiber (gms)
(Rokeach Snack Crackers), 9 pieces	130	2.0	19.0	5.0	n.a.	n.a.	n.a.
rye:							
(Keebler Toasted), 5 pieces	80	1.0	10.0	4.0	n.a.	145	n.a.
(Pepperidge Farm Snack Sticks), 8 pieces	130	2.0	20.0	4.0	n.a.	390	n.a.
(Wasa Golden Rye Crisp Bread), 1 piece	39	1.0	8.0	0	n.a.	43	n.a.
(Wasa Hearty Rye Crisp Bread), 1 piece	52	1.0	11.0	1.0	n.a.	38	.2
(Wasa Lite Rye Crisp Bread), 1 piece	30	1.9	6.9	0	n.a.	20	.1
(Wasa Sport Rye Crisp Bread), 1 piece	44	1.2	9.0	0	n.a.	66	.2
rye-bran *(Kavli)*, 2 pieces	30	1.0	6.0	15.0	0	37	n.a.
saltines:							
(Krispy), 5 pieces	60	1.0	11.0	1.0	0	210	n.a.
(Krispy Unsalted Tops), 5 pieces	60	1.0	11.0	1.0	0	120	n.a.
(Premium), 5 pieces or 1/2 oz.	60	1.0	10.0	2.0	0	180	n.a.
(Premium Unsalted Tops), 5 pieces or 1/2 oz.	60	1.0	10.0	2.0	0	115	n.a.
(Rokeach Kosher), 10 pieces . . .	120	2.0	20.0	3.0	n.a.	n.a.	n.a.
(Zesta), 5 pieces	60	1.0	10.0	2.0	0	205	n.a.
sesame:							
(American Heritage), 4 pieces	70	1.0	8.0	4.0	0	125	n.a.
(FFV Crisp Unsalted), 1 piece or .47 oz.	52	1.3	8.8	1.2	n.a.	95	<.1

Food and Measure	cal.	prot. (gms)	carbo. (gms)	fat (gms)	chol. (mgs)	sod. (mgs)	fiber (gms)
Cracker, sesame *(cont.)*							
(FFV Crisp Unsalted Top), 8 pieces or 1 oz.	120	2.8	19.3	3.4	n.a.	175	<.3
(Great Crisps!), 9 pieces or 1/2 oz.	70	2.0	8.0	4.0	n.a.	190	n.a.
(Keebler Toasted), 5 pieces	80	1.0	10.0	4.0	n.a.	140	n.a.
(Meal Mates), 3 pieces or 1/2 oz.	70	1.0	9.0	3.0	n.a.	140	n.a.
(Pepperidge Farm), 4 pieces	80	2.0	11.0	3.0	n.a.	105	n.a.
(Pepperidge Farm Snack Sticks), 8 pieces	130	2.0	18.0	6.0	n.a.	350	n.a.
(Wasa Sesame Crisp Bread), 1 piece	54	1.9	8.3	1.5	n.a.	63	n.a.
and cheese *(Twigs),* 5 pieces or 1/2 oz.	70	1.0	8.0	4.0	n.a.	200	n.a.
soda and water:							
(Crown Pilot), 1/2-oz. piece	60	1.0	11.0	1.0	n.a.	65	n.a.
(FFV Ocean Crisp), .44-oz. piece . .	39	1.1	8.2	1.2	n.a.	80	<.1
(Pepperidge Farm English), 4 pieces	70	1.0	13.0	1.0	n.a.	90	n.a.
(Royal Lunch), 1/2-oz. piece	60	1.0	10.0	2.0	n.a.	80	n.a.
(Sailor Boy Pilot), .9-oz. piece . .	104	2.1	18.2	2.5	n.a.	142	<.1
(Sea Rounds), 1/2-oz. piece	60	1.0	10.0	2.0	n.a.	140	n.a.
(Sultana), 4 pieces or 1/2 oz.	60	1.0	11.0	1.0	n.a.	115	n.a.
(Sunshine Cafe Crackers), 3 pieces* . .	60	1.0	7.0	3.0	0	135	n.a.

* Smallest portion after breaking on scoreline

Food and Measure	cal.	prot. (gms)	carbo. (gms)	fat (gms)	chol. (mgs)	sod. (mgs)	fiber (gms)
toast:							
(Holland Rusk), 1/2-oz. piece	60	2.0	10.0	1.0	n.a.	35	n.a.
(Planters), 1 oz.	140	4.0	15.0	7.0	n.a.	270	n.a.
(Uneeda Unsalted Tops), 3 pieces or 1/2 oz.	60	1.0	10.0	2.0	n.a.	100	n.a.
(Nabisco Zwieback), 2 pieces or 1/2 oz.	60	2.0	10.0	1.0	n.a.	20	n.a.
tomato and celery (Great Crisps!), 9 pieces or 1/2 oz.	70	1.0	8.0	4.0	n.a.	160	n.a.
vegetable (Nabisco Thins), 7 pieces or 1/2 oz.	70	1.0	8.0	4.0	n.a.	100	n.a.
(Wasa Breakfast Crisp Bread), 1 piece . .	54	2.0	9.0	1.5	n.a.	75	.2
(Wasa Extra Crisp Crackerbread), 1 piece	22	1.0	5.0	.7	n.a.	40	n.a.
(Wasa Fiber Plus Crisp Bread), 1 piece . .	35	1.0	4.0	1.0	n.a.	46	.5
(Waverly), 4 pieces or 1/2 oz.	70	1.0	10.0	3.0	n.a.	160	n.a.
wheat:							
(American Heritage), 4 pieces	60	1.0	8.0	3.0	0	135	n.a.
(FFV Appetize), 11 pieces or 1 oz.	137	2.0	17.0	6.0	n.a.	160	n.a.
(FFV Stoneground), 11 pieces or 1 oz.	116	2.0	20.0	3.0	n.a.	85	n.a.
(FFV Stoneground Wafers), 8 pieces or 1 oz.	116	2.6	20.0	2.9	n.a.	230	.2
(Featherweight), 4 wafers	50	1.0	9.0	1.0	n.a.	2	n.a.
(Keebler Harvest), 3 pieces	70	1.0	8.0	4.0	n.a.	115	n.a.
(Keebler Toasted), 5 pieces	80	1.0	10.0	4.0	n.a.	150	n.a.

Food and Measure	cal.	prot. (gms)	carbo. (gms)	fat (gms)	chol. (mgs)	sod. (mgs)	fiber (gms)
Cracker, wheat *(cont.)*							
(Manischewitz Wheat Tams), 10 pieces	150	2.0	18.0	8.0	0	180	n.a.
(Pepperidge Farm Hearty), 4 pieces	100	2.0	13.0	4.0	n.a.	180	n.a.
(Rich) 8 pieces or 1 oz.	130	3.0	18.0	5.0	n.a.	n.a.	n.a.
(Rich No Salt Added), 8 pieces or 1 oz.	130	3.0	18.0	5.0	n.a.	15	n.a.
(Sociables), 6 pieces or 1/2 oz.	70	1.0	9.0	3.0	n.a.	130	n.a.
(Sunshine Wafers), 8 pieces	80	1.0	10.0	4.0	0	190	n.a.
(Triscuit), 3 pieces or 1/2 oz.	60	1.0	10.0	2.0	n.a.	90	n.a.
(Triscuit Low Salt), 3 pieces or 1/2 oz.	60	1.0	10.0	2.0	n.a.	35	n.a.
(Wheatsworth Stoneground), 5 pieces or 1/2 oz.	70	1.0	9.0	3.0	n.a.	135	n.a.
(Wheat Thins), 8 pieces or 1/2 oz.	70	1.0	9.0	3.0	n.a.	120	n.a.
(Wheat Thins Low Salt), 8 pieces or 1/2 oz.	70	1.0	9.0	3.0	n.a.	35	n.a.
and cheese *(Tom's)*, 1.4 oz.	200	5.0	22.0	10.0	n.a.	480	n.a.
cheese & garlic *(Hain)* 11 pieces or 1 oz.	140	4.0	12.0	8.0	n.a.	470	n.a.
cheese & garlic *(Hain* No Salt Added), 11 pieces or 1 oz.	140	4.0	12.0	8.0	n.a.	10	n.a.
cracked *(Pepperidge Farm)*, 4 pieces	110	2.0	14.0	4.0	n.a.	200	n.a.

Food and Measure	cal.	prot. (gms)	carbo. (gms)	fat (gms)	chol. (mgs)	sod. (mgs)	fiber (gms)
nutty *(Wheat Thins)*, 7 pieces or 1/2 oz.	80	1.0	8.0	5.0	n.a.	250	n.a.
onion *(Hain)*, 11 pieces or 1 oz.	130	3.0	17.0	6.0	n.a.	n.a.	n.a.
onion *(Hain* No Salt Added), 11 pieces or 1 oz.	130	3.0	17.0	6.0	n.a.	5	n.a.
and peanut butter *(Tom's)*, 1.4 oz.	200	6.0	20.0	11.0	n.a.	480	n.a.
pumpernickel *(Hain)*, 10 pieces or 1 oz.	130	3.0	16.0	6.0	n.a.	n.a.	n.a.
pumpernickel *(Hain* No Salt Added), 10 pieces or 1 oz.	130	3.0	16.0	6.0	n.a.	10	n.a.
sesame *(Hain)*, 11 pieces or 1 oz.	140	3.0	16.0	7.0	n.a.	n.a.	n.a.
sesame *(Hain* No Salt Added), 11 pieces or 1 oz.	140	3.0	16.0	7.0	n.a.	5	n.a.
sour cream & chive *(Hain)*, 11 pieces or 1 oz.	130	3.0	15.0	6.0	n.a.	150	n.a.
sour cream & chive *(Hain* No Salt Added), 11 pieces or 1 oz.	130	3.0	15.0	6.0	n.a.	25	n.a.
sourdough *(Hain)*, 11 pieces or 1 oz.	130	3.0	18.0	5.0	n.a.	n.a.	n.a.
sourdough *(Hain* No Salt Added), 11 pieces or 1 oz.	130	3.0	18.0	5.0	n.a.	10	n.a.
toasted, with onion *(Pepperidge Farm)*, 4 pieces	80	3.0	12.0	3.0	n.a.	110	n.a.
vegetable *(Hain)*, 11 pieces or 1 oz.	130	3.0	18.0	5.0	n.a.	n.a.	n.a.
vegetable *(Hain* No Salt Added), 11 pieces or 1 oz.	130	3.0	18.0	5.0	n.a.	50	n.a.

Food and Measure	cal.	prot. (gms)	carbo. (gms)	fat (gms)	chol. (mgs)	sod. (mgs)	fiber (gms)
Cracker *(cont.)*							
wheat and rye *(Hain)*, 11 pieces or 1 oz.	120	3.0	19.0	4.0	n.a.	n.a.	n.a.
wheat and rye *(Hain No Salt Added)*, 11 pieces or 1 oz.	120	3.0	19.0	4.0	n.a.	10	n.a.
whole grain *(Ideal Crisp Bread No Salt)*, 2 pieces	36	1.0	8.0	0	n.a.	<1	.2
Cracker crumbs and meal:							
cracker *(Nabisco)*, 2 tbsp. or 1/2 oz.	50	1.0	12.0	0	0	0	n.a.
graham cracker, see "Cookie crumbs"							
matzo *(Manischewitz Farfel)*, 1 cup	280	6.8	60.0	.8	0	<5	.2
matzo meal *(Manischewitz)*, 1 cup	514	13.0	109.0	1.4	0	3	.5
Cranberry, fresh:							
whole:							
with stems, 1 lb.	210	1.7	54.6	.9	0	5	5.2
1 cup	46	.4	12.1	.2	0	1	1.1
chopped, 1 cup	54	.4	14.0	.2	0	1	1.3
(Ocean Spray), 4 oz.	52	<1.0	12.0	<1.0	0	2	1.4
Cranberry drink, with blended juices:							
(Ocean Spray Crantastic), 8 fl. oz.	143	<1.0	36.0	<1.0	0	8	n.a.
Cranberry juice:							
(Smucker's), 8 fl. oz.	130	0	32.0	0	0	0	n.a.
Cranberry juice cocktail:							
(A&P), 6 fl. oz.	100	<1.0	26.0	<1.0	0	0	n.a.
(Ocean Spray Cocktail), 8 fl. oz.	141	<1.0	35.0	<1.0	0	4	n.a.
(Ocean Spray Low Calorie), 8 fl. oz.	48	<1.0	11.0	<1.0	0	8	n.a.
(P&Q), 6 fl. oz.	100	<1.0	24.0	<1.0	0	0	n.a.

Food and Measure	cal.	prot. (gms)	carbo. (gms)	fat (gms)	chol. (mgs)	sod. (mgs)	fiber (gms)
frozen* *(Welch's)*, 6 fl. oz.	100	0	26.0	0	0	0	n.a.
Cranberry-apple drink:							
(A&P/P&Q), 6 fl. oz.	130	<1.0	32.0	<1.0	0	0	n.a.
(Ocean Spray CranApple), 8 fl. oz. . . .	173	<1.0	43.0	<1.0	0	6	n.a.
(Ocean Spray CranApple Low Calorie), 8 fl. oz.	43	<1.0	10.0	<1.0	0	11	n.a.
Cranberry-apple juice cocktail:							
frozen* *(Welch's)*, 6 fl. oz.	120	0	30.0	0	0	0	n.a.
Cranberry-apricot drink:							
(Ocean Spray Cranicot), 8 fl. oz. . . .	164	<1.0	41.0	<1.0	0	6	n.a.
Cranberry-grape drink:							
(Ocean Spray CranGrape), 8 fl. oz.	144	<1.0	35.0	<1.0	0	8	n.a.
Cranberry-grape juice cocktail:							
frozen* *(Welch's)*, 6 fl. oz.	110	0	27.0	0	0	0	n.a.
Cranberry-orange relish:							
(Ocean Spray), 1 oz.	52	<1.0	13.0	<1.0	0	9	<.1
Cranberry-raspberry drink:							
(Ocean Spray CranRaspberry), 8 fl. oz.	145	<1.0	37.0	<1.0	0	8	n.a.
Cranberry sauce, canned:							
(A&P), 2 oz.	100	<1.0	25.0	<1.0	0	15	n.a.

* Prepared according to package directions

Food and Measure	cal.	prot. (gms)	carbo. (gms)	fat (gms)	chol. (mgs)	sod. (mgs)	fiber (gms)
Cranberry sauce *(cont.)*							
whole *(Ocean Spray)*,							
1 oz.	45	<1.0	11.0	<1.0	0	8	<1.0
whole or jellied *(S&W Old Fashioned)*, 1/4							
cup	90	0	22.0	0	0	20	n.a.
jellied *(Ocean Spray)*,							
1 oz.	44	<1.0	11.0	<1.0	0	8	<1.0
jellied, with raspberry *(Ocean Spray CranRaspberry)*, 1							
oz.	45	<1.0	11.0	<1.0	0	7	<1.0
Crayfish:							
raw, meat only,							
4 oz.	101	21.2	0	1.2	158	60	0
steamed, meat only,							
4 oz.	129	27.1	0	1.5	202	77	0
Cream:							
half and half:							
1 cup	315	7.2	10.4	27.8	89	98	0
1 tbsp.	20	.4	.6	1.7	6	6	0
heavy, whipping:							
1 cup unwhipped or							
2 cups whipped	821	4.9	6.6	88.1	326	89	0
1 tbsp. unwhipped or 2 tbsp.							
whipped	52	.3	.4	5.6	21	6	0
light, coffee or table:							
1 cup	469	6.5	8.8	46.3	159	95	0
1 tbsp.	29	.4	.6	2.9	10	6	0
light, whipping:							
1 cup unwhipped or							
2 cups whipped	699	5.2	7.1	73.9	265	82	0
1 tbsp. unwhipped or 2 tbsp.							
whipped	44	.3	.4	4.6	17	5	0
medium, 25% fat:							
1 cup	583	5.9	8.3	59.8	209	88	0
1 tbsp.	37	.4	.5	3.8	13	6	0

Food and Measure	cal.	prot. (gms)	carbo. (gms)	fat (gms)	chol. (mgs)	sod. (mgs)	fiber (gms)
sour:							
1 cup	493	7.3	9.8	48.2	102	123	0
1 tbsp.	26	.4	.5	2.5	5	6	0
low fat *(Sweet 'n Low)*, 1 oz. . . .	25	1.0	2.0	1.0	n.a.	30	0
sour, half and half, 1 tbsp.	20	.4	.6	1.8	6	6	0
whipped, topping:							
pressurized, 1 cup	154	1.9	7.5	13.3	46	78	0
pressurized, 1 tbsp.	8	.1	.4	.7	2	4	0
frozen *(Kraft Real Cream)*, 1/4 cup	25	0	2.0	2.0	10	10	0
Cream, Imitation (non-dairy):							
powdered:							
1 cup	514	4.5	51.6	33.4	0	170	0
1 tbsp.	33	.3	3.3	2.1	0	12	0
1 tsp.	11	.1	1.1	.7	0	4	0
frozen:							
1 cup	326	2.4	27.3	23.9	0	190	0
1 fl. oz.	40	.3	3.4	3.0	0	24	0
sour, 1 cup	479	5.5	15.3	44.9	0	235	0
(Carnation Coffee Mate), 1 pkg. . . .	16	.1	1.7	1.1	0	5	n.a.
(Carnation Coffee Mate), 1 tsp. . . .	10	.1	1.1	.8	0	4	n.a.
(Carnation Coffee Mate Liquid), 1 fl. oz.	26	.1	2.7	1.7	0	9	n.a.
(Cremora), 1 tsp. . . .	12	0	1.0	1.0	0	5	n.a.
(Mocha Mix), 1/2 fl. oz.	19	.1	1.2	1.6	0	7	0
(N-Rich), 1 tsp. . . .	10	<1.0	2.0	<1.0	0	5	0
(Rich's Coffee Rich), 1/2 oz.	22	<.1	2.1	1.6	0	7	0
(Rich's Poly Rich), 1/2 oz.	22	<.1	2.1	1.4	0	5	0
whipping:							
pressurized, 1 cup	184	.7	11.3	15.6	0	43	0
pressurized, 1 tbsp.	11	<.1	.6	.9	0	2	0

Food and Measure	cal.	prot. (gms)	carbo. (gms)	fat (gms)	chol. (mgs)	sod. (mgs)	fiber (gms)
Cream, imitation , whipping (cont.)							
pressurized							
(Richwhip), 1/4 oz.	20	<.1	1.1	1.7	0	3	0
prewhipped							
(Richwhip), 1							
tbsp.	12	.1	1.0	.9	0	1	0
unwhipped							
(Richwhip), 1/4 oz.	20	n.a.	1.2	1.6	0	4	0
whipped topping:							
semisolid, 1 cup	239	.9	17.3	19.0	0	19	0
semisolid, 1 tbsp.	13	.1	.9	1.0	0	1	0
(Birds Eye Cool							
Whip), 1 tbsp.	14	0	1.0	1.0	n.a.	0	0
(Birds Eye Cool							
Whip Extra							
Creamy), 1 tbsp.	16	0	1.0	1.0	n.a.	0	tr.
(Birds Eye Dover							
Farms), 1 tbsp.	16	0	1.0	1.0	n.a.	0	0
(Kraft), 1/4 cup . .	35	0	2.0	3.0	0	10	n.a.
(La Creme), 1 tbsp.	12	0	1.0	1.0	0	5	n.a.
mix* (Dream Whip),							
1 tbsp.	8	0	1.0	1.0	n.a.	0	tr.
mix* (D-Zerta), 1							
tbsp.	8	0	0	1.0	n.a.	5	tr.
Cream puff, frozen:							
Bavarian (Rich's), 1							
puff	146	2.1	17.0	7.6	35	66	n.a.
chocolate (Rich's), 1							
puff	146	2.0	16.9	7.8	23	83	n.a.
Cress, garden:							
raw, 1/2 cup	8	.7	1.4	.2	0	4	.3
boiled, drained, 1 cup	31	2.6	5.1	.8	0	11	1.2
Cress, water, see							
"Watercress"							
Croaker:							
Atlantic, raw, meat							
only, 4 oz.	118	20.2	0	3.6	69	64	0

* Prepared according to package directions

Food and Measure	cal.	prot. (gms)	carbo. (gms)	fat (gms)	chol. (mgs)	sod. (mgs)	fiber (gms)
white, raw, meat only, 4 oz.	95	20.4	0	.9	n.a.	n.a.	0
yellow, raw, meat only, 4 oz.	101	21.8	0	.9	n.a.	n.a.	0
Croissants,1 piece:							
(Pepperidge Farm), 1.63 oz.	180	4.0	20.0	9.0	n.a.	240	n.a.
frozen:							
all butter (Sara Lee L'Original), 1.5 oz.	170	4.0	19.0	9.0	n.a.	240	n.a.
chocolate (Sara Lee Le Pastrie), 2.6 oz.	320	6.0	34.0	18.0	n.a.	310	n.a.
cinnamon-nut-raisin (Sara Lee Le Pastrie), 3.3 oz. . .	350	7.0	44.0	17.0	n.a.	420	n.a.
fruit, see specific listings							
sandwich, see specific listings							
wheat 'n honey (Sara Lee L'Original), 1.5 oz.	170	4.0	18.0	9.0	n.a.	310	n.a.
Croutons:							
buttery or cheddar (Brownberry), 1 oz.	130	3.0	17.0	6.0	n.a.	n.a.	n.a.
Caesar salad (Brownberry), 1 oz.	130	3.0	18.0	5.0	n.a.	n.a.	n.a.
cheese and garlic (Pepperidge Farm), 1/2 oz.	70	2.0	9.0	3.0	n.a.	180	n.a.
cheese, sexton (Brownberry), 1 oz.	130	3.0	18.0	5.0	n.a.	n.a.	n.a.
onion and garlic:							
(Brownberry), 1 oz.	130	3.0	18.0	5.0	n.a.	n.a.	n.a.
(Pepperidge Farm), 1/2 oz.	70	2.0	9.0	3.0	n.a.	160	n.a.
ranch style (Brownberry), 1 oz.	130	3.0	18.0	5.0	n.a.	n.a.	n.a.

Food and Measure	cal.	prot. (gms)	carbo. (gms)	fat (gms)	chol. (mgs)	sod. (mgs)	fiber (gms)
Croutons *(cont.)*							
seasoned:							
(Brownberry), 1 oz.	130	3.0	17.0	6.0	n.a.	n.a.	n.a.
(Pepperidge Farm),							
1/2 oz.	70	2.0	9.0	3.0	n.a.	210	n.a.
toasted *(Brownberry)*,							
1 oz.	120	3.0	18.0	4.0	n.a.	n.a.	n.a.
Crowder peas, frozen:							
(Southland), 3.3 oz.	130	8.0	24.0	1.0	0	110	n.a.
Cucumber, fresh:							
with skin:							
1 large							
(8 1/4" × 2 1/8")	39	1.6	8.8	.4	0	6	1.8
sliced, 1 cup . . .	14	.6	3.0	.1	0	2	.6
Cumin seed:							
(all brands), 1 tsp.	8	.4	.9	.4	0	4	.2
Cupcake, see "Cake, snack"							
Currant:							
fresh:							
black, trimmed, 1							
cup	71	1.6	17.2	.5	0	2	2.7
red or white,							
trimmed, 1 cup	63	1.6	15.5	.2	0	1	3.8
dried, Zante *(Del Monte)*, 1/2 cup . .	200	2.0	53.0	0	0	<10	n.a.
Curry powder:							
(all brands), 1 tsp.	6	.3	1.2	.3	0	1	.3
Curry sauce:							
dry, 1.2-oz. packet	151	3.3	17.9	8.2	tr.	1444	.5
Cusk:							
raw, meat only, 4 oz.	99	21.5	0	.8	46	35	0

D

Food and Measure	cal.	prot. (gms)	carbo. (gms)	fat (gms)	chol. (mgs)	sod. (mgs)	fiber (gms)
Daiquiri drink mixer:							
(Freeze & Serve), 1 oz.	25	0	6.0	0	0	13	n.a.
(Holland House), 1 pouch	4	0	14.0	0	0	n.a.	n.a.
bottled *(Holland House)*, 1 fl. oz.	31	0	7.0	0	0	16	n.a.
mix* *(Bar-Tender's)*, 3 1/2 fl. oz. with alcohol	177	0	18.0	0	0	50	0
strawberry, bottled *(Holland House)*, 1 fl. oz.	27	0	6.0	0	0	7	n.a.
Dairy Queen/Brazier:							
sandwiches, 1 piece:							
chicken, 7.9 oz.	670	29.0	46.0	41.0	75	870	n.a.
fish, 6 oz.	400	20.0	41.0	17.0	50	875	n.a.
fish, with cheese, 6.3 oz.	440	24.0	39.0	21.0	60	1035	n.a.
hamburger, single, 5.3 oz.	360	21.0	33.0	16.0	45	630	n.a.
hamburger, double, 7.5 oz.	530	36.0	33.0	28.0	85	660	n.a.
hamburger, triple, 9.7 oz.	710	51.0	33.0	45.0	135	690	n.a.
hamburger with cheese, single, 5.8 oz.	410	24.0	33.0	20.0	50	790	n.a.

* Prepared according to package directions

Food and Measure	cal.	prot. (gms)	carbo. (gms)	fat (gms)	chol. (mgs)	sod. (mgs)	fiber (gms)
Dairy Queen/Brazier, sandwiches *(cont.)*							
hamburger with cheese, double, 8.5 oz.	650	43.0	34.0	37.0	95	980	n.a.
hamburger with cheese, triple, 10.8 oz.	820	58.0	34.0	50.0	145	1010	n.a.
hot dog, plain, 3.5 oz.	280	11.0	21.0	16.0	45	830	n.a.
hot dog, with cheese, 4 oz.	330	15.0	21.0	21.0	55	990	n.a.
hot dog, with chili, 4.6 oz.	320	13.0	23.0	20.0	55	985	n.a.
hot dog, super, plain, 6.3 oz. . .	520	17.0	44.0	27.0	80	1365	n.a.
hot dog, super, with cheese, 7 oz.	580	22.0	45.0	34.0	100	1605	n.a.
hot dog, super, with chili, 7.8 oz. . .	570	21.0	47.0	32.0	100	1595	n.a.
side dishes, 1 serving:							
French fries, regular, 2.5 oz. . . .	200	2.0	25.0	10.0	10	115	n.a.
French fries, large, 4 oz.	320	3.0	40.0	16.0	15	185	n.a.
onion rings, 3 oz.	280	4.0	31.0	16.0	15	170	n.a.
desserts and shakes, 1 serving:							
banana split, 13.7 oz.	540	9.0	103.0	11.0	30	150	n.a.
Buster Bar, 5.3 oz.	460	10.0	41.0	29.0	10	175	n.a.
cone, small, 3 oz.	140	3.0	22.0	4.0	10	45	n.a.
cone, regular, 5.1 oz.	240	6.0	38.0	7.0	15	80	n.a.
cone, large, 7.6 oz.	340	9.0	57.0	10.0	25	115	n.a.
cone, dipped, small*, 3.3 oz.	190	3.0	25.0	9.0	10	10	n.a.

* *Chocolate*

Food and Measure	cal.	prot. (gms)	carbo. (gms)	fat (gms)	chol. (mgs)	sod. (mgs)	fiber (gms)
cone, dipped, regular*, 5.6 oz.	340	6.0	42.0	16.0	20	100	n.a.
cone, dipped, large*, 8.4 oz.	510	9.0	64.0	24.0	30	145	n.a.
Dairy Queen frozen dessert, 4 oz.	180	4.0	27.0	6.0	15	65	n.a.
Dilly bar, 3 oz.	210	3.0	21.0	13.0	10	50	n.a.
Double Delight, 9.1 oz.	490	9.0	69.0	20.0	25	150	n.a.
DQ sandwich, 2.1 oz.	140	3.0	24.0	4.0	5	40	n.a.
float, 14.2 oz.	410	5.0	82.0	7.0	20	85	n.a.
freeze, 14.2 oz.	500	9.0	89.0	12.0	30	180	n.a.
hot fudge Brownie Delight, 9.5 oz.	600	9.0	85.0	25.0	20	225	n.a.
malt, small*, 10.4 oz.	520	10.0	91.0	13.0	35	180	n.a.
malt, regular*, 14.9 oz.	760	14.0	134.0	18.0	50	260	n.a.
malt, large*, 21 oz.	1060	20.0	187.0	25.0	70	360	n.a.
Mr. Misty, small, 8.8 oz.	190	0	48.0	0	0	<10	n.a.
Mr. Misty, regular, 11.8 oz.	250	0	63.0	0	0	<10	n.a.
Mr. Misty, large, 15.7 oz.	340	0	84.0	0	0	<10	n.a.
Mr. Misty float, 14.7 oz.	390	5.0	74.0	7.0	20	95	n.a.
Mr. Misty freeze, 14.7 oz.	500	9.0	91.0	12.0	30	140	n.a.
Mr. Misty Kiss, 3.2 oz.	70	0	17.0	0	0	<10	n.a.
parfait, 10.1 oz.	430	8.0	76.0	8.0	30	140	n.a.
Peanut Butter Parfait, 10.9 oz.	740	16.0	94.0	34.0	30	250	n.a.

* Chocolate

Food and Measure	cal.	prot. (gms)	carbo. (gms)	fat (gms)	chol. (mgs)	sod. (mgs)	fiber (gms)
Dairy Queen/Brazier, desserts and shakes *(cont.)*							
shake, chocolate, small, 10.4 oz.	490	10.0	82.0	13.0	35	180	n.a.
shake, chocolate, regular, 14.9 oz.	710	14.0	120.0	19.0	50	260	n.a.
shake, chocolate, large, 21 oz. . .	990	19.0	168.0	26.0	70	360	n.a.
strawberry short-cake, 11.4 oz.	540	10.0	100.0	11.0	25	215	n.a.
sundae, chocolate, small, 3.8 oz.	190	3.0	33.0	4.0	10	75	n.a.
sundae, chocolate, regular, 6.3 oz.	310	5.0	56.0	8.0	20	120	n.a.
sundae, chocolate, large, 8.8 oz. . .	440	8.0	78.0	10.0	30	165	n.a.
Dandelion greens, fresh:							
raw, 1 lb.	204	12.3	41.7	3.2	0	345	7.3
boiled, drained, chopped, 1 cup	35	2.1	6.7	.6	0	46	1.4
Danish pastry:							
butterhorn *(Hostess)*, 1 pastry	330	5.0	39.0	18.0	8	520	n.a.
frozen:							
cheese, see "Cheese danish"							
cinnamon-raisin *(Sara Lee)*, 1.3-oz. roll	150	2.0	17.0	8.0	n.a.	140	n.a.
fruit, see specific listings							
refrigerator:							
caramel, with nuts *(Pillsbury)*, 1 pastry	155	2.0	19.5	8.0	n.a.	245	n.a.
cinnamon raisin, with icing *(Pillsbury)*, 1 pastry	145	1.5	19.5	7.0	n.a.	225	n.a.

Food and Measure	cal.	prot. (gms)	carbo. (gms)	fat (gms)	chol. (mgs)	sod. (mgs)	fiber (gms)
Date, domestic, natural and dry:							
whole, 10 average	228	1.6	61.0	.4	0	2	1.8
whole, 5 pitted *(Dromedary)*	100	1.0	23.0	0	0	0	n.a.
chopped *(Dromedary)*, 1/4 cup	130	1.0	31.0	0	0	0	n.a.
pitted *(Bordo)*, 2 oz.	204	1.2	47.2	1.2	0	5	1.5
diced *(Bordo)*, 2 oz.	203	1.0	47.5	1.1	0	5	1.2
Date, Chinese, see "Jujube"							
Diamondback, see "Terrapin"							
Dill pickle dip:							
(Nalley), 1 oz.	85	.3	.6	9.1	11	408	n.a.
Dill sauce mix, creamy, for fish:							
(Durkee Roastin' Bag), 1.1-oz. pkg.	153	.5	4.0	14.0	n.a.	741	n.a.
Dips (see also specific listings):							
flavored *(Land O'Lakes),* 2 oz.	70	2.0	4.0	5.0	10	315	n.a.
Dock, fresh:							
raw, with stems, 1 lb.	70	6.4	10.2	2.2	0	13	2.5
boiled, drained, 8 oz.	46	4.2	6.6	1.5	0	8	1.7
Domino's Pizza:							
cheese:							
2 slices or 1/4 of 12″ pie	340	18.0	52.0	6.0	10	660	n.a.
2 slices or 1/6 of 16″ pie	400	24.0	58.0	8.0	40	800	n.a.
pepperoni:							
2 slices or 1/4 of 12″ pie	380	20.0	48.0	12.0	30	880	n.a.
2 slices or 1/6 of 16″ pie	440	24.0	56.0	14.0	60	1080	n.a.

Food and Measure	cal.	prot. (gms)	carbo. (gms)	fat (gms)	chol. (mgs)	sod. (mgs)	fiber (gms)
Donut, 1 piece:							
cinnamon:							
(Hostess)	110	1.0	15.0	6.0	6	140	n.a.
(Tastykake)	193	2.8	23.7	9.7	n.a.	225	n.a.
chocolate coated							
(Hostess)	130	1.0	14.0	8.0	4	150	n.a.
chocolate coated, mini							
(Hostess Donettes)	60	1.0	6.0	3.0	4	50	n.a.
coated, mini (Tastykake)	75	.9	7.0	4.9	n.a.	57	n.a.
fudge iced (Tastykake Premium)	339	2.3	39.8	17.9	n.a.	219	n.a.
honey wheat (Tastykake Premium)	302	3.3	39.7	13.5	n.a.	170	n.a.
honey wheat, mini (Tastykake)	66	.7	9.3	2.7	n.a.	53	n.a.
krunch (Hostess) . .	110	1.0	16.0	4.0	4	130	n.a.
old fashioned (Hostess)	180	2.0	22.0	10.0	9	220	n.a.
old fashioned, glazed (Hostess)	230	2.0	30.0	12.0	11	200	n.a.
orange glazed (Tastykake Premium)	336	3.0	44.2	16.4	n.a.	227	n.a.
plain:							
(Hostess)	110	1.0	12.0	7.0	7	135	n.a.
(Tastykake)	197	2.9	21.8	10.9	n.a.	250	n.a.
powdered sugar:							
(Hostess)	110	1.0	15.0	5.0	6	140	n.a.
(Tastykake)	207	2.7	23.4	11.2	n.a.	233	n.a.
(Tastykake, 12 oz.)	118	1.6	14.9	5.9	n.a.	130	n.a.
powdered sugar, mini:							
(Hostess Donettes)	40	0	5.0	2.0	2	40	n.a.
(Tastykake)	59	.7	7.5	2.7	n.a.	55	n.a.
Drum:							
freshwater, raw, meat only, 4 oz.	135	19.9	0	5.6	73	85	0
red, raw, meat only, 4 oz.	91	20.4	0	.5	n.a.	62	0

Food and Measure	cal.	prot. (gms)	carbo. (gms)	fat (gms)	chol. (mgs)	sod. (mgs)	fiber (gms)
Duck:							
domestic:							
raw, meat only, 4 oz.	150	20.7	0	6.7	87	84	0
roasted, meat only, 4 oz.	228	26.6	0	12.7	101	74	0
wild, raw, breast meat only, 4 oz.	140	22.5	0	4.8	n.a.	65	0
Dutch brand loaf:							
pork and beef, 1-oz. slice	68	3.8	1.6	5.1	13	354	n.a.

E

Food and Measure	cal.	prot. (gms)	carbo. (gms)	fat (gms)	chol. (mgs)	sod. (mgs)	fiber (gms)
Eclair, chocolate, frozen:							
(Rich's), 1 piece . .	205	2.3	27.3	9.7	35	113	n.a.
Eel:							
domestic, raw, meat only, 4 oz.	209	20.9	0	13.2	143	58	0
broiled, 4 oz.	268	26.8	0	17.0	183	74	0
Egg, chicken:							
fresh, raw:							
jumbo (A&P Quality), 1 egg . . .	100	8.0	<1.0	7.0	340	75	0
extra large (A&P Grade A), 1 egg	90	7.0	<1.0	6.0	305	70	0
large, 1 egg . . .	79	6.1	.6	5.6	274	69	0
large, white of 1 egg	16	3.4	.4	tr.	0	50	0
large, yolk of 1 egg	63	2.8	<.1	5.6	272	8	0
medium (A&P Grade A), 1 egg	70	6.0	<1.0	5.0	235	55	0
small (A&P Grade A), 1 egg	60	5.0	<1.0	4.0	205	45	0
fresh, hard boiled, large, 1 egg . . .	79	6.1	.6	5.6	274	69	0
fresh, poached, large, 1 egg	79	6.0	.6	5.6	273	146	0
dried:							
whole, 1 oz.	168	13.0	1.4	11.9	544	148	0
whole, 1/2 cup sifted	253	19.5	2.0	17.8	816	222	0
whole, 1 tbsp. . .	30	2.3	.2	2.1	96	26	0

Food and Measure	cal.	prot. (gms)	carbo. (gms)	fat (gms)	chol. (mgs)	sod. (mgs)	fiber (gms)
white, flakes, stabilized, 1 oz.	100	21.8	1.2	<.1	0	328	0
white, powder, stabilized, 1 oz. . . .	107	23.4	1.3	<.1	0	351	0
yolk, 1 oz.	195	8.7	.1	17.4	830	26	0
yolk, 1 tbsp.	27	1.2	<.1	2.5	117	4	0
Egg, duck:							
raw, whole, 1 egg	130	9.0	1.0	9.6	619	102	0
Egg, goose:							
raw, whole, 1 egg	267	20.0	1.9	19.1	n.a.	n.a.	0
Egg, quail:							
raw, whole, 1 egg	14	1.2	<.1	1.0	76	n.a.	0
Egg, turkey:							
raw, whole, 1 egg	135	10.8	.9	9.4	737	n.a.	0
Egg, mix:							
scrambled (Durkee), .8-oz. pkg.	124	8.0	4.0	10.0	n.a.	320	n.a.
scrambled, with bacon (Durkee), 1.3-oz. pkg.	181	12.0	6.0	13.0	n.a.	476	n.a.
omelet, Western (Durkee), 1.3-oz. pkg.	170	11.0	9.0	5.0	n.a.	489	n.a.
freeze-dried, 1/2 pkg.:							
with real bacon (Mountain House)	170	12.0	7.0	10.0	n.a.	n.a.	n.a.
omelet, cheese (Mountain House)	180	13.0	8.0	9.0	n.a.	n.a.	n.a.
precooked, with bacon (Mountain House)	180	12.0	3.0	12.0	n.a.	n.a.	n.a.
scrambled, with butter (Mountain House)	160	11.0	8.0	8.0	n.a.	n.a.	n.a.
Egg, substitute:							
frozen, 1 cup	384	27.1	7.7	26.7	5	479	0
liquid, 1 cup	211	30.1	1.6	8.3	3	444	0
powder, with egg, 1 oz.	126	15.7	6.2	3.7	162	227	0

Food and Measure	cal.	prot. (gms)	carbo. (gms)	fat (gms)	chol. (mgs)	sod. (mgs)	fiber (gms)
Egg, substitute *(cont.)*							
(Fleischmann's Egg Beaters), 1/4 cup	25	5.0	1.0	0	0	80	n.a.
99% real egg, with cheese *(Fleischmann's Egg Beaters)*, 1/2 cup	130	14.0	3.0	6.0	5	440	n.a.
Egg breakfast, frozen:							
omelet:							
with cheese sauce and ham *(Swanson)*, 7 oz. . . .	400	18.0	12.0	31.0	n.a.	1160	n.a.
Spanish *(Swanson)*, 73/4 oz.	250	9.0	14.0	17.0	n.a.	840	n.a.
scrambled, and sausage, with hash brown potatoes *(Swanson)*, 61/4 oz.	410	12.0	17.0	33.0	n.a.	790	n.a.
Egg foo yung, canned:							
(Chun-King Stir Fry), 5 oz.*	138	7.7	9.1	8.2	142	517	.5
Egg foo yung dinner, mix:							
(La Choy), 1/6 pkg.	45	2.0	9.0	0	n.a.	730	n.a.
Egg roll, frozen:							
chicken:							
(Chun King), .65-oz. roll with sauce**	37	1.3	5.0	1.5	2	110	.1
(La Choy), 1 roll	30	1.0	4.0	1.0	n.a.	62	n.a.
lobster:							
(La Choy), 7/16-oz. roll	27	1.0	4.3	.7	n.a.	80	n.a.
(La Choy), 3-oz. roll	180	7.0	25.0	5.0	n.a.	485	n.a.

* *Prepared according to package directions*
** *Mustard packet, prepared with water*

Food and Measure	cal.	prot. (gms)	carbo. (gms)	fat (gms)	chol. (mgs)	sod. (mgs)	fiber (gms)
meat-shrimp:							
(Chun-King), .65-oz. roll with sauce*	40	1.5	5.1	1.7	4	104	.1
(Chun King), 2.6-oz. roll with sauce*	151	5.8	19.1	6.3	14	427	.6
(La Choy, 15 pack), 1 roll	27	1.0	4.0	.7	n.a.	73	n.a.
(La Choy, 30 pack), 1 roll	17	.5	2.5	.5	n.a.	42	n.a.
shrimp:							
(Chun King), .65-oz. roll with sauce*	36	1.0	5.2	1.4	3	105	.1
(La Choy, 7/16-oz. roll	27	1.0	4.3	.7	n.a.	70	n.a.
(La Choy, 3-oz. roll	160	7.0	24.0	4.0	n.a.	575	n.a.
Egg roll entree, Cantonese, frozen:							
(Van de Kamp's Chinese Classic), 5 1/4 oz.	280	10.0	40.0	5.0	n.a.	550	n.a.
Eggnog:							
(Flav-O-Rich), 8 fl. oz.	340	8.0	40.0	17.0	135	125	0
(Land O'Lakes), 8 fl. oz.	300	9.0	32.0	15.0	123	142	n.a.
Eggplant:							
fresh:							
raw, whole, 1 lb.	95	4.0	23.0	.4	0	13	3.7
raw, pieces, 1 cup	22	.9	5.1	.1	0	2	.8
boiled, drained, cubed, 1 cup . .	27	.8	6.4	.2	0	3	.9
frozen, sticks *(Mrs. Paul's),* 3 1/2 oz.	240	4.0	29.0	12.0	n.a.	610	n.a.
Eggplant Parmigiana, frozen:							
(Mrs. Paul's), 11 oz.	540	16.0	40.0	34.0	n.a.	1810	n.a.
Elderberry:							
fresh, 1 cup	105	1.0	23.7	.7	0	n.a.	10.2

* Mustard packet, prepared with water

Food and Measure	cal.	prot. (gms)	carbo. (gms)	fat (gms)	chol. (mgs)	sod. (mgs)	fiber (gms)
Enchilada, frozen:							
beef:							
(Hormel), 1 piece	140	6.0	17.0	5.0	n.a.	573	n.a.
(Patio), 2 pieces	260	8.0	30.0	12.0	n.a.	n.a.	n.a.
beef and beef chili							
gravy (Patio Boil-in-							
Bag), 2 pieces	250	7.0	29.0	12.0	n.a.	n.a.	n.a.
cheese:							
(Hormel), 1 piece	151	6.0	18.0	6.0	n.a.	676	n.a.
(Patio), 2 pieces	170	7.0	26.0	5.0	n.a.	n.a.	n.a.
cheese and chili gravy							
(Patio Boil-in-Bag), 2							
pieces	200	7.0	31.0	5.0	n.a.	n.a.	n.a.
Enchilada dinner, frozen:							
beef:							
(Banquet International Favorites),							
12 oz.	497	19.0	72.0	15.0	n.a.	1805	n.a.
(Patio), 13 oz.	550	17.0	70.0	23.0	n.a.	n.a.	n.a.
(Swanson), 15 oz.	510	18.0	57.0	23.0	n.a.	1400	n.a.
(Van de Kamp's Mexican Holiday),							
12 oz.	390	20.0	45.0	15.0	n.a.	2177	n.a.
beef chili 'n beans							
(Patio), 16 oz.	850	24.0	76.0	50.0	n.a.	n.a.	n.a.
beef and cheese, chili 'n beans (Patio), 16							
oz.	820	31.0	83.0	40.0	n.a.	n.a.	n.a.
cheese:							
(Banquet International Favorites),							
12 oz.	543	22.0	71.0	19.0	n.a.	2166	n.a.
(Patio), 12¾ oz.	470	17.0	68.0	14.0	n.a.	n.a.	n.a.
(Van de Kamp's Mexican Holiday),							
12 oz.	450	20.0	45.0	20.0	n.a.	1664	n.a.
Enchilada dip:							
(Fritos), 3⅛ oz.	120	6.0	13.0	4.0	5	n.a.	n.a.

Food and Measure	cal.	prot. (gms)	carbo. (gms)	fat (gms)	chol. (mgs)	sod. (mgs)	fiber (gms)
Enchilada entree, frozen:							
beef:							
(Banquet Family Entrees), 8 oz. . .	264	11.0	37.0	8.0	n.a.	1477	n.a.
(Swanson), 11¼ oz.	440	16.0	49.0	20.0	n.a.	1190	n.a.
(Swanson Hungry-Man), 16 oz. . .	660	21.0	65.0	35.0	n.a.	2010	n.a.
(Van de Kamp's Mexican Holiday), 7½ oz.	250	10.0	20.0	15.0	n.a.	1201	n.a.
(Van de Kamp's Mexican Holiday 4 pack), 8½ oz.	340	15.0	30.0	15.0	n.a.	1481	n.a.
and cheese, with rice and beans (Van de Kamp's Mexican Combination), 14¾ oz.	540	25.0	60.0	20.0	n.a.	1380	n.a.
shredded (Van de Kamp's Mexican Classics), 5½ oz.	180	10.0	15.0	10.0	n.a.	930	n.a.
shredded, with rice and corn (Van de Kamp's Mexican Combination), 14¾ oz.	490	25.0	60.0	15.0	n.a.	1170	n.a.
cheese:							
(Van de Kamp's Mexican Holiday), 7½ oz.	270	10.0	25.0	15.0	n.a.	963	n.a.
(Van de Kamp's Mexican Holiday 4 pack), 8½ oz.	370	15.0	30.0	20.0	n.a.	1177	n.a.
with rice and beans (Van de Kamp's Mexican Combination), 14¾ oz.	620	25.0	60.0	30.0	n.a.	1460	n.a.

Food and Measure	cal.	prot. (gms)	carbo. (gms)	fat (gms)	chol. (mgs)	sod. (mgs)	fiber (gms)
Enchilada entree, frozen *(cont.)*							
chicken *(Van de Kamp's Mexican Holiday)*, 7 1/2 oz.	250	15.0	25.0	10.0	n.a.	1108	n.a.
chicken, Suiza *(Van de Kamp's Mexican Classic)*, 5 1/2 oz.	220	10.0	20.0	10.0	n.a.	590	n.a.
Ranchero *(Van de Kamp's Mexican Classic)*, 5 1/2 oz.	250	10.0	20.0	15.0	n.a.	540	n.a.
Enchilada sauce:							
canned:							
(Rosarita), 3 oz.	19	<1.0	4.0	<1.0	n.a.	430	n.a.
hot *(Del Monte Cooking Sauce)*, 1/2 cup	45	1.0	11.0	0	0	1090	n.a.
mild *(Del Monte Cooking Sauce)*, 1/2 cup	45	1.0	11.0	0	0	1150	n.a.
mix *(Durkee)*, 1.1-oz. pkg.	89	2.6	18.0	1.8	n.a.	320	n.a.
Endive, curly (escarole), fresh:							
raw, trimmed, 1 head, 18.1 oz.	86	6.4	17.2	1.0	0	115	4.6
chopped, 1 cup . . .	8	.6	1.7	.1	0	12	.5
Endive, French or Belgian, raw:							
trimmed, 1 head, 1.9 oz.	8	.5	1.7	.1	0	4	n.a.
1 cup	14	.9	2.9	.1	0	6	n.a.
Eulachon (smelt):							
raw, meat only, 4 oz.	134	16.6	0	7.0	n.a.	n.a.	0
Escarole, see "Endive, curly"							

F

Food and Measure	cal.	prot. (gms)	carbo. (gms)	fat (gms)	chol. (mgs)	sod. (mgs)	fiber (gms)
Falafel, mix:							
(Casbah), 1 oz. . . .	103	7.0	15.0	2.0	0	n.a.	n.a.
Fat, see specific listings							
Fat substitute:							
(Rokeach Neutral Nyafat), 1 tbsp. . . .	99	0	0	11.0	0	0	0
Fennel leaves, fresh:							
1 lb.	127	12.7	23.2	1.8	0	n.a.	2.3
4 oz.	32	3.2	5.8	.6	0	n.a.	.6
Fennel seed:							
ground (all brands), 1 tsp.	7	.3	1.1	.3	0	2	.3
Fettucini entree, frozen:							
Alfredo *(Stouffer's)*, 5 oz.	280	8.0	17.0	20.0	n.a.	570	n.a.
and meat sauce *(The Budget Gourmet)*, 10 oz.	290	16.0	34.0	10.0	n.a.	980	n.a.
primavera *(Stouffer's)*, 5 1/3 oz.	270	7.0	12.0	21.0	n.a.	520	n.a.
Field peas:							
frozen *(Southland)*, 3.3 oz.	130	9.0	23.0	1.0	0	5	n.a.
Figs:							
fresh:							
with stems, 1 lb.	333	3.4	86.1	1.4	0	5	5.4
1 large	47	.5	12.3	.2	0	1	.8
1 medium	37	.4	9.6	.2	0	1	.6

Food and Measure	cal.	prot. (gms)	carbo. (gms)	fat (gms)	chol. (mgs)	sod. (mgs)	fiber (gms)
Figs *(cont.)*							
candied, 1 oz. . . .	85	1.0	83.6	.2	0	n.a.	n.a.
canned:							
in water, with liquid,							
1 cup	130	1.0	34.7	.3	0	3	1.4
in heavy syrup, with							
liquid, 1 cup . .	228	1.0	59.3	.3	0	3	1.4
Kadota, whole, in							
heavy syrup,							
(S&W Fancy), 1/2							
cup	100	0	28.0	0	0	< 10	n.a.
dried:							
uncooked, 10 figs	477	5.7	122.2	2.2	0	20	9.0
cooked, 1/2 cup	140	1.7	35.9	.6	0	6	2.6
Filberts:							
dried:							
shelled, 4 oz. . . .	717	14.8	17.4	71.0	0	3	4.3
shelled, chopped, 1							
cup	727	15.0	17.6	72.0	0	3	4.4
shelled, ground, 1							
cup	545	11.2	13.2	54.0	0	2	3.3
dry-roasted, 1 oz. . .	188	2.8	5.1	18.8	0	1	1.1
Finnan haddie,							
see "Haddock,							
smoked" **Fish,**							
fresh, see specific							
listings							
Fish, frozen:							
cakes:							
(Mrs. Paul's), 2							
cakes	220	11.0	24.0	8.0	n.a.	669	n.a.
French fried *(Taste							
O' Sea* Crispy							
Light), 4 oz. . .	200	11.0	23.0	8.0	n.a.	790	n.a.
thin *(Mrs. Paul's),* 2							
cakes	300	14.0	25.0	15.0	n.a.	1020	n.a.
fillets:							
(Gorton's Crunchy),							
2 fillets	350	10.0	19.0	26.0	n.a.	440	n.a.

Food and Measure	cal.	prot. (gms)	carbo. (gms)	fat (gms)	chol. (mgs)	sod. (mgs)	fiber (gms)
(Gorton's Potato Crisp), 2 fillets	340	10.0	20.0	24.0	n.a.	460	n.a.
(Van de Kamp's Light & Crispy), 1 fillet	180	5.0	10.0	15.0	n.a.	175	n.a.
(Van de Kamp's Today's Catch), 4 oz.	90	20.0	0	0	n.a.	80	n.a.
in batter (Gorton's Crispy), 1 fillet	250	8.0	18.0	16.0	n.a.	440	n.a.
in batter (Mrs. Paul's), 2 fillets	360	20.0	27.0	19.0	n.a.	830	n.a.
in batter (Mrs. Paul's Crunchy Light), 2 fillets	310	14.0	27.0	16.0	n.a.	855	n.a.
in batter (Mrs. Paul's Supreme Light), 1 fillet . .	220	11.0	19.0	10.0	n.a.	505	n.a.
in batter (Van de Kamp's), 1 fillet	180	10.0	15.0	10.0	n.a.	230	n.a.
breaded (Certi-Fresh Light & Crunchy), 5 oz.	266	16.0	26.0	12.0	n.a.	530	n.a.
breaded (Gorton's Light Recipe), 1 fillet	170	11.0	16.0	7.0	n.a.	380	n.a.
breaded (Mrs. Paul's Crispy Crunchy), 2 fillets	290	14.0	22.0	16.0	n.a.	650	n.a.
breaded (Mrs. Paul's Light & Natural), 1 fillet	290	22.0	21.0	13.0	n.a.	770	n.a.
buttered (Mrs. Paul's), 2 fillets	210	22.0	0	13.0	n.a.	780	n.a.
country seasoned (Van de Kamp's), 1 fillet	200	10.0	10.0	10.0	n.a.	335	n.a.
tempura batter (Gorton's Light Recipe), 1 fillet	190	10.0	10.0	12.0	n.a.	400	n.a.

Food and Measure	cal.	prot. (gms)	carbo. (gms)	fat (gms)	chol. (mgs)	sod. (mgs)	fiber (gms)
Fish, frozen *(cont.)*							
kabobs, in batter *(Van de Kamp's)*, 4 oz.	240	10.0	15.0	15.0	n.a.	430	n.a.
nuggets:							
(Taste O' Sea), 3 oz.	220	9.0	13.0	15.0	n.a.	390	n.a.
(Van de Kamp's Light & Crispy), 2 oz.	130	10.0	10.0	10.0	n.a.	160	n.a.
breaded *(Certi-Fresh Light & Crunchy)*, 4.5 oz.	250	16.0	20.0	12.0	n.a.	430	n.a.
portions, in batter *(Taste O' Sea Batter Dipt)*, 3 oz. . .	200	8.0	14.0	13.0	n.a.	480	n.a.
sticks:							
(Booth), 4 oz. . .	230	13.0	26.0	8.0	n.a.	650	n.a.
(Gorton's Crunchy), 4 sticks	220	7.0	15.0	15.0	n.a.	370	n.a.
(Gorton's Value Pack), 4 sticks	210	9.0	18.0	11.0	n.a.	420	n.a.
(Gorton's Potato Crisp), 4 sticks	280	8.0	17.0	20.0	n.a.	400	n.a.
(Van de Kamp's Light & Crispy), 4 sticks	270	10.0	15.0	20.0	n.a.	300	n.a.
in batter *(Gorton's Crispy)*, 4 sticks	230	9.0	18.0	14.0	n.a.	560	n.a.
in batter *(Mrs. Paul's Crunchy Light)*, 4 sticks	240	9.0	21.0	13.0	n.a.	795	n.a.
in batter *(Taste O' Sea Batter Dipt)*, 4 oz.	310	13.0	26.0	18.0	n.a.	370	n.a.
in batter *(Van de Kamp's)*, 4 oz.	220	10.0	15.0	15.0	n.a.	330	n.a.
breaded *(Certi-Fresh Light & Crunchy)*, 4.5 oz.	269	14.0	22.0	14.0	n.a.	n.a.	n.a.

Food and Measure	cal.	prot. (gms)	carbo. (gms)	fat (gms)	chol. (mgs)	sod. (mgs)	fiber (gms)
breaded (Gorton's), 4 sticks	210	8.0	24.0	9.0	n.a.	480	n.a.
breaded (Mrs. Paul's Crispy Crunchy), 4 sticks	200	11.0	17.0	10.0	n.a.	455	n.a.
Fish and chips, frozen:							
(Taste O' Sea Batter Dipt), 4 oz. fish and 4 oz. chips	500	12.0	46.0	30.0	n.a.	700	n.a.
in batter (Van de Kamp's), 7 oz. . .	440	20.0	35.0	25.0	n.a.	640	n.a.
Fish dinner, frozen:							
(Banquet American Favorites), 8¾ oz.	553	18.0	45.0	33.0	n.a.	927	n.a.
(Morton), 10 oz. . .	320	15.8	48.1	7.1	n.a.	1400	n.a.
(Taste O' Sea), 9 oz.	500	20.0	53.0	23.0	n.a.	1030	n.a.
cake (Taste O' Sea), 8 oz.	420	14.0	46.0	20.0	n.a.	760	n.a.
and chips:							
(Swanson), 10½ oz.	570	21.0	58.0	28.0	n.a.	970	n.a.
(Swanson Hungry-Man), 14¾ oz.	770	36.0	73.0	36.0	n.a.	1350	n.a.
English Country (Taste O' Sea), 9 oz. . .	510	22.0	48.0	26.0	n.a.	870	n.a.
fillet:							
(Van de Kamp's), 12 oz.	300	25.0	25.0	10.0	n.a.	1820	n.a.
divan (Lean Cuisine), 12⅜ oz.	270	31.0	17.0	9.0	85	700	n.a.
Florentine (Lean Cuisine), 9 oz.	240	27.0	13.0	9.0	100	700	n.a.
jardiniere (Lean Cuisine), 11¼ oz.	280	30.0	18.0	10.0	100	840	n.a.
Italian, mild (Taste O' Sea), 9 oz.	510	21.0	51.0	24.0	n.a.	945	n.a.
New England cheddar (Taste O' Sea), 9 oz.	500	20.0	49.0	25.0	n.a.	945	n.a.

Food and Measure	cal.	prot. (gms)	carbo. (gms)	fat (gms)	chol. (mgs)	sod. (mgs)	fiber (gms)
Fish entree, frozen:							
Dijon (Mrs. Paul's Light), 8½ oz. . . .	250	24.0	7.0	14.0	n.a.	650	n.a.
fillet:							
and broccoli Florentine (Freezer Queen Single Serve), 9 oz. . .	200	20.0	9.0	9.0	n.a.	n.a.	n.a.
Newburg sauce (Wakefield), 8 oz.	210	30.0	10.0	5.0	n.a.	820	n.a.
Florentine (Mrs. Paul's Light), 9 oz. . . .	200	23.0	16.0	5.0	n.a.	1025	n.a.
Mornay (Mrs. Paul's Light), 10 oz. . . .	230	25.0	11.0	10.0	n.a.	665	n.a.
Parmesan (Mrs. Paul's Light), 5 oz. . . .	220	15.0	16.0	11.0	n.a.	540	n.a.
Fish flakes:							
canned, 1 oz.	31	7.0	0	.2	n.a.	n.a.	0
Fish flour:							
from whole fish, 1 oz.	95	22.1	0	.1	n.a.	48	n.a.
from fish fillets, 1 oz.	113	26.4	0	<.1	n.a.	11	0
from fish fillet waste, 1 oz.	86	20.1	0	.1	n.a.	62	0
Fish, gefilte, 1 piece or 1 ball:							
jelled broth:							
(Mother's Old Fashioned, 12 oz.)	54	7.0	4.0	.8	n.a.	n.a.	n.a.
(Mother's Old Fashioned, 24 oz.)	70	9.0	5.0	1.0	n.a.	n.a.	n.a.
(Mother's Old World)	70	8.0	7.0	1.0	n.a.	n.a.	n.a.
(Mother's Unsalted)	45	5.0	2.0	1.0	n.a.	10	n.a.
(Rokeach Redi-Jelled)	50	7.0	4.0	1.0	n.a.	n.a.	n.a.
(Rokeach Old Vienna)	70	8.0	8.0	1.0	n.a.	n.a.	n.a.

Food and Measure	cal.	prot. (gms)	carbo. (gms)	fat (gms)	chol. (mgs)	sod. (mgs)	fiber (gms)
in liquid:							
(Mother's Old Fashioned, 12 oz.)	54	7.0	5.0	.8	n.a.	n.a.	n.a.
(Mother's Old Fashioned, 24/31 oz.)	70	9.0	7.0	1.0	n.a.	n.a.	n.a.
in natural broth *(Rokeach)*	50	7.0	4.0	1.0	n.a.	n.a.	n.a.
sweet, jelled broth *(Mother's* Old World)	54	6.0	5.0	.8	n.a.	n.a.	n.a.
whitefish, jelled broth:							
(Mother's, 12 oz.)	46	7.0	3.0	.8	n.a.	n.a.	n.a.
(Mother's, 24/31 oz.)	60	9.0	4.0	1.0	n.a.	n.a.	n.a.
whitefish, in liquid:							
(Mother's, 12 oz.)	54	7.0	5.0	.8	n.a.	n.a.	n.a.
(Mother's, 24/31 oz.)	70	9.0	7.0	1.0	n.a.	n.a.	n.a.
whitefish and pike, jelled broth:							
(Mother's, 12 oz.)	46	7.0	3.0	.8	n.a.	n.a.	n.a.
(Mother's, 24/31 oz.)	60	9.0	4.0	1.0	n.a.	n.a.	n.a.
(Mother's Old World, 12 oz.)	54	6.0	5.0	.8	n.a.	n.a.	n.a.
(Mother's Old World, 24 oz.)	70	8.0	7.0	1.0	n.a.	n.a.	n.a.
(Rokeach/Rokeach Redi-Jelled, 12 oz.)	46	7.0	3.0	1.0	n.a.	n.a.	n.a.
(Rokeach/Rokeach Redi-Jelled, 24/ 31 oz.)	60	9.0	4.0	1.0	n.a.	n.a.	n.a.
whitefish and pike, in liquid *(Mother's)*	70	9.0	7.0	1.0	n.a.	n.a.	n.a.
Flounder:							
fresh, raw, fillets, 4 oz.	103	21.4	0	1.3	54	92	0
frozen:							
(Gorton's Fishmarket Fresh), 4 oz. . .	90	18.0	1.0	1.0	n.a.	140	n.a.

Food and Measure	cal.	prot. (gms)	carbo. (gms)	fat (gms)	chol. (mgs)	sod. (mgs)	fiber (gms)
Flounder, frozen *(cont.)*							
(Van de Kamp's Today's Catch), 4 oz.	90	20.0	0	0	n.a.	130	n.a.
raw *(Taste O' Sea Calorie Watchers)*, 1 portion	60	12.0	0	1.0	n.a.	125	n.a.
breaded *(Van de Kamp's)*, 5 oz.	300	15.0	15.0	15.0	n.a.	412	n.a.
fillets:							
(Booth Light & Tender), 4 oz.	90	19.0	0	1.0	n.a.	88	n.a.
(Gorton's Light Recipe), 1 fillet . . .	260	18.0	23.0	11.0	n.a.	710	n.a.
(Taste O' Sea), 4 oz.	90	19.0	0	1.0	n.a.	150	n.a.
in batter *(Mrs. Paul's Crunchy Light)*, 2 fillets	310	14.0	26.0	17.0	n.a.	1110	n.a.
breaded *(Mrs. Paul's Crispy Crunchy)*, 2 fillets	280	12.0	25.0	15.0	n.a.	800	n.a.
breaded *(Mrs. Paul's Light & Natural)*, 1 fillet	320	21.0	24.0	16.0	n.a.	975	n.a.
with lemon and herbs *(Booth* Light & Tender), 3 oz. . .	170	10.0	12.0	9.0	n.a.	290	n.a.
stuffed *(Gorton's Light Recipe)*, 1 pkg. . .	260	22.0	11.0	14.0	n.a.	880	n.a.
Flounder dinner, frozen:							
(Taste O' Sea), 9 oz.	520	21.0	52.0	27.0	n.a.	800	n.a.
fillet, with salmon mousse *(Le Menu)*, 10 1/2 oz.	340	20.0	26.0	18.0	n.a.	1060	n.a.
provencale *(Taste O' Sea Gourmet)*, 12 oz.	210	22.0	17.0	15.0	n.a.	2290	n.a.

Food and Measure	cal.	prot. (gms)	carbo. (gms)	fat (gms)	chol. (mgs)	sod. (mgs)	fiber (gms)
Flour (see also specific listings):							
all purpose and bread, see "white," below							
buckwheat:							
whole grain, 4 oz.	380	13.3	82.7	2.7	0	n.a.	11.2
dark, 4 oz.	378	13.3	81.7	2.8	0	n.a.	1.8
light, 4 oz.	394	7.3	90.2	1.4	0	n.a.	.6
cake, see "white," below							
carob (St. John's bread), 4 oz. . . .	204	5.1	91.5	1.6	0	n.a.	8.7
corn, 4 oz.	417	8.8	87.1	2.9	0	1	.8
gluten, see "white," below							
(Quaker Masa Harina), 1/3 cup	137	3.5	27.4	1.5	0	2	.7
(Quaker Masa Trigo), 1/3 cup	149	3.5	24.7	4.0	0	794	.1
rye:							
dark, 4 oz.	371	18.5	77.2	2.9	0	1	2.7
light, 4 oz.	405	10.7	88.3	1.0	0	1	.5
medium, 4 oz. . .	397	12.9	84.8	1.9	0	1	1.0
medium (Pillsbury's Best), 1 cup . .	400	12.0	83.0	2.0	0	0	n.a.
rye and wheat (Pillsbury's Best Bohemian Style), 1 cup	400	11.0	86.0	1.0	0	0	n.a.
sauce and gravy (Pillsbury's Best), 2 tbsp.	50	1.0	11.0	0	0	0	n.a.
self-rising:							
4 oz.	399	10.5	84.1	1.1	0	1224	.5
(Aunt Jemima), 1/4 cup	109	3.0	23.6	.3	0	368	.1
(Ballard/Pillsbury's Best), 1 cup . .	380	9.0	84.0	1.0	0	1290	n.a.
(Gold Medal), 4 oz.	380	10.0	83.0	1.0	0	1520	n.a.
(Red Band), 4 oz.	380	9.0	83.0	1.0	0	1520	n.a.

Food and Measure	cal.	prot. (gms)	carbo. (gms)	fat (gms)	chol. (mgs)	sod. (mgs)	fiber (gms)
Flour, self-rising (cont.)							
(Swans Down), 1/4 cup	90	2.0	20.0	0	0	n.a.	n.a.
soybean:							
full-fat, 4 oz. . . .	477	41.6	34.5	23.0	0	n.a.	2.7
low-fat, 4 oz. . . .	404	49.2	41.5	7.6	0	1	2.8
defatted, 4 oz. . .	370	53.3	43.2	1.0	0	1	2.6
sunflower seed, partially defatted, 4 oz.	384	51.3	42.8	3.9	0	56	5.2
white:							
(Wondra), 4 oz. . .	400	11.0	87.0	1.0	0	0	n.a.
all purpose (Ballard), 1 cup . . .	400	10.0	87.0	1.0	0	0	n.a.
all purpose (Gold Medal), 4 oz. . .	400	11.0	87.0	1.0	0	0	n.a.
all purpose (Pillsbury's Best), 1 cup	400	11.0	87.0	1.0	0	0	n.a.
all purpose (Red Band), 4 oz. . .	400	11.0	87.0	1.0	0	0	n.a.
all purpose (White Deer), 4 oz. . .	400	11.0	87.0	1.0	0	0	n.a.
all purpose, unbleached (Pillsbury's Best), 1 cup	400	12.0	86.0	1.0	0	0	n.a.
bread (Gold Medal Better For Bread), 4 oz.	400	14.0	83.0	1.0	0	0	n.a.
bread (Pillsbury's Best), 1 cup . .	400	14.0	83.0	2.0	0	0	n.a.
cake or pastry, 4 oz.	413	8.5	90.0	.9	0	2	.2
cake (Swans Down), 1/4 cup	100	2.0	22.0	0	0	n.a.	n.a.
gluten (45%), 4 oz.	429	46.9	53.5	2.2	0	2	.5
(Drifted Snow), 4 oz.	400	11.0	87.0	1.0	0	0	n.a.
unbleached (Gold Medal), 4 oz. . .	400	11.0	87.0	1.0	0	0	n.a.

Food and Measure	cal.	prot. (gms)	carbo. (gms)	fat (gms)	chol. (mgs)	sod. (mgs)	fiber (gms)
whole wheat:							
(Ceresota/Heckers), 4 oz.	400	15.0	80.0	2.0	0	2	n.a.
(Gold Medal), 4 oz.	370	14.0	84.0	2.0	0	0	n.a.
(Pillsbury's Best), 1 cup	400	15.0	80.0	2.0	0	10	n.a.
(Red Band), 4 oz.	400	13.0	82.0	2.0	0	0	n.a.
Frankfurter wrap, re-frigerator:							
(Wiener Wrap), 1 wrap	60	1.0	10.0	2.0	n.a.	430	n.a.
Frankfurters and weiners, 1 link:							
(Armour Star Jumbo), 2 oz.	190	6.0	2.0	18.0	30	590	n.a.
(Armour Star Jumbo Lower Salt), 2 oz.	170	7.0	2.0	15.0	30	380	n.a.
(Ballpark)	174	6.5	0	16.5	n.a.	545	n.a.
(Eckrich, 12 oz.) . .	120	3.0	2.0	11.0	n.a.	360	n.a.
(Eckrich, 1 lb.) . . .	150	5.0	3.0	13.0	n.a.	470	n.a.
(Eckrich Jumbo) . .	190	6.0	3.0	17.0	n.a.	630	n.a.
(Kahn's Jumbo Weiners), 2 oz. . .	187	6.0	2.0	18.0	n.a.	505	n.a.
(Kahn's Weiners), 1.6 oz.	150	5.0	2.0	14.0	n.a.	505	n.a.
(Lauderdale Jumbo), 2 oz.	184	6.0	2.0	17.0	n.a.	631	n.a.
(Oscar Mayer Little Weiners), 1/3 oz.	28	1.1	.2	2.6	5	91	0
(Oscar Mayer Weiners), 1.6 oz.	144	5.0	1.1	13.4	27	456	0
all meat:							
(Armour Star Giant), 1.6 oz.	150	5.0	n.a.	13.0	25	455	0
(Armour Star Giant), 2 oz.	180	6.0	n.a.	17.0	28	565	0
(Armour Star Great 8), 2 oz.	180	6.0	n.a.	17.0	28	565	0
bacon and cheddar (Oscar Mayer Hot Dogs), 1.6 oz. . .	143	6.1	1.1	12.7	30	515	n.a.

Food and Measure	cal.	prot. (gms)	carbo. (gms)	fat (gms)	chol. (mgs)	sod. (mgs)	fiber (gms)
Frankfurters and weiners *(cont.)*							
beef:							
(Armour Star), 1.6 oz.	150	5.0	n.a.	13.0	20	455	0
(Armour Star), 2 oz.	180	6.0	n.a.	17.0	25	565	0
(Armour Star Giant), 2 oz.	180	6.0	n.a.	17.0	25	565	0
(Armour Star Jumbo), 2 oz.	190	6.0	2.0	18.0	30	590	0
(Armour Star Jumbo Lower Salt), 2 oz.	170	7.0	2.0	15.0	30	390	0
(Ballpark)	167	6.7	0	15.6	n.a.	545	0
(Eckrich—12 oz. pkg.)	110	4.0	2.0	10.0	n.a.	380	0
(Eckrich—1 lb. pkg.)	150	5.0	3.0	13.0	n.a.	480	0
(Eckrich Jumbo)	190	6.0	3.0	17.0	n.a.	620	0
(Hillshire Farms Old Fashioned), 1 oz.	89	3.4	1.4	7.7	7	249	0
(Hormel Wieners— 12 oz. pkg.) . .	100	4.0	1.0	10.0	n.a.	362	0
(Hormel Wieners—1 lb. pkg.)	140	5.0	1.0	13.0	n.a.	463	0
(Kahn's), 1.6 oz.	148	5.0	2.0	17.0	n.a.	494	0
(Kahn's Jumbo), 2 oz.	185	6.0	3.0	17.0	n.a.	618	0
(Oscar Mayer), 1.6 oz.	144	5.0	1.0	13.3	27	460	0
cheese:							
(Eckrich)	190	7.0	3.0	17.0	n.a.	650	n.a.
(Oscar Mayer Hot Dogs), 1.6 oz.	145	5.6	1.0	13.2	30	484	0
nacho style *(Oscar Mayer* Hot Dogs), 1.6 oz.	138	5.4	1.1	12.5	30	558	n.a.
chicken, see "Chicken frankfurters"							
chili *(Hormel* Frank'n Stuff)	165	7.0	2.0	15.0	n.a.	517	n.a.

Food and Measure	cal.	prot. (gms)	carbo. (gms)	fat (gms)	chol. (mgs)	sod. (mgs)	fiber (gms)
meat:							
(Hormel Wieners, 12 oz.)	110	4.0	1.0	10.0	n.a.	378	n.a.
(Hormel Wieners, 1 lb.)	140	5.0	1.0	13.0	n.a.	486	n.a.
smoked:							
(Hormel Range Brand Wranglers)	170	7.0	1.0	16.0	n.a.	600	n.a.
beef (Hormel Wranglers)	170	7.0	2.0	15.0	n.a.	619	n.a.
with cheese (Hormel Wranglers)	180	8.0	1.0	16.0	n.a.	546	n.a.
turkey, see "Turkey frankfurters"							
French toast, frozen, 2 slices or 3 ounces:							
(Aunt Jemima) . . .	170	6.4	26.8	3.9	n.a.	430	.1
cinnamon swirl (Aunt Jemima)	210	6.4	27.6	6.0	n.a.	359	.3
raisin (Aunt Jemima)	190	7.3	29.4	4.2	n.a.	423	.2
French toast breakfast, frozen:							
cinnamon swirl, with sausage (Swanson), 6½ oz.	480	16.0	39.0	29.0	n.a.	710	n.a.
with sausage (Swanson), 6½ oz. . . .	450	17.0	36.0	26.0	n.a.	770	n.a.
Frog's legs, raw:							
whole, 4 oz.	215	48.3	0	.9	n.a.	n.a.	0
meat only, 4 oz. . .	83	18.6	0	.3	n.a.	n.a.	0
Frosting, cake, ready-to-spread, 1/12 can or cake, except as noted:							
butter pecan (Betty Crocker Creamy Deluxe)	160	0	24.0	7.0	n.a.	90	n.a.

Food and Measure	cal.	prot. (gms)	carbo. (gms)	fat (gms)	chol. (mgs)	sod. (mgs)	fiber (gms)
Frosting, cake, ready-to-spread *(cont.)*							
caramel pecan *(Pillsbury Frosting Supreme)*	160	0	21.0	8.0	n.a.	70	n.a.
cherry *(Betty Crocker Creamy Deluxe)*	160	0	26.0	6.0	n.a.	100	n.a.
chocolate:							
(Betty Crocker Creamy Deluxe)	170	<1.0	23.0	8.0	n.a.	100	n.a.
(Duncan Hines)	160	0	24.0	7.0	n.a.	90	n.a.
double Dutch *(Pillsbury Frosting Supreme)*	140	1.0	22.0	6.0	n.a.	45	n.a.
fudge *(Pillsbury Frosting Supreme)*	150	<1.0	24.0	6.0	n.a.	80	n.a.
fudge, dark *(Betty Crocker Creamy Deluxe)*	160	<1.0	23.0	7.0	n.a.	100	n.a.
fudge, dark *(Duncan Hines)*	160	0	24.0	7.0	n.a.	95	n.a.
milk *(Betty Crocker Creamy Deluxe)*	160	<1.0	24.0	7.0	n.a.	100	n.a.
milk *(Duncan Hines)*	160	0	24.0	7.0	n.a.	85	n.a.
milk *(Pillsbury Frosting Supreme)*	150	0	23.0	6.0	n.a.	60	n.a.
mint *(Pillsbury Frosting Supreme)*	150	<1.0	24.0	7.0	n.a.	80	n.a.
nut *(Betty Crocker Creamy Deluxe)*	160	<1.0	22.0	8.0	n.a.	100	n.a.
chocolate chip:							
(Betty Crocker Creamy Deluxe)	160	<1.0	25.0	7.0	n.a.	85	n.a.
(Pillsbury Frosting Supreme) . . .	150	0	27.0	5.0	n.a.	70	n.a.
chocolate *(Betty Crocker Creamy Deluxe)*	160	<1.0	23.0	8.0	n.a.	85	n.a.

Food and Measure	cal.	prot. (gms)	carbo. (gms)	fat (gms)	chol. (mgs)	sod. (mgs)	fiber (gms)
coconut almond (Pillsbury Frosting Supreme)	150	1.0	17.0	9.0	n.a.	60	n.a.
coconut pecan:							
(Betty Crocker Creamy Deluxe)	170	<1.0	19.0	10.0	n.a.	50	n.a.
(Pillsbury Frosting Supreme) . . .	160	0	17.0	10.0	n.a.	60	n.a.
cream cheese:							
(Betty Crocker Creamy Deluxe)	160	0	26.0	6.0	n.a.	100	n.a.
(Pillsbury Frosting Supreme) . . .	160	0	26.0	6.0	n.a.	115	n.a.
decorator:							
all colors except chocolate (Pillsbury), 1 tbsp. . .	70	0	12.0	2.0	n.a.	0	n.a.
chocolate (Pillsbury), 1 tbsp. . .	60	0	11.0	2.0	n.a.	0	n.a.
lemon:							
(Betty Crocker Creamy Deluxe)	160	0	26.0	6.0	n.a.	100	n.a.
(Pillsbury Frosting Supreme) . . .	160	0	26.0	6.0	n.a.	80	n.a.
mocha (Pillsbury Frosting Supreme)	150	<1.0	24.0	6.0	n.a.	60	n.a.
orange (Betty Crocker Creamy Deluxe)	160	0	26.0	6.0	n.a.	90	n.a.
sour cream:							
chocolate (Betty Crocker Creamy Deluxe)	170	<1.0	22.0	8.0	n.a.	100	n.a.
vanilla (Pillsbury Frosting Supreme)	160	0	27.0	6.0	n.a.	80	n.a.
white (Betty Crocker Creamy Deluxe)	160	0	26.0	6.0	n.a.	100	n.a.
strawberry (Pillsbury Frosting Supreme)	160	0	26.0	6.0	n.a.	75	n.a.

Food and Measure	cal.	prot. (gms)	carbo. (gms)	fat (gms)	chol. (mgs)	sod. (mgs)	fiber (gms)
Frosting, cake, ready-to-spread *(cont.)*							
vanilla:							
(Betty Crocker							
Creamy Deluxe)	160	0	27.0	6.0	n.a.	100	n.a.
(Duncan Hines)	160	0	24.0	7.0	n.a.	80	n.a.
(Pillsbury Frosting							
Supreme) ...	160	0	26.0	6.0	n.a.	75	n.a.
Frosting, cake,							
mix*1/12 pkg. or							
cake:							
butter brickle *(Betty*							
Crocker)	170	0	30.0	6.0	n.a.	100	n.a.
butter pecan *(Betty*							
Crocker)	170	0	30.0	6.0	n.a.	100	n.a.
cherry, creamy *(Betty*							
Crocker)	180	0	31.0	6.0	n.a.	100	n.a.
chocolate:							
fudge *(Betty*							
Crocker)	170	0	30.0	6.0	n.a.	50	n.a.
milk *(Betty Crocker)*	170	0	30.0	5.0	n.a.	40	n.a.
coconut almond:							
(Betty Crocker) ..	140	0	18.0	8.0	n.a.	90	n.a.
(Pillsbury)	160	1.0	16.0	10.0	n.a.	85	n.a.
coconut pecan:							
(Betty Crocker) ..	160	0	19.0	9.0	n.a.	45	n.a.
(Pillsbury)	150	1.0	20.0	7.0	n.a.	105	n.a.
cream cheese and nut							
(Betty Crocker) ..	160	0	26.0	6.0	n.a.	100	n.a.
lemon *(Betty Crocker)*	180	0	31.0	6.0	n.a.	100	n.a.
sour cream:							
chocolate fudge							
(Betty Crocker)	180	1.0	30.0	6.0	n.a.	80	n.a.
white *(Betty*							
Crocker)	170	0	31.0	5.0	n.a.	100	n.a.
vanilla *(Betty Crocker)*	190	0	33.0	6.0	n.a.	50	n.a.
white:							
(Betty Crocker) ..	60	0	16.0	0	n.a.	10	n.a.
fluffy *(Pillsbury)* ..	60	0	15.0	0	n.a.	65	n.a.

* *Prepared according to package directions*

Food and Measure	cal.	prot. (gms)	carbo. (gms)	fat (gms)	chol. (mgs)	sod. (mgs)	fiber (gms)
Fructose:							
(Estee), 1 tsp. . . .	12	0	3.0	0	0	0	n.a.
Fruit, see specific listings							
Fruit cocktail, canned, 1/2 cup:							
(Del Monte)	80	0	23.0	0	0	<10	n.a.
(Del Monte Lite) . .	50	0	15.0	0	0	<10	n.a.
(Stokely's Finest) . .	75	0	20.0	0	0	15	n.a.
in juice:							
(S&W Natural Lite)	60	0	15.0	0	0	5	n.a.
(S&W Natural Style)	90	1.0	21.0	0	0	5	n.a.
in heavy syrup *(S&W)*	90	0	24.0	0	0	15	n.a.
Fruit, mixed:							
canned, 1/2 cup, except as noted:							
(Del Monte Fruit Cup), 5 oz. . . .	100	0	27.0	0	0	<10	n.a.
(Mother's), 4 oz.	120	1.0	31.0	1.0	0	4	n.a.
in light syrup *(A&P)*	75	<1.0	20.0	<1.0	0	15	n.a.
chunky *(Del Monte)*	80	0	23.0	0	0	<10	n.a.
chunky *(Del Monte Lite)*	50	0	14.0	0	0	<10	n.a.
chunky, in juice *(S&W)*	90	1.0	21.0	0	0	5	n.a.
cocktail, in pear juice *(A&P)* . . .	50	1.0	14.0	<1.0	0	15	n.a.
cocktail, in heavy syrup *(A&P)* . .	90	<1.0	24.0	<1.0	0	15	n.a.
fruit cup *(Hunt's Snack Pack)*, 5 oz.	120	<1.0	31.0	<1.0	0	5	n.a.
dried:							
(Carnation All Fruit), .9-oz. pouch . .	80	0	18.0	0	0	10	n.a.
(Del Monte), 2 oz.	130	1.0	34.0	0	0	10	n.a.
tropical, with nuts *(Carnation)*, .9-oz. pouch	100	3.0	16.0	3.0	0	10	n.a.

Food and Measure	cal.	prot. (gms)	carbo. (gms)	fat (gms)	chol. (mgs)	sod. (mgs)	fiber (gms)
Fruit, mixed *(cont.)*							
frozen, in light syrup							
(Birds Eye Lite							
Quick Thaw Pouch),							
5 oz.	100	1.0	27.0	0	0	0	.6
Fruit for salad,							
canned, 1/2 cup:							
(Del Monte)	90	0	22.0	0	0	< 10	n.a.
in heavy syrup, quar-							
tered *(S&W)* . . .	100	0	25.0	0	0	15	n.a.
tropical *(Del Monte)*	90	0	26.0	0	0	< 10	n.a.
Fruit bars, frozen,							
1 bar:							
all flavors:							
(Good Humor Lite							
Stix), 1.5 oz. . .	35	0	8.0	0	0	n.a.	n.a.
(Life Savers Flavor							
Pops), 1 pop . .	40	0	10.0	0	0	0	n.a.
banana:							
(Dole Fruit'n Juice),							
21/2 fl. oz. . . .	80	.4	19.7	<.1	0	13	n.a.
and cream							
(Shamitoff's), 3 fl.							
oz.	105	1.0	18.0	3.0	n.a.	20	n.a.
blueberry *(Dole Fruit'n*							
Cream), 21/2 fl. oz.	90	1.1	19.4	1.4	n.a.	20	n.a.
cherry:							
(Shamitoff's), 21/2 fl.							
oz.	60	5.0	14.0	0	0	2	n.a.
(Shamitoff's), 3 fl.							
oz.	75	0	19.0	0	0	2	n.a.
chocolate coconut							
(Shamitoff's), 21/2 fl.							
oz.	195	3.0	23.0	10.0	0	18	n.a.
coconut *(Shamitoff's),*							
3 fl. oz.	150	2.5	18.0	8.0	0	8	n.a.
lemon:							
(Shamitoff's), 21/2 fl.							
oz.	50	.1	13.2	<.1	0	1	n.a.

Food and Measure	cal.	prot. (gms)	carbo. (gms)	fat (gms)	chol. (mgs)	sod. (mgs)	fiber (gms)
(Shamitoff's), 3 fl. oz.	60	0	15.0	0	0	1	n.a.
(Sunkist Lemonade), 3 fl. oz.	70	0	20.0	0	0	5	n.a.
orange:							
(Dole Fruit'n Juice), 2¹/2 fl. oz. . . .	70	.3	16.0	<.1	0	6	n.a.
(Sunkist), 3 fl. oz.	70	<1.0	18.0	0	0	5	n.a.
Mandarin *(Dole Fruit'n Juice)*, 2¹/2 fl. oz.	70	.4	18.2	<.1	0	14	n.a.
peach and cream:							
(Dole Fruit'n Cream), 2¹/2 fl. oz.	90	1.0	19.4	1.4	n.a.	19	n.a.
(Shamitoff's), 2¹/2 fl. oz.	85	1.0	13.0	3.0	n.a.	17	n.a.
pineapple:							
(Dole Fruit'n Juice), 2¹/2 fl. oz. . . .	70	.3	17.0	<.1	0	4	n.a.
(Shamitoff's), 2¹/2 fl. oz.	50	.2	12.0	0	0	2	n.a.
(Shamitoff's), 3 fl. oz.	60	2.0	15.0	0	0	2	n.a.
piña colada *(Shamitoff's)*, 2¹/2 fl. oz.	110	1.5	17.0	4.0	0	17	n.a.
raspberry:							
(Dole Fruit'n Juice), 2¹/2 fl. oz. . . .	70	.2	16.1	<.1	0	14	n.a.
(Shamitoff's), 2¹/2 fl. oz.	60	.1	14.3	0	0	1	n.a.
(Shamitoff's), 3 fl. oz.	70	.1	17.0	0	0	2	n.a.
strawberry:							
(Dole Fruit'n Cream), 2¹/2 fl. oz.	90	1.1	19.3	1.4	n.a.	22	n.a.

Food and Measure	cal.	prot. (gms)	carbo. (gms)	fat (gms)	chol. (mgs)	sod. (mgs)	fiber (gms)
Fruit bars, frozen, strawberry *(cont.)*							
(Dole Fruit'n Juice), 2½ fl. oz. . . .	70	.2	16.0	<.1	0	6	n.a.
(Shamitoff's), 2½ fl. oz.	55	.3	13.2	.2	0	2	n.a.
(Shamitoff's), 3 fl. oz.	70	0	18.0	0	0	2	n.a.
Fruit drinks (see also specific listings):							
all flavors *(Land O'Lakes)*, 8 fl. oz.	120	1.0	27.0	0	0	10	n.a.
canned *(Hi-C Hula Cooler)*, 6 fl. oz.	95	<.1	24.0	<.1	0	17	tr.
Caribbean cooler *(Crystal Light)*, 8 fl. oz.	4	0	0	0	0	0	0
citrus blend *(Crystal Light)*, 8 fl. oz. . .	4	0	0	0	0	0	0
fruit-n apple *(Tree Top Rainbow Blends)*, 6 fl. oz.	90	0	22.0	0	0	10	n.a.
fruit-n berry *(Tree Top Rainbow Blends)*, 6 fl. oz.	80	0	21.0	0	0	10	n.a.
fruit-n cherry *(Tree Top Rainbow Blends)*, 6 fl. oz.	100	0	24.0	0	0	10	n.a.
fruit-n citrus *(Tree Top Rainbow Blends)*, 6 fl. oz.	90	0	22.0	0	0	10	n.a.
fruit-n grape *(Tree Top Rainbow Blends)*, 6 fl. oz.	100	0	25.0	0	0	10	n.a.
punch, canned, 6 fl. oz.:							
(Bama)	90	0	22.0	0	0	n.a.	n.a.
(Hawaiian Punch Low Sugar) . .	30	0	8.0	0	0	20	n.a.
(Hi-C)	95	<.1	24.0	<.1	0	18	tr.

Food and Measure	cal.	prot. (gms)	carbo. (gms)	fat (gms)	chol. (mgs)	sod. (mgs)	fiber (gms)
(Magic Tree) . . .	100	0	25.0	0	0	0	n.a.
berry (Hawaiian Punch)	90	0	22.0	0	0	28	n.a.
island fruit cocktail (Hawaiian Punch)	90	0	22.0	0	0	19	n.a.
red (Hawaiian Punch)	90	0	22.0	0	0	17	n.a.
tropical fruit (Hawaiian Punch) . . .	90	0	22.0	0	0	8	n.a.
wild fruit (Hawaiian Punch)	90	0	23.0	0	0	19	n.a.
punch, chilled (Minute Maid), 6 fl. oz. . .	91	<1.0	23.0	<.1	0	15	n.a.
punch, frozen* (Minute Maid), 6 fl. oz.	91	<1.0	23.0	<.1	0	<1	n.a.
punch, mix*, 8 fl. oz.:							
(Crystal Light Crystals)	4	0	0	0	0	0	0
(Minute Maid Crystals)	99	<1.0	24.0	<.1	0	11	n.a.
(Minute Maid Lite)	16	0	4.0	0	0	7	n.a.
mountain berry (Kool-Aid) . . .	100	0	25.0	0	0	15	tr.
natural flavor (Sunkist Light) . . .	6	0	2.0	0	0	20	n.a.
rainbow, sunshine or tropical (Kool-Aid)	100	0	25.0	0	0	0	tr.
tropical (Wyler's)	90	0	22.0	0	0	n.a.	n.a.
presweetened, mountain berry (Kool-Aid) . . .	90	0	22.0	0	0	15	tr.
presweetened, rainbow or tropical (Kool-Aid) . . .	90	0	24.0	0	0	0	0
presweetened, sunshine (Kool-Aid)	90	0	23.0	0	0	0	0

* Prepared according to package directions

Food and Measure	cal.	prot. (gms)	carbo. (gms)	fat (gms)	chol. (mgs)	sod. (mgs)	fiber (gms)
Fruit drinks, punch, mix* *(cont.)*							
sugar free *(Funny Face)*	4	0	1.0	0	0	0	0
sugar free, mountain berry *(Kool-Aid)*	4	0	0	0	0	35	0
sugar free, rainbow, sunshine or tropical *(Kool-Aid)* . .	4	0	0	0	0	0	0
sugar sweetened *(Funny Face)* . .	88	0	22.0	0	0	< 10	0
Fruit juice, 6 fl. oz.:							
canned or bottled:							
(Welch's Orchard Harvest Blend)	90	0	22.0	0	0	20	n.a.
(Welch's Orchard North Country Blend)	90	0	22.0	0	0	20	n.a.
(Welch's Orchard Vineyard Blend)	120	0	30.0	0	0	5	n.a.
frozen*:							
(Welch's Orchard Harvest Blend)	90	0	22.0	0	0	5	n.a.
(Welch's Orchard North Country Blend)	90	0	22.0	0	0	20	n.a.
Fruit and nut mix:							
(Planters), 1 oz. . . .	150	5.0	13.0	9.0	0	90	n.a.
Fruit punch, see "Fruit drinks"							
Fruit punch roll:							
(Flavor Tree), .75-oz. roll	80	0	18.0	< 1.0	0	15	n.a.

---

* *Prepared according to package directions*

G

Food and Measure	cal.	prot. (gms)	carbo. (gms)	fat (gms)	chol. (mgs)	sod. (mgs)	fiber (gms)
Garden salad, canned:							
(Joan of Arc), 1/2 cup	80	2.0	17.0	<1.0	0	600	n.a.
marinated *(S&W),* 1/2 cup	60	2.0	11.0	0	0	670	n.a.
Garlic:							
raw:							
peeled, 1 oz. . . .	42	1.8	9.4	.1	0	5	.4
peeled, 5 cloves	20	1.0	5.0	.1	0	5	.3
Garlic dip:							
(Kraft), 2 tbsp. . . .	60	1.0	3.0	4.0	0	160	n.a.
(Nalley), 1 oz.	118	.3	.9	12.8	17	400	n.a.
Garlic powder:							
(all brands), 1 tsp.	9	.5	2.0	<.1	0	1	.1
with parsley *(Lawry's),* 1 tsp.	12	.5	2.3	<.1	0	5	<.1
Garlic salt:							
(Lawry's), 1 tsp.	4	<.1	.8	<.1	0	968	<.1
Garlic salt substitute:							
(Featherweight), 1/4 tsp.	0	0	0	0	0	<1	0
Garlic spread:							
concentrate *(Lawry's),* 1 oz.	15	<.1	.2	1.6	n.a.	21	0
Garbanzos, see "Chick peas"							
Gefilte fish, see "Fish, gefilte"							
Gelatin, unflavored:							
(Knox), 1 envelope	25	6.0	0	0	0	10	n.a.

Food and Measure	cal.	prot. (gms)	carbo. (gms)	fat (gms)	chol. (mgs)	sod. (mgs)	fiber (gms)
Gelatin dessert, mix*, 1/2 cup:							
all flavors (Jell-O) . .	80	2.0	19.0	0	0	35–75	0
all flavors (Royal) . .						95–	
	80	2.0	19.0	0	0	100	0
Gelatin drink:							
orange flavor (Knox), 1 envelope	50	6.0	7.0	0	0	20	n.a.
Gin, see "Liquor"							
Ginger, candied:							
crystallized, 1 oz. . .	96	.1	24.7	.1	0	n.a.	.2
Ginger, ground:							
(all brands), 1 tsp. .	6	.2	1.3	.1	0	1	.1
Ginger root, peeled:							
1 oz.	20	.5	4.3	.2	0	4	.3
sliced, 1/4 cup . . .	17	.4	3.6	.2	0	3	.3
Goose, domestic:							
raw, whole, ready-to-cook, 1 lb.	1187	50.8	0	107.6	256	234	0
roasted:							
meat and skin, 4 oz.	346	28.5	0	24.9	103	79	0
meat only, 4 oz.	270	32.9	0	14.4	109	86	0
Gooseberry:							
fresh, 1 cup	67	1.3	15.3	.9	0	1	2.9
canned:							
in water, with liquid, 8 oz.	59	1.1	15.0	.2	0	2	2.9
in light syrup, with liquid, 1 cup . .	185	1.6	47.3	.5	0	6	3.0
Gourd, dishcloth:							
raw:							
whole, 1 gourd, 131/4" × 13/4"	36	2.1	7.8	.4	0	6	.9
1" slices, 1 cup	19	1.1	4.1	.2	0	3	.5
boiled, drained, 1" slices, 1 cup . . .	99	1.2	25.5	.6	0	37	.7

* Prepared according to package directions

Food and Measure	cal.	prot. (gms)	carbo. (gms)	fat (gms)	chol. (mgs)	sod. (mgs)	fiber (gms)
Gourd, white-flowered:							
raw:							
whole, 1 gourd, 17″×3⅛″ . . .	106	4.8	26.1	.2	0	19	4.3
1″ cubes, 1 cup	16	.7	3.9	<.1	0	2	.6
boiled, drained, 1″ cubes, 1 cup . . .	22	.9	5.4	<.1	0	2	.9
Gourmet loaf:							
(Eckrich Calorie Watcher), 1 oz. . .	35	4.0	2.0	1.0	n.a.	390	n.a.
(Eckrich Smorgas Pac), 1 slice . . .	25	3.0	2.0	1.0	n.a.	300	n.a.
Granola and similar snack bars, 1 roll or bar:							
almond:							
(Nature Valley Bars)	120	2.0	17.0	5.0	n.a.	90	n.a.
(Nature Valley Clusters)	160	2.0	28.0	4.0	n.a.	110	n.a.
apple *(Nature Valley Chewy)*	130	2.0	20.0	5.0	n.a.	70	n.a.
apple-cinnamon *(Nature Valley Clusters)*	150	2.0	27.0	4.0	n.a.	100	n.a.
apple or banana nut *(Jack LaLanne)*	85	2.0	13.0	2.0	n.a.	13	n.a.
caramel:							
(Nature Valley Clusters)	150	2.0	28.0	3.0	n.a.	120	n.a.
chocolate chip *(Nature Valley Chewy)*	140	2.0	19.0	6.0	n.a.	80	n.a.
nut *(Quaker Dipps)*, 1.1 oz.	148	1.9	21.0	6.3	n.a.	63	.2
carob chip, chewy *(Nature's Choice)*	90	2.0	15.0	3.0	n.a.	12	n.a.
chocolate:							
(Nature Valley Clusters)	140	2.0	27.0	3.0	n.a.	110	n.a.

Food and Measure	cal.	prot. (gms)	carbo. (gms)	fat (gms)	chol. (mgs)	sod. (mgs)	fiber (gms)
Granola and similar snack bars, chocolate *(cont.)*							
almond *(Nature Valley Dandy Bars)*	170	2.0	22.0	8.0	n.a.	105	n.a.
dark *(Nature Valley Dandy Bars)* . .	160	2.0	23.0	7.0	n.a.	110	n.a.
milk *(Nature Valley Dandy Bars)* . .	160	2.0	23.0	7.0	n.a.	105	n.a.
chocolate chip:							
(Flavor Kist Chewy)	130	2.0	20.0	5.0	n.a.	70	n.a.
(Nature Valley Bars)	110	2.0	16.0	4.0	n.a.	75	n.a.
(Nature Valley Chewy)	150	2.0	19.0	7.0	n.a.	80	n.a.
(Nature Valley Clusters)	150	2.0	27.0	4.0	n.a.	100	n.a.
(New Trail), 1.4 oz.	200	3.0	25.0	10.0	n.a.	110	n.a.
(Quaker Chewy), 1 oz.	129	2.2	19.4	4.7	n.a.	79	.2
(Quaker Dipps), 1 oz.	138	1.8	18.4	6.4	n.a.	65	.3
mint *(Quaker Dipps)*, 1 oz. . .	140	1.8	18.8	6.4	n.a.	56	.2
chocolate graham and marshmallow *(Quaker Chewy)*, 1 oz.	126	1.9	19.6	4.4	n.a.	93	.2
chunky nut and raisin *(Quaker Chewy)*, 1 oz.	133	2.4	17.2	6.1	n.a.	81	.5
cinnamon *(Nature Valley Bars)*	120	2.0	17.0	5.0	n.a.	70	n.a.
cinnamon and raisin, chewy *(Nature's Choice)*	90	2.0	15.0	3.0	n.a.	8	n.a.
coconut *(Nature Valley Bars)*	130	2.0	15.0	7.0	n.a.	65	n.a.
date nut, chewy *(Jack LaLanne)*	85	2.0	13.0	2.0	n.a.	15	n.a.

Food and Measure	cal.	prot. (gms)	carbo. (gms)	fat (gms)	chol. (mgs)	sod. (mgs)	fiber (gms)
honey and oats:							
(Quaker Chewy), 1 oz.	125	2.4	19.0	4.4	n.a.	93	.3
(Quaker Dipps), 1 oz.	137	1.7	18.8	6.1	n.a.	66	.2
oats and honey:							
(Nature's Choice)	90	2.0	15.0	3.0	n.a.	14	n.a.
(Nature Valley Bars)	120	2.0	17.0	5.0	n.a.	65	n.a.
peanut (Nature Valley Bars)	130	3.0	16.0	6.0	n.a.	80	n.a.
peanut butter:							
(Flavor Kist Chewy)	130	2.0	19.0	5.0	n.a.	65	n.a.
(Nature's Choice Chewy)	90	2.0	14.0	4.0	n.a.	21	n.a.
(Nature Valley Bars)	120	2.0	15.0	6.0	n.a.	70	n.a.
(Nature Valley Chewy)	150	3.0	18.0	7.0	n.a.	80	n.a.
(Nature Valley Dandy Bars) . .	160	3.0	22.0	7.0	n.a.	110	n.a.
(New Trail), 1.4 oz.	200	5.0	23.0	10.0	n.a.	105	n.a.
(Quaker Chewy), 1 oz.	130	3.2	18.0	5.0	n.a.	106	.2
(Quaker Dipps), 1 oz.	141	2.5	17.0	7.0	n.a.	89	.3
honey crisp (Peanut Butter Boppers)	160	4.0	14.0	10.0	n.a.	105	n.a.
peanut crunch (Peanut Butter Boppers)	180	5.0	12.0	12.0	n.a.	100	n.a.
peanut butter–chocolate chip:							
(Flavor Kist Chewy)	130	2.0	20.0	5.0	n.a.	60	n.a.
(Nature Valley Chewy)	150	2.0	19.0	7.0	n.a.	80	n.a.
(New Trail), 1.4 oz.	200	4.0	22.0	10.0	n.a.	100	n.a.
(Quaker Chewy), 1 oz.	131	3.0	17.4	5.5	n.a.	92	.3
fudge chip (Peanut Butter Boppers)	160	3.0	15.0	10.0	n.a.	100	n.a.

Food and Measure	cal.	prot. (gms)	carbo. (gms)	fat (gms)	chol. (mgs)	sod. (mgs)	fiber (gms)
Granola and similar snack bars (cont.)							
raisin:							
(Flavor Kist Chewy)	130	2.0	20.0	5.0	n.a.	50	n.a.
(Nature Valley Clusters)	150	2.0	28.0	3.0	n.a.	110	n.a.
almond (Quaker Dipps), 1 oz. ...	139	1.7	18.6	6.4	n.a.	84	.2
cinnamon (Quaker Chewy), 1 oz.	130	2.3	18.6	5.1	n.a.	83	.2
rocky road (Quaker Dipps), 1 oz. ...	148	1.9	21.0	6.3	n.a.	63	.2
Grape:							
fresh, American type (slipskin), Concord, Delaware, Niagara, etc.:							
seeded, whole, 1 lb.	165	1.7	45.1	.9	0	4	2.0
seeded, 1 cup ..	58	.6	15.8	.3	0	2	.7
seeded, 10 grapes	15	.2	4.1	.1	0	0	.2
fresh, European type (adherent skin), Malaga, muscat, Thompson seedless, etc.:							
whole, 1 lb.	309	2.9	77.4	2.5	0	7	2.0
seeded or seedless, 1 cup	114	1.1	28.4	.9	0	3	.7
seedless, 10 grapes, 5/8" diam.	36	.3	8.9	.3	0	1	.2
canned, seedless:							
in water, with liquid, 1 cup	97	1.2	25.2	.3	0	14	.5
in heavy syrup (S&W), 1/2 cup	100	0	25.0	0	0	5	n.a.
in heavy syrup (Thank You), 1 cup	190	1.0	50.0	0	0	15	.5
Grape drink:							
(Magic Tree), 6 fl. oz.	100	0	25.0	0	0	20	n.a.

Food and Measure	cal.	prot. (gms)	carbo. (gms)	fat (gms)	chol. (mgs)	sod. (mgs)	fiber (gms)
canned or bottled, 6 fl. oz.:							
(Hawaiian Punch)	90	0	23.0	0	0	13	n.a.
(Hi-C)	95	<.1	24.0	<.1	0	19	tr.
(Welchade)	90	0	23.0	0	0	20	n.a.
chilled or frozen* (Minute Maid Grapeade), 6 fl. oz.	94	<1.0	24.0	<.1	0	<1	n.a.
frozen* (A&P Grape Beverage), 6 fl. oz.	100	<1.0	50.0	<1.0	0	0	n.a.
mix*, 8 fl. oz.:							
(Crystal Light Crystals)	4	0	0	0	0	0	0
(Kool-Aid)	100	0	25.0	0	0	0	tr.
natural flavor (Sunkist Light Crystals)	6	0	2.0	0	0	25	n.a.
wild (Wyler's) . . .	90	0	22.0	0	0	n.a.	n.a.
presweetened (Kool-Aid) . . .	90	0	23.0	0	0	0	0
sugar free (Funny Face)	4	0	1.0	0	0	0	0
sugar free (Kool-Aid)	4	0	0	0	0	0	tr.
sugar sweetened (Funny Face) . .	88	0	22.0	0	0	0	0
Grape juice, 6 fl. oz.:							
canned or bottled:							
(Seneca)	115	1.0	27.0	0	0	10	n.a.
red or white (Welch's)	120	0	30.0	0	0	15	n.a.
red, sparkling (Welch's)	128	0	32.0	0	0	30	n.a.
regular or purple (Welch's)	120	0	30.0	0	0	5	n.a.
white, sparkling (Welch's)	120	0	30.0	0	0	30	n.a.

* Prepared according to package directions

Food and Measure	cal.	prot. (gms)	carbo. (gms)	fat (gms)	chol. (mgs)	sod. (mgs)	fiber (gms)
Grape juice *(cont.)*							
frozen*:							
(A&P)	200	<1.0	50.0	<1.0	0	0	n.a.
(Minute Maid) . .	98	<1.0	23.0	<1.0	0	2	tr.
(Seneca)	100	0	26.0	0	0	20	n.a.
(Seneca Natural)	115	0	27.0	0	0	20	n.a.
(Welch's)	100	0	25.0	0	0	0	n.a.
(Welch's Orchard)	120	0	30.0	0	0	5	n.a.
Grape juice drink:							
(Welch's), 6 fl. oz.	110	0	27.0	0	0	5	n.a.
Grape roll or bar:							
(Flavor Tree), .75-oz.							
roll	80	0	18.0	<1.0	0	10	n.a.
(Fruit Corners), 1 bar	90	<1.0	17.0	2.0	0	10	n.a.
(Fruit Roll-Ups), 1/2-oz.							
roll	50	0	12.0	<1.0	0	10	n.a.
(Nature's Choice), 1/2-							
oz. bar	50	0	11.0	0	0	1	n.a.
(Pocket Fruit), .7-oz.							
bar	60	0	15.0	0	0	n.a.	n.a.
(Sunkist Fruit Rolls),							
1/2-oz. roll	50	0	12.0	<1.0	0	10	n.a.
(Stretch Island							
Leather), 1/2-oz. bar	40	0	10.0	0	0	1	n.a.
Grapefruit:							
fresh, pink or red, Cal-							
ifornia or Arizona:							
1/2 medium, 33/4"							
diam.	46	.6	11.9	.1	0	1	.3
sections, with juice,							
1 cup	86	1.2	22.3	.2	0	1	.5
fresh, pink or red,							
Florida:							
1/2 medium, 33/4"							
diam.	37	.7	9.2	.1	0	0	.3
sections, with juice,							
1 cup	68	1.3	17.3	.2	0	1	.5

* Prepared according to package directions

Food and Measure	cal.	prot. (gms)	carbo. (gms)	fat (gms)	chol. (mgs)	sod. (mgs)	fiber (gms)
fresh, white, California:							
1/2 medium, 3 3/4" diam.	43	1.0	10.7	.1	0	0	.2
sections, with juice, 1 cup	84	2.0	20.9	.2	0	1	.5
fresh, white, Florida:							
1/2 medium, 3 3/4" diam.	38	.7	9.7	.1	0	0	.2
sections, with juice, 1 cup	75	1.5	18.8	.2	0	1	.5
canned or chilled, 1/2 cup:							
sections (Kraft) . .	50	1.0	12.0	0	0	0	n.a.
sections (Stokely's Finest)	90	1.0	23.0	1.0	0	5	n.a.
in juice, sections (S&W Natural Style)	40	0	9.0	0	0	0	n.a.
in light syrup, sections (S&W) . .	80	<1.0	14.0	0	0	0	n.a.
Grapefruit juice:							
fresh, pink, red or white, 1 cup . . .	96	1.2	22.7	.3	0	2	n.a.
canned, bottled or chilled:							
(Del Monte), 6 fl. oz.	70	1.0	17.0	1.0	0	<10	n.a.
(Kraft), 6 fl. oz. . .	70	1.0	16.0	0	0	0	n.a.
(Minute Maid), 6 fl. oz.	65	<1.0	16.0	<1.0	0	16	n.a.
(Ocean Spray), 8 fl. oz.	95	2.0	22.0	<1.0	0	10	n.a.
(S&W), 6 fl. oz. . .	80	1.0	18.0	0	0	<10	n.a.
(Stokely's Finest), 6 fl. oz.	76	1.0	18.0	1.0	0	5	n.a.
cocktail, pink (Ocean Spray), 8 fl. oz.	131	<1.0	27.0	<1.0	0	20	n.a.
dehydrated, dry form, 1 oz.	107	1.4	25.6	.3	0	3	.1

Food and Measure	cal.	prot. (gms)	carbo. (gms)	fat (gms)	chol. (mgs)	sod. (mgs)	fiber (gms)
Grapefruit juice (cont.)							
frozen*, 6 fl. oz.:							
(A&P)	80	<1.0	18.0	<1.0	0	0	n.a.
(Tropicana)	81	1.5	18.6	.5	0	2	n.a.
pink or white (Minute Maid)	71	<1.0	18.0	<1.0	0	2	n.a.
Grapefruit peel, candied:							
1 oz.	90	.1	22.9	.1	0	n.a.	.7
Grenadine:							
(Rose's), 1 fl. oz. . .	64	0	16.0	0	0	7	n.a.
Ground cherry:							
with husks, 1 lb. . .	226	8.1	47.8	3.0	0	n.a.	11.9
without husks:							
1 lb.	241	8.6	50.9	3.2	0	n.a.	12.7
1 cup	74	2.7	15.7	1.0	0	n.a.	3.9
Grouper:							
raw, fillets, 4 oz. . .	104	22.0	0	1.2	42	60	0
broiled, fillets, 4 oz.	134	28.2	0	1.5	53	60	0
Guacamole dip:							
(Kraft Guacamole), 2 tbsp.	50	1.0	3.0	4.0	0	210	n.a.
(Nalley), 1 oz.	111	.3	.9	12.2	14	380	n.a.
(Nalley Avocado Dip), 1 oz.	108	.3	.9	12.1	14	370	n.a.
Guava, common, fresh:							
1 medium, 4 oz. . .	45	.7	10.7	.5	0	2	5.0
trimmed, 1 cup . . .	83	1.4	19.6	1.0	0	4	9.2
Guava, strawberry, fresh:							
whole, with stems, 1 lb.	268	2.2	66.9	2.3	0	141	24.7
1 medium, .3 oz. . .	4	<.1	1.0	<.1	0	2	.4
trimmed, 1 cup . . .	169	1.4	42.4	1.5	0	89	15.6

* Prepared according to package directions

Food and Measure	cal.	prot. (gms)	carbo. (gms)	fat (gms)	chol. (mgs)	sod. (mgs)	fiber (gms)
Guava juice cocktail:							
(Ocean Spray), 8 fl.							
oz.	131	<1.0	32.0	1.0	0	1	1.0
Guava sauce:							
cooked, 1 cup . . .	87	.8	22.6	.3	0	9	4.7
Guinea hen, raw:							
whole, ready-to-cook,							
1 lb.	568	84.0	0	23.2	n.a.	n.a.	0
meat and skin, 4 oz.	212	26.5	0	7.3	n.a.	n.a.	0

H

Food and Measure	cal.	prot. (gms)	carbo. (gms)	fat (gms)	chol. (mgs)	sod. (mgs)	fiber (gms)
Haddock:							
fresh, fillets:							
raw, 4 oz.	99	21.4	0	.8	65	77	0
broiled, 4 oz. . . .	127	27.5	0	1.1	84	99	0
frozen:							
(Gorton's Fishmarket Fresh), 4 oz. . .	90	20.0	0	1.0	n.a.	100	n.a.
(Van de Kamp's Today's Catch), 4 oz.	90	20.0	0	0	n.a.	70	n.a.
raw (Taste O' Sea Calorie Watcher), 1 portion	70	15.0	0	1.0	n.a.	230	n.a.
in batter (Van de Kamp's), 4 oz.	240	10.0	20.0	10.0	n.a.	430	n.a.
fillets (Booth Light & Tender), 4 oz.	90	21.0	0	1.0	n.a.	70	n.a.
fillets (Gorton's Light Recipe), 1 fillet	260	19.0	23.0	10.0	n.a.	570	n.a.
fillets (Taste O' Sea), 4 oz. . . .	100	22.0	0	1.0	n.a.	160	n.a.
fillets (Van de Kamp's Light & Crispy), 2-oz. fillet	180	5.0	10.0	15.0	n.a.	160	n.a.
fillets, in batter (Mrs. Paul's Crunchy Light), 2 fillets	320	13.0	28.0	17.0	n.a.	935	n.a.
fillets, breaded (Mrs. Paul's Crispy Crunchy), 2 fillets	280	12.0	25.0	15.0	n.a.	800	n.a.

Food and Measure	cal.	prot. (gms)	carbo. (gms)	fat (gms)	chol. (mgs)	sod. (mgs)	fiber (gms)
fillets, breaded (Mrs. Paul's Light & Natural), 1 fillet	320	23.0	25.0	14.0	n.a.	960	n.a.
fillets, with lemon butter sauce (Gorton's Light Recipe), 1 pkg.	240	26.0	8.0	11.0	n.a.	570	n.a.
portions, in batter (Taste O' Sea Batter Dipt), 3 oz.	200	8.0	14.0	12.0	n.a.	370	n.a.
sticks (Taste O' Sea), 4 oz. . . .	240	13.0	21.0	12.0	n.a.	770	n.a.
with Romano cheese (Booth Light & Tender), 3 oz.	190	12.0	12.0	10.0	n.a.	380	n.a.
smoked, meat only, 4 oz.	132	28.6	0	1.1	87	865	0
Haddock dinner:							
frozen (Taste O' Sea), 9 oz.	450	19.0	52.0	18.0	n.a.	890	n.a.
Halibut, Atlantic or Pacific:							
fresh:							
raw, fillets, 4 oz.	125	23.6	0	2.6	36	61	0
broiled, fillets, 4 oz.	159	30.3	0	3.3	46	78	0
frozen:							
steaks (Wakefield), 8 oz.	210	48.0	1.0	1.0	n.a.	160	n.a.
in batter (Van de Kamp's), 4 oz.	260	10.0	15.0	15.0	n.a.	440	n.a.
smoked, 4 oz. . . .	254	23.6	0	17.0	n.a.	n.a.	0
Halibut dinner, Ter- iyaki:							
frozen (Taste O' Sea Gourmet), 12 oz.	300	26.0	36.0	6.0	n.a.	2190	n.a.
Halibut entree:							
in white sauce, frozen (Certi-Fresh), 9 oz.	290	31.0	11.0	13.0	n.a.	n.a.	n.a.

Food and Measure	cal.	prot. (gms)	carbo. (gms)	fat (gms)	chol. (mgs)	sod. (mgs)	fiber (gms)
Ham, retail cuts, meat only:							
leg, whole, roasted with bone and skin:							
lean with fat, 3 oz.							
(5.5 oz. raw) . .	250	21.3	0	17.6	79	51	0
lean with fat, 1 cup	411	35.0	0	29.0	131	83	0
lean (fat trimmed), 3							
oz. (6.5 oz. raw)	187	24.1	0	9.4	80	55	0
lean (fat trimmed), 1							
cup	309	39.7	0	15.4	131	90	0
rump half, roasted with bone and skin:							
lean with fat, 3 oz.							
(5.4 oz. raw) . .	233	22.6	0	15.1	81	52	0
lean with fat, 1 cup	384	37.3	0	24.9	133	85	0
lean (fat trimmed), 3							
oz. (6 oz. raw)	187	24.8	0	9.1	81	55	0
lean (fat trimmed), 1							
cup	309	40.8	0	14.9	134	90	0
shank half, roasted with bone and skin:							
lean with fat, 3 oz.							
(5.6 oz. raw) . .	258	20.7	0	18.8	78	50	0
lean with fat, 1 cup	425	34.0	0	31.0	129	82	0
lean (fat trimmed), 3							
oz., (6.9 oz. raw)	183	24.0	0	8.9	78	54	0
lean (fat trimmed), 1							
cup	301	39.5	0	14.7	129	90	0
cured, blade roll (shoulder), roasted:							
lean with fat, 3 oz.							
(3.6 oz. unheated)	244	14.7	.3	20.0	57	827	0
cured, picnic (shoulder), roasted with bone and skin:							
lean with fat, 3 oz.							
(5.4 oz. unheated)	238	17.4	0	18.2	49	912	0
lean with fat, 1 cup	392	28.6	0	29.9	82	1501	0

Food and Measure	cal.	prot. (gms)	carbo. (gms)	fat (gms)	chol. (mgs)	sod. (mgs)	fiber (gms)
lean (fat trimmed), 3 oz. (7.3 oz. unheated)	145	21.2	0	6.0	41	1046	0
lean (fat trimmed), 1 cup	238	34.9	0	9.9	68	1723	0
Ham, boneless:							
(Armour Lower Salt), 1 oz.	35	5.2	.6	1.4	14	221	0
(Armour Star Speedy Cut), 1 oz.	44	4.5	.6	2.6	15	330	0
(Oscar Mayer Jubilee), 1 oz.	47	5.2	.1	2.9	15	375	0
(Realean), 1 oz. . .	30	4.5	.4	1.1	n.a.	n.a.	0
extra lean, unheated, 1 slice, 6¼″ × 4″ × ¹⁄₁₆″	37	5.5	.3	1.4	13	405	0
extra lean, roasted, 3 oz. (3.4 oz. unheated)	123	17.8	1.3	4.7	45	1023	0
roasted, 3 oz. (3.5 oz. unheated)	151	19.2	0	7.7	50	1275	0
roasted, 1 cup . . .	249	31.7	0	12.7	83	2100	0
slice (Oscar Mayer Jubilee), 1 oz.	29	4.8	0	1.1	13	349	0
steak (Oscar Mayer Jubilee), 2 oz. . .	59	9.7	.1	2.2	27	711	0
Ham, canned:							
(Armour Golden Star), 3 oz.	90	15.0	2.0	3.0	50	970	n.a.
(Armour Star), 3 oz.	120	15.0	2.0	6.0	50	970	n.a.
(Armour Star Nugget), 3 oz.	100	15.0	2.0	3.0	50	970	n.a.
(Black Label, 1½ lb.), 4 oz.	150	21.0	0	7.0	n.a.	1324	0
(Black Label, 3 lb.), 4 oz.	140	20.0	0	7.0	n.a.	1315	0
(Black Label, 5 lb.), 4 oz.	140	20.0	0	7.0	n.a.	1245	0
(EXL), 4 oz.	120	22.0	0	4.0	n.a.	1382	0

Food and Measure	cal.	prot. (gms)	carbo. (gms)	fat (gms)	chol. (mgs)	sod. (mgs)	fiber (gms)
Ham, canned *(cont.)*							
(EXL Deli Ham), 4 oz.	130	20.0	0	6.0	n.a.	1368	0
(Holiday Glaze), 4 oz.	130	21.0	2.0	4.0	n.a.	n.a.	n.a.
(Hormel Bone In), 4 oz.	210	17.0	1.0	15.0	n.a.	n.a.	n.a.
(Hormel Cure 81), 4 oz.	160	22.0	0	8.0	n.a.	1322	n.a.
(Hormel Curemaster), 4 oz.	140	22.0	1.0	5.0	n.a.	1361	n.a.
(Light & Lean Boneless), 2 oz.	60	10.0	0	2.0	n.a.	574	n.a.
(Oscar Mayer Jubilee), 3 oz.	94	15.8	0	3.4	38	860	0
(Patrick Cudahy), 1 oz.	52	4.3	.8	3.4	n.a.	335	n.a.
chopped:							
(Armour Star), 3 oz.	260	11.0	7.0	21.0	50	1100	n.a.
(Hormel, 12 oz.), 2 oz.	120	10.0	0	9.0	n.a.	703	0
(Hormel, 8 lb.), 3 oz.	240	12.0	1.0	21.0	n.a.	1062	n.a.
chunk *(Hormel),* 6³/4 oz.	310	32.0	0	20.0	n.a.	2241	0
extra lean:							
unheated, 3 oz.	102	15.7	0	3.9	33	1068	0
unheated, 1 cup	168	25.9	0	6.4	53	1757	0
roasted, 3 oz., from 3.4 oz. unheated	116	18.0	.4	4.1	25	965	0
roasted, 1 cup . .	191	29.6	.7	6.8	41	1589	0
roasted:							
3 oz., from 3.6 oz. unheated	192	17.5	.4	12.9	52	800	0
1 cup	317	28.7	.6	21.3	86	1317	0
roll *(Hormel),* 4 oz.	170	21.0	0	10.0	n.a.	1338	n.a.
spiced *(Hormel),* 3 oz.	240	13.0	1.0	21.0	n.a.	1093	n.a.
unheated:							
3 oz.	162	14.4	<.1	11.0	33	1056	0
1 cup	266	23.8	<.1	18.2	55	1736	0
Ham, sliced and luncheon:							
(Boar's Head Lower Salt), 1-oz. slice	26	5.0	.6	.6	n.a.	260	n.a.

Food and Measure	cal.	prot. (gms)	carbo. (gms)	fat (gms)	chol. (mgs)	sod. (mgs)	fiber (gms)
barbecue (Light & Lean), 2 slices . .	50	8.0	0	2.0	n.a.	n.a.	n.a.
black or red peppered (Light & Lean), 2 slices	50	9.0	0	2.0	n.a.	n.a.	n.a.
boiled (Boar's Head Short Cut), 1 oz.	26	5.0	.6	.6	n.a.	n.a.	n.a.
chopped:							
(Armour), 1-oz. slice	80	n.a.	n.a.	6.0	15	385	0
(Eckrich Calorie Watcher), 1 slice	45	5.0	1.0	2.0	n.a.	330	n.a.
(Eckrich Smorgas Pac), 3/4-oz. slice	35	4.0	1.0	2.0	n.a.	250	n.a.
(Hormel Perma-Fresh), 2 slices	88	11.0	0	5.0	n.a.	685	n.a.
(Light & Lean), 2 slices	70	8.0	0	4.0	n.a.	n.a.	n.a.
(Oscar Mayer), 1-oz. slice	61	4.7	.8	4.3	14	355	0
cooked:							
(Eckrich Calorie Watcher)	30	6.0	1.0	1.0	n.a.	470	n.a.
(Light & Lean), 2 slices	50	9.0	0	2.0	n.a.	n.a.	n.a.
cracked black pepper (Oscar Mayer), 1-oz. slice	24	3.9	.1	.9	11	269	0
Danish (Eckrich), 1-oz. slice	25	5.0	1.0	1.0	n.a.	390	n.a.
deviled (Hormel), 1 tbsp.	35	2.0	0	3.0	n.a.	108	n.a.
extra lean, 1 slice, 61/4″ × 4″ × 1/16″	37	5.5	.3	1.4	13	405	0
glazed (Light & Lean), 2 slices	50	9.0	0	2.0	n.a.	n.a.	n.a.
honey (Oscar Mayer), 1-oz. slice	27	3.8	.6	1.0	11	272	0
Italian style (Oscar Mayer), 1-oz. slice	24	3.7	.1	.9	9	264	0

Food and Measure	cal.	prot. (gms)	carbo. (gms)	fat (gms)	chol. (mgs)	sod. (mgs)	fiber (gms)
Ham, sliced and luncheon (cont.)							
loaf (Eckrich), 1-oz. slice	70	4.0	1.0	6.0	n.a.	330	n.a.
minced, 4 oz.	300	18.4	2.1	23.4	80	1412	0
smoked:							
(Carl Buddig), 1 oz.	49	5.4	.5	2.8	20	400	0
(Eckrich Calorie Watcher Slender Sliced), 1 oz.	45	5.0	1.0	3.0	n.a.	360	n.a.
cooked (Light & Lean), 2 slices	50	9.0	0	2.0	n.a.	n.a.	n.a.
cooked (Oscar Mayer), 1-oz. slice	23	3.8	.1	.9	10	265	0
sweet (Eckrich Calorie Watcher), 1 slice	25	4.0	1.0	1.0	n.a.	270	n.a.
turkey, see "Turkey ham"							
Ham and Swiss cheese croissant, frozen:							
(Sara Lee Le San*Wich), 4 oz.	320	14.0	25.0	17.0	n.a.	760	n.a.
Ham and cheese loaf:							
(Eckrich), 1-oz. slice	60	4.0	1.0	5.0	n.a.	350	0
(Light & Lean), 2 slices	90	8.0	0	6.0	n.a.	n.a.	0
(Hormel Perma-Fresh), 2 slices	110	11.0	0	7.0	n.a.	668	0
(Oscar Mayer), 1-oz. slice	76	4.5	.5	6.2	17	351	0
canned (Hormel), 3 oz.	260	13.0	1.0	22.0	n.a.	1135	n.a.
Ham and cheese patties:							
canned (Hormel), 1 patty	190	7.0	0	18.0	n.a.	468	n.a.

Food and Measure	cal.	prot. (gms)	carbo. (gms)	fat (gms)	chol. (mgs)	sod. (mgs)	fiber (gms)
Ham and cheese spread:							
(Oscar Mayer), 1 oz.	66	4.5	.6	5.1	16	329	0
Ham crepes, frozen:							
and asparagus *(Stouffer's)*, 6¼ oz. . .	310	14.0	24.0	18.0	n.a.	750	n.a.
and Swiss cheese *(Stouffer's)*, 7½ oz.	410	23.0	21.0	26.0	n.a.	980	n.a.
Ham dinner, frozen:							
(Banquet American Favorites), 10 oz.	532	21.0	61.0	22.0	n.a.	1148	n.a.
(Morton), 10 oz. . .	301	16.0	49.0	4.5	n.a.	700	n.a.
steak *(Le Menu)*, 9¼ oz.	320	19.0	35.0	12.0	n.a.	1510	n.a.
Ham patties:							
(Patrick Cudahy Hamdingers), 1 patty	166	7.3	2.3	14.1	n.a.	529	0
canned *(Hormel)*, 1 patty	180	7.0	0	16.0	n.a.	456	0
Ham salad spread:							
(Oscar Mayer), 1 oz.	62	2.5	3.5	4.2	11	265	n.a.
(The Spreadables), 1.9 oz.	110	5.0	4.0	8.0	n.a.	335	n.a.
Hamburger, see "Beef"							
Hamburger entree, mix*, 1/5 pkg., except as noted:							
beef noodle *(Hamburger Helper)* . .	320	20.0	26.0	15.0	n.a.	1050	n.a.
beef Romanoff *(Hamburger Helper)* . .	350	21.0	30.0	16.0	n.a.	1080	n.a.
cheeseburger macaroni *(Hamburger Helper)*	360	21.0	28.0	18.0	n.a.	1030	n.a.

* *Prepared according to package directions*

Food and Measure	cal.	prot. (gms)	carbo. (gms)	fat (gms)	chol. (mgs)	sod. (mgs)	fiber (gms)
Hamburger entree, mix* *(cont.)*							
chili tomato *(Hamburger Helper)* . .	330	20.0	31.0	14.0	n.a.	1360	n.a.
hash *(Hamburger Helper)*	320	18.0	27.0	15.0	n.a.	1020	n.a.
lasagna *(Hamburger Helper)*	340	20.0	35.0	13.0	n.a.	1070	n.a.
pizzabake *(Hamburger Helper)*, 1/6 pkg.	320	19.0	29.0	14.0	n.a.	840	n.a.
pizza dish *(Hamburger Helper)*	360	21.0	37.0	14.0	n.a.	1010	n.a.
potato au gratin *(Hamburger Helper)* . .	320	19.0	28.0	15.0	n.a.	910	n.a.
potato Stroganoff *(Hamburger Helper)*	320	18.0	28.0	15.0	n.a.	900	n.a.
rice Oriental *(Hamburger Helper)* . .	340	19.0	38.0	14.0	n.a.	1120	n.a.
spaghetti *(Hamburger Helper)*	340	20.0	32.0	15.0	n.a.	1110	n.a.
stew *(Hamburger Helper)*	300	18.0	25.0	14.0	n.a.	1010	n.a.
tacobake *(Hamburger Helper)*, 1/6 pkg.	310	17.0	31.0	13.0	n.a.	940	n.a.
tamale pie *(Hamburger Helper)* . .	380	19.0	39.0	16.0	n.a.	940	n.a.
Hamburger seasoning mix:							
(Durkee), 1-oz. pkg.	110	1.5	15.0	5.0	n.a.	1739	n.a.
Hardee's:							
breakfast, 1 serving:							
bacon and egg biscuit, 4 oz. . . .	405	13.3	30.2	25.7	305	823	n.a.
biscuit, 2.6 oz. . .	257	4.3	32.0	12.4	n.a.	521	n.a.
biscuit, cinnamon 'n raisin, 2.7 oz.	276	3.0	29.5	16.2	<1	346	n.a.
biscuit gravy, 4 oz.	144	5.1	9.6	9.5	21	440	n.a.

* *Prepared according to package directions*

Food and Measure	cal.	prot. (gms)	carbo. (gms)	fat (gms)	chol. (mgs)	sod. (mgs)	fiber (gms)
Canadian sunrise, 5.7 oz.	482	20.7	32.9	29.7	n.a.	1121	n.a.
country ham biscuit, 3.4 oz.	328	14.2	27.8	17.8	12	1038	n.a.
egg, 1.2 oz. . . .	77	4.5	.6	6.3	160	54	n.a.
(Hash Rounds, 2.5 oz.	200	2.0	20.0	13.0	10	310	n.a.
jelly, .6 oz.	49	<.1	12.7	<.1	0	3	n.a.
sausage biscuit, 4 oz.	426	13.9	29.0	28.3	17	831	n.a.
steak biscuit, 5 oz.	491	12.8	46.2	28.3	16	1108	n.a.
sandwiches, 1 serving:							
bacon cheese- burger, 7.3 oz.	556	31.5	33.8	32.8	60	888	n.a.
(Big Deluxe), 7.4 oz.	503	28.7	32.0	28.9	50	903	n.a.
cheeseburger, 4.1 oz.	309	13.9	34.5	12.8	28	825	n.a.
cheeseburger, 1/4 lb., 6.5 oz. . . .	511	29.1	35.3	28.2	77	1112	n.a.
chicken fillet, 6.8 oz.	510	26.9	41.7	26.2	57	360	n.a.
(Fisherman's Fillet), 7 oz.	469	24.6	47.3	20.1	80	1013	n.a.
hamburger, 3.4 oz.	276	13.7	20.8	15.3	n.a.	589	n.a.
hot dog, 4.3 oz.	346	11.6	25.8	21.9	n.a.	678	n.a.
(Hot Ham 'N' Cheese), 5.3 oz.	376	23.0	37.0	15.0	59	1067	n.a.
(Hot Ham 'N' Cheese), with let- tuce and tomato, 6.6 oz.	401	22.9	32.5	19.9	43	1393	n.a.
(Mushroom 'N' Swiss), 7.3 oz.	512	31.8	43.5	23.4	86	1051	n.a.
roast beef, 4.6 oz.	312	20.3	29.8	12.4	46	826	n.a.
(Turkey Club), 6.9 oz.	426	24.4	32.0	22.3	45	1185	n.a.
salads and side dishes, 1 serving:							
chef salad, 12 oz.	277	23.0	9.9	16.1	179	517	n.a.

Food and Measure	cal.	prot. (gms)	carbo. (gms)	fat (gms)	chol. (mgs)	sod. (mgs)	fiber (gms)
Hardee's, salads and side dishes (cont.)							
French fries, small, 2.5 oz.	239	3.1	27.5	12.9	tr.	180	n.a.
French fries, large, 4.3 oz.	406	5.3	46.8	21.9	tr.	306	n.a.
shrimp 'n pasta salad, 11.75 oz.	362	14.4	11.1	28.9	293	941	n.a.
side salad, 4.2 oz.	21	1.3	3.6	.1	<1	42	n.a.
desserts and shakes, 1 serving:							
apple turnover, 3.1 oz.	282	2.5	36.9	13.8	tr.	n.a.	n.a.
big cookie, 1.9 oz.	278	2.5	32.6	15.3	9	258	n.a.
milkshake, 11.6 oz.	391	11.4	62.9	10.4	<1	241	n.a.
Hazelnuts, see "Filberts"							
Head cheese:							
(Oscar Mayer), 1 oz.	55	4.5	0	4.1	21	338	0
Heart, fresh:							
beef, simmered, 4 oz.	199	32.6	.5	6.4	219	71	0
calf, braised, 4 oz.	236	31.5	2.0	10.3	n.a.	128	0
chicken:							
simmered, 4 oz.	210	30.0	.1	9.0	274	54	0
simmered, 1 cup	268	38.3	.2	11.5	350	69	0
hog:							
braised, 4 oz. . . .	168	26.8	.5	5.7	251	40	0
braised, 1 cup . .	214	34.2	.6	7.3	320	51	0
lamb, braised, 4 oz.	294	33.5	.1	16.3	n.a.	n.a.	0
turkey:							
simmered, 4 oz.	201	30.3	2.3	6.9	256	62	0
simmered, 1 cup	257	38.8	3.0	8.8	327	79	0
Herbs, see specific listings							
Herbs, mixed:							
(Lawry's Pinch of Herbs), 1 tsp.	9	.3	.9	.5	0	259	.2
Herring:							
Atlantic, raw, meat only, 4 oz.	179	20.4	0	10.3	68	102	0

Food and Measure	cal.	prot. (gms)	carbo. (gms)	fat (gms)	chol. (mgs)	sod. (mgs)	fiber (gms)
Pacific, raw, meat							
only, 4 oz.	221	18.6	0	15.7	87	84	0
canned:							
plain, with liquid, 4							
oz.	236	22.6	0	15.4	n.a.	n.a.	0
in tomato sauce, 4							
oz.	200	17.9	4.2	11.9	n.a.	n.a.	n.a.
pickled:							
Atlantic, 4 oz. . .	297	16.1	10.9	20.4	15	987	0
Bismarck, 4 oz. . .	253	23.1	0	17.1	n.a.	n.a.	0
smoked:							
bloaters, 4 oz. . .	222	22.2	0	14.1	n.a.	n.a.	0
hard, 4 oz.	340	41.8	0	17.9	n.a.	7066	0
kippered, Atlantic, 4							
oz.	246	27.9	0	14.0	93	1041	0
kippered snacks, Norwegian (King David Brand), 3¹/₄							
oz.	195	20.0	0	12.0	n.a.	n.a.	n.a.
Hickory nuts:							
dried, shelled, 4 oz.	745	14.4	20.7	73.0	0	1	3.7
Hollandaise sauce, mix:							
(Durkee), 1-oz. pkg.	173	9.0	11.0	14.0	n.a.	548	n.a.
(French's), 3 tbsp.*	45	1.0	2.0	4.0	n.a.	290	n.a.
Homestyle gravy, mix:							
(Durkee), .7-oz. pkg.	70	.5	11.0	2.0	n.a.	830	n.a.
(French's), ¹/₄ cup*	20	1.0	4.0	1.0	n.a.	250	n.a.
(Pillsbury/French's), ¹/₄ cup*	15	<1.0	3.0	0	n.a.	300	n.a.
Hominy, see "Corn grits"							
Honey, strained or extracted:							
4 oz.	345	.3	93.3	0	0	6	n.a.
(Sioux), 1 tbsp. . . .	60	0	16.0	0	0	1	n.a.

* Prepared according to package directions, with water

Food and Measure	cal.	prot. (gms)	carbo. (gms)	fat (gms)	chol. (mgs)	sod. (mgs)	fiber (gms)
Honey butter:							
(Downey's), 1/2 tbsp.	50	<1.0	11.0	1.0	n.a.	5	n.a.
Honey loaf, 1 slice, except as noted:							
(Eckrich Calorie Watcher) 1 oz. . .	40	4.0	3.0	2.0	n.a.	350	n.a.
(Eckrich Smorgas Pac, 12 oz.)	30	3.0	2.0	1.0	n.a.	280	n.a.
(Eckrich Smorgas Pac, 1 lb.), 1 oz.	35	4.0	3.0	1.0	n.a.	370	n.a.
(Hormel Perma-Fresh), 2 slices	90	0	1.0	5.0	n.a.	584	n.a.
(Oscar Mayer), 1 oz.	35	5.1	1.0	1.2	12	364	n.a.
Honey roll sausage:							
beef, 1 oz.	52	5.3	.6	3.0	14	375	0
Honeydew melon, fresh:							
1 wedge or 1/10 melon, 7″×2″	46	.6	11.8	.1	0	13	.8
cubed, 1 cup	60	.8	15.6	.2	0	17	1.0
Horseradish:							
fresh, leafy tips:							
raw, whole, 1 lb.	181	26.4	23.3	3.9	0	26	4.2
raw, chopped, 1 cup	13	2.0	1.7	.3	0	2	.3
boiled, drained, chopped, 1 cup	25	2.2	4.7	.4	0	4	.7
fresh, pods:							
raw, whole, 1 lb.	88	5.0	20.1	.5	0	99	3.1
raw, sliced, 1 cup	37	2.1	8.5	.2	0	42	1.3
boiled, drained, sliced, 1 cup . .	42	2.5	9.7	.2	0	51	2.2
prepared:							
1 oz.	11	.4	2.7	.1	0	27	.3
(Kraft), 1 tbsp. . .	4	0	1.0	0	0	50	n.a.
cream style *(Kraft),* 1 tbsp.	8	0	2.0	0	0	150	n.a.
Horseradish sauce:							
(Sauceworks), 1 tbsp.	50	0	2.0	5.0	5	110	n.a.

Food and Measure	cal.	prot. (gms)	carbo. (gms)	fat (gms)	chol. (mgs)	sod. (mgs)	fiber (gms)
Hot dogs, see "Frankfurters and weiners"							
Hot sauce, see "Pepper sauce" and specific listings							
Hull peas, purple, frozen:							
(Frosty Acres), 3.3 oz.	130	9.0	23.0	0	0	6	n.a.
(Southland), 3.3 oz.	130	9.0	22.0	1.0	0	5	n.a.
Hushpuppy:							
frozen (SeaPak), 4 oz.	350	6.0	53.0	13.0	n.a.	750	n.a.
Hummus, mix:							
(Casbah), 1 oz. . . .	110	5.0	10.0	5.0	0	n.a.	n.a.
Hyacinth beans:							
raw, trimmed, 1 cup	37	1.7	7.4	.2	0	2	1.0

Food and Measure	cal.	prot. (gms)	carbo. (gms)	fat (gms)	chol. (mgs)	sod. (mgs)	fiber (gms)
Ice:							
lemon or orange *(Häagen-Dazs)*, 4 fl. oz.	140	<1.0	33.2	0	0	n.a.	n.a.
Ice bars, all flavors:							
(Good Humor Ice Stripes)*, 1 pop . .	40	0	10.0	0	0	0	n.a.
(Eskimo Twin Pops), 3 fl. oz.	70	<1.0	17.0	<1.0	0	0	0
(Eskimo Twin Pops), 2.5 fl. oz.	60	<1.0	14.0	<1.0	0	0	0
(Eskimo Twin Pops), 1.75 fl. oz.	40	<1.0	10.0	<1.0	0	0	0
(Fla-Vor-Ice), 1.5 oz.	30	0	7.4	0	0	n.a.	0
(Fla-Vor-Ice Giant), 3 oz.	59	0	14.8	0	0	n.a.	0
(Fla-Vor-Ice Gigantic), 6 oz.	118	0	29.6	0	0	n.a.	0
(Pop-Ice), 1 oz. . . .	20	0	4.9	0	0	n.a.	0
Ice cream, 1/2 cup, except as noted:							
butter almond *(Flav-O-Rich)*	150	3.0	16.0	8.0	27	60	.1
butter pecan:							
(Flav-O-Rich) . . .	150	3.0	16.0	9.0	27	65	.6
(Good Humor) . .	150	3.0	14.0	9.0	n.a.	n.a.	n.a.
(Häagen-Dazs) . .	316	6.0	20.0	17.2	n.a.	n.a.	n.a.
(Lady Borden) . .	180	3.0	16.0	12.0	n.a.	n.a.	n.a.
carob *(Häagen-Dazs)*	256	6.0	20.0	17.2	n.a.	n.a.	n.a.
cherry, black *(Good Humor)*	130	2.0	14.0	8.0	n.a.	n.a.	n.a.

Food and Measure	cal.	prot. (gms)	carbo. (gms)	fat (gms)	chol. (mgs)	sod. (mgs)	fiber (gms)
cherry vanilla (Flav-O-Rich)	140	2.0	18.0	6.0	25	40	<.1
chocolate:							
(Breyers)	160	3.0	19.0	8.0	n.a.	35	n.a.
(Flav-O-Rich) . . .	150	3.0	18.0	7.0	29	45	0
(Good Humor) . .	130	2.0	15.0	7.0	n.a.	n.a.	n.a.
(Häagen-Dazs) . .	280	6.0	25.2	17.2	n.a.	n.a.	n.a.
(Lady Borden) . .	160	2.0	16.0	10.0	n.a.	n.a.	n.a.
(Oreo Cookies'n Cream), 3 fl. oz.	140	2.0	16.0	8.0	n.a.	100	n.a.
Dutch (Borden) . .	130	2.0	16.0	6.0	n.a.	n.a.	n.a.
Dutch, almond (Borden All Natural)	160	3.0	18.0	9.0	n.a.	n.a.	n.a.
Swiss, almond (Häagen-Dazs)	292	7.2	25.2	20.0	n.a.	n.a.	n.a.
chocolate chip:							
(Flav-O-Rich) . . .	140	3.0	17.0	7.0	27	45	<.1
(Good Humor) . .	150	2.0	15.0	8.0	n.a.	n.a.	n.a.
(Häagen-Dazs) . .	312	7.2	25.2	18.0	n.a.	n.a.	n.a.
coconut (Flav-O-Rich)	150	3.0	18.0	7.0	26	45	.1
coffee:							
(Flav-O-Rich) . . .	130	3.0	16.0	7.0	28	45	.1
(Häagen-Dazs) . .	272	6.0	24.0	17.2	n.a.	n.a.	n.a.
Columbian (Flav-O-Rich Rich & Creamy)	150	3.0	15.0	8.0	34	55	0
cookies 'N cream (Flav-O-Rich) . . .	160	3.0	20.0	8.0	25	80	<.1
cookies & cream (Häagen-Dazs) . .	272	5.2	24.0	17.2	n.a.	n.a.	n.a.
fudge:							
ripple (Flav-O-Rich)	140	3.0	19.0	6.0	25	55	0
royal (Good Humor)	120	2.0	14.0	6.0	n.a.	n.a.	n.a.
heavenly hash (Flav-O-Rich)	160	3.0	19.0	8.0	26	45	.3
honey (Häagen-Dazs)	256	5.2	18.0	18.0	n.a.	n.a.	n.a.
macadamia nut (Häagen-Dazs) . .	260	4.0	20.0	19.2	n.a.	n.a.	n.a.

Food and Measure	cal.	prot. (gms)	carbo. (gms)	fat (gms)	chol. (mgs)	sod. (mgs)	fiber (gms)
Ice cream *(cont.)*							
maple walnut							
(Häagen-Dazs) . .	320	6.0	22.0	23.2	n.a.	n.a.	n.a.
mint *(Oreo* Cookies'n							
Cream), 3 fl. oz.	140	2.0	16.0	8.0	n.a.	100	n.a.
mocha chip *(Häagen-*							
Dazs)	272	5.2	22.0	18.0	n.a.	n.a.	n.a.
moon pie *(Flav-O-*							
Rich)	150	3.0	19.0	7.0	25	60	0
Neopolitan *(Flav-O-*							
Rich)	140	3.0	17.0	7.0	27	45	0
peach:							
(Flav-O-Rich) . . .	130	2.0	17.0	6.0	24	40	0
(Flav-O-Rich Rich &							
Creamy)	140	2.0	18.0	7.0	27	45	0
(Häagen-Dazs) . .	252	5.2	27.2	16.0	n.a.	n.a.	n.a.
pralines & cream:							
(Häagen-Dazs) . .	260	4.0	26.0	16.0	n.a.	n.a.	n.a.
rocky road *(Flav-O-*							
Rich)	160	3.0	19.0	8.0	27	50	<.1
rum raisin *(Häagen-*							
Dazs)	264	4.0	25.2	16.0	n.a.	n.a.	n.a.
spumoni *(Flav-O-Rich)*	140	3.0	17.0	6.0	26	40	0
strawberries 'N cream							
(Flav-O-Rich) . . .	140	2.0	19.0	6.0	20	40	1.0
strawberry:							
(Borden)	120	2.0	17.0	5.0	n.a.	n.a.	n.a.
(Flav-O-Rich) . . .	130	2.0	17.0	6.0	25	40	0
(Good Humor) . .	120	2.0	15.0	6.0	n.a.	n.a.	n.a.
(Häagen-Dazs) . .	268	5.2	25.2	16.0	n.a.	n.a.	n.a.
cheesecake *(Flav-O-Rich* Rich &							
Creamy)	160	3.0	19.0	7.0	31	55	0
toffee fudge twirl							
(Good Humor) . .	130	3.0	18.0	7.0	n.a.	n.a.	n.a.
vanilla:							
(Borden)	130	2.0	15.0	7.0	n.a.	n.a.	n.a.

Food and Measure	cal.	prot. (gms)	carbo. (gms)	fat (gms)	chol. (mgs)	sod. (mgs)	fiber (gms)
(Borden All Natural)	140	3.0	17.0	7.0	n.a.	n.a.	n.a.
(Breyers Natural)	150	3.0	15.0	8.0	n.a.	50	n.a.
(Flav-O-Rich) . . .	140	3.0	16.0	7.0	28	45	0
(Good Humor) . .	140	3.0	14.0	8.0	n.a.	n.a.	n.a.
(Häagen-Dazs) . .	268	5.2	24.0	17.2	n.a.	n.a.	n.a.
(Knudsen's Rich & Natural)	155	2.8	22.0	8.6	n.a.	n.a.	n.a.
(Land O'Lakes) . .	140	2.0	16.0	7.0	30	60	n.a.
(Oreo Cookies'n Cream), 3 fl. oz.	140	2.0	16.0	8.0	n.a.	100	n.a.
chip (Häagen-Dazs)	280	5.2	25.2	17.2	n.a.	n.a.	n.a.
French (Borden All Natural)	150	3.0	16.0	8.0	n.a.	n.a.	n.a.
French (Lady Borden)	170	3.0	20.0	9.0	n.a.	n.a.	n.a.
fudge swirl (Good Humor)	140	3.0	15.0	8.0	n.a.	n.a.	n.a.
old fashioned (Flav-O-Rich Rich & Creamy)	150	3.0	15.0	8.0	34	55	0
slices (Good Humor), 1 slice . .	110	2.0	13.0	6.0	n.a.	45	n.a.
slices (Good Humor Cal-Control), 1 slice	60	2.0	11.0	1.0	n.a.	45	n.a.
Swiss, almond (Häagen-Dazs)	344	7.2	28.0	24.0	n.a.	n.a.	n.a.
Swiss chocolate almond (Flav-O-Rich Rich & Creamy)	170	3.0	16.0	10.0	32	55	0
vanilla-chocolate-strawberry (Good Humor)	130	2.0	14.0	7.0	n.a.	n.a.	n.a.
walnut, black (Flav-O-Rich)	150	3.0	16.0	8.0	27	45	0

Food and Measure	cal.	prot. (gms)	carbo. (gms)	fat (gms)	chol. (mgs)	sod. (mgs)	fiber (gms)
Ice cream, mix*, 1 cup:							
Dutch chocolate *(Salada)*	310	4.0	31.0	19.0	n.a.	75	n.a.
peach, wild strawberry or vanilla *(Salada)*	310	4.0	32.0	19.0	n.a.	60	n.a.
Ice cream, non-dairy, 1/2 cup:							
almond, toasted *(Mocha Mix)* . . .	150	1.0	17.0	9.0	0	80	n.a.
chocolate chip *(Mocha Mix)* . . .	160	1.0	19.0	9.0	0	75	n.a.
Dutch chocolate *(Mocha Mix)* . . .	130	1.0	16.0	8.0	0	75	n.a.
mocha almond fudge *(Mocha Mix)* . . .	150	1.0	20.0	8.0	0	80	n.a.
Neopolitan *(Mocha Mix)*	130	<1.0	16.0	7.0	0	75	n.a.
strawberry swirl *(Mocha Mix)* . . .	140	<1.0	17.0	7.0	0	80	n.a.
vanilla *(Mocha Mix)*	140	<1.0	17.0	7.0	0	80	n.a.
vanilla chocolate almond *(Mocha Mix)*	150	1.0	18.0	9.0	0	95	n.a.
Ice cream bars, 1 bar:							
(Good Humor Fat Frog)*	140	2.0	17.0	7.0	n.a.	45	n.a.
(Good Humor Heart)*	200	3.0	21.0	12.0	n.a.	60	n.a.
(Good Humor Shark)*	70	0	17.0	0	n.a.	0	n.a.
(Nestlé Crunch) . . .	180	2.0	15.0	13.0	n.a.	n.a.	n.a.
(Oreo Cookies'n Cream)*	220	3.0	19.0	15.0	n.a.	100	n.a.
almond, toasted *(Good Humor)* . .	190	1.0	28.0	8.0	n.a.	30	n.a.
assorted *(Good Humor Whammy)* . .	90	1.0	9.0	6.0	n.a.	25	n.a.

* *Prepared according to package directions*

Food and Measure	cal.	prot. (gms)	carbo. (gms)	fat (gms)	chol. (mgs)	sod. (mgs)	fiber (gms)
caramel, toasted (Good Humor) ..	170	2.0	21.0	9.0	n.a.	55	n.a.
chip crunch (Good Humor)	200	2.0	16.0	14.0	n.a.	35	n.a.
chocolate: (Eskimo Pie), 3 fl. oz.	170	2.0	16.0	12.0	n.a.	100	n.a.
(Eskimo Pie Jr.), 1 3/4 oz.	100	2.0	10.0	7.0	n.a.	60	n.a.
chocolate, double: (Eskimo Old Fashioned)	280	4.0	25.0	20.0	n.a.	150	n.a.
(Eskimo Pie Original)	140	2.0	12.0	10.0	n.a.	75	n.a.
chocolate eclair (Good Humor)	180	2.0	24.0	9.0	n.a.	70	n.a.
chocolate fudge cake (Good Humor) ..	260	3.0	25.0	16.0	n.a.	95	n.a.
chocolate malt (Good Humor)	190	2.0	16.0	13.0	n.a.	50	n.a.
crispy (Eskimo Old Fashioned)	290	3.0	24.0	21.0	n.a.	70	n.a.
crunch: (Eskimo Pie), 3 fl. oz.	170	2.0	15.0	12.0	n.a.	55	n.a.
(Eskimo Pie Jr.), 1 3/4 oz.	100	1.0	9.0	8.0	n.a.	30	n.a.
(Eskimo Dietary), 2.5 fl. oz.	110	2.0	10.0	7.0	n.a.	40	n.a.
mint (Eskimo Thin Mints)	130	1.0	10.0	10.0	n.a.	30	n.a.
peanut butter caramel nut (Carnation Heaven)	230	3.0	24.0	13.0	n.a.	55	n.a.
vanilla: (Eskimo Old Fashioned)	280	3.0	23.0	21.0	n.a.	70	n.a.
(Eskimo Pie), 3 fl. oz.	170	2.0	14.0	12.0	n.a.	45	n.a.

Food and Measure	cal.	prot. (gms)	carbo. (gms)	fat (gms)	chol. (mgs)	sod. (mgs)	fiber (gms)
Ice cream bars, vanilla *(cont.)*							
(Eskimo Pie Jr.), 1¾ oz.	100	1.0	9.0	8.0	n.a.	25	n.a.
(Eskimo Pie Original)	140	1.0	11.0	10.0	n.a.	35	n.a.
(GoodHumor) . . .	170	2.0	16.0	11.0	n.a.	40	n.a.
vanilla caramel nut *(Carnation Heaven)*	220	3.0	23.0	13.0	n.a.	50	n.a.
vanilla fudge nut *(Carnation Heaven)* . .	230	2.0	23.0	14.0	n.a.	55	n.a.
Ice cream cones and cups, plain:							
cones, sugar *(Comet)*, 1 cone	40	1.0	9.0	0	0	35	n.a.
cups *(Comet)*, 1 cup	20	0	4.0	0	0	5	n.a.
cups, chocolate flavor *(Comet)*, 1 cup . .	25	0	5.0	0	0	5	n.a.
Ice cream nuggets, chocolate coated:							
chocolate *(Bon Bons)*, 5 nuggets	172	1.5	15.3	12.1	n.a.	53	n.a.
vanilla *(Bon Bons)*, 5 nuggets	167	1.4	13.8	12.0	n.a.	38	n.a.
Ice cream sandwich, 1 sandwich:							
(Oreo Cookies'n Cream)	240	4.0	31.0	11.0	n.a.	300	n.a.
cookie, all flavors:							
(Good Humor), 2.7 oz.	290	4.0	42.0	11.0	n.a.	195	n.a.
(Good Humor), 4 oz.	400	5.0	59.0	16.0	n.a.	270	n.a.
vanilla *(Good Humor)*	170	3.0	28.0	5.0	n.a.	120	n.a.
Ice milk, ½ cup:							
chocolate *(Borden* All Natural)	110	3.0	17.0	3.0	n.a.	n.a.	n.a.
strawberry *(Borden* All Natural)	110	2.0	18.0	3.0	n.a.	n.a.	n.a.
vanilla:							
(Borden All Natural)	100	3.0	16.0	3.0	n.a.	n.a.	n.a.

Food and Measure	cal.	prot. (gms)	carbo. (gms)	fat (gms)	chol. (mgs)	sod. (mgs)	fiber (gms)
(Knudsen's Nice'N Light)	100	2.0	16.0	2.0	n.a.	65	n.a.
(Land O'Lakes) . .	90	3.0	14.0	3.0	10	50	n.a.
Icing, see "Frosting, cake"							
Inconnu (Sheefish):							
raw:							
whole, 1 lb.	417	56.9	0	19.4	n.a.	n.a.	0
meat only, 4 oz.	166	22.6	0	7.7	n.a.	n.a.	0
Italian style dinner:							
frozen (Banquet International Favorites),							
12 oz.	597	21.0	71.0	26.0	n.a.	1783	n.a.

J

Food and Measure	cal.	prot. (gms)	carbo. (gms)	fat (gms)	chol. (mgs)	sod. (mgs)	fiber (gms)
Jack-in-the-Box:							
breakfast, 1 serving:							
bacon, 2 slices . .	70	3.0	0	6.0	10	226	0
breakfast Jack . .	307	18.0	30.0	13.0	203	871	n.a.
Canadian crescent	452	18.6	24.6	31.0	226	851	n.a.
eggs, scrambled,							
breakfast	720	26.0	55.0	44.0	260	1110	n.a.
pancake breakfast	630	16.0	79.0	27.0	85	1670	n.a.
sausage crescent	584	22.0	28.0	43.0	187	1012	n.a.
supreme crescent	547	20.0	27.0	40.0	178	1053	n.a.
sandwiches, salads and dinners, 1 serving:							
bacon cheeseburger							
supreme	724	34.0	44.0	46.0	70	1307	n.a.
cheeseburger . . .	323	16.0	32.0	15.0	42	749	n.a.
chicken strips dinner	689	40.0	65.0	30.0	100	1213	n.a.
chicken supreme	601	31.0	39.0	36.0	60	1582	n.a.
club pita	284	22.0	30.0	8.0	43	953	n.a.
ham and Swiss burger	638	35.6	37.3	38.5	117	1330	n.a.
hamburger	276	13.0	30.0	12.0	29	521	n.a.
jumbo Jack	485	26.0	38.0	26.0	64	905	n.a.
jumbo Jack with cheese	630	32.0	45.0	35.0	110	1665	n.a.
Moby Jack	444	16.0	39.0	25.0	47	820	n.a.
mushroom burger	477	27.7	30.4	27.2	87	906	n.a.
pasta seafood salad	394	15.0	32.0	22.0	48	1570	n.a.
shrimp salad . . .	116	15.0	10.0	1.0	139	460	n.a.

Food and Measure	cal.	prot. (gms)	carbo. (gms)	fat (gms)	chol. (mgs)	sod. (mgs)	fiber (gms)
sirloin steak dinner	699	38.0	75.0	27.0	75	969	n.a.
Swiss and bacon burger	643	33.0	31.0	43.0	99	1354	n.a.
taco, regular . . .	191	8.0	16.0	11.0	21	406	n.a.
taco, super	288	12.0	21.0	17.0	37	765	n.a.
taco salad	377	31.0	10.0	24.0	102	1436	n.a.
nachos and side dishes, 1 serving:							
French fries, regular	221	2.0	27.0	12.0	8	164	n.a.
nachos, cheese	571	15.0	49.0	35.0	37	1154	n.a.
nachos, supreme	718	23.0	66.0	40.0	55	1782	n.a.
onion rings	382	5.0	39.0	23.0	27	407	n.a.
dressings, 1 serving:							
bleu cheese . . .	210	0	11.0	18.0	0	735	n.a.
buttermilk house dressing	290	0	6.0	29.0	0	555	n.a.
1000 dressing . .	250	0	9.0	24.0	0	560	n.a.
desserts and shakes, 1 serving:							
apple turnover . .	410	4.0	45.0	24.0	15	350	n.a.
shake, chocolate	330	11.0	55.0	7.0	25	270	n.a.
shake, strawberry	320	10.0	55.0	7.0	25	240	n.a.
shake, vanilla . . .	320	10.0	57.0	6.0	25	230	n.a.
Jack fruit:							
fresh, peeled and seeded, 4 oz. . . .	107	1.7	27.2	.3	0	3	1.1
Jalapeño pepper, see "Pepper, jalapeño"							
Jalapeño dip:							
(Fritos), 3 1/8 oz. . . .	100	5.0	13.0	4.0	5	640	n.a.
(Kraft), 2 tbsp. . . .	50	1.0	3.0	4.0	0	160	n.a.
(Kraft Premium), 1 oz.	60	1.0	2.0	5.0	15	150	n.a.
(Nalley), 1 oz.	108	.3	.9	11.6	16	286	n.a.
Jams and preserves:							
all flavors:							
(Knotts), 2 tsp. . .	35	0	9.0	0	0	<10	n.a.
(Welch's), 2 tsp.	35	0	9.0	0	0	5	n.a.

Food and Measure	cal.	prot. (gms)	carbo. (gms)	fat (gms)	chol. (mgs)	sod. (mgs)	fiber (gms)
Jams and preserves *(cont.)*							
jams:							
all flavors *(Smucker's)*, 2 tsp. . . .	35	0	9.0	0	0	0	n.a.
all flavors, imitation *(Smucker's Slenderella)*, 2 tsp.	16	0	4.0	0	0	0	n.a.
plum, red *(Bama)*, 2 tsp.	30	0	8.0	0	0	5	n.a.
preserves, all flavors *(Smucker's* Single Service), 1/2-oz. packet	38	0	9.0	0	0	0	n.a.
spread, low sugar, all flavors *(Smucker's)*, 2 tsp.	16	0	4.0	0	0	0	n.a.
strawberry, imitation *(Smucker's)*, 2 tsp.	16	0	4.0	0	0	0	n.a.
Java plum, fresh:							
3 average	5	.1	1.4	<.1	0	1	<.1
1 cup	82	1.0	21.0	.3	0	18	.4
Jellies:							
all flavors:							
(Knotts), 2 tsp. . .	35	0	9.0	0	0	<10	n.a.
(Smucker's), 2 tsp.	35	0	9.0	0	0	0	n.a.
(Smucker's Single Service), 1/2 oz. packet	38	0	9.0	0	0	0	n.a.
(Welch's), 2 tsp.	35	0	9.0	0	0	5	n.a.
all flavors, imitation *(Smucker's)*, 2 tsp.	16	0	4.0	0	0	0	n.a.
apple, mint flavored *(Bama)*, 2 tsp. . .	30	0	8.0	0	0	n.a.	n.a.
grape *(Bama)*, 2 tsp.	30	0	8.0	0	0	5	n.a.
grape, imitation *(Smucker's)*, 2 tsp.	4	0	1.0	0	0	0	n.a.
spread, low sugar, all flavors *(Smucker's)*, 2 tsp.	16	0	4.0	0	0	0	n.a.

Food and Measure	cal.	prot. (gms)	carbo. (gms)	fat (gms)	chol. (mgs)	sod. (mgs)	fiber (gms)
Jerky, meat, see "Sausage sticks"							
Jerusalem artichoke, fresh:							
whole, with skin, 1 lb.	238	6.3	54.6	<.1	0	n.a.	2.5
pared, sliced, 1 cup	114	3.0	26.2	<.1	0	n.a.	1.2
Jujube (Chinese date):							
fresh:							
whole, 1 lb.	331	5.1	85.3	.8	0	11	5.9
without seeds, 4 oz.	90	1.4	22.9	.2	0	3	1.6
dried:							
whole, with seeds, 1 lb.	1157	14.9	297.1	4.4	0	34	12.1
seeded, 4 oz. . . .	326	4.2	83.5	1.2	0	10	3.4

K

Food and Measure	cal.	prot. (gms)	carbo. (gms)	fat (gms)	chol. (mgs)	sod. (mgs)	fiber (gms)
Kale:							
fresh:							
raw, whole, with							
stems, 1 lb. . .	137	9.1	27.7	1.9	0	119	4.2
raw, trimmed, 4 oz.	57	3.7	11.4	.8	0	49	1.7
boiled, drained,							
chopped, 1 cup	41	2.5	7.3	.5	0	30	1.0
frozen:							
chopped (Frosty							
Acres), 3.3 oz.	25	3.0	5.0	0	0	15	1.0
chopped (South-							
land), 3.3 oz. . .	25	3.0	5.0	0	0	15	n.a.
Kale, Scotch, fresh:							
raw:							
whole, 1 lb.	115	7.8	23.0	1.7	0	194	3.4
chopped, 1 cup	28	1.9	5.6	.4	0	47	.8
boiled, drained,							
chopped, 1 cup	37	2.5	7.3	.5	0	59	1.1
Kasha:							
medium or whole							
(Wolff's), 1/3 oz. dry							
or 3/4 cup cooked	145	3.0	30.0	0	0	n.a.	n.a.
Kentucky Fried							
Chicken:							
chicken, original rec-							
ipe:							
breast, center, 3.8							
oz.	257	25.5	8.0	13.7	93	532	n.a.
breast, side, 3.4 oz.	276	20.0	10.1	17.3	96	654	n.a.
drumstick, 2.1 oz.	147	13.6	3.4	8.8	81	269	n.a.

Food and Measure	cal.	prot. (gms)	carbo. (gms)	fat (gms)	chol. (mgs)	sod. (mgs)	fiber (gms)
thigh, 3.4 oz. . . .	278	18.0	8.4	19.2	122	517	n.a.
wing, 2 oz.	181	11.8	5.8	12.3	67	387	n.a.
chicken, extra crispy:							
breast, center, 4.2							
oz.	353	26.9	14.4	20.9	93	842	n.a.
breast, side, 3.5 oz.	354	17.7	17.3	23.7	66	797	n.a.
drumstick, 2.1 oz.	173	12.7	5.9	10.9	65	346	n.a.
thigh, 3.9 oz. . . .	371	19.6	13.8	26.3	121	766	n.a.
wing, 2 oz.	218	11.5	7.8	15.6	63	437	n.a.
chicken, Kentucky							
nuggets,							
.6-oz. piece	46	2.8	2.2	2.9	12	140	n.a.
chicken gravy, 2.8 oz.	59	2.0	4.4	3.7	2	398	n.a.
Kentucky nuggets							
sauces:							
barbecue, 1 oz.	35	.3	7.1	.6	<1	450	n.a.
honey, .5 oz. . . .	49	0	12.1	tr.	<1	<15	n.a.
mustard, 1 oz. . .	36	.9	6.0	.9	<1	346	n.a.
sweet and sour, 1							
oz.	58	.1	13.0	.6	<1	148	n.a.
side dishes, 1 serving:							
baked beans, 3.1							
oz.	105	5.1	18.4	1.2	<1	387	n.a.
buttermilk biscuit,							
2.6 oz. piece . .	269	5.1	31.6	13.6	<1	521	n.a.
cole slaw, 2.8 oz.	103	1.3	11.5	5.7	4	171	n.a.
corn-on-the-cob, 5							
oz.	176	5.1	31.9	3.1	<1	<21	n.a.
Kentucky fries, 4.2							
oz.	268	4.8	33.3	12.8	<2	81	n.a.
mashed potatoes,							
2.8 oz.	59	1.9	11.6	.6	<1	228	n.a.
mashed potatoes							
with gravy, 3 oz.	62	2.1	10.3	1.4	<1	297	n.a.
potato salad, 3.2 oz.	141	1.8	12.6	9.3	11	396	n.a.
Kidneys, fresh:							
beef:							
raw, 8 oz.	242	37.5	4.9	6.9	644	406	0
simmered, 4 oz.	163	28.9	1.1	3.9	439	152	0

Food and Measure	cal.	prot. (gms)	carbo. (gms)	fat (gms)	chol. (mgs)	sod. (mgs)	fiber (gms)
Kidneys *(cont.)*							
calf, raw, 8 oz. . . .	256	37.6	.2	10.4	n.a.	n.a.	0
hog, raw, 8 oz. . . .	240	37.0	2.5	8.2	n.a.	261	0
lamb, raw, 8 oz. . .	238	38.1	2.0	7.5	n.a.	454	0
Kielbasa:							
(Hormel Kolbase), 3 oz.	220	12.0	1.0	19.0	n.a.	904	n.a.
(Hormel Polish Sausage), 2 sausages	170	9.0	0	14.0	n.a.	574	n.a.
beef *(Hillshire Farms),* 3½ oz.	334	13.0	3.0	30.0	29	989	n.a.
endless *(Hillshire Farms),* 3½ oz.	336	13.0	3.6	30.0	23	903	n.a.
skinless *(Hormel* Kielbasa), ½ link	180	12.0	1.0	14.0	n.a.	826	n.a.
Kingfish, fresh:							
raw, whole, 1 lb. . .	210	36.5	0	6.0	n.a.	166	0
raw, meat only, 4 oz.	119	20.8	0	3.4	n.a.	94	0
Kiwifruit, fresh:							
whole, with skin, 1 lb.	237	3.9	58.1	1.7	0	18	4.3
1 large	55	.9	13.5	.4	0	4	1.0
1 medium	46	.8	11.3	.3	0	4	.8
Knockwurst:							
1 lb.	1397	53.9	8.0	125.9	263	4581	0
(Ballpark), 1 link . .	349	13.0	0	33.0	n.a.	1090	n.a.
(Hillshire Farms), 1 oz.	93	3.4	1.1	8.3	12	276	n.a.
beef *(Ballpark),* 1 link	335	13.4	0	31.2	n.a.	1090	n.a.
Kohlrabi, fresh:							
raw:							
whole, without leaves, 1 lb. . .	57	3.6	12.9	.2	0	42	2.1
pared, 4 oz. . . .	31	1.9	7.0	.1	0	23	1.1
pared, sliced, 1 cup	38	2.4	8.7	.1	0	28	1.4
boiled:							
drained, 4 oz. . .	33	2.0	7.6	.1	0	24	1.2
drained, sliced, 1 cup	48	3.0	11.0	.2	0	34	1.8

Food and Measure	cal.	prot. (gms)	carbo. (gms)	fat (gms)	chol. (mgs)	sod. (mgs)	fiber (gms)
Kumquat, fresh:							
whole, with seeds, 1 lb.	266	3.8	69.3	.4	0	25	15.6
trimmed, with seeds, 4 oz.	71	1.0	18.6	.1	0	7	4.2
1 average	12	.2	3.1	<.1	0	1	.7

L

Food and Measure	cal.	prot. (gms)	carbo. (gms)	fat (gms)	chol. (mgs)	sod. (mgs)	fiber (gms)
Lake herring (Cisco):							
fresh, raw,							
meat only, 4 oz. . .	111	21.5	0	2.2	n.a.	62	0
smoked, 4 oz. . . .	201	18.6	0	13.5	36	545	0
Lake trout, raw:							
drawn, 1 lb.	282	30.7	0	16.8	n.a.	n.a.	0
meat only, 4 oz. . .	191	20.8	0	11.3	n.a.	n.a.	0
Lake trout, siscowet, raw:							
under 6.5 lb., whole, 1 lb.	404	24.0	0	33.4	n.a.	n.a.	0
under 6.5 lb., meat only, 4 oz.	273	16.2	0	25.6	n.a.	n.a.	0
over 6.5 lb., whole, 1 lb.	856	12.9	0	88.8	n.a.	n.a.	0
over 6.5 lb., meat only, 4 oz.	594	9.0	0	61.7	n.a.	n.a.	0
Lamb, choice grade, retail trim, meat only:							
leg, roasted, boneless:							
lean with fat, 4 oz.	316	28.7	0	21.4	n.a.	79	0
lean (fat trimmed), 4 oz.	211	32.5	0	7.9	n.a.	79	0
loin chops, broiled with bone:							
lean with fat, 4 oz.	407	24.9	0	33.3	n.a.	79	0
lean (fat trimmed), 4 oz.	213	32.0	0	8.5	n.a.	79	0

Food and Measure	cal.	prot. (gms)	carbo. (gms)	fat (gms)	chol. (mgs)	sod. (mgs)	fiber (gms)
rib chops, broiled with bone:							
lean with fat, 4 oz.	462	22.8	0	40.4	n.a.	79	0
lean (fat trimmed), 4 oz.	239	30.8	0	11.9	n.a.	79	0
shoulder, roasted, boneless:							
lean with fat, 4 oz.	383	24.6	0	30.8	n.a.	79	0
lean (fat trimmed), 4 oz.	232	30.4	0	11.3	n.a.	79	0
Lamb's-quarters:							
raw, trimmed, 1 lb.	195	19.1	33.1	3.6	0	n.a.	9.5
boiled:							
drained, 4 oz.	36	3.6	5.7	.8	0	n.a.	2.0
drained, chopped, 1 cup	58	5.8	9.0	1.3	0	n.a.	3.2
Landjaeger:							
(*Usinger's*), 3-oz. link	310	18.0	n.a.	26.0	n.a.	n.a.	n.a.
Lard:							
8 oz.	2046	0	0	226.8	215	<.1	0
1 cup	1849	0	0	205.0	195	<.1	0
1 tbsp.	116	0	0	12.8	12	0	0
Lasagna, canned:							
(*Hormel* Short Order), 7½ oz.	260	8.0	25.0	14.0	n.a.	1083	n.a.
(*Nalley*), 3½ oz.	100	4.0	11.0	5.0	5	430	n.a.
Lasagna dinner, frozen:							
(*Dinner Classics*), 10 oz.	380	18.0	39.0	17.0	75	1120	n.a.
(*Swanson*), 13 oz.	410	12.0	55.0	16.0	n.a.	800	n.a.
(*Swanson Hungry-Man*), 18¾ oz.	730	25.0	99.0	26.0	n.a.	1510	n.a.
tuna (*Lean Cuisine*), 9¾ oz.	260	18.0	30.0	8.0	25	990	n.a.
vegetable (*Le Menu*), 11 oz.	360	14.0	32.0	20.0	n.a.	1010	n.a.
zucchini (*Lean Cuisine*), 11 oz.	260	21.0	28.0	7.0	20	975	n.a.

Food and Measure	cal.	prot. (gms)	carbo. (gms)	fat (gms)	chol. (mgs)	sod. (mgs)	fiber (gms)
Lasagna entree, frozen:							
(Banquet Family Entrees), 8 oz. . . .	372	21.0	42.0	13.0	n.a.	1190	n.a.
(Freezer Queen, 2 lb.), 8 oz.	290	12.0	41.0	9.0	n.a.	n.a.	n.a.
(Stouffer's), 10 1/2 oz.	370	28.0	34.0	13.0	n.a.	1030	n.a.
(Swanson Main Course), 13 1/4 oz.	450	23.0	50.0	18.0	n.a.	1120	n.a.
beef and mushroom *(Van de Kamp's Italian Classic)*, 11 oz.	430	25.0	30.0	25.0	n.a.	970	n.a.
three cheese *(The Budget Gourmet)*, 1 serving	400	22.0	38.0	17.0	n.a.	760	n.a.
cheese vegetable *(Dining Lite)*, 11 oz.	284	19.3	37.6	7.1	n.a.	720	1.9
Florentine *(Light & Elegant)*, 11 1/4 oz.	280	24.0	34.0	5.0	n.a.	975	n.a.
Italian sausage *(Van de Kamp's Italian Classic)*, 11 oz. . .	440	25.0	35.0	25.0	n.a.	1190	n.a.
with meat sauce *(The Budget Gourmet)*, 10 oz.	290	18.0	32.0	10.0	n.a.	890	n.a.
vegetable *(Stouffer's)*, 10 1/2 oz.	450	26.0	29.0	25.0	n.a.	910	n.a.
zucchini *(Dining Lite)*, 11 oz.	278	22.3	32.6	7.0	n.a.	780	1.3
Leeks:							
fresh:							
raw, 3 average leeks	228	5.6	52.7	1.1	0	75	5.6
raw, trimmed, chopped, 1 cup	64	1.6	14.7	.3	0	20	1.6
boiled, drained, 1 average leek . .	38	1.0	9.5	.3	0	13	1.0
boiled, drained, chopped, 1 cup	32	.8	7.9	.2	0	12	.8

Food and Measure	cal.	prot. (gms)	carbo. (gms)	fat (gms)	chol. (mgs)	sod. (mgs)	fiber (gms)
freeze-dried, 1 tbsp.	1	<.1	.6	<.1	0	0	.1
Lemon, fresh:							
whole, 1 large, 2³/₈″							
diam.	29	1.2	8.7	.3	0	2	n.a.
peeled:							
1 large, 2³/₈″ diam.	25	.9	7.8	.3	0	2	.3
1 medium, 2¹/₈″							
diam.	17	.6	5.4	.2	0	1	.2
1 wedge, ¼ medium	5	.3	2.9	.1	0	1	n.a.
Lemon butter seasoning:							
mix, for fish (Durkee Roastin' Bag), .9-oz.							
pkg.	75	.1	17.0	.7	n.a.	1347	n.a.
Lemon extract:							
(Virginia Dare), 1 tsp.	22	0	0	0	0	0	0
Lemon juice:							
fresh:							
1 cup	60	.9	21.1	0	0	2	n.a.
1 tbsp.	4	.1	1.3	0	0	0	n.a.
frozen (Minute Maid), 6 fl. oz.	22	<1.0	6.0	<.1	0	17	n.a.
reconstituted:							
(A&P), 2 tbsp. or 1 fl. oz.	6	<1.0	2.0	<1.0	0	0	n.a.
(ReaLemon), 2 tbsp. or 1 fl. oz. . . .	6	0	2.0	0	0	10	n.a.
(Seneca), 2 tbsp. or 1 fl. oz.	6	0	2.0	0	0	10	n.a.
Lemon peel, candied:							
1 oz.	90	.1	22.9	.1	0	n.a.	.7
Lemon pepper:							
(Lawry's), 1 tsp. . .	6	.2	1.2	<.1	0	340	.1
Lemon-lime drink, mix*:							
(Country Time), 8 fl. oz.	90	0	22.0	0	0	30	0

* Prepared according to package directions

Food and Measure	cal.	prot. (gms)	carbo. (gms)	fat (gms)	chol. (mgs)	sod. (mgs)	fiber (gms)
Lemon-lime drink, mix* *(cont.)*							
(Country Time Sugar Free), 8 fl. oz. . .	4	0	0	0	0	0	0
(Crystal Light), 8 fl. oz.	4	0	0	0	0	0	0
(Kool-Aid), 8 fl. oz.	100	0	25.0	0	0	0	tr.
Lemon-limeade:							
frozen* *(Minute Maid),* 6 fl. oz.	77	<1.0	19.0	<.1	0	<1	n.a.
Lemonade:							
canned *(Hi-C),* 6 fl. oz.	74	<1.0	19.0	<.1	0	50	n.a.
chilled, pink or white *(Minute Maid),* 6 fl. oz.	81	<1.0	20.0	<.1	0	15	n.a.
freeze-dried *(Mountain House),* 1 cup . .	80	0	20.0	0	0	n.a.	n.a.
frozen*, pink or white:							
(A&P), 8 fl. oz. . .	110	<1.0	28.0	<1.0	0	0	n.a.
(Minute Maid), 6 fl. oz.	77	<1.0	19.0	<.1	0	<1	n.a.
(Sunkist), 6 fl. oz.	110	0	27.0	0	0	0	n.a.
mix*, 8 fl. oz.:							
(Country Time) . .	90	0	22.0	0	0	30	0
(Crystal Light Crystals)	4	0	0	0	0	0	0
(Kool-Aid), ...	100	0	25.0	0	0	0	tr.
(Minute Maid Crystals)	97	<1.0	24.0	<.1	0	4	n.a.
(Minute Maid Lite Crystals)	9	0	2.7	0	0	4	n.a.
(Sunkist Light Crystals)	8	0	2.0	0	0	35	n.a.
(Wyler's Crystals)	90	0	22.0	0	0	n.a.	n.a.
presweetened *(Kool Aid)*	90	0	22.0	0	0	0	tr.
sugar free *(Country Time)*	4	0	0	0	0	0	0
sugar free *(Funny Face)*	4	0	1.0	0	0	0	0

* *Prepared according to package directions*

Food and Measure	cal.	prot. (gms)	carbo. (gms)	fat (gms)	chol. (mgs)	sod. (mgs)	fiber (gms)
sugar free *(Kool-Aid)*	4	0	0	0	0	0	tr.
sugar sweetened *(Funny Face)* . .	88	0	22.0	0	0	0	0
Lentils:							
whole:							
dry, 1 cup	646	46.9	114.2	2.1	0	68	7.4
cooked, 1 cup . .	212	15.6	88.6	tr.	0	n.a.	2.4
split, without seed							
coat, dry, 8 oz. . .	782	56.0	140.1	2.0	0	n.a.	3.9
dry, cooked *(A&P)*, 1							
cup	210	16.0	39.0	1.0	0	0	n.a.
Lentil pilaf mix:							
with rice *(Casbah)*, 1							
oz.	100	5.0	20.0	0	0	n.a.	n.a.
Lettuce:							
Boston or bibb:							
untrimmed, 1 lb.	45	4.3	7.8	.7	0	18	3.2
5"-diam. head . .	21	2.1	3.8	.4	0	8	1.5
2 inner leaves . .	2	.2	.4	<.1	0	1	<.1
iceberg:							
untrimmed, 1 lb.	55	4.3	9.0	.8	0	39	2.3
trimmed, 6"-diam.							
head	70	5.4	11.3	1.0	0	48	2.9
1 leaf, .7 oz. . . .	3	.2	.4	<.1	0	2	.1
1 wedge, 1/4 of 6"							
head	18	1.4	2.8	.3	0	12	.7
loose leaf:							
untrimmed, 1 lb.	52	3.8	10.2	.9	0	26	2.0
2 average leaves	4	.3	.7	.1	0	2	.1
shredded, 1 cup	10	.7	2.0	.2	0	6	.4
romaine or cos:							
untrimmed, 1 lb.	68	6.9	10.1	.9	0	32	3.0
3 inner leaves . .	6	.5	.7	.1	0	3	.2
shredded, 1 cup	8	1.0	1.4	.2	0	4	.4
Lichee nuts:							
raw:							
shelled, 6 average							
nuts	36	.5	9.5	.2	0	0	.1

Food and Measure	cal.	prot. (gms)	carbo. (gms)	fat (gms)	chol. (mgs)	sod. (mgs)	fiber (gms)
Lichee nuts, raw *(cont.)*							
shelled, 1 cup ..	125	1.6	31.4	.8	0	1	.4
dried, shelled, 4 oz.	314	4.3	80.2	1.4	0	3	1.6
Lime, fresh:							
whole, 1 lb.	115	2.7	40.2	.8	0	8	1.9
pulp only of 2″-diam.							
lime	20	.5	7.1	.1	0	1	.3
Lime juice:							
fresh:							
1 cup	66	1.1	22.2	.3	0	2	n.a.
1 tbsp.	4	.1	1.4	<.1	0	0	n.a.
reconstituted:							
(ReaLime), 2 tbsp.	4	0	1.0	0	0	10	n.a.
(Rose's), 1 fl. oz.	41	0	10.0	0	0	n.a.	n.a.
Limeade:							
frozen* *(Minute Maid)*,							
6 fl. oz.	77	<1.0	19.0	<.1	0	<1	n.a.
Ling cod:							
fresh, raw,							
meat only, 4 oz.	96	20.0	0	1.2	59	67	0
Linguine dinner:							
with clam sauce, fro-							
zen *(Lean Cuisine)*,							
9⅝ oz.	260	16.0	32.0	7.0	40	800	n.a.
Linguine entree, fro-							
zen:							
with pesto sauce							
(Stouffer's), 4⅛ oz.	210	9.0	20.0	10.0	n.a.	250	n.a.
with scallops and							
clams *(The Budget*							
Gourmet), 9.5 oz.	280	16.0	28.0	11.0	n.a.	630	n.a.
with bay shrimp and							
clams marinara							
(The Budget Gour-							
met), 1 serving ..	330	15.0	33.0	15.0	n.a.	1250	n.a.

* *Prepared according to package directions*

Food and Measure	cal.	prot. (gms)	carbo. (gms)	fat (gms)	chol. (mgs)	sod. (mgs)	fiber (gms)
Liquor, pure distilled (bourbon, gin, rye, vodka, rum, tequila, etc.), 1 fl. oz.:							
80 proof	65	0	tr.	0	0	tr.	0
86 proof	70	0	tr.	0	0	tr.	0
90 proof	74	0	tr.	0	0	tr.	0
94 proof	77	0	tr.	0	0	tr.	0
100 proof	83	0	tr.	0	0	tr.	0
Liver:							
beef:							
raw, 1 lb.	647	90.7	26.4	17.4	1606	329	0
fried, 4 oz.	246	30.3	8.9	9.1	547	120	0
calves:							
raw, 1 lb.	635	87.1	18.6	21.3	n.a.	331	0
fried, 4 oz.	296	33.5	4.5	15.0	n.a.	134	0
chicken:							
raw, 1 lb.	566	81.5	15.5	17.5	1990	356	0
simmered, 4 oz.	178	27.6	1.0	6.2	716	58	0
simmered, 1 cup	219	34.1	1.2	7.6	883	71	0
goose, raw, 1 lb. . .	826	74.8	24.5	45.4	n.a.	635	0
hog:							
raw, 1 lb.	607	97.0	11.2	16.6	1367	395	0
braised, 4 oz. . . .	187	29.5	4.3	5.0	403	56	0
lamb:							
raw, 1 lb.	617	95.3	13.2	17.7	n.a.	236	0
broiled, 4 oz. . . .	296	36.6	3.2	14.1	n.a.	96	0
turkey:							
raw, 1 lb.	623	90.8	18.7	18.0	2114	436	0
simmered, 4 oz.	192	27.2	3.9	6.7	710	73	0
simmered, 1 cup	237	33.6	4.8	8.3	876	89	0
Liver cheese:							
pork, 1 oz.	86	4.3	.6	7.3	49	347	n.a.
(Oscar Mayer), 13/8- oz. slice	116	5.8	.7	10.0	75	436	0
Liver loaf:							
(Hormel Perma-Fresh), 2 slices	160	9.0	1.0	13.0	n.a.	704	n.a.

Food and Measure	cal.	prot. (gms)	carbo. (gms)	fat (gms)	chol. (mgs)	sod. (mgs)	fiber (gms)
Liver sausage, see "Braunschweiger"							
Liverwurst:							
fresh, 1 oz.	93	4.0	.6	8.1	5	n.a.	n.a.
pork, 1 oz.	92	4.0	.6	8.1	45	n.a.	n.a.
(Armour Star), 1 oz.	90	n.a.	n.a.	8.0	45	325	n.a.
Liverwurst spread:							
canned *(Hormel),* 1/2 oz.	35	2.0	0	3.0	n.a.	n.a.	n.a.
Lobster, northern:							
raw, in shell, 1½lb.	136	28.2	.8	1.4	143	n.a.	0
boiled, meat only, 4 oz.	111	23.2	1.5	.7	82	431	0
Lobster paste:							
canned, 1 oz.	51	5.9	.4	2.7	n.a.	n.a.	n.a.
Lobster Newburg:							
frozen *(Stouffer's),* 6½ oz.	360	15.0	8.0	30.0	n.a.	840	n.a.
Loganberry:							
fresh, trimmed, 4 oz.	70	1.1	16.9	.7	0	1	3.4
canned:							
in water, with liquid, 8 oz.	91	1.6	21.3	.9	0	2	4.5
in heavy syrup, with liquid, 8 oz. . .	202	1.4	50.3	.9	0	2	4.3
Longan:							
fresh, shelled and seeded, 4 oz. . . .	68	1.5	17.2	.1	0	0	.5
dried, shelled and seeded, 4 oz. . . .	324	5.6	83.9	.5	0	54	2.2
Loquat, fresh, without seeds:							
4 oz.	53	.5	13.8	.2	0	1	.6
10 fruits	50	.4	12.0	.2	0	0	.5
Lotus seeds:							
raw, 1 oz.	25	1.2	4.9	.2	0	0	.2
dried:							
1 oz. (47 small or 36 large)	94	4.4	18.3	.6	0	1	.7

Food and Measure	cal.	prot. (gms)	carbo. (gms)	fat (gms)	chol. (mgs)	sod. (mgs)	fiber (gms)
1 cup	106	4.9	20.6	.6	0	1	.8
Luncheon meat (see also specific listings):							
(Oscar Mayer), 1-oz. slice	99	3.5	.6	9.2	16	346	0
(Spam, 7-oz. can), 1¾ oz.	150	7.0	0	14.0	n.a.	756	n.a.
(Spam, 12-oz. can), 2 oz.	170	8.0	0	15.0	n.a.	862	n.a.
with cheese chunks *(Spam)*, 2 oz. . . .	170	8.0	0	16.0	n.a.	811	n.a.
deviled *(Spam)*, 1 tbsp.	35	2.0	0	3.0	n.a.	125	n.a.
smoke flavored *(Spam)*, 2 oz. . . .	170	8.0	0	15.0	n.a.	774	n.a.
spiced:							
(Armour), 1-oz. slice	90	n.a.	n.a.	8.0	20	300	n.a.
(Armour Star), 3 oz.	280	9.0	5.0	25.0	n.a.	n.a.	n.a.
(Hormel), 3 oz. . .	280	11.0	2.0	26.0	n.a.	1110	n.a.
(Hormel Perma-Fresh)*, 2 slices	118	9.0	1.0	9.0	n.a.	702	n.a.
(Light & Lean), 2 slices	120	8.0	1.0	9.0	n.a.	n.a.	n.a.
spiced, with chicken *(Armour Star)*, 3 oz.	280	9.0	7.0	24.0	70	1040	n.a.
spiced, loaf *(Grillmaster)*, 1 slice	83	4.5	.9	6.6	n.a.	404	n.a.
turkey, loaf *(Louis Rich)*, 1-oz. slice	43	4.6	.4	2.6	14	278	n.a.
Luncheon sausage:							
beef and pork, 1 oz.	74	4.4	.5	5.9	18	335	0
Luxury loaf:							
(Oscar Mayer), 1-oz. slice	38	5.2	1.4	1.2	13	302	0

M

Food and Measure	cal.	prot. (gms)	carbo. (gms)	fat (gms)	chol. (mgs)	sod. (mgs)	fiber (gms)
Macadamia nuts:							
dried:							
shelled, 4 oz. . . .	796	9.4	15.6	83.6	0	6	6.0
shelled, 1 cup . .	940	11.1	18.4	98.8	0	6	7.1
oil roasted, 1 oz. . .	204	2.1	3.7	21.7	0	2	.5
Macaroni, plain:							
dry:							
8-oz. pkg.	837	28.4	170.6	2.7	0	5	.7
(Mueller's), 2 oz.	210	7.0	43.0	1.0	0	0	n.a.
(Ronzoni), 2 oz.	210	7.0	41.0	1.0	0	<5	n.a.
spinach ribbons							
(Creamette), 2 oz.	200	8.0	40.0	1.0	0	n.a.	n.a.
cooked:							
8–10 min., firm							
stage, 1 cup . .	192	6.5	39.1	.7	0	1	.1
14–20 min., tender							
stage, 1 cup . .	155	4.8	32.2	.6	0	1	.1
Macaroni and beef,							
canned:							
(Nalley), 3½ oz. . .	110	4.0	13.0	4.0	10	460	n.a.
in tomato sauce							
(Heinz Mac'n'Beef),							
7¼ oz.	200	8.0	23.0	8.0	n.a.	850	n.a.
Macaroni and beef							
dinner, frozen:							
(Morton), 10 oz. . .	245	8.1	30.4	6.1	n.a.	800	n.a.
(Swanson), 12 oz.	360	11.0	46.0	14.0	n.a.	850	n.a.
Macaroni and beef							
entree:							
frozen, with tomatoes							
(Stouffer's), 11½							
oz.	360	21.0	32.0	16.0	n.a.	1600	n.a.

Food and Measure	cal.	prot. (gms)	carbo. (gms)	fat (gms)	chol. (mgs)	sod. (mgs)	fiber (gms)
Macaroni and cheese, canned:							
(Franco-American), 7³/₈ oz.	170	6.0	24.0	5.0	n.a.	960	n.a.
(Heinz), 7¹/₂ oz. . . .	190	5.0	26.0	8.0	n.a.	1105	n.a.
elbow macaroni *(Franco-American),* 7³/₈ oz.	170	6.0	23.0	6.0	n.a.	910	n.a.
Macaroni and cheese, frozen:							
(Banquet Casserole), 8 oz.	344	11.0	36.0	17.0	n.a.	930	n.a.
(Banquet Family Entree), 8 oz.	336	11.0	37.0	16.0	n.a.	871	n.a.
(Freezer Queen, 2 lb.), 8 oz.	240	8.0	38.0	7.0	n.a.	n.a.	n.a.
(Freezer Queen), 8-oz. pkg.	256	11.0	42.0	6.0	n.a.	n.a.	n.a.
(Light & Elegant), 9 oz.	300	15.0	37.0	9.0	n.a.	1015	n.a.
(Morton Casserole), 20 oz.	648	25.9	91.2	19.9	n.a.	2600	n.a.
(Morton Casserole), 32 oz.	1043	39.7	143.7	34.4	n.a.	3600	n.a.
(Stouffer's), 6 oz. . . .	250	11.0	24.0	12.0	n.a.	750	n.a.
(Swanson Main Course), 12 oz. . . .	380	15.0	45.0	16.0	n.a.	1850	n.a.
pie *(Swanson),* 7 oz.	210	8.0	26.0	9.0	n.a.	880	n.a.
Macaroni and cheese, mix:							
(Creamette), 2 oz.	220	9.0	47.0	2.0	n.a.	n.a.	n.a.
Macaroni and cheese dinner:							
frozen:							
(Morton), 11 oz.	278	7.7	45.8	7.3	n.a.	1000	n.a.
(Swanson), 12¹/₄ oz.	380	13.0	46.0	15.0	n.a.	980	n.a.

Food and Measure	cal.	prot. (gms)	carbo. (gms)	fat (gms)	chol. (mgs)	sod. (mgs)	fiber (gms)
Macaroni and cheese dinner *(cont.)*							
mix*:							
(Kraft), 3/4 cup . .	290	9.0	34.0	13.0	5	630	n.a.
(Kraft Deluxe), 3/4 cup	260	11.0	36.0	8.0	20	650	n.a.
(Kraft Family Size), 3/4 cup	290	9.0	34.0	13.0	5	580	n.a.
shells *(Velveeta)*, 3/4 cup	260	12.0	32.0	10.0	25	860	n.a.
spiral *(Kraft)*, 3/4 cup	330	9.0	36.0	17.0	10	670	n.a.
Macaroni-cheese loaf:							
(Eckrich), 1 slice . .	70	3.0	3.0	6.0	n.a.	370	n.a.
(Grillmaster), 1 slice	85	4.2	2.4	6.5	n.a.	482	n.a.
Macaroni salad:							
canned *(Joan of Arc)*, 1/2 cup	200	3.0	19.0	13.0	n.a.	850	n.a.
dairy pack *(Knudsen)*, 1/2 cup	180	4.0	22.0	9.0	n.a.	n.a.	n.a.
Mace:							
ground (all brands), 1 tsp.	8	.1	.9	.6	0	1	.1
Mackerel:							
Atlantic:							
raw, fillets, 4 oz.	232	21.1	0	15.8	79	102	0
broiled, fillets, 4 oz.	297	27.0	0	20.2	85	94	0
canned, with liquid, 8 oz.	415	43.8	0	25.2	n.a.	n.a.	0
jack, canned, drained, 4 oz.	177	26.3	0	7.1	90	430	0
Pacific and jack, raw, meat only, 4 oz.	178	22.8	0	8.9	53	98	0
salted, fillets, 4 oz.	346	21.0	0	26.5	n.a.	n.a.	0
smoked, meat only, 4 oz.	248	27.0	0	14.7	n.a.	n.a.	0

* *Prepared according to package directions*

Food and Measure	cal.	prot. (gms)	carbo. (gms)	fat (gms)	chol. (mgs)	sod. (mgs)	fiber (gms)
Spanish, meat only:							
raw, 4 oz.	158	21.9	0	7.1	86	67	0
broiled, 4 oz. . . .	179	26.8	0	7.2	83	75	0
Mai Tai drink mixer:							
(Holland House), 1							
pouch	4	0	14.0	0	0	n.a.	n.a.
bottled *(Holland*							
House), 1 fl. oz.	29	0	7.0	0	0	11	n.a.
Malt:							
dry, 1 oz.	104	3.7	21.9	.5	0	n.a.	1.6
Malt extract:							
dry, 1 oz.	104	1.7	25.3	tr.	0	23	tr.
Malt liquor, see "Beer, ale and malt liquor"							
Mango, fresh:							
whole, 1 mango, 10.6 oz.	135	1.1	35.2	.6	0	4	1.7
sliced, 1 cup	108	.9	28.1	.5	0	3	1.4
Manhattan drink mixer, bottled:							
(Holland House), 1 fl. oz.	27	0	6.0	0	0	5	n.a.
Maple syrup:							
4 oz.	286	0	73.7	0	0	1	n.a.
maple flavored *(S&W)*, 1 tsp.	4	0	1.0	0	0	25	n.a.
Margarine, 1 tbsp., except as noted:							
(A&P Corn Oil soft bowl)	100	<1.0	<1.0	11.0	0	105	0
(A&P Premium) . . .	100	<1.0	<1.0	11.0	0	110	0
(Ann Page Quarters)	100	<1.0	<1.0	11.0	0	110	0
(Blue Bonnet Light Tasty Spread) . .	60	0	0	7.0	0	100	0
(Blue Bonnet 52% Fat Spread)	80	0	0	8.0	0	110	0
(Blue Bonnet 70% Fat Spread)	90	0	0	10.0	0	95	0

Food and Measure	cal.	prot. (gms)	carbo. (gms)	fat (gms)	chol. (mgs)	sod. (mgs)	fiber (gms)
Margarine *(cont.)*							
(Blue Bonnet 75% Fat Spread)	90	0	0	11.0	0	95	0
(Diet Blue Bonnet)	50	0	0	6.0	0	100	0
(Diet Fleischmann's)	50	0	0	6.0	0	100	0
(Diet Fleischmann's Lite Salt)	50	0	0	6.0	0	50	0
(Miracle Brand) . . .	60	0	0	7.0	0	75	0
(Mother's Spread, 100% corn oil, un-salted)	70	0	0	9.0	0	<10	0
(Mrs. Filbert's Family, quarters)	80	0	0	8.0	0	100	0
(Mrs. Filbert's Family, soft)	70	0	0	7.0	0	85	0
(Mrs. Filbert's 72% Golden Spread)	90	0	0	10.0	0	90	0
(Mrs. Filbert's Spread 25)	80	0	0	8.0	0	105	0
(P&Q Spread, 60% vegetable)	80	<1.0	<1.0	8.0	0	105	0
(Parkay Light Corn Oil Spread)	70	0	0	8.0	0	110	0
(Parkay Light Spread)	60	0	0	7.0	0	110	0
regular, hard or stick, salted:							
1 stick, 4 oz. or 1/2 cup	815	1.0	1.0	91.3	0	1070	0
(Blue Bonnet) . .	100	0	0	11.0	0	95	0
(Blue Bonnet Butter Blend)	90	0	0	11.0	5	95	0
(Country Morning Blend)	100	0	0	11.0	10	115	0
(Diet Mazola) . . .	50	0	0	6.0	0	130	0
(Fleischmann's)	100	0	0	11.0	0	95	0
(I Can't Believe It's Not Butter) . . .	90	0	0	10.0	0	95	0
(Land O'Lakes) . .	100	0	0	11.0	0	115	0

Food and Measure	cal.	prot. (gms)	carbo. (gms)	fat (gms)	chol. (mgs)	sod. (mgs)	fiber (gms)
(Land O'Lakes Premium)*	100	0	0	11.0	0	115	0
(Mazola)	100	0	0	11.0	0	115	0
(Mother's)	100	0	0	11.0	0	n.a.	0
(Mrs. Filbert's Golden or Corn Oil)*	100	0	0	11.0	0	110	0
(Mrs. Filbert's Reduced Calorie)*	50	0	0	6.0	0	120	0
(Nucoa)	100	0	0	11.0	0	160	0
(Parkay regular or soft)*	100	0	0	11.0	0	115	0
regular, hard or stick, unsalted:							
1 stick, 4 oz. or 1/2 cup	810	.6	.5	91.1	0	2	0
(Blue Bonnet Butter Blend)*	90	0	0	11.0	5	0	0
(Country Morning Blend)*	100	0	0	11.0	10	1	0
(Fleischmann's)	100	0	0	11.0	0	0	0
(Mazola)	100	0	0	11.0	0	1	0
(Mother's)	100	0	0	11.0	0	1	0
soft tub, salted:							
8-oz. container ..	1625	1.8	1.1	182.3	0	2446	0
(Blue Bonnet) ..	100	0	0	11.0	0	95	0
(Blue Bonnet Butter Blend)*	90	0	0	11.0	5	95	0
(Country Morning Blend)*	90	0	0	10.0	10	85	0
(Diet Parkay) ...	50	0	0	6.0	0	110	0
(Fleischmann's)	100	0	0	11.0	0	95	0
(I Can't Believe It's Not Butter)* ...	90	0	0	10.0	0	90	0
(Land O'Lakes) ..	100	0	0	11.0	0	115	0
(Mother's)	100	0	0	11.0	0	n.a.	0
(Mrs. Filbert's Golden or Corn Oil)*	100	0	0	11.0	0	110	0

Food and Measure	cal.	prot. (gms)	carbo. (gms)	fat (gms)	chol. (mgs)	sod. (mgs)	fiber (gms)
Margarine, soft tub, salted *(cont.)*							
(Nucoa)	90	0	0	10.0	0	150	0
whipped *(Blue Bonnet)*	70	0	0	7.0	0	70	0
soft tub, unsalted:							
8-oz. container . .	1625	1.8	2.0	182.1	0	62	0
(Country Morning Blend)	90	0	0	10.0	10	1	0
(Fleischmann's)	100	0	0	11.0	0	0	0
(Mother's)	100	0	0	11.0	0	1	0
whipped:							
(Fleischmann's)	70	0	0	7.0	0	60	0
(Fleischmann's Un-salted)	70	0	0	7.0	0	0	0
(Parkay Regular or Soft)	60	0	0	7.0	0	75	0
spread *(Blue Bonnet 60% Fat)* . .	50	0	0	6.0	0	55	0
corn oil spread:							
(Fleischmann's Light)	80	0	0	8.0	0	70	0
(Mrs. Filbert's Family Spread) . . .	70	0	0	7.0	0	95	0
liquid, bottled:							
1 tsp.	34	.1	0	3.8	0	37	0
(Fleischmann's Squeeze)	100	0	0	11.0	0	85	0
(Squeeze Parkay)	100	0	0	11.0	0	100	0
Margarine, imitation:							
1 cup	801	1.2	.9	90.1	0	2226	0
1 tsp.	17	0	0	1.9	0	46	0
Margarita drink mixer:							
(Freeze & Serve), 1 oz.	21	0	5.0	0	0	10	n.a.
(Holland House), 1 pouch	4	0	14.0	0	0	n.a.	n.a.
strawberry *(Holland House)*, 1 pouch	4	0	14.0	0	0	n.a.	n.a.

Food and Measure	cal.	prot. (gms)	carbo. (gms)	fat (gms)	chol. (mgs)	sod. (mgs)	fiber (gms)
Marjoram:							
dried (all brands), 1 tsp.	2	.1	.4	<.1	0	tr.	.1
Marmalade:							
all flavors (Welch's), 2 tsp.	35	0	9.0	0	0	5	n.a.
orange (Smucker's), 2 tsp.	35	0	9.0	0	0	0	n.a.
Mayonnaise, 1 tbsp.:							
(Bama)	100	0	0	11.0	n.a.	70	n.a.
(Best Foods/ Hellmann's)	100	0	0	11.0	5	80	n.a.
(Cains)	100	0	0	11.0	10	80	n.a.
(Kraft)	100	0	0	11.0	5	70	n.a.
(Kraft Light)	45	0	1.0	5.0	5	90	n.a.
(Laura Scudder's)	104	.2	.2	11.5	n.a.	146	0
(Mother's)	100	0	0	11.0	10	n.a.	n.a.
(Mrs. Filbert's)	100	0	0	11.0	10	70	0
(Nalley)	107	.2	.3	11.9	11	100	n.a.
(Rokeach)	100	0	0	11.0	10	70	n.a.
imitation (Mrs. Filbert's)	40	0	1.0	4.0	0	110	0
Mayonnaise substitute:							
(Featherweight Soyamaise), 1 tbsp.	60	0	0	11.0	0	3	n.a.
McDonald's:							
breakfast, 1 serving:							
biscuit, plain, 3 oz.	330	4.9	36.6	18.2	9	786	n.a.
biscuit, with bacon, egg, cheese, 5.2 oz.	483	16.5	33.2	31.6	262	1269	n.a.
biscuit, with sausage, 4.3 oz.	467	12.1	35.3	30.9	48	1147	n.a.
biscuit, with sausage and egg, 6.25 oz.	585	19.8	36.4	39.9	285	1301	n.a.
(Egg McMuffin, 4.9 oz.	340	18.5	31.0	15.8	259	885	n.a.

Food and Measure	cal.	prot. (gms)	carbo. (gms)	fat (gms)	chol. (mgs)	sod. (mgs)	fiber (gms)
McDonald's, breakfast *(cont.)*							
eggs, scrambled, 3.5 oz.	180	13.2	2.5	13.0	514	205	n.a.
English muffin with butter, 2.25 oz.	186	5.0	29.5	5.3	15	310	n.a.
hash brown potatoes, 2 oz. . . .	125	1.5	14.0	7.0	7	325	n.a.
hotcakes with butter, syrup, 7.6 oz.	500	7.9	93.9	10.3	47	1070	n.a.
sausage, 2 oz. . .	210	9.8	.6	18.6	39	423	n.a.
Sausage McMuffin, 4.1 oz.	427	17.6	30.0	26.3	59	942	n.a.
Sausage McMuffin with egg, 5.8 oz.	517	22.9	32.2	32.9	287	1044	n.a.
sandwiches and chicken, 1 serving:							
Big Mac, 7.1 oz.	570	24.6	39.2	35.0	83	979	n.a.
cheeseburger, 4 oz.	318	15.0	28.5	16.0	41	743	n.a.
Chicken McNuggets, 3.8 oz. . .	323	19.1	13.7	21.3	73	512	n.a.
Filet-O-Fish, 5.1 oz.	435	14.7	35.9	25.7	45	799	n.a.
hamburger, 3.5 oz.	263	12.4	28.3	11.3	29	506	n.a.
Quarter Pounder, 5.7 oz.	427	24.6	29.3	23.5	81	718	n.a.
Quarter Pounder with cheese, 6.6 oz.	525	29.6	30.5	31.6	107	1220	n.a.
Chicken McNuggets sauces:							
barbecue, 1.1 oz.	60	.4	13.7	.4	<1	309	n.a.
honey, .5 oz. . . .	50	<.1	12.4	<.1	<1	.2	n.a.
hot mustard, 1.1 oz.	63	.6	10.5	2.1	3	259	n.a.
sweet & sour, 1.1 oz.	64	.2	15.0	.3	<1	186	n.a.
French fries, regular, 2.4 oz.	220	3.0	26.1	11.5	9	109	n.a.
desserts and shakes, 1 serving:							
apple pie, 3 oz.	253	1.9	29.3	14.3	12	398	n.a.

Food and Measure	cal.	prot. (gms)	carbo. (gms)	fat (gms)	chol. (mgs)	sod. (mgs)	fiber (gms)
cherry pie, 3.1 oz.	260	2.0	32.1	13.6	13	427	n.a.
cones, 4 oz.	185	4.3	30.2	5.2	23	109	n.a.
cookies, chocolate chip, 2.4 oz. . .	342	4.2	44.8	16.3	18	313	n.a.
cookies, *McDonaldland*, 2.4 oz. . .	308	4.2	48.7	10.8	10	358	n.a.
milk shake, chocolate, 10.3 oz. . .	383	9.9	65.5	9.0	30	300	n.a.
milk shake, strawberry, 10.3 oz.	362	9.0	62.1	8.7	32	207	n.a.
milk shake, vanilla, 10.3 oz.	352	9.3	59.6	8.4	31	201	n.a.
sundae, caramel, 5.8 oz.	361	7.2	60.8	10.0	31	145	n.a.
sundae, hot fudge, 5.8 oz.	357	7.0	58.0	10.8	27	170	n.a.
sundae, strawberry, 5.8 oz.	320	6.0	54.0	8.7	25	90	n.a.
Meat, see specific listings							
Meat, potted:							
canned *(Hormel* Food Product), 1 tbsp.	30	2.0	0	2.0	n.a.	145	n.a.
Meat-fish-poultry sauce, see "Steak sauce"							
Meat loaf luncheon meat:							
4 oz.	227	18.0	3.7	15.0	n.a.	n.a.	0
Meat loaf mix*:							
with ground beef *(Bell's),* 4½ oz.	300	18.0	14.0	20.0	n.a.	700	n.a.
Meat loaf dinner, frozen:							
(Banquet American Favorites), 11 oz.	437	20.0	30.0	27.0	n.a.	1525	n.a.
(Morton), 11 oz. . .	371	14.5	39.3	17.3	n.a.	1300	n.a.

* *Prepared according to package directions*

Food and Measure	cal.	prot. (gms)	carbo. (gms)	fat (gms)	chol. (mgs)	sod. (mgs)	fiber (gms)
Meat loaf dinner *(cont.)*							
(Swanson), 11 oz.	500	19.0	48.0	26.0	n.a.	970	n.a.
Meat loaf entree, frozen:							
(Banquet Cookin' Bag), 5 oz.	251	14.0	10.0	17.0	n.a.	894	n.a.
with tomato sauce *(Swanson)*, 9 oz.	310	16.0	28.0	15.0	n.a.	950	n.a.
tomato sauce and *(Freezer Queen, 2 lb.)*, 10.67 oz. . .	270	19.0	24.0	11.0	n.a.	n.a.	n.a.
Meat loaf gravy mix:							
(Durkee Roastin' Bag), 1.5-oz. pkg.	129	21.0	18.0	1.0	n.a.	3472	n.a.
Meat loaf sauce:							
canned *(Hunt's Meatloaf Fixins)*, 2 oz.	25	1.0	5.0	0	0	580	n.a.
Meat marinade:							
mix *(Durkee)*, 1-oz. pkg.	47	.9	9.0	.7	0	4104	n.a.
Meat seasoning:							
(Lawry's Natural Choice for Meat), 1 tsp.	6	.4	1.2	.2	0	3	.2
Meatball dinner, frozen:							
stew *(Lean Cuisine)*, 10 oz.	270	21.0	21.0	11.0	65	1120	n.a.
Swedish *(Dinner Classics)*, 11 1/2 oz. . .	470	23.0	32.0	28.0	125	1560	n.a.
Meatball entree, frozen:							
with brown gravy *(Swanson)*, 8 1/2 oz.	290	14.0	19.0	18.0	n.a.	900	n.a.
Italian *(The Budget Gourmet)*, 1 serving	310	20.0	29.0	12.0	n.a.	1120	n.a.
Swedish *(The Budget Gourmet)*, 1 serving	600	23.0	40.0	39.0	n.a.	1085	n.a.

Food and Measure	cal.	prot. (gms)	carbo. (gms)	fat (gms)	chol. (mgs)	sod. (mgs)	fiber (gms)
Swedish, in gravy (Stouffer's), 11 oz.	470	25.0	36.0	25.0	n.a.	1460	n.a.
tomato sauce and (Freezer Queen Cook-in-Pouch), 5 oz.	192	10.0	8.0	10.0	n.a.	n.a.	n.a.
Meatball seasoning mix:							
Italian (Durkee), 1-oz. pkg.	22	4.0	9.0	.7	0	1755	n.a.
Meatball stew, canned:							
(Dinty Moore), 8 oz.	240	13.0	15.0	15.0	n.a.	n.a.	n.a.
(Nalley), 3½ oz. . . .	120	5.0	8.0	7.0	20	485	n.a.
Melon balls:							
(cantaloupe and honeydew), frozen, unthawed, 1 cup . .	55	1.5	13.7	.4	0	53	n.a.
Mettwurst:							
(Hillshire Farms), 1-oz. slice	97	3.7	1.1	8.6	7	272	n.a.
Mexican dinner, frozen:							
(Banquet Extra Helpings), 21¼ oz. . .	777	31.0	105.0	27.0	n.a.	4778	n.a.
(Banquet International Favorites), 12 oz.	483	18.0	62.0	18.0	n.a.	1995	n.a.
(Patio), 12¼ oz. . .	510	16.0	60.0	23.0	n.a.	n.a.	n.a.
(Patio Fiesta), 12¾ oz.	510	17.0	68.0	19.0	n.a.	n.a.	n.a.
(Swanson Hungry-Man), 22 oz. . . .	920	28.0	99.0	46.0	n.a.	2430	n.a.
(Van de Kamp's Mexican Holiday), 11½ oz.	420	20.0	45.0	20.0	n.a.	1040	n.a.
combination:							
(Banquet International Favorites), 12 oz.	518	20.0	72.0	17.0	n.a.	1978	n.a.

Food and Measure	cal.	prot. (gms)	carbo. (gms)	fat (gms)	chol. (mgs)	sod. (mgs)	fiber (gms)
Mexican dinner, combination (cont.)							
(Patio), 11¼ oz.	590	19.0	66.0	28.0	n.a.	n.a.	n.a.
(Swanson), 16 oz.	580	20.0	67.0	26.0	n.a.	1780	n.a.
Milk, fluid, 8 fl. oz.:							
buttermilk:							
sweet cream . . .	464	41.2	58.8	6.9	83	621	0
sweet cream, 1							
tbsp.	25	2.2	3.2	.4	5	34	0
(A&P Cultured)	90	8.0	12.0	1.0	n.a.	260	0
(Borden)	90	8.0	11.0	1.0	n.a.	n.a.	0
(Crowley)	110	9.0	12.0	4.0	n.a.	390	0
(Flav-O-Rich) . . .	90	9.0	12.0	1.0	6	290	0
(Flav-O-Rich 3.25%)	150	8.0	12.0	8.0	35	280	0
(Flav-O-Rich 3.5%)	160	8.0	12.0	9.0	38	280	0
(Knudsen)	120	8.0	11.0	4.0	n.a.	140	0
(Land O'Lakes) . .	100	8.0	12.0	2.0	10	255	0
powder, reconsti-							
tuted (Swiss Miss)	80	5.0	15.0	1.0	n.a.	190	0
salted	99	8.1	11.7	2.2	9	257	0
unsalted	99	8.1	11.7	2.2	9	123	0
condensed, sweet-							
ened:							
1 cup	982	24.2	166.5	26.6	104	389	0
1 fl. oz.	123	3.0	20.8	3.3	13	49	0
(Eagle), ⅓ cup . .	320	7.0	52.0	9.0	n.a.	120	0
filled (Magnolia							
Dairy Blend), ⅓							
cup	320	7.0	54.0	9.0	n.a.	120	0
dry, lowfat, reconsti-							
tuted (Flash) . . .	80	8.0	12.0	<1.0	5	125	0
dry, nonfat, reconsti-							
tuted:							
(Alba)	80	8.0	12.0	0	n.a.	190	0
(Carnation)	80	8.0	12.0	.2	n.a.	125	0
(Mountain House)	90	8.0	11.0	0	n.a.	n.a.	0
evaporated, canned:							
(Carnation), 1 fl. oz.	42	2.0	3.1	2.4	n.a.	33	0
(Pet), ½ cup . . .	170	8.0	12.0	10.0	n.a.	140	0

Food and Measure	cal.	prot. (gms)	carbo. (gms)	fat (gms)	chol. (mgs)	sod. (mgs)	fiber (gms)
lowfat *(Carnation)*, 1							
fl. oz.	27	2.3	3.0	.8	n.a.	35	0
skim, 1 cup	198	19.3	28.9	.5	10	294	0
skim, 1 fl. oz. . . .	25	2.4	3.6	.1	1	37	0
skim *(Carnation)*, 1							
fl. oz.	25	2.3	3.5	.1	n.a.	35	0
whole, 1 cup . . .	338	17.2	25.3	19.1	74	266	0
whole, 1 fl. oz. . .	42	2.1	3.2	2.4	9	33	0
filled, 1 cup	154	8.1	11.6	8.4	4	138	0
lowfat:							
(Flav-O-Rich Sweet							
Acidophilus)* . .	100	8.0	11.0	2.0	13	130	0
(Knudsen)	140	10.0	13.0	5.0	n.a.	150	0
(Knudsen Sweet							
Acidophilus)* . . .	140	10.0	13.0	5.0	n.a.	150	0
.5% *(Flav-O-Rich)*	90	8.0	11.0	1.0	9	130	0
1%	102	8.0	11.7	2.6	10	123	0
1% with nonfat milk							
solids	104	8.5	12.2	2.4	10	128	0
1% protein fortified	119	9.7	13.6	2.9	10	143	0
1% *(A&P)*	100	8.0	12.0	3.0	n.a.	120	0
1% *(Crowley)* . . .	100	8.0	11.0	2.0	n.a.	130	0
1% *(Flav-O-Rich)*	100	8.0	11.0	2.0	13	130	0
1% *(Land O'Lakes)*	100	8.0	12.0	3.0	10	125	0
2%	121	8.1	11.7	4.7	18	122	0
2% with nonfat milk							
solids	125	8.5	12.2	4.7	18	128	0
2% protein fortified	137	9.7	13.5	4.9	19	145	0
2% *(A&P)*	120	8.0	12.0	5.0	n.a.	120	0
2% *(Borden Hi-Pro-*							
tein)*	140	10.0	13.0	5.0	n.a.	n.a.	0
2% *(Crowley Tone)*	120	8.0	11.0	5.0	n.a.	125	0
2% *(Flav-O-Rich)*	120	8.0	11.0	5.0	23	130	0
2% *(Land O'Lakes)*	120	8.0	11.0	5.0	20	120	0
nonfat:							
(Knudsen)	90	9.0	12.0	0	n.a.	130	n.a.
(Skim-line)	100	10.0	13.0	1.0	n.a.	n.a.	0
skim:							
regular	86	8.4	11.9	.4	4	126	0

Food and Measure	cal.	prot. (gms)	carbo. (gms)	fat (gms)	chol. (mgs)	sod. (mgs)	fiber (gms)
Milk, fluid, skim *(cont.)*							
with nonfat milk							
solids	90	8.8	12.3	.6	5	130	0
protein fortified . .	100	9.7	13.7	.6	5	144	0
(A&P)	90	8.0	12.0	<1.0	n.a.	125	0
(Borden)	90	9.0	12.0	0	n.a.	n.a.	0
(Crowley)	90	9.0	12.0	0	n.a.	130	0
(Flav-O-Rich) . . .	90	9.0	12.0	1.0	4	130	0
(Flav-O-Rich Weight							
Watchers) . . .	90	9.0	12.0	0	4	135	0
(Land O'Lakes) . .	90	8.0	12.0	<1.0	5	125	0
whole:							
(A&P)	150	8.0	11.0	8.0	n.a.	120	0
(Borden)	150	8.0	11.0	8.0	n.a.	n.a.	0
(Crowley)	150	8.0	11.0	8.0	n.a.	125	0
(Flav-O-Rich) . . .	150	8.0	11.0	8.0	35	125	0
(Knudsen)	160	8.0	12.0	8.0	n.a.	130	0
(Knudsen Gold Star)	170	8.0	12.0	10.0	n.a.	125	0
(Land O'Lakes) . .	150	8.0	11.0	8.0	35	120	0
3.3% fat	150	8.0	11.4	8.2	33	120	0
3.5% fat *(Flav-O-*							
Rich)	160	8.0	11.0	9.0	37	125	0
low sodium	149	7.6	10.9	8.4	33	6	0
producer, 3.7% fat	157	8.0	11.4	8.9	35	119	0
Milk, fluid, goat's:							
whole, 1 cup	168	8.7	10.9	10.1	28	122	0
Milk, fluid, Indian							
buffalo:							
1 cup	236	9.2	12.6	16.8	46	127	0
Milk, fluid, sheep:							
1 cup	264	14.7	13.1	17.2	n.a.	108	0
Milk, dry:							
buttermilk:							
sweet cream, 1 cup	464	41.2	58.8	6.9	83	621	0
sweet cream, 1							
tbsp.	25	2.2	3.2	.4	5	34	0
nonfat:							
regular, 1 cup . .	435	43.4	62.4	.9	24	642	0
instant, 1 envelope,							
3.2 oz.	326	31.9	47.5	.7	17	499	0

Food and Measure	cal.	prot. (gms)	carbo. (gms)	fat (gms)	chol. (mgs)	sod. (mgs)	fiber (gms)
instant (Alba Dairy Light), 1 envelope	10	1.0	1.0	0	n.a.	15	0
(Carnation), 4 oz.	406	39.7	59.0	.8	n.a.	623	0
instant (Sanalac), ¼ envelope . .	80	8.0	12.0	<1.0	n.a.	125	0
whole, regular, 1 cup	635	33.7	49.2	34.2	124	475	0
Milk, imitation:							
1 cup	150	4.3	15.0	8.3	tr.	191	0
Milk, chocolate, dairy, 8 fl. oz.:							
(Crowley)	220	7.0	30.0	7.0	n.a.	260	n.a.
(Flav-O-Rich/Farm Best)	210	8.0	26.0	8.0	36	220	.7
(Flav-O-Rich/Farm Best 3.5%)	220	8.0	26.0	9.0	38	220	.7
(Land O'Lakes) . . .	210	8.0	26.0	8.0	30	150	n.a.
Dutch (Borden) . . .	210	8.0	26.0	8.0	n.a.	n.a.	n.a.
lowfat:							
(Borden Dutch Brand)	160	8.0	26.0	3.0	n.a.	n.a.	n.a.
(Crowley 1% fat)	180	7.0	32.0	3.0	n.a.	270	n.a.
(Flav-O-Rich/Farm Best 1%)	170	8.0	29.0	3.0	13	220	.7
(Flav-O-Rich/Farm Best 2%)	190	8.0	29.0	5.0	23	220	.7
(Hershey's 2%)	190	8.0	29.0	5.0	n.a.	130	n.a.
(Knudsen)	200	10.0	31.0	4.0	n.a.	370	n.a.
(Land O'Lakes) . .	160	8.0	26.0	3.0	5	150	n.a.
1%	158	8.1	26.1	2.5	7	152	.2
2%	179	8.0	26.0	5.0	17	150	.2
nonfat (Knudsen) . .	160	9.0	31.0	0	n.a.	240	n.a.
skim (Land O'Lakes)	140	8.0	26.0	<1.0	5	155	n.a.
whole	208	7.9	25.9	8.5	30	149	.2
Milk beverages, flavored, 10 fl. oz., except as noted:							
canned:							
banana (Carnation Slender)	220	11.0	34.0	4.0	n.a.	430	n.a.

Food and Measure	cal.	prot. (gms)	carbo. (gms)	fat (gms)	chol. (mgs)	sod. (mgs)	fiber (gms)
Milk beverages, flavored, canned *(cont.)*							
banana *(Sego* Very Banana)	225	11.0	34.0	5.0	n.a.	360	n.a.
chocolate *(Borden Frosted),* 8 fl. oz.	260	5.0	36.0	11.0	n.a.	205	n.a.
chocolate *(Carnation Slender)* . .	220	11.0	34.0	4.0	n.a.	515	n.a.
chocolate *(Sego* Lite)	150	11.0	20.0	3.0	n.a.	475	n.a.
chocolate *(Sego* Very/*Sego* Dutch)	225	11.0	39.0	3.0	n.a.	445	n.a.
chocolate double *(Sego* Lite) . . .	150	11.0	21.0	2.0	n.a.	475	n.a.
chocolate fudge *(Carnation Slender)*	220	11.0	34.0	4.0	n.a.	550	n.a.
chocolate jamoca almond *(Sego* Lite)	150	11.0	20.0	3.0	n.a.	475	n.a.
chocolate malt *(Carnation Slender)*	220	11.0	34.0	4.0	n.a.	530	n.a.
chocolate malt *(Sego* Lite) . . .	150	11.0	20.0	3.0	n.a.	475	n.a.
chocolate malt *(Sego* Very Chocolate Malt) . . .	225	11.0	39.0	3.0	n.a.	445	n.a.
chocolate milk *(Carnation Slender)*	220	11.0	34.0	4.0	n.a.	520	n.a.
peach *(Carnation Slender)*	220	11.0	34.0	4.0	n.a.	430	n.a.
strawberry *(Borden Frosted),* 8 fl. oz.	270	8.0	36.0	10.0	n.a.	190	n.a.
strawberry *(Carnation Slender)* . .	220	11.0	34.0	4.0	n.a.	430	n.a.
strawberry *(Sego* Lite)	150	11.0	17.0	4.0	n.a.	390	n.a.
strawberry *(Sego* Very Strawberry)	225	11.0	34.0	5.0	n.a.	360	n.a.

Food and Measure	cal.	prot. (gms)	carbo. (gms)	fat (gms)	chol. (mgs)	sod. (mgs)	fiber (gms)
vanilla (Carnation Slender)	220	11.0	34.0	4.0	n.a.	550	n.a.
vanilla (Sego Lite/ Lite French) . .	150	11.0	17.0	4.0	n.a.	390	n.a.
vanilla (Sego Very Vanilla)	225	11.0	34.0	5.0	n.a.	360	n.a.
Milk beverages, mix, dry:							
chocolate (see also Cocoa):							
powder, 3 heaping tsp.	83	1.4	17.8	.9	1	49	.1
(Alba Fit 'N Frosty), .8 oz.	76	6.2	12.1	.4	n.a.	206	n.a.
(Carnation Instant Breakfast), 1.3-oz. pkg.	130	7.0	23.0	1.0	n.a.	135	n.a.
(Hershey's Instant), 3 tbsp.	80	1.0	17.0	1.0	0	35	n.a.
(Nestlé Quik), 2 tsp. or .75 oz.	90	1.0	19.0	1.0	0	35	n.a.
(Nestlé Quik Sugar Free), 1 tbsp.	18	1.0	3.0	<1.0	0	40	n.a.
chocolate or Dutch chocolate (Carnation Slender), 1.1- oz. pkg.	110	5.0	21.0	1.0	n.a.	110	n.a.
chocolate malt (Carnation Instant Breakfast), 1.2-oz. pkg.	130	7.0	22.0	1.0	n.a.	160	n.a.
chocolate marshmallow (Alba Fit 'N Frosty), .8 oz. . .	76	5.7	12.4	.3	n.a.	251	n.a.
coffee (Carnation Instant Breakfast), 1.3-oz. pkg.	130	7.0	24.0	n.a.	n.a.	130	n.a.

Food and Measure	cal.	prot. (gms)	carbo. (gms)	fat (gms)	chol. (mgs)	sod. (mgs)	fiber (gms)
Milk beverages, mix *(cont.)*							
eggnog *(Carnation* Instant Breakfast), 1.2-oz. pkg.	130	7.0	23.0	n.a.	n.a.	185	n.a.
strawberry:							
(Alba Fit 'N Frosty), .8 oz.	73	5.7	11.4	.4	n.a.	154	n.a.
(Carnation Instant Breakfast), 1.3-oz. pkg.	130	7.0	24.0	n.a.	n.a.	195	n.a.
vanilla:							
(Alba Fit 'N Frosty), .8 oz.	73	5.6	12.1	.5	n.a.	152	n.a.
(Carnation Instant Breakfast), 1.2-oz. pkg.	130	7.0	24.0	n.a.	n.a.	135	n.a.
French *(Carnation Slender),* 1.1-oz. pkg.	110	5.0	22.0	.5	n.a.	110	n.a.
mix*:							
all flavors *(Carnation Slender),* 6 fl. oz.	90	6.0	9.0	3.5	n.a.	90	n.a.
chocolate or malt *(Pillsbury* Instant Breakfast), 8 fl. oz.	290	14.0	38.0	9.0	n.a.	310	n.a.
chocolate *(Swiss Miss* Milk Makers), 8 fl. oz.**	100	9.0	15.0	<1.0	n.a.	230	n.a.
malted *(Swiss Miss* Milk Makers), 8 fl. oz.**	100	9.0	15.0	<1.0	n.a.	220	n.a.
strawberry *(Pillsbury* Instant Breakfast), 8 fl. oz.	290	14.0	39.0	9.0	n.a.	300	n.a.

* *Prepared according to package directions*

** *Prepared according to package directions, with nonfat milk*

Food and Measure	cal.	prot. (gms)	carbo. (gms)	fat (gms)	chol. (mgs)	sod. (mgs)	fiber (gms)
strawberry *(Swiss Miss* Milk Makers), 8 fl. oz.**	100	9.0	16.0	<1.0	n.a.	170	n.a.
vanilla *(Pillsbury* Instant Breakfast), 8 fl. oz.	300	14.0	41.0	9.0	n.a.	330	n.a.
Milk, malted:							
beverage, 1 cup . .	236	10.8	26.6	9.9	37	215	.1
dry powder, 3 heaping tsp. or 3/4 oz. . . .	86	2.7	15.2	1.8	4	96	.1
natural *(Carnation)*, 3 heaping tsp. . . .	90	3.0	15.6	1.7	n.a.	98	n.a.
chocolate *(Carnation)*, 3 heaping tsp. . .	85	1.0	18.0	1.0	n.a.	19	n.a.
Millet:							
whole grain, 4 oz.	371	11.2	82.7	3.3	0	n.a.	3.6
Mincemeat, see "Pie fillings, canned"							
Molasses:							
first extraction (light), 1 tbsp.	50	n.a.	12.9	n.a.	0	3	n.a.
second extraction (medium), 1 tbsp.	46	n.a.	11.9	n.a.	0	7	n.a.
third extraction (blackstrap), 1 tbsp. . .	42	n.a.	10.9	n.a.	0	19	n.a.
Barbados, 1 tbsp.	54	n.a.	13.9	n.a.	0	n.a.	n.a.
green or yellow *(Grandma's)*, 1 tbsp.	60	0	15.0	0	0	10	n.a.
Mortadella:							
beef and pork, 1 oz.	88	4.6	.9	7.2	16	353	0
(Usinger's), 1 oz. . .	85	3.0	n.a.	8.0	n.a.	n.a.	n.a.
Mostaccioli and meat sauce entree, frozen:							
(Banquet Family Entree), 8 oz.	251	11.0	34.0	8.0	n.a.	1421	n.a.

** *Prepared according to package directions, with nonfat milk*

Food and Measure	cal.	prot. (gms)	carbo. (gms)	fat (gms)	chol. (mgs)	sod. (mgs)	fiber (gms)
Mother's loaf:							
pork, 1 oz.	80	3.4	2.1	6.3	13	320	0
Muffins, 1 piece:							
blueberry *(Thomas' Toast-r-Cakes)* . .	100	2.0	16.0	3.0	0	220	.2
bran *(Thomas' Toast-r-Cakes)*	100	2.0	16.0	3.0	0	240	.3
corn *(Thomas' Toast-r-Cakes)*	110	2.0	17.0	4.0	0	240	.1
English:							
(Pepperidge Farm)	140	5.0	26.0	2.0	n.a.	180	n.a.
(Roman Meal) . .	150	6.0	30.0	1.0	0	150	n.a.
(Thomas'), 2 oz.	130	4.4	25.8	1.4	0	210	.3
(Wonder)	130	4.0	26.0	1.0	0	280	.2
cinnamon raisin *(Pepperidge Farm)*	150	5.0	28.0	2.0	n.a.	180	n.a.
honey wheat *(Thomas')*, 2 oz.	129	5.0	24.0	1.1	0	200	.4
raisin *(Thomas')*, 2.1 oz.	153	4.5	30.4	1.5	0	200	.2
sourdough *(Thomas')*, 2 oz.	130	4.4	25.8	1.4	0	208	.3
raisin *(Wonder* Raisin Rounds)	140	4.0	27.0	2.0	0	280	.2
sourdough *(Wonder)*	130	4.0	27.0	1.0	0	250	.2
Muffins, frozen, 1 piece:							
apple spice *(Pepperidge Farm)*	170	3.0	23.0	8.0	n.a.	230	n.a.
cinnamon *(Sara Lee Hearty Fruit)*, 2.5 oz.	220	3.0	36.0	8.0	0	270	n.a.
banana nut *(Sara Lee Hearty Fruit)*, 2.5 oz.	210	3.0	39.0	7.0	0	280	n.a.
blueberry:							
(Pepperidge Farm)	180	2.0	27.0	7.0	n.a.	250	n.a.
(Sara Lee Hearty Fruit), 2.5 oz. . .	200	3.0	34.0	8.0	0	280	n.a.

Food and Measure	cal.	prot. (gms)	carbo. (gms)	fat (gms)	chol. (mgs)	sod. (mgs)	fiber (gms)
bran with raisin (Pepperidge Farm) ..	180	2.0	28.0	7.0	n.a.	300	n.a.
carrot walnut (Pepperidge Farm)	170	6.0	27.0	4.0	n.a.	220	n.a.
chocolate chip (Pepperidge Farm) ..	200	3.0	28.0	8.0	n.a.	170	n.a.
cinnamon swirl (Pepperidge Farm) ..	190	2.0	30.0	6.0	n.a.	170	n.a.
corn (Pepperidge Farm)	180	3.0	27.0	7.0	n.a.	260	n.a.
oatmeal and fruit (Sara Lee Hearty Fruit), 2.5 oz.	220	4.0	35.0	9.0	0	290	n.a.
Muffins, mix:*							
apple cinnamon (Betty Crocker), 1/12 pkg.	120	2.0	19.0	4.0	n.a.	140	n.a.
apple, spicy (Duncan Hines), 1 muffin	120	2.0	20.0	4.0	n.a.	185	n.a.
banana-nut (Betty Crocker), 1/12 pkg.	150	2.0	21.0	6.0	n.a.	200	n.a.
banana nut (Duncan Hines), 1 muffin	130	2.0	20.0	5.0	n.a.	175	n.a.
blueberry, wild:							
(Betty Crocker), 1/12 pkg.	120	2.0	18.0	4.0	n.a.	150	n.a.
(Duncan Hines), 1 muffin	110	2.0	17.0	3.0	n.a.	155	n.a.
bran and honey (Duncan Hines), 1 muffin	120	2.0	18.0	4.0	n.a.	170	n.a.
cherry, tart (Betty Crocker), 1/12 pkg.	120	2.0	18.0	4.0	n.a.	140	n.a.
corn:							
(Betty Crocker), 1/12 pkg.	160	3.0	25.0	5.0	n.a.	310	n.a.
(Dromedary), 1 piece	120	3.0	20.0	4.0	n.a.	270	n.a.

* Prepared according to package directions

Food and Measure	cal.	prot. (gms)	carbo. (gms)	fat (gms)	chol. (mgs)	sod. (mgs)	fiber (gms)
Muffins, mix*, corn *(cont.)*							
(Martha White), 2-oz. muffin	135	2.3	25.5	3.5	n.a.	n.a.	n.a.
Mulberry, fresh:							
1 cup	61	2.0	13.7	.6	0	14	1.3
10 berries	7	.2	1.5	.1	0	2	.1
Mullet, striped:							
raw, meat only, 4 oz.	133	21.9	0	4.3	56	74	0
Mullet, sucker, see "Sucker"							
Mushroom:							
fresh:							
raw, untrimmed, 1 lb.	111	9.2	20.5	1.9	0	16	3.3
raw, pieces, 1 cup	18	1.5	3.3	.3	0	2	.5
canned:							
drained, 1 cup . .	38	2.9	7.7	.5	0	n.a.	n.a.
(B in B), 2 oz. . .	25	2.0	3.0	<1.0	0	530	n.a.
(Libby/Seneca), 1/4 cup	35	4.0	4.0	0	0	240	n.a.
button, pieces and stems *(Green Giant)*, 2 oz. . . .	14	1.0	2.0	0	0	260	n.a.
in butter sauce *(Green Giant)*, 2 oz.	25	2.0	3.0	<1.0	n.a.	530	n.a.
Mushroom, Shiitake, dried:							
1 lb.	1343	43.5	341.8	4.5	0	60	52.2
4 mushrooms, .5 oz.	44	1.4	11.3	.2	0	2	1.7
cooked, pieces, 1 cup	80	2.3	20.7	.3	0	6	2.8
Mushroom gravy:							
canned:							
(Franco-American), 2 oz.	25	0	3.0	1.0	n.a.	320	n.a.
(Heinz Home Style), 2 oz.	21	.4	2.7	.9	n.a.	200	n.a.

* *Prepared according to package directions*

Food and Measure	cal.	prot. (gms)	carbo. (gms)	fat (gms)	chol. (mgs)	sod. (mgs)	fiber (gms)
mix *(Durkee)*, .7-oz. pkg.	60	2.0	11.0	1.0	n.a.	1170	n.a.
mix* *(French's)*, 1/4 cup	20	1.0	3.0	1.0	n.a.	250	n.a.
Mushroom sauce:							
dehydrated, 1-oz. packet	99	4.1	15.5	2.7	0	1766	.3
Mushrooms Dijon in pastry:							
frozen *(Pepperidge Farm)*, 1 piece . .	220	4.0	19.0	15.0	n.a.	340	n.a.
Muskellunge:							
raw, meat only, 4 oz.	124	22.9	0	2.8	n.a.	n.a.	0
Muskrat:							
roasted, 4 oz.	174	30.8	0	4.6	n.a.	n.a.	0
Mussels:							
fresh, blue, meat only:							
raw, 4 oz.	98	13.5	4.2	2.5	32	324	0
raw, 1 cup	129	17.9	5.5	3.4	42	429	0
poached or steamed, 4 oz. . .	195	27.0	8.4	5.1	64	418	0
canned, drained, meat only, 4 oz.	129	20.6	1.7	3.7	n.a.	n.a.	0
Mustard, prepared:							
(Heinz Pourable), 1 tsp.	5	.3	.5	.2	0	71	n.a.
(Kraft), 1 tsp.	4	0	0	0	0	50	n.a.
(Mr. Mustard), 1 tsp.	11	.5	.4	.8	0	90	n.a.
(Nalley), 1 tbsp. . . .	11	.8	.9	.6	0	204	n.a.
brown *(Heinz)*, 1 tsp.	8	.4	.5	.4	0	58	n.a.
Chinese *(Chun King)*, 4.5-oz. jar	116	7.5	6.8	8.0	0	1667	1.7
Dijon:							
(French's), 1 tbsp.	25	1.0	1.0	2.0	0	460	n.a.
(Grey Poupon), 1 tbsp.	18	<1.0	<1.0	1.0	0	445	n.a.
with horseradish *(French's)*, 1 tbsp.	16	1.0	1.0	1.0	0	265	n.a.

* *Prepared according to package directions*

Food and Measure	cal.	prot. (gms)	carbo. (gms)	fat (gms)	chol. (mgs)	sod. (mgs)	fiber (gms)
Mustard *(cont.)*							
horseradish:							
(Kraft), 1 tsp. . . .	4	0	1.0	0	0	45	n.a.
(Nalley), 1 tbsp.	14	.9	1.1	.9	0	203	n.a.
medford *(French's),* 1 tbsp.	16	1.0	1.0	1.0	0	240	n.a.
mild *(Heinz),* 1 tsp.	5	.3	.5	.2	0	71	n.a.
with onion *(French's),* 1 tbsp.	25	1.0	5.0	1.0	0	190	n.a.
spicy *(French's* Bold'n Spicy),* 1 tbsp. . .	16	1.0	1.0	1.0	0	145	n.a.
yellow *(French's),* 1 tbsp.	10	1.0	1.0	1.0	0	180	n.a.
Mustard greens:							
fresh:							
raw, trimmed, 4 oz.	29	3.1	5.6	.2	0	28	1.3
raw, chopped, 1 cup	14	1.5	2.8	.1	0	14	.6
boiled, drained, chopped, 1 cup	21	3.2	3.0	.3	0	22	1.0
frozen:							
(Frosty Acres), 3.3 oz.	20	2.0	3.0	0	0	20	1.0
(Southland), 3.3 oz.	20	2.0	3.0	0	0	20	n.a.
Mustard sauce:							
creamy *(French's Dip 'Um),* 2 tbsp. . . .	80	1.0	12.0	3.0	n.a.	300	n.a.
hot:							
(French's Dip 'Um), 2 tbsp.	70	1.0	14.0	1.0	n.a.	550	n.a.
(Sauceworks), 1 tbsp.	35	0	4.0	2.0	5	90	n.a.
Mustard seed:							
yellow (all brands), 1 tsp.	15	.8	1.2	1.0	0	tr.	.2
Mustard spinach (tendergreens):							
fresh, boiled, drained, chopped, 1 cup	29	3.1	5.0	.4	0	n.a.	1.4

N

Food and Measure	cal.	prot. (gms)	carbo. (gms)	fat (gms)	chol. (mgs)	sod. (mgs)	fiber (gms)
Nathan's:							
hamburger and roll	360	19.0	18.0	23.0	n.a.	203	n.a.
hot dog and roll . .	290	11.0	19.0	19.0	n.a.	675	n.a.
french fries, 7-oz.							
serving	550	7.0	60.0	31.0	n.a.	151	n.a.
Nectarine, fresh:							
whole, 2½" diam.	67	1.3	16.0	.6	0	0	.5
pitted, sliced, 1 cup	68	1.3	16.3	.6	0	0	.6
New England Brand							
sausage:							
beef and pork, 1 oz.	46	4.9	1.4	2.2	14	346	0
(Oscar Mayer), .82-oz.							
slice	31	3.8	.4	1.6	13	292	0
New England loaf:							
(Light & Lean), 2							
slices	90	10.0	0	6.0	n.a.	n.a.	n.a.
New Zealand spin-							
ach, fresh:							
raw:							
whole, 1 lb.	47	4.9	8.2	.7	0	425	2.3
chopped, 1 cup	8	.8	1.4	.1	0	73	.4
boiled:							
drained, 8 oz. . .	27	2.9	5.0	.4	0	243	1.4
drained, chopped, 1							
cup	22	2.3	4.0	.3	0	193	1.1
Noodle and chicken							
dinner:							
frozen *(Swanson),*							
10½ oz.	270	11.0	37.0	9.0	n.a.	820	n.a.
Noodle, Chinese:							
canned *(Chun King),* 1							
oz.	139	3.5	16.5	6.7	0	n.a.	1.2

Food and Measure	cal.	prot. (gms)	carbo. (gms)	fat (gms)	chol. (mgs)	sod. (mgs)	fiber (gms)
Noodle, Chinese *(cont.)*							
chow mein, canned							
(La Choy), 1/2 cup	150	3.0	17.0	8.0	0	210	n.a.
rice, canned *(La*							
Choy), 1/2 cup ..	130	2.0	22.0	5.0	0	380	n.a.
Noodle, egg:							
(Creamette), 2 oz. dry	220	8.0	40.0	3.0	0	n.a.	n.a.
(Mueller's), 2 oz. dry	220	8.0	41.0	2.0	0	15	n.a.
(Pennsylvania Dutch),							
2 oz. dry	220	8.0	40.0	3.0	0	15	n.a.
(Ronzoni), 2 oz. dry	220	8.0	40.0	3.0	0	75–85	n.a.
cooked, 1 cup . . .	200	6.6	37.3	2.4	0	75–85	n.a.
spinach *(Ronzoni)*, 2							
oz. dry	220	9.0	40.0	3.0	0	75–85	n.a.
Noodle entree:							
canned:							
and beef *(Hormel*							
Short Order), 71/2							
oz.	230	10.0	16.0	14.0	n.a.	974	n.a.
and beef, in sauce							
(Heinz), 71/2 oz.	170	8.0	17.0	8.0	n.a.	825	n.a.
and chicken *(Dinty*							
Moore), 71/2 oz.	210	9.0	15.0	12.0	n.a.	1144	n.a.
and chicken *(Heinz)*,							
71/2 oz.	160	6.0	19.0	7.0	n.a.	930	n.a.
with chicken *(Nal-*							
ley), 31/2 oz. . .	90	4.0	9.0	4.0	n.a.	465	n.a.
with chicken and							
vegetables *(Nal-*							
ley), 31/2 oz. . .	90	5.0	9.0	4.0	n.a.	485	n.a.
with franks *(Van*							
Camp's Noodle							
Weenee), 1 cup	245	9.3	32.9	8.5	n.a.	1245	.5
and tuna *(Heinz)*,							
71/2 oz.	170	11.0	20.0	5.0	n.a.	950	n.a.
freeze-dried:							
and chicken *(Moun-*							
tain House), 1							
cup	135	5.0	17.0	5.0	n.a.	n.a.	n.a.

Food and Measure	cal.	prot. (gms)	carbo. (gms)	fat (gms)	chol. (mgs)	sod. (mgs)	fiber (gms)
with Stroganoff sauce and beef *(Mountain House),* 1/2 cup	135	5.0	13.0	6.0	n.a.	n.a.	n.a.
frozen:							
and beef *(Banquet Family Entree),* 8 oz.	283	10.0	21.0	18.0	n.a.	877	n.a.
Romanoff *(Stouffer's),* 4 oz.	170	8.0	15.0	9.0	n.a.	700	n.a.
Noodle mix, 1/2 cup*, except as noted:							
all flavors *(Maruchan Instant Lunch),* 1 cup*	304	7.0	37.0	14.0	n.a.	1370	n.a.
Alfredo *(Lipton* Deluxe Noodles and Sauce)	220	7.0	22.0	11.0	n.a.	560	n.a.
beef flavor:							
(La Choy Ramen), 1.5 oz.	189	4.6	27.5	6.7	n.a.	1037	n.a.
(Lipton Noodles and Sauce)	190	5.0	26.0	7.0	n.a.	595	n.a.
butter *(Lipton* Noodles and Sauce)	190	5.0	24.0	9.0	n.a.	565	n.a.
butter and herb *(Lipton* Noodles and Sauce)	180	5.0	23.0	9.0	n.a.	525	n.a.
cheese *(Lipton* Noodles and Sauce)	200	5.0	24.0	9.0	n.a.	540	n.a.
chicken flavor:							
(La Choy Ramen), 1.5 oz.	187	4.7	27.3	6.5	n.a.	1156	n.a.
(Lipton Noodles and Sauce)	190	5.0	25.0	9.0	n.a.	465	n.a.
chicken Bombay *(Lipton* Deluxe Noodles and Sauce)	190	6.0	22.0	9.0	n.a.	515	n.a.

* Prepared according to package directions

Food and Measure	cal.	prot. (gms)	carbo. (gms)	fat (gms)	chol. (mgs)	sod. (mgs)	fiber (gms)
Noodle mix *(cont.)*							
fettuccine Alfredo *(Betty Crocker* International), 1/4 pkg.*	230	8.0	25.0	11.0	n.a.	590	n.a.
herb tomato *(Lipton Shells and Sauce)*	170	5.0	25.0	6.0	n.a.	435	n.a.
garlic, creamy *(Lipton Shells and Sauce)*	200	5.0	27.0	9.0	n.a.	535	n.a.
Oriental flavored *(La Choy Ramen)*, 1.5 oz.	189	4.9	27.7	6.5	n.a.	739	n.a.
Parisienne *(Betty Crocker* International), 1/4 pkg.*	190	5.0	22.0	9.0	n.a.	620	n.a.
Parmesano *(Lipton Deluxe Noodles and Sauce)*	210	6.0	22.0	11.0	n.a.	445	n.a.
Romanoff *(Betty Crocker* International), 1/4 pkg.*	220	7.0	24.0	11.0	n.a.	680	n.a.
sour cream and chive *(Lipton Noodles and Sauce)*	190	5.0	23.0	9.0	n.a.	455	n.a.
Stroganoff:							
(Betty Crocker International), 1/4 pkg.*	230	6.0	25.0	11.0	n.a.	730	n.a.
(Lipton Deluxe Noodles and Sauce)	200	6.0	22.0	10.0	n.a.	510	n.a.
Nutmeg:							
ground (all brands), 1 tsp.	12	.1	1.1	.8	0	tr.	.1
Nuts, see specific listings							
Nuts, mixed:							
(Tom's), .7 oz. . . .	120	4.0	5.0	10.0	0	120	n.a.

* *Prepared according to package directions*

Food and Measure	cal.	prot. (gms)	carbo. (gms)	fat (gms)	chol. (mgs)	sod. (mgs)	fiber (gms)
dry-roasted:							
(Flavor House), 1 oz.	180	6.0	5.0	14.0	0	200	n.a.
(Planters), 1 oz.	160	5.0	7.0	14.0	0	270	n.a.
(Planters Unsalted), 1 oz.	170	6.0	7.0	15.0	0	0	n.a.
oil-roasted:							
(Planters), 1 oz.	180	5.0	6.0	16.0	0	130	n.a.
(Planters Deluxe), 1 oz.	180	4.0	6.0	17.0	0	135	n.a.
(Planters Unsalted), 1 oz.	180	5.0	6.0	16.0	0	0	n.a.
Nuts, tavern:							
(Planters), 1 oz. . . .	170	7.0	6.0	15.0	0	65	n.a.

O

Food and Measure	cal.	prot. (gms)	carbo. (gms)	fat (gms)	chol. (mgs)	sod. (mgs)	fiber (gms)
Ocean perch, see "Perch"							
Octopus:							
raw, 4 oz.	93	16.9	2.5	1.8	54	n.a.	0
Oil:							
corn, cottonseed, safflower, sesame or soybean:							
1 cup	1927	0	0	218.0	0	0	0
1 tbsp.	120	0	0	13.6	0	0	0
corn, spray (Mazola No Stick), 2.5 second spray	6	0	0	1.0	0	0	0
olive or peanut:							
1 cup	1909	0	0	216.0	0	<1	0
1 tbsp.	119	0	0	13.5	0	0	0
popcorn:							
(Planters)	130	0	0	14.0	0	0	0
butter flavor (Orville Redenbacher's Gourmet)	120	0	0	14.0	0	0	0
Okra:							
fresh:							
raw, fully trimmed, 4 oz.	43	2.3	8.7	.1	0	9	1.1
raw, sliced, 1 cup	38	2.0	7.6	.1	0	8	.9
boiled, drained, 8 pods, 3″ × 5/8″	27	1.6	6.1	.1	0	5	.8
boiled, drained, sliced, 1 cup . .	50	3.0	11.5	.3	0	8	1.4

Food and Measure	cal.	prot. (gms)	carbo. (gms)	fat (gms)	chol. (mgs)	sod. (mgs)	fiber (gms)
frozen, 3.3 oz.:							
whole *(Birds Eye)*	30	2.0	7.0	0	0	0	.7
whole *(Southland)*	30	2.0	7.0	0	0	0	n.a.
whole, baby *(Frosty Acres)*	30	2.0	7.0	0	0	2	1.0
cut *(Birds Eye)* . .	25	1.0	6.0	0	0	0	.7
cut *(Southland)* . .	25	1.0	6.0	0	0	0	n.a.
Old-fashioned drink mixer:							
bottled *(Holland House)*, 1 fl. oz.	33	0	8.0	0	0	7	n.a.
Old-fashioned loaf:							
(Armour), 1 oz. . . .	80	n.a.	n.a.	7.0	15	320	n.a.
(Eckrich), 1 slice . .	70	3.0	3.0	6.0	n.a.	330	n.a.
(Eckrich Smorgas Pac, 12 oz.), 1 slice . .	50	2.0	2.0	4.0	n.a.	250	n.a.
(Eckrich Smorgas Pac, 1 lb.), 1 slice . . .	70	3.0	2.0	6.0	n.a.	340	n.a.
(Oscar Mayer), 1-oz. slice	64	4.0	2.5	4.2	14	321	n.a.
Olive loaf:							
(Armour), 1-oz. slice	70	n.a.	n.a.	5.0	10	235	n.a.
(Eckrich), 1 slice . .	80	3.0	2.0	7.0	n.a.	370	n.a.
(Hormel Perma-Fresh), 2 slices	110	7.0	5.0	7.0	n.a.	810	n.a.
(Oscar Mayer), 1-oz. slice	63	3.3	2.7	4.4	10	375	n.a.
Olives, pickled, canned or bottled, 10 olives, except as noted:							
green:							
small *(Lindsay)* . .	33	.4	.4	3.6	0	686	.4
large *(Lindsay)* . .	45	.5	.5	4.9	0	926	.6
giant *(Lindsay)* . .	76	.9	.9	8.3	0	1572	1.0
ripe:							
Ascolano, extra large *(Lindsay)*	61	.5	1.2	6.5	0	383	.8

Food and Measure	cal.	prot. (gms)	carbo. (gms)	fat (gms)	chol. (mgs)	sod. (mgs)	fiber (gms)
Olives, ripe *(cont.)*							
Ascolano, mammoth *(Lindsay)*	72	.6	1.5	7.7	0	454	.9
Ascolano, giant *(Lindsay)*	89	.8	1.8	9.5	0	559	1.1
Manzanilla, small *(Lindsay)*	38	.3	.8	4.0	0	237	.5
Manzanilla, medium *(Lindsay)*	44	.4	.9	4.7	0	280	.6
Manzanilla, large *(Lindsay)*	51	.4	1.0	5.5	0	320	.6
Manzanilla, extra large *(Lindsay)*	61	.5	1.2	6.5	0	385	.8
Mission, small *(Lindsay)*	54	.4	.9	5.9	0	219	.5
Mission, medium *(Lindsay)*	63	.4	1.1	6.9	0	258	.6
Mission, large *(Lindsay)*	73	.5	1.3	8.0	0	297	.7
Mission, extra large *(Lindsay)*	87	.6	1.5	9.5	0	355	.8
Sevillano, giant *(Lindsay)*	64	.8	1.9	6.5	0	570	1.0
Sevillano, jumbo *(Lindsay)*	76	.9	2.2	7.8	0	676	1.1
Sevillano, colossal *(Lindsay)*	95	1.1	2.8	9.7	0	847	1.4
Sevillano, supercolossal *(Lindsay)*	114	1.3	3.3	11.6	0	1011	1.7
salt-cured, Greek style:							
medium	65	.4	1.7	6.9	0	631	.9
extra large	89	.6	2.3	9.5	0	868	1.3
all sizes, pitted (S&W), 3½ oz.	163	1.0	1.0	18.0	0	760	n.a.
Onion, mature:							
fresh:							
raw, trimmed, 4 oz.	39	1.3	8.3	.3	0	2	.5

Food and Measure	cal.	prot. (gms)	carbo. (gms)	fat (gms)	chol. (mgs)	sod. (mgs)	fiber (gms)
raw, chopped, 1 cup	54	1.9	11.7	.4	0	4	.7
raw, chopped, 1 tbsp.	3	.1	.7	<.1	0	0	<.1
boiled, drained, chopped, 1 cup	58	1.9	13.2	.3	0	16	.9
boiled, drained, chopped, 1 tbsp.	4	.1	.9	<.1	0	1	.1
canned:							
French fried (Durkee), 1 oz.	175	2.0	9.0	15.0	n.a.	178	n.a.
small, whole (S&W), 1/2 cup	35	1.0	9.0	0	0	345	n.a.
spiced, cocktail (Vlasic), 1 oz.	4	0	1.0	0	0	365	n.a.
dry, minced, with green onion (Lawry's), 1 tsp.	7	.4	1.6	.2	0	1	.6
frozen:							
whole, small (Birds Eye), 4 oz. . . .	40	1.0	10.0	0	0	10	.7
whole, small, with cream sauce (Birds Eye), 3 oz.	110	1.0	11.0	6.0	n.a.	330	.4
chopped (Ore-Ida), 2 oz.	20	0	5.0	0	0	20	n.a.
chopped (Southland), 2 oz. . . .	15	0	4.0	0	0	0	n.a.
rings (Moore's), 3 oz.	180	3.0	25.0	9.0	0	190	n.a.
rings, fried (Mrs. Paul's), 21/4 oz.	150	3.0	20.0	6.0	0	275	n.a.
rings, fried (Ore-Ida), 2 oz. . . .	130	2.0	18.0	7.0	0	8	n.a.
Onion, young green, (scallion), fresh:							
bulb and entire top:							
trimmed, 1 lb. . .	114	7.9	25.2	.6	0	18	3.8
chopped, 1 cup	26	1.7	5.6	.1	0	4	.8
chopped, 1 tbsp.	2	.1	.3	<.1	0	0	.1

Food and Measure	cal.	prot. (gms)	carbo. (gms)	fat (gms)	chol. (mgs)	sod. (mgs)	fiber (gms)
Onion, Welsh:							
raw, trimmed, 4 oz.	39	2.2	7.4	.5	0	n.a.	1.1
Onion dip:							
creamy *(Kraft* Premium), 1 oz. . . .	45	1.0	2.0	4.0	10	125	n.a.
French:							
(Kraft), 2 tbsp. . .	60	1.0	4.0	4.0	0	260	n.a.
(Kraft Premium), 1 oz.	45	1.0	2.0	4.0	10	140	n.a.
(Nalley), 1 oz. . .	105	.3	1.4	11.1	14	359	n.a.
(Thank You), 2 tbsp.	90	2.0	5.0	7.0	1	380	0
green *(Kraft),* 2 tbsp.	60	1.0	3.0	4.0	0	170	n.a.
Onion gravy:							
canned *(Heinz* Home Style), 2 oz. . . .	24	.4	3.6	.8	n.a.	150	n.a.
mix *(Durkee),* 1-oz. pkg.	84	3.0	15.0	.5	n.a.	953	n.a.
mix* *(French's),* 1/4 cup	25	1.0	4.0	1.0	n.a.	270	n.a.
Onion powder:							
(all brands), 1 tsp.	7	.2	1.7	<.1	0	1	.1
Onion salt:							
(Lawry's), 1 tsp. . .	4	.1	.9	<.1	0	918	<.1
Opossum:							
roasted, meat only, 4 oz.	251	34.2	0	11.6	n.a.	n.a.	0
Orange, fresh:							
California navel:							
1 medium, 27/8″ diam.	65	1.4	16.3	.1	0	1	.6
sections, without membranes, 1 cup	76	1.7	19.2	.2	0	1	.8
wedge, 1/4 of medium orange . .	16	.4	4.1	<.1	0	<1	.2
California Valencia:							
1 medium, 25/8″ diam.	59	1.3	14.4	.4	0	0	.6

* *Prepared according to package directions*

Food and Measure	cal.	prot. (gms)	carbo. (gms)	fat (gms)	chol. (mgs)	sod. (mgs)	fiber (gms)
sections, without membranes, 1 cup	88	1.9	21.4	.5	0	0	.9
wedge, 1/4 of medium orange . .	15	.3	3.6	.1	0	0	.2
Florida:							
1 medium, 2 11/16″ diam.	69	1.1	17.4	.3	0	1	.5
sections, without membranes, 1 cup	84	1.3	21.3	.4	0	1	.6
wedge, 1/4 of medium orange . .	17	.3	4.4	.1	0	<1	.1
Orange, Mandarin, canned, 1/2 cup:							
in light syrup:							
(A&P)	80	<1.0	20.0	<1.0	0	0	n.a.
(Dole)	76	.6	20.0	.1	0	8	n.a.
with liquid (Del Monte)	100	0	25.0	0	0	<10	n.a.
in juice (S&W Natural Style)	60	0	15.0	0	0	10	n.a.
in heavy syrup (S&W)	76	0	20.0	0	0	10	n.a.
Orange danish:							
with icing, refrigerated (Pillsbury), 1 danish	145	1.5	19.5	7.0	n.a.	245	n.a.
Orange drink:							
canned or chilled, 6 fl. oz.:							
(Bama)	90	0	22.0	0	0	n.a.	n.a.
(Hawaiian Punch)	100	0	24.0	0	0	19	n.a.
(Hi-C)	94	<1.0	23.0	<.1	0	18	n.a.
imitation (Bright & Early)	90	<1.0	23.0	<.1	0	14	n.a.
freeze-dried* (Mountain House), 1 cup	90	0	23.0	0	0	n.a.	n.a.
frozen*, 6 fl. oz.:							
(Birds Eye Awake)	80	0	21.0	0	0	15	tr.

* Prepared according to package directions

Food and Measure	cal.	prot. (gms)	carbo. (gms)	fat (gms)	chol. (mgs)	sod. (mgs)	fiber (gms)
Orange drink, frozen* *(cont.)*							
(Birds Eye Orange Plus)	100	0	24.0	0	0	10	tr.
(Minute Maid Or-angeade)	85	<1.0	21.0	<.1	0	3	n.a.
imitation *(Bright & Early)*	90	<1.0	22.0	<.1	0	0	n.a.
mix*:							
(Borden Instant Breakfast), 4 fl. oz.	60	0	16.0	0	0	40	n.a.
(Crystal Light), 8 fl. oz.	4	0	0	0	0	0	0
(Kool-Aid), 8 fl. oz.	100	0	25.0	0	0	0	tr.
(Kool-Aid Presweetened), 8 fl. oz.	90	0	22.0	0	0	0	0
(Tang), 6 fl. oz. . .	90	0	22.0	0	0	0	tr.
(Tang Sugar Free), 6 fl. oz.	6	0	1.0	0	0	0	tr.
(Wyler's Soft Drink Mix), 8 fl. oz. . .	100	0	26.0	0	0	n.a.	n.a.
natural flavor *(Sun-kist* Light Crys-tals), 8 fl. oz. with ice	8	0	2.0	0	0	70	n.a.
sugar sweetened *(Funny Face),* 8 fl. oz.	88	0	22.0	0	0	30	0
Orange extract:							
(Virginia Dare), 1 tsp.	22	0	0	0	0	0	0
Orange juice:							
fresh:							
juice of 2⁵/₈″ diam. orange	39	.6	8.9	.2	0	1	.1
1 cup	111	1.7	25.8	.5	0	2	.3

* *Prepared according to package directions*

Food and Measure	cal.	prot. (gms)	carbo. (gms)	fat (gms)	chol. (mgs)	sod. (mgs)	fiber (gms)
canned or chilled, 6 fl. oz.:							
(Citrus Hill)	90	1.0	20.0	<1.0	0	0	n.a.
(Del Monte) . . .	80	1.0	19.0	0	0	<10	n.a.
(Kraft)	90	1.0	19.0	0	0	0	n.a.
(Minute Maid) . .	82	<2.0	21.0	<.1	0	16	n.a.
(S&W)	83	2.0	18.0	0	0	2	n.a.
(Sunkist)	80	1.0	20.0	0	0	5	n.a.
(Tropicana)	76	1.0	18.0	.2	0	2	n.a.
dehydrated, crystals, 1 oz.	108	1.4	25.2	.5	n.a.	2	.2
frozen*, 6 fl. oz.:							
(A&P)	80	1.0	19.0	<1.0	0	0	n.a.
(Minute Maid) . .	82	<2.0	21.0	<.1	0	2	n.a.
(Sunkist)	80	1.0	20.0	0	0	0	n.a.
Orange-grapefruit juice:							
dairy pack *(Kraft)*, 6 fl. oz.	80	1.0	19.0	0	0	0	n.a.
Orange Julius:							
Orange Julius drink:							
small, 12 fl. oz. . .	180	1.0	45.0	1.0	n.a.	10	n.a.
regular, 16 fl. oz. .	265	1.0	66.0	1.0	n.a.	15	n.a.
large, 20 fl. oz. . .	330	2.0	82.0	2.0	n.a.	20	n.a.
pinata colada drink:							
small, 12 fl. oz. . .	200	1.0	49.0	1.0	n.a.	10	n.a.
regular, 16 fl. oz. .	300	2.0	71.0	1.0	n.a.	15	n.a.
large, 20 fl. oz. . .	375	4.0	89.0	2.0	n.a.	20	n.a.
raspberry cream supreme drink:							
small, 12 fl. oz. . .	350	3.0	52.0	16.0	55	25	n.a.
regular, 16 fl. oz. .	510	4.0	76.0	23.0	80	40	n.a.
large, 20 fl. oz. . .	650	5.0	96.0	30.0	105	45	n.a.
strawberry *Julius* drink:							
small, 12 fl. oz. . .	230	1.0	57.0	<1.0	n.a.	10	n.a.
regular, 16 fl. oz.	340	1.0	82.0	1.0	n.a.	15	n.a.

* Prepared according to package directions

Food and Measure	cal.	prot. (gms)	carbo. (gms)	fat (gms)	chol. (mgs)	sod. (mgs)	fiber (gms)
Orange Julius, strawberry *(cont.)*							
large, 20 fl. oz. . .	430	2.0	105.0	1.0	n.a.	20	n.a.
tropical cream supreme drink:							
small, 12 fl. oz. . .	340	4.0	46.0	18.0	65	25	n.a.
regular, 16 fl. oz.	510	5.0	67.0	25.0	95	40	n.a.
large, 20 fl. oz. . .	630	7.0	84.0	32.0	115	50	n.a.
Orange peel:							
candied, 1 oz. . . .	90	.1	22.9	.1	0	n.a.	n.a.
Orange-pineapple juice:							
dairy pack *(Kraft)*, 6 fl. oz.	80	1.0	19.0	0	0	0	n.a.
Orange roll:							
(Fruit Roll-Ups), 1/2-oz. roll	50	0	12.0	<1.0	0	10	n.a.
(Sunkist Fruit Rolls), 1/2-oz. roll	50	0	12.0	<1.0	0	10	n.a.
Orange-pineapple bar:							
(Fruit Corners), 1 bar	90	<1.0	17.0	2.0	0	10	n.a.
Oregano:							
ground (all brands), 1 tsp.	5	.2	1.0	.2	0	tr.	.2
Oyster:							
fresh:							
eastern, raw, in shell, 6 medium	58	5.9	3.3	2.1	46	94	0
eastern, raw, meat only, 4 oz. . . .	78	8.0	4.4	2.8	62	127	0
Pacific/western, meat only, 4 oz.	92	10.7	5.6	2.6	n.a.	120	0
canned:							
(Louisiana Brand), 4 oz.	100	10.0	5.0	4.0	n.a.	n.a.	n.a.
whole *(S&W* Fancy), 4 oz.	95	12.0	4.0	3.0	n.a.	n.a.	n.a.
Oyster stew, see "Soup, canned, condensed"							

P

Food and Measure	cal.	prot. (gms)	carbo. (gms)	fat (gms)	chol. (mgs)	sod. (mgs)	fiber (gms)
P&P loaf:							
(Grillmaster), 1 slice	80	4.0	1.5	6.5	n.a.	421	n.a.
Pancake, frozen, 3 (4-inch) cakes:							
(Aunt Jemima Original)	246	6.7	46.6	3.7	n.a.	777	.2
(Pillsbury Microwave)	260	5.0	46.0	6.0	n.a.	540	n.a.
blueberry (Aunt Jemima)	249	6.8	46.4	4.0	n.a.	789	.2
buttermilk:							
(Aunt Jemima) . .	240	7.0	44.7	3.7	n.a.	778	.2
(Pillsbury Microwave)	220	4.0	43.0	3.0	n.a.	510	n.a.
Pancake batter, frozen, 3 (4-inch) cakes*:							
(Aunt Jemima) . . .	210	6.6	42.2	1.6	n.a.	857	.2
blueberry (Aunt Jemima)	205	6.2	41.5	1.6	n.a.	698	.2
buttermilk (Aunt Jemima)	212	7.1	42.6	1.5	n.a.	733	.1
Pancake and waffle mix:							
(Aunt Jemima Complete), 1/2 cup . .	272	7.5	52.3	3.6	n.a.	881	.2
(Aunt Jemima Original), 1/4 cup . . .	108	3.0	22.5	.6	n.a.	450	.2
(Hungry Jack Extra Lights), 3 cakes, 4"*	210	6.0	30.0	7.0	n.a.	490	n.a.

* Prepared according to package directions

Food and Measure	cal.	prot. (gms)	carbo. (gms)	fat (gms)	chol. (mgs)	sod. (mgs)	fiber (gms)
Pancake and waffle mix *(cont.)*							
(Hungry Jack Extra Lights Complete), 3 cakes, 4″*	190	4.0	37.0	2.0	n.a.	700	n.a.
(Hungry Jack Pan-shakes), 3 cakes, 4″*	250	7.0	43.0	6.0	n.a.	880	n.a.
(Martha White Flap-stax), 1 pkg. . . .	500	11.0	106.0	9.0	n.a.	n.a.	n.a.
blueberry:							
(Hungry Jack), 3 cakes, 4″* . . .	320	7.0	40.0	15.0	n.a.	820	n.a.
(Hungry Jack Complete), 3 cakes, 4″*	180	4.0	35.0	3.0	n.a.	680	n.a.
buttermilk:							
(Aunt Jemima), 1/3 cup	175	5.7	36.5	.7	n.a.	832	.2
(Aunt Jemima Complete), 1/2 cup	264	8.1	51.2	3.0	n.a.	858	.2
(Betty Crocker), 3 cakes, 4″* . . .	280	8.0	39.0	10.0	n.a.	810	n.a.
(Betty Crocker Complete), 3 cakes, 4″*	210	5.0	41.0	3.0	n.a.	500	n.a.
(Hungry Jack), 3 cakes, 4″* . . .	240	7.0	29.0	11.0	n.a.	570	n.a.
(Hungry Jack Complete), 3 cakes, 4″*	180	4.0	39.0	1.0	n.a.	710	n.a.
buckwheat *(Aunt Je-mima)*, 1/4 cup . .	107	3.4	21.3	.8	n.a.	432	.6
whole wheat *(Aunt Je-mima)*, 1/3 cup . .	142	5.9	28.5	.5	n.a.	587	.5

* Prepared according to package directions

Food and Measure	cal.	prot. (gms)	carbo. (gms)	fat (gms)	chol. (mgs)	sod. (mgs)	fiber (gms)
Pancake breakfast, frozen:							
and blueberry sauce *(Swanson)*, 7 oz.	400	9.0	70.0	9.0	n.a.	800	n.a.
and sausage *(Swanson)*, 6 oz.	460	14.0	52.0	22.0	n.a.	940	n.a.
with strawberries *(Swanson)*, 7 oz.	430	8.0	82.0	8.0	n.a.	820	n.a.
Pancake syrup (see also "Maple syrup"):							
(Aunt Jemima), 1 fl. oz.	103	0	25.8	0	0	21	n.a.
(Aunt Jemima Lite), 1 fl. oz.	60	0	15.1	0	0	66	n.a.
(Aunt Jemima Butter Lite), 1 fl. oz. . . .	52	0	12.9	0	0	67	n.a.
(Golden Griddle), 1 tbsp.	50	0	13.0	0	0	20	n.a.
(Karo), 1 tbsp. . . .	60	0	15.0	0	0	35	n.a.
(Nalley Lumberjack), 1 tbsp.	38	n.a.	9.8	0	0	6	n.a.
Pancreas, raw:							
beef, 4 oz.	265	17.7	0	21.0	n.a.	76	0
calf, 4 oz.	183	21.8	0	10.0	n.a.	n.a.	0
Papaw, North American type, fresh:							
whole, 1 lb.	289	17.7	57.2	3.1	0	n.a.	n.a.
peeled and seeded, 4 oz.	96	5.9	19.1	1.0	0	n.a.	n.a.
Papaya, fresh:							
whole, 1-lb. papaya, 3½″ × 5⅛″ . . .	117	1.9	29.8	.4	0	8	2.4
peeled and seeded:							
4 oz.	44	.7	11.1	.2	0	3	1.0
cubed, 1 cup . . .	54	.9	13.7	.2	0	4	1.1
Papaya nectar:							
canned, 1 cup . . .	142	.4	36.3	.4	0	14	n.a.

Food and Measure	cal.	prot. (gms)	carbo. (gms)	fat (gms)	chol. (mgs)	sod. (mgs)	fiber (gms)
Paprika:							
ground (all brands), 1 tsp.	6	.3	1.2	.3	0	1	.4
Parsley:							
fresh:							
whole, 1 lb.	140	9.5	29.8	1.3	0	169	5.2
10 sprigs	3	.2	.7	<.1	0	4	.1
chopped, 1 cup	20	1.3	4.1	.2	0	24	.7
dried (all brands), 1 tsp.	1	.1	.2	<.1	0	1	<.1
freeze-dried, 1 tbsp.	1	.1	.2	<.1	0	2	<.1
Parsnips, fresh:							
raw, whole, 1 lb. ...	289	4.6	69.4	1.2	0	39	7.7
boiled:							
1 parsnip, 9″ × 2¼″	130	2.1	31.3	.5	0	17	3.5
drained, sliced, 1 cup	126	2.1	30.5	.5	0	16	3.4
Passion fruit (purple granadilla), raw:							
whole, in shell, 1 lb.	230	5.2	55.1	1.7	0	66	25.8
shelled, 4 oz.	110	2.5	26.5	.8	0	32	12.4
Passion fruit juice, fresh:							
purple, 1 cup	126	1.0	33.6	.1	0	n.a.	.1
yellow, 1 cup	149	1.7	35.7	.4	0	15	.4
Pasta (spaghetti, vermicelli, linguine, etc.), plain:							
dry:							
8-oz. pkg.	837	28.4	170.6	2.7	0	5	.7
(Creamette), 2 oz.	210	7.0	42.0	1.0	0	<5	n.a.
(Mueller's), 2 oz.	210	7.0	43.0	1.0	0	0	n.a.
(Ronzoni), 2 oz.	210	7.0	41.0	1.0	0	<5	n.a.
cooked firm, 8–10 minutes 1 cup ..	192	6.5	39.1	.7	0	1	.1
cooked tender, 14–20 minutes 1 cup ..	155	4.8	32.2	.6	0	1	.1

Food and Measure	cal.	prot. (gms)	carbo. (gms)	fat (gms)	chol. (mgs)	sod. (mgs)	fiber (gms)
artichoke, Jerusalem, dry *(De Boles)*, 2 oz.	210	7.0	40.0	<1.0	0	10	n.a.
corn, wheat-free, dry *(De Boles)*, 2 oz.	210	4.0	44.0	2.0	0	30	n.a.
whole wheat, organic, dry *(De Boles)*, 2 oz.	200	7.0	40.0	<1.0	0	10	n.a.
Pasta, canned (see also specific listings):							
(Franco-American UFOs), 7 1/2 oz. . . .	180	5.0	35.0	3.0	n.a.	780	n.a.
with meatballs *(Franco-American UFOs with Meteors)*, 7 1/2 oz. . . .	240	9.0	30.0	9.0	n.a.	790	n.a.
Pasta, frozen, see specific listings							
Pasta shells, frozen:							
and beef *(The Budget Gourmet)*, 1 serving	340	20.0	35.0	14.0	n.a.	985	n.a.
and veal with vegetables *(Freezer Queen Single Serve)*, 10 oz.	250	12.0	35.0	8.0	n.a.	n.a.	n.a.
stuffed, 9 oz.:							
with beef and spinach, tomato sauce *(Stouffer's)*	300	21.0	27.0	12.0	n.a.	1100	n.a.
with cheese, meat sauce *(Stouffer's)*	340	23.0	25.0	16.0	n.a.	1200	n.a.
with chicken, cheese sauce *(Stouffer's)* . . .	420	29.0	21.0	24.0	n.a.	810	n.a.
Pastini, dry:							
carrot, 8 oz.	841	27.0	171.7	3.6	n.a.	n.a.	1.4
egg, 8 oz.	869	29.3	162.8	9.3	n.a.	11	.7
spinach, 8 oz.	835	28.1	169.6	3.6	n.a.	n.a.	1.1

Food and Measure	cal.	prot. (gms)	carbo. (gms)	fat (gms)	chol. (mgs)	sod. (mgs)	fiber (gms)
Pastrami:							
(Eckrich Calorie Watcher Slender Sliced), 1-oz. slice	40	5.0	1.0	2.0	n.a.	360	n.a.
(Oscar Mayer), 3/4-oz. slice	21	4.0	.1	.5	8	266	0
smoked *(Carl Buddig),* 1 oz.	42	5.7	.3	2.0	16	320	0
turkey, see "Turkey pastrami"							
Pâté, canned or in jars:							
chicken liver:							
1 oz.	57	3.8	1.9	3.7	n.a.	n.a.	0
1 tbsp.	26	1.8	.9	1.7	n.a.	n.a.	0
de foie gras:							
1 oz.	131	3.2	1.3	12.4	43	n.a.	0
1 tbsp.	60	1.5	.6	5.7	20	n.a.	0
1 tsp.	20	.5	.2	1.9	7	n.a.	0
goose liver:							
smoked, 1 oz. . .	131	3.2	1.3	12.4	43	n.a.	0
smoked, 1 tbsp.	60	1.5	.6	5.7	20	n.a.	0
liver:							
1 oz.	90	4.0	.4	7.9	n.a.	198	0
1 tbsp.	41	1.9	.2	3.6	n.a.	91	0
Patty shell:							
frozen *(Pepperidge Farm),* 1 shell . .	210	2.0	17.0	15.0	n.a.	180	n.a.
Pea pods, Chinese, see "Peas, snow"							
Peach:							
fresh:							
pared, sliced, 1 cup	73	1.2	18.9	.2	0	1	1.1
1 peach, 2 1/2" diam., 4 per lb.	37	.6	9.7	.1	0	0	.6
canned, 1/2 cup, except as noted:							
in heavy syrup *(S&W)*	100	0	26.0	0	0	10	n.a.

Food and Measure	cal.	prot. (gms)	carbo. (gms)	fat (gms)	chol. (mgs)	sod. (mgs)	fiber (gms)
halves or slices (Stokely's Finest)	70	0	18.0	0	0	10	n.a.
diced (Hunt's Snack Pack), 5 oz. . .	110	<1.0	29.0	<1.0	0	5	n.a.
canned, cling, yellow, 1/2 cup, except as noted:							
in water, halves or slices	29	.6	7.5	<.1	0	4	.4
in pear juice (A&P)	50	<1.0	12.0	<1.0	0	10	n.a.
in juice, halves or slices (S&W Natural)	90	0	20.0	0	0	10	n.a.
in juice, slices (S&W Natural Lite) . .	50	0	13.0	0	0	10	n.a.
in heavy syrup, halves (A&P) . .	100	0	25.0	<1.0	0	10	n.a.
in heavy syrup, slices (A&P) . .	100	<1.0	25.0	<1.0	0	10	n.a.
in heavy syrup, halves or slices (S&W)	100	0	26.0	0	0	10	n.a.
in heavy syrup, slices (S&W) Premium)	100	0	25.0	0	0	10	n.a.
halves or slices (Del Monte)	80	0	22.0	0	0	<10	n.a.
halves or slices (Del Monte Lite) . . .	50	0	13.0	0	0	<10	n.a.
diced (Del Monte Fruit Cup), 5 oz. . .	110	0	28.0	0	0	<10	n.a.
spiced, with pits (Del Monte), 31/2 oz.	80	0	20.0	0	0	<10	n.a.
spiced, whole (S&W)	90	0	23.0	0	0	10	n.a.
canned, freestone, 1/2 cup:							
(Del Monte Lite)	60	0	13.0	0	0	<10	n.a.

Food and Measure	cal.	prot. (gms)	carbo. (gms)	fat (gms)	chol. (mgs)	sod. (mgs)	fiber (gms)
Peach, canned, freestone *(cont.)*							
halves or slices *(Del Monte)*	90	0	23.0	0	0	<10	n.a.
dehydrated, sulphured (without sodium bi-sulfite):							
uncooked, 8 oz.	737	11.1	188.7	2.3	0	23	9.0
uncooked, 1 cup	376	5.7	96.5	1.2	0	11	4.6
cooked, 1 cup . .	322	4.9	82.6	1.0	0	10	3.9
dried, sulphured (with-out sodium bisulfite):							
uncooked, 8 oz.	542	8.2	139.1	1.7	0	16	6.7
uncooked, halves, 1 cup	383	5.8	98.1	1.2	0	12	4.7
uncooked, 10 halves	311	4.7	79.7	1.0	0	9	3.8
uncooked *(Del Monte)*, 2 oz.	140	2.0	35.0	0	0	<10	n.a.
cooked, un-sweetened, halves, 1 cup	198	3.0	50.8	.6	0	6	2.4
freeze-dried *(Mountain House)*, 1/4 cup . .	22	1.0	6.0	0	0	n.a.	n.a.
frozen, sliced, sweet-ened, thawed, 1 cup	235	1.6	59.9	.3	0	16	1.0
Peach butter:							
(Smucker's), 2 tsp.	30	0	8.0	0	0	0	n.a.
Peach drink:							
canned *(Hi-C)*, 6 fl. oz.	99	<1.0	25.0	<.1	0	16	n.a.
Peach nectar, canned:							
1 cup	134	.7	34.7	.1	0	17	.4
(S&W), 6 fl. oz. . . .	90	1.0	25.0	0	0	15	n.a.
Peach turnover:							
frozen *(Pepperidge Farm)*, 1 piece . .	320	3.0	34.0	19.0	n.a.	260	n.a.
Peanut, 1 oz., except as noted:							
(Beer Nuts)	180	7.0	7.0	14.0	0	60	n.a.

Food and Measure	cal.	prot. (gms)	carbo. (gms)	fat (gms)	chol. (mgs)	sod. (mgs)	fiber (gms)
(Flavor House Honey Roasted)	180	6.0	9.0	11.0	0	120	n.a.
(Planters Honey Roast)	170	6.0	8.0	13.0	0	180	n.a.
(Planters Sweet 'N Crunchy)	140	4.0	15.0	8.0	0	20	n.a.
dried:							
in shell, 1 lb. . . .	1876	85.0	53.6	162.8	0	53	16.2
shelled, 4 oz. . . .	644	29.2	18.4	55.9	0	20	5.6
shelled, 1 cup . .	827	37.5	23.6	71.8	0	23	7.1
dry-roasted:							
(Eagle Honey Roast)	160	7.0	6.0	13.0	0	135	n.a.
(Flavor House) . .	180	8.0	5.0	14.0	0	200	n.a.
(Flavor House Salt Free)	180	8.0	5.0	14.0	0	0	n.a.
(Frito-Lay's)	170	8.0	5.0	14.0	0	220	n.a.
(Laura Scudder's Snackin')	175	9.1	3.9	14.0	0	247	.7
(Planters)	160	7.0	6.0	14.0	0	250	n.a.
(Planters Lite), 2/3 oz.	90	6.0	5.0	6.0	0	180	n.a.
(Planters Unsalted)	170	7.0	5.0	15.0	0	0	n.a.
(Tom's)	160	9.0	5.0	14.0	0	170	n.a.
oil-roasted:							
unsalted, shelled	165	7.6	5.3	14.0	0	4	.7
unsalted, whole, halves or chopped, 1 cup	841	38.8	26.8	71.3	0	22	3.5
salted, whole, halves or chopped, 1 cup	841	38.8	26.8	71.3	0	626	3.5
(Eagle Honey Roast)	160	7.0	7.0	13.0	0	175	n.a.
(Eagle Salted) . .	170	8.0	5.0	14.0	0	155	n.a.
(Frito Lay's)	170	6.0	6.0	15.0	0	170	n.a.
(Frito-Lay's Salted in the Shell) . . .	160	7.0	6.0	14.0	0	265	n.a.

Food and Measure	cal.	prot. (gms)	carbo. (gms)	fat (gms)	chol. (mgs)	sod. (mgs)	fiber (gms)
Peanut, oil-roasted *(cont.)*							
(Laura Scudder's							
Virginia)	182	8.5	3.2	15.4	0	183	.7
(Planters)	170	7.0	5.0	15.0	0	160	n.a.
cocktail *(Planters)*	170	7.0	5.0	15.0	0	160	n.a.
cocktail *(Planters*							
Unsalted)	170	7.0	5.0	15.0	0	0	n.a.
hot flavored *(Tom's)*	170	7.0	4.0	13.0	0	230	n.a.
redskin *(Planters)*	170	7.0	5.0	15.0	0	150	n.a.
roasted in shell, salted							
(Planters)	160	7.0	6.0	14.0	0	160	n.a.
roasted in shell, un-salted:							
(Laura Scudder's							
Goober)	111	5.0	3.9	9.0	0	1	.5
(Planters)	160	7.0	6.0	14.0	0	0	n.a.
(Tom's), 1.4 oz.	170	7.0	5.0	14.0	0	5	n.a.
Spanish:							
(Laura Scudder's)	181	8.6	3.4	15.2	0	156	.9
(Planters)	170	7.0	5.0	15.0	0	150	n.a.
(Tom's), 1¹⁄8 oz.	190	10.0	5.0	16.0	0	150	n.a.
dry roasted *(Plant-ers)*	160	7.0	6.0	14.0	0	200	n.a.
raw *(Planters)* . .	150	7.0	7.0	12.0	0	0	n.a.
toasted *(Tom's)*, 1¹⁄8 oz.	190	8.0	5.0	16.0	0	120	n.a.
Peanut butter, 2 tbsp.:							
(Adams Old Fash-ioned)	195	9.0	5.0	16.0	0	130	n.a.
(Adams Old Fash-ioned Unsalted)	195	9.0	5.0	16.0	0	<10	n.a.
(Algood No Salt) . .	200	9.0	6.0	16.0	0	10	n.a.
(Laura Scudder's Ho-mogenized)	197	9.2	5.6	15.6	0	150	.7
(Laura Scudder's Old Fashioned)	202	10.9	3.5	16.4	0	214	.7
(Smucker's Natural)	200	8.0	6.0	16.0	0	125	n.a.

Food and Measure	cal.	prot. (gms)	carbo. (gms)	fat (gms)	chol. (mgs)	sod. (mgs)	fiber (gms)
(Smucker's Natural Unsalted)	200	8.0	6.0	17.0	0	0	n.a.
creamy:							
(Algood)	210	9.0	6.0	17.0	0	120	n.a.
(Algood Red Label)	200	9.0	6.0	16.0	0	140	n.a.
(Bama)	200	8.0	7.0	16.0	0	160	n.a.
(Jif)	190	9.0	6.0	16.0	0	155	n.a.
(Peter Pan)	180	8.0	5.0	16.0	0	150	n.a.
(Peter Pan Sodium & Sugar Free)	180	10.0	4.0	17.0	0	0	n.a.
(Skippy)	190	9.0	4.0	17.0	0	150	n.a.
crunchy:							
(Algood)	210	9.0	6.0	17.0	0	100	n.a.
(Algood Red Label)	200	9.0	6.0	16.0	0	130	n.a.
(Bama)	200	8.0	6.0	16.0	0	135	n.a.
(Jif)	190	9.0	6.0	16.0	0	130	n.a.
(Peter Pan)	180	8.0	5.0	16.0	0	150	n.a.
(Peter Pan Salt Free)	180	10.0	4.0	17.0	0	0	n.a.
(Skippy Super Chunk)	190	9.0	4.0	17.0	0	130	n.a.
with grape jam *(Smucker's Goober Grape)*	180	5.0	18.0	10.0	0	120	n.a.
Peanut flour:							
defatted, 1 cup . . .	196	31.3	20.8	.3	0	9	2.4
Peanut spread:							
4 oz.	682	23.0	24.9	59.1	0	677	1.7
Pear nectar, canned:							
1 cup	149	.3	39.4	<.1	0	9	.8
(S&W), 6 fl. oz. . . .	100	0	26.0	0	0	15	n.a.
Pears:							
fresh:							
whole, 1 lb.	247	1.6	63.1	1.7	0	2	5.8
sliced, 1 cup . . .	97	.7	24.9	.7	0	1	2.3
Bartlett, 1 pear, 2 1/2″ × 3 1/2″ . .	98	.7	25.1	.7	0	1	2.3
candied, 1 oz. . . .	86	.4	21.5	.2	0	n.a.	n.a.

Food and Measure	cal.	prot. (gms)	carbo. (gms)	fat (gms)	chol. (mgs)	sod. (mgs)	fiber (gms)
Pears (cont.)							
canned, 1/2 cup:							
in water, halves	36	.3	9.6	<.1	0	3	.8
in juice, (A&P) . .	60	<1.0	15.0	<1.0	0	10	n.a.
in juice, slices (S&W Natural Style)	80	0	20.0	0	0	10	n.a.
in juice, slices, peeled (S&W Natural Lite)	60	0	15.0	0	0	10	n.a.
in light syrup (A&P)	70	<1.0	20.0	<1.0	0	10	n.a.
in heavy syrup (A&P)	95	<1.0	25.0	<1.0	0	10	n.a.
in heavy syrup, Bartlett (S&W)	100	0	25.0	0	0	<10	n.a.
halves (Stokely's Finest)	70	0	20.0	0	0	10	n.a.
halves or slices, Bartlett (Del Monte)	80	0	22.0	0	0	<10	n.a.
halves or slices, Bartlett (Del Monte Lite) . . .	50	0	14.0	0	0	<10	n.a.
dried, sulphured:							
uncooked, 8 oz.	594	4.2	158.1	1.4	0	14	12.9
uncooked, 10 halves	459	3.3	122.0	1.1	0	10	10.0
uncooked, halves, 1 cup	472	3.4	125.5	1.1	0	10	10.2
cooked, un- sweetened, halves, 1 cup	325	2.3	86.2	.8	0	7	7.0
Peas, green, immature:							
fresh:							
raw, in pods, 1 lb.	140	9.3	24.9	.7	0	8	3.8
raw, shelled, 1 cup	118	7.9	21.1	.6	0	7	3.2
boiled, drained, 1 cup	134	8.6	25.0	.3	0	4	3.7

Food and Measure	cal.	prot. (gms)	carbo. (gms)	fat (gms)	chol. (mgs)	sod. (mgs)	fiber (gms)
canned, 1/2 cup:							
(Libby/Seneca) . .	60	4.0	12.0	0	0	320	n.a.
(Libby/Seneca Natural)	60	4.0	12.0	0	0	10	n.a.
(Stokely's Finest, No Salt or Sugar)	50	4.0	9.0	0	0	5	n.a.
early (A&P)	70	4.0	15.0	<1.0	0	350	n.a.
early (A&P No Salt Added)	60	4.0	12.0	<1.0	0	10	n.a.
early (Stokely's Finest, 8 1/2 oz.) . .	60	4.0	12.0	0	0	315	n.a.
early (Stokely's Finest, 17 oz.) . . .	60	4.0	12.0	0	0	320	n.a.
early, June (Joan of Arc)	60	3.0	11.0	<1.0	0	380	n.a.
early, June (S&W Petit Pois) . . .	70	4.0	12.0	0	0	330	n.a.
mixed sizes (A&P)	60	4.0	12.0	<1.0	0	350	n.a.
mixed sizes (A&P No Salt Added)	60	4.0	12.0	<1.0	0	10	n.a.
sweet (Del Monte)	60	3.0	10.0	0	0	355	n.a.
sweet (Green Giant)	60	4.0	11.0	0	0	370	n.a.
sweet (Joan of Arc)	70	4.0	13.0	<1.0	0	240	n.a.
sweet (S&W Veri-Green)	70	4.0	14.0	0	0	320	n.a.
sweet (Stokely's Finest, 8 1/2 oz.)	60	4.0	10.0	0	0	315	n.a.
sweet (Stokely's Finest, 17 oz.)	60	4.0	10.0	0	0	320	n.a.
sweet, medium (S&W Perfection)	70	4.0	12.0	0	0	330	n.a.
sweet, mini (Green Giant)	60	4.0	11.0	0	0	420	n.a.
sweet, small (Del Monte)	50	3.0	9.0	0	0	355	n.a.
sweet, with pearl onions (S&W)	60	3.0	10.0	1.0	0	490	n.a.
sweet, with onions (Joan of Arc) . .	60	3.0	11.0	<1.0	0	550	n.a.

Food and Measure	cal.	prot. (gms)	carbo. (gms)	fat (gms)	chol. (mgs)	sod. (mgs)	fiber (gms)
Peas, green, canned *(cont.)*							
seasoned *(Del Monte)*	60	3.0	11.0	0	0	355	n.a.
freeze-dried *(Mountain House)*, 1/2 cup . .	90	5.0	14.0	1.0	0	n.a.	n.a.
frozen:							
(A&P), 3.3 oz. . .	80	5.0	13.0	< 1.0	0	90	n.a.
(Birds Eye), 3.3 oz.	80	5.0	13.0	0	0	130	1.8
(Frosty Acres), 3.3 oz.	80	5.0	13.0	0	0	91	2.0
early, June *(Green Giant)*, 1/2 cup	60	5.0	10.0	0	0	170	n.a.
early, June *(Green Giant Harvest Fresh)*, 1/2 cup	80	4.0	13.0	1.0	0	170	n.a.
sweet *(Green Giant)*, 1/2 cup . .	60	4.0	11.0	0	0	110	n.a.
sweet *(Green Giant Harvest Fresh)*, 1/2 cup	60	3.0	12.0	0	0	220	n.a.
tiny *(Birds Eye Deluxe)*, 3.3 oz.	60	4.0	11.0	0	0	120	1.9
tiny *(Frosty Acres)*, 3.3 oz.	60	4.0	11.0	0	0	127	2.0
in butter sauce, early *(LeSueur)*, 1/2 cup	90	4.0	15.0	2.0	n.a.	590	n.a.
in butter sauce, sweet *(Green Giant)*, 1/2 cup . .	90	4.0	14.0	1.0	n.a.	490	n.a.
with cream sauce *(Birds Eye)*, 2.6 oz.	130	4.0	14.0	7.0	n.a.	440	1.1
in cream sauce *(Green Giant)*, 1/2 cup	100	4.0	12.0	4.0	n.a.	320	n.a.
Peas, green, combinations, frozen:							
and carrots, see "Peas and carrots"							

Food and Measure	cal.	prot. (gms)	carbo. (gms)	fat (gms)	chol. (mgs)	sod. (mgs)	fiber (gms)
and cauliflower medley *(Green Giant Valley Combination)*, 1/2 cup	30	2.0	5.0	0	0	60	n.a.
with onions and carrots, in butter sauce *(Green Giant)*, 1/2 cup	80	4.0	11.0	3.0	n.a.	470	n.a.
with pea pods and water chestnuts, in butter sauce *(Green Giant)*, 1/2 cup . .	80	4.0	10.0	2.0	n.a.	410	n.a.
with pearl onions: *(Birds Eye)*, 3.3 oz.	70	5.0	13.0	0	0	310	1.7
(Frosty Acres), 3.3 oz.	70	4.0	13.0	0	0	80	n.a.
in cheese sauce *(Birds Eye)*, 5 oz.	140	6.0	18.0	5.0	n.a.	460	1.4
and potatoes, with cream sauce *(Birds Eye)*, 2.6 oz. . . .	140	4.0	15.0	7.0	n.a.	480	.9
Peas, mature seeds, dry:							
whole, 8 oz.	771	54.7	136.8	2.9	0	79	11.1
split: without seed coat, 8 oz.	789	54.9	142.2	2.3	0	91	2.7
without seed coat, cooked, 8 oz. . .	261	18.1	47.2	.7	0	29	.9
cooked *(A&P)*, 1 cup	220	16.0	40.0	<1.0	0	15	n.a.
Peas, snow:							
frozen *(La Choy)*, 1/2 pkg.	35	2.0	6.0	<1.0	0	<10	n.a.
Peas and carrots:							
canned, 1/2 cup: *(Del Monte)* . . .	50	2.0	10.0	0	0	355	n.a.
(Kohl's)	50	3.0	20.0	<1.0	0	330	n.a.
(Libby/Seneca) . .	50	3.0	10.0	0	0	300	n.a.
(S&W)	50	3.0	9.0	0	0	310	n.a.

Food and Measure	cal.	prot. (gms)	carbo. (gms)	fat (gms)	chol. (mgs)	sod. (mgs)	fiber (gms)
Peas and carrots *(cont.)*							
frozen:							
(A&P), 3.3 oz. . .	60	3.0	11.0	<1.0	0	75	n.a.
(Frosty Acres), 3.3 oz.	60	3.0	11.0	0	0	75	n.a.
Pecans:							
(Planters), 1 oz. . . .	190	2.0	5.0	20.0	0	0	n.a.
dried:							
in shell, 1 lb. . . .	1604	18.6	43.8	162.6	0	3	3.8
shelled, 1 lb. . . .	3028	35.2	82.8	307.1	0	5	7.3
shelled, halves, 1 cup	721	8.4	19.7	73.1	0	1	1.7
shelled, 10 mammoth nuts . . .	119	1.4	3.2	12.0	0	0	.3
shelled, 10 jumbo nuts	95	1.1	2.6	9.6	0	0	.2
shelled, 10 large nuts	61	.7	1.7	6.2	0	0	.2
shelled, chopped, 1 cup	794	9.2	21.7	80.5	0	1	1.9
shelled, ground, 1 cup	634	7.4	17.3	64.3	0	1	1.5
dry-roasted:							
shelled, unsalted, 1 oz.	187	2.3	6.3	18.4	0	0	.5
shelled, salted, 1 oz.	187	2.3	6.3	18.4	0	222	.5
oil-roasted:							
shelled, unsalted, 1 oz.	195	2.0	4.6	20.2	0	0	.5
shelled, salted, 1 oz.	195	2.0	4.6	20.2	0	215	.5
(Eagle Honey Roast), 1 oz. . .	200	2.0	6.0	19.0	0	140	n.a.
Pepper, seasoning, 1 tsp.:							
black (all brands) . .	5	.2	1.4	.1	0	1	.3
red or cayenne (all brands)	6	.2	1.0	.3	0	1	.5

Food and Measure	cal.	prot. (gms)	carbo. (gms)	fat (gms)	chol. (mgs)	sod. (mgs)	fiber (gms)
seasoned (Lawry's)	9	.3	1.8	<.1	0	5	.2
white (all brands) . .	7	.3	1.7	.1	0	tr.	.1
Pepper, banana:							
rings (Vlasic), 1 oz.	4	0	1.0	0	0	465	n.a.
Pepper, cherry:							
mild (Vlasic), 1 oz.	8	0	2.0	0	0	410	n.a.
Pepper, chili, green and red:							
raw, without seeds:							
1 medium, 1.6 oz.	18	.9	4.3	.1	0	3	.8
chopped, 1/2 cup	30	1.5	7.1	.2	0	5	1.4
canned:							
with liquid, chopped, 1/2 cup	17	.6	4.2	.1	0	n.a.	.8
green, all styles (Del Monte), 1/2 cup	20	0	5.0	0	0	690	n.a.
green, all styles (Ortega), 1 oz.	10	.4	2.6	.1	0	22	.5
Pepper, sweet:							
fresh, green and red:							
raw, 1 medium (3³/4″ × 3″ diam.)	18	.6	3.9	.3	0	2	.9
raw, chopped, 1 cup	24	.9	5.3	.5	0	4	1.2
boiled, drained, 1 medium (3³/4″)	13	.5	2.8	.2	0	2	.6
boiled, drained, chopped, 1 cup	24	.8	5.3	.4	0	2	1.2
frozen, 2 oz.:							
green and red (Southland) . .	15	0	2.0	0	0	45	n.a.
green, diced (Southland)	15	0	2.0	0	0	45	n.a.
green, and onions (Southland) . .	15	0	2.0	0	0	0	n.a.
Pepper, green, stuffed, dinner:							
frozen (Dinner Classics), 12 oz. . . .	360	16.0	37.0	16.0	70	1750	n.a.

Food and Measure	cal.	prot. (gms)	carbo. (gms)	fat (gms)	chol. (mgs)	sod. (mgs)	fiber (gms)
Pepper, green, stuffed, entree, frozen:							
with beef *(Stouffer's)*, 7¾ oz.	220	11.0	18.0	11.0	n.a.	870	n.a.
with veal *(Weight Watchers)*, 11¾ oz.	270	26.0	29.0	6.0	n.a.	1230	n.a.
Pepper, jalapeño, canned:							
with liquid, chopped, ½ cup	17	.5	3.3	.4	0	995	1.6
(Vlasic Mexican), 1 oz.	8	0	2.0	0	0	380	n.a.
whole or diced *(Ortega)*, 1 oz. . .	10	.4	2.6	.1	0	22	.5
whole or sliced *(Del Monte)*, ½ cup . .	30	1.0	6.0	1.0	0	1690	n.a.
Pepper, pepper-oncini:							
(Vlasic Greek), 1 oz.	4	0	1.0	0	0	450	n.a.
Pepper sauce, hot:							
(Frank's), ½ tsp. . .	<1	<.1	.1	1.0	0	131	n.a.
(Tabasco), ¼ tsp.	0	0	0	0	0	10	0
Peppered loaf, 1 slice:							
(Eckrich Calorie Watcher), 1 oz. . .	40	5.0	1.0	2.0	n.a.	390	n.a.
(Oscar Mayer), 1 oz.	43	4.8	1.3	2.1	13	366	0
Pepperoni:							
(Hormel), 1 oz. . . .	140	6.0	0	13.0	n.a.	462	n.a.
(Hormel Leoni Brand), 1 oz.	130	6.0	0	12.0	n.a.	508	n.a.
(Hormel Perma-Fresh), 2 slices	80	3.0	0	7.0	n.a.	281	n.a.
(Hormel Rosa), 1 oz.	140	6.0	0	13.0	n.a.	626	n.a.
(Hormel Rosa Grande), 1 oz. . .	140	6.0	0	13.0	n.a.	512	n.a.
chunk *(Hormel)*, 1 oz.	140	6.0	0	12.0	n.a.	423	n.a.
sliced or Italian style *(Armour)*, 1 oz. . .	130	n.a.	n.a.	11.0	20	500	0

Food and Measure	cal.	prot. (gms)	carbo. (gms)	fat (gms)	chol. (mgs)	sod. (mgs)	fiber (gms)
sliced (Eckrich), 2 oz.	270	10.0	2.0	24.0	n.a.	n.a.	n.a.
bits, canned (Hormel), 1 tbsp.	35	2.0	0	3.0	n.a.	n.a.	n.a.
Perch:							
fresh, raw:							
ocean, Atlantic, 2.3-oz. fillet	60	11.9	0	1.0	27	48	0
ocean, Atlantic, meat only, 4 oz.	107	21.1	0	1.8	48	85	0
ocean, Pacific, whole, 1 lb. . .	116	23.3	0	1.8	n.a.	77	0
ocean, Pacific, meat only, 4 oz. . . .	108	21.5	0	1.7	n.a.	71	0
white, meat only, 4 oz.	134	21.9	0	4.5	n.a.	n.a.	0
yellow, meat only, 4 oz.	103	22.1	0	1.0	n.a.	77	0
frozen:							
(Van de Kamp's Today's Catch), 4 oz.	110	20.0	0	0	n.a.	180	n.a.
raw, portions (Taste O'Sea Calorie Watcher), 1 portion	100	16.0	0	4.0	n.a.	70	n.a.
in batter (Van de Kamp's), 4 oz.	270	10.0	20.0	15.0	n.a.	510	n.a.
fillets (Booth Light & Tender), 4 oz.	100	19.0	0	2.0	n.a.	80	n.a.
fillets (Taste O'Sea), 4 oz.	100	19.0	0	3.0	n.a.	300	n.a.
fillets (Van de Kamp's Light & Crispy), 2-oz. piece	170	5.0	10.0	10.0	n.a.	115	n.a.
fillets, breaded (Certi-Fresh Light & Crunchy), 5 oz.	265	16.0	26.0	12.0	n.a.	570	n.a.
fillets, breaded (Mrs. Paul's), 2 fillets	290	13.0	21.0	17.0	n.a.	480	n.a.

Food and Measure	cal.	prot. (gms)	carbo. (gms)	fat (gms)	chol. (mgs)	sod. (mgs)	fiber (gms)
Perch, frozen *(cont.)*							
ocean *(Gorton's Fishmarket Fresh)*, 4 oz. . .	100	19.0	1.0	2.0	n.a.	100	n.a.
Perch dinner: frozen *(Taste O'Sea)*, 9 oz.	540	22.0	57.0	25.0	n.a.	890	n.a.
Persimmons, fresh:							
Japanese, or kaki:							
trimmed, 4 oz. . .	79	.7	21.1	.2	0	1	1.7
1 average (2½″ diam.)	118	1.0	31.2	.3	0	3	2.5
dried, 4 oz.	311	1.6	83.3	.7	0	n.a.	4.1
native:							
trimmed and seeded, 4 oz.	144	.9	38.0	.5	0	1	1.7
1 average	32	.2	8.4	.1	0	0	.4
Pheasant, raw:							
whole, ready to cook, 1 lb.	596	95.9	0	20.5	n.a.	n.a.	0
meat only, 4 oz. . .	184	26.8	0	7.7	n.a.	n.a.	0
Picante sauce, canned or in jars:							
(Tostitos), 3⅛ oz.	45	1.0	8.0	1.0	0	520	n.a.
(Ortega Salsa), 1 oz.	10	.4	2.4	.1	0	304	.2
hot *(Del Monte)*, ¼ cup	20	0	4.0	0	0	385	n.a.
hot and chunky *(Del Monte)*, ¼ cup . .	15	0	3.0	0	0	405	n.a.
Pickerel, chain:							
raw, meat only, 4 oz.	95	21.2	0	.6	n.a.	n.a.	0
Pickle, cucumber, 1 oz., except as noted:							
bread and butter:							
fresh	21	.3	5.1	.1	0	191	.1
chunks *(Vlasic* Old Fashioned/*Vlasic* Deli)	25	0	6.0	0	0	120	n.a.

Food and Measure	cal.	prot. (gms)	carbo. (gms)	fat (gms)	chol. (mgs)	sod. (mgs)	fiber (gms)
slices (Heinz) . . .	25	0	6.0	0	0	170	n.a.
sweet, butter chips (Vlasic)	30	0	7.0	0	0	160	n.a.
sweet, butter sticks (Vlasic Stix) . .	18	0	5.0	0	0	110	n.a.
chowchow, with cauli- flower:							
sour	8	.4	1.2	.4	0	379	.2
sweet	33	.4	7.7	.3	0	150	.3
cucumber chips (Nal- ley)	26	.3	6.5	0	0	200	n.a.
dill:							
(Claussen No Gar- lic)	6	.2	1.1	.1	0	300	n.a.
(Heinz Genuine)	2	0	0	0	0	420	n.a.
(Heinz Processed)	2	0	0	0	0	435	n.a.
(Nalley)	3	.3	.6	0	0	386	n.a.
(Vlasic No Garlic)	4	0	1.0	0	0	210	n.a.
(Vlasic Original)	2	0	1.0	0	0	375	n.a.
whole or spears (Heinz Polish Style)	4	0	1.0	0	0	285	n.a.
whole or chips (Nal- ley Banquet) . .	3	.3	.9	0	0	408	n.a.
crunchy (Vlasic Zesty)	4	0	1.0	0	0	250	n.a.
halves (Heinz Deli Style)	4	0	1.0	0	0	280	n.a.
halves (Heinz Old Fashioned Deli Style)	4	0	1.0	0	0	275	n.a.
hamburger chips (Vlasic Half the Salt)	2	0	1.0	0	0	175	n.a.
hamburger slices (Heinz)	2	0	0	0	0	405	n.a.
kosher (Nalley) . .	5	.3	.9	0	0	386	n.a.
kosher (Vlasic Deli)	4	0	1.0	0	0	290	n.a.

Food and Measure	cal.	prot. (gms)	carbo. (gms)	fat (gms)	chol. (mgs)	sod. (mgs)	fiber (gms)
Pickle, cucumber, dill *(cont.)*							
kosher, whole or spears *(Heinz)*	4	0	1.0	0	0	295	n.a.
kosher, whole *(Heinz* Old Fashioned)	4	0	1.0	0	0	280	n.a.
kosher, baby *(Heinz)*	4	0	1.0	0	0	285	n.a.
kosher, chips *(Heinz)*	4	0	1.0	0	0	275	n.a.
kosher, chips *(Heinz* Old Fashioned)	4	0	1.0	0	0	270	n.a.
kosher, baby, crunchy or gherkins *(Vlasic)* . .	4	0	1.0	0	0	210	n.a.
kosher, crunchy *(Vlasic* Half the Salt)	4	0	1.0	0	0	125	n.a.
kosher, fresh pack *(Nalley)*	3	.3	.9	0	0	408	n.a.
kosher, spears *(Vlasic)*	4	0	1.0	0	0	175	n.a.
kosher, spears *(Vlasic* Half the Salt)	4	0	1.0	0	0	120	n.a.
Polish *(Nalley)* . .	3	.3	.6	0	0	395	n.a.
spears *(Vlasic* Zesty)	4	0	1.0	0	0	230	n.a.
hamburger chips *(Nalley)*	3	.3	.6	0	0	420	n.a.
kosher, whole *(Claussen)*, 2-oz. piece	7	.4	1.2	.1	0	558	n.a.
kosher, slices *(Claussen)*	3	.1	.6	<.1	0	319	n.a.
mixed, hot and spicy *(Vlasic)*	4	0	1.0	0	0	380	n.a.
sweet:							
(Claussen)	51	<.1	11.9	.4	0	170	n.a.

Food and Measure	cal.	prot. (gms)	carbo. (gms)	fat (gms)	chol. (mgs)	sod. (mgs)	fiber (gms)
(Heinz/Heinz Gher-kins)	35	0	8.0	0	0	210	n.a.
(Nalley)	37	n.a.	9.6	0	0	227	n.a.
butter chips *(Vlasic Half the Salt)*	30	0	7.0	0	0	80	n.a.
chips *(Nalley)* . . .	31	n.a.	8.5	0	0	196	n.a.
gherkins, midget *(Heinz)*	35	0	8.0	0	0	205	n.a.
mixed *(Heinz)* . .	40	0	9.0	0	0	200	n.a.
mixed *(Nalley)* . .	31	.3	7.9	0	0	207	n.a.
nubbins *(Nalley)*	28	n.a.	7.1	0	0	225	n.a.
salad cubes *(Heinz)*	30	0	7.0	0	0	270	n.a.
slices *(Heinz)* . . .	35	0	8.0	0	0	205	n.a.
slices *(Heinz Cu-cumber Slices)*	20	0	5.0	0	0	195	n.a.
sticks *(Heinz Cu-cumber Stix)* . .	25	0	6.0	0	0	145	n.a.
sweet and sour *(Claussen)*	19	.1	4.3	<.1	0	136	n.a.
Pickle, cucumber, relish, 1 oz.:							
dill *(Vlasic)*	2	0	1.0	0	0	415	n.a.
hamburger:							
(Heinz)	30	0	7.0	0	0	330	n.a.
(Nalley)	28	.3	6.8	0	0	225	n.a.
(Vlasic)	40	0	9.0	0	0	255	n.a.
hot dog:							
(Heinz)	35	0	8.0	0	0	200	n.a.
(Nalley)	31	.6	6.8	.6	0	349	n.a.
(Vlasic)	40	0	8.0	1.0	0	255	n.a.
India *(Heinz)*	35	0	9.0	0	0	211	n.a.
piccalilli *(Heinz)* . . .	30	0	7.0	0	0	140	n.a.
sweet:							
(Heinz)	35	0	9.0	0	0	200	n.a.
(Nalley)	31	.3	7.9	0	0	227	n.a.
(Vlasic)	30	0	8.0	0	0	220	n.a.
Pickle loaf:							
(Eckrich), 1 slice . .	80	3.0	2.0	7.0	n.a.	320	n.a.

Food and Measure	cal.	prot. (gms)	carbo. (gms)	fat (gms)	chol. (mgs)	sod. (mgs)	fiber (gms)
Pickle loaf *(cont.)*							
(Eckrich Smorgas Pac), 1 slice . . .	90	3.0	2.0	8.0	n.a.	320	n.a.
(Hormel Perma-Fresh), 2 slices	102	8.0	3.0	7.0	n.a.	752	n.a.
(Light & Lean), 2 slices	100	8.0	3.0	6.0	n.a.	n.a.	n.a.
beef *(Eckrich Smorgas Pac)*, 1 slice . . .	50	2.0	1.0	5.0	n.a.	260	n.a.
Pickle and pimento loaf:							
(Armour), 1-oz. slice	80	n.a.	n.a.	7.0	10	350	n.a.
(Oscar Mayer), 1-oz. slice	62	4.2	1.4	4.4	12	315	n.a.
Picnic loaf:							
(Oscar Mayer), 1-oz. slice	62	4.2	1.4	4.4	12	315	n.a.
Pie, frozen:							
apple:							
(Banquet), 3¹/3 oz.	253	2.0	37.0	11.0	n.a.	282	n.a.
(Pet-Ritz), 4¹/3 oz.	330	2.0	53.0	12.0	n.a.	n.a.	n.a.
banana cream:							
(Banquet), 2¹/3 oz.	177	2.0	21.0	10.0	n.a.	146	n.a.
(Pet-Ritz), 2¹/3 oz.	170	2.0	22.0	9.0	n.a.	n.a.	n.a.
blackberry *(Banquet)*, 3¹/3 oz.	268	3.0	40.0	11.0	n.a.	342	n.a.
blueberry:							
(Banquet), 3¹/3 oz.	266	3.0	40.0	11.0	n.a.	342	n.a.
(Pet-Ritz), 4¹/3 oz.	370	3.0	50.0	12.0	n.a.	n.a.	n.a.
cherry:							
(Banquet), 3¹/3 oz.	252	3.0	36.0	11.0	n.a.	258	n.a.
(Pet-Ritz), 4¹/3 oz.	300	3.0	48.0	12.0	n.a.	n.a.	n.a.
chocolate cream:							
(Banquet), 2¹/3 oz.	185	2.0	24.0	10.0	n.a.	106	n.a.
(Pet-Ritz), 2¹/3 oz.	190	1.0	27.0	8.0	n.a.	n.a.	n.a.
coconut cream:							
(Banquet), 2¹/3 oz.	187	2.0	22.0	11.0	n.a.	113	n.a.
(Pet-Ritz), 2¹/3 oz.	190	2.0	27.0	8.0	n.a.	n.a.	n.a.

Food and Measure	cal.	prot. (gms)	carbo. (gms)	fat (gms)	chol. (mgs)	sod. (mgs)	fiber (gms)
custard, egg (Pet-Ritz), 4 oz.	200	5.0	28.0	8.0	n.a.	n.a.	n.a.
lemon cream:							
(Banquet), 2¹/₃ oz.	173	2.0	23.0	9.0	n.a.	111	n.a.
(Pet-Ritz), 2¹/₃ oz.	190	2.0	26.0	9.0	n.a.	n.a.	n.a.
mincemeat:							
(Banquet), 3¹/₃ oz.	258	3.0	38.0	11.0	n.a.	364	n.a.
(Pet-Ritz), 4 oz.	280	2.0	48.0	9.0	n.a.	n.a.	n.a.
peach:							
(Banquet), 3¹/₃ oz.	244	3.0	35.0	11.0	n.a.	275	n.a.
(Pet-Ritz), 4¹/₃ oz.	320	2.0	51.0	12.0	n.a.	n.a.	n.a.
pumpkin:							
(Banquet), 3¹/₃ oz.	197	3.0	29.0	8.0	n.a.	341	n.a.
(Pet-Ritz), 4¹/₃ oz.	250	4.0	39.0	9.0	n.a.	n.a.	n.a.
strawberry cream:							
(Banquet), 2¹/₃ oz.	168	2.0	22.0	9.0	n.a.	112	n.a.
(Pet-Ritz), 2¹/₃ oz.	170	2.0	20.0	9.0	n.a.	n.a.	n.a.
Pie, mix:							
chocolate mint (Royal No Bake), ¹/₈ pie*	260	5.0	25.0	15.0	n.a.	280	n.a.
Pie, snack, 1 pie:							
apple:							
(Drake's)	220	2.0	30.0	10.0	n.a.	230	n.a.
(Hostess)	390	5.0	45.0	20.0	18	540	n.a.
(Tastykake)	362	3.9	52.1	14.2	n.a.	458	n.a.
apple, French (Tastykake)	420	4.2	72.4	11.4	n.a.	442	n.a.
berry (Hostess) . . .	390	3.0	48.0	20.0	18	490	n.a.
blueberry:							
(Hostess)	390	3.0	49.0	20.0	18	450	n.a.
(Tastykake)	376	3.4	62.3	11.4	n.a.	406	n.a.
cherry:							
(Hostess)	390	5.0	55.0	20.0	18	530	n.a.
(Tastykake)	356	3.7	61.7	9.5	n.a.	389	n.a.
coconut creme (Tastykake)	507	6.8	44.2	32.1	n.a.	285	n.a.

* Prepared according to package directions

Food and Measure	cal.	prot. (gms)	carbo. (gms)	fat (gms)	chol. (mgs)	sod. (mgs)	fiber (gms)
Pie, snack *(cont.)*							
lemon:							
(Hostess)	400	3.0	53.0	22.0	30	470	n.a.
(Tastykake)	373	4.2	53.6	14.6	n.a.	320	n.a.
peach:							
(Hostess)	400	4.0	53.0	20.0	18	445	n.a.
(Tastykake)	333	3.8	47.8	13.1	n.a.	391	n.a.
pineapple (Tastykake)	369	4.0	58.7	12.1	n.a.	393	n.a.
pumpkin (Tastykake)	358	6.2	55.1	11.5	n.a.	339	n.a.
strawberry (Hostess)	340	3.0	56.0	14.0	13	400	n.a.
(Tastykake Tasty Klair)	446	6.5	64.4	16.6	n.a.	240	n.a.
Pie crust mix:							
(Flako), 1 oz.	244	3.4	14.4	3.4	n.a.	314	.1
(Betty Crocker), 1/16 packet	120	1.0	10.0	8.0	n.a.	140	n.a.
(Pillsbury), 1/6 of 2 crust pie*	270	4.0	25.0	17.0	n.a.	430	n.a.
Pie crust shell, frozen or refrigerated:							
(Pet-Ritz), .8 oz. or 1/6 pie	110	1.0	11.0	7.0	n.a.	n.a.	n.a.
(Pillsbury All Ready), 1/8 pic	240	2.0	24.0	15.0	n.a.	310	n.a.
deep dish (Pet-Ritz), 1 oz. or 1/6 pie . . .	130	1.0	12.0	8.0	n.a.	n.a.	n.a.
Pie crust stick:							
(Betty Crocker), 1/8 stick	120	1.0	10.0	8.0	n.a.	140	n.a.
(Pillsbury), 1/6 of 2 crust pie	270	4.0	25.0	17.0	n.a.	430	n.a.
Pie filling, canned, 3.5 oz. or 1/6 pie, except as noted:							
apple:							
(Comstock)	120	0	30.0	0	0	15	.4
(Comstock Lite)	80	0	20.0	0	0	10	.4

* *Prepared according to package directions*

Food and Measure	cal.	prot. (gms)	carbo. (gms)	fat (gms)	chol. (mgs)	sod. (mgs)	fiber (gms)
(Thank You) . . .	90	0	23.0	0	0	95	.3
(Thank You Reduced Calorie), 3.25 oz.	60	0	14.0	0	0	95	.3
apricot *(Comstock)*	110	0	29.0	0	0	100	.4
banana *(Comstock)*	110	1.0	22.0	2.0	0	300	.5
blueberry:							
(Comstock)	110	0	28.0	0	0	15	.6
(Comstock Lite)	75	0	17.0	0	0	15	.6
cherry:							
(Comstock)	110	0	28.0	0	0	15	.3
(Comstock Lite)	75	0	19.0	0	0	15	.3
(Thank You) . . .	100	0	25.0	0	0	15	.2
(Thank You Reduced Calorie)	85	0	21.0	0	0	10	.1
sweet *(Thank You)*	120	0	29.0	0	0	20	.2
chocolate *(Comstock)*	130	1.0	26.0	3.0	0	240	.2
coconut *(Comstock)*	120	1.0	22.0	3.0	0	290	.2
lemon *(Comstock)*	140	0	34.0	1.0	0	110	.1
mincemeat:							
(Comstock)	150	0	39.0	1.0	0	180	.7
condensed *(None Such)*, 1/3 cup	220	1.0	50.0	2.0	n.a.	330	n.a.
with brandy *(S&W Old Fashioned)*	206	1.0	49.0	2.0	n.a.	206	n.a.
with brandy and rum *(None Such)*, 1/3 cup	220	1.0	48.0	2.0	n.a.	265	n.a.
peach *(Comstock)*	110	0	26.0	0	0	20	.2
pineapple *(Comstock)*	100	0	28.0	0	0	65	.4
pumpkin:							
(Comstock)	100	0	24.0	0	0	180	n.a.
(Stokely's Finest), 1/2 cup	170	1.0	44.0	0	0	420	n.a.
raisin *(Comstock)* . .	120	0	32.0	0	0	80	n.a.
strawberry *(Comstock)*	100	0	25.0	0	0	20	.6
Pie filling, mix, see "Puddings and pie fillings"							

Food and Measure	cal.	prot. (gms)	carbo. (gms)	fat (gms)	chol. (mgs)	sod. (mgs)	fiber (gms)
Pierogies, frozen:							
(Golden), 1 piece . .	90	2.0	13.0	4.0	4	158	n.a.
potato and cheese *(Mrs. Paul's),* 3							
pieces	280	10.0	44.0	7.0	n.a.	720	n.a.
Pigeon peas:							
raw:							
in pods, 1 lb.	296	15.7	52.0	3.6	0	11	5.8
shelled, 1/2 cup . .	105	5.5	18.4	1.3	0	4	2.1
boiled, drained, 1/2							
cup	86	4.6	15.0	1.1	0	3	2.2
Pig's feet:							
pickled, 4 oz.	226	18.9	0	16.8	n.a.	n.a.	0
Pike, raw:							
blue:							
whole, 1 lb.	180	38.1	0	1.8	n.a.	n.a.	0
meat only, 4 oz.	102	21.7	0	1.0	n.a.	n.a.	0
northern:							
whole, 1 lb.	104	21.6	0	1.3	n.a.	n.a.	0
meat only, 4 oz.	100	21.8	0	.8	44	44	0
walleye:							
whole, 1 lb.	240	49.9	0	3.1	n.a.	132	0
meat only, 4 oz.	105	21.7	0	1.4	98	58	0
Pili nuts, dried:							
in shell, 1 lb.	619	9.3	3.4	68.5	0	3	2.4
shelled:							
4 oz.	816	12.3	4.5	90.4	0	4	3.2
1 cup	863	13.0	4.8	95.5	0	4	3.4
Pimentos, canned or in jars:							
with liquid, 4 oz. . .	31	1.0	6.6	.6	0	n.a.	.7
all types, drained *(Dromedary),* 1 oz.	10	0	2.0	0	0	5	n.a.
Pineapple:							
fresh:							
whole, 1 lb.	117	.9	29.2	1.0	0	2	1.3
trimmed, 4 oz. . .	56	.4	14.1	.5	0	1	.6
diced, 1 cup . . .	77	.6	19.2	.7	0	1	.8

Food and Measure	cal.	prot. (gms)	carbo. (gms)	fat (gms)	chol. (mgs)	sod. (mgs)	fiber (gms)
1 slice (3½″ × ¾″ diam.)	42	.3	10.4	.4	0	1	.5
candied, 1 oz. . . .	90	.2	22.7	.1	0	n.a.	.2
canned in water:							
8 oz.	73	1.0	18.8	.2	0	2	1.0
tidbits, 1 cup . . .	79	1.1	20.4	.2	0	3	1.1
canned in juice:							
8 oz.	136	1.0	35.6	.2	0	2	.8
chunks or tidbits, 1 cup	150	1.0	39.2	.2	0	4	.9
all cuts (Del Monte), ½ cup	70	0	18.0	0	0	10	n.a.
all cuts (Dole), ½ cup	70	.5	17.5	.5	0	1	n.a.
chunks or crushed (A&P), ½ cup	70	<1.0	18.0	<1.0	0	10	n.a.
slices (A&P), 2 slices with juice	70	<1.0	18.0	<1.0	0	10	n.a.
slices (S&W 100% Hawaiian), ½ cup	70	0	17.0	0	0	10	n.a.
spears (Del Monte), 2 spears	50	0	14.0	0	0	<10	n.a.
canned in heavy syrup:							
8 oz.	177	.8	45.8	.2	0	2	1.0
chunks, tidbits or crushed, 1 cup	199	.9	51.5	.3	0	3	1.1
all cuts (Del Monte), ½ cup	90	0	23.0	0	0	<10	n.a.
all cuts (Dole), ½ cup	95	.4	24.8	.2	0	2	n.a.
chunks, or crushed (A&P), ½ cup	90	<1.0	23.0	<1.0	0	10	n.a.
slices (A&P), 2 slices with syrup	90	<1.0	23.0	<1.0	0	10	n.a.
slices (S&W 100% Hawaiian), 2 slices	90	0	23.0	0	0	0	n.a.

Food and Measure	cal.	prot. (gms)	carbo. (gms)	fat (gms)	chol. (mgs)	sod. (mgs)	fiber (gms)
Pineapple *(cont.)*							
frozen:							
chunks, sweetened, 8 oz.	193	.9	50.3	.2	0	5	.7
chunks, sweetened, 1 cup	208	1.0	54.4	.3	0	5	.7
Pineapple juice:							
canned:							
(Del Monte), 6 fl. oz.	100	0	25.0	0	0	<10	n.a.
(Dole), 6 fl. oz. . .	103	.8	25.4	.2	0	2	n.a.
(S&W), 6 fl. oz. . .	100	0	25.0	0	0	0	n.a.
frozen* *(Minute Maid)*, 6 fl. oz.	93	<1.0	23.0	<.1	0	2	n.a.
Pineapple juice drink:							
(Magic Tree), 6 fl. oz.	110	0	25.0	1.0	0	0	n.a.
Pineapple-grapefruit juice:							
chilled or frozen* *(Dole)*, 6 fl. oz. . .	90	1.0	23.0	0	0	8	n.a.
Pineapple-grapefruit juice drink, canned:							
(Ocean Spray), 8 fl. oz.	143	<1.0	35.0	<1.0	0	8	n.a.
pink *(Dole)*, 6 fl. oz.	101	.4	25.4	.1	0	tr.	n.a.
pink or white *(Del Monte)*, 6 fl. oz.	90	0	24.0	0	0	50	n.a.
Pineapple-orange juice:							
chilled or frozen* *(Dole)*, 6 fl. oz. . .	100	1.0	23.0	0	0	8	n.a.
frozen* *(Minute Maid)*, 6 fl. oz.	91	<2.0	23.0	<.1	0	2	n.a.
Pineapple-orange juice drink, canned:							
(Del Monte), 6 fl. oz.	90	0	24.0	0	0	20	n.a.

* *Prepared according to package directions*

Food and Measure	cal.	prot. (gms)	carbo. (gms)	fat (gms)	chol. (mgs)	sod. (mgs)	fiber (gms)
(Magic Tree), 6 fl. oz.	100	0	25.0	0	0	0	n.a.
Pine nuts, dried:							
pignolias:							
shelled, 4 oz. . . .	584	27.3	16.2	57.6	0	4	.9
shelled, 1 tbsp. . . .	51	2.4	1.4	5.1	0	0	.1
pinons:							
in shell, 1 lb. . . .	1468	29.9	49.9	157.6	0	186	12.2
shelled, 4 oz. . . .	644	13.2	21.9	69.3	0	80	5.4
shelled, 10 nuts	6	.1	.2	.6	0	1	.1
Pistachio nuts:							
(Planters), 1 oz. . . .	170	5.0	6.0	15.0	0	250	n.a.
dried:							
in shell, 1 lb. . . .	1309	46.7	56.3	109.7	0	13	4.3
shelled, 4 oz. . . .	656	23.4	28.2	55.0	0	8	2.1
shelled, 1 cup . .	739	26.3	31.8	61.9	0	7	2.4
dry-roasted:							
in shell, unsalted, 1 lb.	1429	35.2	64.9	124.5	0	14	4.3
in shell, salted, 1 lb.	1429	35.2	64.9	124.5	0	3541	4.3
shelled, unsalted, 1 cup	776	19.1	35.2	67.6	0	8	2.3
shelled, salted, 1 cup	776	19.1	35.2	67.6	0	998	2.3
(Planters), 1 oz.	170	5.0	6.0	15.0	0	250	n.a.
red *(Planters)*, 1 oz.	170	5.0	6.0	15.0	0	250	n.a.
roasted in shell *(Laura Scudder's)*, 1 oz.	84	2.7	7.6	0	0	n.a.	.3
Pitanga (Surinam cherry), fresh:							
whole, 1 lb.	132	3.2	29.9	1.6	0	11	2.4
whole, 2 average . .	4	.1	1.0	.1	0	0	.1
1 cup	57	1.4	13.0	.7	0	5	1.0
Pizza, frozen:							
Canadian-style bacon:							
(Celeste), 7¾-oz. pie	541	27.3	49.6	26.0	n.a.	1593	.7
(Celeste), ¼ of 19-oz. pie	329	16.6	27.7	16.9	n.a.	976	.5

Food and Measure	cal.	prot. (gms)	carbo. (gms)	fat (gms)	chol. (mgs)	sod. (mgs)	fiber (gms)
Pizza, Canadian-style bacon *(cont.)*							
(Tombstone), 1/8 of							
22-oz. pie . . .	164	10.0	22.0	4.0	n.a.	460	n.a.
(Totino's My Classic), 1/4 pie . . .	320	16.0	38.0	12.0	n.a.	830	n.a.
(Totino's Party Pizza), 1/3 pie	230	10.0	27.0	9.0	n.a.	640	n.a.
(Celeste Deluxe), 81/4-oz. pie	582	22.7	51.2	31.8	n.a.	1308	1.2
(Celeste Deluxe), 1/4 of 221/4-oz. pie . .	378	15.5	29.3	22.1	n.a.	953	.8
(Celeste Suprema), 9-oz. pie	678	26.5	54.0	39.3	n.a.	1693	1.3
(Celeste Suprema), 1/4 of 23-oz. pie . . .	381	16.8	29.2	24.1	n.a.	1043	.8
cheese:							
(Celeste), 61/2-oz. pie	497	21.2	48.0	24.5	n.a.	828	.7
(Celeste), 1/4 of 173/4-oz. pie . .	317	14.2	27.8	16.6	n.a.	673	.5
(Tombstone), 1/8 of 20-oz. pie . . .	164	10.0	21.0	5.0	n.a.	369	n.a.
(Totino's Extra!), 1/4 pie	250	11.0	24.0	12.0	n.a.	450	n.a.
(Totino's Fox Deluxe), 1/3 pie	160	8.0	24.0	4.0	n.a.	430	n.a.
(Totino's Heat 'n Eat), 4.1 oz. . .	270	13.0	31.0	11.0	n.a.	670	n.a.
(Totino's Microwave), 3.9 oz.	250	11.0	31.0	9.0	n.a.	630	n.a.
(Totino's My Classic Deluxe), 1/4 pie	350	15.0	39.0	15.0	n.a.	810	n.a.
(Totino's Party Pizza), 1/3 pie	240	10.0	28.0	10.0	n.a.	480	n.a.
(Totino's Single Serve Microwave), 7.1-oz. pie.	490	20.0	56.0	21.0	n.a.	1170	n.a.

Food and Measure	cal.	prot. (gms)	carbo. (gms)	fat (gms)	chol. (mgs)	sod. (mgs)	fiber (gms)
cheese and hamburger (Tombstone), 1/8 of 22-oz. pie	179	10.0	22.0	6.0	n.a.	437	n.a.
cheese and sausage (Tombstone), 1/8 of 22-oz. pie	178	11.0	20.0	6.0	n.a.	335	n.a.
cheese, sausage and mushroom (Tombstone), 1/8 of 24-oz. pie	178	11.0	20.0	6.0	n.a.	417	n.a.
combination: (Tombstone), 1/8 of 22.5-oz. pie . .	187	11.0	21.0	7.0	n.a.	381	n.a.
(Totino's Heat 'n Eat), 4.8 oz. . .	380	14.0	31.0	21.0	n.a.	1190	n.a.
(Totino's My Classic Deluxe), 1/4 pie	460	18.0	40.0	25.0	n.a.	1040	n.a.
(Totino's Single Serve Microwave), 9-oz. pie	690	24.0	59.0	39.0	n.a.	1750	n.a.
hamburger: (Totino's Fox Deluxe), 1/3 pie	190	8.0	24.0	7.0	n.a.	510	n.a.
(Totino's Party Pizza), 1/3 pie	280	11.0	27.0	14.0	n.a.	630	n.a.
nacho (Totino's Party Pizza), 1/3 pie . . .	230	8.0	20.0	14.0	n.a.	440	n.a.
Mexican style (Totino's Party Pizza), 1/3 pie	250	7.0	21.0	15.0	n.a.	580	n.a.
pepperoni: (Celeste), 63/4-oz. pie	546	20.2	49.7	29.6	n.a.	1417	.8
(Celeste), 1/4 of 19-oz. pie	368	15.0	29.2	21.3	n.a.	1061	.5
(Totino's Extra!), 1/4 pie	250	11.0	24.0	12.0	n.a.	450	n.a.
(Totino's Fox Deluxe), 1/3 pie	190	7.0	24.0	7.0	n.a.	580	n.a.

Food and Measure	cal.	prot. (gms)	carbo. (gms)	fat (gms)	chol. (mgs)	sod. (mgs)	fiber (gms)
Pizza, pepperoni *(cont.)*							
(Totino's Heat 'n Eat), 4.6 oz. . .	350	13.0	31.0	18.0	n.a.	1070	n.a.
(Totino's Microwave), 4.2 oz.	310	11.0	31.0	15.0	n.a.	1090	n.a.
(Totino's My Classic Deluxe), 1/4 pie	410	17.0	40.0	20.0	n.a.	1090	n.a.
(Totino's Party Pizza), 1/3 pie	260	9.0	28.0	12.0	n.a.	700	n.a.
(Totino's Single Serve Microwave), 81/2-oz. pie	610	23.0	59.0	31.0	n.a.	1760	n.a.
sausage:							
(Celeste), 71/2-oz. pie	571	22.6	48.8	31.7	n.a.	1374	1.1
(Celeste), 1/4 of 20-oz. pie	376	15.6	29.7	21.7	n.a.	988	.7
(Totino's Extra!), 1/4 pie	280	10.0	24.0	16.0	n.a.	770	n.a.
(Totino's Fox Deluxe), 1/3 pie	190	7.0	24.0	7.0	n.a.	590	n.a.
(Totino's Heat 'n Eat), 4.8 oz. . .	360	13.0	31.0	20.0	n.a.	1130	n.a.
(Totino's Microwave), 4.2 oz.	300	10.0	31.0	15.0	n.a.	920	n.a.
(Totino's My Classic Deluxe), 1/4 pie	440	16.0	41.0	24.0	n.a.	980	n.a.
(Totino's Party Pizza), 1/3 pie	270	9.0	27.0	14.0	n.a.	750	n.a.
(Totino's Single Serve Microwave), 83/4-oz. pie	660	22.0	59.0	37.0	n.a.	1620	n.a.
smoked, with pepperoni seasoning *(Tombstone),* 1/8 of 22-oz. pie . .	183	11.0	21.0	6.0	n.a.	382	n.a.
sausage and mushroom:							
(Celeste), 81/2-oz. pie	592	23.9	51.3	32.3	n.a.	1347	1.2

Food and Measure	cal.	prot. (gms)	carbo. (gms)	fat (gms)	chol. (mgs)	sod. (mgs)	fiber (gms)
(Celeste), 1/4 of 22 1/2-oz. pie . .	387	16.9	29.4	22.4	n.a.	1033	1.0
sausage and pepperoni:							
(Totino's Extra!), 1/4 pie	290	11.0	25.0	16.0	n.a.	800	n.a.
(Totino's Fox Deluxe), 1/3 pie	190	7.0	24.0	7.0	n.a.	590	n.a.
(Totino's Microwave), 4.2 oz.	310	11.0	31.0	15.0	n.a.	1090	n.a.
(Totino's Party Pizza), 1/3 pie	270	10.0	27.0	13.0	n.a.	740	n.a.
(Tombstone Special Deluxe), 1/8 of 24-oz. pie	182	11.0	22.0	6.0	n.a.	417	n.a.
Pizza, mix*, 1/4 pie:							
thick crust *(Contadina* Pizzeria)	295	8.8	56.0	3.8	n.a.	820	n.a.
thin crust *(Contadina* Pizzeria)	209	6.2	39.2	3.0	n.a.	650	n.a.
Pizza, French bread, frozen:							
cheese *(Stouffer's)*, 5.2 oz.	340	15.0	41.0	13.0	n.a.	840	n.a.
deluxe *(Stouffer's)*, 6.2 oz.	430	18.0	41.0	21.0	n.a.	1130	n.a.
hamburger *(Stouffer's)*, 6.1 oz. . . .	410	21.0	40.0	18.0	n.a.	1040	n.a.
pepperoni *(Stouffer's)*, 5.6 oz.	390	17.0	41.0	18.0	n.a.	1040	n.a.
sausage *(Stouffer's)*, 6 oz.	420	18.0	42.0	20.0	n.a.	1080	n.a.
sausage and mushroom *(Stouffer's)*, 6 1/4 oz.	400	18.0	44.0	17.0	n.a.	1160	n.a.

* *Prepared according to package directions*

Food and Measure	cal.	prot. (gms)	carbo. (gms)	fat (gms)	chol. (mgs)	sod. (mgs)	fiber (gms)
Pizza sauce:							
chunky *(Ragu Pizza Quick)*, 3 tbsp. . . .	45	1.0	6.0	2.0	0	n.a.	n.a.
Plantain (baking banana), fresh:							
whole, 9.7 oz.	218	2.3	57.1	.7	0	7	.9
peeled, 4 oz.	138	1.5	36.2	.4	0	5	.6
cooked, sliced, 1 cup	179	1.2	48.0	.3	0	8	n.a.
Plum:							
fresh:							
whole, 1 lb.	235	3.4	55.5	2.6	0	2	2.6
pitted, 4 oz. . . .	62	.9	14.8	.7	0	0	.7
pitted, sliced, 1 cup	91	1.3	21.5	1.0	0	1	1.0
Japanese or hybrid, 1 average (2¹⁄₈″ diam.)	36	.5	8.6	.4	0	0	.4
canned in water:							
with liquid, 1 cup	102	1.0	27.5	<.1	0	2	.6
3 plums and 2 tbsp. liquid	39	.4	10.5	<.1	0	1	.2
(Thank You), 1/2 cup	50	0	12.0	0	0	<5	0
canned in light syrup:							
(Stokely's Finest), 1/2 cup	100	0	16.0	0	0	20	n.a.
(Thank You), 1/2 cup	80	0	20.0	0	0	10	0
canned in heavy syrup:							
with liquid, 1 cup	230	.9	60.0	.3	0	50	.9
3 plums and 2³⁄₄ tbsp. liquid . . .	119	.5	30.9	.1	0	26	.4
(Stokely's Finest), 1/2 cup	130	0	30.0	0	0	25	n.a.
(Thank You), 1/2 cup	230	1.0	55.0	0	0	30	.9
canned in extra heavy syrup *(S&W Fancy)*, 1/2 cup	135	0	35.0	0	0	25	n.a.
Poi:							
1 cup	269	.9	65.4	.3	0	28	1.3

Food and Measure	cal.	prot. (gms)	carbo. (gms)	fat (gms)	chol. (mgs)	sod. (mgs)	fiber (gms)
Poke shoots (poke-berry):							
raw, 1 cup	37	4.2	5.9	.6	0	n.a.	n.a.
boiled, drained, 1 cup	33	3.8	5.1	.7	0	n.a.	n.a.
Polish sausage, see "Kielbasa"							
Pollock:							
fresh, raw fillets:							
Atlantic, 4 oz. . .	104	22.0	0	1.1	81	98	0
walleye, 4 oz. . .	92	19.5	0	.9	81	112	0
frozen:							
fillets *(Taste O' Sea),* 4 oz. . . .	90	22.0	0	0	n.a.	110	0
sticks *(Taste O' Sea,* 8/14 oz.), 4 oz.	240	13.0	20.0	12.0	n.a.	690	n.a.
sticks *(Taste O' Sea,* 24 oz.), 3.4 oz.	210	11.0	19.0	11.0	n.a.	630	n.a.
Polynesian style dinner:							
frozen *(Swanson),* 12 oz.	360	21.0	52.0	8.0	n.a.	1430	n.a.
Pomegranate, fresh:							
whole, 1 lb.	172	2.4	43.6	.8	0	8	.5
1 average (3³/8″ × 3³/4″ diam.)	104	1.5	26.4	.5	0	5	.3
Pompano:							
raw, meat only, 4 oz.	186	21.0	0	10.7	57	74	0
broiled, fillets, 4 oz.	239	26.9	0	13.8	73	86	0
Popcorn, popped:							
plain, 2 oz.	219	7.2	43.5	2.8	0	2	1.2
with oil and salt, 2 oz.	259	5.6	33.5	12.4	0	1100	1.0
(Bachman), 1 oz. . .	160	2.0	13.0	11.0	0	310	n.a.
(Orville Redenbacher's Gourmet), 4 cups	90	3.0	18.0	1.0	0	0	n.a.
(Pop Secret Natural Flavor), 4 cups . .	230	4.0	27.0	13.0	n.a.	480	n.a.

Food and Measure	cal.	prot. (gms)	carbo. (gms)	fat (gms)	chol. (mgs)	sod. (mgs)	fiber (gms)
Popcorn *(cont.)*							
(Tom's Natural), 3/4							
oz.	110	2.0	13.0	6.0	0	230	n.a.
butter flavor:							
(Pop Secret), 4							
cups	230	4.0	27.0	14.0	n.a.	450	n.a.
(Wise), 1/2 oz. . .	70	1.0	8.0	4.0	n.a.	n.a.	n.a.
caramel, see "Candy"							
cheese:							
(Bachman), 1 oz.	180	2.0	14.0	12.0	0	330	n.a.
(Snyders), 1 oz.	150	3.0	13.0	10.0	n.a.	250	.8
(Tom's), 7/8 oz. . .	130	2.0	15.0	7.0	n.a.	400	n.a.
(Wise), 1/2 oz. . .	90	1.0	7.0	6.0	n.a.	n.a.	n.a.
granola crunch *(Orville*							
Redenbacher's							
Gourmet), 1 oz.	140	2.0	17.0	8.0	0	< 10	n.a.
sesame crunch							
(Orville							
Redenbacher's							
Gourmet), 1 oz.	130	1.0	18.0	6.0	0	190	n.a.
with oil and salt							
(Orville							
Redenbacher's							
Gourmet), 4 cups	160	3.0	21.0	8.0	0	700	n.a.
white:							
(Jolly Time), 4 cups	75	3.0	16.0	1.0	0	n.a.	.5
(Orville							
Redenbacher's							
Gourmet), 4 cups	90	3.0	18.0	1.0	0	0	n.a.
white, with oil and salt							
(Orville							
Redenbacher's							
Gourmet), 4 cups	160	3.0	21.0	8.0	0	700	n.a.
yellow *(Jolly Time),* 4							
cups	88	3.0	19.0	1.0	0	n.a.	.5
microwave:							
(Orville							
Redenbacher's							
Gourmet), 4 cups	140	3.0	16.0	8.0	0	290	n.a.

Food and Measure	cal.	prot. (gms)	carbo. (gms)	fat (gms)	chol. (mgs)	sod. (mgs)	fiber (gms)
(Pillsbury Original), 4 cups	260	4.0	28.0	15.0	0	400	n.a.
(Pops-Rite), 4 cups	167	4.0	21.0	7.0	0	226	n.a.
natural flavor *(Jolly Time),* 4 cups	220	3.0	20.0	14.0	0	240	n.a.
salt free *(Orville Redenbacher's Gourmet),* 4 cups	150	3.0	17.0	9.0	0	0	n.a.
salt free *(Pillsbury),* 4 cups	190	4.0	26.0	8.0	0	5	n.a.
butter flavored *(Orville Redenbacher's Gourmet),* 4 cups	140	2.0	17.0	7.0	n.a.	210	n.a.
butter flavored *(Pillsbury),* 4 cups	260	4.0	29.0	14.0	n.a.	410	n.a.
with butter *(Jolly Time),* 4 cups	220	3.0	20.0	14.0	n.a.	270	n.a.
with cheese *(Pops-Rite),* 4 cups . .	196	4.0	21.0	10.0	n.a.	242	n.a.
Popover mix:							
(Flako), 1.7 oz. . . .	102	3.2	19.6	1.2	n.a.	273	0
Poppy seeds:							
(all brands), 1 tsp.	15	.5	.7	1.3	0	1	.2
Porgy, raw:							
whole, 1 lb.	208	35.3	0	6.3	n.a.	117	0
meat only, 4 oz. . .	127	21.5	0	3.9	n.a.	71	0
Pork, fresh, retail cuts, meat only (see also "Ham"):							
Boston blade (shoulder), lean with fat:							
braised, 3 oz. (5.6 oz. raw with bone)	316	22.4	0	24.4	95	57	0
braised, 1 steak, 6.3 oz. with bone	594	42.2	0	45.9	178	107	0
broiled, 3 oz. (4.9 oz. raw with bone)	297	18.6	0	24.2	87	63	0

Food and Measure	cal.	prot. (gms)	carbo. (gms)	fat (gms)	chol. (mgs)	sod. (mgs)	fiber (gms)
Pork, Boston blade (shoulder), lean with fat *(cont.)*							
broiled, 1 steak, 7.4 oz. with bone	647	40.1	0	52.6	190	138	0
roasted, 3 oz. (4.9 oz. raw with bone)	273	18.5	0	21.5	82	57	0
roasted, 1 steak, 7.5 oz. with bone	594	40.3	0	46.8	179	125	0
Boston blade (shoulder), lean (fat trimmed):							
braised, 3 oz. (6.9 oz. raw with bone and fat)	250	26.5	0	15.0	99	64	0
braised, 1 steak, 6.3 oz. with bone and fat	382	40.5	0	22.9	151	98	0
broiled, 3 oz. (6.0 oz. raw with bone and fat)	233	21.4	0	15.7	89	71	0
broiled, 1 steak, 7.4 oz. with bone and fat	413	38.0	0	27.8	159	126	0
roasted, 3 oz. (5.7 oz. raw with bone and fat)	218	20.7	0	14.3	83	62	0
roasted, 1 steak, 7.5 oz. with bone and fat	404	38.5	0	26.6	155	116	0
center loin, lean with fat:							
braised, 3 oz. (6.0 oz. raw with bone)	301	25.0	0	21.6	91	43	0
braised, 1 chop, 3.2 oz. with bone	266	22.1	0	19.0	81	38	0
broiled, 3 oz. (5.2 oz. raw with bone)	269	23.3	0	18.8	82	59	0

Food and Measure	cal.	prot. (gms)	carbo. (gms)	fat (gms)	chol. (mgs)	sod. (mgs)	fiber (gms)
broiled, 1 chop, 3.7 oz. with bone	275	23.9	0	19.2	84	61	0
pan-fried, 3 oz. (5.1 oz. raw with bone)	318	19.8	0	25.9	87	61	0
pan-fried, 1 chop, 4.0 oz. with bone	333	20.7	0	27.2	92	64	0
roasted, 3 oz. (5.1 oz. raw with bone)	259	21.6	0	18.5	78	54	0
roasted, 1 chop, 3.8 oz. with bone	268	22.4	0	19.1	80	56	0
center loin, lean (fat trimmed):							
braised, 3 oz. (7.4 oz. raw with bone and fat)	231	29.6	0	11.7	95	46	0
braised, 1 chop, 3.2 oz. with bone and fat	166	21.2	0	8.4	68	33	0
broiled, 3 oz. (6.3 oz. raw with bone and fat)	196	27.2	0	8.9	83	66	0
broiled, 1 chop, 3.7 oz. with bone and fat	166	23.0	0	7.5	71	56	0
pan-fried, 3 oz. (6.7 oz. raw with bone and fat)	226	24.5	0	13.5	91	72	0
pan-fried, 1 chop, 4.0 oz. with bone and fat	178	19.3	0	10.7	71	57	0
roasted, 3 oz. (6.0 oz. raw with bone and fat)	204	24.2	0	11.1	78	59	0
roasted, 1 chop, 3.8 oz. with bone and fat	180	21.4	0	9.8	68	52	0

Food and Measure	cal.	prot. (gms)	carbo. (gms)	fat (gms)	chol. (mgs)	sod. (mgs)	fiber (gms)
Pork *(cont.)*							
center rib, lean with fat:							
braised, 3 oz. (6.8 oz. raw with bone)	312	24.3	0	23.1	81	41	0
braised, 1 chop, 3.1 oz. with bone	246	19.2	0	18.2	64	32	0
broiled, 3 oz. (5.9 oz. raw with bone)	291	20.9	0	22.4	79	52	0
broiled, 1 chop, 3.7 oz. with bone	264	18.9	0	20.3	72	47	0
pan-fried, 3 oz. (5.1 oz. raw with bone)	331	18.4	0	28.0	71	38	0
pan-fried, 1 chop, 4.2 oz. with bone	343	19.0	0	29.0	74	40	0
roasted, 3 oz. (5.7 oz. raw with bone)	271	21.0	0	20.1	69	37	0
roasted, 1 chop, 3.8 oz. with bone	252	19.6	0	18.6	64	35	0
center rib, lean (fat trimmed):							
braised, 3 oz. (8.6 oz. raw with bone and fat)	236	29.3	0	12.3	82	44	0
braised, 1 chop, 3.1 oz. with bone and fat	147	18.3	0	7.7	51	28	0
broiled, 3 oz. (7.2 oz. raw with bone and fat)	219	24.5	0	12.7	80	57	0
broiled, 1 chop, 3.7 oz. with bone and fat	162	18.2	0	9.4	59	42	0

Food and Measure	cal.	prot. (gms)	carbo. (gms)	fat (gms)	chol. (mgs)	sod. (mgs)	fiber (gms)
pan-fried, 3 oz. (7.3 oz. raw with bone and fat)	219	23.8	0	13.0	69	43	0
pan-fried, 1 chop, 4.2 oz. with bone and fat	160	17.3	0	9.5	50	31	0
roasted, 3 oz. (6.8 oz. raw with bone and fat)	208	24.0	0	11.7	67	39	0
roasted, 1 chop, 3.8 oz. with bone and fat	162	18.6	0	9.1	52	30	0
loin, blade, lean with fat:							
braised, 3 oz. (6.8 oz. raw with bone)	348	20.4	0	29.0	92	59	0
braised, 1 chop, 3.1 oz. with bone	275	16.1	0	22.8	72	46	0
broiled, 3 oz. (5.9 oz. raw with bone)	334	17.6	0	28.8	83	57	0
broiled, 1 chop, 3.7 oz. with bone	303	15.9	0	26.1	75	52	0
pan-fried, 3 oz. (5.1 oz. raw with bone)	352	16.0	0	31.4	81	52	0
pan-fried, 1 chop, 4.3 oz. with bone	368	16.7	0	32.9	85	55	0
roasted, 3 oz. (5.1 oz. raw with bone)	310	17.9	0	25.9	76	52	0
roasted, 1 chop, 4.2 oz. with bone	321	18.5	0	26.8	79	54	0
loin, blade, lean (fat trimmed):							
braised, 3 oz. (9.1 oz. raw with bone and fat)	266	25.3	0	17.5	96	69	0

Food and Measure	cal.	prot. (gms)	carbo. (gms)	fat (gms)	chol. (mgs)	sod. (mgs)	fiber (gms)
Pork, loin, blade, lean (fat trimmed) *(cont.)*							
braised, 1 chop, 3.1 oz. with bone and fat	156	14.9	0	10.3	57	41	0
broiled, 3 oz. (7.6 oz. raw with bone and fat)	255	21.2	0	18.3	85	65	0
broiled, 1 chop, 3.7 oz. with bone and fat	177	14.7	0	12.7	59	45	0
pan-fried, 3 oz. (7.3 oz. raw with bone and fat)	240	20.7	0	16.9	82	63	0
pan-fried, 1 chop, 4.3 oz. with bone and fat	175	15.1	0	12.3	60	46	0
roasted, 3 oz. (6.4 oz. raw with bone and fat)	238	21.0	0	16.4	76	58	0
roasted, 1 chop, 4.2 oz. with bone and fat	198	17.5	0	13.7	63	48	0
loin, whole, lean with fat:							
braised, 3 oz. (6.4 oz. raw with bone)	312	23.1	0	23.7	87	56	0
braised, 1 chop, 3.1 oz. with bone	261	19.3	0	19.8	73	46	0
broiled, 3 oz. (5.5 oz. raw with bone)	294	20.0	0	23.2	80	56	0
broiled, 1 chop, 3.7 oz. with bone	284	19.3	0	22.3	77	54	0
roasted, 3 oz. (5.5 oz. raw with bone)	271	19.9	0	20.7	77	53	0
roasted, 1 chop, 3.7 oz. with bone	262	19.2	0	19.9	74	52	0

Food and Measure	cal.	prot. (gms)	carbo. (gms)	fat (gms)	chol. (mgs)	sod. (mgs)	fiber (gms)
loin, whole, lean (fat trimmed):							
braised, 3 oz. (8.2 oz. raw with bone and fat)	232	28.0	0	12.4	90	63	0
braised, 1 chop, 3.1 oz. with bone and fat	150	18.1	0	8.0	58	41	0
broiled, 3 oz. (6.9 oz. raw with bone and fat)	218	23.7	0	13.0	81	64	0
broiled, 1 chop, 3.7 oz. with bone and fat	169	18.4	0	10.1	63	49	0
roasted, 3 oz. (6.6 oz. raw with bone and fat)	204	22.9	0	11.8	77	59	0
roasted, 1 chop, 3.7 oz. with bone and fat	166	18.6	0	9.6	62	48	0
picnic (shoulder), lean with fat:							
braised, 3 oz. (6.8 oz. with bone and skin)	293	22.8	0	21.7	93	74	0
braised, 1 cup . .	483	37.5	0	35.7	153	123	0
roasted, 3 oz. (5.5 oz. with bone and skin)	281	19.0	0	22.2	80	59	0
roasted, 1 cup . .	463	31.3	0	36.5	132	97	0
picnic (shoulder), lean (fat trimmed):							
braised, 3 oz. (8.6 oz. raw with bone, skin and fat) . .	211	27.4	0	10.4	97	87	0
braised, 1 cup . .	347	45.2	0	17.1	160	143	0
roasted, 3 oz. (7.1 oz. raw with bone, skin and fat) . .	194	22.7	0	10.7	81	68	0

Food and Measure	cal.	prot. (gms)	carbo. (gms)	fat (gms)	chol. (mgs)	sod. (mgs)	fiber (gms)
Pork, picnic (shoulder), lean (fat trimmed) *(cont.)*							
roasted, 1 cup . .	319	37.4	0	17.7	133	112	0
shoulder, lean with fat:							
roasted, 3 oz. (5.1 oz. raw with bone and skin)	277	18.7	0	21.8	81	58	0
roasted, 1 cup . .	456	30.8	0	36.0	134	96	0
shoulder, lean (fat trimmed):							
roasted, 3 oz. (6.2 oz. raw with bone, skin and fat) . .	207	21.6	0	12.7	82	65	0
roasted, 1 cup . .	341	35.5	0	21.0	135	107	0
sirloin, lean with fat:							
braised, 3 oz. (6.3 oz. raw with bone)	299	23.8	0	21.9	90	45	0
braised, 1 chop, 3.1 oz. with bone	250	19.9	0	18.3	75	38	0
broiled, 3 oz. (5.4 oz. raw with bone)	281	20.5	0	21.5	82	46	0
broiled, 1 chop, 3.7 oz. with bone	278	20.3	0	21.2	81	46	0
roasted, 3 oz. (5.4 oz. raw with bone)	247	21.3	0	17.4	77	50	0
roasted, 1 chop, 3.8 oz. with bone	244	21.0	0	17.1	76	49	0
sirloin, lean (fat trimmed):							
braised, 3 oz. (7.9 oz. raw with bone and fat)	221	28.5	0	11.1	94	50	0
braised, 1 chop, 3.1 oz. with bone and fat	149	19.1	0	7.4	63	34	0
broiled, 3 oz. (6.7 oz. raw with bone and fat)	207	24.0	0	11.5	83	51	0

Food and Measure	cal.	prot. (gms)	carbo. (gms)	fat (gms)	chol. (mgs)	sod. (mgs)	fiber (gms)
broiled, 1 chop, 3.7 oz. with bone and fat	165	19.2	0	9.2	67	41	0
roasted, 3 oz. (6.1 oz. raw with bone and fat)	201	23.4	0	11.2	77	53	0
roasted, 1 chop, 3.8 oz. with bone and fat	175	20.3	0	9.8	67	46	0
sparerib, lean with fat:							
braised, 6.3 oz. (1 lb. raw with bone)	703	51.4	0	53.6	214	165	0
braised, 3 oz. (7.7 oz. raw with bone)	338	24.7	0	25.8	103	79	0
tenderloin, lean:							
roasted, 12.6 oz. (1 lb. raw)	596	103.2	0	17.2	333	238	0
roasted, 3 oz. (3.8 oz. raw)	141	24.5	0	4.1	79	57	0
top loin, lean with fat:							
braised, 3 oz. (6.4 oz. raw with bone)	324	23.5	0	24.8	81	40	0
braised, 1 chop, 3.1 oz. with bone	267	19.4	0	20.4	67	33	0
broiled, 3 oz. (5.5 oz. raw with bone)	306	20.2	0	24.3	79	51	0
broiled, 1 chop, 3.7 oz. with bone	295	19.5	0	23.5	76	49	0
pan-fried, 3 oz. (5.2 oz. raw with bone)	333	18.3	0	28.2	71	38	0
pan-fried, 1 chop, 4.1 oz. with bone	337	18.5	0	28.6	72	39	0
roasted, 3 oz. (5.4 oz. raw with bone)	280	20.5	0	21.4	69	37	0

Food and Measure	cal.	prot. (gms)	carbo. (gms)	fat (gms)	chol. (mgs)	sod. (mgs)	fiber (gms)
Pork, top loin, lean with fat *(cont.)*							
roasted, 1 chop, 3.8 oz. with bone	274	20.1	0	20.9	68	36	0
top loin, lean (fat trimmed):							
braised, 3 oz. (8.4 oz. raw with bone and fat)	236	29.3	0	12.3	82	44	0
braised, 1 chop, 3.1 oz. with bone and fat	147	18.3	0	7.7	51	28	0
broiled, 3 oz. (7.1 oz. raw with bone and fat)	219	24.5	0	12.7	80	57	0
broiled, 1 chop, 3.7 oz. with bone and fat	165	18.4	0	9.6	60	43	0
pan-fried, 3 oz. (7.4 oz. raw with bone and fat)	219	23.8	0	13.0	69	43	0
pan-fried, 1 chop, 4.1 oz. with bone and fat	157	17.1	0	9.3	49	31	0
roasted, 3 oz. (6.7 oz. raw with bone and fat)	208	24.0	0	11.7	67	39	0
roasted, 1 chop, 3.8 oz. with bone and fat	167	19.2	0	9.4	54	31	0
Pork dinner, frozen:							
loin *(Swanson)*, 11¼ oz.	290	22.0	26.0	11.0	n.a.	710	n.a.
sweet and sour *(Dinner Classics)*, 12 oz.	490	36.0	48.0	18.0	95	870	n.a.
Pork entree, canned:							
chow mein *(La Choy Bi-Pack)*, ¾ cup	80	5.0	7.0	4.0	n.a.	950	n.a.
chow mein, drained *(Chun King* Stir-Fry), 6 oz.	116	11.0	11.2	3.8	23	496	.7

Food and Measure	cal.	prot. (gms)	carbo. (gms)	fat (gms)	chol. (mgs)	sod. (mgs)	fiber (gms)
Pork entree, frozen:							
gravy and breaded patties (Freezer Queen, 2 lb.), 10.67 oz.	420	16.0	32.0	25.0	n.a.	n.a.	n.a.
sweet and sour:							
(Chun King Boil-in-Bag), 10 oz. . .	338	13.1	56.8	6.5	43	1104	.9
(La Choy), 2/3 cup	180	7.0	32.0	3.0	n.a.	1100	n.a.
sweet and sour, with rice (Van de Kamp's Chinese Classic), 11 oz.	430	15.0	65.0	15.0	n.a.	790	n.a.
steaks, breaded (Hormel), 3 oz.	220	12.0	11.0	15.0	n.a.	n.a.	n.a.
Pork gravy:							
canned:							
(Franco-American), 2 oz.	40	0	3.0	3.0	n.a.	350	n.a.
(Heinz Home Style), 2 oz.	31	1.8	2.1	1.7	n.a.	130	n.a.
mix:							
(Durkee), 1-oz. pkg.	70	2.0	14.0	.5	n.a.	2175	n.a.
(Durkee Roastin' Bag), 1.5-oz. pkg.	130	3.0	26.0	1.0	n.a.	2579	n.a.
mix* (French's Gravy for Pork), 1/4 cup	20	1.0	4.0	1.0	n.a.	250	n.a.
Pork luncheon meat:							
canned (Hormel), 3 oz.	240	11.0	2.0	21.0	n.a.	1056	n.a.
smoked (Eckrich Calorie Watcher Slender Sliced), 1-oz. slice	45	5.0	1.0	3.0	n.a.	350	n.a.
Pork rind snack:							
(Baken-Ets), 1 oz.	150	17.0	1.0	9.0	n.a.	570	n.a.
(Tom's), 9/16 oz. . .	90	10.0	0	6.0	n.a.	200	n.a.

* Prepared according to package directions

Food and Measure	cal.	prot. (gms)	carbo. (gms)	fat (gms)	chol. (mgs)	sod. (mgs)	fiber (gms)
Pork rind snack *(cont.)*							
barbecue flavor							
(Tom's), 9/16 oz.	90	10.0	0	6.0	n.a.	260	n.a.
Pot roast, Yankee,							
dinner, frozen:							
(Dinner Classics), 11							
oz.	370	31.0	34.0	12.0	n.a.	820	n.a.
(Le Menu), 11 oz.	360	28.0	28.0	15.0	n.a.	810	n.a.
Pot roast gravy, mix,							
1.5-oz. pkg.:							
(Durkee Roastin' Bag)	125	3.0	25.0	1.0	n.a.	2965	n.a.
onion *(Durkee Roas-*							
tin' Bag)	124	4.0	24.0	.1	n.a.	2864	n.a.
Potato, fresh:							
raw:							
weighed with skin, 1							
lb.	269	7.1	61.2	.3	0	21	1.5
peeled, diced, 1 cup	118	3.1	27.0	.2	0	10	.7
baked in skin, 1 po-							
tato, (43/4″ × 21/3″							
diam.)	220	4.7	51.0	.2	0	16	1.3
baked without skin, 1/2							
cup	57	1.2	13.2	.1	0	3	.2
baked, 1 skin							
(43/4″ × 21/3″ diam.)	115	2.5	26.7	.1	0	12	1.3
boiled in skin:							
peeled, 1 round							
(21/2″ diam.) . .	119	2.5	27.4	.1	0	6	.4
peeled, 1 cup . .	136	2.9	31.4	.2	0	6	.5
boiled without skin:							
1 round (21/2″							
diam.)	116	2.3	27.0	.1	0	7	.5
1 cup	134	2.7	31.2	.2	0	8	.6
microwaved:							
in skin, 1 potato,							
(43/4″ × 21/3″							
diam.)	212	4.9	48.7	.2	0	16	1.6
peeled, 1 cup . .	156	3.3	36.3	.2	0	10	.6

Food and Measure	cal.	prot. (gms)	carbo. (gms)	fat (gms)	chol. (mgs)	sod. (mgs)	fiber (gms)
microwaved, 1 skin (4³/₄″ × 2¹/₃″ diam.)	77	2.6	17.2	.1	0	9	1.8
Potato, canned:							
whole, with liquid, 1 cup	120	4.1	26.0	.5	0	904	.7
drained, 1 potato (1″ diam.)	21	.5	4.8	.1	0	n.a.	.1
(Libby/Seneca), ¹/₂ cup	45	2.0	11.0	0	0	310	n.a.
(Stokely's Finest), ¹/₂ cup	50	1.0	11.0	0	0	375	n.a.
whole or sliced (Del Monte) ¹/₂ cup with liquid	45	1.0	10.0	0	0	355	n.a.
small, whole, new (S&W), ¹/₂ cup . .	45	2.0	9.0	0	0	310	n.a.
white, whole or sliced (A&P), ¹/₂ cup . .	45	2.0	11.0	<1.0	0	320	n.a.
au gratin, with bacon (Hormel Short Order), 7¹/₂ oz. . . .	240	9.0	20.0	14.0	n.a.	942	n.a.
scalloped, and ham (Hormel Short Order), 7¹/₂ oz. . . .	260	9.0	19.0	16.0	n.a.	1189	n.a.
scalloped, and pepperoni (Hormel Short Order), 7¹/₂ oz.	246	8.0	21.0	15.0	n.a.	n.a.	n.a.
sliced, and beef (Hormel Short Order), 7¹/₂ oz.	250	11.0	25.0	12.0	n.a.	n.a.	n.a.
Potato, freeze-dried*:							
mashed, instant (Mountain House), ¹/₂ cup	70	2.0	14.0	0	0	n.a.	n.a.

* Prepared according to package directions

Food and Measure	cal.	prot. (gms)	carbo. (gms)	fat (gms)	chol. (mgs)	sod. (mgs)	fiber (gms)
Potato, frozen:							
whole, small *(Ore-Ida)*, 3 oz.	60	2.0	15.0	0	0	60	n.a.
au gratin *(Stouffer's)*, 3.8 oz.	120	3.0	13.0	6.0	n.a.	480	n.a.
fried or frying:							
(Ore-Ida Crispers!), 3 oz.	240	1.0	24.0	16.0	0	540	n.a.
(Ore-Ida Crispy Crowns), 3 oz.	150	1.0	19.0	9.0	0	540	n.a.
(Ore-Ida Country Style Fries), 3 oz.	120	1.0	18.0	5.0	0	45	n.a.
(Ore-Ida Golden Fries), 3 oz. . .	110	1.0	18.0	5.0	0	45	n.a.
(Ore-Ida Homestyle Wedges), 3 oz.	90	1.0	17.0	3.0	0	45	n.a.
with cheese *(Ore-Ida Cheddar Browns)*, 3 oz.	70	2.0	14.0	2.0	10	310	n.a.
cottage fries *(Ore-Ida)*, 3 oz. . . .	110	2.0	18.0	5.0	0	25	n.a.
crinkle cut *(A&P)*, 3.5 oz.	140	2.0	25.0	4.0	0	25	n.a.
crinkle cut *(Ore-Ida Golden Crinkles)*, 3 oz.	110	1.0	18.0	4.0	0	40	n.a.
crinkle cut *(Ore-Ida Lites)*, 3 oz. . .	80	1.0	16.0	2.0	0	30	n.a.
crinkle cut *(Ore-Ida Pixie Crinkles)*, 3 oz.	130	1.0	20.0	6.0	0	40	n.a.
French fries *(A&P)*, 3.5 oz.	140	2.0	25.0	4.0	0	25	n.a.
French fries *(Ore-Ida Lites)*, 3 oz.	80	1.0	15.0	3.0	0	30	n.a.
hash brown *(A&P)*, 3.5 oz.	80	2.0	17.0	0	0	20	n.a.
hash brown *(Ore-Ida Southern Style)*, 3 oz. . .	70	<1.0	17.0	0	0	45	n.a.

Food and Measure	cal.	prot. (gms)	carbo. (gms)	fat (gms)	chol. (mgs)	sod. (mgs)	fiber (gms)
microwave, crinkle cut *(Ore-Ida)*, 3.5-oz. pkg.	170	1.0	26.0	8.0	0	45	n.a.
microwave, French fries *(Simplot Micromagic)*, 3 oz.	243	3.4	30.1	12.1	n.a.	21	n.a.
microwave, puffs *(Ore-Ida Tater Tots)*, 4-oz. pkg.	170	2.0	26.0	8.0	0	655	n.a.
morsels *(A&P)*, 3.5 oz.	140	2.0	23.0	4.0	0	30	n.a.
natural fries *(Ore-Ida Lites)*, 3 oz.	90	1.0	16.0	3.0	0	35	n.a.
O'Brien *(Ore-Ida)*, 3 oz.	60	1.0	14.0	0	0	20	n.a.
with onion *(Ore-Ida Crispy Crowns)*, 3 oz.	160	1.0	19.0	10.0	0	580	n.a.
patties *(Ore-Ida Golden Patties)*, 2.5 oz.	130	1.0	15.0	9.0	0	290	n.a.
puffs *(Ore-Ida Tater Tots)*, 3 oz. . . .	130	1.0	18.0	7.0	0	560	n.a.
puffs, bacon flavor *(Ore-Ida Tater Tots)*, 3 oz. . . .	130	2.0	17.0	7.0	0	630	n.a.
puffs, with onion *(Ore-Ida Tater Tots)*, 3 oz. . . .	130	1.0	19.0	7.0	0	740	n.a.
scalloped *(Stouffer's)*, 4 oz. . . .	110	3.0	11.0	6.0	n.a.	410	n.a.
shoestring *(A&P)*, 3.5 oz.	170	2.0	24.0	6.0	n.a.	50	n.a.
shoestring *(Ore-Ida)*, 3 oz.	130	1.0	20.0	7.0	0	45	n.a.
shoestring *(Ore-Ida Lites)*, 3 oz. . .	90	<1.0	17.0	4.0	0	45	n.a.
steak fries *(A&P)*, 3.5 oz.	140	2.0	24.0	4.0	0	30	n.a.

Food and Measure	cal.	prot. (gms)	carbo. (gms)	fat (gms)	chol. (mgs)	sod. (mgs)	fiber (gms)
Potato, frozen, fried or frying *(cont.)*							
steak fries *(Ore-Ida Lites)*, 3 oz. . .	80	1.0	15.0	2.0	0	40	n.a.
thins *(Ore-Ida Homestyle)*, 3 oz.	120	2.0	18.0	6.0	0	35	n.a.
Potato, mix*, 1/2 cup:							
(Betty Crocker Potato Buds)	130	3.0	17.0	6.0	n.a.	360	n.a.
au gratin:							
(Betty Crocker) . .	150	3.0	21.0	6.0	n.a.	630	n.a.
tangy *(French's)*	140	4.0	19.0	6.0	n.a.	470	n.a.
cheddar with onion, twice baked *(Betty Crocker)*	200	5.0	19.0	12.0	n.a.	630	n.a.
cheese, hickory smoke *(Betty Crocker)*	150	3.0	22.0	6.0	n.a.	700	n.a.
chicken and herb *(Betty Crocker)* . .	120	3.0	19.0	4.0	n.a.	600	n.a.
creamed:							
oven *(Betty Crocker)*	170	4.0	22.0	8.0	n.a.	415	n.a.
saucepan *(Betty Crocker)*	180	4.0	23.0	8.0	n.a.	425	n.a.
parsley *(Betty Crocker)*	180	4.0	22.0	8.0	n.a.	420	n.a.
hash brown, with onion *(Betty Crocker)*	160	2.0	24.0	6.0	n.a.	460	n.a.
Italian style, creamy, with Parmesan sauce *(French's)*	130	3.0	21.0	4.0	n.a.	430	n.a.
julienne *(Betty Crocker)*	140	3.0	19.0	6.0	n.a.	600	n.a.
mashed:							
(French's Idaho)	130	2.0	16.0	6.0	n.a.	340	n.a.
(French's Idaho Spuds)	140	2.0	16.0	7.0	n.a.	370	n.a.

* *Prepared according to package directions, with butter, milk and salt*

Food and Measure	cal.	prot. (gms)	carbo. (gms)	fat (gms)	chol. (mgs)	sod. (mgs)	fiber (gms)
flakes (Hungry Jack)	140	3.0	17.0	7.0	n.a.	380	n.a.
scalloped:							
(Betty Crocker) . .	140	3.0	19.0	6.0	n.a.	570	n.a.
cheese (French's)	140	3.0	20.0	5.0	n.a.	370	n.a.
with onion (French's							
Crispy Top) . . .	140	3.0	20.0	5.0	n.a.	420	n.a.
sour cream and chive:							
(Betty Crocker) . .	200	5.0	19.0	11.0	n.a.	520	n.a.
(French's)	150	3.0	20.0	6.0	n.a.	560	n.a.
Stroganoff, creamy							
(French's)	130	3.0	20.0	4.0	n.a.	520	n.a.
Potato entree:							
freeze-dried, and beef,							
with onions (Moun-							
tain House), 1 cup	290	11.0	27.0	15.0	n.a.	n.a.	n.a.
Potato, stuffed, fro-							
zen:							
baked, with cheese							
flavor topping							
(Green Giant), 5 oz.	200	4.0	33.0	6.0	n.a.	520	n.a.
baked, with sour							
cream and chives							
(Green Giant), 5 oz.	230	5.0	31.0	10.0	n.a.	580	n.a.
seafood (Wakefield), 3							
oz.	100	6.0	13.0	2.0	n.a.	420	n.a.
Potato, sweet, see							
"Sweet potato"							
Potato chips, 1 oz.,							
except as noted:							
(Bachman)	160	2.0	14.0	10.0	0	270	n.a.
(Bachman Ridges)	160	2.0	14.0	10.0	0	260	n.a.
(Bachman Unsalted)	160	2.0	14.0	10.0	0	5	n.a.
(Chipsters)	120	1.0	19.0	5.0	0	580	n.a.
(Delta Gold)	150	2.0	14.0	10.0	0	200	n.a.
(Delta Gold Dip Style)	150	2.0	15.0	10.0	0	200	n.a.
(Eagle)	150	2.0	15.0	10.0	0	200	n.a.
(Eagle Crispy Cut)	150	2.0	14.0	10.0	0	240	n.a.
(Eagle Hawaiian) . .	150	2.0	16.0	8.0	0	120	n.a.
(Eagle Lattice Cut)	150	2.0	14.0	10.0	0	180	n.a.

Food and Measure	cal.	prot. (gms)	carbo. (gms)	fat (gms)	chol. (mgs)	sod. (mgs)	fiber (gms)
Potato chips *(cont.)*							
(Eagle Russet) ...	150	2.0	16.0	8.0	0	175	n.a.
(Laura Scudder's)	150	2.3	15.1	9.1	0	196	.4
(Laura Scudder's Hawaiian)	150	2.0	15.0	9.0	0	100	.4
(Lay's), 1⅛ oz. ...	170	2.0	17.0	11.0	0	230	n.a.
(Lay's Unsalted) ..	160	2.0	14.0	11.0	0	10	n.a.
(Munchos Crisps) ..	150	1.0	16.0	9.0	0	290	n.a.
(Nalley)	161	1.4	14.1	11.3	n.a.	255	n.a.
(O'Grady's)	150	2.0	16.0	9.0	0	160	n.a.
(Pringles Light) ...	150	2.0	17.0	8.0	n.a.	145	n.a.
(Pringles Regular)	170	2.0	12.0	13.0	n.a.	215	n.a.
(Pringles Rippled) ..	170	2.0	13.0	12.0	n.a.	250	n.a.
(Ruffles)	150	2.0	15.0	10.0	0	200	n.a.
(Snyders Regular or Ripple)	150	2.0	15.0	10.0	0	140	.5
(Snyders No Salt Added)	150	2.0	15.0	10.0	0	10	.5
(Tom's Plain or Ruffled),* 1⅛ oz. ...	180	2.0	16.0	12.0	0	210	n.a.
au gratin cheese flavor *(O'Grady's)* ..	170	3.0	17.0	10.0	tr.	330	n.a.
bacon and sour cream flavor *(Ruffles)* ..	160	3.0	14.0	10.0	0	325	n.a.
barbecue flavor:							
(Bachman)	150	2.0	14.0	9.0	0	280	n.a.
(Laura Scudder's)	146	2.3	15.7	8.5	0	232	.5
(Lay's Bar-B-Q)	150	2.0	14.0	10.0	0	360	n.a.
(Nalley)	161	1.7	14.1	11.3	n.a.	284	n.a.
(Ruffles)	150	2.0	15.0	10.0	0	260	n.a.
(Tom's), 1⅛ oz.	180	2.0	15.0	13.0	0	300	n.a.
cheese flavor *(Pringles Cheez-Ums)*	170	2.0	13.0	12.0	n.a.	220	n.a.
hearty seasoning *(O'Grady's)*	140	2.0	17.0	8.0	0	390	n.a.
hot:							
(Bachman)	150	2.0	14.0	9.0	0	200	n.a.
(Tom's), 1⅛ oz.	180	2.0	17.0	11.0	0	350	n.a.

Food and Measure	cal.	prot. (gms)	carbo. (gms)	fat (gms)	chol. (mgs)	sod. (mgs)	fiber (gms)
salt and vinegar flavor:							
(Lay's)	150	2.0	15.0	9.0	0	390	n.a.
(Tom's)	160	1.0	15.0	10.0	0	280	n.a.
sour cream and onion flavor:							
(Bachman)	150	2.0	14.0	9.0	0	200	n.a.
(Laura Scudder's)	150	2.0	14.0	9.0	0	170	.4
(Lay's) 1 1/8 oz. . . .	170	3.0	16.0	11.0	tr.	360	n.a.
(Pringles)	170	2.0	13.0	12.0	n.a.	136	n.a.
(Ruffles)	150	2.0	15.0	9.0	tr.	260	n.a.
(Tom's), 1 1/8 oz.	180	2.0	16.0	12.0	0	300	n.a.
vinegar (Bachman)	150	2.0	15.0	9.0	0	610	n.a.
Potato flour:							
1 cup	628	14.3	143.0	1.4	0	61	2.9
Potato pancake:							
frozen:							
(Golden), 1 piece	70	2.0	12.0	2.0	7	193	n.a.
(Mother's Latka), 2 pieces	120	2.4	20.0	5.6	n.a.	n.a.	n.a.
mix*, dinner							
(French's), 1/2 cup	80	3.0	16.0	1.0		410	n.a.
Potato salad, canned or dairy pack:							
(Knudsen), 1/2 cup	150	2.0	15.0	9.0	n.a.	n.a.	n.a.
German:							
(Joan of Arc), 1/2 cup	120	2.0	24.0	2.0	n.a.	830	n.a.
(Nalley), 3 1/2 oz.	120	2.0	16.0	6.0	n.a.	400	n.a.
home style (Joan of Arc), 1/2 cup . . .	160	2.0	19.0	9.0	n.a.	750	n.a.
Potato starch:							
(Manischewitz), 1 cup	570	.3	137.0	0	0	<2	n.a.
Potato sticks:							
1-oz. pkg.	148	1.9	15.2	9.8	0	71	.3
1 cup	188	2.4	19.2	12.4	0	90	.4
canned (O&C), 1 1/2 oz.	231	2.7	22.0	15.0	n.a.	383	n.a.

* Prepared according to package directions

Food and Measure	cal.	prot. (gms)	carbo. (gms)	fat (gms)	chol. (mgs)	sod. (mgs)	fiber (gms)
Preserves, see "Jams and preserves"							
Pretzels, 1 oz., except as noted:							
(A & Eagle)	110	3.0	21.0	2.0	0	n.a.	n.a.
(Bachman Nutzels)	110	3.0	21.0	2.0	0	470	n.a.
(Laura Scudder's Bavarian)	110	2.0	23.0	1.0	0	475	n.a.
(Laura Scudder's Bavarian Unsalted)	120	2.0	23.0	1.0	0	20	n.a.
(Mister Salty Juniors), 29 pieces or 1 oz.	110	3.0	21.0	1.0	n.a.	510	n.a.
(Mister Salty Mini), 16 pieces or 1 oz. . .	110	3.0	21.0	1.0	n.a.	450	n.a.
(Mister Salty Mini Mix), 23 pieces or 1 oz.	110	3.0	23.0	1.0	n.a.	480	n.a.
(Planters)	110	3.0	22.0	1.0	n.a.	700	n.a.
(Quinlan Big Deals)	110	3.0	22.0	1.0	1	737	.2
(Rokeach Baldies)	110	2.0	20.0	0	n.a.	30	n.a.
(Rold Gold Tiny Tim)	110	2.0	23.0	1.0	0	495	n.a.
beers:							
(Quinlan)	110	3.0	21.0	2.0	1	465	<.1
lightly salted (Quinlan)	110	3.0	23.0	1.0	1	74	.1
Dutch:							
(Mister Salty), 2 pieces or 1 oz.	110	3.0	22.0	1.0	n.a.	440	n.a.
(Rokeach)	110	3.0	24.0	0	n.a.	n.a.	n.a.
(Rokeach No Salt)	110	2.0	20.0	0	n.a.	30	n.a.
hard:							
(Bachman)	102	3.0	23.0	0	0	550	n.a.
(Snyders)	102	2.9	22.7	<.1	0	548	n.a.
logs:							
(Bachman)	110	3.0	21.0	2.0	0	470	n.a.
(Mister Salty), 9 pieces or 1 oz.	110	3.0	21.0	1.0	n.a.	510	n.a.
(Quinlan)	110	3.0	22.0	1.0	1	386	tr.
nachos (Quinlan) . .	115	4.0	19.0	3.0	<5	695	.2

Food and Measure	cal.	prot. (gms)	carbo. (gms)	fat (gms)	chol. (mgs)	sod. (mgs)	fiber (gms)
nuggets *(Mister Salty)*, 21 pieces or 1 oz.	110	3.0	21.0	1.0	n.a.	550	n.a.
petites:							
(Bachman)	110	3.0	21.0	2.0	0	410	n.a.
(Bachman Unsalted)	110	3.0	21.0	2.0	0	0	n.a.
rings:							
(Bachman)	110	3.0	21.0	2.0	0	410	n.a.
(Mister Salty), 22 pieces or 1 oz.	110	3.0	21.0	2.0	n.a.	510	n.a.
rods:							
(Bachman)	110	3.0	21.0	2.0	0	240	n.a.
(Mister Salty), 2 pieces or 1 oz.	110	3.0	21.0	1.0	n.a.	500	n.a.
(Rold Gold)	110	3.0	22.0	1.0	0	510	n.a.
(Quinlan)	100	3.0	21.0	1.0	1	485	tr.
sticks:							
(Bachman Stix) . .	110	3.0	21.0	2.0	0	610	n.a.
(Laura Scudder's Mini)	110	2.0	23.0	1.0	0	570	n.a.
(Mister Salty), 90 pieces or 1 oz.	110	3.0	22.0	1.0	n.a.	620	n.a.
(Mister Salty Veri-Thin), 45 pieces or 1 oz.	110	3.0	22.0	1.0	n.a.	770	n.a.
(Quinlan)	110	3.0	22.0	1.0	1	386	< .1
(Rold Gold)	110	3.0	23.0	1.0	0	685	n.a.
(Snyders Stix) . .	110	3.0	22.0	1.0	1	386	n.a.
thins:							
(Quinlan)	110	3.0	22.0	1.0	1	655	tr.
(Snyders)	110	3.0	22.0	1.0	1	655	n.a.
tiny *(Quinlan)* . . .	110	3.0	21.0	2.0	1	618	tr.
tiny, no salt *(Quinlan)*	120	3.0	22.0	2.0	1	7	.1
twists:							
(Bachman)	110	3.0	21.0	2.0	0	410	n.a.
(Laura Scudder's)	110	2.0	23.0	1.0	0	570	n.a.
(Mister Salty), 5 pieces or 1 oz.	110	3.0	21.0	2.0	n.a.	590	n.a.
(Rold Gold)	110	3.0	23.0	1.0	0	410	n.a.

Food and Measure	cal.	prot. (gms)	carbo. (gms)	fat (gms)	chol. (mgs)	sod. (mgs)	fiber (gms)
Pretzels, twists (cont.)							
(Tom's), 1.6 oz.	160	4.0	35.0	2.0	0	690	n.a.
butter flavored:							
(Mister Salty Juniors), 29 pieces or 1 oz.	110	3.0	21.0	1.0	n.a.	510	n.a.
rings (Mister Salty), 23 pieces or 1 oz.	110	3.0	21.0	2.0	n.a.	570	n.a.
sticks (Mister Salty), 90 pieces or 1 oz.	110	3.0	22.0	1.0	n.a.	620	n.a.
twists (Bachman)	110	3.0	21.0	2.0	0	410	n.a.
twists (Mister Salty), 5 pieces or 1 oz.	110	3.0	22.0	1.0	n.a.	510	n.a.
cheese flavored,							
sticks (Bachman)	110	4.0	21.0	2.0	0	760	n.a.
coated, 3-ring:							
(Tastykake), 1 piece	108	1.8	13.5	4.9	n.a.	69	n.a.
(Tastykake), 1 piece	24	.4	3.0	1.1	n.a.	22	n.a.
Prickly pear:							
peeled and seeded, 4 oz.	46	.8	10.9	.6	0	6	2.1
Prosciutto:							
(Hormel), 1 oz. . . .	90	7.0	0	7.0	n.a.	502	0
Prune:							
canned, with pits, 1 cup	245	2.0	65.1	.5	0	6	1.6
dehydrated (low moisture):							
uncooked, 8 oz.	769	8.4	202.0	1.7	0	11	6.6
uncooked, 1 cup	448	4.9	117.6	1.0	0	7	3.8
cooked, with liquid, 1 cup	317	3.5	83.2	.7	0	5	2.7
dried:							
uncooked, with pits, 8 oz.	472	5.1	123.8	1.0	0	8	4.0
uncooked, with pits, 1 cup	385	4.2	101.0	.8	0	6	3.3
uncooked, with pits (Del Monte), 2 oz.	120	1.0	31.0	0	0	<10	n.a.

Food and Measure	cal.	prot. (gms)	carbo. (gms)	fat (gms)	chol. (mgs)	sod. (mgs)	fiber (gms)
uncooked, pitted							
(Del Monte), 2 oz.	140	1.0	35.0	0	0	< 10	n.a.
cooked, with pits,							
unsweetened, 1							
cup	227	2.5	59.5	.5	0	4	1.9
cooked, with pits,							
sweetened, 1 cup	295	2.6	78.3	.5	0	4	2.0
moist pack *(Del*							
Monte), 2 oz.	120	1.0	30.0	0	0	< 10	n.a.
Prune juice, 6 fl. oz.:							
(Algood Lady Betty)	130	1.0	31.0	0	0	20	n.a.
(Del Monte)	120	1.0	33.0	0	0	< 10	n.a.
(Mott's)	143	1.0	34.0	0	0	20	n.a.
with pulp *(Mott's)* . .	129	1.0	31.0	0	0	20	n.a.
Pudding, ready-to-							
serve:							
banana:							
(Del Monte Pudding							
Cup), 5 oz. . . .	180	3.0	30.0	5.0	n.a.	285	n.a.
(Hunt's Snack							
Pack), 5 oz. . .	210	2.0	26.0	11.0	n.a.	220	n.a.
(Thank You), 1/2 cup	150	2.0	26.0	4.0	1	180	0
butterscotch:							
(Del Monte Pudding							
Cup), 5 oz. . . .	180	3.0	31.0	5.0	n.a.	285	n.a.
(Hunt's Snack							
Pack), 5 oz. . .	210	2.0	30.0	9.0	n.a.	240	n.a.
(Swiss Miss), 4 oz.	140	2.0	21.0	6.0	n.a.	180	n.a.
(Thank You), 1/2 cup	150	2.0	26.0	4.0	1	220	0
chocolate:							
(Del Monte Pudding							
Cup), 5 oz. . . .	190	4.0	31.0	6.0	n.a.	280	n.a.
(Hunt's Snack							
Pack), 5 oz. . .	210	2.0	30.0	9.0	n.a.	160	n.a.
(Swiss Miss), 4 oz.	150	3.0	24.0	6.0	n.a.	180	n.a.
(Thank You), 1/2 cup	190	3.0	36.0	4.0	1	120	0
fudge *(Del Monte*							
Pudding Cup), 5							
oz.	190	4.0	31.0	6.0	n.a.	260	n.a.

Food and Measure	cal.	prot. (gms)	carbo. (gms)	fat (gms)	chol. (mgs)	sod. (mgs)	fiber (gms)
Pudding, ready-to-serve, chocolate (cont.)							
fudge (Hunt's Snack Pack), 5 oz. . .	200	2.0	28.0	10.0	n.a.	170	n.a.
fudge (Swiss Miss), 4 oz.	170	3.0	26.0	6.0	n.a.	190	n.a.
fudge (Thank You), 1/2 cup	190	3.0	36.0	4.0	1	140	0
with fudge topping (Swiss Miss), 4 oz.	170	3.0	25.0	7.0	n.a.	180	n.a.
German (Hunt's Snack Pack), 5 oz.	220	2.0	35.0	9.0	n.a.	160	n.a.
marshmallow (Hunt's Snack Pack), 5 oz. . .	200	2.0	30.0	9.0	n.a.	160	n.a.
custard, egg (Thank You), 1/2 cup . . .	140	3.0	18.0	6.0	70	200	0
lemon:							
(Hunt's Snack Pack), 5 oz. . .	180	n.a.	36.0	4.0	n.a.	80	n.a.
(Thank You), 1/2 cup	170	0	38.0	2.0	11	190	0
rice:							
(Comstock), 1/2 cup	110	2.0	25.0	3.0	n.a.	200	.5
(Hunt's Snack Pack), 5 oz. . .	220	3.0	27.0	12.0	n.a.	230	n.a.
(Thank You), 1/2 cup	150	2.0	29.0	3.0	1	240	0
tapioca:							
(Del Monte Pudding Cup), 5 oz. . . .	180	3.0	30.0	4.0	n.a.	250	n.a.
(Hunt's Snack Pack), 5 oz. . .	140	3.0	27.0	6.0	n.a.	170	n.a.
(Swiss Miss), 4 oz.	130	2.0	22.0	4.0	n.a.	170	n.a.
(Thank You), 1/2 cup	140	2.0	25.0	4.0	1	170	0
vanilla:							
(Del Monte Pudding Cup), 5 oz. . . .	180	3.0	32.0	5.0	n.a.	285	n.a.
(Hunt's Snack Pack), 5 oz. . .	210	2.0	31.0	9.0	n.a.	190	n.a.

Food and Measure	cal.	prot. (gms)	carbo. (gms)	fat (gms)	chol. (mgs)	sod. (mgs)	fiber (gms)
(Swiss Miss), 4 oz.	140	2.0	22.0	6.0	n.a.	190	n.a.
(Thank You), 1/2 cup with fudge topping	150	2.0	26.0	4.0	1	180	0
(Swiss Miss), 4 oz.	160	2.0	24.0	7.0	n.a.	180	n.a.
Pudding, frozen, 3 oz.:							
butterscotch *(Rich's)*	133	1.7	18.3	5.9	n.a.	128	n.a.
chocolate *(Rich's)*	141	1.7	18.2	7.1	n.a.	136	n.a.
vanilla *(Rich's)* . . .	129	1.6	18.4	5.9	n.a.	162	n.a.
Pudding and pie fill- ing, mix*, 1/2 cup, except as noted:							
banana cream:							
(Jell-O Instant) . .	160	4.0	28.0	4.0	n.a.	440	tr.
(Royal)	160	4.0	27.0	4.0	n.a.	210	n.a.
(Royal Instant) . .	180	4.0	27.0	4.0	n.a.	390	n.a.
butter almond, toasted							
(Royal Instant) . .	170	4.0	30.0	4.0	n.a.	350	n.a.
butter pecan *(Jell-O Instant)*	170	4.0	28.0	5.0	n.a.	440	tr.
butterscotch:							
(D-Zerta)**	70	4.0	12.0	0	n.a.	65	tr.
(Jell-O)	170	4.0	30.0	4.0	n.a.	250	tr.
(Jell-O Instant) . .	160	4.0	28.0	4.0	n.a.	480	tr.
(Jell-O Instant Sugar Free)***	90	4.0	13.0	2.0	n.a.	360	tr.
(Royal)	160	4.0	27.0	4.0	n.a.	210	n.a.
(Royal Instant) . .	180	4.0	29.0	5.0	n.a.	390	n.a.
(Royal Instant Sugar Free)***	100	4.0	16.0	2.0	n.a.	470	n.a.
chocolate:							
(D-Zerta)**	60	5.0	11.0	0	n.a.	70	tr.
(Jell-O)	160	5.0	28.0	4.0	n.a.	170	tr.
(Jell-O Instant) . .	180	4.0	30.0	4.0	n.a.	520	tr.

* *Prepared according to package directions, with whole milk, except as noted*
** *Prepared according to package directions, with skim milk*
*** *Prepared according to package directions, with 2% lowfat milk*

Food and Measure	cal.	prot. (gms)	carbo. (gms)	fat (gms)	chol. (mgs)	sod. (mgs)	fiber (gms)
Pudding and pie filling, mix, chocolate *(cont.)*							
(Jell-O Instant Sugar Free)***	100	5.0	14.0	3.0	n.a.	410	tr.
(Royal)	180	5.0	33.0	4.0	n.a.	150	n.a.
(Royal Instant) . .	190	4.0	35.0	4.0	n.a.	390	n.a.
(Royal Instant Sugar Free)***	110	5.0	17.0	3.0	n.a.	480	n.a.
chocolate chip *(Royal* Instant)	190	4.0	35.0	4.0	n.a.	390	n.a.
dark *(Royal* Dark 'n Sweet)	180	5.0	33.0	4.0	n.a.	150	n.a.
dark *(Royal* Dark 'n Sweet Instant)	190	4.0	35.0	4.0	n.a.	390	n.a.
fudge *(Jell-O)* . . .	160	5.0	28.0	4.0	n.a.	170	tr.
fudge *(Jell-O* Instant)	180	5.0	31.0	5.0	n.a.	480	tr.
milk chocolate *(Jell-O)*	160	4.0	28.0	4.0	n.a.	170	tr.
milk chocolate *(Jell-O* Instant) . . .	180	5.0	30.0	5.0	n.a.	510	tr.
mint *(Royal* Instant)	190	4.0	35.0	4.0	n.a.	390	n.a.
mousse pie *(Jell-O)*, 1/8 pie	220	3.0	26.0	12.0	n.a.	400	tr.
coconut:							
(Royal Tembleque)	160	4.0	27.0	4.0	n.a.	210	n.a.
cream *(Jell-O* Instant)	180	4.0	26.0	7.0	n.a.	360	tr.
toasted *(Royal* Instant)	170	4.0	30.0	4.0	n.a.	350	n.a.
custard:							
(Royal)	150	4.0	22.0	5.0	n.a.	115	n.a.
egg *(Jell-O* Golden)	160	5.0	23.0	5.0	n.a.	160	0
flan, with caramel sauce *(Royal)* . .	150	4.0	22.0	5.0	n.a.	115	n.a.
lemon:							
(Jell-O Instant) . .	170	4.0	29.0	4.0	n.a.	390	tr.
(Royal)	160	1.0	30.0	3.0	n.a.	120	n.a.

*** *Prepared according to package directions, with 2% lowfat milk*

Food and Measure	cal.	prot. (gms)	carbo. (gms)	fat (gms)	chol. (mgs)	sod. (mgs)	fiber (gms)
(Royal Instant) ..	180	1.0	29.0	5.0	n.a.	350	n.a.
lime, key *(Royal)* ..	160	1.0	30.0	3.0	n.a.	120	n.a.
pineapple cream							
(Jell-O Instant) ..	160	4.0	29.0	4.0	n.a.	390	tr.
pistachio:							
(Jell-O Instant) ..	170	4.0	28.0	5.0	n.a.	440	tr.
(Royal Instant) ..	170	4.0	30.0	4.0	n.a.	350	n.a.
rennet custard:							
chocolate *(Junket)*	120	5.0	15.0	4.0	n.a.	65	n.a.
strawberry or rasp-							
berry *(Junket)*	120	4.0	16.0	4.0	n.a.	60	n.a.
vanilla *(Junket)* ..	120	4.0	16.0	4.0	n.a.	65	n.a.
rice pudding *(Jell-O*							
Americana)	170	5.0	30.0	4.0	n.a.	160	tr.
tapioca:							
chocolate *(Jell-O*							
Americana) ...	170	5.0	28.0	5.0	n.a.	170	tr.
vanilla *(Jell-O Amer-*							
icana)	160	4.0	27.0	4.0	n.a.	170	tr.
vanilla *(Royal)* ..	160	4.0	27.0	1.0	n.a.	150	n.a.
vanilla:							
*(D-Zerta)***	70	4.0	12.0	0	n.a.	65	tr.
(Jell-O)	160	4.0	27.0	4.0	n.a.	200	tr.
(Jell-O French) ..	170	4.0	30.0	4.0	n.a.	200	tr.
(Jell-O Instant) ..	170	4.0	29.0	4.0	n.a.	420	tr.
(Jell-O Instant							
Sugar Free)***	90	4.0	13.0	2.0	n.a.	420	tr.
(Royal)	160	4.0	27.0	4.0	n.a.	210	n.a.
(Royal Instant) ..	180	4.0	29.0	5.0	n.a.	390	n.a.
(Royal Instant Sugar							
Free)***	100	4.0	16.0	2.0	n.a.	470	n.a.
Pudding bars, fro-							
zen, 1 bar:							
all flavors:							
(Bullwinkle Pudding							
Stix), 2¹/₂ fl. oz.	120	5.0	20.0	2.0	n.a.	n.a.	n.a.

** *Prepared according to package directions, with skim milk*
*** *Prepared according to package directions, with 2% lowfat milk*

Food and Measure	cal.	prot. (gms)	carbo. (gms)	fat (gms)	chol. (mgs)	sod. (mgs)	fiber (gms)
Pudding bars, frozen, all flavors *(cont.)*							
(Good Humor Pudding Stix)	90	4.0	15.0	2.0	n.a.	65	n.a.
chocolate:							
(Jell-O Pudding Pops)	80	2.0	13.0	2.0	n.a.	80	tr.
chocolate covered (Jell-O Pudding Pops)	130	2.0	15.0	8.0	n.a.	75	tr.
chocolate-caramel swirl (Jell-O Pudding Pops)	80	2.0	13.0	2.0	n.a.	65	tr.
chocolate-vanilla swirl (Jell-O Pudding Pops)	80	2.0	13.0	2.0	n.a.	65	tr.
vanilla:							
(Jell-O Pudding Pops)	70	2.0	13.0	2.0	n.a.	50	tr.
chocolate coated (Jell-O Pudding Pops)	130	2.0	15.0	8.0	n.a.	50	tr.
Pummelo, fresh:							
1 medium (5 1/2" diam.)	228	4.6	58.6	.2	0	7	1.1
sections, 1 cup . . .	71	1.4	18.3	.1	0	2	.3
Pumpkin, fresh:							
raw, pulp only, cubed, 1 cup	30	1.2	7.5	.1	0	1	1.3
boiled, drained, mashed, 1 cup . .	49	1.8	12.0	.2	0	3	2.0
Pumpkin, canned:							
(Del Monte), 1/2 cup	35	1.0	9.0	0	0	<10	n.a.
(Joan of Arc), 1/2 cup	50	2.0	11.0	2.0	0	25	n.a.
(Stokely's Finest), 1/2 cup	40	2.0	10.0	0	0	15	n.a.
Pumpkin flowers:							
raw, trimmed, 1 cup	5	.3	1.1	<.1	0	2	.2
boiled, drained, 1 cup	20	1.5	4.4	.1	0	8	1.2

Food and Measure	cal.	prot. (gms)	carbo. (gms)	fat (gms)	chol. (mgs)	sod. (mgs)	fiber (gms)
Pumpkin pie spice:							
1 tsp.	6	.1	1.2	.2	0	1	.3
Pumpkin seed kernels, dry:							
whole, weighed in hull, 4 oz.	464	24.4	12.6	39.2	0	n.a.	1.6
hulled, 4 oz.	627	32.9	17.0	53.0	0	n.a.	2.2
Purslane, fresh:							
raw, whole, with stems, 1 lb.	56	4.5	11.8	.3	0	156	2.8
boiled, drained, 1 cup	21	1.7	4.1	.2	0	51	.9

Q

Food and Measure	cal.	prot. (gms)	carbo. (gms)	fat (gms)	chol. (mgs)	sod. (mgs)	fiber (gms)
Quail, raw:							
whole, ready to cook, 1 lb.	686	102.1	0	27.8	n.a.	n.a.	0
meat and skin only, 4 oz.	195	28.8	0	7.9	n.a.	45	0
giblets, 2 oz.	98	12.4	3.8	3.5	n.a.	n.a.	0
Quiche, 4¹/₃ oz.:							
bacon and onion *(Pour-A-Quiche)*	230	13.0	6.0	18.0	240	380	n.a.
ham *(Pour-A-Quiche)*	230	13.0	4.0	17.0	235	360	n.a.
spinach and onion *(Pour-A-Quiche)*	220	12.0	6.0	16.0	230	365	n.a.
three cheese *(Pour-A-Quiche)*	230	13.0	4.0	18.0	250	385	n.a.
Quince, fresh:							
whole, 1 average, 5.3 oz.	53	.4	14.1	.1	0	4	1.6
peeled and seeded, 4 oz.	65	.5	17.4	.1	0	5	1.9

R

Food and Measure	cal.	prot. (gms)	carbo. (gms)	fat (gms)	chol. (mgs)	sod. (mgs)	fiber (gms)
Rabbit:							
domestic:							
raw, whole, ready to cook, 1 lb. . . .	581	75.0	0	29.0	n.a.	154	0
stewed, meat only, 4 oz.	245	33.2	0	11.5	n.a.	46	0
wild:							
raw, whole, ready to cook, 1 lb. . . .	490	76.0	0	18.0	n.a.	n.a.	0
Raccoon:							
roasted, meat only, 4 oz.	289	33.1	0	16.4	n.a.	n.a.	0
Radish, raw:							
whole, 10 medium (3/4"–1" diam.) . .	7	.3	1.6	.2	0	11	.2
sliced, 1 cup	20	.7	4.2	.6	0	28	.6
Radish, Oriental:							
raw:							
1 radish (7" × 2 1/4" diam.)	62	2.0	13.9	.3	0	71	2.2
pared, sliced, 1 cup	16	.5	3.6	.1	0	18	.6
boiled, drained, sliced, 1 cup	25	1.0	5.1	.4	0	19	.7
dried:							
4 oz.	307	9.0	71.9	.8	0	315	9.5
1/2 cup	157	4.6	36.8	.4	0	161	4.9
Radish, white icicle, raw:							
1 radish, 5.4 oz.	14	1.1	2.6	.1	0	16	.7

Food and Measure	cal.	prot. (gms)	carbo. (gms)	fat (gms)	chol. (mgs)	sod. (mgs)	fiber (gms)
Radish, white icicle *(cont.)*							
pared, sliced, 1/2 cup	7	.6	1.3	.1	0	8	.4
Radish seeds:							
sprouted, raw, 1 cup	16	1.5	1.2	1.0	0	2	n.a.
Raisins:							
seeded:							
8 oz.	671	5.7	178.0	1.2	0	64	1.5
1 cup unpacked	428	3.7	113.8	.8	0	41	1.0
1 cup packed . .	488	4.2	129.5	.9	0	47	1.1
seedless:							
8 oz.	680	7.3	179.5	1.0	0	27	2.9
1 cup unpacked	434	4.7	114.7	.7	0	17	1.9
1 cup packed . .	494	5.3	130.6	.8	0	19	2.1
(Cinderella), 1/2 cup	250	3.0	66.0	0	0	14	.7
(Del Monte), 3 oz.	250	3.0	68.0	0	0	15	n.a.
golden seedless:							
8 oz.	685	7.7	180.4	1.0	0	27	3.2
1 cup unpacked	437	4.9	115.3	.7	0	17	2.1
1 cup packed . .	498	5.6	131.2	.8	0	20	2.4
(Del Monte), 3 oz.	260	3.0	68.0	0	0	< 10	n.a.
with nuts *(Carnation)*, .9-oz. pouch . . .	130	4.0	11.0	7.0	0	10	n.a.
Raja fish, see "Skate"							
Ranch house dip:							
(Nalley), 1 oz.	119	.3	.6	13.0	17	360	n.a.
Raspberry, red:							
fresh:							
trimmed, 1 pint . .	154	2.8	36.1	1.7	0	0	9.4
trimmed, 1 cup . .	61	1.1	14.2	.7	0	0	3.7
canned, red, in heavy syrup, 1 cup . . .	234	2.1	59.8	.3	0	9	n.a.
frozen, red, sweet-ened, 1 cup . . .	256	1.7	65.4	.4	0	1	5.5
frozen, in light syrup *(Birds Eye* Lite Quick Thaw Pouch), 5 oz.	100	1.0	26.0	0	0	0	3.1

Food and Measure	cal.	prot. (gms)	carbo. (gms)	fat (gms)	chol. (mgs)	sod. (mgs)	fiber (gms)
Raspberry danish:							
(Hostess), 1 danish	300	4.0	48.0	10.0	20	360	n.a.
Raspberry drink,							
mix*, 8 fl. oz.:							
(Kool-Aid)	100	0	25.0	0	0	0	0
presweetened *(Kool-Aid)*	90	0	22.0	0	0	0	0
sugar sweetened *(Funny Face)* . . .	88	0	22.0	0	0	0	0
Raspberry juice:							
red *(Smucker's)*, 8 fl. oz.	130	0	32.0	0	0	5	n.a.
Raspberry-cranberry drink:							
(A&P), 6 fl. oz. . . .	110	<1.0	27.0	<1.0	0	0	n.a.
Raspberry roll or bar:							
(Flavor Tree), .75-oz. roll	80	0	18.0	<1.0	0	15	n.a.
(Fruit Roll-Ups), 1/2-oz. roll	50	0	12.0	<1.0	0	10	n.a.
(Pocket Fruit), .7-oz. bar	60	0	16.0	0	0	n.a.	n.a.
(Sunkist Fruit Roll), 1/2-oz. roll	50	0	12.0	<1.0	0	10	n.a.
Raspberry turnover:							
frozen *(Pepperidge Farm)*, 1 piece . .	320	3.0	37.0	18.0	n.a.	270	n.a.
Ratatouille:							
frozen *(Stouffer's)*, 5 oz.	80	2.0	8.0	4.0	n.a.	800	n.a.
Ravioli, canned:							
beef:							
(Franco-American), 71/2 oz.	230	9.0	36.0	5.0	n.a.	1090	n.a.
(Franco-American RavioliOs), 71/2 oz.	250	10.0	35.0	7.0	n.a.	890	n.a.

* *Prepared according to package directions*

Food and Measure	cal.	prot. (gms)	carbo. (gms)	fat (gms)	chol. (mgs)	sod. (mgs)	fiber (gms)
Ravioli, beef *(cont.)*							
(Nalley), 3½ oz.	90	4.0	15.0	2.0	5	510	n.a.
cheese, round							
(Buitoni), 4 oz. . .	230	14.0	26.0	8.0	25	270	n.a.
cheese, square							
(Buitoni), 4 oz. . .	240	13.0	38.0	4.0	95	240	n.a.
chicken *(Nalley)*, 3½							
oz.	100	3.0	15.0	3.0	n.a.	345	n.a.
meat, square *(Buitoni)*,							
4 oz.	270	14.0	41.0	5.0	35	390	n.a.
Red and gray snap-per, meat only:							
raw, 4 oz.	113	23.3	0	1.5	42	73	0
broiled, 4 oz.	145	30.0	0	2.0	53	65	0
Red horse, silver, raw:							
drawn, 1 lb.	204	37.6	0	4.8	n.a.	n.a.	0
meat only, 4 oz. . .	111	20.4	0	2.6	n.a.	n.a.	0
Redfish, see "Perch"							
Reindeer:							
raw, lean meat only, 4 oz.	144	24.7	0	4.3	n.a.	n.a.	0
Relish, see "Pickle, cucumber, relish"							
Rennet:							
(Junket), 1 tablet . .	1	0	0	0	0	165	n.a.
Rennin dessert, dry mix:							
chocolate, 2-oz. pkg.	219	1.6	51.9	1.9	n.a.	40	.5
vanilla, caramel or fruit flavor, 1½-oz. pkg.	163	tr.	42.1	tr.	n.a.	3	n.a.
Rhubarb, raw:							
well trimmed, 1 lb.	95	4.1	20.6	.9	0	18	3.2
diced, 1 cup	26	1.1	5.5	.2	0	5	.9
Rice:							
brown:							
(Mahatma/River), 1 oz. dry	110	2.0	23.0	0	0	<10	n.a.

Food and Measure	cal.	prot. (gms)	carbo. (gms)	fat (gms)	chol. (mgs)	sod. (mgs)	fiber (gms)
cooked (S&W), 3½ oz.	119	2.0	26.0	0	0	<10	n.a.
cooked* (Uncle Ben's), ⅔ cup	152	3.6	26.4	3.6	n.a.	458	.4
cooked** (Uncle Ben's), ⅔ cup	133	3.5	26.4	1.5	0	5	.4
long grain, precooked (S&W Quick), ½ cup	110	2.0	25.0	0	0	<10	n.a.
precooked (Adolphus Instant), ½ cup	110	2.0	22.0	0	0	0	n.a.
precooked (Comet Instant), ½ cup	110	2.0	22.0	0	0	0	n.a.
white:							
(Carolina/Mahatma River/Water Maid), 1 oz. dry	100	2.0	22.0	0	0	<10	n.a.
cooked** (Minute Rice), ⅔ cup	120	3.0	27.0	0	0	0	tr.
cooked* (Uncle Ben's Converted), ⅔ cup	148	3.0	28.9	2.3	n.a.	463	.1
cooked** (Uncle Ben's Converted), ⅔ cup	129	3.0	28.0	.2	0	2	.1
long grain (Comet/ Adolphus), 1 oz.	100	2.0	23.0	0	0	0	n.a.
long grain, cooked (S&W), 3½ oz.	106	2.0	23.0	0	0	<10	n.a.
long grain, parboiled (Comet Extra Fluffy), ½ cup	90	2.0	21.0	0	0	0	n.a.
instant (Carolina/ Mahatma), 1 oz. dry or ½ cup cooked**	110	2.0	23.0	0	0	<10	n.a.

* Prepared according to package direction, with butter and salt
** Prepared according to package directions, without butter and salt

Food and Measure	cal.	prot. (gms)	carbo. (gms)	fat (gms)	chol. (mgs)	sod. (mgs)	fiber (gms)
Rice, canned:							
fried *(La Choy)*, 3/4 cup	190	4.0	41.0	1.0	n.a.	820	n.a.
Spanish:							
(Heinz), 7 1/4 oz.	150	3.0	26.0	5.0	n.a.	1045	n.a.
(Van Camp's), 1 cup	150	3.1	28.2	2.7	n.a.	990	.6
Rice, frozen:							
apple pecan *(Stouffer's)*, 2.9 oz. . . .	130	2.0	22.0	4.0	n.a.	200	n.a.
Chinese fried:							
(Birds Eye), 3.6 oz.	100	3.0	23.0	0	0	430	.4
with meat *(La Choy)*, 3/4 cup	140	5.0	26.0	2.0	n.a.	885	n.a.
with pork *(Chun King* Boil-in-Bag), 10 oz.	306	12.5	46.8	7.4	74	1382	1.1
French style *(Birds Eye)*, 3.6 oz. . . .	120	3.0	25.0	0	0	640	.3
Italian style *(Birds Eye)*, 3.6 oz. . . .	130	3.0	28.0	1.0	0	380	.3
Italian blend and spinach in cheese sauce *(Green Giant Rice Originals)*, 1/2 cup	170	4.0	23.0	7.0	n.a.	400	n.a.
jubilee *(Green Giant Rice Originals)*, 1/2 cup	150	2.0	22.0	6.0	n.a.	340	n.a.
long grain white and wild *(Green Giant Rice Originals)*, 1/2 cup	120	3.0	23.0	2.0	n.a.	550	n.a.
medley:							
(Green Giant Rice Originals), 1/2 cup	120	3.0	21.0	3.0	n.a.	260	n.a.
(Stouffer's), 3 oz.	110	2.0	20.0	2.0	n.a.	340	n.a.
pilaf *(Green Giant Rice Originals)*, 1/2 cup	120	3.0	23.0	2.0	n.a.	520	n.a.

Food and Measure	cal.	prot. (gms)	carbo. (gms)	fat (gms)	chol. (mgs)	sod. (mgs)	fiber (gms)
Spanish style (Birds Eye), 3.6 oz. . . .	120	3.0	26.0	1.0	0	490	.5
and broccoli, in flavored cheese sauce (Green Giant Rice Originals), 1/2 cup	120	3.0	18.0	4.0	n.a.	510	n.a.
with herb and butter sauce (Green Giant Rice Originals), 1/2 cup	150	3.0	22.0	5.0	n.a.	390	n.a.
with peas and mushrooms (Birds Eye), 2.3 oz.	110	4.0	23.0	0	0	320	.6
Rice, mix:							
beef flavor:							
(Comet), 1 oz. . .	100	2.0	21.0	0	0	n.a.	n.a.
(Lipton Rice and Sauce), 1/2 cup*	160	3.0	27.0	4.0	n.a.	665	n.a.
brown and wild, seasoned (Comet), 1 oz.	100	3.0	20.0	0	0	n.a.	n.a.
chicken flavor:							
(Comet), 1 oz. . .	100	2.0	21.0	0	0	n.a.	n.a.
(Lipton Rice and Sauce), 1/2 cup*	150	3.0	26.0	4.0	n.a.	525	n.a.
chicken or beef flavored (Make-It-Easy), 1.3 oz. . .	130	3.0	28.0	1.0	n.a.	n.a.	n.a.
drumstick (Minute), 1/2 cup*	150	3.0	25.0	4.0	n.a.	690	tr.
fried (Minute), 1/2 cup**	160	3.0	25.0	5.0	0	550	tr.
herb and butter (Lipton Rice and Sauce), 1/2 cup*	160	3.0	25.0	5.0	n.a.	500	n.a.

* Prepared according to package directions, with salted butter
** Prepared according to package directions with oil

Food and Measure	cal.	prot. (gms)	carbo. (gms)	fat (gms)	chol. (mgs)	sod. (mgs)	fiber (gms)
Rice, mix *(cont.)*							
long grain and wild:							
(Comet), 1 oz. . .	100	3.0	21.0	0	0	n.a.	n.a.
(Minute), 1/2 cup*	150	3.0	25.0	4.0	n.a.	570	tr.
mushroom *(Lipton Rice and Sauce)*, 1/2 cup*	140	3.0	26.0	3.0	n.a.	560	n.a.
pilaf *(Casbah)*, 1 oz.	90	2.0	20.0	0	0	n.a.	n.a.
pilaf, nutted *(Casbah)*, 1 oz.	160	4.0	30.0	2.0	0	n.a.	n.a.
pilaf, Spanish *(Casbah)*, 1 oz.	90	2.0	20.0	0	0	n.a.	n.a.
rib roast *(Minute)*, 1/2 cup*	150	3.0	25.0	4.0	n.a.	720	tr.
rice medley *(Lipton Rice and Sauce Combinations)*, 1/2 cup*	150	4.0	26.0	3.0	n.a.	400	n.a.
rice and peas *(Lipton Rice and Sauce Combinations)*, 1/2 cup*	150	4.0	26.0	3.0	n.a.	400	n.a.
Spanish *(Lipton Rice and Sauce)*, 1/2 cup*	140	3.0	26.0	3.0	n.a.	520	n.a.
Rice cake:							
(Chico-San), 1 piece	35	1.0	8.0	0	0	10	n.a.
(Chico-San Sodium Free), 1 piece . .	35	1.0	8.0	0	0	0	n.a.
Rice and chicken:							
freeze-dried *(Mountain House)*, 1 cup . .	400	13.0	41.0	13.0	n.a.	n.a.	n.a.
Rice seasoning mix, 1 pkg.:							
beef flavor and onion *(French's Spice Your Rice)*	10	0	2.0	0	n.a.	510	n.a.

* *Prepared according to package directions, with salted butter*

Food and Measure	cal.	prot. (gms)	carbo. (gms)	fat (gms)	chol. (mgs)	sod. (mgs)	fiber (gms)
buttery herb (*French's Spice Your Rice*)	18	1.0	2.0	1.0	n.a.	380	n.a.
cheese and chives (*French's Spice Your Rice*)	14	1.0	2.0	0	n.a.	350	n.a.
chicken and herb (*French's Spice Your Rice*)	12	1.0	1.0	1.0	n.a.	390	n.a.
chicken Parmesan (*French's Spice Your Rice*)	14	1.0	2.0	1.0	n.a.	400	n.a.
fried (*Durkee*), 1-oz. pkg.	62	1.9	11.0	1.1	n.a.	1931	n.a.
Rice, wild:							
raw, 8 oz.	801	32.0	170.8	1.6	0	16	2.3
Rice bran:							
4 oz.	313	15.1	57.6	17.9	0	tr.	13.0
Rice polish:							
4 oz.	301	13.7	65.4	14.5	0	tr.	2.7
Rockfish:							
raw, meat only, 4 oz.	107	21.3	0	1.8	40	68	0
broiled, 4-oz. fillet	137	27.3	0	2.3	50	87	0
Roe (see also "Caviar"):							
mixed species, raw, 4 oz.	159	25.3	1.7	7.3	424	n.a.	0
canned, with liquid, cod, haddock and herring, 4 oz. . . .	134	24.4	.3	3.2	n.a.	n.a.	n.a.
Roll, 1 piece, except as noted:							
brown and serve:							
(*Roman Meal*), 1 oz.	77	3.0	13.0	2.0	0	140	n.a.
(*Wonder* Half & Half)	80	2.0	13.0	2.0	<5	140	.1
(*Wonder* Home Bake)	80	2.0	13.0	2.0	<5	130	.1
with buttermilk (*Wonder*)	80	2.0	13.0	2.0	<5	140	.1

Food and Measure	cal.	prot. (gms)	carbo. (gms)	fat (gms)	chol. (mgs)	sod. (mgs)	fiber (gms)
Roll, brown and serve (cont.)							
club (Pepperidge Farm)	100	3.0	20.0	1.0	n.a.	220	n.a.
gem style (Wonder)	80	2.0	13.0	2.0	<5	140	.1
butter crescent (Pepperidge Farm) . .	110	2.0	13.0	6.0	n.a.	160	n.a.
dinner:							
(Home Pride) . . .	80	2.0	14.0	2.0	<5	170	.1
(Roman Meal), 1 oz.	75	3.0	13.0	1.5	0	140	n.a.
(Wonder)	80	2.0	14.0	1.0	<5	140	.1
French style (Pepperidge Farm)	110	4.0	19.0	1.0	n.a.	250	n.a.
hamburger or hot dog:							
(Pepperidge Farm)	130	4.0	21.0	3.0	n.a.	260	n.a.
(Roman Meal), 1 oz.	75	3.0	13.0	1.5	0	140	n.a.
(Wonder)	80	2.0	14.0	1.0	<5	150	.1
hoagie (Wonder) . .	400	13.0	73.0	7.0	<5	840	.5
Parkerhouse (Pepperidge Farm)	50	2.0	9.0	1.0	n.a.	90	n.a.
party (Pepperidge Farm)	30	1.0	5.0	1.0	n.a.	50	n.a.
sandwich:							
onion and poppyseed (Pepperidge Farm) . . .	150	5.0	26.0	3.0	n.a.	240	n.a.
sesame seed (Pepperidge Farm)	130	5.0	23.0	3.0	n.a.	210	n.a.
sourdough French (Pepperidge Farm)	100	4.0	19.0	1.0	n.a.	240	n.a.
Roll mix*:							
hot (Pillsbury), 1 roll	120	3.5	21.0	2.0	n.a.	215	n.a.
Roll, refrigerated, 1 roll:							
(Pillsbury Butterflake)	110	2.0	16.0	4.0	n.a.	410	n.a.
cinnamon, iced:							
(Hungry Jack Butter Tastin')	145	1.5	18.5	7.0	n.a.	285	n.a.

* Prepared according to package directions

Food and Measure	cal.	prot. (gms)	carbo. (gms)	fat (gms)	chol. (mgs)	sod. (mgs)	fiber (gms)
(Pillsbury)	115	1.5	17.0	4.5	n.a.	260	n.a.
(Pillsbury Best							
Quick)	210	2.0	29.0	9.0	n.a.	260	n.a.
crescent *(Pillsbury)*	100	1.5	11.0	5.5	n.a.	230	n.a.
Roll dough, frozen:							
(Rich's Homestyle), 2							
rolls	152	4.5	28.1	2.4	n.a.	335	n.a.
French *(Bridgford),*							
1 1/2-oz. roll	110	5.0	20.0	1.0	n.a.	247	n.a.
honey wheat							
(Bridgford), 1 1/2-oz.							
roll	110	5.0	20.0	1.0	n.a.	229	n.a.
Parkerhouse							
(Bridgford), 1-oz. roll	90	2.0	14.0	2.0	n.a.	156	n.a.
white *(Bridgford),* 1-oz.							
roll	120	4.0	21.0	1.0	n.a.	245	n.a.
Roseapple, raw:							
trimmed and seeded,							
4 oz.	28	.7	6.5	.3	0	0	1.2
Roselle,							
raw:							
whole, 1 lb.	136	2.7	31.3	1.8	0	16	3.2
1 cup	28	.6	6.5	.4	0	3	.7
Rosemary:							
dried (all brands), 1							
tsp.	4	.1	.8	.2	0	1	.2
Roy Rogers:							
breakfast, 1 serving:							
crescent roll, 2.5-oz.							
roll	287	4.7	27.2	17.7	<5	547	n.a.
crescent sandwich,							
4.5 oz.	401	13.3	25.3	27.3	148	867	n.a.
crescent sandwich							
with bacon, 4.75							
oz.	431	15.4	25.5	29.7	156	1035	n.a.
crescent sandwich							
with ham, 5.9 oz.	557	19.8	25.3	41.7	189	1192	n.a.
crescent sandwich							
with sausage, 5.8							
oz.	449	19.9	25.9	29.4	168	1289	n.a.

Food and Measure	cal.	prot. (gms)	carbo. (gms)	fat (gms)	chol. (mgs)	sod. (mgs)	fiber (gms)
Roy Rogers, breakfast *(cont.)*							
egg and biscuit platter, 5.9 oz. . . .	394	16.9	21.9	26.5	284	734	n.a.
egg and biscuit platter with bacon, 6.2 oz.	435	19.7	22.1	29.6	294	957	n.a.
egg and biscuit platter with ham, 7.15 oz.	442	23.5	22.5	28.6	304	1156	n.a.
egg and biscuit platter with sausage, 7.25 oz.	550	23.4	21.9	40.9	325	1059	n.a.
pancake platter, 5.9 oz.	452	7.7	71.8	15.2	53	842	n.a.
pancake platter with bacon, 6.2 oz.	493	10.4	72.0	18.3	63	1065	n.a.
pancake platter with ham, 7.15 oz.	506	14.3	72.4	17.3	73	1264	n.a.
pancake platter with sausage, 7.25 oz.	608	14.2	71.8	29.6	94	1167	n.a.
chicken, fried:							
breast, 5.15-oz. piece	412	33.0	16.9	23.7	118	609	n.a.
breast and wing, 7-oz. serving . . .	604	43.5	25.4	36.5	165	894	n.a.
leg (drumstick), 1.9-oz. piece	140	11.5	5.5	8.0	40	190	n.a.
thigh, 3.5-oz. piece	296	18.4	11.7	19.5	85	406	n.a.
thigh and leg, 5.4-oz. serving . . .	436	29.9	17.2	27.5	125	596	n.a.
wing, 1.87-oz. piece	192	10.5	8.5	12.8	47	285	n.a.
sandwiches, 1 serving:							
bacon cheeseburger, 6.4 oz.	581	32.3	25.0	39.2	103	1536	n.a.
bar burger, 7.43 oz.	611	36.1	28.0	39.4	115	1826	n.a.
cheeseburger, 6.2 oz.	563	29.5	27.4	37.3	95	1404	n.a.
hamburger, 5.1 oz.	456	23.8	26.6	28.3	73	495	n.a.

Food and Measure	cal.	prot. (gms)	carbo. (gms)	fat (gms)	chol. (mgs)	sod. (mgs)	fiber (gms)
roast beef, 5.5 oz.	317	27.2	29.1	10.2	55	785	n.a.
roast beef, large, 6.5 oz.	360	33.9	29.6	11.9	73	1044	n.a.
roast beef with cheese, 6.5 oz.	424	32.9	29.9	19.2	77	1694	n.a.
roast beef with cheese, large, 7.5 oz.	467	39.6	30.3	20.9	95	1953	n.a.
hot top potatoes, 1 serving:							
plain, 8 oz.	211	5.9	47.9	.2	0	10	n.a.
with oleo, 8.4 oz.	274	5.9	47.9	7.3	0	106	n.a.
with sour cream and chives, 10.6 oz.	408	7.3	47.6	20.9	31	138	n.a.
with bacon 'n cheese, 8.8 oz.	397	17.1	33.3	21.7	34	778	n.a.
with broccoli 'n cheese, 11.1 oz.	376	13.7	39.6	18.1	<19	523	n.a.
with taco beef 'n cheese, 12.8 oz.	463	21.8	45.0	21.8	37	726	n.a.
side dishes, 1 serv- ing:							
biscuit, 2.25 oz.	231	4.4	26.2	12.1	<5	575	n.a.
cole slaw, 3.5 oz.	110	1.0	11.0	6.9	<5	261	n.a.
French fries, 3 oz.	268	3.9	32.0	13.5	42	165	n.a.
French fries, large, 4 oz.	357	5.3	42.7	18.4	56	221	n.a.
macaroni, 3.5 oz.	186	3.1	19.4	10.7	<5	603	n.a.
potato salad, 3.5 oz.	107	2.0	10.9	6.1	<5	696	n.a.
salad dressings:							
bacon 'n tomato, 2 tbsp.	136	<1.0	6.0	12.0	n.a.	150	n.a.
blue cheese, 2 tbsp.	150	2.0	2.0	16.0	n.a.	153	n.a.
Italian lo-cal, 2 tbsp.	70	<1.0	2.0	6.0	n.a.	100	n.a.
ranch, 2 tbsp. . .	155	<1.0	4.0	14.0	n.a.	100	n.a.
thousand island, 2 tbsp.	160	<1.0	4.0	14.0	n.a.	150	n.a.
desserts and shakes:							
brownie, 2.3 oz.	264	3.3	37.3	11.4	10	150	n.a.

Food and Measure	cal.	prot. (gms)	carbo. (gms)	fat (gms)	chol. (mgs)	sod. (mgs)	fiber (gms)
Roy Rogers, desserts and shakes *(cont.)*							
danish, apple, 2.53 oz.	249	4.5	31.6	11.6	15	255	n.a.
danish, cherry, 2.53 oz.	271	4.4	31.7	14.4	11	242	n.a.
danish, cheese, 2.53 oz.	254	4.9	31.4	12.2	11	260	n.a.
shake, chocolate	358	7.9	61.3	10.2	37	290	n.a.
shake, strawberry	315	7.6	49.4	10.2	37	261	n.a.
shake, vanilla . . .	306	8.0	45.0	10.7	40	282	n.a.
strawberry short-cake, 7.3 oz. . .	447	10.1	59.3	19.2	28	674	n.a.
sundae, caramel, 5.2 oz.	293	7.0	51.5	8.5	23	193	n.a.
sundae, hot fudge, 5.4 oz.	337	6.5	53.3	12.5	23	186	n.a.
sundae, strawberry, 5 oz.	216	5.7	33.1	7.1	23	99	n.a.
Rum, see "Liquor"							
Rutabaga (yellow turnip):							
fresh:							
raw, trimmed, 4 oz.	41	1.4	9.2	.2	0	23	1.2
raw, cubed, 1 cup	51	1.7	11.4	.3	0	28	1.5
boiled, drained, cubed, 1 cup . .	58	1.9	13.2	.3	0	30	1.8
boiled, drained, mashed, 1 cup	82	2.6	18.6	.5	0	44	2.5
frozen *(Southland)*, 4 oz.	50	1.0	13.0	0	0	200	n.a.
Rye whiskey, see "Liquor"							

S

Food and Measure	cal.	prot. (gms)	carbo. (gms)	fat (gms)	chol. (mgs)	sod. (mgs)	fiber (gms)
Sablefish:							
raw, meat only, 4 oz.	221	15.2	0	17.4	56	64	0
smoked, 4 oz. . . .	291	20.0	0	22.8	73	836	0
Safflower seed kernels:							
dry, 1 oz.	174	5.4	3.5	16.9	0	n.a.	n.a.
Safflower seed meal:							
partially defatted, 4 oz.	403	44.9	41.4	9.3	0	n.a.	8.4
Saffron:							
(all brands), 1 tsp.	2	.1	.5	<.1	0	1	<.1
Sage:							
ground (all brands), 1 tsp.	2	.1	.4	.1	0	tr.	.1
Salad dressing, bottled, 1 tbsp.:							
(A&P)	70	<1.0	2.0	7.0	8	105	n.a.
(Bama)	50	0	3.0	4.0	n.a.	120	n.a.
(Miracle Whip) . . .	70	0	2.0	7.0	5	85	n.a.
(Miracle Whip Light)	45	0	2.0	4.0	5	95	n.a.
(Mrs. Filbert's) . . .	70	0	2.0	6.0	5	115	0
bacon, creamy (Kraft Reduced Calorie)	30	0	2.0	2.0	0	150	n.a.
bacon and buttermilk (Kraft)	80	0	1.0	8.0	0	125	n.a.
bacon and tomato:							
(Kraft)	70	0	1.0	7.0	0	130	n.a.
(Kraft Reduced Calorie)	30	0	2.0	2.0	0	150	n.a.

Food and Measure	cal.	prot. (gms)	carbo. (gms)	fat (gms)	chol. (mgs)	sod. (mgs)	fiber (gms)
Salad dressing, bottled (cont.)							
blue cheese:							
(Roka Brand) . . .	60	1.0	1.0	6.0	10	170	n.a.
(Roka Brand Reduced Calorie)	14	1.0	1.0	1.0	5	280	n.a.
chunky (Kraft) . .	70	1.0	2.0	6.0	0	230	n.a.
chunky (Kraft Reduced Calorie)	30	0	2.0	2.0	0	240	n.a.
chunky (Wish-Bone)	70	0	< 1.0	8.0	tr.	150	n.a.
chunky (Wish-Bone Lite)	40	0	1.0	4.0	tr.	190	n.a.
blue cheese and bacon (Philadelphia Brand)	70	1.0	1.0	7.0	0	160	n.a.
buttermilk:							
(Wish-Bone Lite)	50	0	2.0	5.0	tr.	150	n.a.
bleu cheese (Hain Naturals)	70	0	0	7.0	n.a.	170	n.a.
creamy (Kraft) . .	80	0	1.0	8.0	5	120	n.a.
creamy (Kraft Reduced Calorie)	30	0	1.0	3.0	0	125	n.a.
old fashioned (Hain Naturals)	70	0	0	7.0	n.a.	100	n.a.
buttermilk and chives, creamy (Kraft) . .	80	0	1.0	8.0	5	125	n.a.
Caesar:							
(Bernstein Extra Rich)	48	.5	.5	5.1	5	93	n.a.
(Wish-Bone) . . .	70	0	< 1.0	8.0	tr.	250	n.a.
creamy (Hain Naturals)	60	0	1.0	6.0	n.a.	220	n.a.
creamy (Hain Naturals No Salt Added)	60	0	1.0	6.0	n.a.	15	n.a.
golden (Kraft) . .	70	0	1.0	7.0	0	180	n.a.
(Catalina Brand Reduced Calorie) . .	16	0	3.0	0	0	125	n.a.
cheese avocado (Hain Naturals)	70	0	0	7.0	n.a.	180	n.a.

Food and Measure	cal.	prot. (gms)	carbo. (gms)	fat (gms)	chol. (mgs)	sod. (mgs)	fiber (gms)
coleslaw (Kraft) . . .	70	0	4.0	6.0	10	200	n.a.
cucumber:							
creamy (Kraft) . .	70	0	1.0	8.0	0	200	n.a.
creamy (Kraft Reduced Calorie)	30	0	1.0	3.0	0	210	n.a.
creamy (Wish-Bone)	80	0	1.0	8.0	tr.	125	n.a.
creamy (Wish-Bone Lite)	40	0	1.0	4.0	0	165	n.a.
dill (Hain Naturals)	80	0	0	8.0	n.a.	210	n.a.
cheddar and bacon (Wish-Bone) . . .	70	<1.0	1.0	7.0	tr.	110	n.a.
French:							
(Catalina Brand)	70	0	4.0	6.0	0	180	n.a.
(Kraft)	60	0	2.0	6.0	0	125	n.a.
(Kraft Reduced Calorie)	25	0	3.0	2.0	0	150	n.a.
(Nalley)	54	.2	2.1	5.3	n.a.	106	n.a.
(Wish-Bone Deluxe)	50	0	2.0	5.0	0	80	n.a.
(Wish-Bone Lite French Style)	30	0	2.0	2.0	0	70	n.a.
garlic (Wish-Bone)	60	0	2.0	6.0	0	150	n.a.
herbal (Wish-Bone)	60	0	2.0	6.0	0	130	n.a.
sweet 'n spicy (Wish-Bone) . .	70	0	3.0	6.0	0	150	n.a.
sweet 'n spicy (Wish-Bone Lite)	30	0	4.0	2.0	0	150	n.a.
vinaigrette (Bernstein)	48	n.a.	.2	5.4	n.a.	112	n.a.
garlic, creamy (Wish-Bone)	80	0	<1.0	8.0	0	170	n.a.
garlic and chives (Philadelphia Brand)	70	0	1.0	7.0	0	115	n.a.
garlic and oil (Hain Naturals)	120	0	0	14.0	0	n.a.	n.a.
garlic and sour cream (Hain Naturals) . .	70	0	0	7.0	n.a.	100	n.a.
herb, savory (Hain Naturals)	90	0	0	10.0	n.a.	25	n.a.
honey and sesame (Hain Naturals) . .	60	0	2.0	5.0	n.a.	210	n.a.

Food and Measure	cal.	prot. (gms)	carbo. (gms)	fat (gms)	chol. (mgs)	sod. (mgs)	fiber (gms)
Salad dressing, bottled *(cont.)*							
Italian:							
(Bernstein Low Calorie)	4	<1.0	1.0	<1.0	n.a.	n.a.	n.a.
(Bernstein Restaurant Recipe) . .	65	.3	.5	7.1	<1	167	n.a.
(Kraft Reduced Calorie)	6	0	1.0	0	0	210	n.a.
(Kraft Zesty) . . .	70	0	1.0	8.0	0	280	n.a.
(Presto)	70	0	1.0	7.0	0	150	n.a.
(Wish-Bone) . . .	70	0	1.0	7.0	0	240	n.a.
(Wish-Bone Lite)	30	0	1.0	3.0	0	210	n.a.
(Wish-Bone Robusto)	80	0	1.0	8.0	0	285	n.a.
with cheese *(Bernstein)*	45	.3	.5	3.3	<1	108	n.a.
with cheese *(Bernstein* Low Calorie)	6	<1.0	1.0	<1.0	n.a.	n.a.	n.a.
with cheese and garlic *(Bernstein)*	50	.3	1.2	5.0	<1	171	n.a.
creamy *(Hain Naturals)*	80	0	0	8.0	n.a.	100	n.a.
creamy *(Kraft* Reduced Calorie)	25	0	1.0	2.0	0	125	n.a.
creamy *(Wish-Bone)*	60	0	1.0	6.0	0	145	n.a.
creamy *(Wish-Bone* Lite)	30	0	1.0	3.0	0	200	n.a.
creamy, with sour cream *(Kraft)* . .	60	0	1.0	6.0	0	120	n.a.
herb *(Philadelphia Brand)*	70	0	1.0	7.0	0	120	n.a.
herbal *(Wish-Bone)*	70	0	1.0	7.0	0	240	n.a.
marinade *(Bernstein)*	51	n.a.	.8	5.6	n.a.	167	n.a.
oil free *(Kraft)* . .	4	0	1.0	0	0	210	n.a.
traditional *(Hain Naturals)*	80	0	0	8.0	n.a.	330	n.a.
oil & vinegar *(Kraft)*	70	0	1.0	7.0	0	220	n.a.
onion and chive:							
(Wish-Bone) . . .	40	0	3.0	3.0	0	160	n.a.

Food and Measure	cal.	prot. (gms)	carbo. (gms)	fat (gms)	chol. (mgs)	sod. (mgs)	fiber (gms)
creamy (Kraft) ..	70	0	1.0	7.0	0	140	n.a.
Romano, robust (Hain Naturals)	70	0	0	8.0	n.a.	105	n.a.
Roquefort (Bernstein)	65	.6	.8	6.6	11	119	n.a.
Russian:							
(Kraft)	60	0	4.0	5.0	0	125	n.a.
(Kraft Reduced Calorie)	30	0	4.0	1.0	0	120	n.a.
(Wish-Bone) ...	45	0	6.0	2.0	0	140	n.a.
(Wish-Bone Lite)	25	0	<1.0	0	0	140	n.a.
tangy (Hain Naturals)	60	0	3.0	5.0	n.a.	120	n.a.
sour cream and bacon (Wish-Bone) ...	70	<1.0	1.0	7.0	tr.	95	n.a.
Thousand Island:							
(Bernstein)	62	.2	1.7	6.2	9	121	n.a.
(Hain Naturals) ..	50	0	0	5.0	n.a.	85	n.a.
(Kraft)	60	0	3.0	5.0	5	150	n.a.
(Kraft Reduced Calorie)	30	0	2.0	2.0	5	140	n.a.
(Nalley)	59	.2	2.3	5.6	8	92	n.a.
(Wish-Bone) ...	70	0	3.0	6.0	5	130	n.a.
(Wish-Bone Lite)	40	0	3.0	3.0	10	110	n.a.
(Wish-Bone Southern Recipe) ..	70	0	3.0	6.0	10	90	n.a.
and bacon (Kraft)	60	0	2.0	6.0	0	95	n.a.
with bacon (Wish-Bone Southern Recipe)	60	0	2.0	6.0	5	95	n.a.
vinaigrette (Bernstein Low Calorie) ...	2	<1.0	<1.0	<1.0	n.a.	n.a.	n.a.
Salad dressing, mix*, 1 tbsp.:							
blue cheese (Hain Natural No Oil) ..	14	1.0	1.0	1.0	n.a.	n.a.	n.a.
buttermilk (Hain Natural No Oil)	11	1.0	2.0	0	n.a.	n.a.	n.a.

* Prepared according to package directions

Food and Measure	cal.	prot. (gms)	carbo. (gms)	fat (gms)	chol. (mgs)	sod. (mgs)	fiber (gms)
Salad dressing, mix* *(cont.)*							
Caesar *(Hain Natural No Oil)*	4	1.0	0	0	0	n.a.	n.a.
French *(Hain Natural No Oil)*	12	9.0	3.0	0	0	n.a.	n.a.
garlic & cheese *(Hain Natural No Oil)* . .	6	0	1.0	0	n.a.	n.a.	n.a.
herb:							
(Good Seasons)	80	<1.0	n.a.	9.0	n.a.	150	tr.
(Hain Natural No Oil)	2	0	1.0	0	0	n.a.	n.a.
Italian:							
(Good Seasons)	80	<1.0	1.0	9.0	n.a.	150	tr.
(Good Seasons Lite)	25	<1.0	1.0	3.0	n.a.	180	tr.
(Good Seasons Low Calorie)	8	<1.0	2.0	tr.	0	30	tr.
(Hain Natural No Oil)	4	0	1.0	0	0	n.a.	n.a.
Salad sprinkles:							
(Lawry's), 1 tsp. . .	10	.6	1.2	.4	0	292	.3
Salami:							
beef *(Hormel Perma-Fresh)*, 2 slices . .	50	3.0	0	5.0	n.a.	219	n.a.
beer:							
(Eckrich), 1 slice	70	4.0	1.0	6.0	n.a.	350	n.a.
(Oscar Mayer), .82-oz. slice	55	3.2	.3	4.5	15	264	0
beef *(Oscar Mayer)*, .82-oz. slice . .	54	3.1	.5	4.4	15	275	0
cooked:							
(Armour), 1 oz. . .	80	n.a.	n.a.	7.0	20	300	0
chub *(Eckrich)*, 1 oz.	70	4.0	1.0	6.0	n.a.	360	n.a.
cotto:							
(Eckrich), 1 slice	70	4.0	1.0	5.0	n.a.	340	n.a.
(Grillmaster), 1 slice	81	4.5	.7	6.6	n.a.	404	n.a.

* *Prepared according to package directions*

Food and Measure	cal.	prot. (gms)	carbo. (gms)	fat (gms)	chol. (mgs)	sod. (mgs)	fiber (gms)
(Hormel Chub), 1 oz.	100	5.0	0	9.0	n.a.	385	n.a.
(Hormel Perma-Fresh), 2 slices	105	9.0	1.0	7.0	n.a.	750	n.a.
(Light & Lean), 2 slices	80	6.0	0	6.0	n.a.	n.a.	n.a.
(Oscar Mayer), .82-oz. slice	54	3.1	.5	4.4	15	275	0
beef *(Eckrich),* 2 slices	100	6.0	2.0	8.0	n.a.	480	n.a.
beef *(Oscar Mayer),* .82-oz. slice . .	45	3.5	.3	3.4	15	274	0
Genoa:							
(Armour), 1 oz. . .	110	n.a.	n.a.	10.0	30	475	0
(Hormel), 1 oz. . .	110	6.0	0	10.0	n.a.	456	n.a.
(Hormel DiLusso), 1 oz.	100	6.0	0	8.0	n.a.	443	n.a.
(Hormel Gran Valore), 1 oz. . .	110	6.0	0	10.0	n.a.	453	n.a.
(Hormel San Remo Brand), 1 oz. . .	118	7.0	0	10.0	n.a.	544	n.a.
(Oscar Mayer), 1/3-oz. slice	35	1.8	.1	3.0	8	157	0
hard:							
(Armour), 1 oz. . .	120	n.a.	n.a.	10.0	20	525	0
(Eckrich), 1 oz. . .	130	5.0	1.0	12.0	n.a.	600	n.a.
(Hormel), 1 oz. . .	110	7.0	0	10.0	n.a.	468	n.a.
(Hormel National Brand), 1 oz. . .	120	6.0	0	11.0	n.a.	463	n.a.
(Hormel Perma-Fresh), 2 slices	80	4.0	0	7.0	n.a.	339	n.a.
(Hormel Sliced), 1 oz.	110	6.0	0	10.0	n.a.	483	n.a.
(Oscar Mayer), 1/3-oz.slice	34	1.9	.1	2.9	7	163	0
Italian *(Armour),* 1 oz.	120	n.a.	n.a.	10.0	20	520	0
(Hormel Party), 1 oz.	90	5.0	0	8.0	n.a.	399	n.a.

Food and Measure	cal.	prot. (gms)	carbo. (gms)	fat (gms)	chol. (mgs)	sod. (mgs)	fiber (gms)
Salami *(cont.)*							
piccolo *(Hormel* stick), 1 oz.	120	6.0	0	11.0	n.a.	512	n.a.
turkey, see "Turkey salami"							
Salisbury steak dinner, frozen:							
(Banquet American Favorites), 11 oz.	395	17.0	24.0	26.0	n.a.	1333	n.a.
(Banquet Extra Helpings), 19 oz. . . .	1024	39.0	72.0	65.0	n.a.	2175	n.a.
(Classic Lite), 10 oz.	290	20.0	25.0	13.0	75	870	n.a.
(Dinner Classics), 11 oz.	470	20.0	39.0	26.0	105	1400	n.a.
(Lean Cuisine), 9½ oz.	270	25.0	14.0	13.0	95	700	n.a.
(Swanson), 11 oz.	460	21.0	44.0	22.0	n.a.	1050	n.a.
(Swanson Hungry-Man), 16½ oz. . .	690	40.0	42.0	40.0	n.a.	1630	n.a.
Salisbury steak entree, frozen:							
(Banquet Cookin' Bag), 5 oz.	251	13.0	5.0	20.0	n.a.	729	n.a.
(Swanson), 5½ oz.	340	18.0	19.0	21.0	n.a.	650	n.a.
(Swanson Main Course), 10 oz. . .	380	26.0	26.0	21.0	n.a.	1400	n.a.
(Swanson Hungry-Man), 11¾ oz. . .	610	39.0	29.0	38.0	n.a.	1340	n.a.
char-broiled, with vegetables *(Freezer Queen* Single Serve),* 10oz. . . .	390	24.0	16.0	25.0	n.a.	n.a.	n.a.
with creole sauce *(Dining Lite),* 9.5 oz.	223	25.1	11.4	9.3	n.a.	1460	1.6
gravy and:							
(Banquet Family Entrees), 32 oz. . .	1004	120.0	36.0	76.0	n.a.	4289	n.a.
(Freezer Queen, 2 lb.), 10.67 oz.	390	20.0	15.0	27.0	n.a.	n.a.	n.a.

Food and Measure	cal.	prot. (gms)	carbo. (gms)	fat (gms)	chol. (mgs)	sod. (mgs)	fiber (gms)
(Freezer Queen Cook-in-Pouch), 5 oz.	180	10.0	7.0	12.0	n.a.	n.a.	n.a.
(Morton Lite), 8 oz.	290	13.0	34.0	12.0	n.a.	670	n.a.
with onion gravy *(Stouffer's)*, 6 oz.	230	20.0	6.0	14.0	n.a.	1120	n.a.
Salmon:							
fresh, meat only:							
Atlantic, raw, 4 oz.	161	22.5	0	7.2	62	50	0
chinook, raw, 4 oz.	204	22.7	0	11.8	75	53	0
chum, raw, 4 oz.	136	22.8	0	4.3	84	57	0
coho, raw, 4 oz.	166	24.5	0	6.7	44	52	0
coho, poached or steamed, 4 oz.	210	31.0	0	8.6	56	67	0
pink (humpback), raw, 4 oz. . . .	132	22.6	0	3.9	59	76	0
red sockeye, raw, 4 oz.	191	24.2	0	9.7	70	53	0
red sockeye, baked or broiled, 4 oz.	245	31.0	0	12.4	99	75	0
canned:							
Atlantic, with liquid, 4 oz.	230	24.6	0	13.8	n.a.	n.a.	0
blueback *(Gill Netters Best)*, 3.5 oz.	170	20.0	0	9.0	62	450	0
chinook (king), with liquid, 4 oz. . .	238	22.2	0	15.9	n.a.	n.a.	0
chum, drained, 4 oz.	160	24.3	0	6.2	44	552	0
chum *(Humpty-Dumpty)*, 3.5 oz.	140	22.0	0	5.0	62	450	0
coho, or silver, with liquid, 4 oz. . .	174	23.6	0	8.1	n.a.	398	0
pink *(Del Monte)*, 1/2 cup	160	22.0	0	7.0	n.a.	660	0
pink, Alaska *(Double "Q")*, 3.5 oz.	140	20.0	0	6.0	62	450	0
red sockeye, drained, 4 oz.	174	23.2	0	8.3	50	610	0

Food and Measure	cal.	prot. (gms)	carbo. (gms)	fat (gms)	chol. (mgs)	sod. (mgs)	fiber (gms)
Salmon, canned *(cont.)*							
red *(Del Monte)*, 1/2 cup	180	23.0	0	9.0	n.a.	660	0
red sockeye *(Deming's/Peter Pan)*, 3.5 oz.	170	20.0	0	9.0	62	450	0
red sockeye, blueback *(S&W Fancy)*, 1/2 cup	190	25.0	0	10.0	n.a.	590	0
frozen, steaks *(Wakefield)*, 3 oz.	110	18.0	0	4.0	n.a.	60	0
smoked, chinook, 4 oz.	133	20.7	0	4.9	26	889	0
Salsa (see also "Chili sauce"):							
(Del Monte Roja), 1/4 cup	20	0	4.0	0	0	510	n.a.
(Ortega Ranchera), 1 oz.	12	.4	2.9	.1	0	244	.3
hot *(Ortega)*, 1 oz.	9	.4	1.9	.1	0	181	.3
medium *(Ortega)*, 1 oz.	7	.3	1.7	.1	0	181	.2
mild:							
(Ortega), 1 oz. . .	7	.3	1.7	.1	0	180	.2
green chili *(Ortega)*, 1 oz.	7	.3	1.7	.1	0	177	.2
picante, see "Picante sauce"							
taco, see "Taco sauce"							
Salsify, fresh:							
raw:							
trimmed, 8 oz. . .	186	7.5	42.2	.5	0	45	4.1
sliced, 1 cup . . .	109	4.4	24.7	.3	0	27	2.4
boiled, drained, sliced, 1 cup	92	3.7	20.7	.2	0	21	2.0
Salt:							
1 tbsp.	0	0	0	0	0	8139	0
1 tsp.	0	0	0	0	0	2713	0

Food and Measure	cal.	prot. (gms)	carbo. (gms)	fat (gms)	chol. (mgs)	sod. (mgs)	fiber (gms)
seasoned *(Lawry's)*, 1 tsp.	4	.1	.6	<.1	0	1367	<.1
Salt pork:							
raw, 1 oz.	212	1.4	0	22.8	25	404	0
Sand dab, raw:							
whole, 1 lb.	118	25.0	0	1.2	n.a.	117	0
meat only, 4 oz. . .	90	18.9	0	.9	n.a.	88	0
Sandwich spread (see also specific listings):							
(Best Foods/ Hellmann's), 1 tbsp.	50	0	2.0	5.0	5	170	n.a.
(Kraft), 1 tbsp. . . .	50	0	3.0	5.0	5	95	n.a.
(Oscar Mayer), 1 oz.	67	2.1	3.6	4.9	10	261	n.a.
Sapodilla, fresh:							
1 fruit (3″ diam.×2½″ high)	140	.7	33.9	1.9	0	20	2.4
pulp only, 1 cup . .	199	1.1	48.1	2.7	0	29	3.4
Sapote (marmalade plum), fresh:							
whole, 1 fruit, 11.2 oz.	301	4.8	76.0	1.4	0	21	4.3
peeled and seeded, 4 oz.	152	2.4	38.3	.7	0	11	2.2
Sardines:							
raw, Pacific, meat only, 4 oz.	181	21.8	0	9.8	n.a.	n.a.	0
canned:							
Atlantic, in oil, 4 oz.	353	23.4	.7	27.7	n.a.	578	n.a.
Atlantic, in oil, drained, 4 oz.	236	27.9	0	13.0	161	573	0
Norwegian Brisling, in oil *(Empress Fancy)*, 3¾ oz.	460	19.0	1.0	42.0	n.a.	n.a.	n.a.
Norwegian Brisling, in oil, drained *(King David Brand)*, 3¾ oz.	293	21.0	0	23.0	n.a.	842	n.a.

Food and Measure	cal.	prot. (gms)	carbo. (gms)	fat (gms)	chol. (mgs)	sod. (mgs)	fiber (gms)
Sardines, canned (cont.)							
Norwegian Brisling, in oil, drained (S&W), 1.5 oz.	130	10.0	0	10.0	n.a.	220	n.a.
Norwegian Brisling, in oil, drained (Queen Helga Brand), 3¾ oz.	310	20.0	0	26.0	n.a.	603	n.a.
skinless, boneless, in oil (Granadaisa Brand), 3¾ oz.	277	24.0	0	19.0	n.a.	526	n.a.
in tomato sauce (Empress Fancy), 3¾ oz.	240	18.0	2.0	18.0	n.a.	n.a.	n.a.
in tomato sauce (Del Monte), ½ cup	360	19.0	45.0	12.0	n.a.	540	n.a.
in tomato sauce Granadaisa Brand), 3¾ oz.	195	19.0	0	13.0	n.a.	434	n.a.
in mustard sauce (Empress Fancy), 3¾ oz.	240	18.0	2.0	18.0	n.a.	n.a.	n.a.
in water (Empress Fancy), 3¾ oz.	190	17.0	1.0	13.0	n.a.	n.a.	n.a.
Sauces, see specific listings							
Sauerkraut, canned, ½ cup, except as noted:							
(A&P)	20	2.0	3.0	<1.0	0	800	n.a.
(Claussen)	17	.7	2.9	.2	0	491	n.a.
(Del Monte)	25	1.0	6.0	0	0	775	n.a.
(Libby/Seneca) . . .	20	1.0	5.0	0	0	780	n.a.
(Silver Floss Bavarian)	40	0	8.0	0	0	600	n.a.
(Stokely's Finest) . .	20	1.0	4.0	0	0	810	n.a.
(Stokely's Finest Bavarian)	30	1.0	7.0	0	0	780	n.a.
(Vlasic), 1 oz.	4	0	1.0	0	0	280	n.a.

Food and Measure	cal.	prot. (gms)	carbo. (gms)	fat (gms)	chol. (mgs)	sod. (mgs)	fiber (gms)
Sauerkraut juice:							
canned *(S&W)*, 5 fl. oz.	14	1.0	3.0	0	0	1120	n.a.
Sauger, raw:							
whole, 1 lb.	133	28.4	0	1.3	n.a.	n.a.	0
meat only, 4 oz. . .	95	20.3	0	.9	n.a.	n.a.	0
Sausage (see also specific listings):							
beef *(Jones Dairy Farm)*, 1-oz. roll	112	3.5	0	10.9	n.a.	177	n.a.
breakfast links or roll *(Jones Dairy Farm Light)*, 1 oz. . . .	70	4.0	.5	5.5	n.a.	220	n.a.
brown and serve:							
(Jones Dairy Farm), 1-oz. link	127	2.9	tr.	12.9	n.a.	189	n.a.
beef *(Swift* Original Brown 'n Serve), 2 links	165	5.0	<1.0	15.0	25	370	n.a.
beef, smoked *(Jones Dairy Farm)*, 1-oz. link	112	3.7	tr.	10.6	n.a.	243	n.a.
breakfast links *(Jones Dairy Farm Light)*, 1-oz. link	70	4.0	.5	5.5	n.a.	200	n.a.
cooked *(Hormel)*, 1 link	70	3.0	0	6.5	n.a.	215	n.a.
pork *(Swift* Original Brown 'n Serve), 2 links	190	5.0	1.0	18.0	30	375	n.a.
pork *(Swift* Brown 'n Serve Country Recipe), 2 links	190	5.0	<1.0	19.0	35	375	n.a.
pork *(Swift* Original Brown 'n Serve), 2 patties	190	6.0	<1.0	18.0	40	365	n.a.
pork and bacon *(Jones Dairy Farm)*, 1-oz. link	107	3.7	tr.	10.0	n.a.	200	n.a.

Food and Measure	cal.	prot. (gms)	carbo. (gms)	fat (gms)	chol. (mgs)	sod. (mgs)	fiber (gms)
Sausage, brown and serve (cont.)							
uncooked (Hormel), 1 link	90	3.5	0	8.5	n.a.	206	n.a.
hot:							
(Grillmaster Red Hots), 1 link	183	9.1	1.2	15.1	n.a.	797	n.a.
(Hormel), 1 patty	150	7.0	0	13.0	n.a.	549	n.a.
Italian:							
5 per lb. raw	217	13.4	1.0	17.2	52	618	0
4 per lb. raw	268	16.6	1.3	21.3	65	765	0
hot (Hillshire Farms), 3 1/2 oz.	317	13.0	1.0	29.0	37	827	n.a.
mild (Hillshire Farms), 3 1/2 oz.	317	13.0	1.0	29.0	26	720	n.a.
pork (Jones Dairy Farm), 1-oz.	92	3.8	tr.	8.4	n.a.	222	n.a.
mild (Hormel), 1 patty	150	7.0	0	13.0	n.a.	541	n.a.
pork, cooked:							
(Eckrich), 2 oz.	260	6.0	1.0	26.0	n.a.	n.a.	n.a.
(Eckrich Link), 2 links	220	7.0	1.0	20.0	n.a.	n.a.	n.a.
(Eckrich Patty), 1 patty	240	6.0	1.0	26.0	n.a.	n.a.	n.a.
(Hormel Little Sizzlers), 2 links	103	6.0	0	9.0	n.a.	172	n.a.
(Hormel Midget Links), 2 links	143	7.0	0	13.0	n.a.	327	n.a.
(Oscar Mayer Little Friers), 3/4-oz. link	77	3.2	.2	7.0	16	206	0
country style, 1 link (4" × 7/8")	48	2.6	.1	4.1	11	168	0
country style, 1 patty (3 7/8" diam. × 1/4" raw)	100	5.3	.3	8.4	22	349	0
hot, fresh, roll (Eckrich), 2 oz.	240	6.0	1.0	26.0	n.a.	n.a.	n.a.

Food and Measure	cal.	prot. (gms)	carbo. (gms)	fat (gms)	chol. (mgs)	sod. (mgs)	fiber (gms)
pork, uncooked:							
(Jones Dairy Farm), 1-oz. link	132	3.0	0	13.2	n.a.	177	n.a.
(Jones Dairy Farm), 1-oz. patty . . .	102	3.8	0	9.4	n.a.	177	n.a.
roll, regular or hot *(Jones Dairy Farm),* 1 oz. . .	102	3.8	0	9.4	n.a.	177	n.a.
smoked:							
(Eckrich), 2-oz. link	190	7.0	1.0	17.0	n.a.	530	n.a.
(Eckrich Skinless), 1 link	180	7.0	2.0	15.0	n.a.	490	n.a.
(Eckrich Skinless), 1-oz. link	90	4.0	1.0	7.0	n.a.	250	n.a.
(Eckrich Smok-Y-Links Skinless), 2 links	150	6.0	2.0	13.0	n.a.	410	n.a.
(Hillshire Farms Endless), 3¹/₂ oz.	334	13.0	3.1	30.0	20	905	n.a.
(Hillshire Farms Links), 3¹/₂ oz.	337	13.0	3.7	30.0	20	905	n.a.
(Hormel), 3 oz. . .	290	12.0	1.0	27.0	n.a.	n.a.	n.a.
(Hormel Smokies), 2 links	160	9.0	2.0	14.0	n.a.	597	n.a.
(Oscar Mayer Little Smokies), ¹/₃-oz. link	28	1.2	.2	2.5	6	92	0
(Oscar Mayer Smokie Links), 1.5-oz. link . . .	124	5.4	.6	11.2	27	432	0
beef *(Eckrich),* 2-oz. link	190	7.0	1.0	17.0	n.a.	520	n.a.
beef *(Eckrich Smok-Y-Links),* 2 links	140	7.0	2.0	12.0	n.a.	400	n.a.
beef *(Hillshire Farms),* 3¹/₂ oz.	331	13.0	3.4	29.5	29	985	n.a.
beef *(Oscar Mayer Smokies),* 1.5-oz. link	122	5.4	.6	10.9	27	425	0

Food and Measure	cal.	prot. (gms)	carbo. (gms)	fat (gms)	chol. (mgs)	sod. (mgs)	fiber (gms)
Sausage, smoked (cont.)							
with cheese (*Eckrich*), 1 link	240	10.0	2.0	20.0	n.a.	670	n.a.
with cheese (*Hormel* Smokie Cheezers), 2 links	168	9.0	1.0	15.0	n.a.	623	n.a.
cheese (*Eckrich*), 2 oz.	180	7.0	2.0	15.0	n.a.	500	n.a.
cheese (*Oscar Mayer* Smokies), 1.5-oz. link . . .	127	5.8	.8	11.2	28	448	0
chicken, see "Chicken sausage"							
cocktail (*Kahn's* Cocktail Smokies), 1 link . . .	29	1.2	.3	2.5	n.a.	97	n.a.
ham (*Eckrich Smok-Y-Links*), 2 links	150	6.0	2.0	13.0	n.a.	560	n.a.
hot (*Eckrich*), 1 link	240	8.0	3.0	21.0	n.a.	640	n.a.
maple flavored (*Eckrich Smok-Y-Links*), 2 links	150	6.0	2.0	13.0	n.a.	400	n.a.
pork, grilled, 1 link (4" × 1 1/8" diam.)	265	15.1	1.4	21.6	46	1020	0
pork, grilled, small, 1 link (2" × 3/4" diam.)	62	3.6	.3	5.1	11	240	0
pork and beef, 1 link (4" × 1 1/8" diam.)	229	9.1	1.0	20.6	48	642	0
pork and beef, small, 1 link (2" × 3/4" diam.)	54	2.1	.2	4.9	11	151	0
turkey, see "Turkey sausage"							
Vienna:							
canned (*Hormel*), 4 links	200	7.0	1.0	18.0	n.a.	479	0

Food and Measure	cal.	prot. (gms)	carbo. (gms)	fat (gms)	chol. (mgs)	sod. (mgs)	fiber (gms)
canned, beef and pork, 1 link (2″ × ⅛″ diam.)	45	1.7	.3	4.0	8	152	0
Sausage sticks:							
beef:							
(Tombstone), 1-oz. stick	136	5.0	.1	13.0	n.a.	312	n.a.
(Tombstone Snappy), 1-oz. stick	129	5.0	.1	12.0	n.a.	284	n.a.
roll (Hormel Lumberjack), 1 oz.	101	5.0	0	9.0	n.a.	304	n.a.
hot (Frito-Lay's), 1 oz.	80	5.0	0	7.0	n.a.	575	n.a.
jerky:							
(Laura Scudder's Natural), 1 oz.	80	15.0	3.0	1.0	n.a.	780	n.a.
(Laura Scudder's Tender), 1 oz.	80	12.0	2.0	2.0	n.a.	755	n.a.
beef (Frito-Lay's), .23 oz.	25	3.0	1.0	1.0	n.a.	150	n.a.
beef (Laura Scudder's), ¼ oz. . .	25	3.0	1.0	1.0	n.a.	200	n.a.
smoked:							
(Laura Scudder's Snack), .54 oz.	80	2.0	1.0	7.0	n.a.	240	n.a.
beef (Frito-Lay's), ½ oz.	80	3.0	0	7.0	n.a.	215	n.a.
Savory:							
ground (all brands), 1 tsp.	4	.1	1.0	.1	0	tr.	.2
Scallop, bay and sea:							
fresh:							
raw, 2 large or 5 small	26	5.0	.7	.2	10	48	0
raw, meat only, 4 oz.	100	19.0	2.7	.9	37	183	0
frozen:							
in batter (Taste O' Sea Batter Dipt), 3½ oz.	190	13.0	20.0	7.0	n.a.	450	n.a.

Food and Measure	cal.	prot. (gms)	carbo. (gms)	fat (gms)	chol. (mgs)	sod. (mgs)	fiber (gms)
Scallop, frozen *(cont.)*							
breaded, French fried *(Mrs. Paul's)*, 3½ oz.	210	13.0	23.0	7.0	n.a.	545	n.a.
French fried *(Taste O' Sea* Crispy Light), 4 oz. . .	230	13.0	24.0	9.0	n.a.	670	n.a.
Scallop dinner, frozen:							
(Taste O' Sea), 8 oz.	470	20.0	49.0	22.0	n.a.	620	n.a.
Oriental *(Lean Cuisine),* 11 oz. . . .	220	15.0	32.0	3.0	20	1100	n.a.
Scallop entree:							
Mediterranean, frozen *(Mrs. Paul's Light),* 11 oz.	250	17.0	36.0	5.0	n.a.	775	n.a.
Scallop and shrimp entree:							
Mariner, frozen *(Stouffer's),* 10¼ oz. . .	390	21.0	35.0	18.0	n.a.	850	n.a.
Schinkenwurst:							
(Usinger's), 1 oz. . .	85	4.0	n.a.	8.0	n.a.	n.a.	n.a.
Scotch, see "Liquor"							
Scrapple:							
(Jones Dairy Farm), 1 oz.	52	2.6	3.4	3.9	n.a.	144	n.a.
Scrod dinner:							
in batter, frozen *(Taste O' Sea* Batter Dipt), 8¾ oz.	500	15.0	48.0	28.0	n.a.	1080	n.a.
Scrod entree:							
baked, stuffed, frozen *(Gorton's Light Recipe),* 1 pkg.	260	26.0	4.0	15.0	n.a.	490	n.a.
Sea bass, see "Bass"							
Seafood dinner, frozen:							
(Taste O' Sea Platter), 9 oz.	520	21.0	52.0	25.0	n.a.	1160	n.a.

Food and Measure	cal.	prot. (gms)	carbo. (gms)	fat (gms)	chol. (mgs)	sod. (mgs)	fiber (gms)
natural herbs (Classic Lite), 11½ oz. . .	250	12.0	38.0	6.0	20	1240	n.a.
Newburg (Dinner Classics), 10½ oz. . .	270	12.0	33.0	10.0	65	1500	n.a.
Seafood entree, frozen:							
breaded (Mrs. Paul's Combination Platter), 9 oz.	510	22.0	49.0	25.0	n.a.	1340	n.a.
Newburg (Mrs. Paul's Light), 8½ oz. . .	310	14.0	34.0	13.0	n.a.	610	n.a.
Seasoned coating mix, ¼ pouch:							
for chicken, barbecue (Shake 'n Bake)	90	1.0	18.0	2.0	0	840	.3
for pork (Shake 'n Bake)	80	1.0	15.0	2.0	0	700	.2
Seasoning, salt-free:							
(Lawry's), 1 tsp. . .	3	.1	.6	<.1	0	7	<.1
Seasonings, see specific listings							
Seaweed:							
agar:							
raw, 4 oz.	29	.6	7.7	<.1	0	10	.5
dried, 4 oz.	347	7.0	91.7	.3	0	116	.8
Irish moss, raw, 4 oz.	56	1.7	14.0	.2	0	76	n.a.
kelp, raw, 4 oz. . . .	49	1.9	10.9	.6	0	264	1.5
laver, raw, 4 oz. . .	40	6.6	5.8	.3	0	54	.3
spirulina:							
raw, 4 oz.	30	6.7	2.8	.5	0	111	.4
dried, 4 oz.	329	65.2	27.1	8.8	0	1189	4.1
wakame, raw, 4 oz.	52	3.4	10.4	.7	0	989	.6
Sesame butter:							
raw, unsalted (Hain), 2 tbsp.	180	6.0	7.0	15.0	0	15	n.a.
Sesame flour:							
high-fat, 4 oz.	596	35.0	30.2	42.2	0	48	7.2
partially defatted, 4 oz.	436	45.8	39.9	13.5	0	48	6.8

Food and Measure	cal.	prot. (gms)	carbo. (gms)	fat (gms)	chol. (mgs)	sod. (mgs)	fiber (gms)
Sesame flour *(cont.)*							
lowfat, 4 oz.	380	57.0	40.3	2.0	0	44	5.7
Sesame paste (see also "Tahini"):							
1 oz.	169	5.1	7.2	14.5	0	3	1.6
1 tbsp.	95	2.9	4.1	8.1	0	2	.9
Sesame seeds, dry:							
whole, 4 oz.	638	21.1	24.5	55.7	0	68	7.1
1 tbsp.	47	2.1	.8	4.4	0	3	.2
1 tsp.	16	.7	.3	1.5	0	1	.1
Sesame snacks:							
(Flavor Tree Party Mix), 1 oz.	160	4.0	11.0	11.0	0	400	n.a.
(Flavor Tree Party Mix Unsalted), 1 oz.	160	4.0	11.0	11.0	0	10	n.a.
(Flavor Tree Sesame Crunch), 1 oz. . .	150	5.0	10.0	10.0	0	70	n.a.
bars *(Sahadi* Sesame Crunch), 3/4 oz. . .	110	4.0	7.0	7.0	0	55	n.a.
chips *(Flavor Tree)*, 1 oz.	150	3.0	13.0	10.0	0	410	n.a.
nut mix, dry roasted *(Planters)*, 1 oz.	160	5.0	8.0	12.0	0	330	n.a.
sticks:							
(Flavor Tree), 1 oz.	150	3.0	13.0	10.0	0	405	n.a.
(Flavor Tree Unsalted), 1 oz. . .	160	3.0	12.0	11.0	0	10	n.a.
sticks, with bran *(Flavor Tree)*, 1 oz. . .	160	4.0	11.0	11.0	0	370	n.a.
Sesbania flower, fresh:							
raw:							
1 flower (23/4″ × 11/8″)	1	<.1	.2	0	0	0	<.1
1 cup	5	.3	1.4	<.1	0	3	.3
steamed, 1 cup . . .	23	1.2	5.4	.1	0	11	1.6
Shad:							
fresh:							
raw, whole, 1 lb.	370	40.5	0	21.8	n.a.	118	0

Food and Measure	cal.	prot. (gms)	carbo. (gms)	fat (gms)	chol. (mgs)	sod. (mgs)	fiber (gms)
raw, meat only, 4 oz.	193	21.1	0	11.3	n.a.	61	0
canned, with liquid, 4 oz.	172	19.2	0	10.0	n.a.	n.a.	0
Shad gizzard:							
raw, meat only, 4 oz.	227	19.5	0	15.9	n.a.	n.a.	0
Shad roe, see "Roe"							
Shallot:							
raw:							
peeled, 1 oz. . . .	20	.7	4.8	<.1	0	3	.2
peeled, chopped, 1 tbsp.	7	.3	1.7	<.1	0	1	.1
freeze-dried, 1 tbsp.	3	.1	.7	0	0	1	<.1
Sheepshead, Atlantic:							
raw, meat only, 4 oz.	128	23.4	0	3.2	n.a.	115	0
Sherbet, 1/2 cup:							
chocolate coconut (*Shamitoff's* Sorbet)	280	5.0	29.0	16.0	0	32	n.a.
all fruit flavors (*Land O'Lakes*)	130	1.0	27.0	2.0	5	25	n.a.
lemon or orange (*Borden*)	110	1.0	25.0	1.0	n.a.	n.a.	n.a.
lemon, raspberry or strawberry (*Shamitoff's* Sorbet)	100	0	25.0	0	0	2	n.a.
orange, 1 cup	270	2.2	58.7	3.8	14	88	tr.
orange, Mandarin (*Dole* Fruit Sorbet)	110	.5	30.0	<.1	0	9	n.a.
peach (*Dole* Fruit Sorbet)	120	.6	29.6	<.1	0	11	n.a.
pineapple (*Dole* Fruit Sorbet)	120	.5	28.0	<.1	0	11	n.a.
raspberry (*Dole* Fruit Sorbet)	110	.4	27.9	<.1	0	12	n.a.
strawberry (*Dole* Fruit Sorbet)	110	.5	27.9	<.1	0	11	n.a.
Sherbet bar, 1 bar:							
chocolate fudge:							
(*Eskimo*), 3 fl. oz.	110	3.0	24.0	0	0	50	0
(*Eskimo*), 2.5 fl. oz.	90	3.0	20.0	0	0	45	0

Food and Measure	cal.	prot. (gms)	carbo. (gms)	fat (gms)	chol. (mgs)	sod. (mgs)	fiber (gms)
Sherbet bar, chocolate fudge *(cont.)*							
(Eskimo), 1.75 fl. oz.	60	2.0	14.0	0	0	30	0
Shortening (see also "Lard"):							
soybean:							
cottonseed or palm, 1 cup	1812	0	0	205.0	0	0	0
cottonseed or palm, 1 tbsp.	113	0	0	12.8	0	0	0
vegetable:							
1 cup	1845	0	0	205.0	0	0	0
1 tbsp.	115	0	0	12.8	0	0	0
(Crisco), 1 tbsp. . .	110	0	0	12.0	0	0	0
(Snowdrift), 1 tbsp.	110	0	0	12.0	0	0	0
butter flavor *(Crisco),* 1 tbsp.	110	0	0	12.0	0	0	0
Shrimp:							
fresh, raw:							
in shell, 1 oz. or 4 large	30	5.7	.3	.5	43	42	0
meat only, 4 oz.	120	23.0	1.0	2.0	172	168	0
canned or in jars, cooked:							
(Louisiana Brand), 2 oz.	58	12.0	0	1.0	n.a.	n.a.	n.a.
(Sau-Sea), 2½ oz.	45	9.0	0	1.0	122	165	0
medium, whole, deveined *(S&W),* 1 oz.	65	13.0	1.0	0	n.a.	n.a.	n.a.
frozen:							
in batter *(SeaPak Shrimp'n Batter),* 4 oz.	260	9.0	26.0	13.0	n.a.	520	n.a.
in batter *(Taste O' Sea* Batter Dipt), 3 oz.	190	8.0	19.0	9.0	n.a.	370	n.a.
breaded *(Mrs. Paul's),* 3 oz. . .	190	9.0	15.0	10.0	n.a.	525	n.a.
breaded *(SeaPak),* 4 oz.	150	14.0	20.0	1.0	n.a.	n.a.	n.a.

Food and Measure	cal.	prot. (gms)	carbo. (gms)	fat (gms)	chol. (mgs)	sod. (mgs)	fiber (gms)
French fried (Taste O' Sea Crispy Light), 4 oz. . .	260	12.0	26.0	12.0	n.a.	790	n.a.
Shrimp cocktail:							
in jars (Sau-Sea), 4 oz.	113	7.0	19.0	1.0	90	1020	n.a.
Shrimp dinner, frozen:							
(Taste O'Sea), 7 oz.	370	16.0	38.0	18.0	n.a.	620	n.a.
baby, in sherried cream sauce (Classic Lite), 10½ oz.	280	17.0	34.0	8.0	110	1220	n.a.
chow mein (La Choy), 12 oz.	220	5.0	47.0	1.0	n.a.	1740	n.a.
Shrimp entree, canned:							
chow mein:							
drained (Chun King Stir-Fry), 7.14 oz.	91	6.8	13.0	2.1	28	258	.8
(La Choy), ¾ cup	45	5.0	4.0	1.0	n.a.	820	n.a.
(La Choy Bi-Pack), ¾ cup*	70	3.0	7.0	3.0	n.a.	620	n.a.
Shrimp entree, frozen:							
baked, stuffed (Gorton's Light Recipe), 1 pkg.	340	15.0	36.0	15.0	n.a.	950	n.a.
chow mein (La Choy), ⅔ cup	70	4.0	11.0	1.0	n.a.	820	n.a.
Creole:							
(Light & Elegant), 10 oz.	200	11.0	31.0	2.0	n.a.	1045	n.a.
with rice (Dining Lite), 10 oz. . .	210	12.1	37.0	1.9	n.a.	820	.9
Oriental:							
(Gorton's Light Recipe), 1 pkg. . . .	350	11.0	72.0	2.0	n.a.	740	n.a.

* Prepared according to package directions

Food and Measure	cal.	prot. (gms)	carbo. (gms)	fat (gms)	chol. (mgs)	sod. (mgs)	fiber (gms)
Shrimp entree, frozen, Oriental *(cont.)*							
(Mrs. Paul's Light), 11 oz.	230	11.0	42.0	2.0	n.a.	940	n.a.
and pasta *(Gorton's Light Recipe)*, 1 pkg.	370	19.0	30.0	19.0	n.a.	550	n.a.
primavera *(Mrs. Paul's Light)*, 11 oz. . . .	310	16.0	42.0	9.0	n.a.	1185	n.a.
scampi *(Gorton's Light Recipe)*, 1 pkg. . .	350	19.0	15.0	24.0	n.a.	420	n.a.
Shrimp paste:							
canned, 1 oz.	51	5.9	.4	2.7	n.a.	n.a.	n.a.
Side dish, mix (see also ''Noodle, Rice, etc.''):							
chicken, meatless:							
(Hain 3 Grain), 1/2 cup*	110	5.0	20.0	1.0	n.a.	525	n.a.
(Hain 3 Grain), 1/2 cup**	140	10.0	18.0	3.0	n.a.	455	n.a.
herb:							
(Hain 3 Grain), 1/2 cup*	90	4.0	17.0	1.0	n.a.	390	n.a.
(Hain 3 Grain), 1/2 cup**	120	8.0	15.0	2.0	n.a.	305	n.a.
Italian:							
(Hain 3 Grain), 1/2 cup*	140	6.0	23.0	2.0	n.a.	530	n.a.
(Hain 3 Grain), 1/2 cup**	130	12.0	11.0	4.0	n.a.	355	n.a.
Spanish:							
(Hain 3 Grain), 1/2 cup*	90	4.0	14.0	2.0	n.a.	415	n.a.
(Hain 3 Grain), 1/2 cup**	140	12.0	14.0	4.0	n.a.	370	n.a.
Skate (Raja fish):							
raw, meat only, 4 oz.	111	24.4	0	.8	n.a.	n.a.	0

* *Prepared according to package directions, without meat*
** *Prepared according to package directions, with meat*

Food and Measure	cal.	prot. (gms)	carbo. (gms)	fat (gms)	chol. (mgs)	sod. (mgs)	fiber (gms)
Sloppy Joe:							
canned *(Nalley)*, 3¹/₂ oz.	164	7.0	11.0	10.0	15	525	n.a.
Sloppy Joe season- ing, mix:							
(Durkee), 1.5-oz. pkg.	118	1.0	29.0	.2	n.a.	3512	n.a.
(French's), ¹/₈ pkg.	16	0	4.0	0	n.a.	390	n.a.
(Hunt's Manwich), .3-oz. pkg.	25	<1.0	5.0	<1.0	n.a.	360	n.a.
(Hunt's Manwich), 4.5 oz.*	200	14.0	10.0	11.0	n.a.	400	n.a.
Italian, *(Durkee)*, 1-oz. pkg.	99	.9	12.0	5.0	n.a.	936	n.a.
Smelt:							
fresh, rainbow:							
raw, meat only, 4 oz.	110	20.0	0	2.7	79	68	0
broiled, meat only, 4 oz.	141	25.6	0	3.5	102	87	0
canned, with liquid, 8 oz.	454	41.7	0	30.6	n.a.	n.a.	n.a.
Smelt, eulachon, see "Eulachon"							
Snails, fresh:							
raw, meat only, 4 oz.	102	18.3	2.3	1.6	n.a.	n.a.	n.a.
giant African, raw, meat only, 4 oz.	83	11.2	5.0	1.6	n.a.	n.a.	n.a.
Snapper, see "Red and gray snap- per"							
Snow peas, see "Peas, snow"							
Soft drinks and mix- ers (see also specific listings), 12 fl. oz., except as noted:							
apple, sparkling *(Welch's)*	180	0	46.0	0	0	55	0

* Prepared according to package directions

Food and Measure	cal.	prot. (gms)	carbo. (gms)	fat (gms)	chol. (mgs)	sod. (mgs)	fiber (gms)
Soft drinks and mixers (cont.)							
bitter lemon:							
(Canada Dry) . . .	150	0	40.0	0	0	26	0
(Schweppes) . . .	156	0	39.0	0	0	13	0
birch beer (Canada Dry)	166	0	42.0	0	0	28	0
blended flavors:							
(Canada Dry Purple Passion)	180	0	46.0	0	0	28	0
(Canada Dry Tahitian Treat) . . .	200	0	52.0	0	0	32	0
(Bubble Up)	145	0	37.0	0	0	32	0
(Bubble Up Diet) . .	2	.2	.4	0	0	32	0
(Bubble Up Sugar Free)	2	0	.4	0	0	95	0
(Canada Dry Cactus Cooler)	180	0	44.0	0	0	32	0
(Canada Dry Hi-Spot)	150	0	38.0	0	0	38	0
(Canada Dry Rooti)	166	0	40.0	0	0	26	0
cherry:							
(Crush)	180	<1.0	50.0	<1.0	0	n.a.	0
black (Shasta) . .	162	0	44.0	0	0	29	0
wild (Canada Dry)	195	0	48.0	0	0	32	0
citrus mist (Shasta)	170	0	46.0	0	0	18	0
club soda:							
(Canada Dry) . . .	0	0	0	0	0	75	0
(Schweppes) . . .	0	0	0	0	0	51	0
(Shasta)	0	0	0	0	0	46	0
chocolate (Yoo-Hoo), 9 fl. oz.	95	<1.0	24.0	<1.0	0	17	0
cola:							
(Canada Dry Diet)	0	0	0	0	0	90	0
(Canada Dry Jamaica)	166	0	40.0	0	0	n.a.	0
(Coca Cola/Coca-Cola Free) . . .	155	0	40.0	0	0	6	0
(Coca-Cola Classic)	144	0	38.0	0	0	14	0
(Coca-Cola Diet)	1	0	.3	0	0	8	0
(Diet Rite Salt Free)	2	0	.4	0	0	<1	0

Food and Measure	cal.	prot. (gms)	carbo. (gms)	fat (gms)	chol. (mgs)	sod. (mgs)	fiber (gms)
(Like)	162	0	40.8	0	0	1	0
(Like Sugar Free)	<1	.2	0	0	0	22	0
(Pepsi-Cola/Pepsi Free)	160	0	39.6	0	0	2	0
(Pepsi Diet)	<1	0	.2	0	0	2	0
(Pepsi Light/Pepsi Free Diet) . . .	1	0	.1	0	0	2	0
(RC Diet/Diet Caffiene Free) . . .	1	0	.4	0	0	<1	0
(RC 100)	171	0	42.8	0	0	<1	0
(RC 100 Diet) . . .	2	0	.4	0	0	<1	0
(Royal Crown/Royal Crown Cherry)	171	0	42.8	0	0	<1	0
(Shasta)	147	0	40.0	0	0	3	0
(Shasta Free) . . .	151	0	41.0	0	0	2	0
(Tab/Tab Free) . .	1	0	.3	0	0	30	0
cherry *(Coca-Cola)*	154	0	40.0	0	0	14	0
cherry *(RC Diet)*	2	0	.4	0	0	<1	0
cherry *(Shasta)* . .	140	0	38.0	0	0	22	0
collins mixer:							
(Canada Dry) . . .	120	0	30.0	0	0	26	0
(Schweppes) . . .	139	0	34.8	0	0	30	0
cream soda:							
(Crush)	160	<1.0	42.0	<1.0	0	n.a.	0
(Shasta)	154	0	42.0	0	0	21	0
(Dr. Diablo)	140	0	38.0	0	0	10	0
(Dr. Nehi)	163	0	40.8	0	0	26	0
(Dr Pepper/Dr Pepper Free)	144	0	37.2	0	0	18	0
(Dr Pepper Diet/Sugar Free)	2	0	.8	0	0	24	0
(Fresca)	4	0	.3	0	0	tr.	0
fruit punch:							
(Nehi)	200	0	49.9	0	0	16	0
(Shasta)	173	0	47.0	0	0	32	0
ginger ale:							
(Canada Dry) . . .	140	0	32.0	0	0	n.a.	0
(Canada Dry Diet)	3	0	0	0	0	90	0
(Canada Dry Golden)	150	0	36.0	0	0	36	0

Food and Measure	cal.	prot. (gms)	carbo. (gms)	fat (gms)	chol. (mgs)	sod. (mgs)	fiber (gms)
Soft drinks and mixers, ginger ale *(cont.)*							
(Fanta)	126	0	32.0	0	0	28	0
(Nehi)	152	0	37.9	0	0	<1	0
(Schweppes) . . .	126	0	31.6	0	0	21	0
(Schweppes Diet)	<4	0	0	0	0	81	0
(Shasta)	120	0	33.0	0	0	22	0
ginger beer (Schweppes)	136	0	34.0	0	0	61	0
grape:							
(Canada Dry Concord)	195	0	48.0	0	0	32	0
(Crush)	180	<1.0	50.0	<1.0	0	n.a.	0
(Fanta)	172	0	44.0	0	0	14	0
(Hi-C)	144	0	40.0	0	0	12	0
(Nehi canned) . .	192	0	47.9	0	0	14	0
(Nehi bottled) . . .	192	0	47.9	0	0	16	0
(Nehi Diet)	3	0	.8	0	0	0	0
(Schweppes) . . .	185	0	46.2	0	0	28	0
(Shasta)	177	0	48.0	0	0	27	0
sparkling (Welch's)	180	0	47.0	0	0	75	0
grapefruit:							
(Schweppes) . . .	153	0	38.4	0	0	56	0
(Wink)	180	0	44.0	0	0	28	0
half and half (Canada Dry)	166	0	40.0	0	0	26	0
(Kick)	195	0	48.7	0	0	49	0
lemon (Hi-C)	146	0	36.0	0	0	12	0
lemon lime:							
(Nehi Diet)	5	0	1.1	0	0	0	0
(Schweppes) . . .	143	0	35.6	0	0	61	0
(Shasta)	146	0	39.0	0	0	18	0
lemon sour (Schweppes)	149	0	37.2	0	0	26	0
lime (Canada Dry Island)	195	0	50.0	0	0	28	0
(Mello Yellow)	172	0	44.0	0	0	28	0
(Mountain Dew) . . .	179	0	44.4	0	0	31	0
(Mr. Pibb)	142	0	38.0	0	0	22	0
(Mr. Pibb Sugar Free)	1	0	.3	0	0	38	0

Food and Measure	cal.	prot. (gms)	carbo. (gms)	fat (gms)	chol. (mgs)	sod. (mgs)	fiber (gms)
orange:							
(Canada Dry Diet)	3	0	0	0	0	90	0
(Canada Dry Sun-							
ripe)	195	0	50.0	0	0	32	0
(Crush)	180	<1.0	50.0	<1.0	0	40	0
(Crush Sugar Free)	4	<1.0	<1.0	<1.0	0	60	0
(Fanta)	176	0	46.0	0	0	14	0
(Hi-C)	144	0	40.0	0	0	14	0
(Nehi Diet)	2	0	.6	0	0	0	0
(Schweppes) ...	172	0	43.0	0	0	31	0
(Shasta)	177	0	48.0	0	0	28	0
peach (Nehi)	203	0	50.8	0	0	33	0
pineapple:							
(Canada Dry) ...	166	0	40.0	0	0	32	0
(Crush)	180	<1.0	50.0	<1.0	0	n.a.	0
punch (Hi-C)	144	0	40.0	0	0	12	0
quinine (Nehi)	142	0	35.5	0	0	0	0
red pop (Shasta) ..	158	0	43.0	0	0	20	0
root beer:							
(Aunt Wicks) ...	4	0	<1.0	0	0	n.a.	0
(Canada Dry Bar-							
relhead)	166	0	40.0	0	0	26	0
(Canada Dry Bar-							
relhead Diet) ..	3	0	0	0	0	90	0
(Dad's)	166	0	41.4	0	0	28	0
(Dad's Diet) ...	2	0	.4	0	0	28	0
(Dad's Sugar Free)	1	0	.4	0	0	82	0
(Fanta)	156	0	40.0	0	0	20	0
(Hires)	160	<1.0	38.0	<1.0	0	50	0
(Hires Sugar Free)	4	<1.0	<1.0	<1.0	0	100	0
(Mug)	168	<1.0	42.0	<1.0	0	40	0
(Mug Diet)	4	<1.0	<1.0	<1.0	0	40	0
(Nehi)	192	0	48.0	0	0	18	0
(Ramblin')	176	0	46.0	0	0	20	0
(Ramblin' Sugar							
Free)	1	0	.4	0	0	58	0
(Schweppes) ...	150	0	37.4	0	0	29	0
(Shasta)	154	0	42.0	0	0	36	0
(Welch's)	170	0	45.0	0	0	65	0

Food and Measure	cal.	prot. (gms)	carbo. (gms)	fat (gms)	chol. (mgs)	sod. (mgs)	fiber (gms)
Soft drinks and mixers (cont.)							
seltzer, plain and flavored:							
(Canada Dry) . . .	0	0	0	0	0	<5	0
(Schweppes) . . .	0	0	0	0	0	<10	0
(7-Up)	144	0	36.3	0	0	25	0
(7-Up Diet)	4	.1	0	0	0	32	0
(Slice)	152	0	39.6	0	0	11	0
(Slice Diet)	26	0	6.0	0	0	11	0
(Sprite)	142	0	36.0	0	0	46	0
(Sprite Diet)	4	0	0	0	0	tr.	0
strawberry:							
(Canada Dry California)	180	0	46.0	0	0	32	0
(Crush)	180	<1.0	44.0	<1.0	0	n.a.	0
(Nehi canned) . .	192	0	47.9	0	0	14	0
(Nehi bottled) . . .	192	0	47.9	0	0	0	0
(Nehi Diet)	3	0	.7	0	0	0	0
(Shasta)	147	0	40.0	0	0	36	0
sparkling (Welch's)	180	0	46.0	0	0	50	0
sour mixer:							
(Canada Dry) . . .	135	0	34.0	0	0	26	0
(Schweppes) . . .	149	0	37.2	0	0	26	0
(Sun-Drop)	180	<1.0	46.0	<1.0	0	n.a.	0
(Sun-Drop Sugar Free)	8	<1.0	<1.0	<1.0	0	17	0
tonic:							
(Canada Dry) . . .	135	0	34.0	0	0	10	0
(Canada Dry Diet)	4	0	0	0	0	90	0
(Schweppes) . . .	128	0	32.0	0	0	13	0
(Schweppes Sugar Free)	<4	0	0	0	0	62	0
(Shasta)	121	0	33.0	0	0	14	0
(Upper 10)	169	0	42.2	0	0	40	0
(Upper 10 Diet/Diet Salt Free)	6	0	1.1	0	0	0	0
(Upper 10 Salt Free)	173	0	43.2	0	0	0	0
vanilla cream (Canada Dry)	195	0	48.0	0	0	28	0
vichy water (Schweppes)	0	0	0	0	0	155	0

Food and Measure	cal.	prot. (gms)	carbo. (gms)	fat (gms)	chol. (mgs)	sod. (mgs)	fiber (gms)
vodka mixer *(Schweppes)*	139	0	34.8	0	0	30	0
Sole:							
fresh, raw, fillets, 4 oz.	103	21.4	0	1.3	54	92	0
frozen:							
(Gorton's Fishmarket Fresh), 4 oz. . .	90	19.0	1.0	1.0	n.a.	110	0
raw, portions *(Taste O' Sea* Calorie Watchers), 1 portion	70	15.0	0	1.0	n.a.	150	0
baby *(Van de Kamp's* Today's Catch), 4 oz. . .	80	15.0	0	0	n.a.	220	n.a.
in batter *(Van de Kamp's),* 4 oz.	280	15.0	25.0	15.0	n.a.	578	n.a.
breaded *(Van de Kamp's),* 5 oz.	300	15.0	15.0	15.0	n.a.	412	n.a.
fillets *(Booth* Light & Tender), 4 oz.	90	19.0	0	1.0	n.a.	88	n.a.
fillets (Taste O' Sea), 4 oz. . . .	90	19.0	0	1.0	n.a.	250	n.a.
fillets, breaded *(Certi-Fresh* Light & Crunchy), 5 oz.	290	18.0	25.0	17.0	n.a.	n.a.	n.a.
fillets, breaded *(Mrs. Paul's),* 1 fillet	280	21.0	19.0	13.0	n.a.	700	n.a.
fillets, with lemon butter sauce *(Gorton's* Light Recipe), 1 pkg.	250	24.0	8.0	13.0	n.a.	730	n.a.
New England style *(Booth* Light & Tender), 3 oz.	160	10.0	18.0	6.0	n.a.	430	n.a.
Sole dinner, frozen:							
(Taste O' Sea), 8 oz.	530	21.0	54.0	25.0	n.a.	880	n.a.
in wine sauce *(Taste O' Sea* Gourmet), 12 oz.	290	22.0	24.0	12.0	n.a.	1920	n.a.

Food and Measure	cal.	prot. (gms)	carbo. (gms)	fat (gms)	chol. (mgs)	sod. (mgs)	fiber (gms)
Sole entree, frozen:							
in butter sauce *(Certi-Fresh)*, 9 oz. . . .	290	29.0	12.0	15.0	n.a.	n.a.	n.a.
crab stuffing in lemon sauce *(Wakefield)*, 8 oz.	220	25.0	19.0	5.0	n.a.	1020	n.a.
Florentine, mornay sauce *(Wakefield)*, 8 oz.	270	28.0	11.0	13.0	n.a.	980	n.a.
Sorghum grain:							
4 oz.	376	12.5	82.8	3.7	0	n.a.	1.9
Soup, canned, ready-to-serve:							
bean *(Grandma Brown's)*, 8 oz. . .	182	8.8	29.1	3.4	n.a.	n.a.	n.a.
bean and ham:							
(Campbell's Chunky), 95/8 oz.	260	12.0	33.0	8.0	n.a.	1010	n.a.
(Campbell's Chunky), 11 oz.	290	14.0	37.0	9.0	n.a.	1150	n.a.
(Progresso), 91/2 oz.	170	11.0	30.0	1.0	n.a.	1170	n.a.
beef:							
(Campbell's Chunky), 91/2 oz.	170	13.0	20.0	4.0	n.a.	970	n.a.
(Campbell's Chunky), 103/4 oz.	190	14.0	23.0	5.0	n.a.	1110	n.a.
(Progresso), 91/2 oz.	150	9.0	19.0	4.0	n.a.	1390	n.a.
and mushrooms *(Campbell's* Chunky Low Sodium)*, 103/4 oz.	210	13.0	23.0	7.0	n.a.	65	n.a.
broth *(Swanson)*, 71/4 oz.	20	2.0	1.0	1.0	n.a.	750	n.a.
minestrone *(Progresso)*, 91/2 oz.	150	11.0	19.0	4.0	n.a.	1040	n.a.
noodle *(Campbell's* Homestyle), 4 oz.	80	6.0	8.0	3.0	n.a.	810	n.a.

Food and Measure	cal.	prot. (gms)	carbo. (gms)	fat (gms)	chol. (mgs)	sod. (mgs)	fiber (gms)
noodle, hearty *(Campbell's Home Cookin)*, 10³/4 oz.	150	17.0	11.0	4.0	n.a.	1130	n.a.
Stroganoff style *(Campbell's Chunky)*, 10³/4 oz.	300	15.0	28.0	15.0	n.a.	1290	n.a.
vegetable *(Progresso)*, 9¹/2 oz.	150	12.0	19.0	2.0	n.a.	1140	n.a.
vegetable *(Progresso)*, 10¹/2 oz.	160	13.0	21.0	3.0	n.a.	1310	n.a.
borscht:							
(Mother's Unsalted), 8 fl. oz.	103	.8	23.0	.2	n.a.	20	n.a.
(Mother's Old Fashioned), 8 fl. oz.	96	.6	26.5	.2	n.a.	n.a.	n.a.
with beets *(Manischewitz)*, 8 fl. oz.	80	1.0	20.0	0	0	660	n.a.
low-calorie *(Manischewitz)*, 8 fl. oz.	20	1.0	4.0	0	0	725	n.a.
low calorie *(Mother's)*, 8 fl. oz. . .	25	1.0	6.0	0	n.a.	n.a.	n.a.
chickarina, with tiny meatballs *(Progresso)*, 9¹/2 oz.	90	8.0	8.0	6.0	n.a.	1060	n.a.
chicken:							
(Campbell's Chunky), 9¹/2 oz.	150	10.0	18.0	4.0	n.a.	1180	n.a.
(Campbell's Chunky), 10³/4 oz.	170	12.0	21.0	5.0	n.a.	1340	n.a.
(Progresso Home Style)*, 9¹/2 oz.	90	9.0	8.0	2.0	n.a.	1190	n.a.
(Progresso Home Style), 10¹/2 oz.	100	10.0	9.0	2.0	n.a.	1320	n.a.
broth *(Campbell's* Low Sodium), 10¹/2 oz.	40	3.0	2.0	2.0	n.a.	70	n.a.

Food and Measure	cal.	prot. (gms)	carbo. (gms)	fat (gms)	chol. (mgs)	sod. (mgs)	fiber (gms)
Soup, canned, ready-to-serve, chicken *(cont.)*							
broth *(Hain Naturals)*, 8³/4 fl. oz.	60	2.0	5.0	3.0	n.a.	870	n.a.
broth *(Swanson)*, 7¹/4 oz.	30	2.0	2.0	2.0	n.a.	910	n.a.
minestrone *(Progresso)*, 9¹/2 oz.	150	10.0	15.0	6.0	n.a.	1210	n.a.
noodle *(Campbell's Home Cookin)*, 10³/4 oz.	140	14.0	11.0	4.0	n.a.	1160	n.a.
noodle *(Campbell's Homestyle)*, 4 oz.	70	3.0	8.0	3.0	n.a.	920	n.a.
noodle *(Hain Naturals)*, 9¹/2 oz.	120	8.0	14.0	3.0	n.a.	1190	n.a.
noodle *(Hain Naturals No Salt Added)*, 9¹/2 oz.	130	8.0	14.0	5.0	n.a.	380	n.a.
noodle *(Progresso)*, 9¹/2 oz.	120	12.0	10.0	4.0	n.a.	980	n.a.
noodle *(Progresso)*, 10¹/2 oz.	130	13.0	11.0	4.0	n.a.	1110	n.a.
noodle, with mushrooms *(Campbell's Chunky)*, 9¹/2 oz.	180	12.0	18.0	6.0	n.a.	1050	n.a.
noodle, with mushrooms *(Campbell's Chunky)*, 10³/4 oz.	200	14.0	20.0	7.0	n.a.	1150	n.a.
with noodles *(Campbell's Low Sodium)*, 10³/4 oz.	160	14.0	15.0	5.0	n.a.	85	n.a.
rice *(Campbell's Chunky)*, 9¹/2 oz.	140	10.0	15.0	4.0	n.a.	1080	n.a.
rice, with vegetables *(Progresso)*, 9¹/2 oz.	140	8.0	22.0	3.0	n.a.	880	n.a.

Food and Measure	cal.	prot. (gms)	carbo. (gms)	fat (gms)	chol. (mgs)	sod. (mgs)	fiber (gms)
vegetable (Campbell's Chunky Low Sodium), 10³/4 oz.	240	15.0	20.0	11.0	n.a.	95	n.a.
vegetable (Hain Naturals), 9¹/2 oz.	130	9.0	15.0	3.0	n.a.	n.a.	n.a.
vegetable (Hain Naturals No Salt Added), 9¹/2 oz.	130	9.0	15.0	3.0	n.a.	100	n.a.
vegetable, with rice (Campbell's Home Cookin), 10³/4 oz.	140	13.0	14.0	3.0	n.a.	1000	n.a.
chili beef:							
(Campbell's Chunky), 9³/4 oz.	260	19.0	33.0	6.0	n.a.	1020	n.a.
(Campbell's Chunky), 11 oz.	290	21.0	37.0	7.0	n.a.	1150	n.a.
clam chowder, Manhattan:							
(Campbell's Chunky), 9¹/2 oz.	150	6.0	22.0	4.0	n.a.	1080	n.a.
(Campbell's Chunky), 10³/4 oz.	160	7.0	24.0	5.0	n.a.	1230	n.a.
(Progresso), 9¹/2 oz.	130	6.0	21.0	3.0	n.a.	1240	n.a.
clam chowder, New England:							
(Campbell's Chunky), 9¹/2 oz.	250	8.0	22.0	15.0	n.a.	1040	n.a.
(Campbell's Chunky), 10³/4 oz.	290	9.0	25.0	17.0	n.a.	1180	n.a.
(Hain Naturals), 9¹/2 oz.	180	10.0	23.0	5.0	n.a.	740	n.a.
(Hain Naturals No Salt Added), 9¹/2 oz.	170	10.0	25.0	3.0	n.a.	380	n.a.
escarole in chicken broth (Progresso), 9¹/2 oz.	35	2.0	3.0	3.0	n.a.	1020	n.a.

Food and Measure	cal.	prot. (gms)	carbo. (gms)	fat (gms)	chol. (mgs)	sod. (mgs)	fiber (gms)
Soup, canned, ready-to-serve *(cont.)*							
fisherman chowder:							
(Campbell's							
Chunky), 9¹/2 oz.	230	10.0	23.0	13.0	n.a.	1160	n.a.
(Campbell's							
Chunky), 10³/4 oz.	260	11.0	26.0	14.0	n.a.	1320	n.a.
Goetta *(Stegner's)*, 4							
oz.	221	13.0	15.0	10.0	n.a.	n.a.	n.a.
ham and butterbean							
(Campbell's							
Chunky), 10³/4 oz.	280	12.0	34.0	10.0	n.a.	1180	n.a.
lentil:							
(Hain Naturals), 9¹/2							
oz.	190	6.0	30.0	5.0	n.a.	970	n.a.
(Hain Naturals No							
Salt Added)*, 9¹/2							
oz.	190	6.0	30.0	5.0	n.a.	55	n.a.
(Progresso), 9¹/2 oz.	170	11.0	26.0	2.0	n.a.	1000	n.a.
(Progresso), 10¹/2							
oz.	180	12.0	28.0	2.0	n.a.	1110	n.a.
macaroni and beef							
(Progresso), 9¹/2 oz.	180	6.0	30.0	3.0	n.a.	1290	n.a.
minestrone:							
(Campbell's							
Chunky), 9¹/2 oz.	140	4.0	21.0	5.0	n.a.	940	n.a.
(Hain Naturals), 9¹/2							
oz.	190	5.0	33.0	4.0	n.a.	1050	n.a.
(Hain Naturals No							
Salt Added)*, 9¹/2							
oz.	190	6.0	33.0	5.0	n.a.	35	n.a.
(Progresso), 9¹/2 oz.	150	7.0	24.0	3.0	n.a.	820	n.a.
(Progresso), 10¹/2							
oz.	160	7.0	27.0	4.0	n.a.	900	n.a.
mushroom:							
(Hain Naturals), 9¹/2							
oz.	120	3.0	16.0	5.0	n.a.	490	n.a.
(Hain Naturals No							
Salt Added)*, 9¹/2							
oz.	120	5.0	17.0	3.0	n.a.	75	n.a.

Food and Measure	cal.	prot. (gms)	carbo. (gms)	fat (gms)	chol. (mgs)	sod. (mgs)	fiber (gms)
cream of							
(Campbell's Low							
Sodium), 10¹/2 oz.	200	3.0	17.0	14.0	n.a.	55	n.a.
onion, French:							
(Campbell's Low							
Sodium), 10¹/2 oz.	80	2.0	8.0	4.0	n.a.	50	n.a.
(Progresso), 9¹/2 oz.	120	4.0	9.0	9.0	n.a.	1270	n.a.
pea (Progresso), 9¹/2							
oz.	190	10.0	31.0	2.0	n.a.	1050	n.a.
pea, split:							
(Hain Naturals), 9¹/2							
oz.	210	9.0	37.0	2.0	n.a.	n.a.	n.a.
(Grandma Brown's),							
8 oz.	184	10.8	28.2	3.0	n.a.	n.a.	n.a.
pea, split, with ham:							
(Campbell's							
Chunky), 9¹/2 oz.	200	11.0	29.0	5.0	n.a.	950	n.a.
(Campbell's							
Chunky), 10³/4 oz.	230	12.0	33.0	6.0	n.a.	1070	n.a.
(Campbell's Low							
Sodium), 10³/4 oz.	240	11.0	38.0	5.0	n.a.	25	n.a.
(Progresso), 9¹/2 oz.	170	10.0	26.0	3.0	n.a.	1030	n.a.
sirloin burger:							
(Campbell's							
Chunky), 9¹/2 oz.	200	11.0	20.0	8.0	n.a.	1130	n.a.
(Campbell's							
Chunky), 10³/4 oz.	220	12.0	23.0	9.0	n.a.	1280	n.a.
steak and potato:							
(Campbell's							
Chunky), 9¹/2 oz.	170	12.0	21.0	4.0	n.a.	1110	n.a.
(Campbell's							
Chunky), 10³/4 oz.	200	14.0	24.0	5.0	n.a.	1250	n.a.
tomato:							
(Campbell's Home-							
style), 4 oz. . .	100	1.0	19.0	3.0	n.a.	860	n.a.
(Hain Naturals), 9¹/2							
oz.	150	2.0	23.0	5.0	n.a.	n.a.	n.a.
(Hain Naturals No							
Salt Added), 9¹/2							
oz.	160	2.0	23.0	6.0	n.a.	80	n.a.

Food and Measure	cal.	prot. (gms)	carbo. (gms)	fat (gms)	chol. (mgs)	sod. (mgs)	fiber (gms)
Soup, canned, ready-to-serve, tomato *(cont.)*							
with macaroni shells *(Progresso)*, 10¹/2 oz.	130	4.0	24.0	2.0	n.a.	1270	n.a.
with tomato pieces *(Campbell's Low Sodium)*, 10¹/2 oz.	180	3.0	29.0	5.0	n.a.	40	n.a.
with vegetables and macaroni *(Progresso)*, 9¹/2 oz.	120	4.0	22.0	2.0	n.a.	1150	n.a.
tortellini *(Progresso)*, 9¹/2 oz.	80	3.0	13.0	2.0	n.a.	1080	n.a.
turkey rice: *(Hain Naturals)*, 9¹/2 oz.	90	7.0	10.0	2.0	n.a.	1020	n.a.
(Hain Naturals No Salt Added), 9¹/2 oz.	110	7.0	11.0	4.0	n.a.	75	n.a.
turkey vegetable *(Campbell's Chunky)*, 9³/8 oz.	150	9.0	16.0	6.0	n.a.	1080	n.a.
turtle, mock *(Stegner's)*, 7¹/2 oz.	168	8.4	17.0	8.0	n.a.	n.a.	n.a.
vegetable: *(Campbell's Chunky)*, 9¹/2 oz.	130	3.0	21.0	4.0	n.a.	970	n.a.
(Campbell's Chunky), 10³/4 oz.	140	4.0	23.0	4.0	n.a.	1100	n.a.
beef *(Campbell's Chunky)*, 9¹/2 oz.	160	11.0	18.0	4.0	n.a.	1070	n.a.
beef *(Campbell's Chunky)*, 10³/4 oz.	180	12.0	20.0	5.0	n.a.	1210	n.a.
beef *(Campbell's Chunky Low Sodium)*, 10³/4 oz.	170	13.0	19.0	5.0	n.a.	60	n.a.
beef, old fashioned *(Campbell's Home Cookin)*, 10³/4 oz.	150	14.0	15.0	3.0	n.a.	1130	n.a.

Food and Measure	cal.	prot. (gms)	carbo. (gms)	fat (gms)	chol. (mgs)	sod. (mgs)	fiber (gms)
country (Campbell's Home Cookin), 10³/4 oz.	120	4.0	21.0	2.0	n.a.	1150	n.a.
Italian (Hain Naturals Vege-Pasta), 9¹/2 oz.	180	4.0	29.0	5.0	n.a.	1110	n.a.
Italian (Hain Naturals Vege-Pasta No Salt Added), 9¹/2 oz.	170	4.0	28.0	5.0	n.a.	60	n.a.
Mediterranean (Campbell's Chunky), 9¹/2 oz.	160	4.0	24.0	5.0	n.a.	1020	n.a.
vegetarian (Hain Naturals), 9¹/2 oz.	180	4.0	25.0	6.0	n.a.	n.a.	n.a.
vegetarian (Hain Naturals No Salt Added), 9¹/2 oz.	160	3.0	25.0	5.0	n.a.	45	n.a.
Soup, canned, con-densed*:							
asparagus, cream of (Campbell's), 8 oz.	90	2.0	11.0	4.0	n.a.	900	n.a.
bean, with bacon (Campbell's), 8 oz.	150	6.0	21.0	5.0	n.a.	860	n.a.
bean, black (Campbell's), 8 oz.	110	5.0	17.0	2.0	n.a.	980	n.a.
beef: (Campbell's), 8 oz.	80	6.0	10.0	2.0	n.a.	850	n.a.
broth/bouillon (Campbell's), 8 oz.	16	3.0	1.0	0	n.a.	860	n.a.
consomme (Campbell's), 8 oz.	25	4.0	2.0	0	n.a.	780	n.a.
noodle (Campbell's), 8 oz.	70	4.0	7.0	3.0	n.a.	770	n.a.
noodle (Campbell's Homestyle), 8 oz.	80	6.0	8.0	3.0	n.a.	810	n.a.

* Prepared with equal amounts soup and water, except as noted

Food and Measure	cal.	prot. (gms)	carbo. (gms)	fat (gms)	chol. (mgs)	sod. (mgs)	fiber (gms)
Soup, canned, condensed* *(cont.)*							
beefy mushroom							
(Campbell's), 8 oz.	60	4.0	5.0	3.0	n.a.	960	n.a.
celery:							
cream of							
(Campbell's), 8							
oz.	100	1.0	8.0	7.0	n.a.	860	n.a.
cream of *(Rokeach)*,							
10 oz.	90	2.0	12.0	4.0	n.a.	n.a.	n.a.
cream of *(Rokeach)*,							
10 oz.**	190	7.0	19.0	9.0	n.a.	n.a.	n.a.
cheddar cheese							
(Campbell's), 8 oz.	130	3.0	10.0	8.0	n.a.	800	n.a.
chicken:							
alphabet							
(Campbell's), 8							
oz.	80	3.0	10.0	3.0	n.a.	870	n.a.
and dumplings							
(Campbell's), 8							
oz.	80	4.0	9.0	3.0	n.a.	980	n.a.
broth *(Campbell's)*,							
8 oz.	35	1.0	3.0	2.0	n.a.	790	n.a.
broth and noodles							
(Campbell's), 8							
oz.	60	2.0	8.0	2.0	n.a.	870	n.a.
broth and rice							
(Campbell's), 8							
oz.	50	1.0	8.0	1.0	n.a.	880	n.a.
cream of							
(Campbell's), 8							
oz.	110	3.0	9.0	7.0	n.a.	850	n.a.
gumbo *(Campbell's)*,							
8 oz.	60	2.0	8.0	2.0	n.a.	910	n.a.
mushroom, creamy							
(Campbell's), 8							
oz.	120	3.0	9.0	8.0	n.a.	940	n.a.

* *Prepared with equal amounts soup and water, except as noted*
** *Prepared with equal amounts soup and whole milk*

Food and Measure	cal.	prot. (gms)	carbo. (gms)	fat (gms)	chol. (mgs)	sod. (mgs)	fiber (gms)
noodle (Campbell's), 8 oz.	70	3.0	8.0	2.0	n.a.	810	n.a.
noodle (Campbell's Homestyle), 8 oz.	70	3.0	8.0	3.0	n.a.	920	n.a.
noodle (Campbell's NoodleOs), 8 oz.	70	3.0	9.0	2.0	n.a.	840	n.a.
with rice (Campbell's), 8 oz.	60	2.0	7.0	2.0	n.a.	840	n.a.
and stars (Campbell's), 8 oz.	60	3.0	7.0	2.0	n.a.	920	n.a.
vegetable (Campbell's), 8 oz.	70	3.0	8.0	3.0	n.a.	870	n.a.
chili beef (Campbell's), 8 oz.	130	5.0	17.0	5.0	n.a.	900	n.a.
clam chowder:							
Manhattan (Campbell's), 8 oz.	70	2.0	11.0	2.0	n.a.	860	n.a.
Manhattan (Snow's), 7½ oz.	70	3.0	9.0	2.0	n.a.	635	n.a.
New England (Campbell's), 8 oz.	80	3.0	11.0	3.0	n.a.	880	n.a.
New England (Campbell's), 8 oz.**	150	7.0	17.0	7.0	n.a.	930	n.a.
New England (Snow's), 7½ oz.**	140	8.0	13.0	6.0	n.a.	665	n.a.
corn chowder (Snow's), 7½ oz.**	150	5.0	18.0	6.0	n.a.	640	n.a.
fish chowder (Snow's), 7½ oz.**	130	9.0	11.0	6.0	n.a.	620	n.a.

** Prepared with equal amounts soup and whole milk

Food and Measure	cal.	prot. (gms)	carbo. (gms)	fat (gms)	chol. (mgs)	sod. (mgs)	fiber (gms)
Soup, canned, condensed* *(cont.)*							
gazpacho							
(Campbell's), 8 oz.	40	0	10.0	0	0	590	n.a.
meatball alphabet							
(Campbell's), 8 oz.	100	5.0	11.0	4.0	n.a.	970	n.a.
minestrone							
(Campbell's), 8 oz.	80	4.0	12.0	2.0	n.a.	930	n.a.
mushroom:							
cream of							
(Campbell's), 8							
oz.	100	1.0	9.0	7.0	n.a.	820	n.a.
cream of *(Rokeach)*,							
10 oz.	150	2.0	13.0	10.0	n.a.	n.a.	n.a.
cream of *(Rokeach)*,							
10 oz.**	240	7.0	20.0	15.0	n.a.	n.a.	n.a.
golden *(Campbell's)*,							
8 oz.	80	2.0	10.0	3.0	n.a.	900	n.a.
noodle, curly, with							
chicken							
(Campbell's), 8 oz.	70	3.0	9.0	3.0	n.a.	960	n.a.
noodles and ground							
beef *(Campbell's)*, 8							
oz.	90	4.0	10.0	4.0	n.a.	840	n.a.
onion:							
cream of							
(Campbell's), 8							
oz.	100	2.0	17.0	5.0	n.a.	830	n.a.
cream of							
(Campbell's), 8							
oz.***	140	4.0	15.0	7.0	n.a.	860	n.a.
French							
(Campbell's), 8							
oz.	60	2.0	9.0	2.0	n.a.	950	n.a.
oyster stew:							
(Campbell's), 8 oz.	80	3.0	5.0	5.0	n.a.	850	n.a.

* *Prepared with equal amounts soup and water, except as noted*
** *Prepared with equal amounts soup and whole milk*
*** *Prepared with 4 oz. soup, 2 oz. water and 2 oz. whole milk*

Food and Measure	cal.	prot. (gms)	carbo. (gms)	fat (gms)	chol. (mgs)	sod. (mgs)	fiber (gms)
(Campbell's), 8 oz.**	150	6.0	10.0	9.0	n.a.	900	n.a.
pea, green							
(Campbell's), 8 oz.	160	8.0	25.0	3.0	n.a.	840	n.a.
pea, split, with ham and bacon							
(Campbell's), 8 oz.	160	8.0	24.0	4.0	n.a.	800	n.a.
pepper pot							
(Campbell's), 8 oz.	90	5.0	9.0	4.0	n.a.	960	n.a.
potato, cream of:							
(Campbell's), 8 oz.	70	1.0	11.0	3.0	n.a.	930	n.a.
(Campbell's), 8 oz.***	110	3.0	14.0	4.0	n.a.	960	n.a.
Scotch broth							
(Campbell's), 8 oz.	80	4.0	9.0	3.0	n.a.	890	n.a.
seafood chowder							
(Snow's), 7½ oz.**	130	8.0	11.0	6.0	n.a.	690	n.a.
shrimp, cream of:							
(Campbell's), 8 oz.	90	2.0	8.0	6.0	n.a.	790	n.a.
(Campbell's), 8 oz.**	160	5.0	13.0	10.0	n.a.	850	n.a.
tomato:							
(Campbell's), 8 oz.	90	1.0	17.0	2.0	n.a.	720	n.a.
(Campbell's), 8 oz.**	160	5.0	22.0	6.0	n.a.	770	n.a.
(Rokeach), 10 oz.	90	2.0	20.0	1.0	n.a.	n.a.	n.a.
(Rokeach), 10 oz.**	190	7.0	27.0	6.0	n.a.	n.a.	n.a.
bisque *(Campbell's)*, 8 oz.	120	1.0	23.0	3.0	n.a.	830	n.a.
cream of *(Campbell's Homestyle)*, 8 oz.	110	1.0	20.0	3.0	n.a.	830	n.a.
cream of *(Campbell's Homestyle)*, 8 oz.**	180	5.0	25.0	7.0	n.a.	780	n.a.

** *Prepared with equal amounts soup and whole milk*
*** *Prepared with 4 oz. soup, 2 oz. water and 2 oz. whole milk*

Food and Measure	cal.	prot. (gms)	carbo. (gms)	fat (gms)	chol. (mgs)	sod. (mgs)	fiber (gms)
Soup, canned, condensed*, tomato *(cont.)*							
rice *(Campbell's)*, 8 oz.	110	1.0	22.0	2.0	n.a.	760	n.a.
rice *(Rokeach)*, 10 oz.	160	3.0	25.0	5.0	n.a.	n.a.	n.a.
turkey noodle *(Campbell's)*, 8 oz.	60	3.0	8.0	2.0	n.a.	910	n.a.
turkey vegetable *(Campbell's)*, 8 oz.	70	2.0	8.0	3.0	n.a.	820	n.a.
vegetable: *(Campbell's)*, 8 oz.	80	3.0	13.0	2.0	n.a.	770	n.a.
(Campbell's Home- style), 8 oz. . .	60	2.0	10.0	2.0	n.a.	880	n.a.
(Campbell's Old Fashioned), 8 oz.	60	2.0	9.0	2.0	n.a.	910	n.a.
beef *(Campbell's)*, 8 oz.	70	4.0	8.0	2.0	n.a.	820	n.a.
beef *(Feather- weight)*, 1 cup	80	4.0	12.0	3.0	n.a.	20	n.a.
vegetarian *(Campbell's)*, 8 oz.	80	2.0	13.0	2.0	0	770	n.a.
vegetarian *(Rokeach)*, 10 oz.	90	2.0	15.0	3.0	0	n.a.	n.a.
won ton *(Campbell's)*, 8 oz.	40	3.0	5.0	1.0	n.a.	870	n.a.
Soup, canned, semi- condensed*, 11 oz.:							
bean with ham *(Campbell's Old Fashioned Soup for One)*	220	8.0	30.0	7.0	n.a.	1400	n.a.
clam chowder, New England: *(Campbell's Soup for One)*	130	6.0	19.0	4.0	n.a.	1360	n.a.

* *Prepared according to package directions*

Food and Measure	cal.	prot. (gms)	carbo. (gms)	fat (gms)	chol. (mgs)	sod. (mgs)	fiber (gms)
with milk (Campbell's Soup for One)	190	9.0	23.0	7.0	n.a.	1410	n.a.
chicken:							
golden, and noodles (Campbell's Soup for One)	120	6.0	14.0	4.0	n.a.	1450	n.a.
vegetable, full flavored (Campbell's Soup for One)	120	4.0	13.0	6.0	n.a.	1500	n.a.
mushroom, cream of (Campbell's Soup for One)	180	3.0	14.0	13.0	n.a.	1500	n.a.
tomato royale (Campbell's Soup for One)	180	3.0	35.0	3.0	n.a.	1080	n.a.
vegetable:							
(Campbell's Old World Soup for One)	130	4.0	18.0	4.0	n.a.	1470	n.a.
beef and bacon (Campbell's Burly Soup for One)	160	8.0	20.0	5.0	n.a.	1480	n.a.
Soup, frozen, ready-to-serve:							
bean, northern (Tabatchnick), 8 oz.	80	8.0	29.0	2.0	n.a.	522	n.a.
bean and barley (Tabatchnick), 8 oz.	63	6.0	22.0	2.0	n.a.	492	n.a.
bean and ham (Myers/Supper Bell), 3½ oz.	82	6.0	14.0	1.0	n.a.	486	n.a.
broccoli, cream of (Myers/Supper Bell), 3½ oz. . . .	62	3.0	4.0	4.0	n.a.	327	n.a.
cabbage (Tabatchnick), 8 oz.	53	2.0	21.0	2.0	n.a.	660	n.a.

Food and Measure	cal.	prot. (gms)	carbo. (gms)	fat (gms)	chol. (mgs)	sod. (mgs)	fiber (gms)
Soup, frozen, ready-to-serve *(cont.)*							
chicken corn *(Myers/ Supper Bell)*, 3¹/2 oz.	47	4.0	5.0	1.0	n.a.	352	n.a.
chicken, with kreplach *(Tabatchnick)*, 8 oz.	78	4.0	11.0	2.0	n.a.	692	n.a.
chicken noodle:							
(Myers/Supper Bell), 3¹/2 oz.	31	3.0	2.0	1.0	n.a.	378	n.a.
(Tabatchnick), 8 oz.	58	3.0	7.0	2.0	n.a.	729	n.a.
chowder, Manhattan *(Tabatchnick)*, 8 oz.	94	4.0	15.0	1.5	n.a.	277	n.a.
chowder, New En- gland *(Tabatchnick)*, 8 oz.	97	4.0	16.0	1.0	n.a.	222	n.a.
clam chowder *(Myers/ Supper Bell)*, 3¹/2 oz.	56	3.0	8.0	2.0	n.a.	329	n.a.
clam chowder, New England *(Stouffer's)*, 8 oz.	200	8.0	16.0	11.0	n.a.	790	n.a.
lentil *(Tabatchnick)*, 8 oz.	173	11.0	27.0	2.0	n.a.	636	n.a.
minestrone *(Tabatchnick)*, 8 oz.	147	8.0	24.0	2.0	n.a.	622	n.a.
mushroom barley:							
(Tabatchnick), 8 oz.	92	2.0	16.0	2.0	n.a.	758	n.a.
(Tabatchnick Salt Free), 8 oz. . .	92	2.0	16.0	2.0	n.a.	180	n.a.
mushroom, cream of *(Myers/Supper Bell)*, 3¹/2 oz. . . .	64	1.0	6.0	4.0	n.a.	377	n.a.
pea:							
(Tabatchnick), 8 oz.	186	11.0	31.0	2.0	n.a.	642	n.a.
(Tabatchnick Salt Free), 8 oz. . .	188	n.a.	31.0	2.0	n.a.	177	n.a.

Food and Measure	cal.	prot. (gms)	carbo. (gms)	fat (gms)	chol. (mgs)	sod. (mgs)	fiber (gms)
split, with ham (My-ers/Supper Bell), 3¹/2 oz.	69	6.0	10.0	1.0	n.a.	392	n.a.
split, with ham (Stouffer's), 8 oz.	200	12.0	30.0	3.0	n.a.	1130	n.a.
potato (Tabatchnick), 8 oz.	95	2.0	19.0	1.0	n.a.	606	n.a.
potato, cream of (My-ers/Supper Bell), 3¹/2 oz.	57	2.0	8.0	2.0	n.a.	335	n.a.
seafood bisque (My-ers/Supper Bell), 3¹/2 oz.	57	3.0	5.0	3.0	n.a.	503	n.a.
seafood chowder (Tabatchnick Salt Free), 8 oz.	100	n.a.	16.0	2.0	n.a.	45	n.a.
spinach, cream of (Stouffer's), 8 oz.	220	7.0	16.0	14.0	n.a.	1020	n.a.
vegetable:							
(Tabatchnick), 8 oz.	97	4.0	18.0	1.0	n.a.	513	n.a.
(Tabatchnick Salt Free), 8 oz. . .	103	n.a.	19.0	1.0	n.a.	175	n.a.
(Myers/Supper Bell), 3¹/2 oz.	42	3.0	3.0	2.0	n.a.	373	n.a.
won ton (Tabatchnick), 8 oz.	78	4.0	11.0	2.0	n.a.	393	n.a.
won ton, chicken (La Choy), ¹/2 pkg. . .	50	4.0	6.0	1.0	n.a.	1050	n.a.
Soup, mix*, 1 cup, except as noted:							
beef:							
barley (Swift Home-made Soup Starter), 12.8 fl. oz.	240	25.0	26.0	4.0	n.a.	1540	n.a.

* Prepared according to package directions

Food and Measure	cal.	prot. (gms)	carbo. (gms)	fat (gms)	chol. (mgs)	sod. (mgs)	fiber (gms)
Soup, mix, beef *(cont.)*							
flavor *(Lipton Cup-A-Soup* Trim), 6 fl. oz.	10	1.0	1.0	0	0	695	n.a.
flavor mushroom *(Lipton)*	40	2.0	7.0	<1.0	n.a.	995	n.a.
flavor noodle *(Lipton Cup-A-Soup),* 6 fl. oz.	45	2.0	8.0	<1.0	n.a.	830	n.a.
ground, vegetable *(Swift Homemade Soup Starter),* 12.8 fl. oz.	372	26.0	24.0	18.0	n.a.	1790	n.a.
noodle *(Swift Homemade Soup Starter),* 12.8 fl. oz.	240	25.0	26.0	5.0	n.a.	1660	n.a.
vegetable noodle *(Lipton Hearty)*	80	3.0	14.0	<1.0	n.a.	905	n.a.
chicken:							
(Quick 'n Tender)	600	17.0	69.0	28.0	n.a.	n.a.	n.a.
(Stir 'n Ready)	190	5.0	21.0	10.0	n.a.	n.a.	n.a.
broth *(Lipton Cup-A-Broth),* 6 fl. oz.	25	1.0	4.0	<1.0	n.a.	780	n.a.
cream of *(Lipton Cup-A-Soup),* 6 fl. oz.	80	2.0	9.0	4.0	n.a.	840	n.a.
flavor *(Lipton Cup-A-Soup* Trim), 6 fl. oz.	10	<1.0	1.0	0	n.a.	560	n.a.
hearty *(Lipton Cup-A-Soup* Country Style), 6 fl. oz.	70	4.0	10.0	1.0	n.a.	970	n.a.
noodle *(Lipton)*	70	3.0	9.0	2.0	n.a.	900	n.a.
noodle *(Lipton Hearty)*	90	4.0	14.0	2.0	n.a.	695	n.a.

Food and Measure	cal.	prot. (gms)	carbo. (gms)	fat (gms)	chol. (mgs)	sod. (mgs)	fiber (gms)
noodle (Swift Homemade Soup Starter), 12.8 fl. oz.	290	22.0	23.0	11.0	n.a.	1450	n.a.
noodle, with meat (Lipton Cup-A-Soup), 6 fl. oz.	45	3.0	6.0	1.0	n.a.	770	n.a.
rice (Lipton Cup-A-Soup), 6 fl. oz.	45	2.0	7.0	<1.0	n.a.	750	n.a.
supreme (Lipton Cup-A-Soup Country Style), 6 fl. oz.	100	3.0	11.0	5.0	n.a.	870	n.a.
vegetable (Lipton Cup-A-Soup), 6 fl. oz.	40	2.0	7.0	<1.0	n.a.	800	n.a.
vegetable (Swift Homemade Soup Starter), 12.8 fl. oz.	290	23.0	22.0	11.0	n.a.	1020	n.a.
minestrone:							
(Hain Old Fashion Natural No Salt Added)	100	3.0	13.0	4.0	n.a.	25	n.a.
(Manischewitz), 6 fl. oz.	50	3.0	9.0	<1.0	0	160	n.a.
mushroom:							
cream of (Hain Old Fashion Natural No Salt Added)	100	4.0	12.0	5.0	n.a.	125	n.a.
cream of (Lipton Cup-A-Soup), 6 fl. oz.	80	2.0	9.0	4.0	n.a.	830	n.a.
golden, chicken broth (Lipton)	60	2.0	8.0	2.0	n.a.	900	n.a.
noodle:							
(Lipton Giggle Noodle)	80	3.0	12.0	2.0	n.a.	925	n.a.

Food and Measure	cal.	prot. (gms)	carbo. (gms)	fat (gms)	chol. (mgs)	sod. (mgs)	fiber (gms)
Soup, mix, noodle (cont.)							
(Lipton Ring-O-Noodle)	60	3.0	9.0	1.0	n.a.	855	n.a.
(Lipton Ring Noodle), 6 fl. oz. . .	50	2.0	9.0	1.0	n.a.	745	n.a.
beef (Cup O'Noodles)	290	8.0	33.0	14.0	n.a.	1790	n.a.
beef (Oodles of Noodles)	390	9.0	49.0	18.0	n.a.	1910	n.a.
beef flavor (Lipton Cup-A-Soup Lots-A-Noodles), 7 fl. oz.	120	5.0	21.0	2.0	n.a.	780	n.a.
chicken (Cup O'Noodles) . . .	300	9.0	32.0	16.0	n.a.	1790	n.a.
chicken (Cup O'Noodles Twin)	150	5.0	19.0	7.0	n.a.	895	n.a.
chicken (Oodles of Noodles)	400	10.0	48.0	18.0	n.a.	1910	n.a.
chicken, cream of (Cup O'Noodles Hearty)	330	9.0	37.0	17.0	n.a.	1790	n.a.
chicken, cream of (Lipton Cup-A-Soup Lots-A-Noodles), 7 fl.oz. . .	150	5.0	22.0	5.0	n.a.	755	n.a.
chicken flavor (Lipton Cup-A-Soup Lots-A-Noodles), 7 fl. oz.	120	5.0	23.0	1.0	n.a.	855	n.a.
with chicken broth (Lipton)	70	2.0	10.0	2.0	n.a.	785	n.a.
Oriental style (Lipton Cup-A-Soup Lots-A-Noodles), 7 fl. oz.	120	5.0	20.0	2.0	n.a.	940	n.a.
shrimp (Cup O'Noodles) . . .	300	10.0	32.0	14.0	n.a.	1790	n.a.

Food and Measure	cal.	prot. (gms)	carbo. (gms)	fat (gms)	chol. (mgs)	sod. (mgs)	fiber (gms)
tomato vegetable *(Lipton Cup-A-Soup Lots-A-Noodles)*, 7 fl. oz. . . .	110	4.0	21.0	1.0	n.a.	885	n.a.
vegetable, garden *(Lipton Cup-A-Soup Lots-A-Noodles)*, 7 fl.oz. . . .	130	5.0	23.0	2.0	n.a.	745	n.a.
with vegetables, chicken broth *(Lipton Hearty)*	80	3.0	12.0	2.0	n.a.	925	n.a.
onion:							
(Hain Old Fashion Natural No Salt Added)	50	1.0	6.0	3.0	n.a.	70	n.a.
(Lipton)	35	1.0	6.0	<1.0	n.a.	640	n.a.
(Lipton Cup-A-Soup), 6 fl. oz.	30	1.0	5.0	1.0	n.a.	870	n.a.
beefy *(Lipton)* . .	35	1.0	5.0	1.0	n.a.	950	n.a.
golden, chicken broth *(Lipton)*	60	1.0	10.0	1.0	n.a.	995	n.a.
mushroom *(Lipton)*	45	2.0	7.0	1.0	n.a.	995	n.a.
pea:							
green *(Lipton Cup-A-Soup)*, 6 fl. oz.	120	4.0	16.0	4.0	n.a.	710	n.a.
split *(Manischewitz)*, 6 fl. oz.	45	3.0	9.0	<1.0	0	320	n.a.
Virginia *(Lipton Cup-A-Soup Country Style)*, 6 fl. oz.	140	5.0	18.0	5.0	n.a.	870	n.a.
tomato:							
(Hain Old Fashion Natural No Salt Added)	90	3.0	14.0	2.0	n.a.	35	n.a.
(Lipton Cup-A-Soup), 6 fl. oz.	80	1.0	17.0	1.0	n.a.	650	n.a.
beefy *(Lipton Cup-A-Soup Trim)*, 6 fl. oz.	10	<1.0	2.0	0	0	440	n.a.

Food and Measure	cal.	prot. (gms)	carbo. (gms)	fat (gms)	chol. (mgs)	sod. (mgs)	fiber (gms)
Soup, mix, tomato *(cont.)*							
onion *(Lipton)* . .	80	1.0	17.0	<1.0	n.a.	900	n.a.
vegetable noodle							
(Lipton Hearty)	80	3.0	15.0	1.0	n.a.	930	n.a.
vegetable:							
(Hain Old Fashion							
Natural No Salt							
Added)	160	6.0	24.0	4.0	n.a.	70	n.a.
(Lipton Country Veg-							
etable)	80	3.0	14.0	1.0	n.a.	995	n.a.
(Lipton Harvest Veg-							
etable), 6 fl. oz.	90	2.0	20.0	<1.0	n.a.	625	n.a.
(Manischewitz), 6 fl.							
oz.	50	3.0	9.0	<1.0	n.a.	25	n.a.
beef *(Lipton Cup-A-*							
Soup), 6 fl. oz.	50	2.0	8.0	<1.0	n.a.	820	n.a.
with beef stock *(Lip-*							
ton)	50	2.0	9.0	<1.0	n.a.	995	n.a.
for dip *(Lipton)* . .	45	2.0	8.0	<1.0	n.a.	995	n.a.
herb *(Lipton Cup-A-*							
Soup Trim), 6 fl.							
oz.	10	1.0	1.0	0	0	560	n.a.
spring *(Lipton Cup-*							
A-Soup), 6 fl. oz.	40	2.0	7.0	1.0	0	865	n.a.
Soup greens:							
(Durkee), 2.5-oz. jar	216	6.0	43.0	3.0	0	408	n.a.
Sour cream, see							
"Cream"							
Sour cream sauce:							
dehydrated, 1.2-oz.							
pkg.	180	5.5	17.0	11.1	28	444	n.a.
Sour cream and on-							
ion sticks:							
(Flavor Tree), 1 oz.	150	3.0	13.0	10.0	n.a.	415	n.a.
Sour drink mix*:							
with whiskey *(Bar-Ten-*							
der's), 3 1/2 fl. oz.	177	0	18.0	0	0	50	0

* *Prepared according to package directions*

Food and Measure	cal.	prot. (gms)	carbo. (gms)	fat (gms)	chol. (mgs)	sod. (mgs)	fiber (gms)
Soursop, raw:							
1 whole, 32.9 oz. . .	416	6.3	105.3	1.9	0	87	6.9
peeled and seeded, 4 oz.	75	1.1	19.1	.3	0	16	1.2
pulp only, 1 cup . .	150	2.3	37.9	.7	0	31	2.5
Soybean, green: raw:							
in pods, 1 lb. . . .	353	31.1	26.6	16.4	0	n.a.	4.9
shelled, 1 lb.	667	58.8	50.2	30.9	0	n.a.	9.3
shelled, 1 cup . .	376	33.2	28.3	17.4	0	n.a.	5.3
boiled, drained, 1 cup	255	22.2	19.9	11.5	0	n.a.	3.3
canned:							
with liquid, 8 oz. .	170	14.7	14.3	7.3	0	535	1.6
drained, 8 oz. . .	234	20.4	16.8	11.3	0	535	3.2
Soybean, fermented:							
natto, 4 oz.	189	19.2	13.0	8.4	0	n.a.	3.6
miso, with cereal, 4 oz.	194	11.9	26.6	5.2	0	3345	2.6
Soybean curd (tofu):							
4 oz.	82	8.8	2.7	4.8	0	8	.1
Soybean flour, see "Flour"							
Soybean kernels, roasted and toasted:							
unsalted:							
1 oz.	129	10.5	8.7	6.8	0	1	1.0
whole kernels, 1 cup	490	40.0	33.0	25.9	0	4	3.8
salted:							
1 oz.	129	10.5	8.7	6.8	0	46	1.0
whole kernels, 1 cup	490	40.0	33.0	25.9	0	176	3.8
Soybean "milk":							
fluid, 4 oz.	37	3.9	2.5	1.7	0	n.a.	0
powder, 4 oz.	486	47.4	31.8	23.0	0	n.a.	.2
dry (Worthington Soyamel Fortified), 1 oz.	130	7.0	10.0	7.0	0	210	n.a.

Food and Measure	cal.	prot. (gms)	carbo. (gms)	fat (gms)	chol. (mgs)	sod. (mgs)	fiber (gms)
Soybean protein:							
4 oz.	365	84.9	17.1	.1	0	238	.5
Soybean proteinate:							
4 oz.	354	91.4	8.7	.1	0	1361	.7
Soybean seeds, mature, dry:							
uncooked, 8 oz. . .	914	77.3	76.0	40.1	0	11	11.1
cooked, 8 oz.	295	24.9	24.5	12.9	0	5	3.6
Soybean sprouts, see "Bean sprouts"							
Soy sauce:							
(Chun King), 1 tsp.	5	.4	.7	.1	0	234	.1
(Kikkoman), 1 tbsp.	10	n.a.	.9	tr.	tr.	892	n.a.
(Kikkoman Lite), 1 tbsp.	10	n.a.	.9	tr.	tr.	599	n.a.
Spaghetti, plain, see "Pasta"							
Spaghetti, canned:							
and beef *(Hormel Short Order)*, 7½ oz.	260	8.0	25.0	14.0	n.a.	1091	n.a.
in meat sauce *(Franco-American)*, 7½ oz.	210	8.0	26.0	8.0	n.a.	1110	n.a.
in tomato sauce, with cheese:							
(Franco-American), 7⅜ oz.	190	5.0	36.0	2.0	n.a.	810	n.a.
(Heinz), 7¾ oz.	160	4.0	30.0	2.0	n.a.	1105	n.a.
in tomato and cheese sauce *(Franco-American SpaghettiOs)*, 7½ oz. . . .	170	4.0	34.0	2.0	n.a.	910	n.a.
in tomato sauce, with meat *(Heinz)*, 7½ oz.	170	8.0	21.0	6.0	n.a.	965	n.a.

Food and Measure	cal.	prot. (gms)	carbo. (gms)	fat (gms)	chol. (mgs)	sod. (mgs)	fiber (gms)
with franks:							
(Van Camp's Skettee Weenee), 1 cup	243	9.4	34.7	7.4	n.a.	1128	.5
in tomato sauce *(Franco-American SpaghettiOs)*, 7³/₈ oz.	210	7.0	28.0	7.0	n.a.	990	n.a.
with meat *(Nalley)*, 3¹/₂ oz.	110	4.0	12.0	5.0	10	600	n.a.
with meatballs:							
(Hormel Short Order)*, 7¹/₂ oz. . .	210	10.0	26.0	8.0	n.a.	n.a.	n.a.
(Nalley), 3¹/₂ oz.	110	4.0	14.0	4.0	10	550	n.a.
with meatballs, in tomato sauce:							
(Franco-American), 7³/₈ oz.	220	9.0	28.0	8.0	n.a.	820	n.a.
(Franco-American SpaghettiOs), 7³/₈ oz.	210	9.0	25.0	8.0	n.a.	910	n.a.
with sausage, Italian *(Hormel* Short Order)*, 7¹/₂ oz. . . .	187	9.0	19.0	9.0	n.a.	1369	n.a.
Spaghetti, freeze-dried:							
with meat sauce *(Mountain House)*, 1 cup	260	12.0	41.0	5.0	n.a.	n.a.	n.a.
Spaghetti, frozen:							
(Morton Casserole)*, 8 oz.	238	13.8	34.0	5.1	n.a.	700	n.a.
Spaghetti dinner, frozen:							
(Morton), 11.5 oz.	444	17.8	67.3	11.4	n.a.	1300	n.a.
with beef and mushroom sauce *(Lean Cuisine)*, 11¹/₂ oz.	280	15.0	38.0	7.0	20	1300	n.a.

Food and Measure	cal.	prot. (gms)	carbo. (gms)	fat (gms)	chol. (mgs)	sod. (mgs)	fiber (gms)
Spaghetti dinner, frozen *(cont.)*							
with meatballs:							
(Dinner Classics),							
11 oz.	380	17.0	25.0	24.0	n.a.	1300	n.a.
(Swanson), 12 1/2							
oz.	360	12.0	44.0	15.0	n.a.	1040	n.a.
Spaghetti dinner mix*:							
American style *(Kraft)*,							
1 cup	310	10.0	51.0	8.0	0	710	n.a.
Italian style *(Kraft)*, 1							
cup	310	11.0	49.0	8.0	5	830	n.a.
with meat sauce							
(Kraft), 1 cup . . .	370	12.0	47.0	14.0	15	860	n.a.
Spaghetti entree, fro-							
zen:							
with beef and mush-							
rooms *(Dining Lite)*,							
11 oz.	286	19.6	35.2	8.3	n.a.	1550	1.9
with meat sauce:							
(Light & Elegant),							
10 1/4 oz.	290	16.0	40.0	8.0	n.a.	700	n.a.
(Morton Lite), 8 oz.	220	9.0	36.0	4.0	n.a.	750	n.a.
(Stouffer's), 14 oz.	440	22.0	53.0	15.0	n.a.	1730	n.a.
casserole *(Ban-*							
quet), 8 oz. . . .	270	14.0	35.0	8.0	n.a.	1242	n.a.
with meatballs *(Stouf-*							
fer's), 12 5/8 oz. . .	370	21.0	43.0	13.0	n.a.	1560	n.a.
and sauce, with							
ground veal and							
mushrooms *(The*							
Budget Gourmet), 1							
serving	320	13.0	33.0	14.0	n.a.	1010	n.a.
in tomato sauce, with							
breaded veal							
(Swanson), 8 1/4 oz.	280	15.0	29.0	12.0	n.a.	810	n.a.
Spaghetti sauce,							
canned or in							
jars:							
(Prego), 4 oz.	140	2.0	20.0	6.0	n.a.	670	n.a.

* *Prepared according to package directions*

Food and Measure	cal.	prot. (gms)	carbo. (gms)	fat (gms)	chol. (mgs)	sod. (mgs)	fiber (gms)
(Prego No Salt Added), 4 oz. . . .	100	2.0	10.0	6.0	n.a.	25	n.a.
(Ragu), 4 oz.	80	2.0	11.0	3.0	0	n.a.	n.a.
(Ragu Homestyle), 4 oz.	70	2.0	12.0	2.0	0	n.a.	n.a.
ground beef sirloin, with onions *(Prego Plus)*, 4 oz.	160	4.0	20.0	7.0	n.a.	420	n.a.
Italian sausage and green peppers *(Prego* Plus), 4 oz.	170	3.0	19.0	9.0	n.a.	480	n.a.
marinara:							
(Aunt Millie's), 1/2 cup	70	1.0	6.0	4.0	<1	250	n.a.
(Ragu), 4 oz. . . .	90	2.0	12.0	4.0	0	n.a.	n.a.
meat flavored:							
(Aunt Millie's), 1/2 cup	70	3.0	7.0	3.0	2	350	n.a.
(P&Q), 1/2 cup . .	70	1.0	11.0	2.0	n.a.	510	n.a.
(Prego), 4 oz. . . .	150	2.0	21.0	6.0	n.a.	680	n.a.
(Ragu Extra Thick & Zesty), 4 oz. . .	100	2.0	14.0	4.0	2	n.a.	n.a.
meatless:							
(Aunt Millie's), 1/2 cup	70	2.0	7.0	3.0	2	350	n.a.
(P&Q), 1/2 cup . .	70	1.0	14.0	1.0	n.a.	540	n.a.
mushroom *(Aunt Millie's)*, 1/2 cup . . .	60	2.0	8.0	3.0	<1	320	n.a.
mushroom flavored *(P&Q)*, 1/2 cup . .	70	1.0	14.0	1.0	n.a.	580	n.a.
mushrooms and chunk tomatoes *(Prego* Plus), 4 oz.	130	2.0	18.0	5.0	n.a.	400	n.a.
with mushrooms:							
(Prego), 4 oz. . . .	140	2.0	21.0	5.0	n.a.	640	n.a.
(Ragu), 4 oz. . . .	90	2.0	9.0	4.0	0	n.a.	n.a.
(Ragu Homestyle), 4 oz.	70	2.0	12.0	2.0	0	n.a.	n.a.

Food and Measure	cal.	prot. (gms)	carbo. (gms)	fat (gms)	chol. (mgs)	sod. (mgs)	fiber (gms)
Spaghetti sauce, canned or in jars *(cont.)*							
with mushrooms and green pepper *(Enrico's)*, 4 oz. . . .	60	2.0	9.0	1.0	n.a.	n.a.	n.a.
pepper and mushroom *(Aunt Millie's)*, 1/2 cup	70	1.0	6.0	4.0	<1	290	n.a.
pepper and onion *(Aunt Millie's)*, 1/2 cup	70	2.0	8.0	3.0	<1	300	n.a.
pepper and sausage *(Aunt Millie's)*, 1/2 cup	70	2.0	7.0	3.0	2	340	n.a.
sausage *(Aunt Millie's)*, 1/2 cup . . .	60	2.0	7.0	3.0	3	310	n.a.
veal and sliced mushrooms *(Prego Plus)*, 4 oz.	150	5.0	20.0	5.0	n.a.	380	n.a.
Spaghetti sauce, mix:							
(Durkee), 1.5-oz. pkg.	85	1.4	20.0	.4	n.a.	3863	n.a.
(Spatini), 1 fl. oz.*	20	1.0	4.0	0	0	130	n.a.
with mushrooms *(Durkee)*, 1.1-oz. pkg.	69	1.6	16.0	.1	n.a.	3042	n.a.
with tomato paste *(Durkee Extra Thick & Rich)*, 1.3-oz. pkg.	72	1.8	24.0	.7	n.a.	1808	n.a.
Spanish mackerel, see "Mackerel"							
Sparerib sauce:							
mix *(Durkee Roastin' Bag)*, 1.9-oz. pkg.	162	.7	37.0	2.0	n.a.	2185	n.a.
Spinach:							
fresh:							
raw, trimmed, 10-oz. pkg.	46	5.8	7.1	.7	0	160	1.8

* *Prepared according to package directions*

Food and Measure	cal.	prot. (gms)	carbo. (gms)	fat (gms)	chol. (mgs)	sod. (mgs)	fiber (gms)
raw, chopped, 1 cup	12	1.6	2.0	.2	0	44	.5
boiled, drained, leaves, 1 cup	41	5.4	6.8	.5	0	126	1.6
canned, 1/2 cup:							
(A&P)	20	2.0	3.0	<1.0	0	350	n.a.
(Libby/Seneca) . .	25	3.0	4.0	0	0	540	n.a.
(S&W Premium Northwest) . . .	25	2.0	3.0	0	0	395	n.a.
(Stokely's Finest)	30	2.0	3.0	0	0	420	n.a.
frozen:							
(Green Giant), 1/2 cup	25	3.0	4.0	0	0	60	n.a.
(Green Giant Harvest Fresh), 1/2 cup	40	4.0	5.0	<1.0	0	360	n.a.
leaf (A&P), 3.3 oz.	25	3.0	4.0	<1.0	0	100	n.a.
leaf (Birds Eye), 3.3 oz.	20	3.0	4.0	0	0	90	.8
leaf (Frosty Acres), 3.3 oz.	20	3.0	4.0	0	0	75	1.0
chopped (A&P), 3.3 oz.	20	3.0	4.0	<1.0	0	90	n.a.
chopped (Birds Eye), 3.3 oz. . .	20	3.0	3.0	0	0	80	.8
chopped (Frosty Acres), 3.3 oz.	20	3.0	4.0	0	0	70	1.0
creamed (Birds Eye), 3 oz. . . .	60	3.0	5.0	3.0	n.a.	280	.7
creamed (Green Giant), 1/2 cup . .	80	3.0	10.0	3.0	n.a.	480	n.a.
creamed (Stouffer's), 41/2 oz.	190	4.0	9.0	15.0	n.a.	440	n.a.
cut leaf, in butter sauce (Green Giant), 1/2 cup . .	60	4.0	6.0	2.0	n.a.	520	n.a.
souffle (Stouffer's), 4 oz.	140	5.0	10.0	9.0	n.a.	560	n.a.

Food and Measure	cal.	prot. (gms)	carbo. (gms)	fat (gms)	chol. (mgs)	sod. (mgs)	fiber (gms)
Spinach, frozen *(cont.)*							
with water chest-							
nuts *(Birds Eye)*,							
3.3 oz.	25	2.0	5.0	0	0	270	.7
Spinach, New Zea-							
land, see "New							
Zealand spinach"							
Spinach crepes:							
frozen, with cheddar							
cheese sauce							
(Stouffer's), 9 1/2 oz.	420	17.0	27.0	27.0	n.a.	1100	n.a.
Spleen, fresh:							
raw:							
beef, 4 oz.	119	20.7	0	3.4	298	97	0
hog, 4 oz.	113	20.2	0	2.9	410	447	0
braised:							
beef, 3 oz.	123	21.3	0	3.6	295	48	0
hog, 3 oz. (4.6 oz.							
raw)	127	24.0	0	2.7	428	n.a.	0
raw, lamb, 4 oz. . .	130	21.3	0	4.4	n.a.	n.a.	0
Sports drink:							
(Max), 6 fl. oz. . . .	35	0	9.0	0	0	4	0
Spot, raw:							
fillets, 4 oz.	139	21.0	0	5.6	n.a.	33	0
Squab (pigeon), raw:							
whole, dressed, ready							
to cook, 1 lb. . . .	872	54.9	0	70.7	n.a.	n.a.	0
meat only, 4 oz. . .	161	19.8	0	8.5	n.a.	n.a.	0
meat only, 1 breast,							
3.6 oz.	135	22.0	0	4.6	n.a.	n.a.	0
Squash, summer,							
fresh:							
crookneck and							
straightneck:							
raw, trimmed, 8 oz.	43	2.1	9.2	.5	0	5	1.2
raw, sliced, 1 cup	24	1.2	5.3	.3	0	2	.7
boiled, drained,							
sliced, 1 cup . .	36	1.6	7.8	.6	0	2	1.1

Food and Measure	cal.	prot. (gms)	carbo. (gms)	fat (gms)	chol. (mgs)	sod. (mgs)	fiber (gms)
scallop:							
raw, trimmed, 8 oz.	41	2.7	8.7	.5	0	2	1.2
raw, sliced, 1 cup	24	1.6	5.0	.3	0	2	.7
boiled, drained,							
sliced, 1 cup . .	28	1.9	5.9	.3	0	2	.9
boiled, drained,							
mashed, 1 cup	38	2.5	7.9	.4	0	2	1.1
zucchini:							
raw, trimmed, 8 oz.	32	2.6	6.6	.3	0	7	1.0
raw, sliced, 1 cup	19	1.5	3.8	.2	0	3	.6
boiled, drained,							
sliced, 1 cup . .	28	1.1	7.1	.1	0	4	.9
boiled, drained,							
mashed, 1 cup	38	1.5	9.4	.1	0	4	.9
Squash, winter, fresh:							
acorn:							
raw, 1 whole							
(4 1/3″ × 4″ diam.)	172	3.5	44.9	.4	0	14	6.0
raw, cubed, 1 cup	56	1.1	14.6	.1	0	5	2.0
baked, cubed, 1 cup	115	2.3	29.9	.3	0	9	4.0
boiled, mashed, 1							
cup	83	1.7	21.5	.2	0	6	2.9
butternut:							
raw, peeled and							
seeded, 8 oz.	102	2.3	26.5	.2	0	9	3.2
raw, cubed, 1 cup	63	1.4	16.4	.1	0	5	2.0
baked, cubed, 1 cup	83	1.8	21.5	.2	0	7	2.6
hubbard:							
raw, peeled and							
seeded, 8 oz.	91	4.5	19.7	1.1	0	16	3.2
raw, cubed, 1 cup	47	2.3	10.1	.6	0	8	1.6
baked, cubed, 1 cup	103	5.1	22.2	1.3	0	16	3.6
boiled, mashed, 1							
cup	70	3.5	15.2	.9	0	12	2.5
spaghetti:							
raw, peeled and							
seeded, 8 oz.	75	1.5	15.7	1.3	0	39	3.2
raw, cubed, 1 cup	33	.7	7.0	.6	0	17	1.4

Food and Measure	cal.	prot. (gms)	carbo. (gms)	fat (gms)	chol. (mgs)	sod. (mgs)	fiber (gms)
Squash, winter, spaghetti *(cont.)*							
baked or boiled and drained, 1 cup	45	1.0	10.0	.4	0	28	2.2
Squash, frozen:							
butternut *(Southland)*, 4 oz.	45	1.0	11.0	0	0	0	n.a.
cooked:							
(Frosty Acres), 3.3 oz.	18	1.0	4.0	0	0	1	1.0
(Kohl's), 4 oz. . .	45	1.0	11.0	<1.0	0	0	n.a.
crookneck, sliced *(Southland)*, 3.3 oz.	20	1.0	4.0	0	0	0	n.a.
prepared *(Southland)*, 3.6 oz.	80	2.0	12.0	2.0	n.a.	430	n.a.
winter, cooked *(Birds Eye)*, 4 oz.	45	1.0	11.0	0	0	260	1.4
Squash seed kernels:							
dry, 4 oz.	627	32.9	17.0	53.0	0	n.a.	2.2
Squid:							
raw, meat only, 4 oz.	104	17.7	3.5	1.6	264	50	0
Steak, see "Beef"							
Steak sauce:							
(A•1), 1 tbsp.	12	<1.0	3.0	<1.0	0	275	n.a.
(Escoffier Sauce Diable), 1 tbsp. . . .	20	<1.0	4.0	<1.0	0	160	n.a.
(Escoffier Sauce Robert), 1 tbsp.	20	<1.0	5.0	<1.0	0	70	n.a.
(Heinz 57), 1 tbsp.	15	.4	2.7	.2	0	265	n.a.
(Heublein Steak Supreme), 1 tbsp. . .	20	<1.0	5.0	<1.0	0	25	n.a.
(Lea & Perrins), 1 oz.	40	<1.0	10.0	<1.0	0	220	n.a.
Stomach, pork:							
raw, 4 oz.	177	18.7	0	10.8	218	59	0
Strawberry:							
fresh:							
whole, fully trimmed, 1 lb.	136	2.8	31.9	1.7	0	5	2.4
whole, 1 pint . . .	97	2.0	22.5	1.2	0	4	1.7

Food and Measure	cal.	prot. (gms)	carbo. (gms)	fat (gms)	chol. (mgs)	sod. (mgs)	fiber (gms)
whole, 1 cup . . .	45	.9	10.5	.6	0	2	.8
freeze-dried (Mountain House), 1/4 cup . .	30	1.0	10.0	0	0	n.a.	n.a.
frozen:							
halves, in syrup (Birds Eye Quick Thaw Pouch), 5 oz.	120	1.0	30.0	0	0	5	.6
halves, in light syrup (Birds Eye Lite Quick Thaw Pouch), 5 oz.	60	1.0	16.0	0	0	5	.6
Strawberry drink:							
canned (Hi-C), 6 fl. oz.	95	<1.0	24.0	<1.0	0	17	n.a.
mix*, 8 fl. oz.:							
(Kool-Aid)	100	0	25.0	0	0	35	tr.
presweetened (Kool-Aid) . . .	90	0	22.0	0	0	0	0
sugar free (Funny Face)	4	0	1.0	0	0	0	0
sugar free (Kool-Aid)	4	0	0	0	0	0	tr.
sugar sweetened (Funny Face) . .	88	0	22.0	0	0	0	0
Strawberry juice:							
(Smucker's), 8 fl. oz.	120	0	30.0	0	0	5	n.a.
Strawberry roll or bar:							
(Flavor Tree), .75-oz. roll	80	0	18.0	<1.0	0	15	n.a.
(Fruit Corners), 1 bar	90	<1.0	17.0	2.0	0	10	n.a.
(Fruit Roll-Ups), 1/2-oz. roll	50	0	12.0	<1.0	0	5	n.a.
(Pocket Fruit), .7-oz. bar	60	0	16.0	0	0	n.a.	n.a.
(Sunkist Fruit Roll), 1/2-oz. roll	50	0	12.0	<1.0	0	10	n.a.

* Prepared according to package directions

Food and Measure	cal.	prot. (gms)	carbo. (gms)	fat (gms)	chol. (mgs)	sod. (mgs)	fiber (gms)
Strawberry syrup:							
(S&W), 1 tsp.	4	0	1.0	0	0	25	n.a.
Stroganoff sauce, mix:							
dehydrated, 1.6-oz. pkg.	161	5.6	26.5	4.4	12	1863	.6
(Durkee), 1.2-oz. pkg.	90	4.0	18.0	.7	n.a.	3002	n.a.
Stuffing, 1/2 cup, ex- cept as noted:							
cornbread *(Pepper- idge Farm),* 1 oz.	110	3.0	22.0	1.0	0	320	n.a.
cube *(Pepperidge Farm),* 1 oz. . . .	110	3.0	22.0	1.0	0	430	n.a.
herb *(Pepperidge Farm),* 1 oz. . . .	110	3.0	22.0	1.0	0	410	n.a.
frozen:							
chicken *(Green Gi- ant Stuffing Origi- nals)*	170	4.0	21.0	7.0	n.a.	670	n.a.
cornbread *(Green Giant Stuffing Originals)*	170	3.0	25.0	6.0	n.a.	660	n.a.
mushroom *(Green Giant Stuffing Originals)*	150	4.0	19.0	7.0	n.a.	780	n.a.
wild rice *(Green Gi- ant Stuffing Origi- nals)*	160	3.0	21.0	7.0	n.a.	540	n.a.
mix*:							
(Bell's Premium Blend)	180	5.0	24.0	6.0	n.a.	420	n.a.
(Bell's Ready Mix)	224	5.0	25.0	13.0	n.a.	660	n.a.
beef flavor *(Stove Top)*	180	4.0	21.0	9.0	n.a.	580	tr.
chicken flavor *(Bell's)*	190	5.0	24.0	8.0	n.a.	536	n.a.

* *Prepared according to package directions, with salted butter*

Food and Measure	cal.	prot. (gms)	carbo. (gms)	fat (gms)	chol. (mgs)	sod. (mgs)	fiber (gms)
chicken flavor (Betty Crocker), 1/6 pkg.	180	4.0	21.0	9.0	n.a.	620	n.a.
chicken flavor (Stove Top) ..	180	4.0	20.0	9.0	n.a.	640	tr.
corn bread (Betty Crocker), 1/6 pkg.	180	3.0	23.0	9.0	n.a.	710	n.a.
corn bread (Stove Top)	170	3.0	21.0	9.0	n.a.	660	tr.
herb (Betty Crocker), 1/6 pkg.	190	4.0	22.0	9.0	n.a.	640	n.a.
New England (Stove Top)	180	4.0	21.0	9.0	n.a.	630	tr.
pork flavor (Betty Crocker), 1/6 pkg.	190	4.0	22.0	9.0	n.a.	640	n.a.
pork flavor (Stove Top), ...	170	4.0	20.0	9.0	n.a.	620	tr.
with rice (Stove Top)	180	3.0	23.0	8.0	n.a.	500	tr.
San Francisco (Stove Top) ..	170	4.0	20.0	9.0	n.a.	640	tr.
turkey flavor (Stove Top)	170	4.0	20.0	9.0	n.a.	630	tr.
Sturgeon:							
fresh:							
raw, meat only, 4 oz.	119	18.3	0	4.6	n.a.	n.a.	0
steamed, meat only, 4 oz.	181	28.8	0	6.5	n.a.	122	0
smoked, 4 oz. ...	196	35.4	0	5.0	n.a.	n.a.	0
Sturgeon roe, see "Caviar"							
Succotash (corn and lima beans):							
fresh:							
raw, 4 oz.	112	5.7	22.2	1.2	0	5	1.5
boiled, drained, 1/2 cup	111	4.9	23.4	.8	0	16	1.3

Food and Measure	cal.	prot. (gms)	carbo. (gms)	fat (gms)	chol. (mgs)	sod. (mgs)	fiber (gms)
Succotash (cont.)							
canned:							
with cream style							
corn, 1/2 cup . .	102	3.5	23.4	.7	0	325	1.7
with whole kernel							
corn, 1/2 cup . .	81	3.3	17.9	.6	0	283	.8
(Libby/Seneca), 1/2							
cup	80	3.0	22.0	1.0	0	270	n.a.
(S&W Country							
Style), 1/2 cup	80	4.0	16.0	1.0	0	250	n.a.
(Stokely's Finest),							
1/2 cup	90	3.0	20.0	0	0	300	n.a.
frozen:							
(Frosty Acres), 3.3							
oz.	100	4.0	19.0	0	0	47	1.0
Sucker, raw:							
carp, meat only, 4 oz.	126	21.8	0	3.6	n.a.	n.a.	0
white or mullet, meat							
only, 4 oz.	104	19.0	0	2.6	46	45	0
Suet (beef kidney fat):							
raw, 1 oz.	242	.4	0	26.6	19	n.a.	0
Sugar, beet or cane:							
brown:							
1 oz.	106	0	27.3	0	0	9	n.a.
1 cup packed . .	793	0	205.0	0	0	64	n.a.
1 tbsp.	53	0	13.7	0	0	4	n.a.
1 tsp.	18	0	4.6	0	0	1	n.a.
granulated:							
1 oz.	109	0	28.2	0	0	<1	n.a.
1 cup	753	0	194.6	0	0	2	n.a.
1 tbsp.	44	0	11.3	0	0	<1	n.a.
1 tsp.	15	0	3.8	0	0	<1	n.a.
powdered (confection-er's):							
1 oz.	109	0	28.2	0	0	<1	n.a.
1 cup	469	0	121.3	0	0	1	n.a.
1 tbsp.	31	0	8.0	0	0	<1	n.a.
1 tsp.	10	0	2.7	0	0	<1	n.a.

Food and Measure	cal.	prot. (gms)	carbo. (gms)	fat (gms)	chol. (mgs)	sod. (mgs)	fiber (gms)
Sugar, maple:							
1 lb.	1579	n.a.	408.0	n.a.	0	64	n.a.
Sugar apple (sweet-sop):							
whole, 1 lb.	236	5.1	59.0	.7	0	24	3.7
1 whole (2⁷/₈″ × ³/₄″ diam.)	146	3.2	36.6	.5	0	15	2.3
peeled and seeded, 4 oz.	107	2.3	26.8	.3	0	10	1.7
pulp only, 1 cup . .	236	5.1	59.1	.7	0	24	3.7
Sugar substitute:							
(Sprinkle Sweet), 1 tsp.	2	0	.5	0	0	1	n.a.
*(Sweet*10)*, 1/8 tsp.	0	0	0	0	0	2	n.a.
Sukiyaki dinner, mix:							
(La Choy), 1/5 pkg.	40	2.0	7.0	0	n.a.	870	n.a.
Sukiyaki entree, canned:							
(Chun King Stir-Fry), 6 oz.	257	18.0	9.6	16.7	52	405	.6
(La Choy Bi-Pack), 3/4 cup*	70	7.0	8.0	1.0	n.a.	740	n.a.
Summer sausage (see also "Thuringer cervelat"):							
(Eckrich), 1 slice . .	90	4.0	1.0	7.0	n.a.	380	n.a.
(Hormel Perma-Fresh), 2 slices	140	10.0	0	11.0	n.a.	706	n.a.
(Hormel Tangy), 1 oz.	90	5.0	0	7.0	n.a.	317	n.a.
(Hormel Thuringer), 1 oz.	90	4.0	0	9.0	n.a.	332	n.a.
(Light & Lean), 2 slices	100	6.0	0	8.0	n.a.	n.a.	n.a.
(Oscar Mayer), .82-oz. slice	73	3.6	.2	6.5	17	327	0
beef:							
(Hormel), 1 oz. . .	100	5.0	0	9.0	n.a.	313	n.a.

* Prepared according to package directions

Food and Measure	cal.	prot. (gms)	carbo. (gms)	fat (gms)	chol. (mgs)	sod. (mgs)	fiber (gms)
Summer sausage, beef *(cont.)*							
(Oscar Mayer), .82-							
oz. slice	73	3.5	.5	6.3	17	316	0
(Usinger's), 1 oz.	95	5.0	n.a.	8.0	n.a.	n.a.	n.a.
cheese *(Armour)*, 1							
oz.	100	n.a.	n.a.	8.0	20	380	0
smoked *(Eckrich*							
Smoky Tang), 1 oz.	80	4.0	1.0	7.0	n.a.	350	n.a.
turkey, see "Turkey							
summer sausage"							
Sunflower butter:							
raw, unsalted *(Hain)*, 2							
tbsp.	180	8.0	6.0	15.0	0	10	n.a.
Sunflower nuts:							
dry roasted:							
(Planters), 1 oz.	160	7.0	5.0	14.0	0	260	n.a.
(Planters Unsalted)*,							
1 oz.	170	7.0	5.0	15.0	0	0	n.a.
oil roasted *(Planters)*,							
1 oz.	170	6.0	5.0	15.0	0	190	n.a.
Sunflower seeds:							
dry:							
in hull, 1 lb.	1372	58.8	48.7	115.8	0	73	n.a.
hulled, 4 oz. . . .	635	27.2	22.6	53.6	0	34	4.3
(Frito-Lay's), 1 oz.	170	8.0	4.0	16.0	0	50	n.a.
(Frito-Lay's Kernels)*, 1							
oz.	180	5.0	5.0	17.0	0	170	n.a.
(Planters), 1 oz. . . .	160	7.0	5.0	14.0	0	30	n.a.
dry roasted:							
(Flavor House), 1							
oz.	180	8.0	4.0	15.0	0	200	n.a.
(Laura Scudder's), 1							
oz.	144	7.0	11.2	8.5	0	215	1.2
oil roasted *(Laura*							
Scudder's), 1 oz.	190	6.9	2.8	17.1	0	125	.7
roasted in shell *(Laura*							
Scudder's), 1 oz.	86	3.7	3.0	7.2	0	5	.6

Food and Measure	cal.	prot. (gms)	carbo. (gms)	fat (gms)	chol. (mgs)	sod. (mgs)	fiber (gms)
Sunflower seed butter:							
salted:							
1 oz.	165	5.6	7.8	13.6	0	147	.4
1 tbsp.	93	3.2	4.4	7.6	0	83	.2
unsalted:							
1 oz.	165	5.6	7.8	13.6	0	1	.4
1 tbsp.	93	3.2	4.4	7.6	0	1	.2
Sunflower seed flour:							
partially defatted, 1 cup	261	38.5	28.7	1.3	0	2	4.2
Swamp cabbage:							
raw:							
trimmed, 1 lb. . .	86	11.8	14.3	.9	0	513	5.0
1 shoot, .6 oz. . .	2	.3	.4	<.1	0	15	.1
boiled, drained, chopped, 1 cup	20	2.0	3.6	.2	0	119	.8
Sweet and sour dinner:							
mix *(La Choy)*, 1/4 pkg.	140	2.0	33.0	0	n.a.	1190	n.a.
Sweet and sour drink mixer, 1 fl. oz.:							
(Holland House) . .	29	0	7.0	0	0	15	n.a.
(Kite-Lem Sweet'N Sour)	29	0	7.0	0	0	15	0
Sweet and sour entree, canned, 3/4 cup:							
Oriental, with chicken *(La Choy)*	230	8.0	47.0	1.0	n.a.	1300	n.a.
Oriental, with pork *(La Choy)*	250	5.0	48.0	4.0	n.a.	1500	n.a.
Sweet and sour sauce:							
(Chun King), 1.8 oz.	57	.4	14.4	.1	0	234	.1
(Contadina), 4 oz.	150	.5	29.6	3.0	0	500	n.a.

Food and Measure	cal.	prot. (gms)	carbo. (gms)	fat (gms)	chol. (mgs)	sod. (mgs)	fiber (gms)
Sweet and sour sauce *(cont.)*							
(French's Dip 'Um), 2							
tbsp.	80	0	20.0	0	0	25	n.a.
(Kikkoman), 1 tbsp.	18	.2	4.0	tr.	0	63	n.a.
(Sauceworks), 1 tbsp.	20	0	5.0	0	0	50	n.a.
mix *(Durkee)*, 2-oz.							
pkg.	230	1.1	45.0	5.7	0	1053	n.a.
Sweetbreads:							
beef (yearling):							
raw, 1 lb.	939	66.2	0	72.6	n.a.	435	0
braised, 4 oz. . . .	363	29.4	0	26.3	n.a.	132	0
calf:							
raw, 1 lb.	426	80.7	0	9.1	n.a.	n.a.	0
braised, 4 oz. . . .	191	37.0	0	3.6	n.a.	n.a.	0
hog, see "Pancreas"							
lamb:							
raw, 1 lb.	426	64.0	0	17.2	n.a.	n.a.	0
braised, 4 oz. . . .	198	31.9	0	6.9	n.a.	n.a.	0
Sweet potato:							
fresh:							
raw, 1 whole (5″							
long×2″ diam.)	136	2.1	31.6	.4	0	17	1.1
raw, cubed, 1 cup	144	2.3	33.3	.4	0	18	1.2
baked in skin, 8 oz.	234	3.9	55.0	.3	0	23	1.8
baked in skin, 1 whole (5″							
long×2″ diam.)	118	2.0	27.7	.1	0	12	.9
baked in skin,							
mashed, 1 cup	206	3.4	48.5	.2	0	20	1.6
boiled, pared, 8 oz.	238	3.7	55.1	.7	0	30	1.9
boiled, pared,							
mashed, 1 cup	344	5.4	79.6	1.0	0	42	2.8
candied, 4 oz. . . .	155	1.0	31.6	3.7	0	79	.4
canned (yams), 1/2 cup:							
whole, in heavy syrup *(Joan of*							
Arc)	150	1.0	35.0	<1.0	0	40	n.a.

Food and Measure	cal.	prot. (gms)	carbo. (gms)	fat (gms)	chol. (mgs)	sod. (mgs)	fiber (gms)
whole, small, in heavy syrup *(S&W Southern)*	139	1.0	31.0	1.0	0	27	n.a.
candied, brown sugar sauce *(S&W)*	180	1.0	44.0	0	0	355	n.a.
cut *(Joan of Arc)*	110	2.0	25.0	<1.0	0	45	n.a.
cut *(Kohl's)*	110	1.0	31.0	<1.0	0	30	n.a.
mashed	129	2.6	29.6	.3	0	96	n.a.
mashed *(Joan of Arc)*	130	2.0	31.0	<1.0	0	60	n.a.
vacuum pack, pieces	92	1.7	21.2	.2	0	54	.7
vacuum pack, mashed	117	2.1	27.0	.3	0	68	.9
in orange pineapple sauce *(Joan of Arc)*	180	1.0	43.0	<1.0	0	60	n.a.
in syrup, with liquid	101	1.1	23.9	.3	0	50	.6
in syrup, drained	107	1.3	24.9	.3	0	38	.6
dehydrated:							
flakes, dry form, 4 oz.	430	4.8	102.1	.7	0	205	3.6
flakes, prepared with water, 8 oz.	215	2.3	51.3	.2	0	102	1.8
frozen (yams):							
and apples *(Stouffer's)*, 5 oz. . . .	160	1.0	33.0	3.0	0	200	n.a.
candied *(Mrs. Paul's)*, 4 oz. . .	181	1.0	44.0	n.a.	0	105	n.a.
candied, and apples *(Mrs. Paul's)*, 4 oz.	150	1.0	36.0	<1.0	0	49	n.a.
Sweet potato leaves, fresh:							
raw:							
whole, 1 lb.	149	17.1	27.2	1.3	0	38	5.1
trimmed, 1 leaf, 12¼″ long . . .	6	.6	1.0	.1	0	1	.2

Food and Measure	cal.	prot. (gms)	carbo. (gms)	fat (gms)	chol. (mgs)	sod. (mgs)	fiber (gms)
Sweet potato leaves, raw *(cont.)*							
chopped, 1 cup	12	1.4	2.2	.1	0	3	.4
steamed, 1 cup . . .	22	1.5	4.7	.2	0	8	.8
Swiss steak, see "Beef dinner, frozen"							
Swiss steak gravy, mix:							
(Durkee), 1-oz. pkg.	68	1.0	16.0	.2	n.a.	2222	n.a.
(Durkee Roastin' Bag), 1.5-oz. pkg.	115	2.0	28.0	.9	n.a.	3008	n.a.
Swordfish: fresh:							
raw, meat only, 4 oz.	137	22.5	0	4.5	44	102	0
baked or broiled, meat only, 4 oz.	176	28.8	0	5.8	57	130	0
canned, with liquid, 8 oz.	231	39.7	0	6.8	n.a.	n.a.	0
frozen, steaks *(Wakefield),* 6 oz.	190	32.0	0	7.0	n.a.	70	n.a.
Swordfish dinner:							
in lemon sauce, frozen *(Taste O' Sea Gourmet),* 12 oz.	350	32.0	24.0	15.0	n.a.	1800	n.a.
Syrup (see also specific listings):							
(Knotts), 1¹/2 fl. oz.	160	0	40.0	0	0	< 10	n.a.

T

Food and Measure	cal.	prot. (gms)	carbo. (gms)	fat (gms)	chol. (mgs)	sod. (mgs)	fiber (gms)
Tabouly, mix:							
(Casbah), 1 oz. . . .	126	4.0	28.0	1.0	0	n.a.	n.a.
Taco, frozen:							
beef *(Patio)*, 2 tacos, 2 oz.	240	10.0	29.0	9.0	n.a.	n.a.	n.a.
beef, snack *(Patio)*, 4 tacos, 1/2 oz. . . .	130	5.0	17.0	5.0	n.a.	n.a.	n.a.
Taco dinner:							
frozen, beef, chili and beans *(Patio)*, 11 oz.	640	26.0	64.0	32.0	n.a.	n.a.	n.a.
Taco dip:							
(Hain Taco Dip & Sauce)*, 1/4 cup . .	20	1.0	4.0	0	0	n.a.	n.a.
(Thank You), 2 tbsp.	90	2.0	4.0	7.0	1	260	0
Taco sauce, canned or in jars:							
hot:							
(Del Monte), 1/4 cup	15	0	4.0	0	0	440	n.a.
(Ortega), 1 oz. . .	13	.3	3.2	.1	0	207	.2
hot salsa *(Ortega)*, 1 oz.	10	.4	2.4	.1	0	304	.2
mild:							
(Del Monte), 1/4 cup	15	0	4.0	0	0	480	n.a.
(Ortega), 1 oz. . .	13	.3	3.1	.1	0	222	.1
mild salsa *(Ortega)*, 1 oz.	9	.3	2.2	0	0	286	.2
western style *(Ortega)*, 1 oz.	8	.3	1.8	.1	0	177	.2

Food and Measure	cal.	prot. (gms)	carbo. (gms)	fat (gms)	chol. (mgs)	sod. (mgs)	fiber (gms)
Taco seasoning mix:							
(Durkee), 1.1-oz. pkg.	67	1.8	15.0	1.0	n.a.	2106	n.a.
(French's), 1/6 pkg.	20	1.0	4.0	0	n.a.	330	n.a.
mild:							
(Ortega), 1 oz. dry	86	1.8	17.6	1.0	0	1966	1.0
(Ortega), 1 oz.*	54	4.3	.9	3.6	18	104	.1
Taco starter:							
(Del Monte), 8 oz.	140	3.0	28.0	1.0	n.a.	2180	n.a.
Tahini (see also "Sesame paste"):							
raw:							
stone ground kernels, 1 oz. . . .	162	5.1	7.4	13.6	0	21	1.4
stone ground kernels, 1 tbsp. . .	86	2.7	3.9	7.2	0	11	.8
unroasted kernels:							
1 oz.	173	5.1	5.1	16.0	0	0	.9
1 tbsp.	85	2.5	2.5	7.9	0	0	.4
roasted or toasted kernels:							
1 oz.	169	4.8	6.0	15.3	0	33	1.4
1 tbsp.	89	2.6	3.2	8.1	0	17	.8
(Sahadi) 2 tbsp. . .	190	6.0	4.0	17.0	0	75	n.a.
mix *(Casbah)*, 1 oz.	25	2.0	2.0	5.0	0	n.a.	n.a.
Tamales, canned:							
(Van Camp's), 1 cup	293	8.3	28.6	16.2	n.a.	1132	2.2
(Wolf), 71/2 oz.	328	8.3	24.9	24.5	n.a.	1181	1.5
beef:							
(Hormel), 2 tamales	140	4.0	8.0	10.0	n.a.	550	n.a.
(Hormel Hot 'n Spicy), 2 tamales	140	4.0	9.0	10.0	n.a.	612	n.a.
Hormel Short Order), 71/2 oz. . .	270	8.0	17.0	19.0	n.a.	1140	n.a.
(Nalley), 31/2 oz.	130	5.0	11.0	6.0	n.a.	n.a.	n.a.
chicken *(Nalley)*, 31/2 oz.	90	3.0	11.0	4.0	n.a.	n.a.	n.a.

* *Prepared according to package directions, with ground beef and water*

Food and Measure	cal.	prot. (gms)	carbo. (gms)	fat (gms)	chol. (mgs)	sod. (mgs)	fiber (gms)
Tamales, frozen:							
beef *(Hormel)*, 1 tamale	140	6.0	13.0	7.0	n.a.	555	n.a.
and beef chili gravy *(Patio)*, 5.3 oz.	280	7.0	27.0	16.0	n.a.	n.a.	n.a.
Tamale Pie:							
canned *(Nalley)*, 3 1/2 oz.	130	4.0	11.0	8.0	15	340	n.a.
Tamarind, fresh:							
1 fruit (3" × 1")	5	.1	1.3	<.1	0	1	.1
pulp only, 1 cup	287	3.4	75.0	.7	0	33	6.1
Tangerine (Dancy variety), **fresh:**							
1 whole (2 3/8" diam.)	37	.5	9.4	.2	0	1	.3
sections, without membranes, 1 cup	86	1.2	21.8	.4	0	3	.7
Tangerine juice:							
fresh, 1 cup	106	1.2	25.0	.5	0	2	.3
canned, sweetened, 6 fl. oz.	96	1.0	22.4	.4	0	0	.2
frozen*, sweetened *(Minute Maid)*, 6 fl. oz.	82	<2.0	21.0	<1.0	0	2	n.a.
Taquito entree:							
shredded beef with guacamole, frozen *(Van de Kamp's Mexican Classic)*, 8 oz.	490	15.0	45.0	25.0	n.a.	990	n.a.
Taro:							
raw, sliced, 1 cup	112	1.6	27.5	.2	0	12	.8
cooked, sliced, 1 cup	187	.7	45.7	.2	0	20	1.1
Taro chips:							
1/2 cup	57	.3	8.1	3.1	0	44	.1
Taro leaves:							
raw:							
whole, 1 lb.	115	13.5	18.3	2.0	0	8	5.5

* *Prepared according to package directions*

Food and Measure	cal.	prot. (gms)	carbo. (gms)	fat (gms)	chol. (mgs)	sod. (mgs)	fiber (gms)
Taro leaves, raw *(cont.)*							
1 cup	12	1.4	1.9	.2	0	1	.6
steamed, 1 cup . . .	35	4.0	5.8	.6	0	3	.8
Taro shoots:							
raw:							
1 shoot							
(15 1/2″ × 1 1/8″							
diam.)	9	.8	1.9	.1	0	1	.5
sliced, 1 cup . . .	10	.8	2.0	.1	0	0	.5
cooked, sliced, 1 cup	19	1.0	4.5	.1	0	3	.8
Taro, Tahitian:							
raw, sliced, 1 cup . .	49	3.5	8.6	1.2	0	62	2.2
cooked, sliced, 1 cup	60	5.7	9.4	.9	0	74	3.1
Tarragon:							
ground (all brands), 1							
tsp.	5	.4	.8	.1	0	1	.1
Tartar sauce:							
(Best Foods/							
Hellmann's), 1 tbsp.	70	0	0	8.0	5	180	n.a.
(Kraft), 1 tbsp. . . .	70	0	1.0	8.0	5	160	n.a.
(Nalley), 1 tbsp. . . .	93	.2	.3	10.2	9	112	n.a.
(Sauceworks), 1 tbsp.	70	0	1.0	8.0	5	160	n.a.
Tautog (blackfish):							
raw:							
whole, 1 lb.	149	31.2	0	1.8	n.a.	n.a.	0
meat only, 4 oz.	101	21.1	0	1.2	n.a.	n.a.	0
Tea, 8 fl. oz., except							
as noted:							
regular or decaf-							
feinated *(Lipton)*	2	0	0	0	0	0	0
regular, flavored:							
all flavors *(Bigelow)*	1	<.1	<.1	<.1	0	<1	0
all flavors *(Lipton)*	2	0	<1.0	0	0	0	0
herbal:							
apple *(Bigelow Ap-*							
ple Orchard) . .	7	<.1	1.7	<.1	0	<1	0
(Bigelow Early							
Riser)	4	<.1	.1	<.1	0	<1	0

Food and Measure	cal.	prot. (gms)	carbo. (gms)	fat (gms)	chol. (mgs)	sod. (mgs)	fiber (gms)
(Bigelow Feeling Free)	1	<.1	<.1	<.1	0	1	0
(Bigelow Looking Good)	2	<.1	.1	<.1	0	2	0
(Bigelow Sweet Dreams)	1	<.1	<.1	<.1	0	2	0
(Bigelow Take-A-Break)	4	<.1	.1	<.1	0	1	0
chamomile *(Lipton)*	4	0	1.0	0	0	0	0
cinnamon apple *(Lipton)*	2	0	<1.0	0	0	0	0
fruit and almond *(Bigelow)*	1	<.1	<.1	<.1	0	<1	0
iced *(Bigelow Nice Over Ice)*	2	<.1	<.1	<.1	0	2	0
lemon *(Bigelow I Love Lemon)* ..	1	<.1	<.1	<.1	0	<1	0
(Lipton Almond Pleasure)	4	0	1.0	0	0	0	0
(Lipton Citrus Sunset)	4	0	1.0	0	0	0	0
(Lipton Gentle/ Tangy Orange)	4	0	1.0	0	0	0	0
(Lipton Lemon Soother)	4	0	1.0	0	0	0	0
(Lipton Toasty Spice)	6	0	1.0	0	0	0	0
mint *(Bigelow Mint Medley)*	1	<.1	<.1	<.1	0	4	0
orange and spice *(Bigelow)*	1	<.1	<.1	<.1	0	<1	0
iced, canned:							
lemon flavor *(Lipton)*	80	0	20.0	0	0	20	0
lemon flavor, sugar free *(Lipton)* ..	2	0	0	0	0	25	0
iced, dairy pack:							
lemon flavor *(Lipton)*	90	0	22.0	0	0	20	0

Food and Measure	cal.	prot. (gms)	carbo. (gms)	fat (gms)	chol. (mgs)	sod. (mgs)	fiber (gms)
Tea, iced, dairy pack *(cont.)*							
lemon flavor, sugar free *(Lipton)* . .	2	0	0	0	0	25	0
iced, mix*:							
(Crystal Light) . .	4	0	0	0	0	0	0
(Lipton Instant) . .	2	0	0	0	0	0	0
lemon flavor *(Lipton* Instant)	2	0	0	0	0	0	0
lemon flavor *(Nestea)*	6	0	0	0	0	0	0
lemon flavor *(Wyler's* Crystals)	80	0	21.0	0	0	n.a.	0
lemon flavor, with NutraSweet *(Lipton)*	4	0	1.0	0	0	0	0
lemon flavor, sugar free *(Lipton)* . .	2	0	0	0	0	5	0
lemon and sugar *(Lipton)*	60	0	16.0	0	0	0	0
lemon and sugar *(Nestea)*, 6 fl. oz.	70	0	9.0	0	0	0	0
instant *(Nestea* 100%)	0	0	n.a.	0	0	0	0
Teawurst:							
(Usinger's), 1 oz. . .	115	4.0	n.a.	11.0	n.a.	n.a.	0
Tequila, see "Liquor"							
Teriyaki sauce:							
(Kikkoman), 1 tbsp.	15	n.a.	2.7	tr.	tr.	630	n.a.
(Kikkoman Baste and Glaze), 1 tsp. . . .	18	.2	2.0	tr.	0	140	n.a.
(La Choy Marinade & Sauce), 1 oz. . . .	30	1.0	5.0	0	0	1640	n.a.
Terrapin (diamond-back),							
raw:							
in shell, 1 lb. . . .	106	17.7	0	3.3	n.a.	n.a.	0
meat only, 4 oz.	126	21.1	0	4.0	n.a.	n.a.	0

* Prepared according to package directions

Food and Measure	cal.	prot. (gms)	carbo. (gms)	fat (gms)	chol. (mgs)	sod. (mgs)	fiber (gms)
Thuringer cervelat							
(see also "Summer sausage"):							
(Hormel Old Smokehouse), 1 oz. . . .	90	4.0	1.0	8.0	n.a.	328	0
(Hormel Old Smokehouse, 11 oz. chub), 1 oz.	100	5.0	0	9.0	n.a.	332	0
(Hormel Old Smokehouse Sliced), 1 oz.	100	5.0	0	9.0	n.a.	321	n.a.
(Hormel Viking Chub Cervelat), 1 oz. . .	90	5.0	0	8.0	n.a.	325	0
Thyme:							
ground (all brands), 1 tsp.	4	.1	.9	.1	0	1	.3
Thymus, beef:							
raw, 4 oz.	266	13.8	0	23.0	252	108	0
braised, 4 oz.	362	24.8	0	28.3	333	132	0
Tilefish:							
raw, meat only, 4 oz.	109	19.8	0	2.6	n.a.	60	0
Toaster pastries and cakes, 1 piece:							
apple:							
(Toast 'Em)	210	3.0	38.0	5.0	n.a.	170	n.a.
(Toastettes) . . .	200	2.0	36.0	5.0	n.a.	170	n.a.
frosted (Toast 'Em)	210	3.0	40.0	5.0	n.a.	170	n.a.
banana-strawberry (Toast 'Em)	200	2.0	39.0	5.0	n.a.	180	n.a.
blueberries 'n cream (Toast 'Em)	210	3.0	40.0	4.0	n.a.	180	n.a.
blueberry:							
(Toast 'Em)	210	2.0	37.0	5.0	n.a.	190	n.a.
(Toastettes) . . .	200	2.0	36.0	5.0	n.a.	200	n.a.
frosted (Toast 'Em)	210	3.0	40.0	4.0	n.a.	180	n.a.
brown sugar-cinnamon:							
(Toast 'Em)	210	3.0	38.0	5.0	n.a.	170	n.a.
frosted (Toast 'Em)	220	2.0	39.0	6.0	n.a.	190	n.a.
frosted (Toastettes)	200	2.0	36.0	5.0	n.a.	170	n.a.

Food and Measure	cal.	prot. (gms)	carbo. (gms)	fat (gms)	chol. (mgs)	sod. (mgs)	fiber (gms)
Toaster pastries and cakes *(cont.)*							
cherry:							
(Toast 'Em)	210	3.0	40.0	4.0	n.a.	190	n.a.
(Toastettes) . . .	200	2.0	36.0	5.0	n.a.	200	n.a.
frosted *(Toast 'Em)*	210	3.0	39.0	5.0	n.a.	170	n.a.
fudge, frosted:							
(Toast 'Em)	210	3.0	38.0	5.0	n.a.	240	n.a.
(Toastettes) . . .	200	2.0	35.0	6.0	n.a.	210	n.a.
strawberry:							
(Toast 'Em)	210	2.0	40.0	5.0	n.a.	180	n.a.
(Toastettes) . . .	200	2.0	36.0	5.0	n.a.	200	n.a.
frosted *(Toastettes)*	200	2.0	36.0	5.0	n.a.	200	n.a.
Tofu, see "Soybean curd"							
Tofu entrees, frozen:							
cannelloni Florentine, with sauce *(Legume)*, 11 oz. . .	260	18.0	30.0	7.0	0	650	n.a.
enchilada, Mexican, with sauce *(Legume)*, 11 oz. . .	300	15.0	41.0	9.0	0	540	n.a.
lasagna:							
with sauce *(Legume Classic)*, 8 oz.	210	15.0	20.0	8.0	0	410	n.a.
vegetable, with sauce *(Legume)*, 12 oz.	240	14.0	26.0	8.0	0	520	n.a.
manicotti, with sauce *(Legume* Classic), 8 oz.	220	17.0	24.0	11.0	0	370	n.a.
pepper steak, whole wheat noodles *(Legume)*, 10 1/2 oz.	210	18.0	27.0	3.0	0	650	n.a.
sesame ginger stir fry, with sauce and brown rice *(Legume)*, 11 1/2 oz.	260	12.0	30.0	10.0	1	460	n.a.

Food and Measure	cal.	prot. (gms)	carbo. (gms)	fat (gms)	chol. (mgs)	sod. (mgs)	fiber (gms)
shells, stuffed, Provencale, with sauce (Legume), 11 oz.	270	15.0	26.0	12.0	0	660	n.a.
sweet and sour, whole wheat noodles (Legume), 11½ oz.	270	16.0	45.0	3.0	0	600	n.a.
Tom Collins drink mixer:							
(Holland House), 1 pouch	4	0	14.0	0	0	n.a.	n.a.
bottled (Holland House), 1 fl. oz.	42	0	10.0	0	0	15	n.a.
Tomato:							
fresh:							
green, 1 whole (2³/₅″ diam.) . .	30	1.5	6.3	.3	0	16	.6
ripe, raw, 1 whole (2³/₅″ diam.) . .	24	1.1	5.3	.3	0	10	.6
ripe, raw, chopped, 1 cup	35	1.6	7.8	.4	0	15	.8
ripe, boiled, 1 cup	60	2.7	13.5	.7	0	25	1.8
canned, ½ cup, except as noted:							
(A&P)	25	1.0	6.0	<1.0	0	220	n.a.
whole (Hunt's), 4 oz.	20	1.0	5.0	0	0	420	n.a.
whole (Stokely's Finest)	25	1.0	5.0	0	0	190	n.a.
whole, peeled, with liquid (Del Monte)	25	1.0	5.0	0	0	220	n.a.
whole, peeled, in juice (S&W) . .	25	1.0	6.0	0	0	220	n.a.
whole, peeled, in juice (S&W 50% Salt Reduced)	25	1.0	6.0	0	0	110	n.a.
cut, in juice (S&W Redi-Cut)	25	1.0	6.0	0	0	220	n.a.
crushed (Hunt's)	25	1.0	5.0	<1.0	0	300	n.a.

Food and Measure	cal.	prot. (gms)	carbo. (gms)	fat (gms)	chol. (mgs)	sod. (mgs)	fiber (gms)
Tomato, canned *(cont.)*							
diced, in puree *(S&W)*	35	1.0	8.0	0	0	290	n.a.
wedges, with liquid *(Del Monte)* . .	30	1.0	8.0	0	0	355	n.a.
Italian style, pear, whole in juice *(S&W)*	25	1.0	5.0	0	0	200	n.a.
Italian style, stewed, in juice *(S&W)*	35	1.0	9.0	0	0	355	n.a.
Mexican style, stewed, in juice *(S&W)*	80	2.0	16.0	0	0	720	n.a.
paste, see "Tomato paste"							
puree *(A&P)* . . .	60	2.0	14.0	<1.0	0	30	n.a.
puree *(Contadina)*	50	2.0	11.0	0	0	90	n.a.
puree *(Hunt's)* . .	45	2.0	10.0	0	0	180	n.a.
puree *(S&W)* . . .	60	2.0	14.0	0	0	35	n.a.
stewed *(A&P)* . .	35	1.0	8.0	<1.0	0	350	n.a.
stewed *(Contadina)*	35	1.0	9.0	0	0	405	n.a.
stewed *(Del Monte)*	35	1.0	8.0	0	0	355	n.a.
stewed *(Hunt's)*, 4 oz.	35	1.0	8.0	0	0	460	n.a.
stewed *(Stokely's Finest)*	35	1.0	8.0	0	0	220	n.a.
stewed, in juice *(S&W 50% Salt Reduced)* . . .	35	1.0	9.0	0	0	180	n.a.
stewed, sliced, in juice *(S&W)* . .	35	1.0	9.0	0	0	355	n.a.
Tomato, pickled:							
(Claussen Kosher), 1 oz.	5	.3	1.1	tr.	0	326	n.a.
Tomato aspic:							
canned, in juice *(S&W Supreme)*, 1/2 cup	60	1.0	16.0	0	0	860	n.a.

Food and Measure	cal.	prot. (gms)	carbo. (gms)	fat (gms)	chol. (mgs)	sod. (mgs)	fiber (gms)
Tomato juice:							
canned, 6 fl. oz., except as noted:							
(A&P)	30	1.0	7.0	0	0	550	n.a.
(Campbell's) . . .	35	1.0	8.0	0	0	570	n.a.
(Hunt's)	30	1.0	7.0	0	0	550	n.a.
(S&W California)	35	1.0	8.0	0	0	600	n.a.
(S&W Lite)	35	1.0	8.0	0	0	300	n.a.
(Stokely's Finest), ½ cup	20	0	4.0	0	0	330	n.a.
(Welch's)	35	1.0	7.0	0	0	550	n.a.
beef cocktail (Beefamato) . .	70	1.0	15.0	0	n.a.	240	n.a.
chili cocktail (Snap-E-Tom)	40	2.0	7.0	0	0	980	n.a.
clam cocktail (Clamato)	80	1.0	20.0	0	0	800	n.a.
dehydrated, crystals, 1 oz.	86	3.3	19.3	.6	0	1115	.9
Tomato paste, canned:							
(A&P), 6 oz.	150	6.0	35.0	<1.0	0	100	n.a.
(Del Monte), ¾ cup	150	6.0	34.0	1.0	0	110	n.a.
(Hunt's), 2 oz. . . .	45	2.0	11.0	0	0	150	n.a.
(S&W), 6 oz.	150	6.0	35.0	0	0	100	n.a.
Italian style (Hunt's), 2 oz.	50	2.0	11.0	0	0	520	n.a.
Tomato powder:							
4 oz.	342	14.6	84.7	.5	0	152	7.5
Tomato sauce, canned:							
(A&P), ½ cup . . .	45	2.0	9.0	<1.0	0	600	n.a.
(Contadina), ½ cup	45	2.0	9.0	0	0	510	n.a.
(Del Monte), 1 cup	70	3.0	16.0	1.0	0	1330	n.a.
(Hunt's), 4 oz. . . .	30	1.0	7.0	0	0	670	n.a.
(S&W), ½ cup . . .	40	2.0	9.0	0	0	620	n.a.
(S&W Lite), ½ cup	40	1.0	9.0	0	0	340	n.a.
(Stokely's Finest), ½ cup	30	2.0	7.0	0	0	810	n.a.

Food and Measure	cal.	prot. (gms)	carbo. (gms)	fat (gms)	chol. (mgs)	sod. (mgs)	fiber (gms)
Tomato sauce *(cont.)*							
chunky *(S&W)*, 1/2 cup	45	2.0	10.0	0	0	615	n.a.
Italian style:							
(Contadina, 1/2 cup	40	1.0	8.0	0	0	620	n.a.
(Hunt's), 4 oz. . .	60	2.0	11.0	2.0	0	520	n.a.
(S&W), 8 oz. . . .	100	3.0	20.0	0	0	1130	n.a.
with onion *(Del*							
Monte), 1 cup	100	3.0	23.0	1.0	0	1150	n.a.
Tomcod, Atlantic:							
raw, meat only, 4 oz.	87	19.5	0	.5	n.a.	n.a.	0
Tongue:							
fresh:							
beef, simmered, 4							
oz.	321	25.1	.4	23.5	121	68	0
calf, braised, 4 oz.	181	27.1	1.1	6.8	n.a.	n.a.	0
hog, braised, 4 oz.	307	27.3	0	21.1	166	124	0
lamb, braised, 4 oz.	288	23.2	.6	20.6	n.a.	n.a.	0
sheep, braised, 4							
oz.	366	22.5	2.7	28.7	n.a.	n.a.	0
canned or cured:							
pickled, 4 oz. . . .	303	21.9	.3	23.0	n.a.	n.a.	0
pork *(Hormel)*, 3 oz.	190	17.0	0	13.0	n.a.	966	0
potted or deviled, 4							
oz.	329	21.1	.8	26.1	n.a.	n.a.	0
Toppings, dessert:							
all flavors *(Smucker's*							
Magic Shell), 2 tbsp.	190	1.0	16.0	15.0	0	25–50	n.a.
all fruit flavors							
(Smucker's), 2 tbsp.	100	0	26.0	0	0	0	n.a.
butterscotch:							
(Kraft), 1 tbsp. . .	.60	0	13.0	1.0	0	70	n.a.
(Smucker's), 2 tbsp.	140	0	33.0	1.0	0	75	n.a.
caramel:							
(Kraft), 1 tbsp. . .	60	1.0	13.0	0	0	45	n.a.
(Smucker's), 2 tbsp.	140	1.0	33.0	1.0	0	110	n.a.
hot *(Smucker's)*, 2							
tbsp.	150	1.0	28.0	4.0	0	75	n.a.
chocolate *(Kraft)*, 1							
tbsp.	50	1.0	12.0	0	0	25	n.a.

Food and Measure	cal.	prot. (gms)	carbo. (gms)	fat (gms)	chol. (mgs)	sod. (mgs)	fiber (gms)
chocolate, syrup:							
(Hershey's), 1 oz. or							
2 tbsp.	80	1.0	17.0	1.0	n.a.	20	n.a.
(Smucker's), 2 tbsp.	130	1.0	27.0	0	0	35	n.a.
chocolate caramel							
(Kraft), 1 tbsp. . .	60	1.0	13.0	0	0	45	n.a.
chocolate fudge:							
(Hershey's), 1 oz. or							
2 tbsp.	100	1.0	14.0	4.0	0	30	n.a.
(Smucker's), 2 tbsp.	130	1.0	31.0	1.0	0	45	n.a.
hot (Kraft), 1 tbsp.	70	1.0	11.0	3.0	0	50	n.a.
hot (Smucker's), 2							
tbsp.	110	1.0	18.0	4.0	n.a.	55	n.a.
Swiss milk (Smucker's), 2 tbsp. . .	140	3.0	31.0	1.0	n.a.	70	n.a.
cream, see "Cream"							
marshmallow creme							
(Kraft), 1 oz. . . .	90	0	23.0	0	0	15	n.a.
(Nestlé Quik Syrup), 1 oz.	80	<1.0	18.0	0	0	35	n.a.
nut (Planters), 1 oz.	180	5.0	9.0	16.0	0	0	n.a.
peanut butter caramel							
(Smucker's), 2 tbsp.	150	3.0	29.0	2.0	0	105	n.a.
pecans, in syrup							
(Smucker's), 2 tbsp.	130	2.0	28.0	1.0	0	0	n.a.
pineapple:							
(Kraft), 1 tbsp. . .	50	0	13.0	0	0	0	n.a.
(Smucker's), 2 tbsp.	130	0	32.0	0	0	0	n.a.
raspberry, red (Kraft),							
1 tbsp.	50	0	13.0	0	0	5	n.a.
strawberry:							
(Kraft), 1 tbsp. . .	50	0	13.0	0	0	0	n.a.
(Smucker's), 2 tbsp.	120	0	30.0	0	0	0	n.a.
walnut:							
(Kraft), 1 tbsp. . .	90	1.0	10.0	5.0	0	0	n.a.
in syrup (Smucker's), 2 tbsp. . .	130	2.0	27.0	1.0	0	0	n.a.

Food and Measure	cal.	prot. (gms)	carbo. (gms)	fat (gms)	chol. (mgs)	sod. (mgs)	fiber (gms)
Tortilla:							
frozen *(Patio)*, 2 tortillas, 3/4 oz.	100	2.0	21.0	1.0	n.a.	n.a.	n.a.
Tortilla chips, see "Corn chips"							
Tostada entree:							
beef, supreme, frozen *(Van de Kamp's Mexican Classic)*, 8 1/2 oz.	530	25.0	40.0	30.0	n.a.	900	n.a.
Towel gourd, see "Gourd, dishcloth"							
Tree fern:							
cooked, chopped, 1/2 cup	28	.2	7.8	.1	0	3	.4
Tripe, beef:							
4 oz.	111	16.5	0	4.5	107	52	0
pickled, 4 oz.	70	13.4	0	1.5	n.a.	52	0
Tropical fruit bar:							
(Fruit Corners), 1 bar	90	<1.0	17.0	2.0	0	10	n.a.
Trout:							
fresh, meat only:							
mixed species, raw, 4 oz.	168	23.6	0	7.5	66	59	0
rainbow, raw, 4 oz.	134	23.3	0	3.8	65	31	0
rainbow, baked or broiled, 4 oz. . .	171	29.9	0	4.9	83	39	0
canned, 4 oz.	237	23.4	0	15.2	n.a.	n.a.	0
Tuna:							
fresh, raw:							
bluefin, meat only, 4 oz.	163	26.5	0	5.6	43	44	0
yellowfin, meat only, 4 oz.	122	26.5	0	1.1	51	42	0
canned in oil:							
chunk light *(A&P)*, 2 oz.	150	13.0	<1.0	13.0	n.a.	310	0

Food and Measure	cal.	prot. (gms)	carbo. (gms)	fat (gms)	chol. (mgs)	sod. (mgs)	fiber (gms)
chunk light *(Bumble Bee)*, 2 oz. . . .	170	12.0	0	14.0	30	310	0
chunk light *(S&W Fancy)*, 2 oz. . .	140	13.0	0	10.0	n.a.	450	0
chunk light *(Star-Kist Low Sodium)*, 2 oz.	170	14.0	<1.0	13.0	31	135	0
solid or chunk light *(Star-Kist)*, 2 oz.	150	13.0	<1.0	13.0	31	310	0
solid white *(A&P)*, 2 oz.	150	13.0	<1.0	10.0	n.a.	310	0
solid white *(Bumble Bee)*, 2 oz. . . .	150	14.0	0	10.0	30	310	0
solid white *(S&W Fancy)*, 2 oz. . .	160	13.0	0	12.0	n.a.	450	0
solid or chunk white *(Star-Kist)*, 2 oz.	140	14.0	<1.0	10.0	31	310	0
canned in water:							
chunk light *(A&P)*, 2 oz.	60	13.0	<1.0	<1.0	n.a.	310	0
chunk light *(Bumble Bee)*, 2 oz. . . .	70	12.0	0	2.0	30	310	0
chunk light *(Empress)*, 6.5 oz.	210	44.0	0	3.0	n.a.	95	0
chunk light *(S&W Fancy)*, 2 oz. . .	60	13.0	0	1.0	n.a.	500	0
chunk light *(Star-Kist)*, 2 oz. . . .	60	13.0	<1.0	<1.0	27	310	0
chunk light *(Star-Kist Low Sodium)*, 2 oz.	65	14.0	<1.0	1.0	27	135	0
chunk white *(A&P)*, 2 oz.	100	12.0	<1.0	5.0	n.a.	310	0
chunk white *(Star-Kist Low Sodium)*, 2 oz.	70	15.0	<1.0	<1.0	27	120	0
chunk white, dietetic *(Star-Kist)*, 2 oz.	70	15.0	<1.0	1.0	27	30	0

Food and Measure	cal.	prot. (gms)	carbo. (gms)	fat (gms)	chol. (mgs)	sod. (mgs)	fiber (gms)
Tuna, canned in water *(cont.)*							
solid light *(Star-Kist)*, 2 oz. . . .	60	14.0	< 1.0	< 1.0	27	310	0
solid white *(A&P)*, 2 oz.	70	15.0	< 1.0	< 1.0	n.a.	310	0
solid white *(Bumble Bee)*, 2 oz. . . .	70	0	0	8.0	5	180	0
solid white, imported albacore *(Star-Kist)*, 2 oz.	70	15.0	< 1.0	1.0	27	310	0
solid white, local albacore *(Star-Kist)*, 2 oz.	100	14.0	< 1.0	5.0	27	310	0
Tuna entree, mix*, 1/5 pkg.:							
au gratin *(Tuna Helper)*	300	16.0	29.0	13.0	n.a.	1110	n.a.
cold salad *(Tuna Helper)*	450	14.0	29.0	30.0	n.a.	1060	n.a.
noodle:							
cheese sauce *(Tuna Helper)*	250	15.0	30.0	8.0	n.a.	910	n.a.
creamy *(Tuna Helper)*	290	14.0	32.0	12.0	n.a.	960	n.a.
tetrazzini *(Tuna Helper)*	270	17.0	26.0	11.0	n.a.	860	n.a.
Tuna noodle casserole:							
frozen *(Stouffer's)*, 5 3/4 oz.	190	11.0	18.0	8.0	n.a.	680	n.a.
Tuna pie:							
frozen *(Banquet)*, 8 oz.	510	17.0	48.0	27.0	n.a.	1305	n.a.
Tuna salad sandwich spread:							
(The Spreadables), 1.9 oz.	100	6.0	3.0	7.0	n.a.	270	n.a.

* Prepared according to package directions

Food and Measure	cal.	prot. (gms)	carbo. (gms)	fat (gms)	chol. (mgs)	sod. (mgs)	fiber (gms)
Turbot:							
frozen, fillets *(Taste O' Sea),* 4 oz.	160	18.0	0	0	n.a.	196	0
Turf and surf dinner:							
frozen *(Classic Lite),* 10 oz.	250	31.0	14.0	7.0	80	890	1.2
Turkey, fresh:							
fryer-roaster, roasted:							
meat and skin, 8.1 oz. (1 lb. raw ready to cook)	395	64.7	0	13.1	241	151	0
meat and skin, 4 oz.	195	32.0	0	6.5	119	75	0
meat only, 1 cup	210	41.4	0	3.7	138	94	0
breast, with skin 1/2 breast, 12.1 oz.	526	100.0	0	11.0	310	182	0
breast, meat only, 1/2 breast, 10.8 oz.	413	92.0	0	2.3	255	159	0
leg, with skin, 8.6 oz.	418	69.9	0	13.3	267	195	0
leg, meat only, 7.9 oz.	355	65.4	0	8.5	171	182	0
wing, with skin, 3.2 oz.	186	24.9	0	8.9	104	65	0
wing, meat only, 2.1 oz.	98	18.5	0	2.1	61	47	0
skin only, 1 oz. . .	85	5.9	0	6.6	41	17	0
young hen, roasted:							
meat and skin, 8.6 oz. (1 lb. raw ready-to-cook)	530	68.3	0	26.4	190	156	0
meat and skin, 4 oz.	247	31.9	0	12.3	88	73	0
meat only, 1 cup	244	41.0	0	7.7	102	93	0
breast, with skin, 1/2 breast, 24.2 oz.	1330	197.5	0	53.9	492	401	0
leg, with skin, 15.8 oz.	955	124.2	0	47.1	365	326	0
wing, with skin, 6.1 oz.	414	47.5	0	23.4	134	98	0

Food and Measure	cal.	prot. (gms)	carbo. (gms)	fat (gms)	chol. (mgs)	sod. (mgs)	fiber (gms)
Turkey, young hen, roasted *(cont.)*							
skin only, 1 oz. . . .	137	5.4	0	12.6	30	12	0
young tom, roasted:							
meat and skin, 8.4 oz. (1 lb. raw ready to cook)	482	67.1	0	21.6	197	173	0
meat and skin, 4 oz.	229	31.9	0	10.3	93	82	0
meat only, 1 cup	235	41.1	0	6.6	108	104	0
breast, with skin, 1/2 breast, 46.9 oz.	2510	380.3	0	98.3	1002	892	0
leg, with skin, 28.4 oz.	1660	224.9	0	77.5	727	648	0
wing, with skin, 8.4 oz.	524	65.1	0	27.3	192	157	0
skin only, 1 oz. . . .	120	5.7	0	10.6	33	17	0
Turkey, frozen:							
breast:							
(Land O'Lakes), 3 oz.	100	20.0	0	1.0	50	55	0
(Weaver Gourmet), 3 oz.	105	18.6	.3	4.1	n.a.	560	0
roll *(Weaver)*, 3 oz.	98	19.8	2.3	1.0	n.a.	600	0
broth baste:							
(Armour Star), 4 oz.	180	22.0	0	10.0	n.a.	185	0
young *(Land O'Lakes* Self-Basting)*, 3 oz.	120	18.0	<1.0	5.0	77	145	0
butter baste:							
(Armour Star), 4 oz.	190	22.0	0	10.0	n.a.	155	0
(Land O'Lakes), 3 oz.	140	17.0	<1.0	8.0	85	135	0
cured, breast *(Armour)*, 4 oz. . . .	120	24.0	1.0	2.0	65	1320	0
roasted, white meat, no skin:							
10–12-lb. hen *(Beatrice Butterball)*, 31/2 oz.	160	29.0	0	4.0	80	125	0

Food and Measure	cal.	prot. (gms)	carbo. (gms)	fat (gms)	chol. (mgs)	sod. (mgs)	fiber (gms)
14–16-lb. tom *(Beatrice Butterball)*, 3 1/2 oz.	160	30.0	0	4.0	80	130	0
roasted, dark meat, no skin:							
10–12-lb. hen *(Beatrice Butterball)*, 3 1/2 oz.	190	26.0	0	10.0	125	90	0
14–16-lb. tom *(Beatrice Butterball)*, 3 1/2 oz.	200	26.0	0	10.0	130	90	0
roasted, white and dark meat and skin:							
10–12-lb. hen *(Beatrice Butterball)*, 3 1/2 oz.	190	27.0	0	9.0	95	110	0
14–16-lb. tom *(Beatrice Butterball)*, 3 1/2 oz.	200	27.0	0	10.0	100	115	0
roasted, skin only:							
10–12-lb. hen *(Beatrice Butterball)*, 3 1/2 oz.	410	21.0	0	37.0	140	90	0
14–16-lb. tom *(Beatrice Butterball)*, 3 1/2 oz.	430	21.0	0	38.0	135	100	0
white meat, with gravy *(Armour Star)*, 3.7 oz.	140	16.0	4.0	6.0	50	655	n.a.
white and dark meat, with gravy *(Armour Star)*, 3.7 oz. . . .	150	15.0	4.0	8.0	50	655	0
young *(Land O'Lakes)*, 3 oz.	130	17.0	<1.0	7.0	65	55	n.a.
Turkey, boneless, cooked:							
breast:							
(Louis Rich), 1 oz.	51	8.5	0	1.9	12	21	0

Food and Measure	cal.	prot. (gms)	carbo. (gms)	fat (gms)	chol. (mgs)	sod. (mgs)	fiber (gms)
Turkey, boneless, breast (cont.)							
oven roasted (Louis Rich), 1 oz. . .	36	6.2	.3	1.1	n.a.	306	n.a.
with skin (Boar's Head), 1 oz. . .	40	7.0	.1	1.0	n.a.	n.a.	n.a.
skinless (Boar's Head), 1 oz. . .	32	5.7	1.4	.4	n.a.	n.a.	n.a.
slices (Louis Rich), 1 slice	44	8.9	0	.9	13	29	0
tenderloin (Louis Rich), 1 oz. . .	41	9.0	0	.5	9	22	0
barbecued (Louis Rich), 1 oz. . .	39	6.2	.5	1.3	n.a.	316	n.a.
with cheese (Land O'Lakes), 5 oz.	300	25.0	16.0	16.0	35	835	n.a.
butter added (Golden Star), 4 oz.	163	20.0	0	8.6	68	512	0
ground (Louis Rich), 1 oz.	61	7.3	0	3.5	24	30	0
smoked:							
(Carl Buddig), 1 oz.	47	5.1	1.0	2.5	6	400	0
(Eckrich Calorie Watcher Slender Sliced), 1-oz. slice	40	5.0	2.0	2.0	n.a.	400	n.a.
(Louis Rich), 1-oz. slice	33	5.5	.2	1.1	12	279	n.a.
breast (Hormel Perma-Fresh), 2 slices	60	10.0	0	2.0	n.a.	540	n.a.
breast (Louis Rich), 1 oz.	35	6.2	.2	1.1	13	227	n.a.
breast (Oscar Mayer), 3/4-oz. slice	20	4.2	.1	.3	7	294	0
breast, chunk (Louis Rich), 1 oz. . .	34	5.8	.3	1.0	11	260	n.a.
breast, sliced (Louis Rich), .7-oz. slice	21	4.5	.1	.3	7	194	n.a.

Food and Measure	cal.	prot. (gms)	carbo. (gms)	fat (gms)	chol. (mgs)	sod. (mgs)	fiber (gms)
with barbecue sauce (Armour Star), 4 oz. . . .	140	16.0	8.0	5.0	50	840	n.a.
with spiced sauce (Armour Star), 4 oz.	140	15.0	9.0	5.0	50	610	n.a.
white meat:							
with gravy (Armour Star), 4 oz. . . .	130	17.0	5.0	4.0	50	650	n.a.
roast, with gravy (Land O'Lakes Buttermoist), 3 oz.	110	14.0	1.0	5.0	20	510	n.a.
roll (Avondale), 3 oz.	130	18.0	0	7.0	45	865	0
roll (Gold Band), 3 oz.	110	16.0	1.0	5.0	45	605	0
roll (Land O'Lakes Blue Label), 3 oz.	110	14.0	2.0	5.0	50	560	n.a.
roll (Land O'Lakes Red Label), 3 oz.	110	14.0	3.0	5.0	50	530	n.a.
roll (Magic Slice), 3 oz.	120	18.0	0	5.0	50	685	0
white and dark meat:							
diced (Land O'Lakes), 3 oz.	120	15.0	<1.0	6.0	35	590	n.a.
with gravy (Armour Star), 4 oz. . . .	120	16.0	5.0	5.0	50	660	n.a.
roast, with gravy (Land O'Lakes Buttermoist), 3 oz.	120	13.0	1.0	7.0	20	490	n.a.
roll (Avondale), 3 oz.	140	17.0	0	7.0	50	860	0
roll (Gold Band), 3 oz.	120	15.0	0	6.0	50	690	0
roll (Land O'Lakes Blue Label), 3 oz.	120	14.0	1.0	6.0	50	550	n.a.
roll (Land O'Lakes Red Label), 3 oz.	110	13.0	4.0	5.0	50	510	n.a.

Food and Measure	cal.	prot. (gms)	carbo. (gms)	fat (gms)	chol. (mgs)	sod. (mgs)	fiber (gms)
Turkey, boneless, white and dark meat *(cont.)*							
roll *(Magic Slice)*, 3 oz.	120	16.0	0	5.0	50	695	0
with dressing and gravy *(Armour Star)*, 4 oz.	160	12.0	11.0	8.0	35	650	n.a.
Turkey, canned:							
boned, with broth, 5-oz. can	231	33.6	0	9.7	n.a.	663	0
chunk *(Hormel)*, 6³/₄ oz.	230	37.0	0	10.0	n.a.	1278	0
Turkey bologna:							
2 slices or 2 oz. . .	113	7.8	.5	8.6	56	498	n.a.
(Armour), 4 oz. . . .	220	14.0	6.0	16.0	95	1070	n.a.
(Louis Rich), 1-oz. slice	58	3.6	.5	4.6	19	225	n.a.
Turkey dinner, frozen:							
(Banquet American Favorites), 11 oz.	320	19.0	41.0	9.0	n.a.	1416	n.a.
(Banquet Extra Helpings), 19 oz. . . .	723	31.0	98.0	23.0	n.a.	2165	n.a.
(Morton), 11 oz. . .	279	17.0	41.7	4.9	n.a.	1100	n.a.
(Swanson), 11¹/₂ oz.	330	21.0	39.0	10.0	n.a.	1260	n.a.
(Swanson Hungry-Man), 18¹/₂ oz. . .	590	40.0	66.0	18.0	n.a.	2150	n.a.
Dijon *(Lean Cuisine)*, 9¹/₂ oz.	280	25.0	20.0	11.0	70	1030	n.a.
Parmesan *(Classic Lite)*, 11 oz. . . .	240	19.0	25.0	8.0	70	480	1.6
sliced breast, with mushrooms *(Le Menu)*, 11¹/₄ oz. . .	460	28.0	34.0	24.0	n.a.	1140	n.a.
tetrazzini *(Morton Lite)*, 11 oz. . . .	280	13.0	47.0	4.0	n.a.	900	n.a.
Turkey entree, freeze-dried:							
tetrazzini, *(Mountain House)*, 1 cup . .	200	13.0	20.0	8.0	n.a.	n.a.	n.a.

Food and Measure	cal.	prot. (gms)	carbo. (gms)	fat (gms)	chol. (mgs)	sod. (mgs)	fiber (gms)
Turkey entree, frozen:							
(Swanson), 8¾ oz.	250	17.0	24.0	10.0	n.a.	1090	n.a.
(Swanson Hungry-Man), 13¼ oz. . . .	390	30.0	36.0	14.0	n.a.	1740	n.a.
a la king, with rice *(The Budget Gourmet)*, 1 serving . .	390	20.0	36.0	18.0	n.a.	740	n.a.
casserole *(Stouffer's)*, 9¾ oz.	380	24.0	28.0	19.0	n.a.	1250	n.a.
with gravy *(Swanson Main Course)*, 9¼ oz.	300	28.0	24.0	10.0	n.a.	1120	n.a.
gravy and:							
breaded croquettes *(Freezer Queen, 2 lb.)*, 10.67 oz.	210	14.0	13.0	11.0	n.a.	n.a.	n.a.
sliced *(Banquet Cookin' Bag)*, 5 oz.	137	10.0	4.0	8.0	n.a.	471	n.a.
sliced *(Banquet Family Entree)*, 8 oz.	296	17.0	7.0	22.0	n.a.	734	n.a.
sliced *(Freezer Queen Cook-in-Pouch)*, 5 oz.	80	9.0	5.0	3.0	n.a.	n.a.	n.a.
sliced *(Freezer Queen, 2 lb.)*, 8 oz.	320	16.0	28.0	16.0	n.a.	n.a.	n.a.
sliced *(Freezer Queen Single Serve)*, 10 oz.	265	21.0	32.0	5.0	n.a.	n.a.	n.a.
sliced *(Morton Lite)*, 8 oz.	270	14.0	45.0	4.0	n.a.	1310	n.a.
sliced *(Light & Elegant)*, 8 oz.	230	20.0	25.0	5.0	n.a.	1020	n.a.
tetrazzini:							
(Freezer Queen Single Serve), 9 oz.	270	20.0	30.0	8.0	n.a.	n.a.	n.a.
(Stouffer's), 6 oz.	230	13.0	14.0	14.0	n.a.	650	n.a.

Food and Measure	cal.	prot. (gms)	carbo. (gms)	fat (gms)	chol. (mgs)	sod. (mgs)	fiber (gms)
Turkey frankfurters, 1 link:							
(Armour Star), 2 oz.	110	7.0	3.0	8.0	50	580	n.a.
(Louis Rich)	103	5.6	1.1	8.5	39	482	n.a.
cheese (Louis Rich)	108	6.0	1.6	8.6	40	514	n.a.
Turkey gravy: canned:							
(Franco-American), 2 oz.	30	0	3.0	2.0	n.a.	300	n.a.
(Heinz Home Style), 2 oz.	29	.8	2.1	2.0	n.a.	140	n.a.
mix:							
(Durkee), 1-oz. pkg.	87	2.8	14.0	.1	n.a.	1010	n.a.
(French's Gravy for Turkey), 1/4 cup	25	1.0	4.0	1.0	n.a.	290	n.a.
Turkey ham:							
(Armour), 4 oz. . . .	140	22.0	2.0	4.0	60	1210	0
(Land O'Lakes), 3 oz.	100	18.0	2.0	2.0	55	845	n.a.
(Louis Rich), 1 oz.	34	5.5	.3	1.2	18	278	n.a.
(Louis Rich Water Added), 1 oz. . . .	34	5.0	.2	1.4	21	281	n.a.
(Weaver), 3 oz. . . .	142	19.7	1.3	6.4	n.a.	1060	n.a.
chopped (Louis Rich), 1 oz.	42	5.1	.2	2.3	17	254	n.a.
smoked (Carl Buddig), 1 oz.	40	5.7	.3	1.7	19	435	0
Turkey loaf, breast:							
6-oz. pkg.	187	38.3	0	2.7	69	2433	0
2 slices or 1.5 oz.	47	9.6	0	.7	17	608	0
Turkey meat loaf:							
(Armour), 3 oz. . . .	160	10.0	8.0	8.0	50	470	n.a.
Turkey pastrami:							
8-oz. pkg.	320	41.7	3.8	14.1	n.a.	2372	n.a.
2 slices or 2 oz. . .	80	10.4	.9	3.5	n.a.	593	n.a.
(Armour), 4 oz. . . .	140	22.0	1.0	5.0	65	1305	n.a.
(Louis Rich), 1-oz. slice	33	5.4	.1	1.2	17	276	n.a.

Food and Measure	cal.	prot. (gms)	carbo. (gms)	fat (gms)	chol. (mgs)	sod. (mgs)	fiber (gms)
Turkey patties:							
(Land O'Lakes), 2¹/₄ oz.	170	8.0	10.0	11.0	30	330	n.a.
battered or breaded, fried, 2.3 oz. . . .	181	9.0	10.1	11.5	n.a.	512	n.a.
frozen *(Tyson Chick 'N Quick)*, 3 oz.	220	13.0	12.0	14.0	n.a.	n.a.	n.a.
Turkey pie, frozen:							
(Banquet), 8 oz. . .	526	18.0	41.0	32.0	n.a.	1111	n.a.
(Stouffer's), 10 oz.	540	20.0	36.0	35.0	n.a.	1260	n.a.
(Swanson), 8 oz. . .	430	12.0	41.0	24.0	n.a.	800	n.a.
(Swanson Chunky), 10 oz. . . . . . . : . .	530	19.0	45.0	31.0	n.a.	950	n.a.
(Swanson Hungry-Man), 16 oz. . . .	740	27.0	66.0	41.0	n.a.	1590	n.a.
Turkey salad sandwich spread:							
(The Spreadables), 1.9 oz.	110	7.0	3.0	8.0	n.a.	245	n.a.
Turkey salami:							
(Louis Rich), 1-oz. slice	52	4.5	.1	3.7	19	245	n.a.
cotto:							
(Armour), 4 oz. . .	180	17.0	4.0	11.0	70	1080	n.a.
(Louis Rich), 1-oz. slice	52	4.4	.3	3.7	22	257	n.a.
Turkey sausage:							
breakfast *(Louis Rich)*, 1 oz.	60	6.2	0	3.9	23	200	n.a.
smoked *(Louis Rich)*, 1 oz.	55	4.6	.4	3.8	19	230	n.a.
Turkey sticks:							
(Land O'Lakes), 2 sticks or 2 oz. . .	150	7.0	9.0	10.0	25	295	n.a.
Turkey summer sausage:							
(Louis Rich), 1-oz. slice	52	4.7	.4	3.5	22	311	n.a.

Food and Measure	cal.	prot. (gms)	carbo. (gms)	fat (gms)	chol. (mgs)	sod. (mgs)	fiber (gms)
Turmeric:							
ground (all brands), 1 tsp.	8	.2	1.4	.2	0	1	.2
Turnip:							
fresh:							
raw, whole, un-trimmed, 1 lb.	100	3.3	22.9	.4	0	248	3.3
raw, cubed, 1 cup	35	1.2	8.1	.1	0	88	1.2
boiled, drained, cubed, 1 cup . .	28	1.1	7.7	.1	0	100	1.1
boiled, drained, mashed, 1 cup	42	1.6	11.3	.2	0	116	1.6
frozen, mashed (Southland), 3.6 oz.	90	1.0	9.0	6.0	n.a.	60	n.a.
Turnip greens:							
fresh:							
raw, trimmed, 1 lb.	123	6.8	26.0	1.4	0	182	3.6
raw, chopped, 1 cup	15	.8	3.2	.2	0	22	.4
boiled, drained, chopped, 1 cup	29	1.6	6.3	.3	0	41	.9
canned, 1/2 cup:							
with liquid	17	1.6	2.9	.4	0	325	.7
chopped (Stokely's Finest)	20	2.0	3.0	0	0	350	n.a.
with turnips, diced (Stokely's Finest)	20	2.0	0	0	0	340	n.a.
frozen, chopped, 3.3 oz.:							
(Frosty Acres) . .	20	2.0	4.0	0	0	10	1.0
(Southland)	20	2.0	4.0	0	0	10	n.a.
with diced turnips (Southland) . .	20	3.0	3.0	0	0	35	n.a.
Turtle, green:							
raw:							
in shell, 1 lb. . . .	97	21.6	0	.5	n.a.	n.a.	0
meat only, 4 oz.	101	22.5	0	.6	n.a.	n.a.	0
canned, 4 oz.	120	26.5	0	.8	n.a.	n.a.	0

V

Food and Measure	cal.	prot. (gms)	carbo. (gms)	fat (gms)	chol. (mgs)	sod. (mgs)	fiber (gms)
Vanilla extract:							
pure *(Virginia Dare)*, 1 tsp.	10	0	.3	0	0	0	0
Veal, fresh, retail cuts, meat only:							
chuck cuts and boneless for stew, lean with fat, stewed, 4 oz.	267	31.6	0	14.5	n.a.	56	0
loin cuts, lean with fat, broiled, 4 oz. . . .	265	29.9	0	17.0	n.a.	74	0
plate (breast), lean with fat, stewed, 4 oz.	344	29.6	0	24.1	n.a.	52	0
rib roast, lean with fat, roasted, 4 oz. . .	305	30.9	0	19.2	145	76	0
round with rump (roasts and leg cutlets), lean with fat, broiled, 4 oz. . . .	245	30.7	0	12.6	n.a.	75	0
Veal, steaks, frozen:							
(Hormel), 4 oz. . . .	130	22.0	2.0	4.0	n.a.	n.a.	0
breaded *(Hormel),* 4 oz.	240	17.0	13.0	13.0	n.a.	n.a.	0
Veal dinner, frozen:							
Parmigiana:							
(Banquet International Favorites), 11 oz.	413	14.0	43.0	21.0	n.a.	1310	n.a.

Food and Measure	cal.	prot. (gms)	carbo. (gms)	fat (gms)	chol. (mgs)	sod. (mgs)	fiber (gms)
Veal dinner, Parmigiana *(cont.)*							
(Banquet Extra Helpings), 20 oz.	1092	30.0	116.0	57.0	n.a.	2123	n.a.
(Dinner Classics), 10³/₄ oz.	380	17.0	36.0	20.0	85	1430	n.a.
(Morton), 12 oz.	320	11.3	50.2	8.2	n.a.	1300	n.a.
(Morton), 20 oz.	570	28.8	79.1	15.3	n.a.	2300	1.0
(Morton Lite), 11 oz.	290	17.0	39.0	7.0	n.a.	1300	n.a.
(Swanson), 12³/₄ oz.	470	22.0	49.0	21.0	n.a.	1120	n.a.
(Swanson Hungry-Man), 20 oz. . .	640	35.0	62.0	28.0	n.a.	2010	n.a.
pepper steak *(Classic Lite)*, 11 oz. . . .	280	26.0	25.0	8.0	n.a.	540	2.1
Veal entree, Parmigiana, frozen:							
(Banquet International Favorites Cookin' Bag), 5 oz.	293	11.0	23.0	17.0	n.a.	853	n.a.
(Banquet Family Entrees), 6.4 oz. . .	282	15.0	21.0	18.0	n.a.	961	n.a.
(Freezer Queen Cook-in-Pouch), 5 oz.	250	9.0	18.0	15.0	n.a.	n.a.	n.a.
(Freezer Queen, 2 lb.), 8 oz.	370	15.0	26.0	23.0	n.a.	n.a.	n.a.
Veal loaf:							
(Usinger's), 1 oz. . .	65	3.0	n.a.	6.0	n.a.	n.a.	n.a.
Vegetable entree:							
chow mein, canned:							
(La Choy Bi Pack), ³/₄ cup*	50	2.0	8.0	2.0	n.a.	640	n.a.
(La Choy Meatless), ³/₄ cup	35	2.0	6.0	1.0	n.a.	780	n.a.
stew, canned *(Dinty Moore)*, 8 oz. . . .	170	5.0	20.0	8.0	n.a.	1047	n.a.

* Prepared according to package directions

Food and Measure	cal.	prot. (gms)	carbo. (gms)	fat (gms)	chol. (mgs)	sod. (mgs)	fiber (gms)
stew, freeze-dried, with beef *(Mountain House)*, 1 cup . .	230	11.0	27.0	7.0	n.a.	n.a.	n.a.
Vegetable juice, canned, 6 fl. oz.:							
("V-8")	35	1.0	8.0	0	0	345	n.a.
("V-8" No Salt Added)	40	1.0	9.0	0	0	30	n.a.
cocktail *(S&W Spring Vegetable)*	35	1.0	8.0	0	0	600	n.a.
spicy hot *("V-8")* . .	35	1.0	8.0	0	0	345	n.a.
Vegetable seasoning:							
(Lawry's Natural Choice for Vegetables), 1 tsp. . . .	6	.3	1.3	.2	0	4	.4
Vegetable sticks: breaded, fried, frozen *(Farm Rich)*, 4 oz. . .	240	4.0	32.0	10.0	n.a.	625	n.a.
Vegetables, see specific listings							
Vegetables, mixed (see also specific listings):							
canned, 1/2 cup, except as noted:							
(A&P No Salt Added)	40	1.0	9.0	< 1.0	0	20	n.a.
(A&P/P&Q Chunky Eastern)	40	2.0	8.0	< 1.0	0	330	n.a.
(A&P/P&Q Chunky Western)	40	1.0	9.0	< 1.0	0	380	n.a.
(Del Monte) . . .	40	2.0	7.0	0	0	355	n.a.
(S&W Old Fashioned Harvest Time)	35	1.0	6.0	0	0	380	n.a.
(Stokely's Finest)	40	2.0	8.0	0	0	300	n.a.
(Stokely's Finest No Salt or Sugar)	40	2.0	8.0	0	0	25	n.a.

Food and Measure	cal.	prot. (gms)	carbo. (gms)	fat (gms)	chol. (mgs)	sod. (mgs)	fiber (gms)
Vegetables, mixed, canned *(cont.)*							
Chinese, fancy, drained *(La Choy)*	12	1.0	2.0	0	0	30	n.a.
chop suey, drained *(La Choy)* . . .	10	1.0	2.0	0	0	320	n.a.
chow mein, drained *(Chun-King)*, 8 oz.	64	5.7	12.7	.5	0	41	1.6
frozen:							
(A&P), 3.3 oz. . .	65	3.0	13.0	<1.0	0	55	n.a.
(Birds Eye), 3.3 oz.	60	3.0	13.0	0	0	45	1.1
(Frosty Acres), 3.3 oz.	65	3.0	13.0	0	0	50	1.0
(Green Giant), 1/2 cup	50	2.0	11.0	0	0	30	n.a.
(Green Giant Harvest Fresh), 1/2 cup	45	2.0	9.0	0	0	170	n.a.
breaded, fried *(Chill Ripe)*, 4 oz. . .	233	3.6	31.0	9.2	0	397	n.a.
American style, *(Green Giant Valley Combination)*, 1/2 cup	90	3.0	16.0	2.0	n.a.	340	n.a.
in butter sauce *(Green Giant)*, 1/2 cup	80	3.0	13.0	2.0	n.a.	370	n.a.
California blend *(A&P)*, 3.3 oz.	25	2.0	5.0	<1.0	0	25	n.a.
Chinese style *(Birds Eye Stir-Fry)*, 3.3 oz.	30	2.0	7.0	0	0	480	.8
Chinese style *(La Choy)*, 1/2 cup	25	1.0	5.0	<1.0	0	540	n.a.
Chinese style with sauce *(Birds Eye)*, 3 oz.	80	2.0	8.0	5.0	n.a.	360	.2
Dutch style *(Frosty Acres)*, 3.2 oz.	30	2.0	5.0	0	0	30	n.a.

Food and Measure	cal.	prot. (gms)	carbo. (gms)	fat (gms)	chol. (mgs)	sod. (mgs)	fiber (gms)
Far Eastern, with sauce (Birds Eye), 3.3 oz.	80	2.0	8.0	5.0	n.a.	390	.8
gumbo mix (Southland), 3.2 oz. . .	40	2.0	9.0	0	0	10	n.a.
Italian style (A&P), 3.3 oz.	40	2.0	8.0	<1.0	0	35	n.a.
Italian style (Frosty Acres), 3.2 oz.	40	3.0	8.0	0	0	20	n.a.
Italian style with sauce (Birds Eye), 3.3 oz.	110	2.0	11.0	7.0	n.a.	570	.6
Italian style with sauce (Green Giant Valley Combination), 1/2 cup	50	3.0	5.0	2.0	n.a.	310	n.a.
Japanese style (Birds Eye Stir-Fry), 3.3 oz. . .	30	2.0	6.0	0	0	570	.7
Japanese style with sauce (Birds Eye), 3.3 oz.	100	2.0	10.0	6.0	n.a.	500	.6
Japanese style with sauce (Green Giant Valley Combination), 1/2 cup	45	2.0	7.0	1.0	n.a.	420	n.a.
Mexican style (Green Giant Valley Combination), 1/2 cup	150	5.0	22.0	5.0	n.a.	540	n.a.
Mexicana style, with sauce (Birds Eye), 3.3 oz.	120	3.0	16.0	6.0	n.a.	470	1.0
New England style, with sauce (Birds Eye), 3.3 oz. . .	130	3.0	14.0	7.0	n.a.	410	.7
with onion sauce (Birds Eye), 2.6 oz.	100	2.0	11.0	5.0	n.a.	350	.7

Food and Measure	cal.	prot. (gms)	carbo. (gms)	fat (gms)	chol. (mgs)	sod. (mgs)	fiber (gms)
Vegetables, mixed, frozen *(cont.)*							
Oriental style *(A&P)*, 3.3 oz.	25	2.0	5.0	<1.0	0	15	n.a.
Oriental style *(Frosty Acres)*, 3.2 oz.	25	2.0	5.0	0	0	15	n.a.
San Francisco style, with sauce *(Birds Eye)*, 3.3 oz. . .	100	2.0	11.0	5.0	n.a.	400	.5
with sauce *(LeSueur Valley Combination)*, 1/2 cup . .	90	4.0	13.0	2.0	n.a.	340	n.a.
soup mix *(Frosty Acres)*, 3 oz. . .	45	4.0	11.0	0	0	35	n.a.
soup mix *(Southland)*, 3.2 oz. . .	50	2.0	11.0	0	0	40	n.a.
stew *(A&P)*, 4 oz.	60	1.0	13.0	<1.0	0	30	n.a.
stew *(Frosty Acres)*, 3 oz.	42	3.0	10.0	0	0	21	n.a.
stew *(Kohl's)*, 3.3 oz.	50	1.0	10.0	<1.0	0	30	n.a.
stew *(Ore-Ida)*, 3 oz.	60	1.0	12.0	0	0	35	n.a.
stew *(Southland)*, 3.2 oz.	45	1.0	10.0	0	0	20	n.a.
Swiss mix *(Frosty Acres)*, 3 oz. . .	25	2.0	5.0	0	0	36	1.0
winter blend *(A&P)*, 3.3 oz.	24	2.0	6.0	<1.0	0	20	n.a.
Vegetarian foods, canned and dry:							
"beef":							
bits *(Loma Linda)*, 4 pieces	80	8.0	4.0	3.0	0	340	1.0
roast *(Loma Linda)*, 2 oz.	150	11.0	2.0	11.0	0	670	<1.0
slices *(Worthington)*, 2 oz.	105	8.0	4.0	6.0	0	550	n.a.
steak *(Worthington Prime Stakes)*, 1 piece	180	10.0	8.0	12.0	0	585	n.a.

Food and Measure	cal.	prot. (gms)	carbo. (gms)	fat (gms)	chol. (mgs)	sod. (mgs)	fiber (gms)
steak *(Worthington Vegetable Steaks)*, 2.5 oz. piece	100	17.0	4.0	2.0	0	505	n.a.
biscuits *(Loma Linda Ruskets)*, 2 pieces	110	4.0	23.0	< 1.0	0	85	< 1.0
"burgers" and "burger" granules:							
(Loma Linda Burger-Like), 4 oz. . . .	90	13.0	8.0	.2	0	440	.3
(Loma Linda Burger-Mix), 1 oz. . . .	90	10.0	12.0	.7	0	368	.4
(Loma Linda Patty Mix), 1/4 cup . .	50	9.0	4.0	1.0	0	320	< 1.0
(Loma Linda Redi-Burger), 1/2" slice	130	14.0	5.0	6.0	0	370	< 1.0
(Loma Linda Vege-Burger), 1/2 cup	110	22.0	4.0	1.0	0	190	1.0
(Loma Linda Vege-Burger, granules), 1/2 cup	110	20.0	3.0	1.7	0	450	.2
(Loma Linda Vege-Burger, no salt added), 1/2 cup	140	27.0	4.0	2.0	0	55	1.0
(Loma Linda Vita-Burger, chunks or granules), 3 tbsp.	70	10.0	7.0	< 1.0	0	150	< 1.0
(Worthington Granburger), 6 tbsp.	110	19.0	7.0	1.0	0	700	n.a.
(Worthington Vegetarian Burger), 1/2 cup	130	19.0	7.0	3.0	0	630	n.a.
(Worthington Vegetarian Burger No Salt Added), 1/2 cup	130	19.0	7.0	3.0	0	500	n.a.
(Loma Linda Vita-Burger), 1/4 cup	70	10.0	7.0	< 1.0	0	150	< 1.0

Food and Measure	cal.	prot. (gms)	carbo. (gms)	fat (gms)	chol. (mgs)	sod. (mgs)	fiber (gms)
Vegetarian foods *(cont.)*							
"chicken":							
diced *(Worthington)*, 1/4 cup	90	6.0	3.0	6.0	0	490	n.a.
fried *(Loma Linda)*, 2-oz. piece . . .	180	13.0	2.0	14.0	0	510	<1.0
fried *(Worthington Fri Chik)*, 2 pieces	170	10.0	5.0	12.0	0	590	n.a.
fried, with gravy *(Loma Linda)*, 2 pieces or 3 oz.	140	9.0	4.0	10.0	0	340	<1.0
sliced *(Worthington)*, 2 slices	110	9.0	5.0	6.0	0	390	n.a.
supreme *(Loma Linda)*, 1/4 cup dry	50	9.0	4.0	<1.0	0	450	<1.0
chili *(Worthington)*, 2/3 cup	230	12.0	21.0	11.0	0	930	n.a.
"chops" *(Worthington Choplets)*, 2 slices	100	17.0	4.0	2.0	0	480	n.a.
"cold cuts":							
(Loma Linda Nuteena), 1/2" slice	160	8.0	5.0	12.0	0	120	1.0
(Loma Linda Proteena), 1/2" slice	140	17.0	6.0	5.0	0	460	1.0
(Loma Linda Vegelona), 1/2" slice	100	18.0	6.0	1.0	0	210	<1.0
(Worthington Numete), 1/2" slice	160	7.0	7.0	11.0	0	480	n.a.
(Worthington Protose), 1/2" slice	180	17.0	8.0	9.0	0	660	n.a.
"cutlets" *(Worthington)*, 1.5 oz. slice	100	17.0	4.0	2.0	0	625	n.a.
"fish" *(Loma Linda Ocean Platter)*, 1/4 cup	50	8.0	5.0	<1.0	0	260	<1.0

Food and Measure	cal.	prot. (gms)	carbo. (gms)	fat (gms)	chol. (mgs)	sod. (mgs)	fiber (gms)
"franks":							
(Loma Linda Big Franks), 1 frank	100	10.0	4.0	5.0	0	220	1.0
(Loma Linda Sizzle Franks), 2 franks	170	10.0	3.0	13.0	0	340	1.0
fries *(Loma Linda Wheat Fries)*, 2.5 oz.	60	12.0	2.4	.9	0	180	.1
"links":							
(Loma Linda Linketts), 2 links	150	15.0	5.0	8.0	0	340	1.0
(Loma Linda Little Links), 2 links	80	8.0	2.0	5.0	0	210	< 1.0
(Worthington Saucettes), 2 links	160	10.0	5.0	11.0	0	450	n.a.
(Worthington Super Links), 1 link . .	100	6.0	3.0	7.0	0	430	n.a.
(Worthington Vege-Links), 2 links	120	7.0	6.0	7.0	0	380	n.a.
(Loma Linda Dinner Cuts), 3.5 oz. . . .	110	21.0	4.0	1.0	0	550	< 1.0
(Loma Linda Dinner Cuts, No Salt Added), 3.5 oz. . .	110	21.0	4.0	1.0	0	30	< 1.0
(Loma Linda Savorex), 1 tsp.	16	3.0	1.0	1.0	0	320	< 1.0
(Loma Linda Tasty Cuts), 2 cuts . . .	70	12.0	2.0	1.0	0	230	1.0
(Loma Linda Tender Cuts), 3.6 oz. . . .	80	14.0	3.3	1.2	0	410	.2
"meat" balls:							
(Worthington), 3 pieces	110	7.0	6.0	6.0	0	165	n.a.
with gravy *(Loma Linda Tender Rounds)*, 6 pieces	120	15.0	7.0	4.0	0	310	< 1.0
"meat" loaf:							
(Loma Linda), 1 oz.	90	9.9	12.0	.8	0	380	.6

Food and Measure	cal.	prot. (gms)	carbo. (gms)	fat (gms)	chol. (mgs)	sod. (mgs)	fiber (gms)
Vegetarian foods, "meat" loaf *(cont.)*							
(Loma Linda Savory Dinner Loaf), 1/4 cup dry	50	9.0	4.0	< 1.0	0	380	< 1.0
nut meat *(Loma Linda)*, 2.5 oz.	150	7.2	6.6	10.0	0	280	1.0
sandwich spread *(Loma Linda)*, 3 tbsp.	70	4.0	4.0	4.0	0	300	1.0
"scallops":							
(Loma Linda Vege-Scallops), 6 pieces	70	14.0	2.0	1.0	0	180	< 1.0
(Worthington Skallops), 1/2 cup	80	14.0	3.0	1.0	0	420	n.a.
(Worthington Skallops, No Salt Added), 1/2 cup	80	14.0	3.0	1.0	0	135	n.a.
stew:							
(Loma Linda Stew Pac), 2 oz.	70	10.0	4.0	2.0	0	220	< 1.0
(Worthington Country Stew), 9.5 oz.	240	10.0	22.0	12.0	0	950	n.a.
Stroganoff *(Worthington)*, 6.7 oz.	160	7.0	18.0	7.0	0	1578	n.a.
Swiss "steak," with gravy *(Loma Linda)*, 1 steak	140	9.0	8.0	8.0	0	350	2.0
"turkey" *(Worthington '209')*, 2 slices	140	9.0	5.0	9.0	0	620	n.a.
Vegetarian foods, frozen:							
"bacon":							
(Morningstar Farms), 3 pieces	80	3.0	3.0	6.0	0	330	n.a.
(Worthington Stripples), 4 pieces	120	4.0	4.0	10.0	0	435	n.a.
"beef":							
corned, sliced *(Worthington)*, 4 slices	130	9.0	8.0	7.0	0	980	n.a.

Food and Measure	cal.	prot. (gms)	carbo. (gms)	fat (gms)	chol. (mgs)	sod. (mgs)	fiber (gms)
smoked, sliced *(Worthington)*, 6 slices	110	10.0	8.0	4.0	0	1005	n.a.
"beef" pot pie *(Worthington)*, 8 oz. . . .	420	9.0	42.0	24.0	0	1310	n.a.
"bologna":							
(Loma Linda), 2 oz. or 2 slices . . .	150	14.0	5.0	9.0	0	490	< 1.0
(Worthington Bologno), 2 slices	60	7.0	2.0	3.0	0	520	n.a.
"burger" *(Loma Linda Sizzle Burger)*, 1 burger	210	15.0	13.0	11.0	0	320	< 1.0
"chicken":							
(Loma Linda), 2 oz. or 2 slices . . .	160	10.0	1.0	13.0	0	330	< 1.0
(Worthington Chic-Ketts), 1/2 cup	180	20.0	6.0	8.0	0	720	n.a.
(Worthington Chik-Stiks), 1 piece	120	8.0	4.0	8.0	0	425	n.a.
diced *(Worthington)*, 1/2 cup	175	13.0	6.0	11.0	0	1195	n.a.
nuggets *(Loma Linda Chik-Nuggets)*, 5 pieces	230	14.0	15.0	13.0	0	640	< 1.0
patties *(Loma Linda Chik-Patties)*, 1 patty	230	14.0	15.0	13.0	0	640	< 1.0
sliced *(Worthington)*, 2 slices	120	9.0	4.0	7.0	0	725	n.a.
"chicken" pot pie *(Worthington)*, 8 oz.	375	7.0	37.0	22.0	0	1175	n.a.
corn dog *(Loma Linda)*, 1 piece . .	200	7.0	21.0	10.0	0	620	< 1.0
"egg" roll *(Worthington)*, 1 roll	170	6.0	20.0	7.0	0	475	n.a.
"eggs" *(Morningstar Farms Scramblers)*, 1/4 cup	60	6.0	3.0	3.0	0	130	n.a.

Food and Measure	cal.	prot. (gms)	carbo. (gms)	fat (gms)	chol. (mgs)	sod. (mgs)	fiber (gms)
Vegetarian foods *(cont.)*							
fillets *(Worthington)*, 2 pieces	180	15.0	9.0	9.0	0	1050	n.a.
"fish" *(Loma Linda Ocean Fillet)*, 1 fillet	130	11.0	4.0	8.0	0	230	<1.0
"franks" *(Worthington Dixie Dogs)*, 1 piece	180	8.0	20.0	7.0	0	780	n.a.
grillers *(Morningstar Farms)*, 1 piece	180	14.0	5.0	12.0	0	320	n.a.
"ham" sliced *(Worthington Wham)*, 3 slices	120	11.0	5.0	6.0	0	1155	n.a.
"links":							
(Morningstar Farms Breakfast), 3 links	180	13.0	5.0	12.0	0	480	n.a.
(Worthington Leanies), 1 link	120	7.0	3.0	9.0	0	595	n.a.
(Worthington Prosage), 3 links	190	13.0	4.0	14.0	0	620	n.a.
"meat" balls, Swedish *(Loma Linda)*, 8 pieces	190	22.0	7.0	8.0	0	420	<1.0
"patties":							
(Morningstar Farms Breakfast), 2 patties	190	16.0	7.0	11.0	0	870	n.a.
(Worthington FriPats), 1 piece	180	14.0	5.0	12.0	0	300	n.a.
(Worthington Prosage), 2 patties	220	16.0	5.0	15.0	0	800	n.a.
"roast" *(Worthington Dinner Roast)*, 2 oz.	120	8.0	5.0	8.0	0	465	n.a.
roll *(Worthington Prosage)*, 2 slices, 3/8"	190	13.0	4.0	14.0	0	600	n.a.
"salami":							
(Loma Linda), 2 oz. or 2 slices . . .	130	13.0	2.0	7.0	0	640	<1.0

Food and Measure	cal.	prot. (gms)	carbo. (gms)	fat (gms)	chol. (mgs)	sod. (mgs)	fiber (gms)
(Worthington), 2 slices	80	7.0	3.0	4.0	0	675	n.a.
"steak":							
(Loma Linda Griddle Steaks), 1 steak	190	13.0	5.0	13.0	0	460	<1.0
(Worthington Stakelets), 1 piece	140	12.0	8.0	7.0	0	705	n.a.
"tuna" *(Worthington Tuno Roll)*, 2 oz.	90	7.0	3.0	5.0	0	400	n.a.
"turkey":							
(Loma Linda), 2 oz. or 2 slices . . .	160	10.0	3.0	12.0	0	1350	<1.0
smoked, sliced *(Worthington)*, 4 slices	180	13.0	8.0	11.0	0	985	n.a.
Venison:							
raw, lean meat only, 4 oz.	143	23.8	0	4.5	n.a.	n.a.	0
Vine spinach:							
raw, 4 oz.	22	2.0	3.9	.3	0	n.a.	.8
Vinegar, 2 tbsp. or 1 fl. oz.:							
all varieties *(Heinz)*	4	0	0	0	0	<20	0
apple cider *(White House)*	4	0	2.0	0	0	5	0
distilled *(White House)*	4	0	2.0	0	0	<5	0
wine:							
red *(Regina)* . . .	4	<1.0	<1.0	<1.0	0	2	0
red, garlic *(Regina)*	4	<1.0	<1.0	<1.0	0	2	0
white *(Regina)* . .	4	<1.0	<1.0	<1.0	0	3	0
Vodka, see "Liquor"							

W

Food and Measure	cal.	prot. (gms)	carbo. (gms)	fat (gms)	chol. (mgs)	sod. (mgs)	fiber (gms)
Waffles:							
mix, see "Pancake and waffle mix"							
frozen:							
(Eggo), 1 waffle	120	3.0	17.0	5.0	n.a.	n.a.	n.a.
(Roman Meal), 2 waffles or 3 oz.	280	5.0	33.0	14.0	n.a.	680	.7
bran (Eggo), 1 waffle	170	4.0	20.0	8.0	n.a.	n.a.	n.a.
with imitation blueberries (Eggo), 1 waffle	130	3.0	17.0	5.0	n.a.	n.a.	n.a.
with imitation strawberries (Eggo), 1 waffle	120	2.0	17.0	5.0	n.a.	n.a.	n.a.
nutri-grain (Eggo), 1 waffle	130	3.0	18.0	5.0	n.a.	n.a.	n.a.
Walnuts:							
black, dried:							
in shell, 1 lb. . . .	661	26.5	13.2	61.6	0	2	7.0
shelled, 4 oz. . . .	688	27.6	13.7	64.2	0	1	7.3
shelled, chopped, 1 cup	759	30.4	15.1	70.7	0	2	8.1
shelled, finely ground, 1 cup	486	19.5	9.7	64.2	0	1	5.2
(Planters), 1 oz.	180	7.0	3.0	17.0	0	0	n.a.
English or Persian:							
in shell, 1 lb. . . .	1310	29.2	37.4	126.3	0	21	9.4
shelled, 4 oz. . . .	728	16.2	20.8	70.2	0	11	5.2
shelled, 1 oz. or 14 halves	182	4.1	5.2	17.6	0	3	1.3
shelled, halves, 1 cup	642	14.3	18.3	61.9	0	10	4.6

Food and Measure	cal.	prot. (gms)	carbo. (gms)	fat (gms)	chol. (mgs)	sod. (mgs)	fiber (gms)
shelled, pieces or chips, 1 cup	770	17.2	22.0	74.2	0	12	5.5
(Planters), 1 oz.	190	4.0	3.0	20.0	0	0	n.a.
Water chestnuts:							
raw:							
whole, 1 lb.	369	4.9	83.6	.4	0	50	2.8
4 chestnuts (1¼"– 2" diam.)	38	.5	8.6	<.1	0	5	.3
peeled, 4 oz.	120	1.6	27.1	.1	0	16	.9
peeled, sliced, 1 cup	132	1.7	29.7	.1	0	18	1.0
canned:							
whole, drained *(Chun King)*, 8.5 oz.	190	3.4	45.8	.5	0	157	1.9
sliced, with liquid, 1 cup	70	1.2	17.4	.1	0	12	.8
sliced, drained *(Chun King)*, 8 oz.	179	3.2	43.1	.5	0	147	1.8
Watercress, fresh:							
whole:							
with stems, 1 lb.	46	9.6	5.4	.4	0	170	2.9
1 sprig, 11¼" long	0	.1	<.1	0	0	1	<.1
chopped, 1 cup	4	.8	.4	<.1	0	14	.2
Watermelon, fresh:							
whole, with rind, 1 lb.	74	1.5	16.9	1.0	0	5	.7
1 wedge (10" diam. × 1" thick)	152	3.0	34.6	2.1	0	10	1.5
diced, 1 cup	50	1.0	11.5	.7	0	3	.5
Watermelon seed kernels, dried:							
shelled, 4 oz.	632	32.2	17.4	53.8	0	112	3.4
shelled, 1 cup	602	30.6	16.5	51.2	0	107	3.3
Wax gourd (Chinese preserving melon):							
raw:							
whole, 1 lb.	42	1.3	9.7	.6	0	358	1.6
cubed, 1 cup	17	.5	4.0	.3	0	147	.7

Food and Measure	cal.	prot. (gms)	carbo. (gms)	fat (gms)	chol. (mgs)	sod. (mgs)	fiber (gms)
Wax gourd *(cont.)*							
boiled, drained, cubed, 1 cup	23	.7	5.3	.4	0	186	.9
Weakfish, raw:							
whole, 1 lb.	263	35.9	0	12.2	n.a.	163	0
meat only, 4 oz.	137	18.7	0	6.4	n.a.	85	0
Weiners, see "Frank-furters"							
Welsh rarebit:							
frozen *(Stouffer's),* 5 oz.	360	13.0	9.0	30.0	n.a.	700	n.a.
sauce, canned *(Snow's),* 1/2 cup	170	9.0	10.0	11.0	n.a.	460	n.a.
Wendy's:							
breakfast, 1 serving:							
bacon, 2 strips	110	5.0	<1.0	10.0	15	445	n.a.
breakfast sandwich, 4.6 oz.	370	17.0	33.0	19.0	200	770	n.a.
danish, 3 oz.	360	6.0	44.0	18.0	n.a.	340	n.a.
eggs, scrambled, 3.25 oz.	190	14.0	7.0	12.0	450	160	n.a.
French toast, 2 slices	400	11.0	45.0	19.0	115	850	n.a.
home fries, 3.7 oz.	360	4.0	37.0	22.0	20	745	n.a.
omelet, ham and cheese, 4 oz.	250	18.0	6.0	17.0	450	405	n.a.
omelet, ham, cheese, mush-room, 4.2 oz.	290	18.0	7.0	21.0	355	570	n.a.
omelet, ham, cheese, onion, green pepper, 4.6 oz.	280	19.0	7.0	19.0	525	485	n.a.
omelet, mushroom, onion, green pep-per, 4 oz.	210	14.0	7.0	15.0	460	200	n.a.
sausage, 1 patty	200	9.0	<1.0	18.0	30	410	n.a.
toast with marga-rine, 2 slices	250	6.0	35.0	9.0	0	410	n.a.

Food and Measure	cal.	prot. (gms)	carbo. (gms)	fat (gms)	chol. (mgs)	sod. (mgs)	fiber (gms)
chili, 8 oz.	260	21.0	26.0	8.0	30	1070	n.a.
sandwiches, 1 serving:							
bacon cheese- burger, white bun, 5.25 oz.	460	29.0	23.0	28.0	65	860	n.a.
chicken, wheat bun, 4.6 oz.	320	25.0	31.0	10.0	59	500	n.a.
hamburger, single, wheat bun, 4.25 oz.	340	25.0	20.0	17.0	67	290	n.a.
hamburger, single, white bun, 4.2 oz.	350	21.0	27.0	18.0	65	410	n.a.
hamburger, double, white bun, 7 oz.	560	41.0	24.0	34.0	125	575	n.a.
hamburger, *Kids' Meal,* 2.7 oz. . .	220	13.0	11.0	8.0	20	265	n.a.
condiments:							
American cheese, .6-oz. slice . . .	70	4.0	<1.0	6.0	15	260	n.a.
bacon, 3 1/2 slices	90	4.0	<1.0	8.0	10	335	n.a.
dill pickles, 4 slices	1	<1.0	<1.0	<1.0	0	125	n.a.
ketchup, 1 tsp. . .	6	<1.0	1.0	<1.0	0	65	n.a.
lettuce, 1 piece . .	2	<1.0	<1.0	<1.0	0	0	n.a.
mayonnaise, 1 tbsp.	100	<1.0	<1.0	11.0	10	80	n.a.
mustard, 1 tsp. . .	4	<1.0	<1.0	<1.0	0	50	n.a.
onion rings, 1/3 oz.	4	<1.0	<1.0	<1.0	0	0	n.a.
relish, 1/3 oz.	14	<1.0	3.0	<1.0	0	70	n.a.
tomato, 1 slice . .	2	<1.0	<1.0	<1.0	0	0	n.a.
baked potato, hot stuffed, 1 serving:							
plain, 8.8 oz. . . .	250	6.0	52.0	2.0	1	60	n.a.
bacon and cheese, 12.5 oz.	570	19.0	57.0	30.0	22	1180	n.a.
broccoli and cheese, 13 oz.	500	13.0	54.0	25.0	22	430	n.a.
cheese, 12.5 oz.	590	17.0	55.0	34.0	22	450	n.a.
chicken a la king, 12.8 oz.	350	15.0	59.0	6.0	20	820	n.a.

Food and Measure	cal.	prot. (gms)	carbo. (gms)	fat (gms)	chol. (mgs)	sod. (mgs)	fiber (gms)
Wendy's, baked potato, hot stuffed *(cont.)*							
chili and cheese, 14.2 oz.	510	22.0	63.0	20.0	22	610	n.a.
sour cream and chives, 11 oz.	460	6.0	53.0	24.0	15	230	n.a.
Stroganoff and sour cream, 14.5 oz.	490	14.0	60.0	21.0	43	910	n.a.
salads and side dishes, 1 serving:							
French fries, regular, 3.5 oz. . . .	280	4.0	35.0	14.0	15	95	n.a.
pick-up window side salad, 18.2 oz.	110	8.0	5.0	6.0	15	540	n.a.
taco salad, 12.75 oz.	390	23.0	36.0	18.0	40	1100	n.a.
dessert, dairy, frosty, 12 fl. oz.	400	8.0	59.0	14.0	50	220	n.a.
Western style dinner, frozen:							
(Banquet American Favorites), 11 oz.	513	22.0	43.0	29.0	n.a.	1548	n.a.
(Morton), 11.1 oz.	347	16.9	36.7	14.7	n.a.	1400	n.a.
(Morton Lite), 11 oz.	290	13.0	31.0	12.0	n.a.	1010	n.a.
(Swanson), 12¼ oz.	440	23.0	45.0	19.0	n.a.	1150	n.a.
(Swanson Hungry-Man), 17½ oz. . .	750	41.0	71.0	34.0	n.a.	1930	n.a.
Whale:							
raw, meat only, 4 oz.	177	23.4	0	8.5	n.a.	88	0
Wheat, parboiled, see "Bulgur"							
Wheat, whole-grain:							
durum, 4 oz.	376	14.4	79.5	2.8	0	3	2.0
hard red spring, 4 oz.	374	15.9	78.4	2.5	0	3	2.6
hard red winter, 4 oz.	374	13.9	81.3	2.0	0	3	2.6
soft winter, 4 oz. . .	370	11.6	81.8	2.3	0	3	2.6
white, 4 oz.	380	10.7	85.5	2.3	0	3	2.2
Wheat bran:							
crude, commercially milled, 4 oz. . . .	242	18.1	70.2	5.2	0	10	10.3

Food and Measure	cal.	prot. (gms)	carbo. (gms)	fat (gms)	chol. (mgs)	sod. (mgs)	fiber (gms)
toasted *(Kretschmer)*, 1 oz.	60	5.0	18.0	1.0	0	0	n.a.
unprocessed *(Quaker)*, 2 tbsp.	21	1.1	3.6	.2	0	0	.8
Wheat germ:							
crude, commercially milled, 4 oz. . . .	314	30.2	53.0	12.4	0	3	2.8
(Kretschmer), 1/4 cup	110	9.0	13.0	3.0	0	0	n.a.
honey *(Kretschmer)*, 1/4 cup	110	7.0	17.0	2.0	0	0	n.a.
Wheat "nuts":							
(Flavor Tree), 1 oz.	200	4.0	5.0	18.0	0	185	n.a.
Wheat pilaf, mix:							
(Casbah), 1 oz. . . .	100	3.0	20.0	0	0	n.a.	n.a.
Whey:							
dry, 4 oz.	396	14.6	83.3	1.2	n.a.	n.a.	0
fluid, 8 oz.	59	2.0	11.6	.7	n.a.	n.a.	0
Whiskey, see "Liquor"							
Whiskey sour drink mixer:							
(Holland House), 1 fl. oz.	32	0	8.0	0	0	15	n.a.
White Castle:							
sandwiches, 1 serving:							
bun only, .89 oz.	74	2.2	13.9	.9	0	131	.5
cheese only, .31 oz.	31	1.5	2.3	1.6	n.a.	154	.2
cheeseburger, 2.29 oz.	200	7.8	15.5	11.2	n.a.	361	2.7
chicken, 2.25 oz.	186	6.7	20.5	7.5	n.a.	497	1.7
fish, without tartar sauce, 2.09 oz.	155	5.8	20.9	5.0	n.a.	201	1.4
hamburger, 2.06 oz.	161	5.9	15.4	7.9	n.a.	266	2.1
sausage, 1.72 oz.	196	6.7	13.3	12.3	n.a.	488	1.9
sausage and egg, 3.39 oz.	322	12.6	16.1	22.0	n.a.	698	3.0

Food and Measure	cal.	prot. (gms)	carbo. (gms)	fat (gms)	chol. (mgs)	sod. (mgs)	fiber (gms)
White Castle *(cont.)*							
side dishes, 1 serving:							
French fries, 3.42							
oz.	301	2.5	37.7	14.7	n.a.	193	4.6
onion chips, 3.29							
oz.	329	3.7	38.8	16.6	n.a.	823	3.5
onion rings, 2.12 oz.	245	2.9	26.6	13.4	n.a.	566	2.6
White sauce, mix:							
(Durkee), 1-oz. pkg.	155	1.9	11.0	11.0	n.a.	617	n.a.
dehydrated, 1.8-oz.							
pkg.	230	5.4	25.1	13.2	tr.	1691	.1
Whitefish:							
raw, meat only, 4 oz.	152	21.6	0	6.6	68	58	0
smoked, 4 oz. . . .	122	26.5	0	1.1	37	1156	0
Whiting:							
fresh, fillets:							
raw, 4 oz.	102	20.8	0	1.5	76	82	0
broiled, 4 oz. . . .	130	26.6	0	1.9	95	150	0
frozen fillets *(Taste O'*							
Sea), 4 oz.	80	21.0	0	0	n.a.	140	n.a.
Wine, 4 fl. oz., except							
as noted:							
barbera, white *(Col-*							
ony)	91	0	3.5	0	0	4	0
Burgundy:							
(Bravo)	91	0	1.7	0	0	4	0
(Carlo Rossi) . . .	92	0	1.6	0	0	n.a.	0
(Colony Classic)	90	0	1.2	0	0	4	0
(Gallo)	88	0	.8	0	0	n.a.	0
(Gallo Hearty) . .	92	0	1.6	0	0	n.a.	0
(Gambarelli &							
Davitto Parma)	91	0	1.7	0	0	4	0
(Petri)	91	0	1.7	0	0	4	0
white *(Colony* Clas-							
sic)	80	0	.8	0	0	4	0
Cabernet Sauvignon:							
(Colony)	88	0	.7	0	0	4	0
(Gallo)	88	0	0	0	0	n.a.	0

Food and Measure	cal.	prot. (gms)	carbo. (gms)	fat (gms)	chol. (mgs)	sod. (mgs)	fiber (gms)
carbonated:							
almond *(Jacques Bonet)*	104	0	7.7	0	0	4	0
apricot or peach *(Jacques Bonet)*	111	0	9.5	0	0	4	0
raspberry or cherry *(Jacques Bonet)*	106	0	8.3	0	0	4	0
(Carlo Rossi Paisano)	92	0	1.6	0	0	n.a.	0
Chablis:							
(Bravo)	86	0	1.7	0	0	4	0
(Carlo Rossi) ...	84	0	2.0	0	0	n.a.	0
(Colony Classic)	84	0	1.8	0	0	4	0
(Gallo Blanc) ...	80	0	.6	0	0	n.a.	0
(Gambarelli & Davitto Parma)	86	0	1.7	0	0	4	0
(Petri Chablis Blanc)	86	0	1.7	0	0	4	0
emerald *(Colony)*	102	0	5.3	0	0	4	0
gold *(Colony)* ...	97	0	4.3	0	0	4	0
pink *(Carlo Rossi)*	92	0	3.6	0	0	n.a.	0
pink *(Colony)* ...	98	0	4.5	0	0	4	0
pink *(Gallo)*	80	0	4.0	0	0	n.a.	0
pink *(Petri)*	98	0	4.5	0	0	4	0
ruby *(Colony)* ...	104	0	5.9	0	0	4	0
champagne:							
brut *(Jacques Bonet)*	92	0	2.1	0	0	4	0
brut *(Lejon)*	92	0	3.4	0	0	4	0
extra dry *(Jacques Bonet)*	97	0	3.4	0	0	4	0
extra dry *(Lejon)*	97	0	2.1	0	0	4	0
pink *(Jacques Bonet)*	98	0	3.7	0	0	4	0
pink *(Lejon)*	98	0	3.7	0	0	4	0
Chardonnay *(Gallo)*	88	0	0	0	0	n.a.	0
chenin blanc:							
(Colony)	86	0	2.4	0	0	4	0
(Gallo)	88	0	1.6	0	0	n.a.	0
Chianti:							
(Carlo Rossi Light)	92	0	2.4	0	0	n.a.	0

Food and Measure	cal.	prot. (gms)	carbo. (gms)	fat (gms)	chol. (mgs)	sod. (mgs)	fiber (gms)
Wine, Chianti *(cont.)*							
(Petri)	91	0	1.7	0	0	4	0
cold duck:							
(Jacques Bonet)	108	0	5.9	0	0	4	0
(Lejon)	108	0	5.9	0	0	4	0
French colombard							
(Colony)	84	0	1.8	0	0	4	0
(Gallo French							
Colombard)	88	0	2.0	0	0	n.a.	0
(Gallo Gewurztra-							
miner)	88	0	1.6	0	0	n.a.	0
Marsala *(Gambarelli &*							
Davitto)	77	0	4.0	0	0	4	0
(Mission Bell Arriba), 2							
fl. oz.	95	0	6.8	0	0	4	0
(Mission Bell Diamond							
Red), 2 fl. oz. . . .	95	0	6.8	0	0	4	0
(Mission Bell Silver							
Satin), 2 fl. oz. . .	83	0	5.4	0	0	4	0
(Mission Bell Silver							
Satin Bitter Lemon),							
2 fl. oz.	83	0	5.5	0	0	4	0
(Mission Bell Swiss							
Up), 2 fl. oz. . . .	84	0	5.6	0	0	4	0
Moselle *(Colony*							
Rhineskeller) . . .	97	0	4.3	0	0	4	0
muscatel *(Italian*							
Swiss Colony), 2 fl.							
oz.	122	0	5.9	0	0	4	0
pastoso *(Petri)* . . .	92	0	1.8	0	0	4	0
port, 2 fl. oz.:							
(Gallo)	64	0	2.0	0	0	n.a.	0
(Italian Swiss Col-							
ony)	85	0	5.7	0	0	4	0
tawney *(Livingston*							
Cellars)	86	0	6.4	0	0	n.a.	0
white *(Gallo)* . . .	86	0	5.6	0	0	n.a.	0
white *(Italian Swiss*							
Colony)	86	0	6.3	0	0	4	0

Food and Measure	cal.	prot. (gms)	carbo. (gms)	fat (gms)	chol. (mgs)	sod. (mgs)	fiber (gms)
Riesling (Gallo Johannisberg)	84	0	1.6	0	0	n.a.	0
Rhine:							
(Bravo)	97	0	4.3	0	0	4	0
(Carlo Rossi) . . .	84	0	4.4	0	0	n.a.	0
(Colony Classic)	89	0	3.8	0	0	4	0
(Gallo)	80	0	4.0	0	0	n.a.	0
(Gambarelli & Davitto Parma)	92	0	1.2	0	0	4	0
(Petri)	97	0	4.3	0	0	4	0
rosé:							
(Bravo)	92	0	3.1	0	0	4	0
(Carlo Rossi Vin Rosé)	88	0	2.8	0	0	n.a.	0
(Colony Classic)	89	0	3.0	0	0	4	0
(Gallo Grenache)	88	0	2.4	0	0	n.a.	0
(Gallo Red Rosé)	112	0	6.4	0	0	n.a.	0
(Gallo Vin Rosé)	88	0	2.8	0	0	n.a.	0
(Gambarelli & Davitto Parma)	92	0	3.1	0	0	4	0
(Petri)	92	0	3.1	0	0	4	0
sauvignon blanc (Gallo)	80	0	.8	0	0	n.a.	0
sherry, 2 fl. oz.:							
(Gallo)	64	0	2.0	0	0	n.a.	0
cream (Italian Swiss Colony)	85	0	6.8	0	0	4	0
cream (Livingston Cellars)	78	0	5.6	0	0	n.a.	0
dry (Italian Swiss Colony)	63	0	1.2	0	0	4	0
dry (Livingston Cellars Very Dry)	60	0	1.0	0	0	n.a.	0
straight (Italian Swiss Colony)	67	0	2.1	0	0	4	0
Tokay (Italian Swiss Colony), 2 fl. oz.	82	0	5.1	0	0	4	0
vermouth, 2 fl. oz.:							
dry (Gallo)	56	0	.8	0	0	n.a.	0

Food and Measure	cal.	prot. (gms)	carbo. (gms)	fat (gms)	chol. (mgs)	sod. (mgs)	fiber (gms)
Wine, vermouth *(cont.)*							
dry *(Gambarelli & Davitto)*	64	0	1.5	0	0	4	0
dry *(Lejon)*	64	0	1.5	0	0	4	0
sweet *(Gallo)* . . .	90	0	9.4	0	0	n.a.	0
sweet *(Gambarelli & Davitto)*	77	0	8.4	0	0	4	0
sweet *(Lejon)* . . .	77	0	8.4	0	0	4	0
Zinfandel:							
(Colony)	91	0	.7	0	0	4	0
(Gallo)	92	0	0	0	0	n.a.	0
white *(Colony)* . .	82	0	2.7	0	0	4	0
Wine, cooking:							
Burgundy *(Regina),* 1/4 cup	2	<1.0	<1.0	<1.0	0	365	n.a.
Sauterne *(Regina),* 1/4 cup	2	<1.0	<1.0	<1.0	0	365	n.a.
sherry *(Regina),* 1/4 cup	20	<1.0	5.0	<1.0	0	70	n.a.
Winged bean:							
raw:							
whole, 1 lb.	218	30.9	19.2	3.9	0	17	11.4
sliced, 1 cup . . .	22	3.1	1.9	.4	0	2	1.1
boiled, drained, 1 cup	23	3.3	2.0	.4	0	3	.9
Winged bean leaves:							
raw, 4 oz.	84	6.6	16.0	1.2	0	n.a.	2.8
Winged bean tuber:							
raw, 4 oz.	180	13.2	31.9	1.0	0	n.a.	8.4
Worcestershire sauce:							
(French's), 1 tbsp.	10	0	2.0	0	0	200	n.a.
(Lea & Perrins), 1 tsp.	5	<1.0	1.0	<1.0	0	55	n.a.
Wreckfish:							
raw, meat only, 4 oz.	129	20.9	0	4.4	n.a.	n.a.	0

Y

Food and Measure	cal.	prot. (gms)	carbo. (gms)	fat (gms)	chol. (mgs)	sod. (mgs)	fiber (gms)
Yachtwurst:							
(Usinger's), 1 oz. . . .	70	4.0	n.a.	6.0	n.a.	n.a.	n.a.
Yams,fresh:							
raw:							
whole, with skin, 1							
lb.	460	6.0	108.8	.7	0	37	n.a.
cubed, 1 cup . . .	177	2.3	41.8	.3	0	14	n.a.
cooked, drained,							
cubed, 1 cup . . .	158	2.0	37.5	.2	0	11	n.a.
Yams, canned or fro-zen, see "Sweet potato"							
Yam bean, tuber:							
raw:							
whole, with skin, 1							
lb.	170	5.8	36.5	.8	0	26	2.9
pared, 4 oz. . . .	47	1.6	9.9	.2	0	7	.8
sliced, 1 cup . . .	49	1.7	10.5	.2	0	8	.8
boiled, drained, 4 oz.	52	1.3	11.8	.1	0	7	1.3
Yardlong bean:							
raw:							
whole, 1 lb.	203	12.1	36.0	1.7	0	17	n.a.
sliced, 1 cup . . .	43	2.6	7.6	.4	0	4	n.a.
boiled, drained, sliced,							
1 cup	49	2.6	9.5	.1	0	4	1.6
Yeast, baker's:							
active dry:							
1 oz.	80	10.5	11.0	.5	0	15	n.a.
(Fleischmann's), 1							
packet	20	3.0	3.0	0	0	10	n.a.

Food and Measure	cal.	prot. (gms)	carbo. (gms)	fat (gms)	chol. (mgs)	sod. (mgs)	fiber (gms)
Yeast, baker's *(cont.)*							
compressed:							
1 oz.	24	3.4	3.1	.1	0	5	n.a.
(Fleischmann's), 1							
cube	15	2.0	2.0	0	0	5	n.a.
rapid rise:							
(Fleischmann's), 1							
packet	20	3.0	3.0	0	0	10	n.a.
Yeast, brewer's:							
debittered, 1 oz. . .	80	11.0	10.9	.3	0	34	.5
Yellowtail:							
raw, meat only, 4 oz.	166	26.2	0	5.9	n.a.	44	0
Yogurt:							
plain:							
(Columbo), 8 oz.	150	9.0	13.0	7.0	15	70	n.a.
(Columbo Natural							
Lite), 8 oz. . . .	110	11.0	17.0	0	2	80	n.a.
(Crowley Whole							
Milk), 8 oz. . . .	170	11.0	15.0	8.0	n.a.	150	n.a.
(Crowley Lowfat), 8							
oz.	140	12.0	17.0	2.0	n.a.	180	n.a.
(Dannon Lowfat), 8							
oz.	140	10.0	16.0	4.0	12	160	n.a.
(Knudsen), 8 oz.	180	11.0	15.0	9.0	n.a.	160	n.a.
(Knudsen Lowfat), 8							
oz.	260	8.0	45.0	5.0	n.a.	140	n.a.
(Lite-line Lowfat							
Swiss Style), 8							
oz.	180	11.0	24.0	4.0	n.a.	145	n.a.
(Yoplait), 6 oz. . .	130	9.0	13.0	5.0	n.a.	120	n.a.
apple:							
(Yoplait), 6 oz. . .	190	7.0	32.0	4.0	n.a.	105	n.a.
cinnamon *(Yoplait*							
Breakfast), 6 oz.	220	8.0	38.0	4.0	n.a.	90	n.a.
crisp *(New Country)*,							
6 oz.	150	5.0	30.0	2.0	n.a.	85	n.a.
Dutch *(Dannon*							
Lowfat), 8 oz.	240	9.0	43.0	3.0	<11	120	n.a.

Food and Measure	cal.	prot. (gms)	carbo. (gms)	fat (gms)	chol. (mgs)	sod. (mgs)	fiber (gms)
banana:							
(Dannon Lowfat), 8 oz.	240	9.0	43.0	3.0	<11	120	n.a.
(Yoplait Custard Style), 6 oz. . .	190	7.0	32.0	4.0	n.a.	95	n.a.
and strawberries *(Dannon Supreme)*, 6 oz.	190	6.0	33.0	4.0	n.a.	n.a.	n.a.
banana-strawberry *(Columbo)*, 8 oz.	235	7.0	38.0	6.0	20	70	n.a.
berry:							
(Yoplait Breakfast), 6 oz.	230	8.0	40.0	4.0	n.a.	95	n.a.
mixed *(Dannon* Lowfat), 8 oz.	240	9.0	43.0	3.0	<11	120	n.a.
mixed *(Dannon* Hearty Nuts & Raisins), 8 oz.	260	11.0	48.0	3.0	9	<100	n.a.
mixed *(Dannon* Mini-Pack), 4.4 oz.	130	5.0	23.0	2.0	n.a.	n.a.	n.a.
mixed *(Dannon* Y.E.S.), 6 oz. . .	190	7.0	33.0	4.0	<9	100	n.a.
mixed *(New Country* Supreme), 6 oz.	150	5.0	31.0	2.0	n.a.	85	n.a.
mixed *(Yoplait)*, 6 oz.	190	7.0	32.0	4.0	n.a.	105	n.a.
mixed *(Yoplait* Custard Style), 6 oz.	180	7.0	30.0	4.0	n.a.	95	n.a.
mixed *(Yoplait* Fruit-on-the-Bottom), 6 oz.	180	7.0	34.0	2.0	n.a.	95	n.a.
mixed, and blueberries *(Dannon Supreme)*, 6 oz.	190	6.0	33.0	4.0	n.a.	n.a.	n.a.
wild *(Columbo)*, 8 oz.	250	8.0	45.0	5.0	20	70	n.a.

Food and Measure	cal.	prot. (gms)	carbo. (gms)	fat (gms)	chol. (mgs)	sod. (mgs)	fiber (gms)
Yogurt *(cont.)*							
blackberry, and							
raspberries *(Dannon*							
Supreme), 6 oz.	190	6.0	33.0	4.0	n.a.	n.a.	n.a.
blueberry:							
(Columbo), 8 oz.	250	8.0	38.0	7.0	20	70	n.a.
(Crowley Sundae							
Style), 8 oz. . .	250	9.0	47.0	2.0	n.a.	160	n.a.
(Crowley Swiss), 8							
oz.	240	9.0	48.0	2.0	n.a.	150	n.a.
(Dannon Lowfat), 8							
oz.	240	9.0	43.0	3.0	< 11	120	n.a.
(Dannon Mini-Pack),							
4.4 oz.	130	5.0	23.0	2.0	n.a.	n.a.	n.a.
(Dannon Y.E.S.), 6							
oz.	190	7.0	33.0	4.0	< 9	100	n.a.
(New Country Su-							
preme), 6 oz.	150	5.0	31.0	2.0	n.a.	90	n.a.
(Sweet 'n Low), 6							
oz.	110	5.0	24.0	0	n.a.	80	n.a.
(Yoplait), 6 oz. . .	190	7.0	32.0	4.0	n.a.	105	n.a.
(Yoplait Custard							
Style), 6 oz. . .	190	7.0	32.0	4.0	n.a.	95	n.a.
(Yoplait Fruit-on-the-							
Bottom), 6 oz.	180	7.0	34.0	2.0	n.a.	95	n.a.
boysenberry:							
(Dannon Lowfat), 8							
oz.	240	9.0	43.0	3.0	< 11	120	n.a.
(Yoplait), 6 oz. . .	190	7.0	32.0	4.0	n.a.	105	n.a.
cherry:							
(Dannon Lowfat), 8							
oz.	240	9.0	43.0	3.0	< 11	120	n.a.
(Dannon Y.E.S.), 6							
oz.	190	7.0	33.0	4.0	< 9	100	n.a.
(New Country Su-							
preme), 6 oz.	150	5.0	32.0	2.0	n.a.	90	n.a.
(Sweet 'n Low), 6							
oz.	110	5.0	24.0	0	n.a.	85	n.a.
(Yoplait), 6 oz. . .	190	7.0	32.0	4.0	n.a.	105	n.a.

Food and Measure	cal.	prot. (gms)	carbo. (gms)	fat (gms)	chol. (mgs)	sod. (mgs)	fiber (gms)
(Yoplait Fruit-on-the-Bottom), 6 oz.	180	7.0	34.0	2.0	n.a.	95	n.a.
black (Crowley Sundae Style), 8 oz.	250	9.0	47.0	2.0	n.a.	160	n.a.
black (Crowley Swiss), 8 oz. . .	240	9.0	48.0	2.0	n.a.	150	n.a.
with almonds (Yoplait Breakfast), 6 oz. . . .	230	8.0	40.0	4.0	n.a.	110	n.a.
cherry-vanilla:							
(Borden Swiss Style), 8 oz. . .	270	9.0	54.0	2.0	n.a.	160	n.a.
(Columbo), 8 oz.	250	8.0	40.0	7.0	20	70	n.a.
(Crowley Swiss), 8 oz.	240	9.0	48.0	2.0	n.a.	150	n.a.
citrus fruits (Yoplait Breakfast), 6 oz.	250	8.0	45.0	4.0	n.a.	95	n.a.
coconut, and cherries (Dannon Supreme), 6 oz.	190	6.0	33.0	4.0	n.a.	n.a.	n.a.
coffee (Dannon Lowfat), 8 oz. . .	200	10.0	34.0	3.0	<11	140	n.a.
fruit crunch (New Country), 6 oz. . .	150	5.0	30.0	2.0	n.a.	90	n.a.
granola (Columbo Breakfast), 8 oz.	240	8.0	40.0	6.0	20	70	n.a.
Hawaiian salad (New Country), 6 oz. . .	150	5.0	31.0	2.0	n.a.	90	n.a.
honey vanilla (Columbo), 8 oz.	220	8.0	30.0	7.0	20	60	n.a.
lemon:							
(Borden Swiss Style), 8 oz. . .	320	9.0	69.0	2.0	n.a.	115	n.a.
(Columbo), 8 oz.	220	8.0	30.0	7.0	20	60	n.a.
(Crowley Swiss), 8 oz.	240	9.0	48.0	2.0	n.a.	150	n.a.
(Dannon Lowfat), 8 oz.	240	9.0	43.0	3.0	<11	120	n.a.

Food and Measure	cal.	prot. (gms)	carbo. (gms)	fat (gms)	chol. (mgs)	sod. (mgs)	fiber (gms)
Yogurt, lemon *(cont.)*							
(New Country Supreme), 6 oz.	150	5.0	31.0	2.0	n.a.	90	n.a.
(Yoplait), 6 oz. . .	190	7.0	32.0	4.0	n.a.	105	n.a.
(Yoplait Custard Style), 6 oz. . .	190	7.0	32.0	4.0	n.a.	95	n.a.
orchard fruits:							
(Dannon Hearty Nuts & Raisins), 8 oz.	260	11.0	48.0	3.0	9	< 100	n.a.
(Yoplait Breakfast), 6 oz.	230	8.0	41.0	4.0	n.a.	90	n.a.
orange:							
(New Country Supreme), 6 oz.	150	5.0	31.0	2.0	n.a.	90	n.a.
(Yoplait), 6 oz. . .	190	7.0	32.0	4.0	n.a.	105	n.a.
passion fruit, and peaches *(Dannon* Supreme), 6 oz.	190	6.0	33.0	4.0	n.a.	n.a.	n.a.
peach:							
(Crowley Sundae Style), 8 oz. . .	250	9.0	47.0	2.0	n.a.	160	n.a.
(Crowley Swiss), 8 oz.	240	9.0	48.0	2.0	n.a.	150	n.a.
(Dannon Lowfat), 8 oz.	240	9.0	43.0	3.0	< 11	120	n.a.
(Dannon Y.E.S.), 6 oz.	190	7.0	33.0	4.0	< 9	100	n.a.
(Sweet 'n Low), 6 oz.	110	5.0	24.0	0	n.a.	80	n.a.
(Yoplait), 6 oz. . .	190	7.0	32.0	4.0	n.a.	105	n.a.
and cream *(New Country),* 6 oz.	150	5.0	31.0	2.0	n.a.	90	n.a.
Melba *(Columbo),* 8 oz.	230	8.0	37.0	6.0	20	70	n.a.
sunrise *(Yoplait* Breakfast), 6 oz.	230	8.0	42.0	3.0	n.a.	90	n.a.

Food and Measure	cal.	prot. (gms)	carbo. (gms)	fat (gms)	chol. (mgs)	sod. (mgs)	fiber (gms)
piña colada:							
(Borden Swiss Style), 8 oz. . .	260	9.0	51.0	2.0	n.a.	115	n.a.
(Columbo), 8 oz.	240	7.0	40.0	6.0	20	70	n.a.
(Dannon Lowfat), 8 oz.	240	9.0	43.0	3.0	<11	120	n.a.
(Dannon Y.E.S.), 6 oz.	190	7.0	33.0	4.0	<9	100	n.a.
(Yoplait), 6 oz. . .	190	7.0	32.0	4.0	n.a.	105	n.a.
pineapple:							
(Crowley Swiss), 8 oz.	230	8.0	45.0	2.0	n.a.	180	n.a.
(Yoplait), 6 oz. . .	190	7.0	32.0	4.0	n.a.	105	n.a.
(Yoplait Fruit-on-the-Bottom), 6 oz.	180	7.0	34.0	2.0	n.a.	95	n.a.
pineapple-cherry (Crowley Swiss), 8 oz.	240	9.0	48.0	2.0	n.a.	150	n.a.
raspberry:							
(Columbo), 8 oz.	250	7.0	39.0	7.0	20	70	n.a.
(Crowley Sundae Style), 8 oz. . .	250	9.0	47.0	2.0	n.a.	170	n.a.
(Crowley Swiss), 8 oz.	240	9.0	48.0	2.0	n.a.	150	n.a.
(Dannon Lowfat), 8 oz.	240	9.0	43.0	3.0	<11	120	n.a.
(Dannon Mini-Pack), 4.4 oz.	130	5.0	23.0	2.0	n.a.	n.a.	n.a.
(Dannon Y.E.S.), 6 oz.	190	7.0	33.0	4.0	<9	100	n.a.
(New Country Supreme), 6 oz.	150	5.0	31.0	2.0	n.a.	90	n.a.
(Sweet 'n Low), 6 oz.	110	5.0	24.0	0	n.a.	90	n.a.
(Yoplait), 6 oz. . .	190	7.0	32.0	4.0	n.a.	105	n.a.
(Yoplait Custard Style), 6 oz. . .	190	7.0	32.0	4.0	n.a.	95	n.a.
(Yoplait Fruit-on-the-Bottom), 6 oz.	180	7.0	34.0	2.0	n.a.	95	n.a.

Food and Measure	cal.	prot. (gms)	carbo. (gms)	fat (gms)	chol. (mgs)	sod. (mgs)	fiber (gms)
Yogurt *(cont.)*							
strawberry:							
(Borden Swiss Style), 8 oz. . .	230	9.0	46.0	2.0	n.a.	145	n.a.
(Columbo), 8 oz.	230	8.0	36.0	6.0	20	70	n.a.
(Crowley Sundae Style), 8 oz. . .	250	9.0	47.0	2.0	n.a.	170	n.a.
(Crowley Swiss), 8 oz.	240	9.0	48.0	2.0	n.a.	150	n.a.
(Dannon Lowfat), 8 oz.	240	9.0	43.0	3.0	<11	120	n.a.
(Dannon Mini-Pack), 4.4 oz.	130	5.0	23.0	2.0	n.a.	n.a.	n.a.
(Dannon Y.E.S.), 6 oz.	190	7.0	33.0	4.0	<9	100	n.a.
(New Country Supreme), 6 oz.	150	5.0	30.0	2.0	n.a.	90	n.a.
(New Country Fruit Cup), 6 oz. . . .	150	5.0	30.0	2.0	n.a.	85	n.a.
(Sweet 'n Low), 6 oz.	110	5.0	24.0	0	n.a.	85	n.a.
(Yoplait), 6 oz. . .	190	7.0	32.0	4.0	n.a.	95	n.a.
(Yoplait Custard Style), 6 oz. . .	190	7.0	32.0	4.0	n.a.	95	n.a.
(Yoplait Fruit-on-the-Bottom), 6 oz.	180	7.0	34.0	2.0	n.a.	95	n.a.
with almonds *(Yoplait* Breakfast), 6 oz. . . .	230	8.0	40.0	4.0	n.a.	110	n.a.
and strawberries *(Dannon Supreme),* 6 oz.	190	6.0	33.0	4.0	n.a.	n.a.	n.a.
strawberry-banana:							
(Crowley Swiss), 8 oz.	240	9.0	48.0	2.0	n.a.	150	n.a.
(Dannon Lowfat), 8 oz.	240	9.0	43.0	3.0	<11	120	n.a.
(Dannon Y.E.S.), 6 oz.	190	7.0	33.0	4.0	<9	100	n.a.

Food and Measure	cal.	prot. (gms)	carbo. (gms)	fat (gms)	chol. (mgs)	sod. (mgs)	fiber (gms)
(New Country), 6 oz.	150	5.0	31.0	2.0	n.a.	85	n.a.
(Sweet 'n Low), 6 oz.	110	5.0	24.0	0	n.a.	80	n.a.
(Yoplait), 6 oz. . .	190	7.0	32.0	4.0	n.a.	105	n.a.
(Yoplait Breakfast), 6 oz.	240	8.0	43.0	4.0	n.a.	90	n.a.
strawberry-vanilla *(Columbo)*, 8 oz.	260	7.0	45.0	6.0	20	70	n.a.
tropical fruits:							
(Crowley Sundae Style), 8 oz. . .	250	9.0	47.0	2.0	n.a.	160	n.a.
(Sweet 'n Low), 6 oz.	110	5.0	24.0	0	n.a.	80	n.a.
(Yoplait Breakfast), 6 oz.	230	8.0	41.0	4.0	n.a.	90	n.a.
vanilla:							
(Crowley Lowfat), 8 oz.	200	12.0	33.0	2.0	n.a.	170	n.a.
(Dannon Lowfat), 8 oz.	200	10.0	34.0	3.0	< 11	140	n.a.
(Dannon Hearty Nuts & Raisins), 8 oz.	260	11.0	48.0	3.0	9	< 100	n.a.
(Knudsen), 8 oz.	260	9.0	48.0	4.0	n.a.	140	n.a.
(Yoplait Custard Style), 6 oz. . .	180	7.0	30.0	4.0	n.a.	95	n.a.
French *(Colombo)*, 8 oz.	210	8.0	29.0	7.0	20	60	n.a.
French *(New Country)*, 6 oz.	150	5.0	31.0	2.0	n.a.	90	n.a.
Yogurt, frozen:							
blueberry *(Danny)*, 1 cup	210	7.0	42.0	2.0	n.a.	115	n.a.
chocolate:							
(Danny), 1 cup . .	190	9.0	32.0	3.0	n.a.	115	n.a.
(Danny-Yo), 3½ oz.	120	5.0	23.0	1.0	n.a.	n.a.	n.a.
piña colada *(Danny)*, 1 cup	230	6.0	44.0	4.0	n.a.	105	n.a.

Food and Measure	cal.	prot. (gms)	carbo. (gms)	fat (gms)	chol. (mgs)	sod, (mgs)	fiber (gms)
Yogurt, frozen *(cont.)*							
raspberry:							
(Danny), 1 cup . .	210	7.0	42.0	2.0	n.a.	105	n.a.
red *(Danny-Yo)*, 3¹/2							
oz.	110	4.0	21.0	1.0	n.a.	n.a.	n.a.
strawberry:							
(Danny), 1 cup . .	210	7.0	42.0	2.0	n.a.	105	n.a.
(Danny-Yo), 3¹/2 oz.	110	4.0	21.0	1.0	n.a.	n.a.	n.a.
vanilla:							
(Danny), 1 cup . .	180	8.0	33.0	2.0	n.a.	105	n.a.
(Danny-Yo), 3¹/2 oz.	110	4.0	21.0	1.0	n.a.	n.a.	n.a.
Yogurt bars, frozen,							
2¹/2 fl.-oz. bar:							
boysenberry, carob							
coated *(Danny)*,	140	2.0	15.0	8.0	n.a.	30	n.a.
chocolate *(Danny)*	60	3.0	10.0	1.0	n.a.	30	n.a.
chocolate, chocolate							
coated *(Danny)* . .	130	3.0	12.0	8.0	n.a.	35	n.a.
piña colada *(Danny)*	70	2.0	14.0	1.0	n.a.	30	n.a.
raspberry, chocolate							
coated *(Danny)* . .	130	2.0	15.0	7.0	n.a.	30	n.a.
strawberry, chocolate							
coated *(Danny)* . .	130	2.0	15.0	7.0	n.a.	30	n.a.
vanilla *(Danny)* . . .	60	2.0	11.0	1.0	n.a.	30	n.a.
vanilla, chocolate							
coated *(Danny)* . .	130	2.0	11.0	8.0	n.a.	30	n.a.

Z

Food and Measure	cal.	prot. (gms)	carbo. (gms)	fat (gms)	chol. (mgs)	sod. (mgs)	fiber (gms)
Ziti dinner:							
Italian style, frozen							
(*Morton* Lite), 11 oz.	280	12.0	43.0	6.0	n.a.	790	n.a.
Zucchini:							
fresh, see "Squash, summer"							
canned, 1/2 cup:							
in tomato sauce							
(*Del Monte*) . .	30	1.0	8.0	0	0	485	n.a.
Italian style, in							
sauce (*S&W*) . .	45	2.0	7.0	1.0	0	467	n.a.
frozen:							
sliced (*Southland*), 3.2 oz.	15	1.0	3.0	0	0	0	n.a.
sticks, in batter (*Mrs. Paul's*), 3 oz.	180	3.0	23.0	9.0	n.a.	630	n.a.